AF358634

Dual-Pivot Quicksort and Beyond:

Analysis of Multiway Partitioning
and Its Practical Potential

Vom Fachbereich Informatik der
Technischen Universität Kaiserslautern
zur Verleihung des akademischen Grades
Doktor der Naturwissenschaften (Dr. rer. nat.)
genehmigte

Dissertation

von

Sebastian Wild

Datum der wissenschaftlichen Aussprache: 8. Juli 2016

Dekan:　　　　　　　Prof. Dr. Klaus Schneider

Berichterstatter:　　Prof. Dr. Markus Nebel,
　　　　　　　　　　Prof. Robert Sedgewick und
　　　　　　　　　　Prof. Dr. Martin Dietzfelbinger

D 386

To Lydia

Abstract

Multiway Quicksort, i.e., partitioning the input in one step around several pivots, has received much attention since Java 7's runtime library uses a new dual-pivot method that outperforms by far the old Quicksort implementation. The success of dual-pivot Quicksort is most likely due to more efficient usage of the memory hierarchy, which gives reason to believe that further improvements are possible with multiway Quicksort.

In this dissertation, I conduct a mathematical average-case analysis of multiway Quicksort including the important optimization to choose pivots from a sample of the input. I propose a parametric template algorithm that covers all practically relevant partitioning methods as special cases, and analyze this method in full generality. This allows me to analytically investigate in depth what effect the parameters of the generic Quicksort have on its performance. To model the memory-hierarchy costs, I also analyze the expected number of *scanned elements*, a measure for the amount of data transferred from memory that is known to also approximate the number of cache misses very well. The analysis unifies previous analyses of particular Quicksort variants under particular cost measures in one generic framework.

A main result is that multiway partitioning can reduce the number of scanned elements significantly, while it does not save many key comparisons; this explains why the earlier studies of multiway Quicksort did not find it promising. A highlight of this dissertation is the extension of the analysis to inputs with equal keys. I give the first analysis of Quicksort with pivot sampling and multiway partitioning on an input model with equal keys.

Zusammenfassung

Seit in Version 7 der Java runtime library ein neuer dual-pivot Quicksort zum Einsatz kommt, der deutlich schneller als die vorherige Implementierung arbeitet, hat *multiway Quicksort*, also das Partitionierung bzgl. mehrerer Pivotelemente zugleich, einige Aufmerksamkeit auf sich gezogen. Der Erfolg von dual-pivot Quicksort ist höchstwahrscheinlich auf eine effizientere Verwendung der Speicherhierarchie zurückzuführen, was Grund zu der Annahme gibt, dass weitere Verbesserungen mit multiway Quicksort möglich sind.

In dieser Dissertation wird die mathematische Average-Case-Analyse von multiway Quicksort beschrieben, wobei ausdrücklich die wichtige Optimierung, die Pivotelemente aus einem Sample der Eingabe zu ziehen, das sogenannte *pivot sampling*, berücksichtigt wird. Dazu wird ein parametrischer Algorithmus vorgestellt und symbolisch in seinen Parametern analysiert, der alle in der Praxis relevanten Partitionierungsmethoden als Spezialfall abdeckt. Das ermöglicht eine detaillierte analytische Untersuchung des Effekts, den die Wahl der verschiedenen Parameter auf die Effizienz des Verfahrens hat. Um Kosten bzgl. der Speicherhierarchie zu modellieren, wird das Kostenmaß "scanned elements" verwendet, dem die mit dem Hauptspeicher ausgetauschte Datenmenge zugrunde liegt, und das bekanntermaßen die Anzahl an cache misses gut approximiert. Die Analyse in dieser Arbeit vereinheitlicht frühere Untersuchungen konkreter Partitionierungsmethoden bzgl. bestimmter Kostenmaße unter dem Dach einer vereinheitlichten Theorie.

Ein Ergebnis dieser Arbeit ist, dass multiway Quicksort deutliche Vorteile bzgl. des Kostenmaßes scanned elements bringen kann, während die Anzahl Schlüsselvergleiche nicht wesentlich verbessert wird. Das ist eine mögliche Erklärung, warum multiway Quicksort nicht schon in der Vergangenheit als vielversprechende Variante angesehen wurde.

Darüber hinaus gelang in dieser Dissertation erstmals die Verallgemeinerung der Analyse von Quicksort mit multiway partitioning und pivot sampling auf Eingaben mit gleichen Schlüsseln.

Contents

Foreword

In some sense, sorting is the *Drosophila* of computer science: On one hand, the task of rearranging elements into sorted order is simple enough to allow a focused and confined treatment. It thus is an ideal example to teach undergraduates the design and analysis of algorithms. On the other hand, sorting still motivates challenging algorithmic and mathematical research problems. One such problem is covered by the present book.

The underlying research started when we were working on our tool *MaLiJan* which aims at a semi-automated average-case analysis of algorithms. After we were able to rediscover well-known results like, e.g., the expected number of comparisons performed by the classic Quicksort algorithm on random permutations, we were looking for similar yet unsolved problems in order to tackle them by using our tool. It was then that we became aware of a new Quicksort variant that was about to replace the sorting algorithm in Sun's Java library.

The new algorithm has experimentally shown a superior runtime behavior. However, it surprisingly makes use of a well-known idea—using several pivots—that in theoretical investigations had proven to be of no advantage. This of course attracted our attention and a new research question was born: why is Java's dual-pivot Quicksort faster than former single-pivot implementations? The problem became the subject of the master and doctoral thesis of my former student Sebastian Wild. I vividly remember our first related discussion on a plane in 2012—years of inspiring work were to follow.

Over the years other researchers joined our quest to answer this question and various parameters like the number of comparisons, memory accesses, branch misses etc. were studied. Finally the memory hierarchy (caches) of modern computers was identified to be responsible. The present book derives from Sebastian's thesis and summarizes the related research. It generalizes our early findings to a parameterized Quicksort algorithm that, e.g., uses an arbitrary number of pivots. Choosing the parameters properly allows to apply the presented results to any of the Quicksort variants that have gained attention in the past. This book is thus one of the most general treatments of Quicksort available. It furthermore draws a nice picture of many state-of-the-art methods for the average-case analysis of algorithms and the beautiful mathematical patterns they create.

Markus E. Nebel

Preface

Dear Reader,

By the time you are reading these words, I may call myself *doctor rerum naturalium* on the basis of the present dissertation, and of course this was a primary objective for me to write this work. However, I tried hard to make it useful beyond that.

Purpose of this Book.   I believe that when one computational method is significantly faster than another, there must be an intrinsic reason for that, one that persists in a simplified model that we can analyze mathematically. And I believe that we make progress in understanding what makes one algorithm faster than another from exactly such analyses.

The goal of my research hence is to rigorously derive mathematical theorems about the performance of practical algorithms in a realistic, but clean and well-defined model of reality. When a generic analysis of a parametric template algorithm is possible, we can then reason analytically about good choices for the parameters and obtain a solid machine-independent basis for tuning practical implementations.

In this work I present a unified analysis of multiway Quicksort and give tentative advise on which Quicksort variants to use in practice (Chapters 7 and 9). In particular, I demonstrate that there is genuine potential in multiway partitioning to speed up Quicksort w.r.t. efficient use of memory references that cannot easily be obtained by other optimizations.

Apart from those results on Quicksort many of which did not appear in the literature before, this book also serves as a reference for mathematical tools and techniques used in obtaining these results. It naturally happened that my analysis makes use of several mathematical techniques and facts. I found that—once things are viewed from the right angle—I could replace more and more specific own arguments by general properties of existing notions, from discrete math to real analysis, a bit of complex analysis and a good deal of stochastics. That way Chapter 2 which introduces the mathematical preliminaries grew by itself to its 80-odd pages.

While there are good books with comprehensive surveys on techniques for the analysis of algorithms, e.g., references [165, 64, 103, 73, 97], and others focusing on the analysis of a specific class of algorithms or data structures, e.g., [112, 113, 47], I know only a single source that discusses in breadth and depth analytical tools to analyze Quicksort: Robert Sedgewick's dissertation [162], finished 1975.

I tried to continue the story of the analysis of Quicksort in Sedgewick's spirit: eternal truths derived in a clear model of reality using techniques thoroughly introduced from the basics; and not forgetting to discuss their practical implications. The techniques are math, the subject is computer science.

I can merely tell one further chapter of the story—a lot has happened since 1975—but I tried to give a broader overview of the field in Section 1.7.

Intended Audience. The imaginary reader I had in mind when writing this book is a mathematically inclined computer scientist who knows about basic algorithms and data structures covered in a typical introductory course and has some proficiency in real analysis and elementary math, but who is not an expert in the analysis of algorithms.

Concepts from complex analysis and stochastics appear in this work, but an intuitive understanding suffices to follow the presentation. I try to give these intuitions and indeed the arguments used in this work are mostly elementary.

Chapter 2 collects all (mathematical) facts used in this work that are not derived on the spot. Instead of reproducing formal proofs of these statements I mostly refer to external sources; I rather devote the space to share an intuition why a statement holds and how it relates to the analysis of Quicksort or other mathematical results. I sorely missed such comments escaping the tight corset of definition-theorem-proof purism from many math textbooks and lectures, so I put special effort in providing them in my own work.

My Highlights. I would like to point out my two favorite results in this book: Section 7.3 shows how to compute for any multi-pivot sampling scheme an equivalent one for single-pivot Quicksort that produces pivots of the "same quality" (it is made precise there what I mean by this). This allows us to separate savings that are truly coming from multiway partitioning from those that are merely a consequence of better pivots. I have long had this in mind as a vague concept, but only the generic setup in this work finally made it possible to formalize the idea.

My second highlight is the analysis of Quicksort with equal keys (Chapter 8). Although there are some technical nuisances left, the simplicity and elegance of the final result (Theorem 8.17) is very pleasing. Shortly after finishing this dissertation, I could generalize the result for single-pivot Quicksort to any expected-profile input [183], thus confirming Conjecture 8.5 of Sedgewick and Bentley. The foundations for that are laid in Chapter 8 of this work.

A Remark on Style. I tried to keep the style of writing as formal as appropriate for a dissertation, but as vivid and flowery as possible whenever when I felt this would help conveying the facts at hand more clearly and effectively.

Wherever possible I try to "look into the box" of used techniques and results: provide an idea for why they hold instead of using them as a black box.

> **Digressions.** I found that interesting connections to other areas suggested themselves quite insistently during the preparation of this material. Unlike the look-into-the-box comments, such connections had no direct contribution to the purpose of this work. The same is true for the historical contexts, discussions about notations and names, and blind alleys of thought I spend quite some of my time on. Yet these side paths were among the most rewarding parts for me and felt reluctant doing away with them altogether.
>
> I finally settled for a compromise: I would keep digressions like this one, but typeset them separately from the main text; the latter is written so that digressions may be skipped without disturbing the main line of thought. I hope the reader will find my digressions helpful; but if not, they are at least easy enough to spot and skip.

For these reasons many parts are longer than ultimately necessary, but I think it made them much better, too—in terms of the content they present and in terms of efficiency of reading: I am convinced that a slightly longer text will guide the reader in *less* time through a complicated argument than a shorter one that leaves parts unclear or implicit.

> **Elegant Proofs.** This is especially true for mathematical proofs. Like many mathematicians I find elegance in a proof that is short, but sometimes brevity of the presentation is mistaken for elegance of the argument. E. W. Dijkstra suspected that this might even be done on purpose: *"I should point out that my ideal of crisp clarity is not universally shared. Some consider the puzzles that are created by their omissions as spicy challenges, without which their texts would be boring; others shun clarity lest their work is considered trivial."* ([45], p. 1).
>
> It might not be far-fetched to assume that someone who mistakes brevity for clarity also mixes up confusing presentation with depth of a topic.

If the proofs in this work are found trivial to understand, I will take it as the greatest compliment: it means I succeeded in presenting my thesis the way I intended to.

History of this Work. I started working on the analysis of Quicksort almost five years ago, when I was in my last year as computer science student. Quite coincidentally I got to know of the success of a new dual-pivot Quicksort implementation in Java 7, and I started digging through the immense literature on Quicksort . . . but no theoretical analysis of this algorithm was known! Since I had already been working regularly as „*Hiwi*" (student research assistant) in the group of my later advisor Markus Nebel, I discussed this topic with him and we decided to make it my master's thesis project. Since the initial analysis of YBB Quicksort was so well received in the algorithms community, I stuck to the topic for further research towards my *Doktor* (Ph. D.).

The articles I coauthored in that time extended the analysis in various directions, but mostly dealt with YBB Quicksort only. The analytical tools however extend naturally to a whole class of algorithms, and for my dissertation I finally tackled the unified analysis of a very general class of Quicksort variants, covering all practically relevant implementations. My work has taken this transition from concrete to general in several respects:

- ▶ from very concrete algorithms (even assembly implementations)
  to generic, parametric templates,
- ▶ from counting comparisons and swaps
  to analyzing a generic class of cost measures,
- ▶ from specific methods to solve particular recurrences exactly
  to methods for asymptotic approximations of sweeping generality,
- ▶ from counting configurations combinatorially
  to stochastic characterizations of the main mechanisms, and
- ▶ from computing specific terms ad hoc
  to reusing more and more known results from mathematics.

Since I started analyzing Quicksort almost five years ago, a lot has also changed for myself. Instead of a student, I am now an employee of the university with teaching duties; visiting conferences, giving talks and collaborating with other researchers have become routine. My two kids were born in this time, and the third one will be with us before this book will be available in print. Priorities have shifted and views have changed.

Although this happened in parallel to and quite independently of my work on Quicksort, many happy personal memories will remain entangled with certain stages of this work. In that sense, Quicksort will always be a part of my life.

Acknowledgments.   A lot has happened in the years while I worked towards this dissertation. I wish to thank all my family, friends and colleagues for accompanying and supporting me in this time.

Without my advisor and mentor, Markus Nebel, I would be nowhere near where I am today. His open-door policy always invited discussions and digressions and I am deeply thankful for his continuous support and his professional and personal advice.

I am also much obliged to my two external reviewers, Robert Sedgewick and Martin Dietzfelbinger, for their rigorous scrutiny of this work and their fair and precise reports. Martin Dietzfelbinger and Markus Nebel provided me with lists of thoughtful comments and detailed corrections, which improved this work a lot. I am also very thankful for the comments of Raphael Reitzig and my wife Lydia who proof-read substantial parts of this work and contributed numerous corrections and improvements.

I greatly profited from the experience, expertise and advice of my coauthors Ralph Neininger, Hosam M. Mahmoud and Conrado Martínez. The discussions with Hosam on language and style had lasting influence on my writing. Many of the ideas underlying Chapter 7 are synergistic outcomes of extensive whiteboard sessions with Conrado and Markus, and I am sure our fruitful collaboration will continue.

I also enjoyed the stimulating atmosphere in the "theory hallway" of our group in Kaiserslautern. With Raphael Reitzig, Ulrich Laube, Frank Weinberg, and Wolfgang

Schlauch, we had countless late-afternoon discussions on research, teaching, typography, politics, technology, history, and psychology. These were not exactly the most productive moments, but they shaped and sharpened my thinking in many subtle ways. These were good times that kept me motivated, and I will miss them.

Finally, I am greatly indebted to my family, most importantly my wife Lydia, for her never-ending support and love, and my kids, Theodor and Aurelia, for their amazing energy and creativity. I share my time between my passions, research and family, but my love is fully yours. You are the joy and solid root of my life, this work would never have been finished without you!

Kaiserslautern, October 2016   *Sebastian Wild*

Curriculum Vitae

Contact

Name	Sebastian Wild
Date of Birth	11 April 1987
Email	`wild@cs.uni-kl.de`
Mail Address	Building 48, Room 660 Postfach 3049 67663 Kaiserslautern, Germany

Research

Oct 2012 – Jul 2016	Doctoral candidate and scientific employee Algorithms and Complexity Group of Prof. Dr. Markus Nebel Department of Computer Science University of Kaiserslautern
Mar 2009 – Sep 2012	Research Assistant in Prof. Dr. Markus Nebel's group

Awards and Scholarships

Jun 2013	*Preis des Freundeskreises der TU Kaiserslautern* Best Master's Thesis of the Department 2012
Sep 2012	Best Paper Award at the *European Symposium on Algorithms* 2012
Feb 2009 – Apr 2012	Scholarship of German National Academic Foundation
winter term 2009/10	Best Student Tutor Award of Fachschaft Informatik (Student Council) for lectures in applied computer science

Teaching

since Oct 2012	Teaching Assistance for lectures *Algorithm Engineering, Computational Biology 1, Computational Biology 2, Entwurf und Analyse von Algorithmen, Beweistechniken* and *Kombinatorische Algorithmen*
Oct 2008 – Feb 2011	Student Tutor for lectures: *Softwareentwicklung 1, Softwareentwicklung 3* and *Formale Grundlagen der Programmierung*

Education

Oct 2010 – Sep 2012	Master of Science in Computer Science (major algorithmics, minor math) at University of Kaiserslautern
Apr 2007 – Sep 2010	Bachelor of Science in Computer Science (major algorithmics, minor math) at University of Kaiserslautern
Apr 2006	Abitur Kurfürst-Ruprecht-Gymnasium Neustadt a. d. Weinstraße

Publications

The following peer-reviewed articles were published while working towards this dissertation. The articles in this list appear in reverse chronological order of (initial) submission, the order of publication dates differs. Preprints of all papers can be found on my website: `wwwagak.cs.uni-kl.de/home/staff/sebastian-wild`. As university websites might cease to exist, all articles that are not freely available from the original publishers are also deposited in an open-access archive server for perpetual availability.

[137]

▶ *Analysis of Pivot Sampling in Dual-Pivot Quicksort*
Markus E. Nebel, Sebastian Wild and Conrado Martínez,
Algorithmica 75, 4, pp 632-683 (August 2016)

[117]

▶ *Analysis of Branch Misses in Quicksort*
Conrado Martínez, Markus E. Nebel and Sebastian Wild,
Meeting on Analytic Algorithmics and Combinatorics (ANALCO15)
in Sedgewick R., Ward M.D. (eds.) ANALCO15, SIAM, pp 114–128

[136]

▶ *Pivot Sampling in Dual-Pivot Quicksort*
Markus E. Nebel and Sebastian Wild,
International Conference on Probabilistic, Combinatorial and Asymptotic Methods for the Analysis of Algorithms 2014 (AofA14),
In: Bousquet-Mélou M., Soria M. (eds.): DMTCS-HAL Proceedings Series, vol. BA, pp 325–338

[187]

▶ *Analysis of Quickselect under Yaroslavskiy's Dual-Pivoting Algorithm*
Sebastian Wild, Markus E. Nebel and Hosam Mahmoud,
Algorithmica 74, 1, pp 485-506 (January 2016)

[186]

▶ *Average Case and Distributional Analysis of Dual Pivot Quicksort*
Sebastian Wild, Markus E. Nebel and Ralph Neininger,
ACM Transactions on Algorithms 11, 3, Article 22 (January 2015)

[185]

▶ *Engineering Java 7's Dual Pivot Quicksort Using MaLiJAn*
Sebastian Wild, Markus E. Nebel, Raphael Reitzig and Ulrich Laube,
SIAM Meeting on Algorithm Engineering and Experiments 2013 (ALENEX13)
in Sanders P., Zeh N. (eds.) ALENEX13, SIAM, pp 55–69

[184]

▶ *Average Case Analysis of Java 7's Dual Pivot Quicksort*
Sebastian Wild and Markus E. Nebel,
European Symposium on Algorithms 2012 (ESA12),
in Epstein L. and Ferragina P. (eds.): ESA 2012, LNCS 7501, Springer, 2012, pp 825–836.
The article won one of two Best Paper Awards.

0   Appetizer

A SILENT REVOLUTION has been taking place in sorting: within the last decade, *all* sorting methods in Oracle's widely used Java runtime library have been rewritten entirely; other libraries are likely to follow. Always concerned about breaking existing client programs, maintainers of programming libraries are very conservative in adopting new trends; so how come two youngsters among the sorting algorithms, dual-pivot Quicksort and Timsort, have taken over from the old guard so quickly?

Sorting. Sorting is fundamental to computer science in several respects. Sorting algorithms are widely used to demonstrate techniques and concepts, both in a technical and an educational sense. The problem is easy to state,

> rearrange a list of elements $A[1], \ldots, A[n]$ from a totally ordered universe, so that $A[1] \leqslant \cdots \leqslant A[n]$,

yet is rich enough to allow for many different solutions with different qualities. Writing a sorting method is easy enough to be one of the first programming exercises, yet devising a robust, efficient library implementation still is a challenging task for experts.

Sorting is also fundamental in the sense that it is used as a subroutine in many applications and more sophisticated algorithms: we sort lists to facilitate searching, both for humans and computers; we use sorting to solve the *togetherness problem,* bringing equal items of one category together; various algorithms rely on sorted inputs to simplify their invariants and speed up further processing. The extensive use has been fostered by the ubiquitous availability of good library sorting methods.

Despite the large number of sorting algorithms that most algorithms textbooks discuss, library implementations use only very few of them: unless a stable sort is required, in which case Mergesort variants, including Timsort, are preferred, the vast majority of sorting methods is based on *Quicksort*.

The purpose of this work is to deepen our understanding of what makes this sorting method so efficient, and to guide the development of future library implementations.

Quicksort. In its simplest form Quicksort works as follows. We select an arbitrary element to act as *pivot*. The remaining elements are split into two groups: those smaller than the pivot go to the left, the others to the right. This step is called *partitioning*. After partitioning, we can put the pivot element between the two groups; this is its correct position in the final sorted output. The two segments left and right of the pivot are sorted by repeating this procedure, until segments contain at most one element.

This strategy can be realized on a computer as a recursive procedure and is particularly efficient because the part of the code that is executed most often is extremely short and fast. Implementing Quicksort is also simple in principle, but the devil is in the details when it comes to maximum efficiency and robustness against degenerate cases.

Multiway Quicksort.   It has long been thought that using more than one pivot, i.e., directly splitting elements into more than two groups, would not make Quicksort more efficient. This is true if we count how many comparisons between elements we use. Nevertheless does Oracle's Java runtime library nowadays contain a dual-pivot Quicksort that clearly outperforms single-pivot Quicksort, which raises the following questions:

> *What makes Java's dual-pivot Quicksort fast?*
>
> *What can be gained from multiway partitioning in general?*

These are the driving questions behind this thesis. Our method is the mathematical analysis of algorithms; we derive mathematical statements in well-defined models of reality. By choosing models that are independent of specific hardware, but still reflect common behavior of modern computers, we derive lasting truths about Quicksort that help settling the above questions.

1 Introduction

Contents

SORTING is a very practical task and several sorting algorithms had long been known and used when the first computers were built [103]. Not so Quicksort. Its recursive nature makes it inconvenient to execute Quicksort physically by hand. Quicksort was only discovered in the early 1960s and first published by Hoare [79, 82]; with its fifty-odd years, it is the youngster among the classic sorting methods—and just about the right age for a midlife crisis.

1.1 History

Quicksort's youth was turbulent. A humongous collection of potential improvements to the basic algorithm have been proposed and tested [162]. A few turned out very successful and have found their way into basically all productive-use implementations; most notably choosing pivots from a small sample, e.g., the median-of-three strategy, and using a special purpose method for small subproblems. Many others were found to be detrimental to overall performance, both in experiments and by mathematical analysis. After final changes to Quicksort in the 1990s, almost all programming libraries used almost identical versions of the algorithm: classic Quicksort had reached calm waters. Or so it seemed.

One of the variations of Quicksort that used to be deemed not helpful is *multiway partitioning*: splitting the array into more than two parts at once, using several pivot elements. Sedgewick [162], Hennequin [77] and Tan [173] analyzed this idea; they all discarded it on the basis of inferior comparison and swap counts. Multiway Quicksort was put in the dustbin of history.

The Dual-Pivot Era.   It was to lie there for almost two decades, until Vladimir Yaroslavskiy, software developer at Sun Microsystems at that time, experimented with a dual-pivot Quicksort variant. Together with Jon Bentley and Joshua Bloch, he developed a Java version that was 10 % faster in practice than the state-of-the-art implementation of classic Quicksort used in the Java runtime library at that time. This finding was so surprising that fellow developers were initially reluctant to believe it, but the *Yaroslavskiy-Bentley-Bloch (YBB) algorithm* was deployed to millions of devices with the release of Java 7 in 2011, which offers it as the default sorting method for primitive-type arrays.

And Besides . . .   I first got to know about the advent of dual-pivot Quicksort from an article on Java 7 in the German computer magazine *c't* [110]. It contains a small paragraph entitled „Und außerdem . . . " ("And besides . . . ") which states that, oh, by the way, Oracle replaced the Quicksort implementation with a new dual-pivot Quicksort that seems to run twice as fast on many inputs. Here is the original paragraph of the mentioned German article:

„Für die Sortierung numerischer Arrays, für die bisher eine optimierte Quicksort-Variante benutzt wurde, kommt nun der Dual-Pivot-Quicksort-Algorithmus von Vladimir Yaroslavskiy zum Einsatz, der in der Regel ungefähr doppelt so schnell ist wie der alte Algorithmus. Auch für den Spezialfall der stabilen Sortierung von Object-Arrays und Collections, für den bisher einfach Mergesort

> *benutzt wurde, gibt es einen neuen, schnelleren Algorithmus namens TimSort, der seine Stärken insbesondere dann ausspielt, wenn Teile der Eingabedaten bereits vorsortiert sind."* (Lau [110], p. 177)
>
> Remarkably, this news did *not* create a stir among software developers. It might be taken as sign of a good programming library that users do not have to be interested in its implementation. For an algorithms researcher, its success is nothing less than a sensation.

Apart from its superior performance in running time studies, little was known about YBB Quicksort at the time of its deployment in Java 7. How could this substantial improvement to the well-studied Quicksort algorithm have escaped the eyes of generations of researchers? Why had YBB Quicksort not been discovered much earlier?

I devoted my master's thesis [182] to a classical average-case analysis of basic variants of dual-pivot Quicksort. The results seemed conclusive: YBB Quicksort needs *5 % less comparisons* in the asymptotic average than classic single-pivot Quicksort, and also less than the other dual-pivot partitioning algorithms studied earlier. The savings result from subtle asymmetries in YBB partitioning. This effect might have been overlooked in the past, so that using two pivots was discarded because the right partitioning method had not yet been found; the contribution of Yaroslavskiy, Bentley and Bloch was to finally devise such a method. This makes a nice, coherent story, but the true reasons for the success of YBB Quicksort are not that simple.

Results in the second classical cost measure for sorting, the number of element *swaps*, clearly favor classic Quicksort: YBB Quicksort needs over *one and a half times* the number of swaps of classic Quicksort. Similar results hold for the number of primitive instructions of typical low-level implementations of the algorithms.

But if the YBB Quicksort actually uses more instructions, how come it is still faster in practice? And why was this discrepancy between theory and practice not noticed earlier? In my master's thesis, I could not settle these questions.

1.2 Little Glossary of Quicksort Terms

At this point, a few remarks are in order about the meaning of certain phrases, some of which we already used above. Many concepts remain vague here; we put the relevant ones in more concrete terms later.

Partitioning is the process of splitting a set of elements into the equivalence **classes** w.r.t. their relation to the pivot element(s). In a linear arrangement of the elements, all elements of one class form a **segment**. How we obtain this rearrangement procedurally is left unspecified for now.

Quicksort means all methods that follow the abstract idea to sort by repeatedly partitioning a sublist around pivot elements. It is unspecified still how partitioning is achieved, how many pivots are used, how these are chosen, in what order sublists are processed, and how the bookkeeping for the latter is done.

Pivot Sampling is the process of selecting pivot values from a sample of elements of the input. We may use any selection scheme that uses only the relative ranking of the sample elements; most common choices pick pivots as specific order statistics of the sample. A well-known example is the **median-of-three** scheme.

Single-pivot / dual-pivot / four-way / multiway Quicksort are all Quicksort variants with the indicated number of pivots or segments per partitioning step. How partitioning is achieved and how pivots are selected is unspecified.

> **Multiway vs. Multi-pivot.** Even though k-pivot Quicksort is a coined term in the Quicksort literature, I will mainly use *s-way Quicksort* in this work, since the number of segments is a much more convenient parameter than the number of pivots for the notation introduced later. The reader might moreover appreciate the similarity between multiway Quicksort and multiway Mergesort, and the correspondence of s-way Quicksort to s-ary search trees.
>
> I am not the first researcher to speak of *multiway Quicksort*; Flajolet [61] used the same term in a 2001 editorial.

Classic Quicksort is a single-pivot Quicksort with the crossing-pointer partitioning method of Sedgewick and Hoare as given in Algorithm 2. Classic Quicksort may or may not be combined with pivot sampling.

YBB Quicksort is a dual-pivot Quicksort with the three-way partitioning method of Yaroslavskiy, Bentley and Bloch **(YBB partitioning)** as given in Algorithm 4. The pivot-sampling strategy is left unspecified.

Java 7's dual-pivot Quicksort (Java 7 Quicksort) means the concrete code used for `Array.sort(int[])` in version 7 (b147) of Oracle's Java runtime library. It is an implementation of YBB Quicksort, but adds further optimizations: pivots are chosen as tertiles of five elements, sublists with less than 47 elements are sorted by Insertionsort, inputs consisting of at most 67 runs (correctly ordered subranges) are sorted with a Mergesort variant instead of Quicksort, and equal pivots are treated specially, to name the most important ones.

> **Rectification of Names.** Vladimir Yaroslavskiy re-initiated research on Quicksort with two pivots, and I concluded from the publicly available documents[a] that he was also the main driving force in its development, and hence referred to the partitioning method simply as *Yaroslavskiy's algorithm* in my previous works. Only recently have I learned from personal communication that the new dual-pivot Quicksort algorithm should rightfully be attributed to the trio of Vladimir Yaroslavskiy, Jon Bentley and Joshua Bloch, since all were involved in the development of the algorithm very early on. This is also documented in the Javadoc of the OpenJDK sources.[b]

In creative projects, a team often develops ideas that none of its members would have had alone, and separating contributions is hardly possible. By no means was I trying to do so in using the name *Yaroslavskiy's algorithm,* and I wish to replace it by *Yaroslavskiy-Bentley-Bloch (YBB) Quicksort.*

One could have used Java 7's (or JDK/JRE 7's) dual-pivot Quicksort for the algorithmic principle, as well, but I prefer to give credit to the creators of the algorithm instead of emphasizing the algorithmically irrelevant fact that it was first implemented in Java. It has been demonstrated independently by several authors that YBB Quicksort performs just as well if implemented in C/C++ [182, 105, 9], and certainly other programming languages will follow.

---

[a] See in particular the discussions on the OpenJDK mailing list *core-libs-dev,* archived online:
`http://mail.openjdk.java.net/pipermail/core-libs-dev/2009-September/002630.html`.

[b] In class `java.util.DualPivotQuicksort`, see, e.g., `http://grepcode.com/file/repository.`
`grepcode.com/java/root/jdk/openjdk/7-b147/java/util/DualPivotQuicksort.java`.

1.3 Recent Developments

Together with my advisor Markus Nebel, I continued the study of YBB Quicksort. It turns out that even for comparisons, the lead of YBB Quicksort evaporates if we take into consideration how pivots are selected in practice (ninther for classic Quicksort, tertiles-of-five for dual-pivot Quicksort): YBB Quicksort actually needs *more* comparisons [136, 137].

After I presented the results of my master's thesis at the *European Symposium on Algorithms (ESA) 2012* [184], the intriguing questions caught the interest of other researchers. One group from Ilmenau, Germany, around Martin Aumüller and Martin Dietzfelbinger, has addressed the question of how many comparisons can be saved with *any* dual-pivot partitioning method [8].

A Plausible Answer. Another group from Waterloo, Canada, around Alejandro López-Ortiz and Ian Munro, first suggested a plausible explanation for the success of dual-pivot Quicksort. They argue that what makes YBB faster is that it incurs *fewer cache misses,* see [105]: Kushagra et al. determine *20 % savings* over classic Quicksort in the asymptotic average for the basic versions of the algorithms. Taking pivot sampling into account, the savings drop to something slightly below 10 %, but this is still a significant improvement over classic Quicksort [137]. It even matches the observed speedup in running times.

I would like to see the term *cache misses* being used with caution, as its meaning is rather narrow and tied to a specific hardware event. But I am confident that Kushagra et al. are right: *the influence of the memory hierarchy makes the difference for dual-pivot Quicksort.* The reason is a long-lasting trend in computer hardware design that has been referred to, somewhat dramatically, as the "memory wall" — and was predicted 20 years ago [189, 125].

1.4 The Memory Wall

Since the earliest electronic computers in the middle of the 20th century, processor manufacturing techniques have improved dramatically. *Moore's law* has become folklore, predicting a doubling of the number of transistors in integrated circuits roughly every two years. Net CPU speed increased at a similar rate, and still does, partly because more transistors can be used, partly because transistors become more efficient individually, and partly because more sophisticated processor architectures have been invented. Memory capacity has increased at a similar rate.

Memory Bandwidth.   Ample memory to hold data and ample computing power to process it are both in vain if computation has to wait for data to arrive. Backus [12] called this the *von-Neumann bottleneck,* and there is considerable evidence that this bottleneck is tightening.

Based on the extensive data for the STREAM benchmark [119, 118], CPU speed has increased with an average annual growth rate of 46 % over the last 25 years, whereas *memory bandwidth*, the net amount of data transferable between RAM and CPU in a given amount of time, has increased by only 37 % per year in the same period. One should not be too strict about the exact numbers since they are averages over different architectures and measurements are not evenly distributed over time. Still, processor speed has been growing considerably faster than memory bandwidth for a long time. Figure 1 shows how *machine balance,* the ratio of speed over bandwidth, has developed over time for the STREAM data.

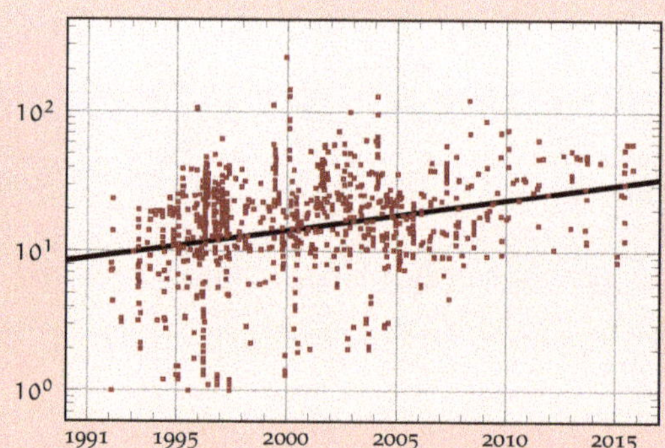

Figure 1: Development of *machine balance*, the ratio of CPU speed over memory bandwidth, in the last 25 years. Each point shows one reported result of the STREAM benchmark. Dates are given on the x-axis and machine balance (peak MFLOPS divided by bandwidth in MW/s in the "triad" benchmark) on the logarithmic y-axis. The fat line shows the linear regression (on log-scale).

Data. McCalpin [119, 118] describes the STREAM benchmark itself. The machine-balance data is taken from `www.cs.virginia.edu/stream/by_date/Balance.html`, accessed on 2015-12-15. Entries from 1991, when STREAM was first released, have been removed. The reported dates are the dates of submission to the STREAM mailing list, not the years of construction of the machines. These initial entries could thus skew the picture. Three entries with machines balance larger than 500 were treated as outliers. They had a measured bandwidth of 0.0, so suitable accuracy cannot be guaranteed there, so they have likewise been removed.

A significant increase in *imbalance* is undeniable. Note that Figure 1 is on a logarithmic scale, so the difference between CPU and memory transfer speed grows *exponentially*. The linear regression indicates a little over 5 % annual increase in imbalance. Wulf and McKee [189] warned in 1995 that if this trend continues like this, at some point in the future any further improvements of CPUs will be futile: the processor is waiting for data *all* the time; we hit a "memory wall". It is debatable if and when this extreme will be reached [57, 125], and consequences certainly depend on the application. In fact, net bandwidth has grown much faster than predicted in the mid 1990s [189], but it still does not keep pace with CPU speed improvements. We bought some time.

Implications for Sorting.   Wall or no wall—the relative costs of memory accesses have increased significantly over the last two decades: in 1993, when Bentley and McIlroy designed the gold standard of classic Quicksort implementations [20], the average machine balance was still below ten; 20 years later, their implementation has to compete with dual-pivot Quicksort on machines with balance around 30. *The model of computation has changed.*

In this respect it is quite plausible why the improvement of dual-pivot Quicksort went unnoticed for so many years: it was not there! In the computational model of their time, the researchers correctly concluded that the use of several pivots does not pay off. What may now be the most efficient way to sort, was really no good when the aforementioned studies on dual-pivot Quicksort were conducted. But computers have changed since then, and so should our algorithms: nowadays it pays off to save memory transfers, even at the cost of (slightly) increased effort inside the CPU.

Scanned Elements: A Model for Bandwidth.   If we compare algorithms for today's machines with the yardsticks of yesterday, our conclusions will not be accurate. We should not expect to find YBB Quicksort outperform classic Quicksort, if we measure efficiency by comparison and swap counts only. We have to take bandwidth consumption into account. We need a simple abstract model for that, one that is independent of specific machines and suitable for the mathematical analysis of algorithms.

Scanned elements can serve this purpose for Quicksort [137]. Scanned elements are closely related to cache misses for an idealized cache and roughly proportional to the amount of memory transferred on a typical machine, but defined abstractly as the number of steps of scanning indices. We discuss this model in depth later.

1.5 Multiway Quicksort

From the observations discussed above, a natural question arises: if dual-pivot Quicksort is faster nowadays because of a better balance of CPU costs and memory bandwidth demands, are more pivots even better?

As mentioned above, the idea of s-way Quicksort, i.e., partitioning the input into s segments at once (using $s - 1$ pivots), is not novel at all. Hennequin [77] and Tan [173] considered such Quicksort variants more than 20 years ago, but their comparison-focused analysis showed no compelling advantages of using $s > 2$.

Kushagra et al. [105] revived that question recently. They proposed a three-pivot Quicksort implementation that indeed uses even less memory transfers than YBB Quicksort and performed very well in preliminary running-time studies.

This shows that multiway partitioning is practical nowadays, but it is merely a start. Do improvements continue if we increase s further? What are good multiway partitioning algorithms? Should we favor asymmetric partitioning schemes, such as in YBB Quicksort, over symmetric procedures? How does multiway partitioning interact with tried-and-tested optimizations of classic Quicksort? The game is afoot—again.

1.6 Aim and Scope of this Dissertation

This work is concerned with *practical* variants of Quicksort, i.e., methods that could readily be implemented in a low-level procedural language, and perform reasonably well on realistic input sizes. A handful of such Quicksort versions are known for binary partitioning, and many options are conceivable for multiway Quicksort. Moreover, there are strategies that can be combined orthogonally with any such partitioning method: choosing better pivots by sampling, truncating recursion and using a special-purpose sort for small subproblems, precautions against rare bad cases, and special handling of equal keys, to name the most important ones. Among all possible combinations, which are the most efficient ones? What is it that makes them efficient? And how sensitive is efficiency to (small) changes of these parameters?

Only analytically can we explore this vast design space in its generality. In the work at hand, I thus approach answers to these questions by means of *mathematical* analysis of algorithms as opposed to doing running time studies. We will derive *provably correct* statements about the performance of Quicksort. As traditionally done in the field, the results will be of an asymptotic kind, i.e., about the limiting behavior for large input sizes. I do this to keep both calculations and the interpretation of results tractable.

We confine our statements to a well-defined, theoretical model of computation and consider corresponding measures of cost. For analyzing memory-bandwidth costs in Quicksort, we will use the number of scanned elements.

We will analyze a parametric template algorithm: The partitioning step divides the array into s parts and the $s - 1$ pivots are chosen as order statistics from a sample of k elements of the input. Some additional degrees of freedom concern how the rearrangement of elements itself is done. The only fixed part is that partitioning should proceed in *one pass* over the array and *in place*, i.e., using only a constant amount of additional working memory.

This covers basically all practically relevant partitioning algorithms: Hoare's original crossing-pointers scheme [82], later revised by Sedgewick [161], Lomuto's partitioning [18], the dual-pivot method studied in Sedgewick's Ph.D. thesis [162], YBB Quicksort [191, 184] and the recently proposed Waterloo four-way Quicksort [105]. In this work, we unify the analyses of these algorithms, including the option to choose pivots from a sample, and extend them to the new cost measure of scanned elements. This allows us to reason analytically about promising candidates for a *21st century Quicksort* which will have to excel both in terms of used CPU cycles as well as required memory transfers.

Most statements concern the random-permutation model, i.e., all permutations of input elements are equally likely, and elements are distinct. But we also go beyond that; we consider the practically relevant situation of *duplicate keys* in the input. An early version of the Unix system sort gained notoriety for its dramatic failure in the presence of duplicates: it had quadratic running time on binary inputs [20]. Under a natural random model for inputs with many equal keys, we will analyze how much can be gained by collecting elements equal to pivots during partitioning. Our analysis is the first ever for generalized Quicksort with equal keys, and we show that the same relative speedup is achieved with pivot sampling and multiway partitioning as for the random-permutation case.

For a qualification work, which is what this dissertation is to be after all, it should be clarified what my original contributions are. I extracted the algorithmic core of YBB Quicksort from the original Java code, and provided the first average-case analysis of the basic YBB Quicksort without pivot sampling and Insertionsort cutoff in my master's thesis. New contributions in this dissertation are

1. the introduction of *generic one-pass partitioning* as a parametric algorithm template generalizing all known practical partitioning methods (Chapter 4),

2. the analysis of generic one-pass partitioning with pivot sampling under various cost measures (Chapter 5), unifying previous analyses in the common framework of *element-wise charging schemes*,

3. the precise analysis of branch misses,

4. the systematic computation of expectations involving Dirichlet distributed random variables arising in the analysis of partitioning using *Dirichlet calculus* (Chapter 2),

5. the distinction between *scanned elements* and cache misses (Chapter 3), which allows us to separate errors from asymptotic approximations from inaccuracies of the cost model,

6. the resolute use of distributional formulations for recurrences and partitioning costs throughout this work and

7. the direct extraction of asymptotic approximations of expected costs from the distributional recurrence with the *distributional master theorem (DMT)* (Chapter 6), a version of Roura's continuous master theorem rephrased in distributional terms;

8. the first analysis of Quicksort with pivot sampling and multiway partitioning on inputs with equal keys (Chapter 8), and

9. a comprehensive discussion of the influence of the parameters of generic one-pass partitioning on the performance of Quicksort (Chapter 7).

I have always found collaborative research efforts most enjoyable and rewarding on many levels, and some results are genuine group efforts for which I cannot claim sole authorship: **1** Generic one-pass partitioning was inspired by discussions with Martin Aumüller and Timo Bingmann at the Dagstuhl seminar 14091; Martin Aumüller worked independently and concurrently on a similar partitioning scheme afterwards. **3** The analysis of branch misses was done together with Conrado Martínez and Markus Nebel. **5** The idea to have a clean cost measure to approximate cache misses was mine, but the final definition and name was formed in extensive discussions with Conrado Martínez and Markus Nebel. **6** Discussions with Hosam Mahmoud and Ralph Neininger and the elegance of their work lead to my fondness for distributional formulations. Without their guidance during our cooperative work on the distributional analysis of YBB Quicksort and Quickselect, I would not have been courageous enough to extensively use distributional recurrences for my work. **8** The work on equal keys originated in a discussion with Conrado Martínez, Markus Nebel, Martin Aumüller and Martin Dietzfelbinger. First attempts to obtain $\mathbb{E}[A_q]$ were a joint effort with Conrado Martínez, which laid the ground for the solution now presented in this work. **9** The discussion chapter includes many insights that emerged while exchanging thoughts with numerous researchers, most notably Conrado Martínez, Markus Nebel and Martin Aumüller. Instead of tracing all these ideas to their origins, I briefly list what is solely my contribution in that chapter: the optimality criterion for sampling vectors in the case of finite-size samples, the heuristic rule for finding good sampling vectors, the optimality criteria for comparison trees based on the Hu-Tucker algorithm, the considerations regarding the benefit of two comparison trees, and the discovery of the *jellyfish paradox*.

◆   ◆   ◆

Outline. In the remainder of this first chapter we give a rather comprehensive literature overview on the analysis of Quicksort. In Chapter 2, I introduce all mathematical tools used in the analysis. Most techniques and results are well-known, but I made an effort to collect them all in consistent notation and convey at least the intuition behind the results; where helpful, I included detailed proofs.

In Chapter 3, we discuss the model assumptions for the analysis: what are the costs of an execution, and how are random inputs for the average-case analysis drawn. I then present in Chapter 4 my parametric template algorithm for multiway Quicksort, *generic one-pass partitioning*. The main part of this work then is the analysis of this generic algorithm when pivots are chosen from a sample. This is done in two steps. First, we analyze a single partitioning step in Chapter 5. Then we set up and solve a recurrence equation for overall costs based on that in Chapter 6.

We obtain the expected costs of Quicksort under generic one-pass partitioning symbolically in the parameters of the algorithm. In Chapter 7, we discuss in detail how to choose the various parameters wisely.

The main analysis assumes the random-permutation model. In Chapter 8, we leave this familiar environment and consider inputs with equal keys. We describe Quicksort versions that take advantage of such inputs, and we give the first ever analysis of Quicksort on equal keys with pivot sampling and multiway partitioning. Chapter 9 gives concrete hints for finding sensible Quicksort variants, and lists directions for future research.

In the appendix, you find a comprehensive index of notations and details on bibliographic references.

1.7 Related Work

Some work directly related to YBB Quicksort and the latest twists of Quicksort history have already been mentioned in the introduction above. This work has been influenced by many other papers on Quicksort and related topics. We summarize the most important ones in this section, and how they interface with our work. Likewise, we attempt to put the present work in a wider context. Much more is known about Quicksort than can be covered in a sensibly sized section; the collection has to remain selective. The present selection puts a clear emphasis on the mathematical analysis of Quicksort. We mostly ignore literature on empirical results on Quicksort and we do not discuss parallel versions, implementations on specific hardware or specialized variants for certain data types like strings.

1.7.1 Towards Classic Quicksort

The first published version of Quicksort is due to Hoare [80] and appeared in the algorithms columns of the *Journal of the ACM* in 1961. Hoare also first described the average-case analysis of the number of comparisons in Quicksort, and anticipated the most relevant optimizations of the basic algorithm in his 1962 journal article [82]; however, he did not foresee a reason to partition around *several* pivot elements (or bounds, as he calls them) at once. In an independent and concurrent work, Hibbard [78] discussed binary search trees under the random permutation model. He was the first to note the close correspondence between them and Quicksort; he solved essentially the same recurrence equation when analyzing the external path length of binary search trees.

Hoare suggested to choose the median of a small sample as pivot to improve performance. Singleton [170] devised a careful implementation in 1969 that puts this into practice. It uses the median of three elements, namely the first, the last and the middle element of the input.

Hoare's partitioning method works by advancing two pointers *outside-in;* they start at opposite ends of the array and move towards each other until they have met—as Knuth puts it, this is *"burning the candle at both ends"* ([103], p. 114). Singleton was the first to note that stopping pointers on elements equal to the pivot prevents quadratic behavior on inputs with many equal keys.

Bentley [17] proposed a simpler, *one-way* partitioning method in 1984; Bing-Chao and Knuth [24] described essentially the same method two years later. They also analyzed it in detail. Bentley attributes the method to Nico Lomuto, and it is thus referred to as *Lomuto partitioning*. In direct competition, Hoare's crossing pointer method is slightly faster than Lomuto partitioning, and thus remained the method of choice.

The details of how to implement Hoare's crossing pointer scheme remained subject of discussions, until Robert Sedgewick came up with an implementation that unites the advantages of all previous versions, see Knuth's digression on Quicksort (pp 287–289) in his 1974 article [101] on structured programming. We refer to Sedgewick's code as Sedgewick-Hoare partitioning, and it is this method that we have in mind when we speak of *classic Quicksort*, see Algorithm 2 in this work.

1.7.2 Sedgewick's Work

Sedgewick devoted his Ph.D. thesis [158], finished in 1975, to the meticulous analysis of some ten Quicksort variants. A reprint of Sedgewick's thesis [162] appeared five years later; when giving page numbers etc. in the following, I always refer to the 1980 publication. Sedgewick's thesis is probably the most comprehensive source on Quicksort to this day, in particular in terms of techniques for its mathematical analysis. We sum up Sedgewick's contributions in the following.

Sedgewick derives the precise expected costs of his Quicksort variants, including the variations

- ▶ to truncate recursion and switch to Insertionsort, either directly on each small sub-problem, or in one pass over the whole array at the very end,

- ▶ a generic scheme to select the pivot from a fixed-size sample,

- ▶ and to unroll inner loops of the partitioning method.

Moreover, he studies in detail the Samplesort algorithm of Frazer and McKellar [66] and an adaptive sampling strategy by van Emden [55] which tries to postpone the choice for a pivot as long as possible.

In passing, Sedgewick extends the mathematical toolbox for the analysis of algorithms. Even though not all of the following tools are his sole invention, it is his contribution to give a detailed account on how to apply them to Quicksort.

- ▶ Sedgewick describes the solution of the generalized Quicksort recurrence, i.e., with the pivot chosen from a sample. He uses the differential-operator method for Euler differential equations; a sketch of this method is also given in the first edition of *The Art of Computer Programming* [100] from 1973, see solutions to Exercise 5.2.2–29.

- ▶ He also covers the computation of variances from a recurrence for the probability generating function of the complete distribution.

Sedgewick proposed and discussed a dual-pivot Quicksort: Program 5.1 in [162]. To my knowledge this is the first ever published implementation of multiway Quicksort, and probably the most *under*appreciated contribution of Sedgewick's work. Sedgewick pro-moted dual-pivot partitioning mainly as an efficient method to deal with many duplicate

keys; but when he determined the swap cost of his method and found that it needs *140 %
more swaps* than single-pivot Quicksort, he deemed it unworthy of further study.

Sedgewick presented parts of his thesis, in more condensed and digested form, in two journal articles: one focusing on analysis [159] and another dealing with implementation issues [161]. A third article [160] adds a detailed treatment of inputs with equal keys; we discuss it in detail in Section 1.7.9.

1.7.3 Practical Tweaks in the Nineties

Bentley and McIlroy [20] made noteworthy progress on the practical side. Besides setting a good example for how to design and evaluate running-time studies, they devised a practical implementation of *fat-pivot partitioning*, a method that divides the array into three segments: elements strictly smaller than the pivot, elements strictly larger than the pivot, and elements *equal* to the pivot. At that time, many practical implementations exhibited quadratic behavior on inputs with many equal keys, although Sedgewick [162] recognized and discussed this problem in detail, and the method to avoid it by stopping pointers on equal elements had been known at least since the 1969 implementation of Singleton [170]. Removing elements equal to the pivot had been deemed too costly before, but the method of Bentley and McIlroy achieves this without excessive overhead in case there are no duplicates.

They also introduced *ninther* sampling, which picks the median of three elements, each of which is chosen independently as the median of three elements. It took ten years before Durand published the first rigorous mathematical analysis of Quicksort with ninther sampling [49].

Introsort. The combination of its ubiquitous use and its quadratic worst-case make Quicksort a possible target of denial-of-service attacks by making the server sort a worst-case input. McIlroy describes an elegant method to compute such an adversarial input for *any* Quicksort variant [124].

Shuffling inputs before they are sorted protects against this attack; another possibility is to make Quicksort *self-monitoring*. With an additional parameter that we decrement in each recursive call, we can check before partitioning if we are already further down in the recursion tree than we should ever get in a usual case, e.g., at depth more than $2\,\mathrm{ld}(n)$, and if so, resort to a method with linearithmic worst-case guarantee before things get out of hand. The idea for this *introspective sort* is due to Musser [133] and has been widely adopted in practice; interestingly enough, not in the Java library.

1.7.4 Off-the-Shelf Theorems for Solving Recurrences

Classical *master theorems*, as presented, e.g., by Cormen et al. [35] can help to analyze divide-and-conquer algorithms that divide a problem into a fixed number of equal-sized parts whose size is a *fixed* fraction of the overall problem size. For Quicksort and similar algorithms, subproblem sizes are *not* fixed fractions. Roura [154, 153] derived two generalized versions of the master theorem which he calls the *discrete* master theorem and the *continuous* master theorem (CMT). The former applies to algorithms that split a problem into a fixed number of subproblems with fixed relative sizes, but not all subproblems need to be of the same size. The latter covers algorithms like Quicksort that produce a fixed number of subproblems, whose relative subproblem sizes are *random variables* whose distribution is well approximated by a fixed continuous distribution.

An important contribution of Roura's is the precise error analysis when the above assumptions hold only in the limit for large n. This makes the theorems widely applicable. In many cases, Roura's improved master theorems yield the leading-term coefficient of the solution instead of only an order-of-growth statement. Martínez and Roura [116] exemplify the use of the CMT in a detailed study of different sampling strategies for Quicksort and Quickselect. We discuss the CMT in detail in Section 2.6.

In a similar vein, Chern et al. [30] derive a general solution for recurrences that correspond to a Cauchy-Euler differential equation for the generating function of the sequences. The costs in Quicksort are again the prime example for such a sequence. The set of recurrences to which their solution applies is smaller than for Roura's theorems, but Chern et al. can give more precise solutions, in particular if the toll function is relatively small. For such cases, the overall solution is dominated by contributions of initial values, which Roura's theorems ignore completely. Their statement is inherently limited to an order of growth in such cases. In contrast, Chern et al. explicitly include initial conditions.

Recurrences like the one for costs in Quicksort can be seen as a *transformation:* given a sequence of toll costs, e.g., the cost of one partitioning step in Quicksort, the recurrence transforms this into the sequence of total costs. In fact, for costs of divide-and-conquer algorithms, this transformation is a *linear* operator. Fill et al. [60] adopt this view and transfer it to the realm of generating functions: the recurrence induces a transformation that turns the generating function of the toll sequence into the generating function of total costs. For Quicksort-type recurrences, this transformation involves integration and differentiation to solve the Cauchy-Euler differential equation discussed by Chern et al. [30]. Fill et al. [60] then show that these operations, and also the Hadamard product, can be applied to a *singular expansion* of the generating function, instead of the function itself, and then yield a corresponding singular expansion of the generating function for the total cost. From the latter, one can then extract an asymptotic expansion of the coefficients by classical singularity analysis [62].

1.7.5 Analysis of Pivot Sampling

In his 1962 article on Quicksort, Hoare already suggested to choose the pivot as *"the median of a small random sample of the items in the segment. [. . .] It is very difficult to estimate the savings which would be achieved by this"* ([82], p. 12). It took almost a decade to approach these savings analytically; van Emden [55] gave the first derivation of the leading term of costs of median-of-$(2t + 1)$ sampling strategy in 1970. He does not rigorously address error terms in this article, though.

Sedgewick [159] solved the recurrence explicitly for the median-of-three case and gave an asymptotic approximation for the general case. He used generating-function techniques, namely the operator method to solve the Cauchy-Euler differential equation for the generating function of costs.

In his Ph.D. thesis [162], Sedgewick also considered the more general case that we pick the Rth smallest element from a sample of k elements, where R is randomly chosen, as well, according to a given distribution. For his MIX implementation of Quicksort the optimal choice among all distributions for R is to *deterministically* select the median, i.e., fix $R = \lfloor k/2 \rfloor - 1$.

Hennequin [77] extends Sedgewick's techniques to multiway Quicksort: he analyzes the generic model that we pick random order statistics from a sample, and shows that it is optimal w.r.t. comparisons for his multiway Quicksort to deterministically pick pivots as equidistant quantiles.

The widely used *ninther* a.k.a. *pseudo-median-of-nine* proposed by Bentley and McIlroy [20] can be seen as a special case of selecting a randomly chosen rank from a sample of nine elements; but it was only in 2000 that Durand first computed the resulting cost explicitly in her *mémoire de DEA* [48] (master's thesis). She presented the result in an English article [49] that was published in 2003.

Chern et al. further extended the generating-function based analysis and derived a general theorem to solve recurrences arising, e.g., in the analysis of pivot sampling, in a journal article [30] from 2002; we already discussed their work in Section 1.7.4. They apply their theorem to the generalized *remedian* strategy: the remedian of order zero is simply one random element, the remedian of order $t + 1$ is the median of three elements, each of which is a remedian of order t. The cases $t = 0$, $t = 1$ and $t = 2$ thus correspond to a random pivot, median-of-three resp. ninther sampling. Chern et al. do not give closed forms for expected costs, but they show that their framework applies, so coefficients can in principle be given at least for any fixed t. Similarly, Chern et al. briefly discuss alternative pivot-selection strategies, e.g., using the maximum of a number of minima, each chosen from a sample.

Chern and Hwang [29] addressed a related question: what happens if we do not use median-of-three pivots in all partitioning steps, but only for the first k levels of the recursion, switching back to random pivots after that? They showed that the improvement is essentially linear in k until $k \approx \frac{12}{7} \ln(n)$; for larger k, costs are asymptotically the same as for median-of-three Quicksort. In a similar vein, they considered a hybrid strategy that does k levels of Quicksort partitioning before switching to Insertionsort, irrespective of the current subproblem size.

1.7.6 Quicksort and Search Trees

Hibbard noted the intimate relation between classic Quicksort and binary search trees in his article [78] on BSTs published in 1962; he had been working concurrently with Hoare who published his article on Quicksort in the same year, and he immediately saw the connection to Hoare's work: averaged over all permutations, the number of comparisons in Quicksort and the internal path length of a binary search tree are the same.

Fringe-Balanced Trees. The correspondence of Quicksort and BSTs is lost when we consider Quicksort with median-of-three pivot selection, but we can restore it with a modification of BSTs that is interesting in its own right: *fringe-balancing.*

In a fringe-balanced search tree, leaves have buffers that hold up to k elements. If a new element is to be inserted into a leaf, it is simply added to the buffer. If the buffer becomes full, the median of the k buffered elements is selected as key for a new internal node which takes the place of the leaf. Two new leaves with the smaller and larger elements from the overflown buffer are attached to the new internal node in the tree. This effectively enforces a local rebalancing of subtrees near the leaves, i.e., at the *fringe* of the tree.

> **One Idea, Five Names?** Fringe-balanced trees appear under various names in the literature; the idea seems to have been rediscovered several times. Walker and Wood [176] traced the origin of fringe-balanced trees to the 1965 dissertation of Bell [16]. They discussed them under the name k-*locally balanced BSTs* in 1976. Instead of an explicit leaf with a buffer, they use binary nodes and keep the k-node subtrees at the fringe balanced by rotations.
>
> Apparently independently, Greene developed fringe-balanced trees as we introduced them above in his Ph.D. thesis [74], finished in 1983. Greene calls them *diminished trees* and analyzes them in detail.
>
> Concurrently to Greene, Huang and Wong worked on two articles [88, 89] on search trees whose fringe subtrees must be complete BSTs; their *SR trees* are fringe-balanced with $k = 3$, which they generalized to *iR trees*, whose parameter i corresponds to k, the leaf buffer size. Like Walker and Wood [176], Huang and Wong enforce trees at the bottom to be balanced instead of introducing special leaf nodes.
>
> The name *fringe-balanced trees* derives from the term *fringe analysis* that Eisenbarth et al. coined in an article [52] from 1982. Fringe analysis approximates the evolution of the shape of a tree by only considering how often a fixed number of small subtrees occurs at the *fringe*, i.e., at the leaves, of a tree. One then studies how the multiplicities of these fringe subtrees change upon random insertions. Yao first used this idea in a 1978 article [190] to study the average number of nodes in 2–3 trees and B-trees; the earliest appearance of a fringe-analysis idea seems to be in the 1973 edition of Knuth's book *The Art of Computer Programming* [100] in Exercise 6.2.4–10 on a B-tree variant (it became Exercise 6.2.4–8 in the second edition [103]).
>
> Although initially invented to study balanced trees, fringe analysis is a perfect fit for the analysis of fringe-balanced trees; Poblete and Munro [145] did that in 1985. They used the term *fringe heuristic* to describe local rebalancing rules, but they did not use the term fringe-balanced tree. The first use of that term I could find was in a paper by Devroye [39] from 1993 with the title "On the expected height of fringe-balanced trees"; interestingly Devroye did *not* use the term fringe-balanced anywhere in the text of the article. In more recent literature, the name fringe-balanced (binary search) trees has become widely accepted, see, e.g., Mahmoud [114] and Drmota [47].

I think *fringe-balanced* aptly describes the idea underlying these trees, and I will use this term throughout this work. Fringe-balancing has the same effect on the internal path length of a search tree as median-of-k pivot selection has on the comparison count of Quicksort, see, e.g., Hennequin [77] and Section 8.7 of this work.

It is not per se easier to analyze path lengths of search trees than comparisons in Quicksort, but some reasoning is more comfortable in one world, and some tricks work only in the other world; see, e.g., the surprisingly simple derivation of the path length for BSTs given by Knuth [103] in his Section 6.2.2 (page 430). We will make heavy use of the connection between Quicksort and search trees in Chapter 8, when we study Quicksort (and search trees) with equal keys.

> **Fringe-Balanced Trees: A Natural Model.** Devroye and Kruszewski [41] devised methods to synthesize graphics of naturally looking trees. Their method works by first generating a random generalized binary search tree, which is then drawn according to certain rules: internal nodes become branches of the tree whose length, width and branching angle depends mostly on the subtree size that is attached to that node. The trees they generate are essentially fringe-balanced trees with a second parameter: when a leaf buffer overflows, we do not necessarily choose the median as value for the new node, but any fixed order statistic of the sample. They simulate this by their random splitting process using beta distributed relative subtree sizes.

s-Ary Search Trees. As we can partition into s segments at once instead of only two in Quicksort, we can have s-way branching nodes instead of only binary search trees. Mahmoud [112] described the resulting *s-ary search trees* in detail. Note that in the literature on search trees, the branching factor s is often called m. Hennequin [77] made the connection between s-ary search trees and s-way Quicksort explicit.

Random Split Trees. Devroye noted in an article published in 1998 that the analysis of many random tree variants can be unified in a single framework: *random split trees*. His framework covers BSTs, s-ary search trees, fringe-balanced trees, quadtrees and tries, and under mild assumptions Devroye obtains asymptotic approximations to D_n, the depth of the last inserted element.

This extension is not directly relevant for Quicksort, but noteworthy in its own right. Moreover, the result of Devroye's analysis has technical similarities with our solution of the Quicksort recurrence: Devroye [40, Theorem 2] shows that $\mathbb{E}[D_n] = \frac{1}{\mu} \ln n$ where μ is the expected entropy of his *splitter* random variable V. We derive a very similar result using quite different techniques in Chapter 6.

1.7.7 Limit Distributions

Computing the *expected* costs of Quicksort would be pointless if actual realizations of the random costs were not likely to be close to it. Deriving statements about the distribution of Quicksorts cost has hence been an active field of research.

Variance. The distribution of the number of comparisons is characterized by the number of permutations of size n on which Quicksort needs exactly k comparisons. These numbers fulfill a recurrence similar to the average number of comparisons. For each n, we get a different distribution over the number of comparisons whose probability generating functions $G_n(z) = \sum_k p_{nk} z^k$ fulfill a recurrence similar to that for the expected number of comparisons: $G_n(z) = z^{n-1} \sum_{k=1}^{n} G_{k-1}(z) G_{n-k}(z)/n$ with $G_0(z) = 1$; see Exercise 6.2.2–8 of Knuth [103]. Taking derivatives and extracting coefficients, Knuth determines the variance for the number of comparisons in classic Quicksort as $7n^2 - 4(n+1)^2 H_n^{(2)} - 2(n+1)H_n + 13n$.

Concentration. Since the standard deviation is thus bounded by a linear function in n, we find with *Chebyshev's inequality* that for any fixed probability $p \in (0,1)$ and deviation $\varepsilon > 0$, there is a minimum size n_0 such that for $n \geqslant n_0$, the costs deviate from the mean by less than ε percent with probability p. Such an existential guarantee is already reassuring, but the values of n_0 from Chebyshev's inequality will usually be very large, since the mean is only by a logarithmic factor larger that the standard deviation. This result is known at least since the early 1970s.

Exploiting much more of the specific structure in Quicksort, McDiarmid and Hayward [121, 122] showed in 1992 that the probability for large deviations is in fact much smaller than that. They explicitly included median-of-$(2t+1)$ Quicksort in their work.

From a practitioner's point of view, it is reassuring that not only the average performance of Quicksort is good, but also that chances are low to deviate much from it on every single input, as long as it is a random permutation. The actual *distribution* of costs in Quicksort is not as important from a practical point of view, but it has many interesting features from a mathematical point of view, and its study has fostered the development of useful methodology.

Existence of a Limit Law. Regnier [148] first showed in 1989 that the normalized number of comparisons $(C_n - \mathbb{E}[C_n])/n$ converges in distribution to a limit distribution. Her martingale-based proof is not constructive. Hennequin [76, 77] showed that the first twelve *cumulants* of the distributions converge for $n \to \infty$, and he formulates a conjecture for all others. The existence of all cumulants is known to imply that the limit distribution is characterized by cumulants or moments, which extends Regnier's finding also for Hennequin's multiway Quicksort.

The Contraction Method. A relatively new and successful tool for the analysis of algorithms had its premiere in giving the first characterization of the limit distribution of Quicksort: the *contraction method*. Rösler [151] showed that the distribution of normalized costs for sorting an input of size n with Quicksort can be described by a *distributional recurrence* that transforms distributions with smaller parameters into the distribution for n. This mapping of probability distributions is a contraction in the complete metric space of centered distributions with the minimal ℓ_2 metric (a.k.a. Wasserstein metric or Mallow's metric), so if we iterate the mapping from any starting point, it converges to a unique fixed-point by *Banach's fixed-point theorem*.

The limit law is the unique solution of the fixed-point equation among all centered distributions, and the normalized cost distribution of Quicksort converges to it in the ℓ_2 metric, which is known to imply convergence in distribution and in first and second moments. As we do not have a simple, explicit representation for the solution of the fixed-point equation, the limit distribution is only given implicitly. We can nevertheless compute, e.g., asymptotic variances directly from the fixed-point equation with much less computational effort than a direct recurrence for the variance.

Rösler on one hand, and Rachev and Rüschendorf on the other hand independently developed the general methodology behind this idea in two articles, [152] and [146], that appeared in 1992 resp. 1995. The name *contraction method* is due to Rachev and Rüschendorf. In a joint effort, Rösler and Rüschendorf [150] reviewed the method systematically in 2001, including many examples and the abstraction of *weighted branching systems*. In the same year, Neininger [138] extended the method to multivariate random variables, which allowed him to compute, e.g., covariances between different cost measures; Neininger and Rüschendorf [140] further developed the contraction method on the basis of Zolotarev metrics in 2004. This allows them to handle recurrences with a normal limit law, which usually do not yield a contracting map in the ℓ_2 metric.

Non-Uniform Input. Eddy and Schervish [50] describe the remarkable fact that for *any* distribution of pivot ranks, i.e., any choice for probabilities $q_j^{(n)}$ for the pivot to have rank j in an array of n elements, one can recursively identify a family of distributions over the permutations of $[1..n]$, so that classic Quicksort with a deterministic pivot choice has the given probability to select a pivot of a certain rank. What is more, they show that recursive calls operate on inputs drawn from the same family of distributions, i.e., randomness is preserved. This means that, e.g., any pivot-sampling scheme can be simulated by changing the input distribution accordingly instead.

> Since in the recursion we always have segment sizes $j-1$ and $n-j$ if the pivot has rank j, (comparison) costs only depend on $q_j^{(n)} + q_{n-(j-1)}^{(n)}$, and any distribution for which this equals $2/n$ implies the *same* costs as uniformly random permutations. For example, the distribution $q_j^{(n)} = \frac{2j}{n(n+1)}$, which at first sight seems to imply unbalanced partitioning, yields the same distribution of costs as does the random-permutation model.

Limit Density. The characterization of limit distributions as fixed point of a mapping is still implicit. Eddy and Schervish [50] used the fixed-point equation to numerically approximate the limit distribution of Quicksort, by successively substituting an initial guess for the characteristic function, the moment generating function or the density into the fixed-point equation.

A succinct precise description of, e.g., the density of the Quicksort limit law is still not known; in fact, even the *existence* of a density is not obvious a priori. Tan showed in his Ph.D. thesis [173] in 1993 that the limit distribution of Quicksort indeed has a positive continuous density with support $\mathbb{R}_{\geqslant 0}$; he published the result in a joint article with Hadjicostas [174] in 1995.

Phase Changes. Limit distributions for normalized costs of divide-and-conquer algorithms usually fall into one of only a few classes: they can be normal distributions (with a certain mean and variance), an otherwise unknown distribution like Quicksort (non-normal case), or they might not exist at all, e.g., because of fluctuations of the costs in n. Other well-known distributions do not seem to occur often in such applications. Mahmoud [113] analyzed many classical sorting algorithms and reports asymptotic normality for almost all of them. Interestingly, as one varies certain parameters, limit distributions exhibit a *phase transition* from one class to another.

Chern and Hwang [29] studied a collection of different cost measures with linear expectation, e.g., the number of partitioning steps in (generalized) Quicksort or the number of nodes in m-ary search trees. For such cost measures there is a phase transition from normality to non-existence as either the number of pivots or the size of the sample for pivot selection exceed certain thresholds. Chern and Hwang characterize these thresholds.

Another type of phase transition happens when one varies the order of growth of the toll function in a Quicksort-like recurrence. Hwang and Neininger [91] study limit laws in the setting of the classic Quicksort. Roughly speaking for tolls smaller than $\sqrt{n}$, limit laws are normal, for larger tolls they are non-normal.

Limit Law of Multiway Quicksort. The contraction method works for multiway Quicksort as well as in the single-pivot case; but one has to fix a partitioning method.

Tan shows the existence of a density in his Ph.D. thesis [173] for his multiway Quicksort based on iterative binary partitioning; see Section 1.7.8 for details on the algorithm. He also extends the contraction-method argument for his multiway Quicksort and generalizes the numerical approximations of Eddy and Schervish [50] for the limit density.

For the normalized number of comparisons in Hennequin's generalized Quicksort [77], Chern et al. [30] sketch the derivation of the limit distribution with the *method of moments*, using their transfer theorem to asymptotically solve the recurrence for all moments.

For YBB Quicksort, we obtained the limit distribution of the normalized number of comparisons, swaps, and number of Bytecode instructions with the contraction method after noting that, conditioned on pivot values, partitioning costs are sufficiently concentrated; this was a joint work with Ralph Neininger and Markus Nebel [186].

1.7.8 Multiway Quicksort

Hoare anticipated almost all modifications of his basic algorithm that actually improve its practical efficiency in his 1962 article on Quicksort [82]; but partitioning around more than one pivot at the same time was not on his list. In fact until recently, only few researchers studied multiway Quicksort.

Sedgewick's Dual-Pivot Quicksort.   To my knowledge, Sedgewick gave the first ever implementation of a multiway Quicksort in his Ph. D. thesis [162] in 1975. His "two-partition" Quicksort (Program 5.1 on page 150) is a three-way Quicksort, splitting the input around two pivots. Sedgewick proposed it as a method to efficiently deal with many equal keys, generalizing from a fat-pivot method with one pivot. He analyzed and discarded it for its excessive swap count. As we will discuss in this work, Sedgewick's original dual-pivot Quicksort needs more comparisons, more swaps, and also more scanned elements, i.e., memory bandwidth, than classic Quicksort.

Hennequin's Generalized Quicksort.   Over a decade later, Hennequin studied in detail a *generalized Quicksort* with an arbitrary number of pivots chosen from a sample in his doctoral thesis [77] finished in 1991. He focused on the analysis of comparisons and left some implementation details of his framework unspecified. Hennequin's partitioning method conceptually operates on linked lists, which makes it hard to determine, e.g., sensible swap counts; some more details are given in Chapter 4.

His analysis results in slight savings for multiway Quicksort, but they are so small that Hennequin comes to the following conclusion: *"Il apparaît ainsi que l'utilisation de la médiane apporte asymptotiquement un gain significatif sur les coûts moyens en particulier pour les premières valeurs* $t = 1$ *ou* $t = 2$. *Le multipartitionnement semble par contre beaucoup moins intéressant dans la pratique sauf si on peut réduire de façon significative la valeur de* $\bar{a}(s)$ *(par exemple par hachage sur les nœuds). On note de plus que la constante* $K_{s,t}$ *n'est pas monotone en* s *; les cas* $s = 3$ *ou* $s = 5$ *sont ainsi moins bons que les multipartitionnements avec* $s = 2$ *ou* $s = 4$.*"* (Hennequin [77], p. 54) (Using the median seems to bring, asymptotically, a significant gain for the average costs, especially for the first values $t = 1$ or $t = 2$. Multiway partitioning, on the other hand, seems much less interesting in practice unless one can significantly reduce the value of $\bar{a}(s)$ [the leading-term coefficient of partitioning costs] (for example by hashing nodes). One further notes that the constant $K_{s,t}$ is not monotonic in s; the cases $s = 3$ and $s = 5$ are thus worse than multiway partitioning with $s = 2$ and $s = 4$, respectively.)

Apart from his French doctoral thesis, Hennequin never published his results on multiway Quicksort; his 1989 article [76] on the analysis of Quicksort considers the case $s = 2$ only.

Tan's Iterative Binary Partitioning Quicksort.   A second doctoral thesis, finished two years after Hennequin's, also covers the analysis of a multiway Quicksort variant: Tan [173] considered the cost of *iterative binary partitioning:* Initially we choose $s - 1$ pivots, for s a power of two, and then perform a binary partition of the array around the *median* of these $s - 1$ pivots. Afterwards we partition the left segment using the *first quartile* of the $s - 1$ pivots and the right segment likewise around the *third quartile,* and so on, until we have s segments after $ld(s)$ levels of partitioning.

With respect to the number of comparison, Tan's algorithm is equivalent to Hennequin's generalized Quicksort, but unlike that, iterative binary partitioning clearly works in-place on an array. Tan reported on a small running time study where his multiway Quicksort performed slightly better than classic Quicksort; it has to be noted, however, that he did not use pivot sampling, which might have changed the picture. Tan focused in his work on the distribution of the number of comparisons; we already discussed his corresponding results in Section 1.7.7.

Tan published a journal article [174] in 1995 with results from his thesis, wherein he considers the single-pivot case only—exactly as Hennequin did. This indicates that in the mid 1990s, the algorithms community still saw multiway Quicksort more as a gimmicky generalization, a training ground for (graduate) students to exercise and demonstrate their skills on, rather than as a helpful optimization of practical use.

Dual-Pivot Quicksort in Java.

It so happened that the extraordinarily successful revival of dual-pivot Quicksort in practice remained unnoticed by the algorithms community for years. Starting in the fall of 2008, Russian Java developer Vladimir Yaroslavskiy started experimenting with Quicksort variants using two pivots in his free time at Sun Microsystems. Over the course of one year, he refined his sorting program so as to perform well on many types of inputs. With the help of experienced Java library developer Joshua Bloch and expert for practical algorithms Jon Bentley, Yaroslavskiy developed a sorting method that consistently outperformed the existing library implementation. In September 2009, Yaroslavskiy announced to the Java mailing list that the Yaroslavskiy-Bentley-Bloch (YBB) Quicksort was to be included in the OpenJDK sources [94].

Shortcomings in Early Analyses of YBB Quicksort.

While otherwise relying entirely on running time experiments, Yaroslavskiy's announcement [94] also contains a mathematical analysis of YBB Quicksort (without sampling); he also gave this analysis as part of an article [191] that he posted on his personal website. Unfortunately, the presented analysis is based on overly simplistic assumptions and so does not give the correct results. Concerning the number of comparisons during partitioning, Yaroslavskiy assumed the following: *"for elements from left part (one comparison), center and right parts (2 comparisons)"* ([191], p. 4); in other words, elements are always compared to the small pivot first. This is actually not the case in YBB Quicksort [184], so they erroneously obtain the same number of comparisons as for classic Quicksort.

In terms of swaps, Yaroslavskiy wrote about classic Quicksort: *"We assume that average number of swaps during one iteration is $1/2 * (n - 1)$. It means that in average one half of elements is swapped only."* ([191], p. 4) This is far too pessimistic; it is known that on average, only every sixth comparison is followed by a swap; see, e.g., Knuth [103], p. 121. So the obtained result is roughly thrice the actual swap count. Similarly, the number of swaps in one dual-pivot partitioning round is assumed to be $\frac{2}{3}(n - 2)$, which is the swap count for Sedgewick's dual-pivot Quicksort; YBB Quicksort needs only about $\frac{1}{2}n$ swaps per partitioning step [184].

Iliopoulos and Penman [92] published a paper on dual-pivot Quicksort concurrently to my analysis of YBB Quicksort. They claim to analyze Sedgewick's dual-pivot Quicksort, but without commenting on the important difference, they actually count comparisons under the same simplistic scheme that Yaroslavskiy [191] assumed: Small elements *"only need to be compared with one of the pivots. However if an element is greater than i then it needs to be compared with the other pivot as well, to determine whether or not it is greater than j. We refer to Sedgewick [4] for code for a version of this scheme."* (Iliopoulos and Penman [92], p. 3) For the number of swaps they reproduce Sedgewick's analysis of his dual-pivot Quicksort. Later they refer to running time studies of the dual-pivot Quicksort in Java, which does not fit their analysis, though.

Waterloo Four-Way Quicksort.   Kushagra et al., a group of four researchers from Waterloo, Canada, analyzed multiway Quicksort variants with respect to caches misses; we discuss this part of their work in Section 1.7.11. They note that Tan's iterative binary partitioning is suboptimal w.r.t. cache misses, and they propose an alternative partitioning scheme that works in one pass over the array with a similar invariant as Sedgewick's dual-pivot Quicksort. It is worth noting that the number of comparisons coincides with both Hennequin's and Tan's algorithms for three pivots, but the number of scanned elements is substantially smaller.

Swaps in Tan's and Waterloo Quicksort.   In terms of swaps, Tan's method is very efficient. Its first pass partitions into two segments around a pivot chosen as median of three. This entails $\frac{n}{5} \pm O(1)$ swaps in expectation [159]. The second pass subdivides both ranges into two segments each, using a pivot that is distributed randomly among its segment. The second pass then needs another $\frac{n}{6} \pm O(1)$ swaps. This makes an overall leading-term coefficient of $\frac{22}{65} \approx 0.338462$, which compares quite favorably to the coefficient $\frac{1}{3}$ of classic Quicksort. The leading-term coefficient for Waterloo partitioning is $\frac{42}{65} \approx 0.646154$, almost twice as much.

Note that there is a mistake in the analysis of Kushagra et al. [105]: They count only $\frac{n-2}{6}$ swaps for the crossing-pointer part of their algorithm, since the *"swaps made during partitioning using single pivot was analysed by Sedgewick in 1977 [6] and their number is given by $\frac{n-2}{6}$"* ([105], p. 49). It apparently escaped their notice that the pivot here has a different distribution, so this result is not applicable. As in the first pass of Tan's method, the pivot is effectively chosen as the median of the three pivots, and the correct number of crossing-pointer swaps is thus $\frac{n-4}{5}$.

Generic k-Pivot Quicksort of Aumüller et al.   Aumüller studied a generic multiway Quicksort implementation under different cost models, both mathematically and experimentally, in his doctoral thesis [7] finished in 2015. His work emerged independently of my thesis and some parts are similar. We discuss the differences in detail in Section 4.6.4. Aumüller's algorithmic framework is a subclass of generic one-pass partitioning considered herein.

1.7.9 Equal Keys

By *equal keys,* we mean the possibility to have duplicate elements in the input. In applications, these might actually be keys for whole records of data, so that equal keys not necessarily means equal records. When I started my thesis, surprisingly little was known about Quicksort's performance under input models with duplicates, and some of the results are not very well known; to the best of my knowledge, this section lists all relevant works on Quicksort with equal keys. We give a brief summary of them here; Chapter 8 contains a more detailed discussion.

Burge [27] first analyzed binary search trees under a model with equal keys in 1976. He inspired Sedgewick to his seminal article [160] on Quicksort with equal keys in 1977. Sedgewick derived bounds on the performance of Quicksort programs in the *exact-profile model*, where the multiplicities of all keys are fixed and all orderings are equally likely, and the *random-u-ary-word model*, where keys are chosen i.i.d. *uniformly* from the universe $\{1, \dots, u\}$. He analyzed three concrete implementations in detail; the winner of his competition was the classic Quicksort that stops scanning on equal elements. This algorithm's performance on random permutations is good and it does degrade in the presence of duplicates.

If we consider only the number of comparisons, we should actually be able to take *advantage* of duplicates: there are less than $n!$ different orderings, so from an information-theoretic perspective, finding the right one is an *easier* problem than for n distinct elements. In an article [178] from 1985, Wegner proposed several Quicksort variants intended to do so. Unfortunately, he only partly analyzed his algorithms, and did not give detailed implementations.

Only with the engineering article of Bentley and McIlroy [20] eight years later has a *fat-pivot* partitioning method found widespread use in practice. Sedgewick and Bentley [163, 164] reported on the detailed analysis of this algorithm in the exact-profile model in two talks given in 1999 and 2002; they apparently never published these results in an article. They show that fat-pivot Quicksort is optimal in the sense that it achieves an information-theoretic lower bound up to constant factors; the analysis only applies to a randomly chosen single pivot. Sedgewick and Bentley uttered the conjecture that this constant approaches one as $k \to \infty$ when the pivot is chosen as median of k. The same duo previously adapted fat-pivot Quicksort to obtain an efficient string sorting algorithm [21].

On the analytical side, Kemp [98] studied binary search trees from inputs with duplicates in much more detail. He considered BSTs built by successively inserting inputs under the exact-profile model and derives expected values for typical measures of the trees. Kemp transfers these results to the *expected-profile model*, where keys are chosen i.i.d. from a given *discrete* distribution. Archibald and Clément [3] extend this work by deriving variances.

Notably, all these results on equal keys concern single-pivot Quicksort without pivot sampling, and the used methodology seems hard to generalize. In Chapter 8, we will hence seek a new way to analyze Quicksort on inputs with duplicates, one that allows us to handle multiway partitioning and pivot sampling.

1.7.10 Bit Complexity and Symbol Comparisons

The efficiency of Quicksort in the comparison model is well understood, but how does Quicksort compete with, e.g., Radixsort? This is essentially a question of models. To determine the relative order of two elements, Radixsort uses several *symbol comparisons* and effectively treats elements as *strings* over some alphabet with lexicographic order. For Quicksort, we usually assume that key comparisons are atomic operations, and count each of these comparisons as one unit of cost. When sorting strings, the cost of one comparisons is no longer constant.

The word-RAM model offers a way to smoothly transition from *uniform operation costs* to *logarithmic operation costs:* The usual arithmetic and bitwise operations on words of w bits can be done in constant time, larger numbers have to be treated as strings of words. By letting w be a function of n, the number of elements, we obtain different classical models as special cases: a constant w corresponds to logarithmic operation costs, and with a word size large enough to hold all occurring numbers, we obtain the uniform cost model.

In other words, the comparison model corresponds to sorting single *words*; as we assume n distinct elements, w must be at least $ld(n)$ in this case. For Radixsort, one usually assumes a smaller, typically constant, word size w; how would Quicksort perform with such word sizes?

Analysis of Fill and Janson.   Fill and Janson first addressed this question in a conference paper [58] in 2004; in 2012 they published a more comprehensive full version [59] of it. In their setting, we draw input elements i.i.d. from a continuous distribution over the unit interval, and interpret them as infinite bit-strings given by their binary representation. Comparing two such elements proceeds bitwise from the beginning of the two strings, and continues until the first differing bit is found. The cost measure is the number of bit comparisons needed.

For a uniform distribution, Fill and Janson reported an expected value of asymptotically $n \ln(n) \, ld(n)$ bit comparisons, which means that a single key comparison inspects $ld(n)/2 = ld(\sqrt{n})$ bits on average. For this case they proceeded in two steps: First they derived the *precise* expectation by summing over all pairs (i, j) of indices the probability that the ith and jth smallest elements are directly compared, times the expected number of leading bits these numbers have in common. This is an extension of the well-known technique for counting comparisons without solving recurrences; see, e.g., Section 7.4.2 of Cormen et al. [35]. The exact result is

$$2 \sum_{k=2}^{n} (-1)^k \binom{n}{k} \frac{1}{k(k-1)(1 - 2^{-(k-1)})}.$$

They then applied *Rice's method* [63] to the exact expression to obtain an asymptotic expansion.

For non-uniform distributions whose density fulfills a certain condition, Fill and Janson determined the expected number of bit comparisons. Here, they took a different route, which I will call *prefix-wise analysis:* For any fixed common prefix of bit strings, the number of times the rightmost bit of this prefix is compared and found equal in two keys is the overall number of key comparisons between two keys with this given prefix. To get the total number of bit comparisons, Fill and Janson thus summed this, i.e., the expected number of key comparisons between keys with a given fixed prefix, over all possible prefixes. To simplify analysis they used the *poissonization trick* here.

> **Poissonization.**   Instead of a fixed size n, we consider an input of *random* size N, where N is *Poisson distributed*. The mean of the distribution is left as parameter and takes the role of n. It is a well-known property of the Poisson distribution that a random variable that has a binomial $\mathrm{Bin}(N, p)$ marginal distribution *conditional* on N, has, upon unconditioning, again a Poisson distribution, with mean pN. For algorithms like Quicksort and data structures like tries, where subproblem sizes are multinomially distributed, we thus get Poisson-sized subproblems again.
>
> The big advantage of the Poisson model is that after poissonization, subproblem sizes are *independent* of each other. This is what simplifies analysis. To obtain results in the usual model, with fixed n, there are rules for *analytic depoissonization,* see Section VIII.5.3 of *Analytic Combinatorics* [64].

With Poisson-sized inputs, the number of key comparisons between elements from a given interval only depends on the probability that elements are drawn from this interval; the numbers are independent for all prefixes of the same length, so it suffices to determine this number to sufficient precision. Fill and Janson omit the depoissonization step.

Seidel's Trie-Argument.   Seidel [167] rephrased the prefix-wise analysis of Fill and Janson in terms of *tries*. He also assumes infinite strings as input. Although the strings are infinite, there is only a finite number of common prefixes that is shared by at least two input strings. Since subproblems with a single element entail no key comparisons, we can restrict our attention to common prefixes shared by at least two elements, of which we only have finitely many. These prefixes correspond exactly to the internal nodes of the trie built from the input strings. By proving matching upper and lower bounds on additive parameters of tries built from uniform memoryless sources, Seidel obtains the leading term in the uniform case without sophisticated analytical machinery.

Seidel's analysis extends to any *strongly faithful* sorting algorithm, i.e., to any algorithm for which the expected number of key comparison between elements of a given subrange of the input depends only the *number* of elements in this range. Subrange here means the set of elements of ranks $i, i+1, \ldots, j$ for some $1 \leqslant i \leqslant j \leqslant n$. Quicksort's faithfulness follows from the well-known fact that it directly compares the elements of rank i and j with probability $\frac{2}{j-i+1}$, namely if and only if one of these two elements is the first element from the corresponding subrange that is chosen as pivot. Since pivots are chosen uniformly at random, this probability depends only on the difference $j - i$, not on i or j itself.

Unfaithful Sampling. The bit complexity of Quicksort with *pivot sampling* is still an open question. Simple analyses in the style of Seidel [167] are not possible; single-pivot Quicksort with median-of-three is already *not strongly faithful* in the sense of Seidel: when sorting all 6! permutations of $\{1, \ldots, 6\}$, we in total do 3432 key comparisons among keys $\{1, 2, 3, 4\}$, but slightly more, namely 3456, comparisons among the keys $\{2, 3, 4, 5\}$. This means that the average number of key comparisons in subranges of the input depends not only on the size of the subrange, but also on its location in the input. Therefore Quicksort with pivot sampling is not strongly faithful.

Note that the analysis of Clément et al. [31] sketched below does not rely on faithfulness, so there is still hope.

Dynamical Sources. Vallée et al. [175] extend the results of Fill and Janson [59] to a wider class of input models, namely suitably tamed *dynamical sources;* the n input strings are still drawn i.i.d., but the next symbols of a single string can depend on the already generated prefix almost arbitrarily. The analysis is given in more detail by Clément et al. [32], an extended article for which the authors were joined by Nguyen Thi. They essentially follow the analysis of Fill and Janson [58], but generalize it in two ways: for the algorithm under consideration, they only need the expected number of key comparisons performed between elements from specific ranges of the universe; for the source, some analytical *tameness* property is required. They also include Insertionsort and Bubblesort in their analysis, and the class of sources contains all memoryless and Markov sources.

For Quicksort, the leading term of the number of symbol comparisons is $\frac{\ln 2}{\mathcal{H}(S)} n \ln(n) \, \mathrm{ld}(n)$, where $\mathcal{H}(S)$ is the (binary) entropy of the source S. Clément et al. also extend a lower bound argument of Seidel [167] to find that *any* sorting algorithm that does not make use of the fact that we are sorting strings needs at least $\frac{1}{2\mathcal{H}(S)} n \ln(n) \, \mathrm{ld}(n)$ symbol comparisons in the asymptotic average to sort n i.i.d. strings emitted by the source S. Exactly as for ordinary key comparisons on random permutations, and as in the case of equal keys, Quicksort uses only $2 \ln 2 \approx 1.38629$ times the number of symbol comparisons required by any comparison-based sorting algorithm.

1.7.11 Memory Hierarchy

The growing influence of the memory hierarchy on the design of algorithms has been known for a long time; since Aggarwal and Vitter [1] proposed the *external-memory model (EMM)* at ICALP 1987, many researchers studied classic algorithmic problems in the context of memory hierarchies. Meyer et al. [129] edited a monograph on the topic.

In the context of sorting, LaMarca conducted a systematic study in his Ph. D. thesis [108] in 1996; extended versions are published as joint work with Ladner [106, 107]. LaMarca proposed memory-tuned versions of most classical sorting algorithms and demonstrates that they often run faster than versions classically optimized for CPU efficiency only. He also derived the number of cache miss counts of his algorithms in a simplified model; he argued that in the context of such analyses, one can assume a direct-mapped cache without degrading prediction accuracy considerably.

For classic Quicksort, LaMarca and Ladner [107] reported approximately

$$\frac{2n}{B} \ln\left(\frac{n}{M}\right) + \frac{5n}{8B} + \frac{3M}{8B}$$

cache misses for a cache that can hold M keys and works with blocks of B keys. According to their measurements, this was very accurate in predicting the number of cache misses in their setup, but some parts of their analysis are heuristic.

Their optimization of Quicksort chooses a linear number of pivots and a linked-list based multiway partitioning implementation to split up the input in one step into segments that fit into the cache with high probability. While this increased the number of executed instructions, it significantly reduced the number of cache misses according to LaMarca and Ladner; overall running times were slightly better, as well. They note that since classic Quicksort already has decent cache behavior, the *"improvements in overall performance for heapsort and mergesort are significant, while the improvement for quicksort is modest."* ([107], p. 67).

Their core idea to memory-tune Quicksort was to use multiway partitioning. Since they used a very large number of pivots, partitioning became much more expensive and was no longer sensibly doable in place. Interestingly, the idea to partition (repeatedly) into a *moderate* fixed number of segments, but one that is also larger than two, seems not to have been considered promising.

Multiway Quicksort.   Kushagra et al. [105] apparently were the first to recognize the potential of multiway Quicksort with a modest number of pivots in reducing memory accesses and cache misses. In their 2014 article, they determined, in a manner similar to LaMarca and Ladner [107], the approximate number of cache misses of YBB Quicksort and a natural new four-way Quicksort implementation, see Section 1.7.8 for details on the *Waterloo four-way Quicksort*.

They reported that the expected number of cache misses in classic, YBB and Waterloo Quicksort are at most $a\frac{n+1}{N}\ln\left(\frac{n+1}{M+2}\right) \pm O\left(\frac{n}{B}\right)$, where $a = 2$, $a = \frac{8}{5} = 1.6$ resp. $a = \frac{18}{13} \approx 1.38$, so significant savings result from using three- or four-way partitioning. According to their experiments, these savings seemed to directly translate into running-time improvements if compiler optimizations are turned off.

Aumüller and Dietzfelbinger [9] conducted extensive running-time experiments, including hardware performance counter measurements for cache misses with several Quicksort variants including YBB and Waterloo Quicksort. Their results confirmed earlier findings of running-time speedups: Waterloo four-way Quicksort and YBB Quicksort are fastest and have essentially the same running time, whereas classic Quicksort is roughly 10 % slower. They also found that scanned elements are in very good accordance with L1 cache misses. However, in their experiments, Waterloo Quicksort needed less instructions and incurred less cache misses than any of the other algorithms they tested, in particular significantly less than YBB Quicksort; but still was YBB Quicksort as fast as Waterloo

Quicksort, even faster in some runs. They thus conclude: *"in the light of our experiments, neither the average number of instructions nor the average number of cache misses can fully explain empirical running time."* (Aumüller and Dietzfelbinger [9], p. 25)

All works discussed above only consider random pivots in the analysis; my joint article with Conrado Martínez and Markus Nebel seems to be the first to cover the influence of pivot sampling in the analysis of caching behavior [137]. In that article, we focused on YBB Quicksort, but the methodology is not limited to that; I will extend these results to generic one-pass partitioning in this work.

1.7.12 Branch Misses

Pipelined execution leads to enormous speedups for programs that are computation-intensive. Conditional branches interfere with that, since the next instruction to be executed becomes known only after the branching condition has been evaluated. CPUs thus try to *predict* the outcome of branches; if the predictor errs, we have a branch miss, which is a costly event.

As an extreme example, in 2006 Kaligosi and Sanders [96] observed on a CPU with a long pipeline and thus high branch miss costs that a very skewed pivot choice outperformed the typically optimal median pivot, even though the latter leads to much less executed instructions in total. The reason is that a skewed pivot makes the inner loop branches much more predictable. Kaligosi and Sanders also derive upper bounds on the number of branch misses. Note that their results for the 2-bit predictor are not tight [117].

Two years later, Biggar et al. [23] conducted an extensive study of branch prediction in typical sorting algorithms, paralleling the study of LaMarca and Ladner [107] for caching. They could not reproduce the extreme behavior of Quicksort observed by Kaligosi and Sanders on another processor; in fact, in their study, classic Quicksort was faster than the multiway Quicksort of LaMarca and Ladner [107] and their variants optimized for branch misses. Biggar et al. reported from experiments that choosing the pivot as median of a sample raises the overall number of branch misses, even though at the same time the number of executed branches significantly drops. The reason is that a pivot closer to the median makes branches less predictable.

The analyses of Kaligosi and Sanders [96] and Biggar et al. [23] are both based on the heuristic assumption that there is a *fixed* branching probability if the rank of the pivot is fixed. They then used this probability in the steady-state distribution of the branch-prediction automata to obtain average misprediction rates. By conditioning on pivot *values* instead of ranks, we could make this argument rigorous [117].

Brodal and Moruz [26] showed that there is a general trade-off in comparison-based sorting: One can only save comparisons at the price of additional branch misses, this is unless one can avoid the conditional branch altogether.

The latter is always possible [53], but only at a large penalty in terms of executed instructions in general. Elmasry et al. [54] noted that in this respect, Lomuto's partitioning scheme is superior to Hoare's classic crossing-pointers technique, since one can easily make the conditional swap in Lomuto's method a predicated move instruction, thereby eliminate the branch.

1.7.13 Academic Quicksort Variants

Although successful in practice, many variants of Quicksort do not meet all criteria for a theoretically optimal sorting method: they do not achieve lower bounds, e.g., in terms of time and space. Researchers have been trying to answer the question if such shortcomings are inherent limitations of the Quicksort idea or if they can be circumvented. The resulting algorithms are often of mostly academic interest.

Some sorting algorithms have been inspired by Quicksort, but the final algorithm does not really feel *Quicksortish* any more; e.g., Cantone and Cincotti [28] presented the QuickHeapsort algorithm, which mixes a partitioning step and Heapsort. We will not discuss these derivatives and distant relatives here.

Worst-Case Efficiency. Quadratic worst-case complexity is a well-known shortcoming of classic Quicksort. We can obtain linearithmic worst-case complexity without affecting average performance by much using introspective sorting [133]; see Section 1.7.3. One might argue though that Introsort is no longer a true Quicksort, since it passes control to an entirely different algorithm for hard inputs. Quadratic worst cases can also be avoided in a more Quicksortish way by selecting pivots as exact medians using a worst-case linear-time selection algorithm. This approach is much slower than classic Quicksort except for very few inputs, but we can say that Quicksort is not inherently quadratic in the worst-case.

Stable Sorting. In the presence of equal keys, the issue of stability arises: with a *stable* sorting method, elements with equal keys appear in the output in the same relative order as they did in the input. Without trickery, Quicksort on arrays is not stable. Motzkin [130] and Wegner [177] concurrently presented a simple and stable implementation of Quicksort based on linked lists. So Quicksort is not unstable per se, but all efficient array-based implementations are.

Constant Extra Space. Wegner [179] demonstrated that Quicksort can be implemented stack-less, i.e., with $O(1)$ additional memory. He described a clever trick to remember boundaries of segments in the array using an element that we put temporarily out of order. The algorithm strictly operates from left to right, always sorting left subproblems first, so that we only need to detect the right boundary of subproblems. To do so, we put the largest element of the subproblem *preceding* the current subproblem at the right end of the current subproblem; this element is smaller than all elements in the current subarray, and was smaller than the pivot in the previous partitioning phase. We then continue partitioning, until we find the first element that is (weakly) smaller than the element one position left of the beginning of the current subarray, which is the pivot of the previous partitioning phase; this element must hence be the boundary of this subproblem. Since it was the largest element of its subproblem, we can easily put it back in place.

Bing-Chao and Knuth [24] presented a simpler version of this idea one year earlier. They used negation of integers to mark boundaries, which allows only inputs with positive keys. Bing-Chao and Knuth precisely analyzed their algorithm and found it to be 60 % slower than classic Quicksort in terms of MIX instructions.

Asymptotically Comparison-Optimal Quicksort. It is a fundamental open question of theoretical computer science whether it is possible to sort any permutation with at most $\lceil ld(n!) \rceil$ comparisons, the information-theoretic lower bound (Knuth [103], Section 5.3.1). A much simpler task is to achieve this asymptotically, i.e., to sort with $\sim ld(n!) \sim n\,ld(n)$ comparisons as $n \to \infty$; Mergesort attains this bound for example.

Classic Quicksort is quite far away from this; even the expected number on random permutations is $\sim 2n\ln(n) \approx 1.38629\,n\,ld(n)$, i.e., almost 40 % more than the lower bound. This number can be made smaller using median-of-k pivots, and if k grows with n, i.e., $k = \omega(1)$ and $k = o(n)$ as $n \to \infty$, Quicksort needs $\sim n\,ld(n)$ comparisons [123, 116].

Comparison-Optimal Multiway Partitioning. Asymmetries allow YBB Quicksort to save comparisons; Aumüller and Dietzfelbinger [8, 9] addressed the question how much can be saved by this with any conceivable dual-pivot partitioning method. They prove a lower bound and also devise schemes to attain this bound asymptotically. Very recently, they analyzed their algorithms precisely in a joint work [11] with Clemens Heuberger, Daniel Krenn, and Helmut Prodinger.

Aumüller extended the comparison-optimal partitioning schemes to any number of pivots in his doctoral thesis [7] finished in 2015; the results also appear in a recent pre-print [10] written with his advisor Martin Dietzfelbinger. They found diminishing returns as the number of pivots k gets larger; in fact, they reported that classic Quicksort with median-of-k pivots has a very similar expected comparisons count as the comparison-optimal classification scheme for k pivots. They did however not consider the case of choosing these k pivots from a sample, as well.

1.7.14 My Previous Work

I mentioned some of my work on Quicksort in the introduction, but did not give a systematic summary; this section does so.

Analysis of YBB Quicksort. When I noticed the discrepancies between existing analyses and the JDK code mentioned in Section 1.7.8 in the spring of 2012, I set out to redo the analysis as part of my master's thesis [182], which I finished in the summer of 2012. The analysis revealed important differences between Sedgewick's dual-pivot Quicksort and YBB Quicksort; in particular, the latter outperforms the former w.r.t. comparisons *and* swaps. YBB Quicksort even saves a few comparisons over classic Quicksort using a strategy that was apparently not widely understood at that time: which pivot we compare an element first with depends on whether it is reached by the left-bound or the right-bound scanning index. Since the distance traveled by each of these pointers depends on the pivot rank, YBB partitioning introduces a positive correlation between the event of a cheap classification (only one comparison), and the event that more elements are reached by this index than by the other one. This reduces the overall expectation.

Apart from the operation counts, my thesis contains a running time study that confirms the roughly 10 % speedup observed between the Java 6 and Java 7 libraries. The speedup remains of the same order for basic versions of the algorithms (instead of the tuned library implementations), and for C++ ports of the Java code. I computed the precise number of executed instructions for implementations in Java Bytecode and MMIX assembly; in both cases, classic Quicksort needs fewer instructions. I also included a preliminary treatment of pivot sampling, but could only obtain results for a few concrete values for the sample size.

With Markus Nebel, my advisor for both my master's thesis and this dissertation, I presented the operation counts at the *European Symposium on Algorithms 2012* [184]. We added the use of Insertionsort for small subproblems in an extended journal version [186] written with Ralph Neininger, who obtained a characterization of the limit distribution of costs.

The instruction counts with pivot sampling suggest that the tertiles-of-five scheme used in Java 7 entails more executed instructions on random permutations than using the first and third smallest elements of a sample of five as pivots instead. With Raphael Reitzig and Ulrich Laube, we experimentally investigated whether this translates into faster Java code [185]. However, any anticipated advantage of the asymmetric sampling scheme is dwarfed by another, quite peculiar effect: as the experiments clearly indicate, it depends on the input how Oracle's just-in-time compiler (JIT) translates Java Bytecode to machine code: it either produces a fast version, or a slow version. The JIT chooses code optimizations based on profiling data from early executions, and the choice of the pivot-sampling scheme influences those. The running time for the *same* input changes dramatically, depending on which input was used during the JIT warmup phase to trigger compilation.

While we could not give a convincing explanation of what caused these differences, we succeeded with the mathematical analysis of pivot-sampling in YBB Quicksort: we computed expected comparison, swap and Bytecode instruction counts as functions of the pivot-sampling parameter t [136].

Scanned Elements.   We introduced the cost measure of *scanned elements* in a joint work with Martínez [137], extending our conference article [136]. The number of scanned elements serves as an intermediate, abstract measure that approximates the number of cache misses, but can be precisely defined and analyzed mathematically and is hardware-independent. Both LaMarca and Ladner [107] and Kushagra et al. [105] determine essentially the number of scanned elements in their analyses of the caching behavior of Quicksort, but do not make the distinction between scanned elements and cache misses: they mix exact mathematical parts with heuristic simplifications in their analyses, making it impossible to tell for sure if observed differences in measurements are due to differences in the algorithms or due to inaccuracies of their model.

By distinguishing scanned elements and cache misses, and counting both in experiments, we can separately account for two sources of discrepancies between measurements and analytical results:

▶ we measure the *analysis error* that comes from asymptotic approximations by comparing scanned element counts from experiments with the analysis results;

▶ we determine the *modeling error* by comparing measured scanned element and cache miss counts.

We showed for an idealized LRU cache that indeed the analysis error is often *larger* than the modeling error [137]. To within the predictive quality of our asymptotic analysis, we can thus safely compare Quicksort variants by their scanned elements counts instead of actual cache miss counts.

YBB Quickselect. We can use three-way partitioning also as basis for a dual-pivot Quick*select*. In a joint project with Hosam Mahmoud, we analyzed this idea [187]: we determined expectation and limit distribution of the number of comparisons needed by YBB Quickselect to find an element of random rank (a.k.a. *grand average*). In terms of key comparisons, dual-pivot Quickselect is clearly worse than the traditional single-pivot method.

> **Quickselect and Scanned Elements.** As discussed in the introduction, there is compelling evidence for a shift in computational models. Since memory bandwidth has not grown as quickly as processing speed, a reduction in scanned elements can outweigh an increase in the number of executed instructions. Unfortunately, the Quickselect article was published before I became aware of this; in terms of scanned elements, dual-pivoting actually *improves* Quickselect in the grand average by 12.5 %!
>
> According to my preliminary tests, however, there is no measurable difference between YBB Quickselect and classic Quickselect in terms of running time; if anything, classic Quickselect is very slightly *faster*. The reduction in scanned elements of 12.5 % might just be too little to compensate for the increase in the number of swaps and comparisons, and instructions in general. Recall that for sorting, the savings in terms of scanned elements are twice as big and the difference in other measures is smaller, which might explain why Quicksort profits from YBB partitioning but Quickselect does not.

Branch Misses. Memory bandwidth can become a bottleneck of execution speed, but branch mispredictions can also slow down execution as they thwart the efficient use of instruction pipelines. As discussed in Section 1.7.12, this can be a significant factor for running time in certain scenarios. Interestingly, the expected number of branch misses in Quicksort was not known even for classic Quicksort with median-of-three pivot. The analysis of classic and YBB Quicksort including pivot sampling was again a cooperation with Conrado Martínez [117]. It turned out that classic and YBB Quicksort perform almost exactly the same in this respect; this eliminates expected branch miss counts from the list of plausible causes for the systematic running-time advantage of dual-pivot Quicksort.

2 Mathematical Tools

Contents

WE COLLECT IN THIS CHAPTER the mathematical tools we use later on in this work. The first four sections serve mainly as a *formulary,* a collection of statements given here once in consistent notation for later reference. Most are basic facts that appear or could appear in textbooks, but since they come from a variety of fields, not every reader will be familiar with all results. I made an effort to provide appropriate references for all results. Readers who are familiar with this kind of mathematics may skip Sections 2.1–2.4 and only consult them on demand.

Section 2.4 contains some results on the Dirichlet distribution often not covered in standard references, in particular the rules of *Dirichlet-calculus* introduced in Section 2.4.5.

The last two sections present some original material. We will use them in our analysis of Quicksort, but the results therein are to a good extent independent of Quicksort and thus given in this chapter. Section 2.5 considers the *discrete entropy,* the function that appears in the leading-term coefficient of the solution of the Quicksort recurrence. It has intuitive meaning and properties that are not directly tied to Quicksort and could be of independent interest.

In Section 2.6, we translate the conditions for Roura's Continuous Master Theorem (CMT) [154] to the language of probability. I found it often more natural to set up a *distributional* recurrence instead of expressing the expectation recursively, even if when I was only interested in the latter. With the presented master theorems for distributional recurrences one can conveniently obtain an asymptotic approximation for the expectation directly from the distributional recurrence.

A Note on Notation. This chapter also serves the purpose to fix notations for the presented mathematical tools. A respectable body of notation is built up successively throughout this chapter, and in fact also the next two chapters. Please note that we collect all introduced notation in Appendix A in one place.

I tried hard to choose memorizable notations, and to explain underlying mnemonics upon definition (watch out for $\underline{\text{underlines}}$!), but I gave preference to consistency with existing literature, whenever possible and applicable.

Vectorized Notation. A valuable convention for concise notation is to work with vectors and apply operations element-wise by default. To avoid confusion, we always write vectors in bold font: $\mathbf{x} = (x_1, \ldots, x_n)$. Element-wise application then means that we understand $\mathbf{x} + 5$ to mean the vector $(x_1 + 5, \ldots, x_n + 5)$, i.e., we have applied the operation *add five* to each component of the vector. If we have a second vector $\mathbf{y}$ of same dimension, we write $\mathbf{x} - \mathbf{y}$ for $(x_1 - y_1, \ldots x_n - y_n)$. We have applied the binary operation *difference* element-wise to the vectors. For a scalar $\alpha \in \mathbb{R}$, the usual scalar multiplication notation $\alpha\mathbf{x}$ is simply a special case.

The same convention is also used for relations, which we require to hold *for all* components. $\mathbf{x} \geqslant 0$ means all components are at least zero, $\mathbf{x} = 0$ means $\mathbf{x} = (0, \ldots, 0)$, $\mathbf{x} < \mathbf{y}$ means $x_i < y_i$ for all i etc. Some authors use relations on vectors with existential semantics; this is never done in this work.

There is one problem with this conventions: most mathematically inclined readers will understand an expression $x \cdot y$ as the *dot product* of x and y (a.k.a. the *scalar product* or *inner product*). Fortunately, there is no need for element-wise products in this work, so we define that *products of vectors are not meant element-wise;* to the contrary, we will occasionally use dot products for concise notation. To avoid confusion with an element-wise product, we always write $x^\mathsf{T}y$ instead of $x \cdot y$ when we mean $\sum_{i=1}^{n} x_i y_i$. By convention, all our vectors are *column vectors,* even though we write their components in a row for brevity; the inner product is the only place in this work where the orientation of vectors is relevant.

Dot products remain the only exception to our rule of element-wise application.

Vectorized Notation in Programming Languages. The idea of vectorized notation has been used in programming languages for scientific programming for a long time. Unlike for mathematical formulas, the notion of *types* of variables is widely accepted and understood by programmers, which helps to clarify the semantics of the vectorized syntax.

Matlab is probably the language that follows this convention most rigorously. Other tools have mimicked the syntax, e.g., the numpy package for Python. In Mathematica, most built-in functions are defined to automatically thread over lists, by having the Listable attribute. I have come to like this notation a lot.

It is interesting to note that all the above examples use the ordinary multiplication operator for the element-wise product (remember: unlike the notation of this work). For inner products a.k.a. dot products, they usually define another operator or function.

We will regularly refer to the *total* of a vector $x = (x_1, \ldots, x_n)$, which we write as

$$\Sigma x \;=\; \sum_{i=1}^{n} x_i. \tag{2.1}$$

Once we are accustomed to this, the multiplicative version naturally suggests itself; we write

$$\Pi x \;=\; \prod_{i=1}^{n} x_i. \tag{2.2}$$

Iverson Bracket. For any boolean expression, i.e., any statement P, we write

$$[P] \;=\; \begin{cases} 1, & \text{if P is true;} \\ 0, & \text{if P is false.} \end{cases} \tag{2.3}$$

This often avoids the need to address several special cases separately and also clearly shows in which part of a formula the cases differ.

Sets. We reserve $\mathbb{N}$ for the natural numbers without zero, and write $\mathbb{N}_0$ when it is included. More generally, we attach predicate expressions in the subscript of sets to denote the restricted sets, e.g., $\mathbb{R}_{>5}$ denotes $(5, \infty)$, the reals strictly greater five. Closed intervals are written as $[0,1] = \mathbb{R}_{\geqslant 0} \cap \mathbb{R}_{\leqslant 1}$. Occasionally, we use the open resp. closed neighborhoods or balls $B_{<\varepsilon}(x) = \{y : |y - x| < \varepsilon\}$ and $B_{\leqslant\varepsilon}(x) = \{y : |y - x| \leqslant \varepsilon\}$.

We write $[m..n]$ for the *integer interval* $\{m, m+1, \ldots, n\}$ and $[n] = [1..n]$. We use element-wise notation also for sets, e.g., $2\mathbb{N}$ means the set of even numbers $\{2, 4, 6, 8, \ldots\}$ and $[3..6] + \frac{1}{2}$ is $\{3.5, 4.5, 5.5, 6.5\}$.

We denote by $\mathbb{1}_{\mathfrak{I}}^{(n)}$ the characteristic vector of a subset $\mathfrak{I} \subseteq [n]$, i.e.,

$$\mathbb{1}_{\mathfrak{I}} = \mathbb{1}_{\mathfrak{I}}^{(n)} = \Big([1 \in \mathfrak{I}], \ldots, [n \in \mathfrak{I}] \Big). \tag{2.4}$$

If n is clear from the context, we drop the superscript.

Weakly Increasing.   If $x \leqslant y < z$, we say x is *weakly smaller* than y and y is *strictly smaller* than z. Similarly, a number $x \geqslant 0$ is *weakly positive*, whereas $y > 0$ is said to be strictly positive or just positive. Similarly we call a function f *weakly* (or *strictly*) *increasing* if $x < y$ implies $f(x) \leqslant f(y)$ (resp. $f(x) < f(y)$).

More generally, we use the qualifiers weakly and strictly to refine any property that has a less-or-equal flavor: A is a strict/weak subset of B, $\prec$ is a strictly/weakly partial order, $a_1 \leqslant a_2 \leqslant a_3$ is a weakly sorted (ascendingly), etc.

What is nondecreasing?   Instead of saying that x is weakly smaller than y, it has become customary in mathematics to say that x is *not larger* than y. (The only established alternative I know is to say x is less than or equal to y, which is quite verbose.) While logically fine, this tradition of using negated notations makes reading much harder than necessary. $x \leqslant y$ is a really fundamental statement, and we should have a first-class expression for it, instead of forcing readers to mentally undo the negation.

However, x is not larger than y is at least unambiguous, and people have become used to it, so is it worth breaking a tradition? Well, first of all, x is not larger than y is not unambiguous at all, as soon as we deal with an order relation that is strictly partial! It might then mean that either $x < y$ or x and y are incomparable.

Similarly, what exactly is a *nondecreasing* function? One that is not (strictly/weakly) decreasing? Of course not; think of $\sin(x)$ for example. Rather, we have to move the negation behind the quantifier: strictly decreasing means $\forall x < y : f(x) > f(y)$, and nondecreasing means $\forall x < y : \neg f(x) > f(y)$, which is a different thing than not decreasing $\neg \forall x < y : f(x) > f(y)$. We have become used to the term, but it is really a bad notation; on top of the needless negation, the literal meaning is misleading as it does not say where to put the negation.

Weakly increasing in contrast is positive and naturally suggests to transfer the less-or-equal flavor from an order relation to the function: a function is weakly increasing if and only if the values of the function get weakly larger.

I was convinced to convert to positive notation by a post on math.stackexchange.com, and I'd like to quote the nicely written answer there: *"if you want to be precise, it is better to say what you mean rather than to say what you don't mean (or even to not say what you are nonmeaning)"* (van Leeuwen [111])

2.1 Continuous Basics

In this section, we collect basics from (real) analysis and properties of special functions.

2.1.1 Asymptotic Notation

Landau notation, in particular the *"Big-Oh" notation* is very widely used in computer science nowadays to describe asymptotic bounds on a term. Despite being in widespread use—or is it *because* of that?—there has been considerable dissension about proper definitions and recommended syntax for Big-Oh and its relatives.

Big Uh-Oh. Let us briefly recapitulate the story with its most recent twists. Knuth [102] traces the origins of the O-notation to works on number theory around 1900, more precisely to the German mathematicians Edmund Landau and Paul Bachmann. Landau [109, p. 59] defines $f(x) = O(g(x))$ as abbreviation for

$$\limsup_{x \to \infty} \frac{|f(x)|}{g(x)} < \infty,$$

requiring g to be (asymptotically) positive. He also defines $f(x) = o(g(x))$ to mean $\lim_{x \to \infty} f(x)/g(x) = 0$. If the above limit is 1 instead, Landau writes $f(x) \sim g(x)$.

Knuth bemoans the widespread abuse of O when actually a *lower* bound on the order of growth is meant—a bad habit that has been resisting all attempts to eradicate it to this day. A notation expressing lower bounds does not appear in the works of Landau and Bachmann; according to Knuth [102], the symbol Ω first appeared in a work of G. H. Hardy and J. E. Littlewood, but they used it with the meaning that a function is larger than another *infinitely often*. Knuth advocates the use of Ω in the sense of *all but finitely often*, symmetrical to O, and proposes to use Θ if both O and Ω hold.

It is interesting that Knuth's formal definition is, however, *not* symmetric; Knuth [102] defines O as upper bound on the growth rate of the *absolute value* of a function, but introduces Ω *without* absolute values. In his sense, we would have $-n^2 \neq \Omega(n)$ and $-n^2 = \Omega(-n^3)$. I welcome the fact that these asymmetric versions have not won through.

Modern textbooks on algorithms, e.g., the classic by Cormen et al. [35], restrict Big-Oh definitions to weakly positive functions; with the justification that in the analysis of algorithms, the resource counts are never negative. This effectively precludes us from using O to bound error terms in truncated asymptotic expansions, as those may well be negative or oscillating around 0, even when the overall function is positive. In line with Landau's original context, I consider the use of O for error terms very appropriate—even more important than overall bounds—so negative functions definitely have to be handled sensibly by bounding the *absolute value*.

One persisting bone of contention is whether statements of the form "$f(n) = O(g(n))$" are to be discouraged in favor of "$f(n) \in O(g(n))$." Brassard [25] argues vigorously for the proper set-theoretic notation, as formal definitions of O consider sets of functions. Knuth says w.r.t. this discussion that his *"feeling is that we should continue to use one-way equality together with O-notations, since it has been common practice of thousands of mathematicians for so many years now, and since we understand the meaning of our existing notation sufficiently well."* ([102], p. 20) I am in line with Knuth, and stick to one-way equalities in this work.

Gurevich [75] even argues that "$O(f(n)n)$" could be seen as a "common name," an abstract representative for a class of functions with some common property. In his sense, "$O(n) = O(n^2)$." should be seen as analog to the statement "a square is a rectangle," making $O(f(n))$ a first-class object. Gurevich draws a parallel to the widely accepted use of indefinite integrals $\int f(x)\,dx$, omitting the constant of integration in antiderivatives.

Howell [85] demonstrates that one has to be very careful in using O-terms with several variables. He generalizes a few natural desirable properties for Big-Oh to that case—and shows them to be contradictory! Rutanen et al. [155] recently proposed an axiomatization of asymptotic notation with a list of properties the notion should have. It builds on Howell's work. The main property that notions like the original one by Landau [109] fail to fulfill is what Rutanen et al. call *sub-composability*: It requires $g(n) \in O(f(n))$ to imply $g(h(n)) = O\big(f(h(n))\big)$ for *all* functions h.

It is clear that sub-composability *cannot* hold if we ignore behavior *for small n*, i.e., for all $n \leqslant n_0$, where n_0 is a constant: function h might concentrate attention to exactly this disregarded region that we know nothing about; say $h(n) = 0$ for the most extreme case. To resolve this issue Rutanen et al. propose to define O based on "linear dominance," i.e., requiring $f(n) \leqslant cg(n)$ for *all* n. Howell suggests to use a more complicated definition that takes maximal function values into account.

Expecting an *asymptotic* bound to continue to hold after inserting constant values for n does not seem natural to me. Howell and Rutanen et al. both argue that sub-composability is especially desirable for O-terms involving functions in *several* variables. Composition might there hold only one parameter constant, while another keeps growing.

Asymptotics with several variables are delicate, the proposed solutions feel like throwing the baby out with the bathwater. *They propose to take the asymptotics out of asymptotic notation!* It would make O quite cumbersome to use; if we fail to show linear dominance right away, we would have to explicitly restrict the domain of our functions first.

Bounds that are valid everywhere are certainly desirable, but neither is their statement an *asymptotic* notation, nor will their proof be truly asymptotic in nature. (Proofs via limits of quotients are possible if the function in the O-term is never zero, cf. Theorem 9.13 of Rutanen et al. [155, v22]. This latter requirement does not feel "asymptotic" to me.) Having a concise notation to express linear dominance might be beneficial; *replacing* Big-Oh by it is something I would disapprove of.

In light of this ongoing dispute, I reached the conclusion that it should become best practice to briefly state which flavor of Big-Oh is used in any piece of work; of course, I should set a good example here.

Definition of O used in this work.   We use the notations O, o, Ω ω, Θ and $\sim$ as they are defined by Flajolet and Sedgewick [64], i.e., we require the ratio of absolute values to stay bounded resp. converge to 0, except for $\sim$, where we require the ratio to converge to 1 without taking absolute values. For convenience, here is their definition.

Definition 2.1 (Asymptotic Notation, Section A.2 of *Analytic Combinatorics* [64]):
Let $\mathcal{X}$ be a set and $x_0 \in \mathcal{X}$ a particular element of $\mathcal{X}$. We assume a notion of neighborhood to exist on $\mathcal{X}$. Examples are $\mathcal{X} = \mathbb{N} \cup \{+\infty\}$ with $x_0 = +\infty$, $\mathcal{X} = \mathbb{R}$ with x_0 any point

in $\mathbb{R}$; $X = \mathbb{C}$ or a subset of $\mathbb{C}$ of $\mathbb{C}$ with $x_0 = 0$, and so on.
For two functions f and g from $X \setminus \{x_0\}$ to $\mathbb{R}$ or $\mathbb{C}$, we write

- ▶ $f(x) = O(g(x))$ *as $x \to x_0$,*
  if there is a neighborhood N of x_0 and a constant $C > 0$, such that for all $x \in N$ except $x = x_0$ holds $|f(x)| \leqslant C|g(x)|$;

- ▶ $f(x) = o(g(x))$ *as $x \to x_0$,*
  if for any $\varepsilon > 0$ there is a neighborhood N of x_0, such that for all $x \in N$ except $x = x_0$ holds $|f(x)| \leqslant \varepsilon|g(x)|$;

- ▶ $f(x) \sim g(x)$ *as $x \to x_0$,*
  if $\lim_{x \to x_0} f(x)/g(x) = 1$;

- ▶ $f(x) = \Omega(g(x))$ *as $x \to x_0$,*
  if there is a neighborhood N of x_0 and a constant $C > 0$, such that for all $x \in N$ except $x = x_0$ holds $|f(x)| \geqslant C|g(x)|$;

- ▶ $f(x) = \Theta(g(x))$ *as $x \to x_0$,*
  if $f(x) = O(g(x))$ and $f(x) = \Omega(g(x))$ as $x \to x_0$. ◀

We allow ourselves to write $f(n) = O(g(n))$, but formally think of $O(g(n))$ etc. as sets of functions. If $O(g(n))$ appears in the middle of an expression, that term stands for the set of functions obtained by inserting any function $f(n) \in O(g(n))$ in place of $O(g(n))$.

Positive Errors.   Error terms are customarily written as $+O(h)$. A positive attitude towards errors should be welcomed, but I would like to syntactically emphasize that the sign in error terms is really not specified, therefore I write $f(n) = g(n) \pm O(h(n))$. The error bound might be positive, negative, zero, or any mixture. We only bound its absolute value.

Even though it deviates from established notation, this change is harmless, in that it can hardly be misunderstood, whereas $+O(h(n))$ might be mistaken for a positive quantity where it is not.

Uniform Big-Oh Bounds.   According to the definition above, bounds expressed by Big-Oh only hold in the limit: if we write $f(x) = O(x^{-1})$ as $x \to 0$, we mean that there is a *neighborhood* around the limit point, $x = 0$, and a constant C so that $|f(x)| \leqslant C|x^{-1}|$ for all x *in that neighborhood*. Usually this is what we have in mind for an asymptotic notation.

However, some authors use Big-Oh also in a wider meaning (equivalent to linear dominance): the statement "$f(x) = O(x^{-1})$ *uniformly* for $|x| < 1$" is to be understood as there is a constant C such that *for all x with $|x| < 1$ holds $|f(x)| \leqslant C|x^{-1}|$*. Again: for *all* such x. This extended use is advocated, e.g., by Graham et al. [72, Section 9.2]; when they write

$$f(x) \;=\; O(x^{-1}), \qquad |x| < 1, \tag{2.5}$$

they mean the above statement.

I find this syntax unfortunate since it can be mistaken to mean only the usual in-the-limit bound. When we use Big-Oh in the meaning of such a uniform bound, we explicitly put the keyword *uniformly*, to emphasize the extended scope.

Similarly, we say that $f(x, y) = O(g(x, y))$ as $x \to x_0$ holds *uniformly in* $y \in \mathcal{Y}$ if the constants in the O-term do not depend on y.

Multivariate Big-Oh.   We will mostly work with univariate asymptotics, but in Chapter 8, we use bivariate Big-Oh as well. As discussed in the digression above, multivariate asymptotics can be dangerous, so we had better state formally what we mean by it.

Definition 2.2 (Multivariate Big-Oh): *As before, let $\mathcal{X}$ and $\mathcal{Y}$ be two sets with a notion of neighborhood, and let $x_0 \in \mathcal{X}$ and $y_0 \in \mathcal{Y}$. We say that*

$$f(x, y) = O(g(x, y)) \qquad \text{as } x \to x_0 \text{ and } y \to y_0,$$

if for all functions $x : \mathbb{R} \to \mathcal{X}$ and $y : \mathbb{R} \to \mathcal{Y}$ with $x(z) \to x_0$ and $y(z) \to y_0$ as $z \to \infty$ holds

$$f\big(x(z), y(z)\big) = O\big(g(x(z), y(z))\big) \qquad \text{as } z \to \infty. \qquad \blacktriangleleft$$

This definition reduces the question to univariate asymptotics by introducing a *hidden variable z* that drives the limiting process; both variables have to converge to their limit, but the relative speed of convergence is not restricted.

This definition makes it easy to incorporate side conditions on the relative growth of the variables, and we will always add such restrictions explicitly to our statements. The formal meaning is that we require the side conditions to hold for the functions $x(z)$ and $y(z)$ from Definition 2.2; let us consider an example to make this clear.

Example.   Running time complexities of graph algorithms typically depend on the number of nodes n and the number of edges m, and both go to infinity. If the graph is simple and connected, we have the restrictions $m = \Omega(n)$ and $m = O(n^2)$ as $n \to \infty$. We then write

$$f(n, m) = O(g(n, m)) \qquad \text{as } n \to \infty \text{ with } m = \Omega(n) \text{ and } m = O(n^2) \qquad (2.6)$$

to mean that for *all* functions $n : \mathbb{R} \to \mathbb{N}$ and $m : \mathbb{R} \to \mathbb{N}$ with $n(z) \to \infty$ and $m(z) = \Omega(n(z))$ and $m(z) = O(n^2(z))$ as $z \to \infty$ holds

$$f\big(n(z), m(z)\big) = O\big(g(n(z), m(z))\big) \qquad \text{as } z \to \infty. \qquad (2.7)$$

2.1.2 Special Functions

The Gamma Function.   The *gamma function* $\Gamma(z)$ is defined by

$$\Gamma(z) = \int_0^\infty e^{-t} t^{z-1} \, dt, \qquad \Re z > 0, \qquad (2.8)$$

and elsewhere by analytic continuation; it has poles at $z \in \mathbb{Z}_{\leqslant 0}$. It is a continuous extension of the factorial function $n! = 1 \cdot 2 \cdot 3 \cdots n$ to any real (in fact complex) number z; we have

$$\Gamma(n+1) = n!, \qquad n \in \mathbb{N}_0, \qquad (2.9)$$

see Equation (5.4.1) of the DLMF [46].

The NIST Digital Library of Mathematical Functions (DLMF). The *digital library of mathematical functions (DLMF)* is the online version of the successor of *"the Abramowitz and Stegun,"* i.e., the *Handbook of Mathematical Functions with Formulas, Graphs, and Mathematical Tables* first published in 1964. The handbook had since become the standard reference for facts on special functions, widely referred to by naming its two editors Milton Abramowitz and Irene A. Stegun. In 2010, its successor was published, both as a traditional printed handbook [143] and as a freely accessible website, the DLMF [46]. References in this work will refer to the online version but equation numbers are that same in the printed version. In the PDF-version of this work, equation and section numbers from the DLMF are clickable links that point directly to the referenced part on the website.

It is in fact easy to see by partial integration that $\Gamma(z+1) = z\Gamma(z)$, so we have (by induction) the relation

$$z^{\overline{n}} = \frac{\Gamma(z+n)}{\Gamma(z)}, \qquad n \in \mathbb{N}_0 \text{ and } z \notin \mathbb{Z}_{\leqslant 0}, \tag{2.10}$$

where $z^{\overline{n}}$ is the nth rising factorial power of z, see Section 2.2. We can give a handy asymptotic expansion for such quotients, where we assume that z is real:

$$\frac{\Gamma(z+a)}{\Gamma(z+b)} = z^{a-b} \pm O(z^{a-b-1}), \qquad (z \to \infty). \tag{2.11}$$

This follows from Equation (5.11.13) of the DLMF [46]. In fact, a full asymptotic expansion is given there, but for our purposes the simple form in Equation (2.11) suffices.

The Digamma Function. A close relative of the gamma function is the *digamma function* $\psi(z)$ defined via

$$\psi(z) = \frac{\Gamma'(z)}{\Gamma(z)} = \frac{d}{dz}\ln(\Gamma(z)). \tag{2.12}$$

Many multiplicative properties of $\Gamma(z)$ have additive analogs for $\psi(z)$, for example the fundamental equation

$$\psi(z+1) = \psi(z) + \frac{1}{z}, \qquad z \notin \mathbb{Z}_{\leqslant 0}, \tag{2.13}$$

which is Equation (5.5.2) of the DLMF [46]. (It also follows directly from the definition upon inserting $\Gamma(z+1) = z\Gamma(z)$.) Iterating Equation (2.13), we find that what $\Gamma(z)$ is to $n!$, is $\psi(z)$ to $H_n = \frac{1}{1} + \frac{1}{2} + \cdots + \frac{1}{n}$, the harmonic numbers (see Section 2.2.2):

$$\psi(n+1) = H_n - \gamma, \qquad n \in \mathbb{N}_0, \tag{2.14}$$

where

$$\gamma \approx 0.57721\,56649\,01532\,86061 \tag{2.15}$$

is the *Euler-Mascheroni constant* a.k.a. *Euler-gamma*.

Order of Growth Check   At first sight, this connection might be a bit obscure and seemingly appears out of thin air. The following back-of-the-envelope computation immediately shows that the order of growth checks out: $\ln(\Gamma(n+1)) = \ln(n!) \sim n \ln n$, and the derivative of that is $\ln n \pm O(1) \sim H_n$.

The Beta Function.   The beta function is usually defined with two parameters as $B(\alpha, \beta) = \int_0^1 z^{\alpha-1}(1-z)^{\beta-1}\, dz$ for $\alpha, \beta > 0$. For our application, in particular for the Dirichlet distribution, it is more convenient to directly work with the d-*dimensional beta function* $B(\alpha_1, \ldots, \alpha_d)$. To conveniently express it, we let Δ_d for $d \in \mathbb{N}_{\geqslant 2}$ denote the *standard* $(d-1)$-*dimensional open simplex,* i.e.,

$$\Delta_d := \left\{ x \in \mathbb{R}^{d-1} : x > 0 \ \wedge\ \Sigma x < 1 \right\} \subseteq (0,1)^{d-1}. \tag{2.16}$$

Note the (deliberate) mismatch in dimension: Δ_d has dimension $d-1$. For convenience and to allow symmetric notation, we formally write $\int_{\Delta_d} f(x)\, dx$ for an integrable function $f : \mathbb{R}^d \to \mathbb{R}$ to mean the integral

$$\int_{\Delta_d} f(x_1, \ldots, x_d)\, dx := \int_{\Delta_d} f\left(x_1, \ldots, x_{d-1}, 1 - \sum_{i=1}^{d-1} x_i \right) d(x_1, \ldots, x_{d-1}) \tag{2.17}$$

$$= \int_0^1 \int_0^{1-x_1} \cdots \int_0^{1-\sum_{i=1}^{d-2} x_i} f\left(x_1, \ldots, x_{d-1}, 1 - \sum_{i=1}^{d-1} x_i \right) dx_{d-1} \cdots dx_2\, dx_1 .$$

$$\tag{2.18}$$

Simplex: Open or Closed?   Two different sets are known under the name *standard simplex*. Both describe the set of stochastic vectors in $\mathbb{R}^d$, i.e., vectors with positive entries that sum to one. The first one is our Δ_d, the *open simplex*. It describes stochastic vectors by leaving out the last component x_d, which is indirectly given by the others as $x_d = 1 - x_1 - \cdots - x_{d-1}$ anyway. For example, $\Delta_2 = (0,1)$. It is clear that the set of stochastic vectors has dimension $d-1$, so representing it by a subset of $\mathbb{R}^{d-1}$ instead of $\mathbb{R}^d$ is natural.

However, the choice of leaving out x_d is arbitrary; we could eliminate any other component instead. This introduces asymmetry in the notation, which can be avoided using the *closed simplex* $\blacktriangle_d = \{x \in \mathbb{R}^d : x > 0 \wedge \Sigma x = 1\}$ instead. For example, $\blacktriangle_2 = \{(t, 1-t) : t \in (0,1)\}$. $\blacktriangle_d$ is formally a subset of $\mathbb{R}^d$, but it has dimension $d-1$. This makes it very inconvenient for integration: it has measure zero.

Our convention from above tries to combine the best of both worlds: by introducing the syntactic abbreviation x_d for $1 - x_1 - \cdots - x_{d-1}$, we can write integrals in the symmetric form as if they were taken over $\blacktriangle_d$, but we compute them by separating the components of Δ_d as in Equation (2.18).

We adopt here the naming convention of Ng et al. [141]; it is a bit unfortunate since as a subset of $\mathbb{R}^d$, $\blacktriangle_d$ is neither open nor closed in the topological sense, and is indeed an *open* subset of the containing $(d-1)$-dimensional affine subspace of $\mathbb{R}^d$. Δ_d is sometimes also called *standard (open) orthogonal simplex*, or *corner* of the $(d-1)$-dimensional hypercube.

With this convention, we define the beta function by the integral

$$B(\boldsymbol{\alpha}) = B(\alpha_1, \ldots, \alpha_d) := \int_{\Delta_d} x_1^{\alpha_1-1} \cdots x_d^{\alpha_d-1} \, d\mathbf{x}, \qquad \boldsymbol{\alpha} > 0. \tag{2.19}$$

The beta function can be written in terms of the gamma function as

$$B(\alpha_1, \ldots, \alpha_d) = \frac{\Gamma(\alpha_1) \cdots \Gamma(\alpha_d)}{\Gamma(\alpha_1 + \cdots + \alpha_d)}, \tag{2.20}$$

see Equation (5.12.1) of the DLMF [46] for $d = 2$, and Equation (2.3) of Ng et al. [141] for the general case. If we take the case $d = 2$ for granted, the generalization follows by induction:

Proof of (2.20): Assume $d \geqslant 3$. Writing the integral for $B(\boldsymbol{\alpha})$ in the form of Equation (2.18), we have as innermost integral

$$\int_{x_{d-1}=0}^{1-x_1-\cdots-x_{d-2}} x_{d-1}^{\alpha_{d-1}-1} (1 - x_1 - \cdots - x_{d-2} - x_{d-1})^{\alpha_d-1} \, dx_{d-1}. \tag{2.21}$$

This is $i_{\alpha_{d-1}, \alpha_d}(x_1 + \cdots + x_{d-2})$ when we abbreviate

$$i_{a,b}(z) := \int_{x=0}^{1-z} x^{a-1} (1 - z - x)^{b-1} \, dx. \tag{2.22}$$

This can be rewritten with the substitution $y = x/(1-z)$, i.e., $x = y(1-z)$ as

$$= (1-z)^{a+b-1} \int_{y=0}^{1} y^{a-1} (1-y)^{b-1} \, dy \tag{2.23}$$

$$= (1-z)^{a+b-1} B(a, b). \tag{2.24}$$

We thus have

$$B(\boldsymbol{\alpha}) = B(\alpha_{d-1}, \alpha_d) \cdot B(\alpha_1, \ldots, \alpha_{d-2}, \alpha_{d-1} + \alpha_d), \tag{2.25}$$

and using the induction hypothesis on both yields

$$= \frac{\Gamma(\alpha_1) \cdots \Gamma(\alpha_d)}{\Gamma(\alpha_1 + \cdots + \alpha_d)}. \tag{2.26}$$

$\blacksquare$

Incomplete Beta Function. For the binary case $d = 2$ we also use the *regularized incomplete beta function* where the limits of integration are variable:

$$I_{x,y}(\alpha, \beta) = \frac{1}{B(\alpha, \beta)} \int_x^y t^{\alpha-1} (1-t)^{\beta-1} \, dt. \tag{2.27}$$

If the parameters α and β are integers, we can express the incomplete beta function more explicitly. With Equation (8.17.5) of the DLMF [46] we find the form

$$I_{x,y}(\alpha,\beta) \;=\; \sum_{b=0}^{\beta-1} \binom{\alpha-1+b}{\alpha-1}\left(y^{\alpha}(1-y)^{b} - x^{\alpha}(1-x)^{b}\right), \qquad \begin{array}{l} \alpha,\beta \in \mathbb{N} \text{ and } \alpha \geqslant \beta, \\ 0 \leqslant x,y < 1 . \end{array}$$

$$(2.28)$$

If we need $\beta > \alpha$, we can exploit the symmetry of beta integrals:

$$I_{x,y}(\alpha,\beta) \;=\; I_{1-y,1-x}(\beta,\alpha), \qquad \alpha,\beta > 0 \text{ and } 0 \leqslant x,y < 1. \tag{2.29}$$

A Logarithmic Beta Integral.

$$\int_{0}^{1} z^{a-1}(1-z)^{b-1}\ln(z)\,dz \;=\; B(a,b)\big(\psi(a)-\psi(a+b)\big), \qquad a,b > 0. \tag{2.30}$$

This is a special case of Equation (4.253-1), p. 540, of Gradshteyn and Ryzhik [71] with $r = 1$, but there is also a nice direct argument.

Proof of (2.30): A simple computation shows that

$$\frac{\partial}{\partial a}B(a,b) \;=\; B(a,b)\left(\frac{\Gamma'(a)}{\Gamma(a)} - \frac{\Gamma'(a+b)}{\Gamma(a+b)}\right) \tag{2.31}$$

$$=\; B(a,b)\big(\psi(a)-\psi(a+b)\big). \tag{2.32}$$

On the other hand, using *Leibniz's rule* for differentiation under the integral sign, we have

$$\frac{\partial}{\partial a}B(a,b) \;=\; \int_{0}^{1}(1-x)^{b-1}\frac{\partial}{\partial a}x^{a-1}\,dx \tag{2.33}$$

$$=\; \int_{0}^{1}(1-x)^{b-1}x^{a-1}\ln(x)\,dx. \tag{2.34}$$

$\blacksquare$

2.1.3 Convexity

The unrestricted set of (real) functions contains many hideous creatures, traditionally used in introductory math courses to tame students' tendencies to eagerly jump to general conclusions that seem intuitive, since they are true for *typical* examples. Most functions in this work are, however, really harmless. It is then desirable to tame the class of functions instead, so that intuitive statements hold. Restricting attention to *continuous* functions already saves some of them as in the *intermediate value theorem;* for other properties continuity alone is not sufficient, e.g., the existence of a derivative.

In the next two section, we will consider two constrained classes of functions whose properties are often helpful in our analyses. We consider definitions and properties only in so far as we need them; most results have been generalized further. This section considers *convex* functions. They fulfill a few fundamental inequalities that we state here for reference.

Definition 2.3 (Convex Function): *Let $I \subseteq \mathbb{R}$ be an interval and $f : I \to \mathbb{R}$ a function. f is called convex if*

$$\forall x, y \in I \; \forall \mu \in (0,1) \; : \; f\big(\mu x + (1-\mu)y\big) \;\leqslant\; \mu f(x) + (1-\mu)f(y).$$

If the inequality is strict for all $x \neq y$, f is said to be strictly convex.
Likewise, f is (strictly) concave if we have $\geqslant$ (resp. $>$) in the inequality instead. ◄

Geometrically speaking, *a convex function lies below its chords,* a concave one lies above. Note that f is concave if and only if $-f$ is convex, so most properties of convex functions directly carry over to concave ones. We hence only need to discuss them for the convex case. In the following, I denotes a real interval.

The most convenient way to check convexity is usually via the following characterization.

Proposition 2.4 (Convexity via Derivatives, Thms. 12B,C of Roberts and Varberg [149]):

Let $f : I \to \mathbb{R}$ be a function.

(a) *Suppose f' exists in the interior of I.*
Then f is (strictly) convex if and only if f' is (strictly) increasing.

(b) *Suppose f'' exists in the interior of I.*
Then f is convex if and only if $f''(x) \geqslant 0$ for all x inside I.
If even $f''(x) > 0$ for all such x, then f is strictly convex. ■

For differentiable convex functions, we have the tangent inequality: *a convex function lies above all its tangents.*

Lemma 2.5 (Tangent Inequality, Theorem 12E of Roberts and Varberg [149]):
Let $f : I \to \mathbb{R}$ be a convex function and $x_0 \in I$ a point where $f'(x_0)$ exists. Then

$$\forall x \in I \; : \; f(x) \;\geqslant\; f(x_0) + f'(x_0)(x - x_0).$$

If f' exists on all of I and f is strictly convex, equality holds only for $x = x_0$. ■

While a convex functions lies above its tangents, it lies below its chords. If we extend a chord to a secant, the function lies below the secant between the two points, but above the secant elsewhere:

Lemma 2.6 (Secant Inequalities):
Let $f : I \to \mathbb{R}$ be convex and $x, y \in I$ be two points $x \neq y$. Then

(a) $f\big(\mu x + (1-\mu)y\big) \leqslant \mu f(x) + (1-\mu)f(y)$ *for $\mu \in [0,1]$ and*

(b) $f\big(\mu x + (1-\mu)y\big) \geqslant \mu f(x) + (1-\mu)f(y)$ *for $\mu \notin [0,1]$.*
If f is strictly convex, the inequality is strict. ◄

Proof: The first part is the definition of convexity, the second follows directly from the *three chords lemma*, see, e.g., Proposition 6.7.3 of Sohrab [171].   ∎

A classic inequality follows by iteratively using the definition of convexity.

Lemma 2.7 (Jensen's Inequality, Proposition 6.7.2 of Sohrab [171]):
Let $f : I \to \mathbb{R}$ be convex and n points $x_1, \ldots, x_n \in I$ be given. For any $\mu_1, \ldots, \mu_n \geq 0$ with $\mu_1 + \cdots + \mu_n = 1$ holds

$$f\left(\sum_{i=1}^{n} \mu_i x_i\right) \leq \sum_{i=1}^{n} \mu_i f(x_i).$$

∎

2.1.4 Lipschitz- and Hölder-Continuity

Continuity alone is not enough for many intuitive properties of nice functions, as this notion of smoothness is too localized. In this section we consider more restrictive forms of continuity that guarantee us some handy properties, collected in Proposition 2.12 below.

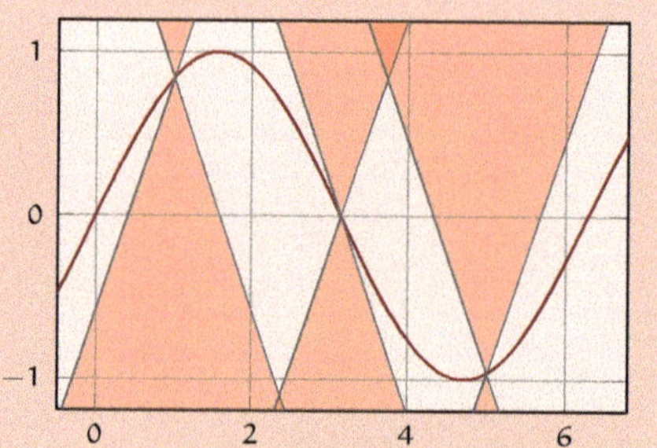

Figure 2: Illustration of Lipschitz continuity. A function f (here $f(x) = \sin(x)$) is Lipschitz-continuous if its graph lies "within any bow tie ⋈" centered at a point of the graph; in the picture, the function may not enter the red area. The slope of the bow ties is the Lipschitz constant.

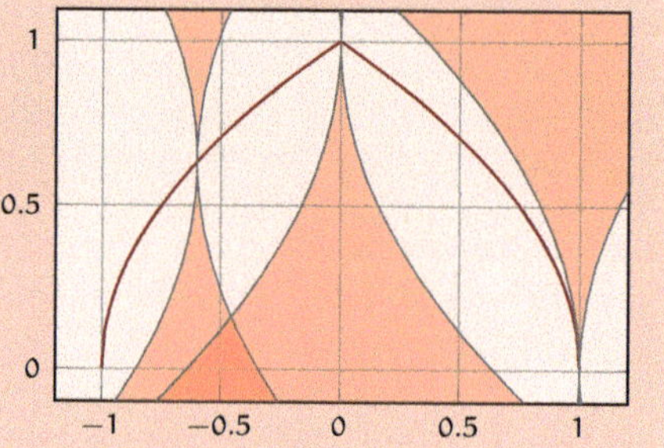

Figure 3: Illustration of Hölder continuity. A function f (here $f(x) = \sqrt{1 - |x|}$) is Hölder-continuous if its graph lies "within any diabolo ⤬" centered at a point of the graph. The Hölder-exponent and constant control the shape of the diabolo.

Definition 2.8 (Lipschitz- and Hölder-continuity): *Let I be a real interval, $f : I \to \mathbb{R}$ be a function and $0 < \alpha \leq 1$. f is Hölder-continuous with exponent α when*

$$\exists C \; \forall x, y \in I \; : \; \left|f(x) - f(y)\right| \leq C|x - y|^{\alpha}.$$

If $\alpha = 1$, then f is called Lipschitz-continuous.   ◀

Hölder-continuity is also called *Lipschitz of order* α by some authors, e.g., Sohrab [171, Definition 4.6.9]. Figures 2 and 3 illustrate the notations.

> **The Unspeakable.** With these pictures in mind, I was strongly tempted to refer to Lipschitz-continuity as ⋈-*continuity* and likewise to Hölder-continuity as ⋊⋉-*continuity*; but in the end I did not dare to deprive Rudolf Lipschitz and Otto Hölder of their right to give their name to these important concepts.
>
> Moreover, while ⋈- and ⋊⋉-continuous is somewhat pleasing to write, the spoken versions, *bow-tie-continuous* resp. *diabolo-continuous*, sounded a bit too much like a children's birthday party. The picture, however, got stuck in my mind.

Note that Hölder- and Lipschitz-continuity are *global* properties: the inequality in Definition 2.8 has to hold for any pair of values from the domain. This leads to some peculiar properties on unbounded domains: the function $x \mapsto x^\alpha$, $\alpha \in (0, 1]$ is Hölder-continuous with exponent α on $[0, \infty)$, but not for any other exponent, so each exponent defines its own class of Hölder-continuous functions.

We will mostly work with *bounded* domains, and there the exponent can be seen as the lower bound on the degree of smoothness: we can shrink the exponent without affecting continuity. This is formally stated in the following proposition.

Proposition 2.9 (Lipschitz implies Hölder on Bounded Domains): *Let* I *be bounded. If* $f : I \to \mathbb{R}$ *is Lipschitz-continuous on* I, *it is also Hölder-continuous on* I *for any exponent* $0 < \alpha \leqslant 1$. *If* f *is Hölder-continuous on* I *with exponent* α, *then it is also Hölder-continuous for any exponent* $\alpha' \in (0, \alpha]$. ◀

Proof: We only prove the second claim; it implies the first with $\alpha = 1$. We have $x^{\alpha'} \geqslant x^\alpha$ for $x \in [0, 1]$ and $0 < \alpha' \leqslant \alpha \leqslant 1$. Now let f be Hölder-continuous with constant C and exponent α, then we have for $x, y \in I$ that $|x - y| \leqslant |I|$ and $\frac{|x-y|}{|I|} \leqslant 1$. Then

$$
\begin{align}
|f(x) - f(y)| &\leqslant C|x - y|^\alpha \tag{2.35}\\
&= C|I|^\alpha \cdot \left(\frac{|x-y|}{|I|}\right)^\alpha \tag{2.36}\\
&\leqslant C|I|^\alpha \cdot \left(\frac{|x-y|}{|I|}\right)^{\alpha'} \tag{2.37}\\
&\leqslant C|I|^{\alpha-\alpha'} \cdot |x-y|^{\alpha'}. \tag{2.38}
\end{align}
$$

Hence, f is Hölder-continuous with constant $C|I|^{\alpha-\alpha'}$ and exponent α'. ∎

The following simple observation is usually the most convenient way to prove Lipschitz-continuity.

Proposition 2.10 (Bounded Derivative Implies Lipschitz): *A differentiable function* $f : I \to \mathbb{R}$ *is Lipschitz-continuous on* I *if* f' *is bounded on* I. *In particular if* I *is compact,* f *is Lipschitz if* f' *is continuous on* I. *The Lipschitz constant is* $\sup_{x \in I} f'(x)$. ◀

Proof: Let $C = \sup_{x \in I} f'(x)$. Assume there were $x, y \in I$ with $|f(x) - f(y)| > C|x - y|$. Then the secant connecting $(x, f(x))$ and $(y, f(y))$ has slope $C' = |f(x) - f(y)|/|x - y| > C$. By the *mean-value theorem*, there would be a z in between with $f'(z) = C' > C$, a contradiction to the choice of C. ∎

Hölder-continuity is maintained by many operations.

Lemma 2.11 (Stability of Hölder-Continuity, Theorem 4.6.14 of Sohrab [171]):

(a)   *Linear combinations of (finitely many) Hölder-continuous functions, all with the same exponent α, are again Hölder-continuous with exponent α.*

(b)   *The product of (finitely many) bounded-domain Hölder-continuous functions, all with the same exponent α, is again Hölder-continuous with exponent α.*

(c)   *The composition of two Hölder-continuous functions is again Hölder-continuous, where the exponents multiply.* ∎

In the following proposition, we collect for reference a few consequences of Hölder-continuity, in particular guarantees on the convergence speed of the Riemann sum for the integral. We will regularly use these facts.

Proposition 2.12 (Hölder Error Bounds):
Let $f(z)$ be Hölder-continuous with exponent α on $[a, b]$.

(a)   *Then holds uniformly for $z \in [a, b]$ with $z + \varepsilon \in [a, b]$ the approximation*

$$f(z + \varepsilon) \;=\; f(z) \pm O(\varepsilon^{\alpha}), \qquad (\varepsilon \to 0). \tag{2.39}$$

(b)   *Moreover we have for fixed limits a and b the approximation*

$$\int_a^b f(z)\,dz \;=\; \frac{b - a}{n} \sum_{i=0}^{n-1} f\big((1 - \tfrac{i}{n})a + \tfrac{i}{n}b\big) \;\pm\; O(n^{-\alpha}), \qquad (n \to \infty), \tag{2.40}$$

(c)   *and a similar relation for thin integrals*

$$n \cdot \int_a^{a + \frac{1}{n}} f(z)\,dz \;=\; f(a) \;\pm\; O(n^{-\alpha}), \qquad (n \to \infty). \tag{2.41}$$

◀

Although a trivial consequence, let us remark once more that for Lipschitz-continuous functions the above statements hold with $\alpha = 1$.

Proof: The first statement follows directly from the definition with $x = z + \varepsilon$ and $y = z$. It holds in fact without restriction on ε, as long as we do not leave the domain of f.

The integral exists as f is continuous on the compact interval. We split the integral at the equidistant points $a = a_0, a_1, a_2, \ldots, a_n = b$ with $a_i = (1 - \tfrac{i}{n})a + \tfrac{i}{n}b$ for $0 \leqslant i \leqslant n$, and use the Hölder condition on each of the integral slices:

$$\left| \int_{a_i}^{a_{i+1}} f(z)dz - \frac{b-a}{n} f(a_i) \right| = \int_{a_i}^{a_{i+1}} \left| f(z) - f(a_i) \right| dz \tag{2.42}$$

$$\leqslant \int_{a_i}^{a_{i+1}} C|z - a_i|^\alpha dz \tag{2.43}$$

$$= \frac{C}{1+\alpha} \cdot \left(\frac{b-a}{n} \right)^{1+\alpha}. \tag{2.44}$$

Summing this inequality over all i yields the second claim, since for fixed a and b, we have $n \cdot \frac{C}{1+\alpha} \left(\frac{b-a}{n} \right)^{1+\alpha} = O(n^{-\alpha})$.

The last claim follows from Equation (2.44) for $i = 0$, upon setting $n = 1$ and $b = a + \frac{1}{\tilde{n}}$; then the error term is $\frac{C}{1+\alpha} \left(\frac{1}{\tilde{n}} \right)^{1+\alpha} = O(\tilde{n}^{-1-\alpha})$. Multiplying by $\tilde{n}$ yields the claim in the given form. ■

◆   ◆   ◆

Most applications in this work refer to bounded intervals and list Hölder-continuity as the minimal requirement for the given proofs. When actually using the statement it will in most cases be sufficient to show Lipschitz-continuity with Proposition 2.10 and then apply Proposition 2.9.

There is one case however, where we actually need the flexibility since some functions are Hölder-, but *not* Lipschitz-continuous:

Lemma 2.13: $f : [0,1] \to \mathbb{R}$ with $f(x) = x \ln(1/x)$ *is Hölder-continuous for any exponent* $\alpha \in (0,1)$, *but not Lipschitz-continuous.* ◀

Proof: Intuitively, the derivative $f'(x) = \ln(1/x) - 1$ of f approaches infinity as $x \to 0$, so there is no constant bound for the steepness and f cannot be Lipschitz. But the growth is only logarithmic, so it is smaller than x^α for $\alpha < 1$ as $x \to 0$, so it is Hölder-continuous. The formal arguments uses Hölder's inequality and seems to be folklore, but I could not find a formal proof to cite; so here are the details.

We start by showing that for any $q > 1$, the following improper integral exists:

$$\int_0^1 \left| \ln(x) + 1 \right|^q dx = \int_0^{1/e} \left(-\ln(x) - 1 \right)^q dx + \int_{1/e}^1 \left(\ln(x) + 1 \right)^q dx. \tag{2.45}$$

The second integral is bounded since $\log(x) + 1 \leqslant 1$ in that range. For the range of the first one, there is an antiderivative; using $\frac{\partial}{\partial z} \Gamma(a,z) = -z^{a-1} e^{-z}$ (Equation (8.8.13) of the DLMF [46]), where $\Gamma(a,z) = \int_z^\infty t^{a-1} e^{-t} dt$ is the incomplete gamma function:

$$\frac{\partial}{\partial x} \frac{\Gamma(q+1, -\ln(x) - 1)}{e} = \left(-\ln(x) - 1 \right)^q. \tag{2.46}$$

Thereby, we find

$$\int_0^{1/e} \left(-\ln(x) - 1 \right)^q dx = \frac{\Gamma(q+1)}{e}. \tag{2.47}$$

We thus know that

$$\int_0^1 \left| \ln(x) + 1 \right|^q dx \; = \; C < \infty, \tag{2.48}$$

for a constant C depending only on q.

> Similarly as above, we can explicitly compute the second integral and thus C:
>
> $$\int_{1/e}^a \left(\ln(x) + 1 \right)^q dx \; = \; \frac{(-1)^q}{e} \left(\Gamma(q+1, -1) - \Gamma(q+1) \right),$$
>
> where for $q \in \mathbb{Z}$ we have $\Gamma(q+1, -1) = e \cdot D_q$ for $D_n = n! \cdot \left(1 - \frac{1}{1!} + \frac{1}{2!} - \cdots + \frac{(-1)^n}{n!} \right)$ the number of *derangements* of n objects (see Bergeron et al. [22] for the connection to $\Gamma(n+1, -1)$ and Example II.14 of Flajolet and Sedgewick [64] for the expression for D_n).

The second ingredient to our proof is *Hölder's inequality* (Equation (1.7.5) of the DLMF [46]): For $p > 1$ and $\frac{1}{p} + \frac{1}{q} = 1$ and two weakly positive functions f and g holds

$$\int_a^b f(x)g(x)\,dx \; \leqslant \; \left(\int_a^b \left(f(x) \right)^p dx \right)^{1/p} \cdot \left(\int_a^b \left(g(x) \right)^q dx \right)^{1/q}. \tag{2.49}$$

Now towards proving the Hölder-condition for exponent $\alpha \in (0,1)$, we express the difference $f(x) - f(y)$ as integral via the *fundamental theorem of calculus*. Setting $p = 1/\alpha$ it holds for $x, y \in [0,1]$

$$\left| f(y) - f(x) \right| \; = \; \left| \int_x^y f'(t)\,dt \right| \tag{2.50}$$

$$\leqslant \; \int_x^y 1 \cdot \left| \ln(1/t) - 1 \right| dt \tag{2.51}$$

$$\underset{(2.49)}{\leqslant} \; \left(\int_x^y 1^p\,dt \right)^{1/p} \cdot \left(\int_x^y \left| \ln(t) + 1 \right|^q dt \right)^{1/q} \tag{2.52}$$

$$\leqslant \; |y - x|^{1/p} \cdot \left(\int_0^1 \left| \ln(t) + 1 \right|^q dt \right)^{1/q} \tag{2.53}$$

$$\underset{(2.48)}{=} \; C^{1/q} \cdot |y - x|^\alpha, \tag{2.54}$$

so f is indeed Hölder-continuous on $[0,1]$ with exponent α.

To see that f is not Lipschitz-continuous, note that for any constant $C \geqslant 0$, there is a $x \in (0,1]$ with $Cx = f(x) = x \ln(1/x)$, namely $x = e^{-C}$. This means that Cx is the *chord* through points $x = 0$ and $x = e^{-C}$, and the strictly concave function f thus lies strictly above Cx for $x \in (0, e^{-C})$. $\blacksquare$

The above proof can be extended to functions $f(x) = x^a \ln(1/x)$.

Lemma 2.14: *Let $f_a : [0,1] \to \mathbb{R}$ with $f_a(x) = x^a \ln(1/x)$. For $a \in (0,1]$, f_a is Hölder-continuous on $[0,1]$ for any exponent $\alpha \in (0, a)$. For $a > 1$, f_a is even Lipschitz-continuous.* ◄

Proof: For $a > 1$, the claim follows simply from Proposition 2.10 since the derivative $f'(x) = x^{a-1}(\ln(1/x) - 1)$ then exists for all $x \in [0, 1]$. For $a < 1$, we proceed as in the proof of Lemma 2.13, only the integral $\int_0^1 |f'(t)|^q\, dt$ changes. We have to argue that it exists and is finite, for suitable values of q; we do so by showing that it is dominated by a convergent integral.

First observe that given any $\varepsilon > 0$, we can split

$$\int_0^1 |f'(t)|^q\, dt \;=\; \int_0^\varepsilon t^{q(a-1)}(\ln(1/t) - 1)^q\, dt + \int_\varepsilon^1 t^{q(a-1)}\big|\ln(1/t) - 1\big|^q\, dt, \qquad (2.55)$$

and the integrand is clearly bounded over the range of the second integral; it is therefore bounded by a constant depending only on q and a. It thus suffices to find ε so that the left integral is dominated.

For constants $c_1, c_2 \geqslant 0$ holds $n^{c_1}\ln^{c_2} n = O(n^{c_1 + \delta})$ for any $\delta > 0$ as $n \to \infty$. Hence, as long as $q(a - 1) > -1$, so that we find a $\delta > 0$ with $q(a - 1) > -1 + \delta$, we have

$$x^{q(a-1)}(\ln(1/x) - 1)^q \;=\; O(x^{-1+\delta}), \qquad (x \to 0). \qquad (2.56)$$

Let C and $\varepsilon > 0$ be the constants hidden in O, i.e., for $x \leqslant \varepsilon$, holds

$$\left| x^{q(a-1)}(\ln(1/x) - 1)^q \right| \;\leqslant\; Cx^{-1+\delta}. \qquad (2.57)$$

Then we find for the integral

$$\int_0^\varepsilon t^{q(a-1)}(\ln(1/t) - 1)^q\, dt \;\leqslant\; \int_0^\varepsilon Ct^{-1+\delta}\, dt \;=\; \frac{C \cdot \varepsilon^\delta}{\delta} \;<\; \infty. \qquad (2.58)$$

The condition $q(a - 1) > -1$ means $\frac{1}{q} > 1 - a$, and with $\alpha = \frac{1}{p} = 1 - \frac{1}{q} < a$, the claim follows. $\blacksquare$

2.2 Discrete Basics

This section forms the counterpart of Section 2.1 for basics of discrete mathematics. Here we collect useful notations and relations from combinatorics.

2.2.1 Binomial Coefficients

Binomial coefficients are one of the most fundamental quantities of combinatorics, and they are very well studied.

Definition and Factorial Powers. For $z \in \mathbb{C}$ and $k \in \mathbb{Z}$ we denote by $z^{\overline{k}}$ and $z^{\underline{k}}$ the *rising* and *falling factorial powers*:

$$z^{\overline{k}} = \begin{cases} \displaystyle\prod_{i=0}^{k-1}(z+i), & \text{integer } k \geqslant 0; \\[2.5ex] \displaystyle\prod_{i=1}^{-k}\frac{1}{z-i}, & \text{integer } k \leqslant -1; \end{cases} \qquad z^{\underline{k}} = \begin{cases} \displaystyle\prod_{i=0}^{k-1}(z-i), & \text{integer } k \geqslant 0; \\[2.5ex] \displaystyle\prod_{i=1}^{-k}\frac{1}{z+i}, & \text{integer } k \leqslant -1. \end{cases} \qquad (2.59)$$

Based on these, we define *binomial coefficients* as

$$
\binom{z}{k} = \begin{cases} \dfrac{z^{\underline{k}}}{k!}, & \text{integer } k \geqslant 0; \\[2ex] 0, & \text{integer } k < 0, \end{cases} \tag{2.60}
$$

where only integral k are allowed. z may be any complex number.

Relations. Binomial coefficients satisfy a great number of relations; we only need a few basic ones in this work. The first is the *binomial theorem,* see, e.g., Equation (5.12) and (5.13) of Graham et al. [72]:

$$
(x+y)^r = \sum_k \binom{r}{k} x^k y^{r-k}, \qquad \begin{array}{l} \text{integer } r \geqslant 0 \\ \text{or } |x/y| < 1; \end{array} \tag{2.61}
$$

$$
(1+z)^r = \sum_k \binom{r}{k} z^k, \qquad |z| < 1. \tag{2.62}
$$

As second useful relation is known as *negating the upper index:*

$$
\binom{r}{k} = (-1)^k \binom{k-r-1}{k}, \qquad \text{integer } k. \tag{2.63}
$$

This is Equation (5.14) of Graham et al. [72]. Finally, here is the generating function of binomial coefficients [72, (5.57)]:

$$
\frac{z^n}{(1-z)^{n+1}} = \sum_{k \geqslant 0} \binom{k}{n} z^k, \qquad \text{integer } n \geqslant 0. \tag{2.64}
$$

Multinomial Coefficients. Let $d \in \mathbb{N}_{\geqslant 2}$, $n \in \mathbb{N}$ and $k_1, \dots, k_d \in \mathbb{N}$. *Multinomial coefficients* are the multidimensional extension of binomials:

$$
\binom{n}{k_1, k_2, \dots, k_d} := \begin{cases} \dfrac{n!}{k_1! k_2! \cdots k_d!}, & \text{if } n = \sum_{i=1}^{d} k_i \, ; \\[2ex] 0, & \text{otherwise.} \end{cases} \tag{2.65}
$$

In vector notation, we briefly write $\binom{n}{\mathbf{k}}$ for $\mathbf{k} = (k_1, \dots, k_d)$. Combinatorially, $\binom{n}{k_1, \dots, k_d}$ is the number of ways to partition a set of n objects into d subsets of respective sizes $k_1, \dots, k_d$ and thus they appear naturally in the *multinomial theorem:*

$$
(x_1 + \cdots + x_d)^n = \sum_{\substack{i_1, \dots, i_d \in \mathbb{N} \\ i_1 + \cdots + i_d = n}} \binom{n}{i_1, \dots, i_d} x_1^{i_1} \cdots x_d^{i_d}, \qquad \text{for } n \in \mathbb{N}. \tag{2.66}
$$

Inequalities.

Lemma 2.15: *For* $r \in [0, 1]$ *and* $n \in \mathbb{N}_0$ *holds* $\binom{n+r}{n} \geqslant n^r$.   ◄

Proof: We first show the following *generalized Bernoulli inequality:*

$$\forall r \in [0,1], n \in \mathbb{N}_0 : (1+1/n)^r \leqslant 1 + r/n. \tag{2.67}$$

To prove Equation (2.67), we observe that for any n, both terms are 1 for $r = 0$ and $1 + 1/n$ for $r = 1$. The term $1 + r/n$ describes the straight line connecting these two points, and thus a secant of the graph of $(1+1/n)^r$. The second derivative of the latter $\frac{\partial^2}{\partial r^2}(1+1/n)^r = \ln^2(1+1/n)(1+1/n)^r > 0$, so $r \mapsto (1+1/n)^r$ is convex on $[0,1]$. As convex functions lie below their chords (Lemma 2.6), this completes the proof of Equation (2.67).

We are now ready to prove the main claim. For $r = 0$, both terms are constant 1, for $r = 1$, we have $\binom{n+r}{n} = n+1 > n = n^r$. For the other values of r, we prove by induction on n that $1 + r/n \geqslant (n+1)^r$, where we fix $r \in (0,1)$. The claim then follows as $(n+1)^r \geqslant n^r$. For the induction basis, consider $n = 0$; then $\binom{n+r}{n} = 1 \geqslant 1 = (n+1)^r$.

Now assume that the claim holds for $n - 1 \geqslant 0$, i.e., $\binom{n-1+r}{n-1} \geqslant n^r$. Then

$$\binom{n+r}{n} \; = \; \frac{n+r}{n}\binom{n+r-1}{n-1} \; \geqslant \; (1+r/n)n^r \; \underset{(2.67)}{\geqslant} \; \left(\frac{n+1}{n}\right)^r n^r \; = \; (n+1)^r, \tag{2.68}$$

which concludes the inductive step and thus the proof. $\blacksquare$

2.2.2 Harmonic Numbers

The harmonic numbers are defined as follows:

$$H_n \; = \; \sum_{i=1}^{n} \frac{1}{i}, \qquad n \in \mathbb{N}_0. \tag{2.69}$$

It is well-known that this sequence diverges and behaves asymptotically like the natural logarithm. This relation stems from the fact that H_n is a Riemann-sum-approximation for the integral $\int_1^n \frac{1}{t}\,dt = \ln(n)$. By a diligent analysis of the error term for this approximation, one can derive the following extremely precise approximations for the harmonic numbers (Equations (6.66) and (9.89) of Graham et al. [72]):

$$\forall n \in \mathbb{N} : \exists \varepsilon \in (0,1) : \quad H_n \; = \; \ln n + \gamma + \frac{1}{2n} - \frac{1}{12n^2} + \frac{\varepsilon}{120n^4}, \tag{2.70.1}$$

$$\forall n \in \mathbb{N} : \exists \varepsilon \in (0,1) : \quad H_n \; = \; \ln n + \gamma + \frac{1}{2n} - \frac{1}{12n^2} + \frac{1}{120n^4} - \frac{\varepsilon}{252n^6}. \tag{2.70.2}$$

Here γ is the *Euler-Mascheroni constant,* see Equation (2.15). Of course, the order of the quantifiers in Equation (2.70) is important: ε can have a different value for each n, but it is restricted to $(0,1)$. Equation (2.70.1) nails H_n down to an interval of length $\frac{1}{120n^4}$, which determines H_1 to an absolute error of $0.8\overline{3}\,\%$. For larger values of n the error becomes extremely small.

It is often desirable to extend the definition of the harmonic numbers to non-integral arguments, mostly for technical reasons so that we can apply the machinery of Section 2.1. By rewriting

$$H_n \; = \; \sum_{i=1}^{n} \frac{1}{i} \; = \; \sum_{i=0}^{n-1} \left[\frac{t^{i+1}}{i+1}\right]_0^1 \; = \; \int_0^1 \sum_{i=0}^{n-1} t^i \, dt \; = \; \int_0^1 \frac{1-t^n}{1-t}\, dt, \tag{2.71}$$

where the last step uses the telescoping property $(1 + t + t^2 + \cdots + t^{n-1})(1 - t) = 1 - t^n$, we have syntactically moved the parameter n from the upper limit of a sum—where non-integral values are senseless—to an exponent, where non-integral values have a well-defined meaning. The latter integral is indeed the well-known continuation of the harmonic numbers (see, e.g., Equations (5.9.16) and (5.4.14) of the DLMF [46]) and we set herein

$$H_z \;=\; \int_0^1 \frac{1 - t^z}{1 - t}\, dt, \qquad z \in \mathbb{R}_{\geqslant 0}. \tag{2.72}$$

Of course, the canceling trick from above does not work in general, and computing the integral becomes quite involved. Figure 4 shows a plot of the values. We can even let z be complex, but we will not need that in this work.

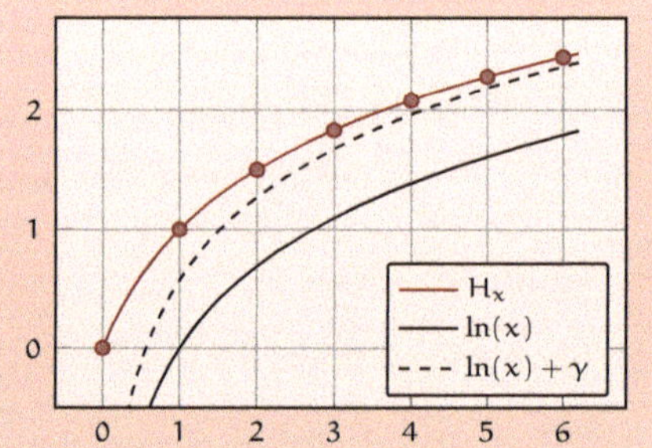

Figure 4: The harmonic numbers extended to the weakly positive reals. The plot shows H_x as defined in Equation (2.72) for x between 0 and 6; integer values of x are shown by marks. The natural logarithm is shown for comparison.

The connection between harmonic numbers and the digamma function from Equation (2.14) is in fact valid for all z:

$$\psi(z + 1) \;=\; H_z - \gamma, \qquad z \in \mathbb{R}_{\geqslant 0}. \tag{2.73}$$

This is Equation (5.9.16) of the DLMF [46]. Via this fundamental connection, we can generalize the approximation from Equation (2.70) using known asymptotic expansions for $\psi(z)$.

Proposition 2.16: *With the continuation of H_z from Equation (2.72) holds*

$$\forall z \in \mathbb{R}_{>0} : \exists \varepsilon \in [0, 1] : \quad H_z \;=\; \ln z + \gamma + \frac{1}{2z} - \frac{1}{12z^2} + \frac{\varepsilon}{120z^4}, \tag{2.74.1}$$

$$\forall z \in \mathbb{R}_{>0} : \exists \varepsilon \in [0, 1] : \quad H_z \;=\; \ln z + \gamma + \frac{1}{2z} - \frac{1}{12z^2} + \frac{1}{120z^4} - \frac{\varepsilon}{252z^6}. \tag{2.74.2}$$

◄

Proof: Equation (5.11.2) of the DLMF [46] states the following asymptotic expansion for the digamma function $\psi(z)$

$$\psi(z) \;\sim\; \ln z - \frac{1}{2z} - \sum_{k=1}^{\infty} \frac{B_{2k}}{2k z^{2k}} \tag{2.75}$$

$$= \; \ln z - \frac{1}{2z} - \frac{1}{12z^2} + \frac{1}{120z^4} - \frac{1}{252z^6} + \frac{1}{240}z^8 - \frac{1}{132z^{10}} + \cdots, \tag{2.76}$$

where B_n is the nth *Bernoulli number*. Moreover §5.11 (ii) of the DLMF [46] states that for real $x > 0$, *"the remainder terms are bounded in magnitude by the first neglected terms and have the same sign."* We thus get

$$\forall z \in \mathbb{R}_{>0} : \exists \varepsilon \in [0,1] : \quad \psi(z) \;=\; \ln z - \frac{1}{2z} - \frac{1}{12z^2} + \frac{\varepsilon}{120z^4}, \tag{2.77.1}$$

$$\forall z \in \mathbb{R}_{>0} : \exists \varepsilon \in [0,1] : \quad \psi(z) \;=\; \ln z - \frac{1}{2z} - \frac{1}{12z^2} + \frac{1}{120z^4} - \frac{\varepsilon}{252z^6}. \tag{2.77.2}$$

With Equations (2.73) and (2.13) we have for $z > 0$ that $H_z = \psi(z+1) + \gamma = \psi(z) + \gamma + \frac{1}{z}$ and so the claim follows. ∎

We collect here for reference bounds for the difference of two harmonic numbers. They follow rather straight-forwardly from Proposition 2.16.

Lemma 2.17: *For reals $x \geqslant 1$ and $y \geqslant x + 1$, we have*

$$\ln\!\left(\frac{x}{y}\right) + \frac{1}{2}\left(\frac{1}{x} - \frac{1}{y}\right) - \frac{1}{12}\left(\frac{1}{x^2} - \frac{1}{y^2}\right) \;\leqslant\; H_x - H_y \;\leqslant\; \ln\!\left(\frac{x}{y}\right) + \frac{1}{2}\left(\frac{1}{x} - \frac{1}{y}\right). \quad \blacktriangleleft$$

Remark: The conditions on x and y are vital, but not the only possible versions. We can trade a smaller difference between x and y for a larger minimal value for x and vice versa. ◀

Proof: With Equation (2.74.1) we find

$$H_x - H_y - \left(\ln\!\left(\frac{x}{y}\right) + \frac{1}{2}\left(\frac{1}{x} - \frac{1}{y}\right)\right) \;\leqslant\; -\frac{1}{12x^2} + \frac{1}{120x^4} + \frac{1}{12y^2} \tag{2.78}$$

$$\leqslant\; -\frac{1}{12x^2} + \frac{1}{120x^4} + \frac{1}{12(x+1)^2}. \tag{2.79}$$

The latter function has only one real root, namely at $x \approx 0.33$, it is clearly continuous on $\mathbb{R}_{>0}$ and converges to 0 as $x \to \infty$. Moreover, it is negative at, e.g., $x = 1$. Therefore, we must have $-\frac{1}{12x^2} + \frac{1}{120x^4} + \frac{1}{12(x+1)^2} \leqslant 0$ for all $x > 0.33$ by the *intermediate value theorem*. This proves the second inequality.

For the first inequality, we use Equation (2.74.2) to find

$$H_x - H_y - \left(\ln\!\left(\frac{x}{y}\right) + \frac{1}{2}\left(\frac{1}{x} - \frac{1}{y}\right) - \frac{1}{12}\left(\frac{1}{x^2} - \frac{1}{y^2}\right)\right) \;\geqslant\; \frac{1}{120x^4} - \frac{1}{252x^6} - \frac{1}{120y^4} \tag{2.80}$$

$$\geqslant\; \frac{1}{120x^4} - \frac{1}{252x^6} - \frac{1}{120(x+1)^4} \tag{2.81}$$

$$\geqslant\; 0, \tag{2.82}$$

where the last step follows similarly as above, noting that $\frac{1}{120x^4} - \frac{1}{252x^6} - \frac{1}{120(x+1)^4}$ has its only real root at $x \approx 0.70$ and is positive for $x = 1$. ∎

Generalized Harmonic Numbers. We occasionally also use *generalized harmonic numbers*

$$H_n^{(r)} \;=\; \sum_{i=1}^{n} \frac{1}{i^r}, \qquad n \in \mathbb{N}_0, r \in \mathbb{Z}. \tag{2.83}$$

$r = 1$ corresponds to the ordinary harmonics. Unlike those, $H_n^{(2)}$ converges to a finite limit, namely

$$\lim_{n \to \infty} H_n^{(2)} \;=\; \zeta(2) \;=\; \frac{\pi^2}{6}, \tag{2.84}$$

where $\zeta(z)$ is the *Riemann zeta function,* whose value at $z = 2$ is given in Equation (25.6.1) of the DLMF [46]. We can extend them to any real (even complex) argument setting

$$H_x^{(2)} \;=\; \frac{\pi^2}{6} - \psi'(x+1) \;=\; \sum_{k=1}^{\infty} \frac{1}{k^2} - \sum_{k=1}^{\infty} \frac{1}{(k+z)^2}, \qquad x \in \mathbb{R}_{>0}, \tag{2.85}$$

which coincides with Equation (2.83) for $x \in \mathbb{N}$.

2.3 Generating Functions

Generating functions are the ubiquitous tool of *analytic combinatorics,* the study of asymptotic properties of combinatorial classes. They provide the link between recursively defined quantities and tools from complex analysis to obtain asymptotic estimates. For this work, we only need the basic tools described below. Flajolet and Sedgewick [64] give a comprehensive treatment of the field.

For a sequence of real or complex numbers $(a_n)_{n \in \mathbb{N}_0} = a_0, a_1, \ldots$, we define its *generating function* $A(z)$ by the power series

$$A(z) \;=\; \sum_{n=0}^{\infty} a_n z^n. \tag{2.86}$$

By $[z^n]A(z)$ we denote the inverse operation, extracting the *coefficient at z^n,* i.e., we have $a_n = [z^n]A(z)$ for all n. If understood as complex function, the power series defines an analytic function inside its circle of convergence. Then we can extract coefficients by *Taylor's theorem:* $[z^n]A(z) = A^{(n)}(0)/n!$.

Since they are analytic functions, we can differentiate and integrate generating functions term-wise, we can add or multiply them, take powers, etc. All these operations in the generating-function world have corresponding counterparts in the world of sequences.

Often a complicated sequence results from a simpler sequence by applying such operations, that are conveniently expressed on the generating functions, but not on the sequences. For our application the complicated sequence is the total cost of Quicksort on inputs of size n. It can be expressed as a transformation of the corresponding cost sequence for a single partitioning step (see Chapter 6).

In fortunate cases, we can translate back from generating function to coefficients precisely, but even if we cannot, not all hope is lost. Researchers of the *analysis-of-algorithms* community have developed techniques for extracting coefficient asymptotics directly from generating functions, allowing intermediate approximations already in the world of generating functions. We will use one such technique to solve the Quicksort recurrence, which we sketch in the following: *singularity analysis.*

2.3.1 Singularity Analysis

Seen as complex functions, the power series in Equation (2.86) often has a finite radius of convergence. This means that there is a singular point on the circle of convergence, and it is known that the coefficient growth rate is determined by the behavior of $A(z)$ near such singularities. We can thus approximate $A(z)$ with an expression capturing its behavior only there and extract coefficients from this much simpler function.

The technical condition of Δ-*analyticity* guarantees that we have only a single, isolated singularity on the circle of convergence. This is sufficient for this work.

Definition 2.18 (Δ-Analyticity): *A function f is Δ-analytic, if there are $r > 1$ and $\phi \in (0, \frac{\pi}{2})$ such that f is analytic for all (complex) z in the Δ-domain*

$$\{z : |z| < r\} \setminus \{z : |\arg(z - 1)| \leqslant \phi\}. \tag{2.87}$$

(We set $\arg(0) = 0$, *so in particular* $z = 1$ *is excluded.)* ◄

A *singular expansion* of a Δ-analytic function f is an asymptotic approximation of the form

$$f(z) \;=\; g(z) \pm O(h(z)), \qquad (z \to 1), \tag{2.88}$$

that is valid in the intersection of a neighborhood of 1 and a Δ-domain. If we can prove such an expansion with g and h from the *standard function scale*

$$\mathcal{S} \;=\; \left\{ (1-z)^{-\alpha} \left(\tfrac{1}{z} \ln\left(\tfrac{1}{1-z} \right) \right)^{\beta} : \alpha, \beta \in \mathbb{C} \right\}, \tag{2.89}$$

we directly know the coefficient asymptotics by the following theorem.

Theorem 2.19 (Singularity Analysis, Theorem VI.4 of Flajolet and Sedgewick [64]): *Assume $f(z)$ is Δ-analytic and admits the singular expansion*

$$f(z) \;=\; g(z) \pm O\big((1-z)^{-\alpha}\big), \qquad (z \to 1), \tag{2.90}$$

Then

$$[z^n]f(z) \;=\; [z^n]g(z) \pm O(n^{\Re\alpha - 1}), \qquad (n \to \infty). \tag{2.91}$$

> *The coefficients in the standard function scale* $g(z) = (1-z)^{-\alpha}\left(\frac{1}{z}\ln\left(\frac{1}{1-z}\right)\right)^{\beta}$ *are given by*
>
> $$[z^n]g(z) = \begin{cases} \dfrac{n^{\alpha-1}}{\Gamma(\alpha)} \pm O(n^{\alpha-2}), & \text{for } \alpha \notin \mathbb{Z}_{\leqslant 0} \text{ and } \beta = 0; \\[3mm] \dfrac{n^{\alpha-1}}{\Gamma(\alpha)} \ln^{\beta}(n) \pm O(n^{\alpha-1}\log^{\beta-1}(n)), & \text{for } \alpha \notin \mathbb{Z}_{\leqslant 0} \text{ and } \beta \neq 0. \end{cases}$$
>
> $$(2.92)$$

This is a simplified form of the theorem of Flajolet and Sedgewick; the error term may also contain logarithmic factors, and coefficients for the standard scale are known as full asymptotic expansion, see their Theorems VI.1 and VI.2. For simple cases, we can even give *exact* expressions for the coefficients:

$$[z^n]\frac{1}{(1-z)^{m+1}} = \binom{n+m}{n}, \qquad m \in \mathbb{N}_0, \tag{2.93}$$

$$[z^n]\frac{\ln\left(\frac{1}{1-z}\right)}{(1-z)^{m+1}} = (H_{n+m} - H_m)\binom{n+m}{n}, \qquad m \in \mathbb{N}_0. \tag{2.94}$$

The first is merely Equation (2.64), the second is Equation (7.43) from Table 352 of Graham et al. [72].

Manipulation of Singular Expansions. If we extract coefficients only asymptotically anyway, we would like to truncate precision also on the level of generating functions as early as possible in the process. The only missing piece of the puzzle is which transformations are valid on a singular expansion of a generating function.

By the standard calculus of error terms, sums and products are fine; and in fact, many other operations are as well: Flajolet and Sedgewick [64] add inverse functions, polylogarithms, compositions, derivatives, antiderivatives and Hadamard products to the list, see their Sections VI.7 – VI.10. We only need the calculus operations, for which we cite the corresponding result.

Proposition 2.20 (Singular Differentiation and Integration, Thms. VI.8 and VI.9 of [64]): *Let f be Δ-analytic with the singular expansion*

$$f(z) = c_1(1-z)^{\alpha_1} + \cdots + c_k(1-z)^{\alpha_k} \pm O\big((1-z)^{\gamma}\big), \qquad (z \to 1). \tag{2.95}$$

Then we have that

(a) $f'(z)$ *is Δ-analytic and its singular expansion results from term-wise differentiation of Equation (2.95), and*

(b) $\int f(z)\,dz$ *is Δ-analytic, as well. If $\gamma \neq -1$, its singular expansion results from term-wise integration of Equation (2.95).*

Remark (Uniform Error Bounds in Singular Expansions): In their original formulation of Proposition 2.20, Fill et al. [60] require the error term in the singular expansion to hold *uniformly* in the whole Δ-domain. With our error term $O((1-z)^{-\alpha})$, it suffices to require the error bound in a neighborhood of 1, since we can always extend it to hold uniformly in a Δ-domain:

Assume the error bound holds in the intersection of the Δ-domain and an ε-ball around 1. First, we can always shrink a Δ-domain a bit by decreasing r and increasing ϕ slightly, and obtain another Δ-domain. We can also add the boundary to that smaller domain, except for the point $z = 1$, and are still completely within the original Δ-domain.

If we subtract from such a smaller, closed Δ-domain the ε-ball around 1, we obtain a bona fide closed domain G. Our function is analytic in G, hence continuous, and thus bounded from above in absolute value. Since $(1-z)^{-\alpha}$ is never 0 in G, the ratio of the function and $(1-z)^{-\alpha}$ remains bounded (in absolute value) in the whole of G. Combining the error bounds in G and the ε-ball around 1, we find that the $O((1-z)^{-\alpha})$ bound actually holds uniformly in a Δ-domain. ◀

2.3.2 Euler Differential Equations and the Operator Method

The Quicksort recurrence transforms the sequence of toll costs into the sequence of sorting costs. On the corresponding generating functions, this transformation turns out to be a special form of differential equation, one that is luckily easy to solve.

Cauchy-Euler differential equation are linear ordinary differential equations with variable coefficients, where the latter follow a specific pattern:

$$c_m x^m f^{(m)}(x) + c_{m-1} x^{m-1} f^{(m-1)}(x) + \cdots + c_0 f(x) \;=\; R(x). \tag{2.96}$$

Such equations are also known as *equidimensional* equations, because the exponent of x and the order of the derivatives are equal in each term. They can be solved systematically by the operator method we discuss below. The operator method and possible alternatives are described, e.g., by Ince [93] in his Section 6.3[1]. Chern et al. [30] provide a shortcut to directly obtain knowledge about the coefficients of a generating function, but it is a little too specialized for our goal; we have to go the long way.

The Operator Method. Let the *differential operator* Θ be defined by

$$\Theta\, f(x) \;=\; x \tfrac{d}{dx} f(x) \,. \tag{2.97}$$

We trivially have $\Theta[f(x) + g(x)] = \Theta\, f(x) + \Theta\, g(x)$ and $\Theta[\alpha f(x)] = \alpha\, \Theta\, f(x)$ for $\alpha \in \mathbb{C}$, so Θ is a *linear operator*. Denoting by $\Theta^0\, f(x) = f(x)$ and $\Theta^{i+1}\, f(x) = \Theta[\Theta^i\, f(x)]$ *successive* applications of the operator, we can extend the definition to $P(\Theta)[f(x)]$ for arbitrary polynomials P in Θ. As easily shown by induction, we have

$$\binom{\Theta}{k} f(x) \;=\; \frac{1}{k!}\Theta(\Theta-1)\cdots(\Theta-k+1)f(x) \;=\; \frac{x^k f^{(k)}(x)}{k!}. \tag{2.98}$$

---

[1] An electronic version is available in the public domain:
http://archive.org/stream/ordinarydifferen029666mbp#page/n148

Proposition 2.21: *Let* P *be a polynomial and* Θ *the operator defined via Equation (2.97).
We have* $P(\Theta)x^\beta = P(\beta)x^\beta$. ◀

Proof: The proof is by induction over the degree of P. If P is a constant $P(y) = c$, then the
claim holds trivially. If P has degree at least one, it has a root $\alpha \in \mathbb{C}$ and can be written as
$P(y) = (y - \alpha)Q(y)$. As Q has degree one less than P, we get by the inductive hypothesis
that $Q(\Theta)x^\beta = Q(\beta)x^\beta$. Putting everything together we have

$$
\begin{aligned}
P(\Theta)x^\beta &= (\Theta - \alpha)Q(\beta)x^\beta & (2.99)\\
&= Q(\beta)\left(x\tfrac{d}{dx}x^\beta - \alpha x^\beta\right) & (2.100)\\
&= Q(\beta)\left((\beta - \alpha)x^\beta\right) & (2.101)\\
&= P(\beta)x^\beta. & (2.102)
\end{aligned}
$$

∎

Explicit Solution With Differential Operator. Let us first consider the effect of a single
factor $(\Theta - \alpha)$. We are only interested in the behavior of generating functions near 1, the
dominant singularity. We thus directly work on singular expansions instead of the function
itself, hiding irrelevant detail as early as possible in the computation. Proposition 2.20
guarantees us that we can work on singular expansions *term-wise*, only requiring that the
involved functions be Δ-analytic.

Hennequin [77] does not make this point very clear. He considers the solution of
the differential equation for an explicitly given function in his Proposition III.4, and gives
the case with an asymptotic approximation on the right-hand side as corollary; he states:
"Le principe de la preuve et les propriétés de l'intégration vis-à-vis de $O()$, $o()$ *et* $\sim$ *donnent le
corollaire suivant"* ([77], p. 43). (The principle of the proof and the properties of integration
with respect to $O()$, $o()$ and $\sim$ give the following corollary.) Let us state the needed side
conditions explicit, in particular regarding the domain of validity of error terms in singular
expansions.

Following Hennequin, we make a change of variables $x = 1 - z$ in the generating functions while solving the differential equations. This allows us to directly use the classical
choice of Θ; working with $\vartheta f(z) = (1 - z)\tfrac{d}{dz}f(z)$ is also possible, but introduces annoying
powers of -1.

Lemma 2.22: *Let* Θ *the operator defined via Equation (2.97) and let* $c \neq 0$ *and* α *be complex
constant and* $\gamma \in \mathbb{R}$ *with* $\gamma \neq \mathfrak{R}(\alpha)$. *Let* $R(z)$ *be a* Δ-*analytic function.*

(a) *Let* $f(x)$ *be given by the ordinary first-order differential equation*

$$(\Theta - \alpha)f(x) = R(1 - x) = cx^\beta \pm O(x^\gamma), \qquad (2.103)$$

where $R(z)$ *admits the given singular expansion as* $z \to 1$, *i.e., for* $x \to 0$. *Then* $f(1 - z)$
is Δ-*analytic and also admits a singular expansion as* $z \to 1$, *i.e., for* $x \to 0$, *of the*

form

$$f(x) \;=\; \begin{cases} \dfrac{c}{\beta-\alpha}x^\beta \;+\; \lambda x^\alpha \;\pm\; O(x^\gamma), & \text{for } \alpha \neq \beta; \\[2ex] c\,x^\beta \ln(x) + \lambda x^\alpha \;\pm\; O(x^\gamma), & \text{for } \alpha = \beta, \end{cases} \tag{2.104}$$

where λ is a constant determined by initial conditions.

(b) *Assume $\alpha \neq \beta$ and let $f(x)$ be given by the ordinary first-order differential equation*

$$(\Theta - \alpha)f(x) \;=\; R(1-x) \;=\; c x^\beta \ln(x) \pm O(x^\gamma), \qquad (x \to 0), \tag{2.105}$$

where $R(z)$ admits the given singular expansion as $z \to 1$, i.e., for $x \to 0$. Then $f(1-z)$ is Δ-analytic and also admits a singular expansion as $z \to 1$, i.e., for $x \to 0$, of the form

$$f(x) \;=\; \frac{c}{\beta-\alpha}x^\beta \ln(x) \;-\; \frac{c}{(\beta-\alpha)^2}x^\beta \;+\; \lambda x^\alpha \;\pm\; O(x^\gamma), \tag{2.106}$$

with constant λ determined by initial conditions. ◄

Proof: Apart from checking the formal conditions to integrate singular expansions, the proof is an exercise in calculus of moderate complexity. As the functions on the right are Δ-analytic by assumption, we can apply Proposition 2.20 with the substitution $x = 1 - z$. The resulting functions are then again Δ-analytic and their expansions are obtained by term-wise integration of the expansion of the right-hand sides. We start with the proof of the first part. Using the *integrating factor* $x^{-\alpha}$, we compute

$$\frac{d}{dx}x^{-\alpha}f(x) \;=\; x^{-\alpha}f'(x) - \alpha x^{-\alpha-1}f(x) \tag{2.107}$$
$$=\; x^{-\alpha-1}\big((\Theta - \alpha)f(x)\big) \tag{2.108}$$
$$=\; x^{-\alpha-1}\big(cx^\beta \pm O(x^\gamma)\big) \tag{2.109}$$
$$=\; cx^{\beta-\alpha-1} \pm O(x^{\gamma-\Re(\alpha)-1}), \tag{2.110}$$

whence integrating using $\gamma \neq \Re(\alpha)$ yields

$$f(x) \;=\; cx^\alpha \int t^{\beta-\alpha-1}\, dt \;\pm\; x^\alpha \int O(t^{\gamma-\Re(\alpha)-1})\, dt \tag{2.111}$$

$$=\; \begin{cases} \dfrac{c}{\beta-\alpha}x^\beta \;+\; \lambda x^\alpha \;\pm\; O(x^\gamma), & \text{for } \alpha \neq \beta; \\[2ex] c\,x^\beta \ln(x) + \lambda x^\alpha \;\pm\; O(x^\gamma), & \text{for } \alpha = \beta, \end{cases} \tag{2.112}$$

which proves the first statement. For the second part of the claim, the same approach gives

$$\frac{d}{dx}x^{-\alpha}g(x) \;=\; cx^{\beta-\Re(\alpha)-1}\ln(x) \pm O(x^{\gamma-\alpha-1}), \tag{2.113}$$

which we integrate under $\beta \neq \alpha$ and $\gamma \neq \Re(\alpha)$ to

$$g(x) \;=\; cx^\alpha \int t^{\beta-\Re(\alpha)-1}\ln(t)\,dt \;\pm\; x^\alpha \int O(t^{\gamma-\Re(\alpha)-1})\,dt \tag{2.114}$$

$$=\; \frac{c}{\beta-\alpha}x^\beta \ln(x) \;-\; \frac{c}{(\beta-\alpha)^2}x^\beta \;+\; \lambda x^\alpha \;\pm\; O(x^\gamma). \tag{2.115}$$

Now that we know how a single factor of the operator polynomial transforms a singular expansion, we can easily iterate that process to obtain an explicit solution.

Theorem 2.23:
Let Θ be the operator defined via Equation (2.97), α, β, and c be complex constants and $\gamma \in \mathbb{R}$ with $\gamma \neq \Re(\alpha)$. Assume that $R(z)$ is a Δ-analytic function with the expansion

$$R(z) \;=\; c(1-z)^\beta \;\pm\; O((1-z)^\gamma) \tag{2.116}$$

as $z \to 1$. Let further Q be a polynomial with $Q(\alpha) \neq 0$, and let $f(x)$ be given by the Euler differential equation

$$Q(\Theta)(\Theta-\alpha)f(x) \;=\; R(1-x). \tag{2.117}$$

Then $f(1-z)$ is Δ-analytic and admits a singular expansion as $z \to 1$, i.e., as $x \to 0$ of the form

$$f(x) \;=\; \begin{cases} \dfrac{c}{Q(\alpha)}x^\beta \;+\; \lambda x^\alpha \;\pm\; O(x^\gamma), & \text{for } \alpha \neq \beta; \\[2mm] \dfrac{c}{Q(\alpha)}x^\beta \ln(x) \;+\; \lambda x^\alpha \;\pm\; O(x^\gamma), & \text{for } \alpha = \beta. \end{cases} \tag{2.118}$$

Proof: An induction over the degree of Q, using Lemma 2.22 to solve the first-order equations, yields the claim.

2.4 Random Basics

In this section we recapitulate a few basic results from stochastics. We also introduce a handful (or two) of more and some less widely used probability distributions that will arise at various points in our analysis of s-way Quicksort. Many nontrivial, but well-studied properties of these distributions can be put to good use in the analysis. We then profit twice from these basics of stochastics: we can apply known results, and we get acquainted to the random face of Quicksort.

Taking Appropriate Measures. I assume familiarity with elementary notions of probability, but not more. We will work exclusively with discrete distributions and continuous distributions with a Lebesgue-density, there is no reason to use general measure-theoretic notions and notations. Similarly, we leave the probability spaces our random variables live in implicit; the usual choices are sufficient: for discrete variables the power-set σ-algebra of the domain with a density, i.e., probability weights, w.r.t. the counting measure, and for continuous variables the Borel σ-algebra restricted to the domain with the probability measure given as density w.r.t. the Lebesgue measure.

Notation.   We briefly describe the probability-related notation used in this work. Together with all other notations, it is summarized in Appendix A.

The *probability* of an event E is denoted by $\mathbb{P}[E]$. We write $\mathbb{1}_E$ for its *indicator random variable,* which is 1 if the event occurs and 0 otherwise. If an event E is given by a boolean expression involving other random variables, e.g., $X \leqslant 5$, we write $E = \{X \leqslant 5\}$ for the induced event.

> **Iverson Bracket in Stochastics?**   We could write the indicator variable of an event defined by a boolean expression also as $[X \leqslant 5]$ instead of $\mathbb{1}_{\{X \leqslant 5\}}$, using the *Iverson bracket* notation defined in Equation (2.3). This notation seems very uncommon; the Iverson bracket has not (yet?) entered the stochastics literature. Since the notation $\mathbb{1}_{\{X \leqslant 5\}}$ is so common that it will probably be readily understood by most readers, we will stick to it in this work.

For a random variable X, let $\mathbb{E}[X]$ and $\mathrm{Var}(X)$ denote its *expectation* and *variance,* respectively. As traditionally done in stochastics, random variables are written in uppercase letters; corresponding lower-case letters usually represent a fix value for the random variable.

By $X \overset{\mathcal{D}}{=} Y$ we mean that X and Y have the same distribution, i.e., their *cumulative distribution functions (CDF)* $F_X = F_Y$ coincide, where $F_X(x) = \mathbb{P}[X \leqslant x]$. Random variable $X \in \mathbb{R}^d$ admits a *density* $f_X : \mathbb{R}^d \to \mathbb{R}$ if for any measurable set $A \subseteq \mathbb{R}^d$ holds

$$\mathbb{P}[X \in A] \;=\; \int_A f_X(x)\,dx \;=\; \int_{\mathbb{R}^d} [x \in A] f_X(x)\,dx\,. \tag{2.119}$$

A *stochastic vector* is a vector whose components are at least zero and sum to one.

Conditioning.   The *conditional probability* that an event E occurs when we already know that another event E' has occurred is denoted as $\mathbb{P}[E \mid E']$, which fulfills $\mathbb{P}[E \text{ and } E'] = \mathbb{P}[E \mid E'] \cdot \mathbb{P}[E']$. Conditioning can often simplify arguments and computations, but one has to be careful: if $\mathbb{P}[E'] = 0$, the above equation leaves $\mathbb{P}[E \mid E']$ undefined.

> **Dangers of Conditioning: The Borel-Kolmogorov Paradox.**   Conditioning can be dangerous, if applied to events with zero probability. At first sight one might be tempted to say that such events are not interesting anyway, but for a continuous random variable X it is natural to condition another quantity on the event $\{X = x\}$. These single-value events $\{X = x\}$ have "smaller dimension" than the full probability space and thus probability zero.

In many cases, we can still assign proper conditional distributions in such cases, but we may not let intuition lead us astray in precisely defining what we condition on. This is illustrated by the *Borel-Kolmogorov paradox:*

We start with a uniform distribution over the unit sphere, and ask for the conditional distribution, given that we lie on a given *great circle* of the sphere, i.e., any circle of maximal diameter. Intuitively, and by symmetry, we expect a uniform distribution to be the answer. But this is not the only one!

Say the uniform distribution over the sphere means we specify longitude and latitude of a point. If the great circle we condition on is the equator w.r.t. these coordinates, i.e., latitude is fixed to 0, the longitude is indeed uniformly distributed. If the great circle is however a line of longitude, say 0, the distribution of the latitude is *not* uniform, for larger latitudes near 0 correspond to larger circles than those farther from 0. We obtain two different conditional distributions, although they really only differ in their coordinate system, and intuitively, one feels they should be the same by symmetry.

The resolution of the paradox is that this symmetry exists only *before* we decide for a coordinate system. Formally, we have to fix a probability space, and we did so by choosing longitude and latitude as two components of the random point on the sphere. Then the marginal distribution of the latitude is not uniform in the first place, so why should it become so after conditioning?

The lesson to be learned is that events we condition on have to be tied to values of given random variables; we shall not use isolated events of probability zero.

We heavily use *conditional expectations* of a random variable X, given that a (discrete or continuous) random variable Y has a fixed value y, written as $\mathbb{E}[X\,|\,Y = y]$. In the discrete case with $\mathbb{P}[Y = y] > 0$, we have $\mathbb{E}[X\,|\,Y = y] = \sum_{x \in \mathcal{X}} x \cdot \mathbb{P}[X = x\,|\,Y = y]$. Since the event $\{Y = y\}$ has probability zero when Y is continuous, the elementary definition with conditional probability does not work, and in light of the Borel-Kolmogorov paradox, we should state clearly what is meant by $\mathbb{E}[X\,|\,Y = y]$ then. Assume $(X, Y) \in \mathcal{X} \times \mathcal{Y}$ has a joint density $f(x, y)$, and denote the marginal density of Y by $f_Y(y) = \int_{\mathcal{X}} f(x, y)\, dx$. Then the *conditional density* of X given $Y = y$ is

$$f_{X|Y}(x\,|\,y) \;=\; \frac{f(x, y)}{f_Y(y)} \tag{2.120}$$

for any y with $f_Y(y) > 0$. The expectation of X conditional on $Y = y$ is then

$$\mathbb{E}[X\,|\,Y = y] \;=\; \int_{\mathcal{Y}} x\, f_{X|Y}(x\,|\,y)\, dx. \tag{2.121}$$

In both cases, discrete and continuous, the $\mathbb{E}[X\,|\,Y = y]$ depends on y, so with the function $g(y) = \mathbb{E}[X\,|\,Y = y]$, we obtain the random variable $g(Y)$. This is the conditional expectation of X given Y, denoted by $\mathbb{E}[X\,|\,Y] = g(Y)$. Note that still $\mathbb{P}[Y = y] = 0$ for a continuous distribution, but it suffices for the marginal *density* to be positive to have a well-defined conditional expectation. If we take the expectation of $\mathbb{E}[X\,|\,Y]$, simply plugging in the definitions shows that we obtain again the *unconditional expectation* of X:

$$\mathbb{E}\big[\mathbb{E}[X\,|\,Y]\big] \;=\; \mathbb{E}[X]. \tag{2.122}$$

This is known as the *law of total expectation.*

2.4.1 Categorical Distribution

Let us start with a simple generic discrete distribution. For a stochastic vector $\mathbf{p} \in [0,1]^u$ with $\Sigma\mathbf{p} = 1$, the *categorical distribution* $\mathcal{D}(\mathbf{p})$ with u choices is a discrete distribution over $[u] = \{1,\ldots,u\}$ with the given weights. For $X \stackrel{\mathcal{D}}{=} \mathcal{D}(\mathbf{p})$, we have

$$\mathbb{P}[X = x] \;=\; \begin{cases} p_x, & \text{if } x \in \{1,\ldots,u\}\,; \\ 0, & \text{otherwise.} \end{cases} \tag{2.123}$$

The categorical distribution with two choices $\mathcal{D}(p, 1-p)$ is also called *Bernoulli distribution* and written as $B(p)$.

2.4.2 Exponential Distribution

The exponential distribution does *not* directly arise in the analysis of Quicksort; rather it appears as building block for the gamma distribution that we will discuss in the next section. The gamma distribution does not directly arise in Quicksort, either; it enters the game through a very helpful stochastic characterization of the Dirichlet-distribution, which we address in Section 2.4.4. The Dirichlet distribution, finally, will be the distribution of our pivot values, as we discuss in detail in Section 5.2. Some properties of the Dirichlet distribution seem to hold magically if we look at it as black box, but with the representation via gamma variables, they follow naturally. A black box remains black until we open it and let some light in.

A random variable X has an exponential distribution with rate $\lambda > 0$ if its cumulative distribution function is given by

$$\mathbb{P}[X \leqslant x] \;=\; \left(1 - e^{-\lambda x}\right) \cdot [x \geqslant 0]. \tag{2.124}$$

We then write $X \stackrel{\mathcal{D}}{=} \mathrm{Exp}(\lambda)$. We will mostly use the standard exponential distribution $\mathrm{Exp}(1)$, whose density then simply is e^{-x}.

2.4.3 Gamma Distribution

The gamma distribution arises in the stochastic characterization of the Dirichlet-distribution discussed below. To exploit this connection, we only need one basic property of the gamma distribution, Corollary 2.25 below.

X is gamma-distributed with shape parameter $k \in \mathbb{R}_{>0}$, $X \stackrel{\mathcal{D}}{=} \mathrm{Gamma}(k)$, if its cumulative distribution function is given by

$$\mathbb{P}[X \leqslant x] \;=\; \frac{1}{\Gamma(k)} \int_0^x e^{-t} t^{k-1} \, dt, \tag{2.125}$$

which is exactly a regularized lower incomplete gamma function, giving the distribution its name. Recall that $\Gamma(k)$ is exactly the integral in Equation (2.125) with $x = \infty$. The gamma distribution is usually introduced with a second parameter, the rate λ. We only need the special case $\lambda = 1$.

The core property of the gamma distribution is that sums of i.i.d. gamma variates follow a gamma distribution again.

Lemma 2.24: *Let* $X \overset{\mathcal{D}}{=} \mathrm{Gamma}(k)$ *and* $Y \overset{\mathcal{D}}{=} \mathrm{Gamma}(l)$ *be independent random variables, then* $X + Y \overset{\mathcal{D}}{=} \mathrm{Gamma}(k+l)$. ◄

Proof: The lemma is a simple calculation exercise. It is obvious from Equation (2.125) that the densities of X and Y are $f_X(x) = e^{-x}x^{k-1}/\Gamma(k)$ and $f_X(x) = e^{-x}x^{l-1}/\Gamma(l)$, respectively. The density of their sum is, by independence, the convolution of these two.

$$f_{X+Y}(z) \;=\; \int_0^z f_X(x) f_Y(z-x)\,dx \tag{2.126}$$

$$=\; \frac{e^{-z}}{\Gamma(k)\Gamma(l)} \int_0^z x^{k-1}(z-x)^{l-1}\,dx, \tag{2.127}$$

substituting $x = zt$ and using Equation (2.20),

$$=\; \frac{e^{-z}z^{k+l-1}}{B(k,l)\Gamma(k+l)} \int_0^1 t^{k-1}(1-t)^{l-1}\,dt \tag{2.128}$$

$$=\; \frac{e^{-z}z^{k+l-1}}{\Gamma(k+l)}, \tag{2.129}$$

which is the density of the $\mathrm{Gamma}(k+l)$ distribution. ∎

Iterating Lemma 2.24 immediately generalizes the statement to any finite sum.

Corollary 2.25: *Let* $G_i \overset{\mathcal{D}}{=} \mathrm{Gamma}(\sigma_i)$ *for* $i = 1, \ldots, s$ *be independent random variables, then* $G_1 + \cdots + G_s \overset{\mathcal{D}}{=} \mathrm{Gamma}(\sigma_1 + \cdots + \sigma_s)$. ∎

Corollary 2.25 is useful, because it also applies backwards. With the following simple fact that $k = 1$ reduces the gamma distribution to the standard exponential distribution, this yields the promised connection.

Lemma 2.26: *For* $k \in \mathbb{N}$ *we have* $\mathrm{Gamma}(k) \overset{\mathcal{D}}{=} E_1 + \cdots + E_k$, *where* $E_1, \ldots, E_k$ *are i.i.d.* $\mathrm{Exp}(1)$ *distributed.* ◄

Proof: It suffices to prove the claim for $k = 1$, i.e., that $\mathrm{Gamma}(1) \overset{\mathcal{D}}{=} \mathrm{Exp}(1)$; the general claim then follows from Corollary 2.25. So let $X \overset{\mathcal{D}}{=} \mathrm{Gamma}(1)$ and $Y \overset{\mathcal{D}}{=} \mathrm{Exp}(1)$. We have

$$\mathbb{P}[X \leqslant x] \;=\; \int_0^x e^{-t}\,dt \;=\; 1 - e^{-x} \;=\; \mathbb{P}[Y \leqslant x], \tag{2.130}$$

so the distributions are the same. ∎

2.4.4 Beta and Dirichlet Distributions

Dirichlet-distributed vectors are our key tool to analyzing Quicksort with its pivots chosen from a sample. Therefore, this section lists a whole collection of properties of this distribution. In particular, we develop a little *Dirichlet-calculus* to compute expectations involving Dirichlet-vectors.

The Dirichlet Distribution. Let $d \in \mathbb{N}_{\geq 2}$ and $\alpha = (\alpha_1, \ldots, \alpha_d) \in \mathbb{R}_{>0}$. A random variable $X \in \mathbb{R}^d$ is said to have the *Dirichlet distribution* with *shape parameter* α, abbreviated as $X \overset{\mathcal{D}}{=} \mathrm{Dir}(\alpha)$, if it has a density given by

$$f_X(x_1, \ldots, x_{d-1}) := \begin{cases} \dfrac{1}{B(\alpha)} \cdot x_1^{\alpha_1 - 1} \cdots x_d^{\alpha_d - 1}, & \text{if } x \in \Delta_d \ ; \\ 0, & \text{otherwise} \ , \end{cases} \tag{2.131}$$

where we write $x_d = 1 - x_1 - \cdots - x_{d-1}$. Recall that Δ_d denotes the open $(d-1)$-dimensional simplex, see Equation (2.16). We allow ourselves to formally include this superfluous component as parameter of the function, so that $f_X(x)$ with $x \in \mathbb{R}^d$ and $\Sigma x = 1$ is understood as $f_X(x_1, \ldots, x_{d-1})$. Courageously using our concise vector notation, we write $\Pi(x^{\alpha-1})$ for $x_1^{\alpha_1 - 1} \cdots x_d^{\alpha_d - 1}$, so that the Dirichlet density becomes $f_X(x) = \Pi(x^{\alpha-1})/B(\alpha)$.

Recall that B, the d-dimensional beta function (Section 2.1.2), is defined as an integral whose integrand is exactly $\Pi(x^{\alpha-1})$, so $\int f_X(x)dx = 1$ as needed for a probability distribution.

The domain of a Dirichlet-variable is Δ_d, the set of all d-dimensional stochastic vectors, or equivalently, all categorical distributions with d choices. An important special case is then $\mathrm{Dir}(1, \ldots, 1)$, the *uniform* distribution over all categorical distributions.

The Beta Distribution. The *beta distribution* is simply the special case of a Dirichlet distribution with $d = 2$. It is customary to rename $(\alpha_1, \alpha_2) = (\alpha, \beta)$ in this case and to abbreviate the distribution as $\mathrm{Beta}(\alpha, \beta)$. Usually, a beta-variable is considered a real random variable, i.e., the redundant $x_d = x_2$ is dropped: $\mathrm{Beta}(\alpha, \beta) \in (0, 1)$ and has density

$$f(x) = \frac{x^{\alpha-1}(1-x)^{\beta-1}}{B(\alpha, \beta)} . \tag{2.132}$$

Stochastic Representation. There is an insightful stochastic representation for the Dirichlet distribution that allows us to easily compute expected values.

> **Theorem 2.27 (Dirichlet via Gamma, Theorem XI-4.1 of Devroye [38]):**
> Let $X = (X_1, \ldots, X_d)$ be $\mathrm{Dir}(\alpha)$ distributed with $\alpha \in \mathbb{R}_{>0}^d$ and let $G_1, \ldots, G_d$ be d independent gamma-distributed variables with parameters α, i.e., $G_i \overset{\mathcal{D}}{=} \mathrm{Gamma}(\alpha_i)$ for $i = 1, \ldots, d$. Further define $S = G_1 + \cdots + G_d$. Then
>
> $$X \overset{\mathcal{D}}{=} \left(\frac{G_1}{S}, \ldots, \frac{G_d}{S} \right) . \qquad \blacksquare$$

We will fully exploit this representation in the following section to compute expectations. Another application is the relation to spacings that we briefly explore in the following.

Relation to Exponential Spacings. Let us assume an integral parameter vector $\alpha \in \mathbb{N}^s$ for $D \stackrel{\mathcal{D}}{=} \text{Dir}(\alpha)$. By Theorem 2.27, we have $G = (G_1, \ldots, G_s)$ with $G_i \stackrel{\mathcal{D}}{=} \text{Gamma}(\alpha_i)$ so that

$$D \stackrel{\mathcal{D}}{=} \frac{G}{\Sigma G}. \tag{2.133}$$

Moreover, the s gamma variates are each a sum of i.i.d. standard exponential variables by Lemma 2.26, i.e., $G_i \stackrel{\mathcal{D}}{=} \Sigma(E^{(i)})$, where $E^{(i)} = (E_1^{(i)}, \ldots, E_{\alpha_i}^{(i)})$ with $E_j^{(i)} \stackrel{\mathcal{D}}{=} \text{Exp}(1)$. Unfolding, we thus have

$$D \stackrel{\mathcal{D}}{=} \frac{\left(E_1^{(1)} + \cdots + E_{\alpha_1}^{(1)}, \; \ldots, \; E_1^{(s)} + \cdots + E_{\alpha_s}^{(s)} \right)}{E_1^{(1)} + \cdots + E_{\alpha_1}^{(1)} + \cdots + E_1^{(s)} + \cdots + E_{\alpha_s}^{(s)}}. \tag{2.134}$$

This means that a $\text{Dir}(\alpha)$ vector can be obtained, by drawing $A = \Sigma \alpha$ i.i.d. standard exponential variables, summing them up in s groups of α_1 elements, α_2 elements and so on, up to the last α_s elements, and dividing them by the sum of all A variables. A Dirichlet variable corresponding to normalized spacings, i.e., successive differences, of exponential order statistics.

Even though interesting in its own right as it provides a good model for reasoning about simplifications, the connection to exponential spacings does not directly fit our needs. However, it can be translated also to uniform spacings.

Relation to Uniform Order Statistics. It turns out that the normalized vector $E/\Sigma E$ for E a vector of k i.i.d. standard exponential variables corresponds to the partition of the unit interval induced by $k - 1$ i.i.d. uniform in $(0, 1)$ distributed random variables, see, e.g., Theorem V-2.2 of Devroye [38]. Together with the relation to exponential spacings, this proves the following correspondence.

Proposition 2.28 (Dirichlet as Uniform Spacings, Sect. 6.4 of David and Nagaraja [37]): *Let $\alpha \in \mathbb{N}^s$ be a vector of positive integers and set $k := \Sigma \alpha - 1$. Further let $V_1, \ldots, V_k$ be k random variables i.i.d. uniformly in $(0, 1)$ distributed. Denote by $V_{(1)} \leqslant \cdots \leqslant V_{(k)}$ their corresponding order statistics. We select some of the order statistics according to α: for $j = 1, \ldots, s - 1$ define $W_j := V_{(p_j)}$, where $p_j := \sum_{i=1}^{j} \alpha_i$. Additionally, we set $W_0 := 0$ and $W_d := 1$.*

Then the consecutive distances (or spacings) $D_j := W_j - W_{j-1}$ for $j = 1, \ldots, s$ induced by the selected order statistics $W_1, \ldots, W_{s-1}$ are Dirichlet distributed with parameter α:

$$(D_1, \ldots, D_s) \stackrel{\mathcal{D}}{=} \text{Dir}(\alpha_1, \ldots, \alpha_s) . \qquad\blacksquare$$

So for integral parameters $\alpha \in \mathbb{N}^s$, $\text{Dir}(\alpha)$ is the distribution of *consecutive differences* induced by appropriate order statistics of i.i.d. $\mathcal{U}(0, 1)$ variables. This will match our process to select pivot elements from a sample as detailed in Section 5.2. Therefore, we consider next some tools to work with expectations over such variables.

Smooth Density. The following lemma states a smoothness condition for the beta density that simplifies later proofs.

Lemma 2.29: *The density of the Beta(α, β) distribution with $\alpha, \beta \in \{1\} \cup \mathbb{R}_{\geqslant 2}$ is Lipschitz-continuous (and hence Hölder-continuous with exponent 1) on $[0, 1]$.* ◄

Proof: Let f be the density of the Beta(α, β) distribution with $\alpha, \beta \in \{1\} \cup \mathbb{R}_{\geqslant 2}$. We have $g(x) = B(\alpha, \beta) f(x) = x^{\alpha-1}(1-x)^{\beta-1}$ whose derivative

$$g'(x) \;=\; (\alpha-1)x^{\alpha-2}(1-x)^{\beta-1} + (\beta-1)x^{\alpha-1}(1-x)^{\beta-1} \tag{2.135}$$

exists for all $x \in [0, 1]$ as long as α and β are either 1 or at least 2, and is continuous. So f is continuously differentiable on the closed unit interval and thus also Lipschitz-continuous [171, Corollary 6.4.20]. ■

2.4.5 Dirichlet-Calculus

In the analysis of s-way partitioning under pivot sampling, we are faced with expectations involving Dirichlet-variables. The following set of rules, and their mnemonic abbreviations are indispensable tools for that; they form the "Dirichl-$\mathbb{E}$-Calculus".

Terms. Dirichlet-calculus operates on terms of the form $\mathbb{E}_{D(\boldsymbol{\alpha})}[f(\mathbf{X})]$, where $f : \Delta_d \to \mathbb{R}$ is a function and $\boldsymbol{\alpha} \in \mathbb{R}_{>0}^d$ is a parameter vector. Its meaning or semantic is the expectation of $f(\mathbf{X})$ when $\mathbf{X} \stackrel{\mathcal{D}}{=} \mathrm{Dir}(\boldsymbol{\alpha})$; formally we understand $\mathbb{E}_{D(\boldsymbol{\alpha})}[f(\mathbf{X})]$ as the syntactic abbreviation

$$\mathbb{E}_{D(\boldsymbol{\alpha})}[f(\mathbf{X})] \;=\; \int_{\Delta_d} f(x) \frac{\Pi(x^{\boldsymbol{\alpha}-1})}{B(\boldsymbol{\alpha})}\, dx\,. \tag{2.136}$$

Here we use the integral-syntax from Equation (2.17) on page 46, and the vector notation $\Pi(x^{\boldsymbol{\alpha}-1}) = x_1^{\alpha_1-1} \cdots x_d^{\alpha_d-1}$. The variable $\mathbf{X}$ is to be understood as a formal parameter, i.e., a local, bound variable whose distribution potentially differs between two terms.

One could extend the notation to include vector-valued functions f, but since the expectation of a vector is simply the vector of expectations of the components, there is no need to.

Rules. There are rules governing the work with Dirichlet-terms. First we inherit, of course, the rules

$$\mathbb{E}_{D(\boldsymbol{\alpha})}[cf(\mathbf{X})] \;=\; c \cdot \mathbb{E}_{D(\boldsymbol{\alpha})}[f(\mathbf{X})], \tag{2.137}$$
$$\mathbb{E}_{D(\boldsymbol{\alpha})}[f(\mathbf{X}) + g(\mathbf{X})] \;=\; \mathbb{E}_{D(\boldsymbol{\alpha})}[f(\mathbf{X})] + \mathbb{E}_{D(\boldsymbol{\alpha})}[g(\mathbf{X})], \tag{2.138}$$

by the linearity of the expectation. For the more interesting rules, we profit from our abbreviations. In that syntax, we can specify the rules of Dirichlet-calculus in very terse form. For our first nontrivial rule, we give the verbalized form alongside for clarity.

Lemma 2.30 ("Powers-to-Parameters"-Rule of Dirichlet Calculus):

$$\mathbb{E}_{D(\alpha)}\left[\Pi(\mathbf{X^m})\cdot f(\mathbf{X})\right] \;=\; \frac{\Pi(\alpha^{\overline{m}})}{(\Sigma\alpha)^{\overline{\Sigma m}}}\cdot\mathbb{E}_{D(\alpha+m)}[f(\mathbf{X})], \qquad \begin{array}{l}\alpha\in\mathbb{R}^d_{>0},\\[4pt] m\in\mathbb{Z}^d \text{ and } m>-\alpha.\end{array} \qquad \text{(P2P)}$$

Verbalized form: Let $\mathbf{X}=(X_1,\dots,X_d)\in\mathbb{R}^d$ *be a* $\mathrm{Dir}(\alpha)$ *distributed random variable with parameter* $\alpha=(\alpha_1,\dots,\alpha_d)$. *Let further* $m=(m_1,\dots,m_d)\in\mathbb{Z}^d$ *be an integer vector with* $m>-\alpha$ *(componentwise) and abbreviate the sums* $A:=\sum_{i=1}^d\alpha_i$ *and* $M:=\sum_{i=1}^d m_i$. *Then we have for an arbitrary (real-valued) function* $f:\Delta_d\to\mathbb{R}$ *the identity*

$$\mathbb{E}\left[X_1^{m_1}\cdots X_d^{m_d}\cdot f(\mathbf{X})\right] \;=\; \frac{\alpha_1^{\overline{m_1}}\cdots\alpha_d^{\overline{m_d}}}{A^{\overline{M}}}\cdot\mathbb{E}\left[f(\tilde{\mathbf{X}})\right],$$

where $\tilde{\mathbf{X}}=(\tilde{X}_1,\dots,\tilde{X}_d)$ *is* $\mathrm{Dir}(\alpha+m)$ *distributed.* ◄

Proof: Using $\frac{\Gamma(z+n)}{\Gamma(z)}=z^{\overline{n}}$, see Equation (2.10), we compute

$$\mathbb{E}\left[X_1^{m_1}\cdots X_d^{m_d}\cdot f(\mathbf{X})\right] \;=\; \int_{\Delta_d} x_1^{m_1}\cdots x_d^{m_d}\, f(\mathbf{x})\cdot\frac{x_1^{\alpha_1-1}\cdots x_d^{\alpha_d-1}}{B(\alpha)}\,dx \tag{2.139}$$

$$=\; \frac{B(\alpha+m)}{B(\alpha)}\cdot\int_{\Delta_d} f(\mathbf{x})\cdot\frac{x_1^{\alpha_1+m_1-1}\cdots x_d^{\alpha_d+m_d-1}}{B(\alpha+m)}\,dx \tag{2.140}$$

$$=\; \frac{B(\alpha_1+m_1,\dots,\alpha_d+m_d)}{B(\alpha_1,\dots,\alpha_d)}\cdot\mathbb{E}\left[f(\tilde{\mathbf{X}})\right] \tag{2.141}$$

$$\underset{(2.20)}{=}\; \frac{\alpha_1^{\overline{m_1}}\cdots\alpha_d^{\overline{m_d}}}{A^{\overline{M}}}\cdot\mathbb{E}\left[f(\tilde{\mathbf{X}})\right]. \tag{2.142}$$

∎

The powers-to-parameter rule is obvious when writing out the integrals as in the proof above, but it is helpful to not have to explicitly go this way each time. Despite its simplicity it is a very handy tool.

Below we give some further rules that are not immediately visible from the integrals, but exploit the stochastic representation of the Dirichlet distribution in terms of gamma-distributed variables (Theorem 2.27). An immediate consequence is that we can permute components.

Corollary 2.31 ("Permutation"-Rule of Dirichlet Calculus):

$$\mathbb{E}_{D(\alpha)}[f(\mathbf{X})] \;=\; \mathbb{E}_{D(\alpha_{\pi(1)},\dots,\alpha_{\pi(d)})}[f(X_{\pi(1)},\dots,X_{\pi(d)})], \qquad \textit{permutation } \pi. \qquad \text{(Perm)}$$

∎

Even though the permutation rule is almost obvious, the freedom to renumber indices allows the following more interesting rules to be stated in a concise way. The first one allows us to aggregate components that we do not distinguish in our term, anyway.

Lemma 2.32 ("Aggregation"-Rule of Dirichlet Calculus):

$$\mathbb{E}_{D(\alpha)}[f(X_1,\dots,X_{d-2},X_{d-1}+X_d)] \;=\; \mathbb{E}_{D(\alpha_1,\dots,\alpha_{d-2},\alpha_{d-1}+\alpha_d)}[f(\mathbf{X})], \qquad \alpha\in\mathbb{R}^d_{>0}.$$
$$\text{(Agg)}$$

◄

Proof: Using Theorem 2.27, we have $\mathbf{X} \overset{\mathcal{D}}{=} \mathbf{G}/S$ for $\mathbf{G} = (G_1, \ldots, G_d)$ with $G_i \overset{\mathcal{D}}{=} \mathrm{Gamma}(\alpha_i)$ for $i = 1, \ldots, d$ and $S = G_1 + \cdots + G_d$.

$$(X_1, \ldots, X_{d-2}, X_{d-1} + X_d) \overset{\mathcal{D}}{=} \left(\frac{G_1}{S}, \ldots, \frac{G_{d-2}}{S}, \frac{G_{d-1} + G_d}{S} \right) \tag{2.143}$$

$$\underset{\text{Corollary 2.25}}{\overset{\mathcal{D}}{=}} \left(\frac{G_1}{S}, \ldots, \frac{G_{d-2}}{S}, \frac{\mathrm{Gamma}(\alpha_{d-1} + \alpha_d)}{S} \right) \tag{2.144}$$

$$\underset{\text{Theorem 2.27}}{\overset{\mathcal{D}}{=}} \mathrm{Dir}(\alpha_1, \ldots, \alpha_{d-2}, \alpha_{d-1} + \alpha_d). \tag{2.145}$$

This shows that the involved terms are in fact equal *in distribution*, which of course implies that they are equal in expectation. ∎

The last rule of Dirichlet-calculus allows us to remove unused components, when we only consider relative size of some components. The stated rule is the simplest of this kind, where we only relate two components. It could be generalized further, if needed; for this work the given zoom rule is sufficient.

Lemma 2.33 ("Zoom"-Rule of Dirichlet Calculus):

$$\mathbb{E}_{D(\boldsymbol{\alpha})} \left[f \left(\frac{X_1}{X_1 + X_2} \right) \right] = \mathbb{E}_{D(\alpha_1, \alpha_2)} [f(X_1)], \qquad \boldsymbol{\alpha} \in \mathbb{R}_{>0}^d. \tag{Zoom}$$

◀

Proof: As in the proof of Lemma 2.32, we use Theorem 2.27 to write $\mathbf{X} \overset{\mathcal{D}}{=} \mathbf{G}/S$ for $\mathbf{G} = (G_1, \ldots, G_d)$ with $G_i \overset{\mathcal{D}}{=} \mathrm{Gamma}(\alpha_i)$ for $i = 1, \ldots, d$ and $S = G_1 + \cdots + G_d$. Then $G_1/(G_1 + G_2) \overset{\mathcal{D}}{=} \mathrm{Dir}(\alpha_1, \alpha_2)$ by Theorem 2.27 again. ∎

◆   ◆   ◆

Example. A very simple first example for the use of our Dirichlet-calculus is the computation of the mean of the Dirichlet distribution.

Fact 2.34 (Mean of Dirichlet Distribution): With $\mathbf{X} \overset{\mathcal{D}}{=} \mathrm{Dir}(\boldsymbol{\alpha})$ with $\boldsymbol{\alpha} \in \mathbb{R}_{>0}^d$ holds

$$\mathbb{E}[\mathbf{X}] = \frac{\boldsymbol{\alpha}}{\Sigma \boldsymbol{\alpha}}.$$

◀

Proof: Let $\mathbf{X} \overset{\mathcal{D}}{=} \mathrm{Dir}(\boldsymbol{\alpha})$ with $\boldsymbol{\alpha} \in \mathbb{R}_{>0}^d$. Recall that we use $\mathbb{1}_{\mathcal{J}}$ for the characteristic vector of a subset of $[s]$, see Equation (2.4). We compute

$$\mathbb{E}[X_r] = \mathbb{E}_{D(\boldsymbol{\alpha})}[X_r] \underset{\text{(P2P)}}{=} \frac{\alpha_r^{\overline{1}}}{(\Sigma\boldsymbol{\alpha})^{\overline{1}}} \cdot \mathbb{E}_{D(\boldsymbol{\alpha} + \mathbb{1}_{\{r\}})}[1] = \frac{\alpha_r}{\Sigma\boldsymbol{\alpha}}. \tag{2.146}$$

∎

2.4.6 Binomial and Multinomial Distributions

When we repeatedly draw from a categorical distribution and only keep the class counts, we obtain the multinomial distribution. If we take the Bernoulli distribution as basis, it coincides with the more well-known binomial distribution.

Formally, we have $\mathbf{p} \in [0,1]^d$ such that $\Sigma\mathbf{p} = 1$. A random variable $\mathbf{X} \in \mathbb{N}_0^d$ is said to have *multinomial distribution* with parameters n and $\mathbf{p}$, written shortly as $\mathbf{X} \overset{\mathcal{D}}{=} \mathrm{Mult}(n, \mathbf{p})$, if for any $\mathbf{i} = (i_1, \ldots, i_d) \in \mathbb{N}_0^d$ holds

$$
\mathbb{P}[\mathbf{X} = \mathbf{i}] \;=\; \binom{n}{i_1, \ldots, i_d} p_1^{i_1} \cdots p_d^{i_d} \;=\; \binom{n}{\mathbf{i}} \Pi(\mathbf{p}^{\mathbf{i}}) . \tag{2.147}
$$

The probability weights include multinomial coefficients (recall Equation (2.65)), hence the name. For $d = 2$, the binomial distribution, we write $X \overset{\mathcal{D}}{=} \mathrm{Bin}(n, p)$ instead of $(X, n - X) \overset{\mathcal{D}}{=} \mathrm{Mult}(n, (p, 1 - p))$.

Properties. It is clear form the definition that we can permute indices aggregate components of a multinomial variable, if we do likewise on the parameter vector. In particular, the *marginal distribution* of X_r for $\mathbf{X} \overset{\mathcal{D}}{=} \mathrm{Mult}(n, \mathbf{p})$ is $X_r \overset{\mathcal{D}}{=} \mathrm{Bin}(n, p_r)$. The mean of the $\mathrm{Mult}(n, \mathbf{p})$ distribution is simply $n \cdot \mathbf{p}$.

It is well-known that binomial variables, which are sums of i.i.d. variables, are highly concentrated around their mean. This fact is formally expressed in *Chernoff bounds*, which provide an exponentially shrinking bound on the probability of large deviations from the mean. In this work, we only need the most basic variant of Chernoff bounds, given in the following lemma.

Lemma 2.35 (Chernoff Bound, Theorem 2.1 of McDiarmid [120]):
Let $X \overset{\mathcal{D}}{=} \mathrm{Bin}(n, p)$ *and* $\delta \geqslant 0$. *Then*

$$
\mathbb{P}\left[\left|\frac{X}{n} - p\right| \geqslant \delta\right] \;\leqslant\; 2\exp(-2\delta^2 n). \tag{2.148}
$$

■

In applications, we often encounter terms of the form $\mathbb{E}[f(\frac{X}{n})]$, which we would like to approximate by $f(p)$ plus some error term. For arbitrary functions f, this is not possible since f might amplify small variations of X arbitrarily much. But the Chernoff bound is strong enough to dominate the variations introduced by a large class of sufficiently smooth functions.

Lemma 2.36: *Let* $s \in \mathbb{N}$ *and* $\mathbf{p} \in (0,1)^s$, $\Sigma\mathbf{p} = 1$, *be fixed, and assume* $\mathbf{X} \overset{\mathcal{D}}{=} \mathrm{Mult}(n, \mathbf{p})$. *Let* $f : [0,1]^s \to \mathbb{R}$ *be a bounded function that is Hölder-continuous with exponent* $h \in (0,1]$ *in a neighborhood of* $\mathbf{p}$, *i.e., there are constants* $\rho > 0$ *and* C *such that* $|f(\mathbf{y}) - f(\mathbf{x})| \leqslant C\|\mathbf{y} - \mathbf{x}\|_\infty^h$ *for all* $\mathbf{x}$ *and* $\mathbf{y}$ *with* $\|\mathbf{x} - \mathbf{p}\|_\infty < \rho$ *and* $\|\mathbf{y} - \mathbf{p}\|_\infty < \rho$. *Then for all fixed* $\varepsilon > \frac{1-h}{2}$ *holds*

$$
\mathbb{E}\left[f\left(\frac{\mathbf{X}}{n}\right)\right] \;=\; f(\mathbf{p}) \pm o(n^{-1/2+\varepsilon}).
$$

If f *is Hölder-continuous with exponent* h *over the whole domain* $[0,1]^s$, *then the error bound holds uniformly in* $\mathbf{p}$. ◀

Proof: Using *subadditivity,* also known as the *union bound* or *Boole's inequality,* we have

$$\mathbb{P}\left[\left\|\frac{\mathbf{X}}{n} - \mathbf{p}\right\|_\infty \geq \delta\right] \;=\; \mathbb{P}\left[\bigvee_{r=1}^{s}\left|\frac{X_r}{n} - p_r\right| \geq \delta\right] \tag{2.149}$$

$$\leq\; \sum_{r=1}^{s}\mathbb{P}\left[\left|\frac{X_r}{n} - p_r\right| \geq \delta\right] \tag{2.150}$$

$$\underset{\text{Lemma 2.35}}{\leq}\; 2s\exp(-2\delta^2 n). \tag{2.151}$$

To use this in bounding $\mathbb{E}\left[\left|f\left(\frac{\mathbf{X}}{n}\right) - f(\mathbf{p})\right|\right]$, we divide the domain $[0,1]^s$ of $\frac{\mathbf{X}}{n}$ into the region of values with $\|\cdot\|_\infty$-distance at most δ from $\mathbf{p}$, and all others. So let $\varepsilon > \frac{1-h}{2}$ be given, i.e., $h = 1 - 2\varepsilon + \lambda$ for a constant $\lambda > 0$. We may further assume $\varepsilon < \frac{1}{2}$; for larger values the claim is vacuous. Using the boundedness of f and Equation (2.151), we find

$$\mathbb{E}\left[\left|f\left(\frac{\mathbf{X}}{n}\right) - f(\mathbf{p})\right|\right]n^{1/2-\varepsilon} \tag{2.152}$$

$$\leq\; \sup_{\boldsymbol{\xi}:\|\boldsymbol{\xi}\|_\infty<\delta}\left|f(\mathbf{p}+\boldsymbol{\xi}) - f(\mathbf{p})\right|n^{1/2-\varepsilon}\cdot\left(1 - 2s\exp(-2\delta^2 n)\right)$$

$$+\; \underbrace{\max_{\mathbf{x},\mathbf{y}\in[0,1]^s}\left|f(\mathbf{x}) - f(\mathbf{y})\right|}_{A\in\mathbb{R}}n^{1/2-\varepsilon}\cdot 2s\exp(-2\delta^2 n); \tag{2.153}$$

with any $\delta = o(1)$, we have $\delta < \rho$ for n large enough, so using Hölder-continuity, this is

$$\leq\; C\delta^h n^{1/2-\varepsilon}\cdot\left(1 - 2s\exp(-2\delta^2 n)\right) + An^{1/2-\varepsilon}\cdot 2s\exp(-2\delta^2 n), \tag{2.154}$$

and choosing $\delta = \frac{\ln(n)}{\sqrt{n}} = o(1)$ this is

$$=\; \underbrace{C\ln^h(n)n^{-\lambda/2}}_{\to 0}\cdot\big(1 - \underbrace{2s\exp(-2\ln^2(n))}_{\to 0}\big) + \underbrace{2sA\exp\big((\tfrac{1}{2}-\varepsilon)\ln(n) - 2\ln^2(n)\big)}_{\to 0} \tag{2.155}$$

$$\to\; 0 \tag{2.156}$$

for $n \to \infty$, which implies the claim. The error bound is uniform in $\mathbf{p}$ if the constant C from the Hölder-condition applies uniformly for all $\mathbf{p}$. ■

In our application, the multinomial distribution is used *on top of a Dirichlet distribution:* We first draw $\mathbf{D} \overset{\mathcal{D}}{=} \mathrm{Dir}(\boldsymbol{\sigma})$, which is then used as the class probabilities in a multinomial distribution: $\mathbf{I} \overset{\mathcal{D}}{=} \mathrm{Mult}(n, \mathbf{D})$. Formally, this means that the distribution of $\mathbf{I}$ depends on the value of $\mathbf{D}$; conditionally on the event that $\mathbf{D} = \mathbf{d}$ for a stochastic vector $\mathbf{d} \in [0,1]^s$, we have $\mathbf{I} \overset{\mathcal{D}}{=} \mathrm{Mult}(n, \mathbf{d})$. In case we are only interested in the final result $\mathbf{I}$ of this process, we can *hide* the intermediate variable $\mathbf{D}$. This case is common enough to warrant a name of its own: the Dirichlet-multinomial distribution.

2.4.7 Beta-Binomial and Dirichlet-Multinomial Distributions

The *Dirichlet-multinomial distribution* is a multidimensional discrete distribution. A random variable $\mathbf{I} \in \mathbb{N}_0^s$ has the Dirichlet-multinomial distribution, $\mathbf{I} \overset{\mathcal{D}}{=} \mathrm{DirMult}(n, \sigma)$, with parameters $n \in \mathbb{N}_0$ and $\sigma \in \mathbb{R}_{>0}^s$, if

$$\mathbb{P}[\mathbf{I} = \mathbf{i}] \;=\; \binom{n}{\mathbf{i}} \frac{B(\sigma + \mathbf{i})}{B(\sigma)}, \qquad \mathbf{i} \in \mathbb{N}_0^s . \tag{2.157}$$

Recall that the multinomial coefficient is zero unless $\Sigma \mathbf{i} = n$. An alternative representation of the weights is often used:

$$\binom{n}{\mathbf{i}} \frac{B(\sigma + \mathbf{i})}{B(\sigma)} \;=\; \binom{n}{\mathbf{i}} \frac{\Gamma(\Sigma\sigma)}{\Gamma(\Sigma(\sigma + \mathbf{i}))} \cdot \prod_{r=1}^{s} \frac{\Gamma(\sigma_r + \mathbf{i}_r)}{\Gamma(\sigma_r)} \tag{2.158}$$

$$\;=\; \binom{n}{\mathbf{i}} \frac{\prod_{r=1}^{s} \sigma_r^{\overline{\mathbf{i}_r}}}{(\Sigma\sigma)^{\overline{\Sigma \mathbf{i}}}} . \tag{2.159}$$

In the binary case $s = 2$, the Dirichlet-multinomial distribution $\mathbf{I} \overset{\mathcal{D}}{=} \mathrm{DirMult}(n; \sigma)$ corresponds to the *beta-binomial distribution*: $I_1 \overset{\mathcal{D}}{=} \mathrm{BetaBin}(n, \sigma_1, \sigma_2)$. For the special case $\sigma = (1, 1)$, we obtain $\mathrm{BetaBin}(n, 1, 1) \overset{\mathcal{D}}{=} \mathcal{U}[0..n]$: for $i \in [0..n]$ then holds

$$\mathbb{P}[I_1 = i] \;=\; \binom{n}{i} \frac{1^{\overline{i}}\, 1^{\overline{n-i}}}{2^{\overline{n}}} \;=\; \frac{n!}{i!(n-i)!} \frac{i!(n-i)!}{(n+1)!} \;=\; \frac{1}{n+1} . \tag{2.160}$$

Urn Model. The weights of the Dirichlet-multinomial distribution look quite arbitrary at first sight, but they stem from a very natural urn process if $\sigma \in \mathbb{N}^s$: Assume we have an urn filled with balls of the s different *colors*, named $1, \ldots, s$. Initially, we have σ_r balls of color r for $r = 1, \ldots, s$, which makes a total of $\Sigma\sigma$ balls initially in the urn. In each step, we uniformly draw one ball from the urn, put it back, and additionally add one *new* ball of the *same* color we have just drawn. If we now denote by I_r the number of balls of color r added to the urn in n drawings (for $r = 1, \ldots, s$), we have $\mathbf{I} = (I_1, \ldots, I_s) \overset{\mathcal{D}}{=} \mathrm{DirMult}(n, \sigma)$.

The key observation to see this is that the results of individual drawings are *exchangeable* random variables; what this means is best seen in an example. So, pick $\sigma = (2, 1, 5)$ and let us determine the probability to draw balls colors 3313231, in that order:

$$\begin{aligned}
\mathbb{P}[\text{color sequence } 3313231] &= \frac{5}{8} \cdot \frac{6}{9} \cdot \frac{2}{10} \cdot \frac{7}{11} \cdot \frac{1}{12} \cdot \frac{8}{13} \cdot \frac{3}{14} \\[4pt]
&= \frac{2 \cdot 3 \cdot 1 \cdot 5 \cdot 6 \cdot 7 \cdot 8}{8 \cdot 9 \cdot 10 \cdot 11 \cdot 12 \cdot 13 \cdot 14} \\[4pt]
&= \frac{2^{\overline{2}} \cdot 1^{\overline{1}} \cdot 5^{\overline{4}}}{8^{\overline{7}}} .
\end{aligned}$$

As is obvious from the example, the probability of a color sequence depends only on its *profile*, i.e., how often each color occurs, but not on the order. In other words, it only depends on the final contents of the urn. Since there are $\binom{n}{\mathbf{i}}$ different color sequences with profile $\mathbf{i}$, the probability $\mathbb{P}[\mathbf{I} = \mathbf{i}]$ is as given in Equation (2.159).

The above urn model is known as the *classical Pólya urn* which is the father of a whole family of generalized models nowadays known as Pólya urns, see, e.g., Mahmoud [114]. The beta-binomial distribution with integral parameters is also called *Pólya distribution,* and was studied by Eggenberger and Pólya [51] in 1923. Their urn model, the Pólya-Eggenberger urns, include as additional parameter how many additional balls are put into the urn after each drawing. According to Johnson and Kotz [95], Markov already studied the version with one additional ball in 1906.

For our analysis of Quicksort, Pólya urns are not the most convenient vehicle, although very recently Aumüller et al. [11] used them for the analysis of comparison-optimal three-way partitioning methods. The following stochastic representation of the Dirichlet-multinomial distribution as mixed distribution plays the central role in this work.

Stochastic Representation.   As hinted at above, there is a second way to obtain Dirichlet-multinomial distributed random variables: we first draw random probabilities $\mathbf{D} \stackrel{\mathcal{D}}{=} \mathrm{Dir}(\boldsymbol{\sigma})$ according to a Dirichlet distribution, and then use this as parameter of a multinomial distribution, i.e., $\mathbf{I} \stackrel{\mathcal{D}}{=} \mathrm{Mult}(n; \mathbf{d})$ *conditional* on $\mathbf{D} = \mathbf{d}$. In other words, the Dirichlet-multinomial distribution is a *mixed* multinomial distribution, using a Dirichlet *mixer* $\mathbf{D}$ to determine the parameter of the multinomial, written deceptively concisely as $\mathrm{DirMult}(n; \boldsymbol{\sigma}) \stackrel{\mathcal{D}}{=} \mathrm{Mult}(n; \mathrm{Dir}(\boldsymbol{\sigma}))$

It makes a good exercise for Dirichlet-calculus (Section 2.4.5) to verify that the probability weights of the Dirichlet-multinomial distribution from the stochastic representation, $\mathbf{I} \stackrel{\mathcal{D}}{=} \mathrm{Mult}(n, \mathrm{Dir}(\boldsymbol{\sigma}))$ coincide with those in Equation (2.157). We have

$$
\begin{aligned}
\mathbb{P}[\mathbf{I} = \mathbf{i}] \;&=\; \mathbb{E}_{\mathbf{D}}\big[\mathbb{P}[\mathbf{I} = \mathbf{i} \mid \mathbf{D}]\big] && (2.161)\\[4pt]
&=\; \mathbb{E}_{\mathbf{D}(\boldsymbol{\sigma})}[\mathbb{P}[\mathbf{I} = \mathbf{i} \mid \mathbf{D} = \mathbf{X}]] && (2.162)\\[4pt]
&\underset{(2.147)}{=}\; \mathbb{E}_{\mathbf{D}(\boldsymbol{\sigma})}\Big[\tbinom{n}{\mathbf{i}}\Pi(\mathbf{X}^{\mathbf{i}})\Big] && (2.163)\\[4pt]
&=\; \binom{n}{\mathbf{i}} \cdot \mathbb{E}_{\mathbf{D}(\boldsymbol{\sigma})}\Big[\Pi(\mathbf{X}^{\mathbf{i}})\Big] && (2.164)\\[4pt]
&\underset{(\mathrm{P2P})}{=}\; \binom{n}{\mathbf{i}} \frac{\Pi(\boldsymbol{\sigma}^{\bar{\mathbf{i}}})}{(\Sigma\boldsymbol{\sigma})^{\overline{\Sigma\mathbf{i}}}} \cdot \mathbb{E}_{\mathbf{D}(\boldsymbol{\sigma})}[1] && (2.165)\\[4pt]
&=\; \binom{n}{\mathbf{i}} \frac{\Pi(\boldsymbol{\sigma}^{\bar{\mathbf{i}}})}{(\Sigma\boldsymbol{\sigma})^{\bar{n}}}. && (2.166)
\end{aligned}
$$

So indeed, the Dirichlet-multinomial distribution is the mixed multinomial distribution, conditional on a Dirichlet variable.

Permuting and Aggregating.   Lemma 2.31 shows that we can permute indices in a Dirichlet variables, and we obtain the distribution where the same permutation is applied to the parameter vector. By the stochastic representation, it is clear that we can likewise permute indices in a Dirichlet-multinomial distribution. The same holds for aggregating components using Lemma 2.32:

Lemma 2.37: *If* $\mathbf{I} \overset{\mathcal{D}}{=} \mathrm{DirMult}(n, \sigma)$ *for* $\sigma \in \mathbb{R}^s_{>0}$, *then*

$$(I_1, \ldots, I_{s-2}, I_{s-1} + I_s) \;\overset{\mathcal{D}}{=}\; \mathrm{DirMult}(n; \sigma_1, \ldots, \sigma_{s-2}, \sigma_{s-1} + \sigma_s). \qquad\blacksquare$$

This implies that the marginal distributions of $\mathbf{I} \overset{\mathcal{D}}{=} \mathrm{DirMult}(n, \sigma)$ are beta-binomial: $I_r \overset{\mathcal{D}}{=}$ $\mathrm{BetaBin}(n, \sigma_r, \Sigma\sigma - \sigma_r)$.

Mean. The expectation of $\mathbf{I} \overset{\mathcal{D}}{=} \mathrm{DirMult}(n, \sigma)$ with $\sigma \in \mathbb{R}^s_{>0}$ is easily computed using the stochastic representation. Conditional on $\mathbf{D}$, we have $\mathbb{E}[\mathbf{I} \mid \mathbf{D}] = n \cdot \mathbf{D}$, and from Fact 2.34, we know $\mathbb{E}[\mathbf{D}] = \sigma/\Sigma\sigma$, so together

$$\mathbb{E}[\mathbf{I}] \;=\; \frac{n \cdot \sigma}{\Sigma\sigma}. \qquad\qquad (2.167)$$

A computation in Dirichlet-calculus is also possible, but much more tedious in this case than the above argument.

Convergence to Beta Distribution. If we normalize a Dirichlet-multinomial variable $\mathbf{I}$ by dividing it by n, we essentially remove the multinomial part, and what remains should be a Dirichlet variable again: $\mathrm{DirMult}(n, \sigma)/n \approx \mathrm{Dir}(\sigma)$. If it were not for the random probabilities $\mathbf{D}$, this would simply be an application of the law of large numbers; but the convergence holds also with random $\mathbf{D}$. Mahmoud [114] shows that $\mathrm{DirMult}(n, \sigma)/n$ converges in distribution to $\mathrm{Dir}(\sigma)$ (Theorem 3.2, page 53).

For our application later in this work, convergence in distribution is too weak, and we can in fact show a stronger statement. We only need the binary case $s = 2$; but a similar computation is possible for the multidimensional case. The precise type of stochastic convergence we use is a little unusual; it is chosen to match the requirement of the distributional master theorem introduced in Section 2.6 below. We call the type of convergence in this work *convergence in density*.

Lemma 2.38 (Local Limit Law for Beta-Binomial): *Let* $(I^{(n)})_{n \in \mathbb{N}_{\geqslant 1}}$ *be a family of random variables with beta-binomial distribution,* $I^{(n)} \overset{\mathcal{D}}{=} \mathrm{BetaBin}(n, \alpha, \beta)$ *where* $\alpha, \beta \in \{1\} \cup \mathbb{R}_{\geqslant 2}$, *and let* $f_B(z)$ *be the density of the* $\mathrm{Beta}(\alpha, \beta)$ *distribution. Then as* $n \to \infty$, *we have uniformly in* $z \in (0, 1)$ *that*

$$n \cdot \mathbb{P}\big[I = \lfloor z(n+1) \rfloor\big] \;=\; f_B(z) \pm O(n^{-1}), \qquad (n \to \infty).$$

That is, $I^{(n)}/n$ *converges to* $\mathrm{Beta}(\alpha, \beta)$ *in distribution, and the probability weights converge uniformly to the limiting density at rate* $O(n^{-1})$. $\qquad\blacktriangleleft$

Proof: Let $z \in (0, 1)$ be arbitrary and write $i = i(z) = \lfloor z(n+1) \rfloor \in [0..n]$. We note for reference that

$$\left| \frac{i}{n} - z \right|^c \;<\; n^{-c}, \qquad (c > 0 \text{ and } n \geqslant 1). \qquad\qquad (2.168)$$

Moreover, we will make use of the asymptotic expansion of quotients of the gamma function, see Equation (2.11). We compute

$$\mathbb{P}[I^{(n)} = i] = \binom{n}{i} \frac{B(i+\alpha, n-i+\beta)}{B(\alpha,\beta)} \tag{2.169}$$

$$= \frac{1}{B(\alpha,\beta)} \cdot \frac{\Gamma(n+1)}{\Gamma(i+1)\Gamma(n-i+1)} \cdot \frac{\Gamma(\alpha+i)\Gamma(\beta+(n-i))}{\Gamma(\alpha+\beta+n)} \tag{2.170}$$

$$= \frac{1}{B(\alpha,\beta)} \cdot \frac{\Gamma(n+1)}{\Gamma(\alpha+\beta+n)} \cdot \frac{\Gamma(i+\alpha)}{\Gamma(i+1)} \cdot \frac{\Gamma((n-i)+\beta)}{\Gamma((n-i)+1)} \tag{2.171}$$

$$\underset{(2.11)}{=} \frac{1}{B(\alpha,\beta)} \cdot \frac{\left(i^{\alpha-1} \pm O(i^{\alpha-2})\right)\left((n-i)^{\beta-1} \pm O((n-i)^{\beta-2})\right)}{n^{\alpha+\beta-1} \pm O(n^{\alpha+\beta})} \tag{2.172}$$

$$= \frac{1}{B(\alpha,\beta)} \cdot \frac{\left(\left(\frac{i}{n}\right)^{\alpha-1} \pm O\left(\frac{i^{\alpha-2}}{n^{\alpha-1}}\right)\right)\left(\left(\frac{n-i}{n}\right)^{\beta-1} \pm O\left(\frac{(n-i)^{\beta-2}}{n^{\beta-1}}\right)\right)}{n \pm O(n^2)}, \tag{2.173}$$

assuming $\alpha, \beta \geqslant 2$,

$$\underset{(2.168)}{=} \frac{1}{B(\alpha,\beta)} \cdot \frac{\left(z^{\alpha-1} \pm O(n^{-\alpha+1})\right)\left((1-z)^{\beta-1} \pm O(n^{-\beta+1})\right)}{n \pm O(n^2)} \tag{2.174}$$

$$= \frac{z^{\alpha-1}(1-z)^{\beta-1}}{B(\alpha,\beta)} \cdot \left(n^{-1} \pm O(n^{-2})\right). \tag{2.175}$$

For $\alpha = 1$, we do not need the error term from Equation (2.168), since the term $\left(\frac{i}{n}\right)^{\alpha-1} = 1$ then, and the same result follows from the error term $O\left(\frac{i^{\alpha-2}}{n^{\alpha-1}}\right) = O(n^{-1})$ then. The case for $\beta = 1$ is similar. Finally, multiplying the equation above by n yields the claim. ∎

Convergence Speed: Barry-Esseen Theorems and Local Limit Laws. Regarding the relation between the beta-binomial and beta distribution, it might be tempting to condition on the beta variable D. Then we have the conditional distribution $I \overset{\mathcal{D}}{=} \mathrm{Bin}(n, D)$, a much simpler thing to deal with, especially because the law of large numbers immediately implies (almost sure) convergence $\frac{I}{n} \to D$, and so much is known about this convergence.

The most promising route is using *local limit laws*, which prove $n^{-1/2}$ convergence rates for densities (Laplace's theorem as given in the Encyclopedia of Mathematics [56], or in fact, for any sum of i.i.d. variables, Theorem 6, p. 197, of Petrov [144]). However, this merely transforms a beta-binomial distribution into a beta-normal distribution, i.e., a mixed normal distribution, where conditional on D, mean and standard deviation are nD and $\sqrt{nD(1-D)}$, respectively. The density of the latter is

$$f(z) = \int_{x=0}^{1} \frac{x^{\alpha-1}(1-x)^{\beta-1}}{B(\alpha,\beta)} \frac{1}{\sqrt{2\pi nx(1-x)}} \exp\left(-\frac{(z-nx)^2}{2nx(1-x)}\right) dx$$

$$= \frac{1}{B(\alpha,\beta)\sqrt{2\pi n}} \int_{x=0}^{1} x^{\alpha-3/2}(1-x)^{\beta-3/2} \exp\left(-\frac{(z-nx)^2}{2nx(1-x)}\right) dx,$$

where the integral seems very tough to deal with. (Mathematica does not even solve it for $\alpha = \beta = 1$, the uniform case.)

Even for convergence of CDFs (where the maximal point-wise difference is called *Kolmogorov-Smirnov distance* or *total variation distance*), the route via fixing D does not allow as strong an error bound as in Lemma 2.38, as the best error bound between a binomial and its normal approximation is $O(n^{-1/2})$, obtained from the classical *Berry-Esseen theorem* for i.i.d. variables, whereas for the difference between a normalized beta-binomial and the corresponding beta distribution, we could show $O(n^{-1})$ error rate in Lemma 2.38.

The moral of the story is that even though we excessively use conditioning on the hidden Dirichlet variable, it is not always the way to go.

This concludes our review of probability distributions that arise in this work. There is one last concept related to probability that plays an important role in our analysis: the entropy function of information theory.

2.4.8 Shannon Entropy

Can one random variable be *more random* than another? Shannon's classical information theory [168] answers this question in the affirmative, and it provides a quantitative measure for the amount of randomness or surprise: *entropy.*

For $X \stackrel{\mathcal{D}}{=} \mathcal{D}(\mathbf{p})$ any finitely supported discrete random variable, $\mathbf{p} \in [0,1]^u$ and $\Sigma\mathbf{p} = 1$, we define its base b Shannon entropy, $b > 1$, as

$$\mathcal{H}_{\log_b}(X) \;=\; \sum_x \mathbb{P}[X = x] \log_b\left(\frac{1}{\mathbb{P}[X = x]}\right) \;=\; -\sum_{i=1}^{u} p_i \log_b(p_i) \;=\; \mathcal{H}_{\log_b}(\mathbf{p}). \quad (2.176)$$

Here we define $0 \log_b(0) = 0$, the smooth continuation of $x \log_b x$ as $x \to 0$. The entropy is really a property of the *distribution* of X, therefore we write also $\mathcal{H}_{\log_b}(\mathbf{p})$ instead of $\mathcal{H}_{\log_b}(X)$. We will mostly use $b = 2$ and $b = e$, the *binary entropy* and the *natural entropy,* respectively.

For the above definition, it does not make a difference whether X is a vector or a scalar, we also do not need an order on its values. One can also extend the above definition to any countable domain, provided the sum in Equation (2.176) converges absolutely.

Usually the Shannon entropy is written without the $\log_b$ in the subscript, but we reserve this for the *discrete entropy* defined below. It is convenient to define a generic syntax for entropy-like functions.

Definition 2.39 (Entropy-Like Functions): *For* $f : [0,1] \to \mathbb{R}$ *a function and* $\mathbf{p} \in [0,1]^s$ *with* $\Sigma\mathbf{p} = 1$ *we define the* f-*entropy of* $\mathbf{p}$ *as*

$$\mathcal{H}_f(\mathbf{p}) \;=\; -\sum_{r=1}^{s} p_r \cdot f(p_r). \qquad \blacktriangleleft$$

Lower Bounds. It is well-known that the binary entropy $\mathcal{H}_{\mathrm{ld}}(\mathbf{p})$ is a lower bound for the number of bits needed on average to transmit the outcome of $\mathcal{D}(\mathbf{p})$; see Theorem 9 of Shannon [168] for the formal statement in terms of message transmission. For our purposes, the following formulation as a classification problem is more adequate, which is an immediate corollary of Shannon's theorem.

Fact 2.40 (Entropy Bound for Classification): Let $\mathcal{X} = \{x_1, \dots, x_u\}$ be a domain with u values and $f : [u] \to \mathcal{X}$ be a bijection. Let further $\mathbf{p} \in [0,1]^u$ with $\Sigma \mathbf{p} = 1$ be a stochastic vector. The random variable $X = f(I)$ for $I \overset{\mathcal{D}}{=} \mathcal{D}(\mathbf{p})$ attains the values in $\mathcal{X}$ with probabilities $\mathbf{p}$.

A *classification algorithm* may only use *element-queries* of the form "$X \in \mathcal{Y}$?", with a subset $\mathcal{Y} \subset \mathcal{X}$ to find out the value of X. Then any classification algorithm needs at least $\mathcal{H}_{\mathrm{ld}}(\mathbf{p})$ queries in expectation to classify $X \overset{\mathcal{D}}{=} f(\mathcal{D}(\mathbf{p}))$. ∎

Entropy and Interval Bisections. There is a nice graphical intuition behind binary entropy for finitely supported distributions: If draw the probability weights p_i as contiguous segments of $[0,1]$ with respective lengths, classifying a randomly drawn element is best done by binary searching the unit interval, bisecting the remaining range in the middle each time, until our range of possible values is contained completely in one of the segments.

The number of bisections, i.e., yes-no-questions a.k.a. bits of information, needed to single out p_i, is the number of times we have to halve $[0,1]$ until the range fits into the segment for p_i, which is at least $\log_{1/2} p_i = -\mathrm{ld}\, p_i$ times. With $I \overset{\mathcal{D}}{=} \mathcal{D}(\mathbf{p})$ the expected number of bisections is thus at least $\mathbb{E}[\log_{1/2}(p_I)] = \mathcal{H}_{\mathrm{ld}}(\mathbf{p})$.

For certain probability weights p_i, the number of bisections computed above is actually achieved, namely if any bisection point lies at a segment boundary. For that to happen, it is necessary that all p_i are multiples of an integer power of $\frac{1}{2}$, for example with $\mathbf{p} = (\frac{1}{2}, \frac{1}{8}, \frac{1}{8}, \frac{1}{4})$, we need exactly one bisection to identify p_1, one more bisection for p_4 and a third one to separate p_2 from p_3. On average, this makes $\frac{1}{2} \cdot 1 + \frac{1}{4} \cdot 2 + 2 \cdot \frac{1}{8} \cdot 3 = \frac{7}{4} = \mathcal{H}_{\mathrm{ld}}(\frac{1}{2}, \frac{1}{8}, \frac{1}{8}, \frac{1}{4})$.

Entropy of Independent Variables. Shannon's entropy has many noteworthy properties; see, e.g., the comprehensive introduction by Cover and Thomas [36]. We collect here only the properties that we need in this work.

Lemma 2.41: *Let $X_1, \dots, X_n$ be i.i.d. $\mathcal{D}(\mathbf{p})$ distributed and $\mathbf{X} = (X_1, \dots, X_n)$. Then holds*

$$\mathcal{H}_{\mathrm{ld}}(\mathbf{X}) \;=\; \mathcal{H}_{\mathrm{ld}}(X_1) + \dots + \mathcal{H}_{\mathrm{ld}}(X_n) \;=\; n \cdot \mathcal{H}_{\mathrm{ld}}(\mathbf{p}). \qquad \triangleleft$$

Proof: This follows from the *chain rule for conditional entropy* , Theorem 2.2.1 of Cover and Thomas [36], which states $\mathcal{H}_{\mathrm{ld}}(X, Y) = \mathcal{H}_{\mathrm{ld}}(X) + \mathcal{H}_{\mathrm{ld}}(Y \mid X)$. Here, the latter is the conditional entropy

$$\mathcal{H}_{\mathrm{ld}}(Y \mid X) \;=\; -\sum_{x,y} \mathbb{P}\big[(X,Y) = (x,y)\big]\, \mathrm{ld}\big(\mathbb{P}[Y = y \mid X = x]\big). \tag{2.177}$$

For independent variables X and Y, we have $\mathcal{H}_{\mathrm{ld}}(Y \mid X) = \mathcal{H}_{\mathrm{ld}}(Y)$; knowing X does not reduce the surprise from the independent Y. The claim follows by iteratively using the rule. ∎

Since the entropy is a continuous function, it changes only slightly if we change the probabilities vector a little bit; this is quantified in following statement.

Proposition 2.42 (Effect of Perturbations on Entropy): *Let* $\mathbf{p}, \mathbf{q} \in [0,1]^s$ *with* $\Sigma\mathbf{p} = \Sigma\mathbf{q} = 1$ *with* $\|\mathbf{p} - \mathbf{q}\|_\infty \leqslant \delta$. *Then for any* $\varepsilon \in (0,1)$ *there is a constant* C *such that*

$$\left|\mathcal{H}_{\ln}(\mathbf{p}) - \mathcal{H}_{\ln}(\mathbf{q})\right| \;\leqslant\; C \cdot s\delta^{1-\varepsilon}. \qquad \blacktriangleleft$$

Proof: By Lemma 2.13, the function $x\ln(x)$ is Hölder-continuous for any exponent $\alpha = 1 - \varepsilon$ for $\varepsilon \in (0,1)$. Let C be the corresponding Hölder-constant. Then

$$\left|\mathcal{H}_{\ln}(\mathbf{p}) - \mathcal{H}_{\ln}(\mathbf{q})\right| \;\leqslant\; \sum_{r=1}^{s} \left|p_r \ln(p_r) - q_r \ln(q_r)\right| \tag{2.178}$$

$$\leqslant\; sC \cdot \delta^{1-\varepsilon}. \tag{2.179}$$

$$\blacksquare$$

Inequalities. *Gibb's inequality* is an elementary tool for working with Shannon's entropy. The proof is elementary, but we include it here because we will transfer Gibb's inequality to the discrete entropy in the following section.

Lemma 2.43 (Gibb's Inequality): *Let* $\mathbf{p}, \mathbf{q} \in [0,1]^s$ *with* $\Sigma\mathbf{p} = 1$ *and* $\Sigma\mathbf{q} \leqslant 1$. *Then*

$$\mathcal{H}_{\ln}(\mathbf{p}) \;=\; -\sum_{i=1}^{s} p_i \ln(p_i) \;\leqslant\; -\sum_{i=1}^{s} p_i \ln(q_i),$$

and equality holds only for $\mathbf{p} = \mathbf{q}$. $\qquad \blacktriangleleft$

Proof: Rewrite the difference

$$-\sum_{i=1}^{s} p_i \ln(q_i) + \sum_{i=1}^{s} p_i \ln(p_i) \;=\; -\sum_{i=1}^{s} p_i \ln(q_i/p_i). \tag{2.180}$$

By strict concavity, $\ln$ lies below any of its tangents, in particular $\ln(x) \leqslant x - 1$ for all $x \geqslant 0$, and equality holds only for $x = 1$. We thus find

$$-\sum_{i=1}^{s} p_i \ln(q_i/p_i) \;\geqslant\; -\sum_{i=1}^{s} p_i(q_i/p_i - 1) \;=\; -\Sigma\mathbf{q} + 1 \;\geqslant\; 0, \tag{2.181}$$

and equality holds only if $q_i/p_i = 1$ for all $i \in [s]$, i.e., only for $\mathbf{q} = \mathbf{p}$. $\qquad \blacksquare$

As a simple consequence we can give the maximum of the entropy.

Corollary 2.44 (Maximum of Shannon Entropy): *The unique maximum for* $\mathcal{H}_{\ln}(\mathbf{p})$ *over all* $\mathbf{p} \in [0,1]^s$ *with* $\Sigma\mathbf{p} = 1$ *is attained for* $\mathbf{p} = (\frac{1}{s}, \ldots, \frac{1}{s})$ *and has value* $\ln(s)$. $\qquad \blacktriangleleft$

Proof: Set $\mathbf{q} = (\frac{1}{s}, \ldots, \frac{1}{s})$ and let $\mathbf{p} \in [0,1]^s$ with $\Sigma\mathbf{p} = 1$. We have

$$\mathcal{H}_{\ln}\left(\frac{1}{s}, \ldots, \frac{1}{s}\right) \;=\; \ln(s) \;=\; -\sum p_i \ln(q_i) \;\geqslant\; \mathcal{H}_{\ln}(\mathbf{p}), \tag{2.182}$$

where the last step follows by Lemma 2.43, and equality holds only for $\mathbf{p} = \mathbf{q}$. $\qquad \blacksquare$

Schur-convexity. The above proof using Gibb's inequality is appealingly simple, but we can actually make a much stronger and more general statement with the machinery of *Schur convexity*. For a complete introduction to the theory of Schur-convex functions the reader is referred to the books of Marshall et al. [115] and Roberts and Varberg [149]; we only need two definitions and a simple lemma from the theory.

Definition 2.45 (Majorization): *For a vector $x \in \mathbb{R}^s$, let sort(x) denote the vector with the components of x in descending order.*

We say a vector $x \in \mathbb{R}^s$ is majorized by another vector $y \in \mathbb{R}^s$, written as $x \preccurlyeq y$, if $\Sigma x = \Sigma y$ and for $r = 1, \ldots, s$ holds $\sum_{i=1}^{r} (sort(x))_i \leqslant \sum_{i=1}^{r} (sort(y))_i$. ◀

For example, we have $(3,3,3) \preccurlyeq (4,4,1)$; indeed, a vector with all equal components is majorized by any vector with the same total. We further have $(4,4,1) \not\preccurlyeq (5,2,2)$ and $(5,2,2) \not\preccurlyeq (4,4,1)$, so some vectors are incomparable w.r.t. majorization.

Geometrically speaking, we have $x \preccurlyeq y$ if and only if x lies in the *convex hull* of all vectors obtained by permuting the coordinates of y.

Note that the majorization relation is in the literature commonly denotes as $\prec$ instead of $\preccurlyeq$. This is unfortunate since majorization clearly has a *less-or-equal* meaning, so we will stick to $\preccurlyeq$ in this work.

Definition 2.46 (Schur-convexity): *A function $f : \mathbb{R}^s \to \mathbb{R}$ is called Schur-convex if $x \preccurlyeq y$ implies $f(x) \leqslant f(y)$. f is strictly Schur-convex, if additionally $f(x) < f(y)$ holds for all $x \preccurlyeq y$ with sort$(x) \neq$ sort(y).* ◀

The notion of Schur-convexity is a little awkward at first, and one might wonder how to find Schur-convex functions. For a simple class of functions, we can reduce this question to ordinary convexity.

Lemma 2.47 (Sums of convex functions, Proposition C.1 of Marshall et al. [115], p. 92): *Let $I \subset \mathbb{R}$ be an interval and $g : I \to \mathbb{R}$ be a function. For $s \in \mathbb{N}$ define $f : I^s \to \mathbb{R}$ as $f(x) = \sum_{r=1}^{s} g(x_r)$. Then holds:*

(a) *If g is convex on I, then f is Schur-convex on I^s.*

(b) *g is strictly convex on I if and only if f is strictly Schur-convex on I^s.* ■

This class of functions covers in particular our entropy-like functions. We therefore obtain the following corollary that generalizes Corollary 2.44 from above.

Corollary 2.48 (Schur-concavity): *Let $f : [0,1] \to \mathbb{R}$ be a function so that $x \mapsto -x \cdot f(x)$ is a strictly concave function on $[0,1]$. Then $\mathcal{H}_f(p) = -\sum_{r=1}^{s} p_r f(p_r)$ is a strictly Schur-concave function on $[0,1]^s$.*

Moreover, $\mathcal{H}_f(p)$ attains a strict global maximum of $-f(1/s)$ at $p = (\frac{1}{s}, \ldots, \frac{1}{s})$. ■

2.4.9 Entropy and Binary Search Trees

Fact 2.40 states a general lower bound for any classification algorithm. One important family of such classification algorithms is to use a binary search tree, where the possible outcomes, the classes, are in the leaves. The entropy lower bound applies in this case, as well, but since binary search trees are a more restricted class, one might ask whether an even stronger lower bound holds. In general, this is not the case; in fact we can precisely characterize, when search trees achieve the entropy bound. The statements in this section are close to folklore, but we refer often enough to them to properly state them here, once and for all.

(Extended) Binary Search Trees — Terminology.   We assume familiarity with *binary search trees;* a suitable introduction is given, e.g., by Mahmoud [113, Section 1.6]. An *extended binary search tree* is a binary search tree, where we attach *external (leaf) nodes* to all nodes of the BST that do not already have two children; the original BST nodes are called *internal nodes* to make the distinction clear. We also call the external nodes simply *leaves;* after all, this is what they are. For $s \in \mathbb{N}$ we denote by Λ_s set of all these extended binary search trees over s leaves.

For a fixed s, let $\mathbf{q} \in [0,1]^s$ with $\Sigma\mathbf{q} = 1$ be the probability weights of a discrete distribution over $[1..s]$. Let λ be an extended binary search tree (BST) with the s leaves $1,\ldots,s$. To be specific, assume the inner nodes of the BST to be labeled with the $s-1$ numbers $1.5, 2.5, \ldots, s-0.5$.

Figure 5: Example of an extended binary search tree $\lambda \in \Lambda_s$ over $s = 7$ leaves. We draw internal nodes as circle and leaves as squares. The depth vector is $\lambda = (2,3,3,2,3,4,4)$. With $\mathbf{q} = (0.301, 0.022, 0.267, 0.156, 0.206, 0.028, 0.020)$, we have the expected search costs of $C_\lambda(\mathbf{q}) = 2.591$ comparisons for finding a random leaf.

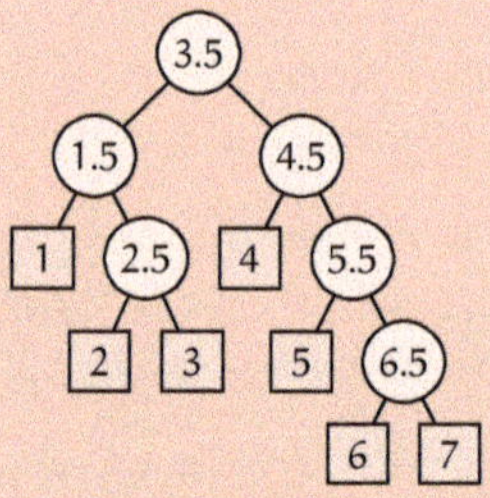

For a given tree $\lambda \in \Lambda$, we write $\lambda(i)$ for the depth of leaf i, which is the number of internal nodes on the path from the root to leaf i, or the number of comparisons with keys in internal nodes to find i in λ. If now I is randomly chosen in $[s]$ with $\mathbb{P}[I = i] = q_i$, i.e., $I \overset{\mathcal{D}}{=} \mathcal{D}(\mathbf{q})$, we call $C_\lambda(\mathbf{q}) = \mathbb{E}[\lambda(I)]$ the *expected cost* of tree λ under distribution $\mathcal{D}(\mathbf{q})$. Moreover, we write $\lambda = (\lambda(1), \ldots, \lambda(s))$ for the vector of *leaf depths;* then $C_\lambda(\mathbf{q}) = \lambda^\top \cdot \mathbf{q}$. Figure 5 illustrates the definitions.

Proposition 2.49 (Entropy-Bound for Weighted External Path Length):
For any distribution $\mathbf{q}$ and any extended binary search tree (BST) $\lambda \in \Lambda$ holds

$$C_\lambda(\mathbf{q}) \;\geqslant\; \mathcal{H}_{\mathrm{ld}}(\mathbf{q}). \tag{2.183}$$

Equality holds if and only if for every internal node in λ, the probabilities of going left and right are equal. (We will call such trees entropy-tight.)
Moreover, there is a tree $\lambda^* \in \Lambda$ with $C_{\lambda^*}(\mathbf{q}) < \mathcal{H}_{\mathrm{ld}}(\mathbf{q}) + 2$.   ◀

Proof: Our costs coincide exactly with the cost studied by Knuth [103], see his Equation (14) in Section 6.2.2. The p_i are all zero in our case; our search never stops in internal nodes. Then our Equation (2.183) follows from Knuth's Theorem B (page 444), noting that $P = 0$. Likewise, the moreover part is a simple consequence of his Theorem M (page 445).

For characterization of entropy-tight trees let $\lambda \in \Lambda$ be a tree. For any internal node v of λ, we define $p(v)$ as the sum of the probabilities of leaves in the subtree rooted at v and $H(v)$ as the base-2 Shannon entropy of these probabilities after dividing them all by $p(v)$. Let the internal node v have the two children l and r and let $p_l = \frac{p(l)}{p(v)}$ and $p_r = \frac{p(r)}{p(v)}$. Then holds

$$H(v) \;=\; \mathcal{H}_{\mathrm{ld}}(p_l, p_r) + p_l H(l) + p_r H(r), \tag{2.184}$$

i.e., the entropy of the subtree of v is the entropy of the two child subtrees plus the entropy of the local decision at v, whether to go left or right. This identity is tantamount to Knuth's Lemma E (page 444); it is easy to show if we assume the leaves below l have probabilities $q_i, \ldots, q_k$ and those below r have $q_{k+1}, \ldots, q_j$. Then

$$p(v)\mathcal{H}_{\mathrm{ld}}\left(\frac{p(l)}{p(v)}, \frac{p(r)}{p(v)}\right) + p(l)H(l) + p(r)H(r) \tag{2.185}$$

$$= \; p(l)\,\mathrm{ld}\left(\frac{p(v)}{p(l)}\right) + p(r)\,\mathrm{ld}\left(\frac{p(v)}{p(r)}\right)$$

$$+ \sum_{r=i}^{k} q_r \,\mathrm{ld}\left(\frac{p(l)}{q_r}\right) + \sum_{r=k+1}^{j} q_r \,\mathrm{ld}\left(\frac{p(r)}{q_r}\right) \tag{2.186}$$

$$= \; p(v) \sum_{r=1}^{j} \frac{q_r}{p(v)} \,\mathrm{ld}\left(\frac{p(v)}{q_r}\right) \tag{2.187}$$

$$= \; p(v)H(v). \tag{2.188}$$

Dividing by $p(v)$ yields Equation (2.184).

Now define $C(v)$ as the expected leaf depth in the subtree rooted at v, where depth means the number of internal nodes on the path from v to the leaf. Using Equation (2.183) and that the entropy of a binary variable $\mathcal{H}_{\mathrm{ld}}(p, 1-p)$ is at most 1 and attains 1 only for $p = \frac{1}{2}$, we find for any internal node v

$$C(v) \;=\; p_l C(l) + p_r C(r) + 1 \tag{2.189}$$

$$\geq \; p_l H(l) + p_r H(r) + \mathcal{H}_{\mathrm{ld}}(p_l, p_r) \tag{2.190}$$

$$\underset{(2.184)}{=} \; H(v), \tag{2.191}$$

and equality holds if and only if $C(l) = H(l)$, $C(r) = H(r)$ and $p_l = p_r$. Unfolding these conditions shows that the costs of the whole tree are equal to $\mathcal{H}_{\mathrm{ld}}(q)$ if and only if $p_l(v) = p_r(v)$ for all v in λ. ∎

As noted by Knuth [103], his Theorem B and Lemma E hold for *any* binary tree. This property carries over to our Proposition 2.49. The upper bound can be improved slightly to $a_C < \mathcal{H}_{\mathrm{ld}}(q) + 1 - q_1 - q_s + \max q_i$ according to Nagaraj [134, page 12].

Entropy-tight Trees.   The trees that fulfill Equation (2.183) with equality are quite special creatures. The following simple characterization is indirectly used in the proof above, but it is helpful enough to make it explicit.

Fact 2.50: A binary tree λ is entropy-tight w.r.t. leaf probabilities q if and only if

$$q_i \;=\; \frac{1}{2^{\lambda(i)}}, \qquad \text{for } i = 1,\ldots,s. \tag{2.192}$$

◀

Proof: If λ is entropy-tight, we have equal probability of going left and right in any internal node by Proposition 2.49. For a leaf at depth i, we thus have halved its probability i times. If conversely q fulfills Equation (2.192), we have $q_i \operatorname{ld}(1/q_i) = q_i \lambda(i)$ for $i = 1,\ldots,s$; summing up yields the claim, if we can show that $\Sigma q = 1$. This is easy to see inductively. It is certainly true for a tree with only one internal node. In any larger BST, there is one internal node with two leaves. By collapsing these two leaves into their father and assigning it the sum of their weights, we do not change the total of q, but have reduced the number of internal nodes. ■

Fact 2.50 implies in particular that q is κ-discretized (in the sense of Definition 2.51 below) for a κ that is a power of two. It is clear that given a distribution, we can easily construct the unique entropy-tight BST by recursively picking as root the element that divides the leaf probabilities exactly in half—or conclude there is no such tree if no such root exists— see Algorithm 1. Whenever it exists, this tree is the unique optimal tree for the given distribution.

Algorithm 1: Pseudocode for constructing entropy-tight binary search trees. The initial call takes the form $\textsc{EntropyTightBST}(q, 1, s, 1)$.

```
ENTROPYTIGHTBST(q, i, j, S)
 1   if i == j then return Leaf(i) end if
 2   sum := 0;  k := i
 3   repeat
 4              sum := sum + q_k
 5              k := k + 1
 6   until sum ⩾ S/2
 7   if sum == S/2
 8       l := ENTROPYTIGHTBST(q, i, k, S/2)
 9       r := ENTROPYTIGHTBST(q, k + 1, j, S/2)
10       return Node(k + 0.5, l, r)
11   else return "No entropy-tight BST exists."
```

Equation (2.192) can also be used in the converse direction. If we fix a tree $\lambda \in \Lambda$, then Equation (2.192) *defines* a probability distribution q for which λ is entropy-tight. This means, for any tree we have a distribution for which the given tree has optimal cost. Note that this distribution is *not* in general the distribution under which λ has minimal cost! The distributions minimizing $\mathbb{E}[\lambda(I)]$ simply put all weight to the highest leaves.

2.5 Discrete Entropy

A special instance of an entropy-like function appears in the analysis of the Quicksort recurrence. It can be seen as a discrete, combinatorial approximation of the (base e) Shannon entropy of a distribution that is not only discrete in its domain, but also has *discretized values for the probability weights*. The definition below makes this restriction formal. In this section, we use the same symbols that will later appear in the analysis of generalized Quicksort, but we do not refer to or rely on their algorithmic meaning here.

Definition 2.51 (κ-discretized): *Let $\tau = (\tau_1, \ldots, \tau_s)$ be the weights of a discrete probability distribution. For $\kappa \in \mathbb{N}$, we call a distribution (or its vector of weights) κ-discretized if $\kappa \cdot \tau \in \mathbb{N}_0^s$, i.e., $\tau \in \frac{1}{\kappa}\mathbb{N}_0^s$.* ◀

A κ-discretized distribution τ is characterized by the integer vector $t = \kappa \cdot \tau - 1$, or equivalently by the vector $\sigma = \kappa \cdot \tau$. The former is the parameter traditionally used to describe the sampling process to choose pivots in Quicksort (Section 4.4) and we will stick to parameter t for consistency with the literature. From the point of view of discretized distributions, σ would have been the more fortunate and convenient choice. τ will represent the probabilities of an element to belong to a certain recursive call.

Definition 2.52 (Discrete Entropy): *For $t \in \mathbb{N}_0^s$ and $k = \Sigma(t+1) - 1$ we define the discrete entropy of t as*

$$\mathcal{H}(t) \;=\; \sum_{r=1}^s \frac{t_r + 1}{k+1}\left(H_{k+1} - H_{t_r+1}\right). \tag{2.193}$$

We simply write $\mathcal{H}$ when t is clear from the context. ◀

In the discrete entropy for the κ-discretized distribution $\tau = \frac{t+1}{\kappa}$, with $\Sigma(t+1) = \kappa$, the logarithm $\ln(\tau_r)$ used in Shannon's entropy is thus replaced by $H_{\tau_r \cdot \kappa} - H_\kappa$, the difference of two harmonic numbers. This term is important enough to deserve a notation of its own: the harmonic-difference function.

Definition 2.53 (Harmonic-Difference Function):
We define the harmonic-difference function as

$$\mathrm{hd}_\kappa(x) \;:=\; H_{x\kappa} - H_\kappa, \qquad \kappa, x \in \mathbb{R}_{\geqslant 0}. \tag{2.194}$$

◀

Although not strictly needed for our application in the discrete entropy, it is technically convenient to define $\mathrm{hd}_\kappa(x)$ also for values x where $x\kappa \notin \mathbb{N}$. There we understand $H_{x\kappa}$ as the integral in Equation (2.72) which smoothly continues the harmonic numbers. The same is true for κ itself. Using the notation for generalized entropy-like functions (Definition 2.39), we may now write

$$\mathcal{H}(\mathbf{t}) \;=\; \mathcal{H}_{\mathrm{hd}_\kappa}(\boldsymbol{\tau}). \tag{2.195}$$

We next show that the discrete entropy arises naturally in the context of Dirichlet-distributed random vectors, and it is due to this fact that $\mathcal{H}$ plays such an important role in the analysis of Quicksort. The subsequent two sections then collect various helpful properties of $\mathrm{hd}_\kappa(x)$ and $\mathcal{H}_{\mathrm{hd}_\kappa}(\boldsymbol{\tau})$.

2.5.1 Entropy of Dirichlet Vectors

As pointed out above, a Dirichlet-distributed random variable $\mathbf{D} \stackrel{\mathcal{D}}{=} \mathrm{Dir}(\boldsymbol{\sigma})$ is a stochastic vector which can be seen as (random) probability weights of a discrete distribution $\mathcal{D}(\mathbf{D})$. We know that the expected value of $\mathbf{D}$ is simply the distribution induced by the parameter vector $\boldsymbol{\sigma}$:

$$\mathbb{E}[\mathbf{D}] \;=\; \frac{\boldsymbol{\sigma}}{\Sigma\boldsymbol{\sigma}} \;=\; \boldsymbol{\tau}. \tag{2.196}$$

We now show that *the expected (Shannon) entropy of $\mathbf{D}$ is the discrete entropy of $\boldsymbol{\tau}$*.

Proposition 2.54 (Expected Entropy): *Let $\boldsymbol{\sigma} \in \mathbb{R}^s_{>0}$ and $\mathbf{D} \stackrel{\mathcal{D}}{=} \mathrm{Dir}(\boldsymbol{\sigma})$. Then holds*

$$\mathbb{E}\big[\mathcal{H}_{\ln}(\mathbf{D})\big] \;=\; \mathcal{H}_{\mathrm{hd}_\kappa}(\boldsymbol{\tau}),$$

where $\kappa = \Sigma\boldsymbol{\sigma}$ and $\boldsymbol{\tau} = \boldsymbol{\sigma}/\kappa$.   ◄

Proof: The proof is simply by computing, using several of the results presented earlier in this chapter; in particular using the notation of Dirichlet calculus (Section 2.4.5), we find for $r = 1,\ldots,s$ the relation

$$\mathbb{E}[D_r \ln(D_r)] \;=\; \mathbb{E}_{D(\boldsymbol{\sigma})}[X_r \ln(X_r)] \tag{2.197}$$

$$\underset{(\mathrm{Agg})}{=}\; \mathbb{E}_{D(\sigma_r,\kappa-\sigma_r)}[X_1 \ln(X_1)] \tag{2.198}$$

$$\underset{(\mathrm{P2P})}{=}\; \frac{\sigma_r}{\kappa} \cdot \mathbb{E}_{D(\sigma_r+1,\kappa-\sigma_r)}[\ln(X_1)] \tag{2.199}$$

$$=\; \frac{\sigma_r}{\kappa} \cdot \int_0^1 \ln(x)\,\frac{x^{\sigma_r}(1-x)^{\kappa-\sigma_r-1}}{B(\sigma_r+1,\kappa-\sigma_r)}\,dx \tag{2.200}$$

$$\underset{(2.30)}{=}\; \frac{\sigma_r}{\kappa} \cdot \big(\psi(\sigma_r+1) - \psi(\kappa+1)\big) \tag{2.201}$$

$$\underset{(2.73)}{=}\; \frac{\sigma_r}{\kappa} \cdot \big(H_{\sigma_r} - H_\kappa\big) \tag{2.202}$$

$$=\; \tau_r\,\mathrm{hd}_\kappa(\tau_r)\,. \tag{2.203}$$

Summing this up over all r and negating yields the claim.   ∎

The discrete entropy thus deserves its name not only because it has the form of an entropy-like function, but also because it gives the expected entropy of random distributions based on its argument.

How Much Entropy Should We Expect? For the special case $\sigma = (1,\ldots,1)$, we have that $\mathbf{D} \overset{\mathcal{D}}{=} \mathrm{Dir}(\sigma)$ is chosen uniformly among all discrete probability distributions over $[s]$. Proposition 2.54 tells us that its average entropy is

$$\mathbb{E}[\mathcal{H}_{\ln}(\mathbf{D})] = \mathcal{H}_{\mathrm{hd}_s}\left(\tfrac{1}{s},\ldots,\tfrac{1}{s}\right) = H_s - 1 = \ln(s) - \underbrace{(1-\gamma)}_{\approx 0.42278} \pm O(s^{-1}); \quad (2.204)$$

this is only slightly less than $\ln(s)$, the maximal value of $\mathcal{H}_{\ln}(\mathbf{p})$ for *any* stochastic vector $\mathbf{p} \in [0,1]^s$. Most distributions thus have high entropy. Bayer [15] made this observation in his Section 5.0; the same result appears also as Exercise 6.2.2–37 of Knuth [103].

2.5.2 Properties of the Harmonic-Difference Function

The discrete entropy of Definition 2.52 and thus the harmonic-difference function will play an important role in this work; it therefore pays to study a few of its properties up front. This is the purpose of this section. Figure 6 shows a plot of hd_κ for a few exemplary values of κ.

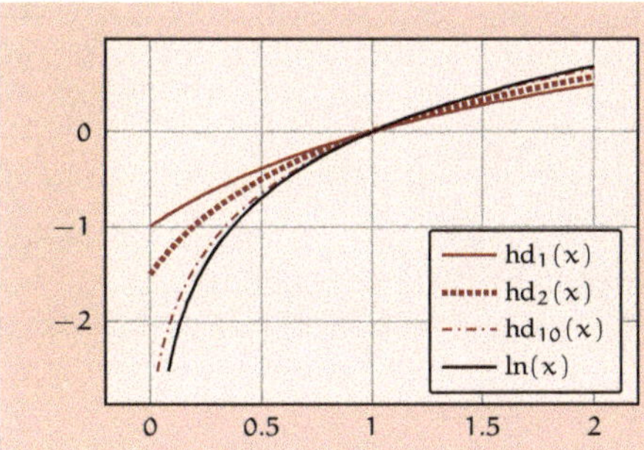

Figure 6: Exemplary plot of the harmonic difference function $\mathrm{hd}_\kappa(x)$, for $\kappa = 1$, 2 and 10 in the range for x from 0 to 2. The plot also shows $\ln(x)$. It is visible that hd_κ is approximates the natural logarithm quite well when κ is not too small.

Relation to Logarithm. As hinted at above, $\mathrm{hd}_\kappa(x)$ can be interpreted as a discrete approximation to $\ln x$, and indeed, we have the following relation.

Proposition 2.55: *Let $\kappa \in \mathbb{N}$ and $x \in [\tfrac{1}{\kappa}, 1 - \tfrac{1}{\kappa}]$. Then*

$$\mathrm{hd}_\kappa(x) = \ln(x) + \frac{1}{2}\left(\frac{1}{x\kappa} - \frac{1}{\kappa}\right) + R_{x,\kappa}, \quad (2.205)$$

where

$$-\frac{1}{12}\left(\frac{1}{(x\kappa)^2} - \frac{1}{\kappa^2}\right) \leqslant R_{x,\kappa} \leqslant 0. \quad (2.206)$$

Proof: We have $\mathrm{hd}_\kappa(x) = H_{x\kappa} - H_\kappa$ where $x\kappa \geqslant 1$ and $\kappa \geqslant x\kappa + 1$, so the claim follows from Lemma 2.17. ■

Corollary 2.56: *For any fixed* $x \in (0,1)$ *holds*

$$\mathrm{hd}_\kappa(x) \;=\; \ln(x) \pm O(\kappa^{-1}), \qquad (\kappa \to \infty). \tag{2.207}$$

(Note that the error is not uniformly bounded; the constant in $O(\kappa^{-1})$ depends on x!) ◄

Proof: Let $x \in (0,1)$ be fixed. For κ large enough, we will have $x \geqslant \frac{1}{\kappa}$, then the claim follows from Proposition 2.55. ■

hd Algebra. We collect a few elementary properties of the harmonic-difference function for reference. They all directly follow by unfolding the definition, but it pays to familiarize with their looks in terms of the new—and most likely unfamiliar—notation $\mathrm{hd}_\kappa(x)$. The reader is encouraged to mentally replace $\mathrm{hd}_{\langle\circ\rangle}$ by $\ln$ and check which properties are analogs of properties of the logarithm. Note that despite many similarities, qualitative differences between the two do exist, most notably, the harmonic-difference function remains finite for $x = 0$, whereas $\ln(0) = -\infty$. Unless further restrictions are given, the following relations hold for all $x, y, \kappa \in \mathbb{R}_{\geqslant 0}$.

$$\mathrm{hd}_0(x) \;=\; 0\,, \tag{2.208}$$

$$\mathrm{hd}_\kappa(0) \;=\; -H_\kappa\,, \tag{2.209}$$

$$\mathrm{hd}_\kappa(1) \;=\; 0\,, \tag{2.210}$$

$$\mathrm{hd}_\kappa(x) \;=\; -\mathrm{hd}_{x\kappa}(1/x)\,, \qquad\qquad x > 0; \tag{2.211}$$

$$\mathrm{hd}_{y\kappa}(x/y) \;=\; \mathrm{hd}_\kappa(x) - \mathrm{hd}_\kappa(y)\,, \qquad\qquad y > 0; \tag{2.212}$$

$$\mathrm{hd}_\kappa(x^2) \;=\; \mathrm{hd}_{x\kappa}(x) + \mathrm{hd}_\kappa(x)\,, \tag{2.213}$$

$$\mathrm{hd}_\kappa(x^n) \;=\; \sum_{i=0}^{n-1} \mathrm{hd}_{x^i\kappa}(x)\,, \qquad\qquad n \in \mathbb{N}; \tag{2.214}$$

$$\mathrm{hd}_\kappa(x^y) \;=\; \mathrm{hd}_\kappa(x^{\{y\}}) + \sum_{i=0}^{\lfloor y\rfloor-1} \mathrm{hd}_{x^{i+\{y\}}\kappa}(x)\,, \qquad \{y\} = y - \lfloor y\rfloor. \tag{2.215}$$

The last two rules show that certain operations are by far not as convenient as for the logarithm.

Analytic Properties. We have defined $\mathrm{hd}_\kappa(x)$ for all $x \geqslant 0$. Indeed $\mathrm{hd}_\kappa(x)$ is a smooth function in x.

Lemma 2.57: $\mathrm{hd}_\kappa(x)$ *is continuously differentiable w.r.t.* x *on* $\mathbb{R}_{\geqslant 0}$ *with*

$$\mathrm{hd}'_\kappa(x) \;=\; \kappa \cdot \left(\frac{\pi^2}{6} - H_{x\kappa}^{(2)} \right). \tag{2.216}$$

◄

Here $H_n^{(r)} = \sum_{i=1}^{n} n^{-r}$ are the generalized harmonic numbers, see Equation (2.83).

Proof: The derivative of $hd_\kappa(x)$ w.r.t. x is given by

$$hd_\kappa'(x) \;=\; \frac{\partial}{\partial x}(H_{x\kappa} - H_\kappa) \underset{(2.73)}{=} \frac{\partial}{\partial x}\psi(x\kappa + 1) \;=\; \kappa\psi'(x\kappa + 1), \qquad (2.217)$$

where $\psi(z) = \Gamma'(z)/\Gamma(z)$ is the digamma function. Using

$$\psi'(n+1) \;=\; \sum_{k \geqslant 0} \frac{1}{(k+n+1)^2} \;=\; \frac{\pi^2}{6} - H_n^{(2)}, \qquad (2.218)$$

which is Equation (5.15.1) of the DLMF [46], we find that $hd_\kappa'(x) = \kappa(\frac{\pi^2}{6} - H_{x\kappa}^{(2)})$. ∎

Corollary 2.58: *Let $\kappa > 0$. Then $x \mapsto hd_\kappa(x)$ is strictly concave, monotonically increasing and Lipschitz-continuous with Lipschitz constant $\kappa\frac{\pi^2}{6}$ on $\mathbb{R}_{\geqslant 0}$.* ◄

Proof: The harmonic number of second order, $H_n^{(2)}$ are strictly increasing and converge to $H_n^{(2)} \to \frac{\pi^2}{6}$ as $n \to \infty$. Thus, the derivative $hd_\kappa'(x) = \kappa(\frac{\pi^2}{6} - H_x^{(2)})$ is positive and strictly decreasing. Hence $hd_\kappa(x)$ is strictly concave and increasing in x. As the derivative is bounded, hd_κ is Lipschitz-continuous by Proposition 2.10 and the Lipschitz constant is $\max_{x \geqslant 0} hd_\kappa'(x) = \kappa\frac{\pi^2}{6}$. ∎

Lemma 2.59: *Let $\kappa \geqslant 0$. $x \mapsto x\,hd_\kappa(x)$ is a strictly convex function in $[0, \infty)$.* ◄

Proof: We show that the derivative w.r.t. x is strictly increasing (cf. Proposition 2.4). We have

$$\frac{d}{dx}x\,hd_\kappa(x) \;=\; \underbrace{hd_\kappa(x)}_{\text{strictly increasing}} + x\kappa\left(\frac{\pi^2}{6} - H_{x\kappa}^{(2)}\right), \qquad (2.219)$$

so it suffices to show that

$$z\left(\frac{\pi^2}{6} - H_z^{(2)}\right) \underset{(2.218)}{=} z\psi'(z+1) \qquad (2.220)$$

is increasing for $z \in [0, \infty)$. To do so, we will show that its derivate is positive, using two auxiliary results. The first one is a sandwich bound for $\psi'(z)$, similar to the ones for $\psi(z)$ in our Equation (2.70). We reproduce Equation (5) of Merkle [128]:

$$\frac{1}{x} + \frac{1}{2x^2} + \sum_{k=1}^{2N}\frac{B_{2k}}{x^{2k+1}} \;<\; \sum_{k=0}^{\infty}\frac{1}{(x+k)^2} \;<\; \frac{1}{x} + \frac{1}{2x^2} + \sum_{k=1}^{2N+1}\frac{B_{2k}}{x^{2k+1}}, \qquad \begin{array}{l} x \in \mathbb{R}_{>0} \text{ and} \\ N \in \mathbb{N}_{\geqslant 1}. \end{array}$$

$$(2.221)$$

Here B_k is the kth *Bernoulli number*. Recall that $\sum_{k=0}^{\infty}\frac{1}{(x+k)^2} = \psi'(z)$, this is Equation (5.15.1) of the DLMF [46], so we obtain our sandwich bound for $\psi'(x)$. For our needs, $N = 1$ is sufficient:

$$\frac{1}{x} + \frac{1}{2x^2} + \frac{1}{6x^3} - \frac{1}{30x^5} \;<\; \psi'(x) \;<\; \frac{1}{x} + \frac{1}{2x^2} + \frac{1}{6x^3} - \frac{1}{30x^5} + \frac{1}{42x^7}, \qquad x \in \mathbb{R}_{>0}.$$

$$(2.222)$$

The second auxiliary fact is Equation (1.4) of Batir [14], which for $n = 1$ yields

$$\psi''(x) \; > \; -\psi'(x)^2, \qquad x \in \mathbb{R}_{>0}\,; \tag{2.223}$$

With these preparations, we proceed to show that $z\psi'(z+1)$ is an increasing function. Let $z \geqslant 0$ be given and consider the derivative:

$$\frac{d}{dz}z\psi'(z+1) \;=\; \psi'(z+1) + z\psi''(z+1) \tag{2.224}$$

$$\underset{(2.223)}{>}\; \psi'(z+1) + z\bigl(-\psi'(z+1)^2\bigr) \tag{2.225}$$

$$=\; \psi'(z+1)\bigl(1 - z\psi'(z+1)\bigr) \tag{2.226}$$

$$\underset{(2.222)}{>}\; \left(\frac{1}{z+1} + \frac{1}{2(z+1)^2} + \frac{1}{6(z+1)^3} - \frac{1}{30(z+1)^5}\right)\cdot$$

$$\left(1 - z\cdot\left(\frac{1}{z+1} + \frac{1}{2(z+1)^2} + \frac{1}{6(z+1)^3} - \frac{1}{30(z+1)^5} + \frac{1}{42(z+1)^7}\right)\right) \tag{2.227}$$

$$=\; \frac{30z^4 + 135z^3 + 230z^2 + 175z + 49}{30(z+1)^5}\cdot$$

$$\frac{105z^6 + 700z^5 + 1960z^4 + 2947z^3 + 2499z^2 + 1122z + 210}{210(z+1)^7} \tag{2.228}$$

$$>\; 0, \qquad z \in \mathbb{R}_{\geqslant 0}\,. \tag{2.229}$$

The analytic properties reveal further similarities between $\mathrm{hd}_\kappa(x)$ and $\ln(x)$: Both are smooth, increasing and concave functions, and for both the product with x gives a convex function. There are also differences: the logarithm and its derivatives are unbounded as $x \to 0$, whereas for any finite κ, $\mathrm{hd}_\kappa(0)$ and its derivatives are finite, hence hd_κ is Lipschitz-continuous on $[0, \infty)$, which $\ln(x)$ is not.

Inequalities. For the natural logarithm, we have the well-known bound $\ln(x) \leqslant x - 1$ for all $x \in \mathbb{R}_{\geqslant 0}$: the logarithm is a concave function, so it lies below its tangents; and $x - 1$ is the tangent at $x = 1$. This bound is at the core of the proof of *Gibb's inequality*, our Lemma 2.43, which is helpful in proving lower bounds for costs of Quicksort in the limit case of sampling pivots from a very large sample, see Section 7.5. The following lemma transfers this bound to $\mathrm{hd}_\kappa(x)$—or rather, as much of it as possible.

Lemma 2.60: *We have the following upper bound for the harmonic-difference function:*

$$\mathrm{hd}_\kappa(x) \;\leqslant\; x - 1, \qquad \kappa \in \mathbb{N} \text{ and } x \in \mathbb{R}_{\geqslant 0}\setminus(1 - \tfrac{1}{\kappa}, 1). \tag{2.230}$$

(In particular, the bound holds for $x \in \tfrac{1}{\kappa}\mathbb{N}_0$.)
Equality holds in Equation (2.230) exactly for $x = 1$ and $x = 1 - \tfrac{1}{\kappa}$. ◄

Proof: It is easily checked that $\mathrm{hd}_\kappa(x) = x - 1$ for $x = 1$ and $x = 1 - \tfrac{1}{\kappa}$, so $x - 1$ is the *secant* of hd_κ through $x = 1$ and $x = 1 - \tfrac{1}{\kappa}$. The secant $x - 1$ is *below* a strictly concave function between the two crossing points, so we have $\mathrm{hd}_\kappa(x) > x - 1$ for $x \in (1 - \frac{1}{\kappa}, 1)$. As the derivative of a concave function is strictly decreasing (Proposition 2.4), the tangent slopes $\mathrm{hd}'_\kappa(1 - \frac{1}{\kappa})$ and $\mathrm{hd}'_\kappa(1)$ satisfy $\mathrm{hd}'_\kappa(1 - \frac{1}{\kappa}) \leqslant 1 \leqslant \mathrm{hd}'_\kappa(1)$. Hence, the *tangent* at $x = 1$ lies below $x - 1$ for $x \geqslant 1$ and the tangent $1 - \frac{1}{\kappa}$ lies below $x - 1$ for $x \leqslant 1 - \frac{1}{\kappa}$. The claim then follows since hd_κ lies below all its tangents by concavity (Lemma 2.5). ∎

It is explicitly mentioned in the proof, but let us repeat once more: The condition $x \notin (1 - \frac{1}{\kappa}, 1)$ in Lemma 2.60 is best possible; *for $x \in (1 - \frac{1}{\kappa}, 1)$ the reverse inequality holds.* This idiosyncrasy of hd_κ will resurface several times, in disguise: the discrete entropy inherits many properties from Shannon entropy, but some are disfigured beyond recognition by the above fact.

Lemma 2.61: *Let $\kappa \in \mathbb{N}$ and $x \in [0, 1)$. Then $\mathrm{hd}_\kappa(x) > \ln x$.* ◄

Proof: The claim looks innocent, but I could not find a more elegant way than to deal separately with the three regions $[0, \frac{1}{\kappa})$, $[\frac{1}{\kappa}, 1 - \frac{1}{\kappa}]$ and $(1 - \frac{1}{\kappa}, 1)$. Let first $x \in [\frac{1}{\kappa}, 1 - \frac{1}{\kappa}]$. For those x Proposition 2.55 gives

$$\mathrm{hd}_\kappa(x) - \ln(x) \;\geqslant\; \frac{1}{2}\left(\frac{1}{x\kappa} - \frac{1}{\kappa}\right) - \frac{1}{12}\left(\frac{1}{(x\kappa)^2} - \frac{1}{\kappa^2}\right).$$

The latter is zero for $x = 1$ and $x = \frac{1}{6\kappa - 1}$ and positive in between, and because $\frac{1}{6\kappa - 1} \leqslant \frac{1}{\kappa}$ for $\kappa \geqslant \frac{1}{5}$ this covers the whole range $x \in [\frac{1}{\kappa}, 1 - \frac{1}{\kappa}]$.

Now assume $x < \frac{1}{\kappa}$. The tangent of $\ln(x)$ at $x = 1/\kappa$ is $\mathrm{l}(x) := \ln(1/\kappa) + (x - \frac{1}{\kappa})\ln'(1/\kappa) = x\kappa - \ln(\kappa) - 1$. If we can show that $\mathrm{hd}_\kappa(x) \geqslant \mathrm{l}(x)$ for $x = 0$ and $x = \frac{1}{\kappa}$, we have $\mathrm{hd}_\kappa(x) \geqslant \mathrm{l}(x) > \ln(x)$ for all $x \in [0, \frac{1}{\kappa})$; the first inequality follows by concavity of hd_κ and the second one by strict concavity of $\ln$ and Lemma 2.5. Now, we have $\mathrm{hd}_\kappa(0) = -H_\kappa$ and $\mathrm{l}(0) = -\ln(\kappa) - 1$. For $\kappa = 1$, both are -1. For $\kappa \geqslant 2$, we have by Equation (2.74.1) on page 58

$$H_\kappa \;\leqslant\; \ln(\kappa) + \gamma + \frac{1}{2\kappa} \;\leqslant\; \ln(\kappa) + \gamma + \underbrace{\frac{1}{4}}_{\approx 0.83} \;<\; \ln(\kappa) + 1, \tag{2.231}$$

so $\mathrm{hd}_\kappa(0) \geqslant \mathrm{l}(0)$ for all $\kappa \in \mathbb{N}$. The second point uses the very same computation: $\mathrm{hd}_\kappa(1/\kappa) = -H_\kappa + 1 > \ln(\kappa) = \mathrm{l}(1/\kappa)$. Hence $\mathrm{hd}_\kappa(x) > \ln(x)$ for all $\kappa \in \mathbb{N}$ and $x \in [0, \frac{1}{\kappa})$.

Finally, let $x \in (1 - \frac{1}{\kappa}, 1)$. We follow the same lines of argumentation as above, this time using the tangent of $\ln(x)$ at $x = 1$, which is $x - 1$. $\mathrm{hd}_\kappa(1) = 0$ and $\mathrm{hd}_\kappa(1 - \frac{1}{\kappa}) = H_{\kappa-1} - H_\kappa = -\frac{1}{\kappa}$, so $x - 1$ is the *chord* of hd_κ through $x = 1$ and $x = 1 - \frac{1}{\kappa}$, which always lie *below* a strictly concave function. We thus have $\mathrm{hd}_\kappa(x) > x - 1 > \ln(x)$ also for $x \in (1 - \frac{1}{\kappa}, 1)$, which concludes the proof. ∎

2.5.3 Properties of the Discrete Entropy

We collect a few properties of the discrete entropy here for later reference.

Corollary 2.62: *For any $\kappa \geqslant 0$ is $\mathcal{H}_{\mathrm{hd}_\kappa}(\mathbf{p})$ a strictly Schur-concave function, and it attains a unique global maximum of $-\mathrm{hd}_\kappa(1/s)$ at $\mathbf{p} = (\frac{1}{s}, \ldots, \frac{1}{s})$.* ◄

Proof: By Lemma 2.59, $-x\,\mathrm{hd}_\kappa(x)$ is strictly concave, so the claim follows with Corollary 2.48 (page 85). ∎

Lemma 2.63 (Bounds on Discrete Entropy): *For any κ-discretized distribution $\boldsymbol{\tau}$ holds*

$$\mathcal{H}_{x\mapsto x-1}(\boldsymbol{\tau}) \;\leqslant\; \mathcal{H}_{\mathrm{hd}_\kappa}(\boldsymbol{\tau}) \;\leqslant\; \mathcal{H}_{\ln}(\boldsymbol{\tau}), \tag{2.232}$$

where equality holds if and only if $\tau_i = 1$ for some $i \in [s]$. The upper bound $\mathcal{H}_{\mathrm{hd}_\kappa}(\boldsymbol{\tau}) \leqslant \mathcal{H}_{\ln}(\boldsymbol{\tau})$ holds for any $\kappa \in \mathbb{N}$ and $\boldsymbol{\tau} \in [0,1)^s$ with $\Sigma\boldsymbol{\tau} = 1$. ◄

Proof: The claim follows by bounding $\mathrm{hd}_\kappa(x)$ using Lemma 2.60 resp. Lemma 2.61, where we assume w.l.o.g. that all $\tau_i > 0$; otherwise we can drop these components without affecting the three entropies. If by dropping all zero-entries, only the degenerate vector (1) is left, we find that all three entropies are 0. ∎

The bounds above are tight for degenerate distributions, but lie far apart from each other in general. For large values of κ, the upper bound becomes tight. We can prove that even in a slightly more general setting.

Lemma 2.64 (Limit of Discrete Entropy): *Let $(\boldsymbol{\tau}^{(\kappa)})$ be a sequence of vectors with $\boldsymbol{\tau}^{(\kappa)} \in [0,1]^s$ and $\Sigma\boldsymbol{\tau}^{(\kappa)} = 1$, and assume it converges to a limit vector $\lim_{\kappa\to\infty}\boldsymbol{\tau}^{(\kappa)} = \boldsymbol{\tau}^* \in [0,1]^s$. Denote by $\delta(\kappa) = \|\boldsymbol{\tau}^{(\kappa)} - \boldsymbol{\tau}^*\|_\infty$ the difference of the κth vector to the limit. Then*

$$\mathcal{H}_{\mathrm{hd}_\kappa}(\boldsymbol{\tau}^{(\kappa)}) \;=\; \mathcal{H}_{\ln}(\boldsymbol{\tau}^*) \pm O\big(\delta(\kappa) + \kappa^{-1}\big), \qquad (\kappa \to \infty), \tag{2.233}$$

so the discrete entropy converges to the base-e Shannon entropy with rate κ^{-1}. ◄

Proof: As s is finite and fixed, it suffices to consider the summands of the entropy in isolation. Assume first that $\tau_r^* \in (0,1)$. By definition of $\delta = \delta(\kappa)$ and Lipschitz-continuity of hd_κ (Corollary 2.58) we have

$$\tau_r^{(\kappa)} \cdot \mathrm{hd}_\kappa(\tau_r^{(\kappa)}) \;=\; \big(\tau_r^* \pm O(\delta)\big)\big(\mathrm{hd}_\kappa(\tau_r^*) \pm O(\delta)\big) \tag{2.234}$$

$$=\; \tau_r^* \cdot \mathrm{hd}_\kappa(\tau_r^*) \pm O(\delta) \tag{2.235}$$

$$\underset{\text{Corollary 2.56}}{=}\; \tau_r^* \cdot \ln(\tau_r^*) \pm O(\delta + \kappa^{-1}). \tag{2.236}$$

If $\tau_r^* \in \{0,1\}$, we cannot apply Corollary 2.56, but we have $\tau_r^* \cdot \ln(\tau_r^*) = 0 = \tau_r^* \cdot \mathrm{hd}_\kappa(\tau_r^*)$. ∎

Thereby, the upper bound of $\mathcal{H}_{\ln}(\boldsymbol{\tau})$ cannot be improved in general. For the lower bound, there is room for improvement, if $\boldsymbol{\tau}$ is not degenerate.

Lemma 2.65 (Refined Lower Bound): *Let $\boldsymbol{\tau}$ be a κ-discretized distribution, where for every component τ_i holds*

$$\tau_i \;\leqslant\; \frac{-\ln(\kappa)/\kappa}{W_0(-\ln(\kappa)/\kappa)} \;=\; \exp\big(W_0(-\ln(\kappa)/\kappa)\big), \tag{2.237}$$

with W_0 the (principal branch of the) Lambert-W-function, a.k.a. the product logarithm. Then holds

$$\mathcal{H}_{\mathrm{hd}_\kappa}(\boldsymbol{\tau}) \;\geqslant\; \mathcal{H}_{\ln}(\boldsymbol{\tau}) \cdot \left(1 - \frac{1}{2\ln\kappa}\right). \tag{2.238}$$

◄

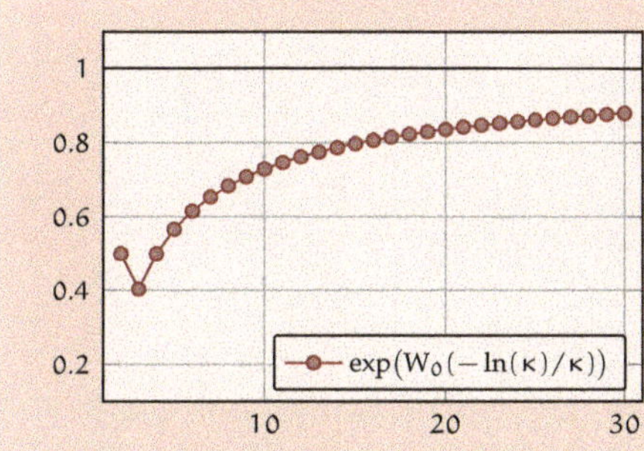

Figure 7: The upper bound $\exp(W_0(-\ln(\kappa)/\kappa))$ on the probabilities τ_i from Lemma 2.65 for κ between 2 and 30. It approaches 1 with increasing κ.

Proof: We first show that for $a \in [-\frac{1}{e}, 0]$ the equation $x \ln x = a$ has two real solutions, which coincide for $a = -\frac{1}{e}$, and are given by $x_1 = \frac{a}{W_{-1}(a)}$ and $x_2 = \frac{a}{W_0(a)}$.

Recall that $W(a)$ is a number so that $we^w = a$. For $a \in \mathbb{R}$ there are no real solutions if $a < -\frac{1}{e}$, two solutions for $-\frac{1}{e} \leqslant a < 0$, which coincide at $a = -\frac{1}{e}$, and one real solution for $a \geqslant 0$. By $W_0(a)$, we denote the larger real solution (if one exists), and by $W_{-1}(a)$, we denote the second, smaller real solution (where two solutions exist). For complex a, W has further branches; see Corless et al. [34] for further information.

Inserting and using $\ln(W(z)) = \ln(z) - W(z)$, (Equation (3.8) of Corless et al. [34]), we find

$$x_{1,2} \ln(x_{1,2}) = \frac{a}{W(a)} \ln\left(\frac{a}{W(a)}\right) \tag{2.239}$$

$$= \frac{a}{W(a)} \Big(\ln(a) - \ln(W(a))\Big) \tag{2.240}$$

$$= \frac{a}{W(a)} \Big(\ln(a) - \ln(a) + W(a)\Big) \tag{2.241}$$

$$= a. \tag{2.242}$$

The alternative form in the claim follows by dividing $we^w = a$ by w.

Set $W := \frac{-\ln(\kappa)/\kappa}{W_0(-\ln(\kappa)/\kappa)}$. By the fact above we have $W \ln W = \frac{1}{\kappa} \ln(\frac{1}{\kappa})$. (The other, smaller solution of that equation is of course $W = \frac{1}{\kappa}$.) For the unimodal function $x \ln(1/x) = -x \ln x$, this means

$$x \ln(1/x) \geqslant \frac{\ln(\kappa)}{\kappa}, \qquad \text{for } x \in [\tfrac{1}{\kappa}, W]. \tag{2.243}$$

Let $x \in [\frac{1}{\kappa}, W]$. We have by Proposition 2.55

$$\mathrm{hd}_\kappa(x) \leqslant \ln(x) + \frac{1}{2}\left(\frac{1}{x\kappa} - \frac{1}{\kappa}\right) \tag{2.244}$$

$$\leqslant \ln(x) + \frac{1}{2x\kappa}, \tag{2.245}$$

and by dividing by $\ln(x)$

$$\frac{hd_\kappa(x)}{\ln(x)} \;\geqslant\; 1 - \frac{1}{2\kappa \cdot x \ln(1/x)} \tag{2.246}$$

$$\underset{(2.243)}{\geqslant} \; 1 - \frac{1}{2\ln(\kappa)}. \tag{2.247}$$

Using this in the entropy gives the claim

$$\sum_{r=1}^{s} -\tau_r \, hd_\kappa(\tau_r) \;\geqslant\; \sum_{r=1}^{s} -\tau_r \ln(\tau_r) \cdot \left(1 - \frac{1}{2\ln(\kappa)}\right) \;=\; \mathcal{H}_{\ln}(\tau) \cdot \left(1 - \frac{1}{2\ln(\kappa)}\right). \tag{2.248}$$
$$\blacksquare$$

$$\blacklozenge \qquad \blacklozenge \qquad \blacklozenge$$

We obtain an analog of Gibb's inequality for hd_κ when we restrict the scope to discretized vectors, in fact, to κ-discretized vectors.

Lemma 2.66 (Gibb's Inequality for Discrete Entropy):
For $p, q \in (\frac{1}{\kappa}\mathbb{N})^s$ with $\Sigma p = 1$ and $\Sigma q \leqslant 1$. We have

$$-\sum_{i=1}^{s} p_i \, hd_\kappa(p_i) \;\leqslant\; -\sum_{i=1}^{s} p_i \, hd_\kappa(q_i), \tag{2.249}$$

and equality holds only if $p = q$. ◄

Proof: Rewrite the difference

$$-\sum_{i=1}^{s} p_i \, hd_\kappa(q_i) + \sum_{i=1}^{s} p_i \, hd_\kappa(p_i) \underset{(2.212)}{=} -\sum_{i=1}^{s} p_i \, hd_{p_i\kappa}(q_i/p_i). \tag{2.250}$$

By assumption, q_i is a multiple of $\frac{1}{\kappa}$, so q_i/p_i is a multiple of $\frac{1}{p_i\kappa}$ and we can apply Lemma 2.60 to find

$$-\sum_{i=1}^{s} p_i \, hd_{p_i\kappa}(q_i/p_i) \;\geqslant\; -\sum_{i=1}^{s} p_i(q_i/p_i - 1) \;=\; -\Sigma q + 1 \;\geqslant\; 0. \tag{2.251}$$

Equality holds only when $q_i = p_i$ or $q_i = p_i - \frac{1}{\kappa}$ for all i and $\Sigma q = 1$, i.e., when $q = p$. $\blacksquare$

Remark: The proof of Gibb's inequality actually only requires vectors where $q_i/p_i \notin (1 - \frac{1}{p_i\kappa}, 1)$ to apply Lemma 2.60, i.e., $q_i \notin (p_i - \frac{1}{\kappa}, p_i)$ for all $i = 1, \ldots, s$. This is obviously fulfilled for κ-discretized vectors, but one could generalize the statement a little. ◄

There is another property that the discrete entropy shares with the Shannon entropy: *aggregation preserves entropy.* What we mean by this is expressed formally in Lemma E (page 444) of Knuth [103] for the Shannon entropy. We used Knuth's Lemma E in our proof of Proposition 2.49, see Equation (2.184) on page 87; we reproduced the main argument for its proof there, as well.

We now adapt Knuth's description for our scenario. Consider a not-necessarily-binary tree in which the positive reals $\sigma_1, \ldots, \sigma_s \in \mathbb{R}_{>0}$ have been assigned to the leaves. The access probability of a leaf is proportional to its weight σ_r; we only have to normalize σ_r/κ, where $\kappa = \Sigma\sigma$ for $\sigma = (\sigma_1, \ldots, \sigma_s)$. The branching at each internal node corresponds to a local probability distribution based on the subtree probabilities, i.e., the sums of leaf probabilities below each edge. For any such node v, we denote by $\kappa(v)$ the sum of weights of leaves in the subtree rooted at v, and by $\sigma(v)$ the vector of sums of leaf weights for all its direct children. Clearly $\Sigma(\sigma(v)) = \kappa(v)$, so $\tau(v) = \sigma(v)/\kappa(v)$ is the local probability distribution for the branch at v. As usual, we set $\tau = \sigma/\kappa$ for the global leaf probabilities.

We then have the following analog to Knuth's Lemma E for discrete entropy.

Lemma 2.67 (Aggregation Preserves Entropy): *Let a (not-necessarily-binary) tree T with leaf weights $\sigma_1, \ldots, \sigma_s \in \mathbb{R}_{>0}$ be given and let $\kappa(v)$ and $\tau(v)$ be defined as above. Then*

$$\sum_{\substack{v \text{ internal} \\ \text{node of } T}} \frac{\kappa(v)}{\kappa} \cdot \mathcal{H}_{\mathrm{hd}_{\kappa(v)}}\big(\tau(v)\big) = \mathcal{H}_{\mathrm{hd}_\kappa}(\tau). \tag{2.252}$$

■

We omit a formal inductive proof, and instead consider an example; it is easy to see that the cancellations in the example generalize to any branching degree and any number of nodes. Consider the following tree with four leaves.

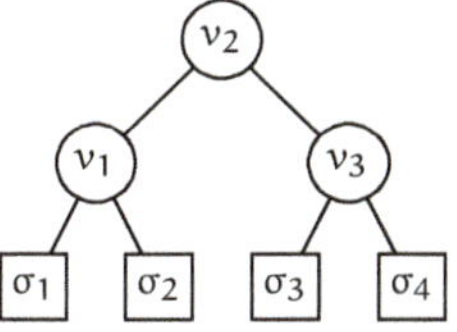

Here we have for example $\sigma(v_1) = (\sigma_1, \sigma_2)$, $\kappa(v_1) = \sigma_1 + \sigma_2$ and thus $\tau(v_1) = \left(\frac{\sigma_1}{\sigma_1+\sigma_2}, \frac{\sigma_1}{\sigma_1+\sigma_2}\right) = \left(\frac{\tau_1}{\tau_1+\tau_2}, \frac{\tau_1}{\tau_1+\tau_2}\right)$. The lemma then asserts that

$$\mathcal{H}_{\mathrm{hd}_\kappa}(\tau_1, \tau_2, \tau_3, \tau_4) = \mathcal{H}_{\mathrm{hd}_\kappa}(\tau_1 + \tau_2, \tau_3 + \tau_4)$$
$$+ (\tau_1 + \tau_2)\mathcal{H}_{\mathrm{hd}_{(\tau_1+\tau_2)\kappa}}\left(\frac{\tau_1}{\tau_1+\tau_2}, \frac{\tau_2}{\tau_1+\tau_2}\right)$$
$$+ (\tau_3 + \tau_4)\mathcal{H}_{\mathrm{hd}_{(\tau_3+\tau_4)\kappa}}\left(\frac{\tau_3}{\tau_3+\tau_4}, \frac{\tau_4}{\tau_3+\tau_4}\right); \tag{2.253}$$

and in fact we find by expanding definitions that the right-hand is

$$- (\tau_1 + \tau_2)\, \mathrm{hd}_\kappa(\tau_1 + \tau_2) - (\tau_3 + \tau_4)\, \mathrm{hd}_\kappa(\tau_3 + \tau_4)$$

$$- (\tau_1 + \tau_2) \cdot \frac{\tau_1}{\tau_1 + \tau_2}\, \mathrm{hd}_{(\tau_1 + \tau_2)\kappa}\left(\frac{\tau_1}{\tau_1 + \tau_2} \right)$$

$$- (\tau_1 + \tau_2) \cdot \frac{\tau_2}{\tau_1 + \tau_2}\, \mathrm{hd}_{(\tau_1 + \tau_2)\kappa}\left(\frac{\tau_2}{\tau_1 + \tau_2} \right)$$

$$- (\tau_3 + \tau_4) \cdot \frac{\tau_3}{\tau_3 + \tau_4}\, \mathrm{hd}_{(\tau_3 + \tau_4)\kappa}\left(\frac{\tau_3}{\tau_3 + \tau_4} \right)$$

$$- (\tau_1 + \tau_2) \cdot \frac{\tau_4}{\tau_3 + \tau_4}\, \mathrm{hd}_{(\tau_3 + \tau_4)\kappa}\left(\frac{\tau_4}{\tau_3 + \tau_4} \right) \tag{2.254}$$

$$\underset{(2.212)}{=} -(\tau_1 + \tau_2)\, \mathrm{hd}_\kappa(\tau_1 + \tau_2) - (\tau_3 + \tau_4)\, \mathrm{hd}_\kappa(\tau_3 + \tau_4)$$

$$- \tau_1 \big(\mathrm{hd}_\kappa(\tau_1) - \mathrm{hd}_\kappa(\tau_1 + \tau_2) \big)$$

$$- \tau_2 \big(\mathrm{hd}_\kappa(\tau_2) - \mathrm{hd}_\kappa(\tau_1 + \tau_2) \big)$$

$$- \tau_3 \big(\mathrm{hd}_\kappa(\tau_3) - \mathrm{hd}_\kappa(\tau_3 + \tau_4) \big)$$

$$- \tau_4 \big(\mathrm{hd}_\kappa(\tau_4) - \mathrm{hd}_\kappa(\tau_3 + \tau_4) \big) \tag{2.255}$$

$$= -\sum_{r=1}^{4} \tau_r\, \mathrm{hd}_\kappa(\tau_r) \tag{2.256}$$

$$= \mathcal{H}_{\mathrm{hd}_\kappa}(\boldsymbol{\tau}) \tag{2.257}$$

as claimed. We will use Lemma 2.67 in the context of Quicksort to show that we can simulate the effect of multiway partitioning for the Quicksort recurrence using several levels of binary decisions. This is especially valuable to judge potential benefits of multiway Quicksort over classic Quicksort with pivot sampling, see Section 7.3.

We have seen that the discrete entropy arises naturally as the expected entropy of Dirichlet vectors. We have also seen that the discrete entropy shares many, but not all, of the properties of the ordinary entropy. In the next section, we will explore how the expected entropy arises in solutions of recurrence equations.

2.6 A Master Theorem for Distributional Recurrences

Roura's *continuous master theorem (CMT)* allows us to asymptotically solve certain *full-history recurrences*, typically with explicit leading-term constants, using only elementary methodology [153, 154]. Such recurrences result when analyzing the average cost of divide-and-conquer algorithms with *random* subproblem sizes. Quicksort is of this type, but there are many more examples [154]. We give Roura's CMT in Section 2.6.1.

Roura lists such divide-and-conquer scenarios as initial motivation for his master theorems; in his final formulations this connection is somewhat concealed. One reason is that we obtain the most general theorems when we only assume the technical conditions that are needed for the proof. Roura's formulations are perfectly sensible for his endeavor to give improved master theorems, but I have always pitied a lack of user-friendliness in his formal statements. As a first step, we state simple sufficient conditions for the applicability of the CMT, see Lemma 2.69 below.

Another reason is that we simply *cannot* translate the recursive structure of an algorithm directly to a recurrence for its expected costs if the sizes of subproblems are random: we have to include all possible subproblem sizes in the recurrence in some way. The direct correspondence between recursive calls in the algorithm and recursive cost terms in the recurrence equation is thereby lost. We can recover this direct correspondence, if we dare to set up a recurrence of the full *distribution* of the cost, instead of its mean only. This is often *not* more work, and allows an elegant description of an algorithm's cost, directly mimicking its recursive nature. Section 2.6.2 discusses usual hurdles of distributional recurrences and how to overcome them.

In the remainder of this section, we derive a *distributional CMT (DMT)*, which is a reformulation of Roura's theorem in the language of distributional recurrences. The attribute *distributional* here refers to the *input*, i.e., the recurrence, not to the *output*. Our theorems provide a convenient shortcut to compute *expected* costs directly from the *distributional* recurrence.

We do not extend the applicability of Roura's theorem; but we ease its application. And we bring back the direct correspondence between a random-subproblem-size recursive algorithm and the recursive description of its costs. Instead of the weights of the expected-cost recurrence, we make the *distribution of relative subproblem sizes* the central object of study.

2.6.1 The Continuous Master Theorem

We begin by restating Roura's CMT and presenting a few shortcuts to checking its technical conditions for relevant special cases.

Theorem 2.68 (Roura's Continuous Master Theorem (CMT)):
Let F_n be recursively defined by

$$F_n = \begin{cases} b_n, & \text{for } 0 \leqslant n < N; \\ t_n + \displaystyle\sum_{j=0}^{n-1} w_{n,j}\, F_j, & \text{for } n \geqslant N, \end{cases} \qquad (2.258)$$

where t_n, the toll function, satisfies $t_n \sim K n^\alpha \log^\beta(n)$ as $n \to \infty$ for constants $K \neq 0$, $\alpha \geqslant 0$ and $\beta > -1$. Assume there exists a function $w : [0,1] \to \mathbb{R}_{\geqslant 0}$, the shape function, with $\int_0^1 w(z)\,dz \geqslant 1$ and

$$\sum_{j=0}^{n-1} \left| w_{n,j} - \int_{j/n}^{(j+1)/n} w(z)\,dz \right| = O(n^{-d}), \qquad (n \to \infty), \qquad (2.259)$$

---

for a constant $d > 0$. With $H := 1 - \int_0^1 z^\alpha w(z)\, dz$, we have the following cases:

1. *If $H > 0$, then $F_n \sim \dfrac{t_n}{H}$.*

2. *If $H = 0$, then $F_n \sim \dfrac{t_n \ln n}{\tilde{H}}$ with $\tilde{H} = -(\beta + 1)\int_0^1 z^\alpha \ln(z)\, w(z)\, dz$.*

3. *If $H < 0$, then $F_n = O(n^c)$ for the unique $c \in \mathbb{R}$ with $\int_0^1 z^c w(z)\, dz = 1$.* ∎

Several similar theorems are called CMT, so a few remarks are in order.

a) Theorem 2.68 is the "reduced form" of the CMT, which appears as Theorem 1.3.2 in Roura's doctoral thesis [153], and as Theorem 18 of Martínez and Roura [116]. The full version (Theorem 3.3 in [154]) allows us to handle sublogarithmic factors in the toll function, as well, which we do not need here. The ideas below could easily be extended to the full-power CMT.

b) In Case 3 actually holds $F_n = \Theta(n^c)$ if either $K > 0$ and $F_n \geqslant 0$ for all n, or if $K < 0$ and $F_n \leqslant 0$. We will not make use of this refinement though.

c) Roura [153, 154] requires for shape functions $w(z)$ additionally that there is $\mu > 0$ so that also $\int_0^1 w(z)z^\mu\, dz$ exists. We understand the conditions involving such integrals as not fulfilled if the integral does not exist.

To apply the CMT, one first has to identify the so-called *shape function* $w(z)$ which smoothly approximates the weights $w_{n,j}$. A good starting point to try is $\lim_{n\to\infty} n \cdot w_{n,zn}$ for $w(z)$. Then one has to verify the condition (2.259). There is a convenient shortcut for this step if our function is smooth enough. We assume here that $w_{n,zn}$ can be analytically continued to a real function in $z \in [0, 1]$.

Lemma 2.69: *Let $w(z)$ be Hölder-continuous on $[0, 1]$ with exponent $\alpha \in (0, 1]$ and assume*

$$n \cdot w_{n,zn} \;=\; w(z) \pm O(n^{-\delta}) \tag{2.260}$$

uniformly for $z \in (0, 1)$ for a constant $\delta > 0$. Then $w(z)$ fulfills Equation (2.259) with $d = \min\{\alpha, \delta\}$. ◀

Recall that in particular if $w(z)$ has bounded derivative on $[0, 1]$, it is Lipschitz- and thus Hölder-continuous with exponent 1 (Proposition 2.10).

Proof of Lemma 2.69: Let $z \in (0, 1)$ be fixed and write $j = j(n) = \lfloor zn \rfloor \in [0..n - 1]$. By Proposition 2.12 we have

$$n \cdot \int_{j/n}^{(j+1)/n} w(z)\, dz \;=\; w(j/n) \pm O(n^{-\alpha}), \tag{2.261}$$

and by the assumption

$$w(j/n) \;=\; nw_{n,j} \pm O(n^{-\delta}). \tag{2.262}$$

Putting both together, dividing by n and summing over all j yields

$$\sum_{j=0}^{n-1} \left| w_{n,j} - \int_{j/n}^{(j+1)/n} w(z)\, dz \right| \;=\; O(n^{-\alpha} + n^{-\delta}). \tag{2.263}$$

$\blacksquare$

2.6.2 Distributional Recurrences

In analogy to recursive definitions of ordinary sequences, we can define sequences of probability distributions recursively, representing one distribution as the result of some transformation of distributions with smaller indices: a distributional recurrence. This section is a user's manual for such distributional recurrences. We discuss technicalities of the approach and how to cope with them.

In particular, independence assumptions for distributional recurrences are usually stated in a well-chosen, concise wording. While precise and sufficient for the expert, details can remain blurry to the untrained eye. We have a little closer look and emphasize potentially unclear aspects.

Stand-In Random Variables.   Here comes a first peculiarity in notation: instead of stating a recursive relations on the distributions, it is customary to state a distributional recurrence on a sequence of *random variables*. This is convenient because the recursive description usually involves *computing* a distribution from others. Arithmetic operations are readily understood on (real) random variables, but for two distributions, it is not a priori clear what it means to add them up. We could define operations to be lifted from random variables to distributions, but working with random variables is just as fine.

Recall that a *stochastic representation* $X \overset{\mathcal{D}}{=} f(Y)$ of random variable X by a term $f(Y)$ means that for any event A, we have $\mathbb{P}[X \in A] = \mathbb{E}_Y[\mathbb{P}[f(Y) \in A]]$. We have seen such representations before, e.g., for Dirichlet-variables. A distributional recurrence is then just a stochastic representation using other members of the same family.

Joint Distributions.   Consider the following simplistic distributional recurrence for the sequence $(C_n)_{n \in \mathbb{N}}$ of random variables:

$$C_1 \overset{\mathcal{D}}{=} T_1\,, \tag{2.264.1}$$

$$C_n \overset{\mathcal{D}}{=} T_n \cdot C_{n-1}\,, \qquad n \geqslant 2, \tag{2.264.2}$$

where $(T_n)_{n \in \mathbb{N}}$ is a family of *toll random variables* with known distributions. The recurrence telescopes and C_n is distributed like the product of the first n toll terms, of which we know the distributions—but only as marginal distributions! We do *not* know the *joint* distribution of $(T_1, \dots, T_n)$, and we cannot even say what $\mathbb{E}[C_n]$ is in this case.

Let us make this point explicit. Assume for all T_n holds $\mathbb{P}[T_n = 0] = \frac{2}{3}$ and $\mathbb{P}[T_n = 1] = \frac{1}{3}$. C_n then also attains values 0 and 1 only. If we assume all variables to be independent, then $\mathbb{P}[C_n = 1] = \left(\frac{1}{3}\right)^n$. If, however in the representation of $C_2 \overset{\mathcal{D}}{=} T_1 \cdot C_1$ the joint distribution of C_1 and T_1 is given by

$$\mathbb{P}\big[(C_1, T_1) = (0,1)\big] \;=\; \tfrac{1}{3}, \qquad \mathbb{P}\big[(C_1, T_1) = (1,0)\big] \;=\; \tfrac{1}{3}, \qquad (2.265.1)$$

$$\mathbb{P}\big[(C_1, T_1) = (0,0)\big] \;=\; \tfrac{1}{3}, \qquad \mathbb{P}\big[(C_1, T_1) = (1,1)\big] \;=\; 0, \qquad (2.265.2)$$

the marginal distributions are the same, but of course $\mathbb{P}[C_n = 1] = 0$ for all $n \geqslant 2$. Without information about the joint distribution of all involved variables, a stochastic representation does not identify a distribution uniquely.

It is therefore part of every distributional recurrence to specify the relation of the variables on the right-hand side.

Quicksort Declaration of Independence.   Let us see how joint distributions are stated for a prototypical divide-and-conquer recurrence: the costs of single-pivot Quicksort on a random permutation. The algorithm works by splitting an input of size $n \geqslant 2$ into two parts of random sizes $J_1^{(n)}, J_2^{(n)} \in [0..n-1]$, with $J_1^{(n)} + J_2^{(n)} = n - 1$. This process incurs random costs T_n. By analyzing the partitioning algorithm, we obtain the joint distribution of $(J_1^{(n)}, J_2^{(n)}, T_n)$.

Moreover, we found that, if implemented carefully, partitioning *preserves randomness*, i.e., partitioning a random permutation produces subproblems that are themselves random permutations of the respective elements. For the costs, this means that if we fix the subproblem sizes $(J_1^{(n)}, J_1^{(n)}) = (j_1, j_2)$, then the partitioning costs and the costs for sorting the two subproblems are (mutually) independent.

> **Mutual Independence.**   Mutual independence, also called total independence or joint independence means that probabilities for joint events factor for any finite subset of a given collection of events. This is a strictly stronger requirement than pairwise independence, so to make clear that not only the latter is meant, one should always say mutually independent. Unless explicitly stated otherwise, we always mean mutually independence.

Unconditionally, they are all dependent because partitioning cost and recursive costs depend on subproblem sizes in general.

With that we can set up the distributional recurrence for the sequence of random variables $(C_n)_{n \in \mathbb{N}_0}$, the cost of Quicksort:

$$C_0 \overset{\mathcal{D}}{=} C_1 \overset{\mathcal{D}}{=} 0 \qquad\qquad (2.266.1)$$

$$C_n \overset{\mathcal{D}}{=} T_n + C_{J_1^{(n)}}^{(1)} + C_{J_2^{(n)}}^{(2)}, \qquad n \geqslant 2, \qquad (2.266.2)$$

with the following conditions:

1 $(C_n^{(1)})_{n \in \mathbb{N}_0}$ and $(C_n^{(2)})_{n \in \mathbb{N}_0}$ are *independent copies* of $(C_n)_{n \in \mathbb{N}_0}$, i.e., for all $n \in \mathbb{N}_0$ holds $C_n^{(1)} \overset{\mathcal{D}}{=} C_n^{(2)} \overset{\mathcal{D}}{=} C_n$, and for all $i_1, i_2, i_3 \in \mathbb{N}_0$ are $C_{i_1}^{(1)}$, $C_{i_2}^{(2)}$ and C_{i_3} mutually independent.

2 For fixed subproblem sizes, the remaining variables are *conditionally independent*, i.e., for all $j_1, j_2 \in \mathbb{N}_0$ with $j_1 + j_2 = n - 1$ holds: if we fix $(J_1^{(n)}, J_2^{(n)}) = (j_1, j_2)$, we have that T_n, $C_{j_1}^{(1)}$ and $C_{j_2}^{(2)}$ are mutually independent.

Similar conditions result for most divide-and-conquer algorithms. The space-economic formulation of the above conditions is as follows: $(C_n^{(1)})_{n \in \mathbb{N}}$ and $(C_n^{(2)})_{n \in \mathbb{N}}$ are independent copies of $(C_n)_{n \in \mathbb{N}}$, which are also independent of $(J_1^{(n)}, J_2^{(n)})$ and T_n.

In Praise Of Distributional Recurrences.   The expression for C_n in Equation (2.266.2) follows exactly the structure of Quicksort: one partitioning step, a recursive call to the left, and one to the right. It is much simpler to argue why this distributional recurrence describes Quicksort than it would be for a direct full-history recurrence for expected costs. The ordinary recurrence for the expected costs can be derived *mechanically* from the distributional recurrence. The same is true for recurrences for the variance or higher moments [113].

On the other hand, the reader might have the impression that distributional recurrences make analyses much more complicated. In general this is true; if for example costs for recursive calls are not independent, we might still obtain a recurrence for the mean by linearity of the expectation, whereas a statement about the distribution may be out of reach. For Quicksort, the distributional analysis mostly makes conditions explicit that already existed for the average-case analysis. In particular, the property of randomness preservation is now part of the statement of the recurrence, instead of a side note in a sub-clause.

2.6.3 A Simple Distributional Master Theorem

Now, starting with the original CMT (Theorem 2.68), the main idea towards a distributional master theorem is that Equation (2.259) can be rephrased in terms of random variables. For that, assume that J is the random vector of subproblem sizes, then $w_{n,j} = \sum_r \mathbb{P}[J_r = j]$. If we further assume that $\frac{J_r}{n}$ converges to a limit variable Z_r^* with density $f_{Z_r^*}$ (where the precise sense of stochastic convergence is given below), we expect $w(z) = \sum_r f_{Z_r^*}(z)$, and therefore the above condition will in this case be valid separately for the r components, i.e., it is sufficient to have for all r that

$$\sum_{j=0}^{n-1} \left| \mathbb{P}[J_r = j] - \int_{j/n}^{(j+1)/n} f_{Z_r^*}(z)\, dz \right| = O(n^{-d}). \tag{2.267}$$

There might be recurrences where the original CMT applies, but which do not have such a separable shape. We trade generality applicability for ease of application here.

The following statement is an immediate corollary of our more general DMT given as Theorem 2.76 in the following section. The weaker form below is easier to state and to apply, so it serves as good starting point and is of independent interest.

Theorem 2.70 (Distributional Master Theorem (DMT)):
Let $(C_n)_{n \in \mathbb{N}_0}$ be a family of random variables that satisfies the distributional recurrence

$$C_n \overset{\mathcal{D}}{=} T_n + \sum_{r=1}^{s} C_{J_r^{(n)}}^{(r)}, \qquad (n \geqslant n_0), \tag{2.268}$$

where $(C_n^{(1)})_{n \in \mathbb{N}}, \ldots, (C_n^{(s)})_{n \in \mathbb{N}}$ are independent copies of $(C_n)_{n \in \mathbb{N}}$, which are also independent of $\mathbf{J}^{(n)} = (J_1^{(n)}, \ldots, J_s^{(n)}) \in \{0, \ldots, n-1\}^s$ and T_n. Define $\mathbf{Z}^{(n)} = \mathbf{J}^{(n)}/n$ and assume that the components $Z_r^{(n)}$ of $\mathbf{Z}^{(n)}$ fulfill uniformly for $z \in (0,1)$

$$n \cdot \mathbb{P}[Z_r^{(n)} \in (z - \tfrac{1}{n}, z]] = f_{Z_r^*}(z) \pm O(n^{-\delta}), \qquad (n \to \infty), \tag{2.269}$$

for a constant $\delta > 0$ and a Hölder-continuous function $f_{Z_r^*} : [0,1] \to \mathbb{R}$. Then $f_{Z_r^*}$ is the density of a random variable Z_r^* and $Z_r^{(n)} \overset{\mathcal{D}}{\longrightarrow} Z_r^*$.

Moreover, assume $\mathbb{E}[T_n] \sim K n^\alpha \log^\beta(n)$, as $n \to \infty$, for constants $K \neq 0$, $\alpha \geqslant 0$ and $\beta > -1$. Then, with $H = 1 - \sum_{r=1}^{s} \mathbb{E}[(Z_r^*)^\alpha]$, we have the following cases.

1. *If $H > 0$, then $\mathbb{E}[C_n] \sim \dfrac{\mathbb{E}[T_n]}{H}$.*

2. *If $H = 0$, then $\mathbb{E}[C_n] \sim \dfrac{\mathbb{E}[T_n] \ln n}{\tilde{H}}$ with $\tilde{H} = -(\beta + 1) \sum_{r=1}^{s} \mathbb{E}[(Z_r^*)^\alpha \ln(Z_r^*)]$.*

3. *If $H < 0$, then $\mathbb{E}[C_n] = O(n^c)$ for the unique $c \in \mathbb{R}$ with $\sum_{r=1}^{s} \mathbb{E}[(Z_r^*)^c] = 1$.* ◀

The technical conditions in the theorem might look scary, so a few remarks are in order:

▶ The functions $z \mapsto n\mathbb{P}[Z_r = z]$ can be seen as a *discrete density* of Z_r, obtained as the *difference quotient* (in contrast with the *differential quotient*, which would give the continuous derivative)

$$n\mathbb{P}[Z_r = z] = n\mathbb{P}[Z_r \in (z - \tfrac{1}{n}, z]] = \frac{F_{Z_r}(z) - F_{Z_r}(z - \tfrac{1}{n})}{1/n}, \tag{2.270}$$

so intuitively, condition (2.269) requires *convergence of densities with polynomial speed,* which is a local limit law with a guarantee for the speed of convergence.

▶ To find $f_{Z_r^*}$, we need a good guess for the distribution of the limit variables Z_r^*. Convergence of the joint distribution $\mathbf{Z}^{(n)} \to \mathbf{Z}^*$ is sufficient, but not needed, only the marginal distributions have to converge.

▶ Recall that a real function f is Hölder-continuous with constant C and exponent h, if $|f(x) - f(y)| \leqslant C|x - y|^h$ for all x and y in the domain of f. A sufficient condition for Hölder-continuity on a bounded domain is a continuous derivative; then $h = 1$ and the function is called Lipschitz-continuous. These notions of continuity are discussed in Section 2.1.4.

We will subsequently drop the superscript n from $\mathbf{J}$ and $\mathbf{Z}$ when it is clear from the context.

2.6.4 Self-Contained Proof of an Educational DMT

Some researchers might shy away from using Roura's theorems, since their proofs are, although elementary in nature, quite lengthy and thus hard to read. We here give a self-contained and elementary proof of a restricted version of our DMT; in particular, no logarithmic factors in the toll function are allowed. This simplifies the arguments. We directly derive stronger error bounds from stricter assumptions on the toll function; one can get the same with Roura's original theorems by applying them twice. We dub the streamlined version an *educational DMT*, even though it is still powerful enough to solve the generalized Quicksort recurrence, see Chapter 6.

> **Theorem 2.71 (Educational DMT):**
> *We assume the setting of Theorem 2.70, i.e., the assumptions on $C_n, T_n, \mathbf{J}, \mathbf{Z}, \mathbf{Z}^*$ and $f_{Z_r^*}$ made there. Let $c \in \mathbb{R}$ be the unique number with $\sum_{r=1}^{s} \mathbb{E}[(Z_r^*)^c] = 1$, and assume the following additional assumptions hold:*
>
> ▶ $\mathbb{E}[T_n] = Kn^\alpha \pm O(n^{\alpha-\varepsilon})$ *for constants $\alpha \geqslant 0$ and $\varepsilon > 0$.*
>
> ▶ *If $c = 0$, then $\alpha > 0$.*
>
> ▶ *The Hölder-exponent of f_{Z_r} is $\zeta \in (0, 1]$.*
>
> *Then we have for any $\tilde{\varepsilon} > 0$*
>
> ☐1 *if $c < \alpha$, then* $\mathbb{E}[C_n] = \dfrac{K}{1 - \sum_{r=1}^{s} \mathbb{E}[(Z_r^*)^\alpha]} n^\alpha \pm O(n^b),$
>
> *where $b = \max\{c, \alpha - \delta + \tilde{\varepsilon}, \alpha - \zeta + \tilde{\varepsilon}, \alpha - \varepsilon + \tilde{\varepsilon}, \tilde{\varepsilon}\}$,*
>
> ☐2 *if $c = \alpha$, then* $\mathbb{E}[C_n] = -\dfrac{K}{\sum_{r=1}^{s} \mathbb{E}[(Z_r^*)^\alpha \ln(Z_r^*)]} n^\alpha \ln n \pm O(n^c),$ *and*
>
> ☐3 *if $c > \alpha$, then* $\mathbb{E}[C_n] = O(n^c + n^{\tilde{\varepsilon}}).$ ◀

The proof is entirely elementary in that we only need basic real analysis; it uses almost exclusively properties of Hölder-continuous functions, in particular the bounds on the difference between sums and integrals listed in Proposition 2.12.

Proof: The proof of Theorem 2.71 consists of the following three steps, which we address in the remainder of this section.

_I_ First, we study a simple *equilibrium equation* obtained by replacing in the recurrence $J_r^{(n)}$ by $Z_r^* n$, and *canceling* all n's. This equation is simple to solve, and its equilibrium solutions are candidates for the leading terms of $\mathbb{E}[C_n]$.

_II_ Next, we show that the equilibrium solution fulfills the actual recurrence *approximately*, i.e., we can explicitly bound the error that results from unfolding the recurrence once.

III Finally, we prove a bound on the difference between exact and equilibrium solution by induction. To do so, we need the error bound obtained in step two.

Notation. With a few preparations we can follow the above route without distractions. So we collect a few notations and preliminaries first.

As usual, we drop the upper index n for brevity where it is clear from context, in particular we write $J_r = J_r^{(n)}$ in this proof. We also write here Z_r instead of Z_r^* for the limit variable since they appear so often; but this collides with the above convention, so here is the exception: Z_r without upper index is the limit variable, whereas $Z_r^{(n)} = J_r^{(n)}/n$, with the upper index, is a different quantity. It converges to, but is in general not equal to $Z_r = Z_r^*$.

As in Theorem 2.70 we assume that all limit densities f_{Z_r} are Hölder-continuous on $[0,1]$. Since we are on the bounded domain $[0,1]$, we can use the minimum of all their Hölder exponents, see Proposition 2.9; let us name this minimum $\zeta \in (0,1]$, the common Hölder-exponent of f_{Z_r} for $r = 1, \ldots, s$.

The distributional recurrence (2.268) implies the following relation for the expected value $c(n) = \mathbb{E}[C_n]$:

$$c(n) \;=\; \mathbb{E}[T_n] + \sum_{r=1}^{s} \mathbb{E}[c(J_r^{(n)})], \qquad (n \geqslant n_0). \tag{2.271}$$

Notation-wise, we keep on the right the s recursive calls with their random sizes $J_r^{(n)}$.

The z Functions. We define the following two functions,

$$z(a) \;=\; \sum_{r=1}^{s} \mathbb{E}[Z_r^a], \quad \text{and} \quad z_{\ln}(a) \;=\; \sum_{r=1}^{s} \mathbb{E}\big[Z_r^a \ln(Z_r)\big], \tag{2.272}$$

which play an important role in the solution of the recurrence. $z(\alpha)$, with α the exponent of the toll function, is vital for the growth rate of $c(n)$, and the constant c from the statement of the theorem is the solution of $z(c) = 1$. Let us look at z a little closer.

Lemma 2.72: *The expectation $z(a) = \sum_{r=1}^{s} \mathbb{E}[Z_r^a]$ exists for all $a \geqslant 0$, and $a \mapsto z(a)$ is an strictly decreasing and weakly positive function in a.* ◀

Proof: Since f_{Z_r} is (Hölder)-continuous by assumption, $f_{Z_r}(z)z^a$ is continuous on $z \in [0,1]$ for any $a \geqslant 0$, hence bounded and integrable.

For any $a \in (0,1)$, the function $x \mapsto a^x$ is strictly decreasing and positive. Since $Z_r \in (0,1)$ almost surely by Equation (2.269), this means for $a < b$ that $Z_r^a > Z_r^b$ almost surely, and so

$$\sum_{r=1}^{s} \mathbb{E}[Z_r^a] \;>\; \sum_{r=1}^{s} \mathbb{E}[Z_r^b] \;>\; 0. \tag{2.273}$$

Hölder-Continuity and Expectations. The following error estimate is used below; it is essentially a consequence of Proposition 2.12, which gives an error guarantee for approximating a sum by an integral over a Hölder-continuous function.

Lemma 2.73: *Assume Equation (2.269), the density convergence condition, holds and that f_{Z_r} is Hölder-continuous on $[0,1]$ with exponent ζ. Let further $f : [0,1] \to \mathbb{R}$ be a Hölder-continuous function with exponent ϕ. Then holds*

$$\mathbb{E}\left[f\left(\frac{J_r^{(n)}}{n}\right)\right] \;=\; \mathbb{E}[f(Z_r)] \;\pm\; O(n^{-\min\{\delta,\zeta,\phi\}}), \qquad (n \to \infty). \tag{2.274}$$

Proof: f and f_{Z_r} are both Hölder-continuous with exponent $\min\{\phi,\zeta\}$ by Proposition 2.9; on the compact interval $[0,1]$ they are bounded, so their product is Hölder-continuous as well by Lemma 2.11–(b). We thus have

$$\mathbb{E}[f(J_r/n)] \;=\; \sum_{j=0}^{n-1} f(j/n) \cdot \frac{1}{n} \cdot n\mathbb{P}[J_r = j] \tag{2.275}$$

$$\underset{(2.269)}{=}\; \frac{1}{n} \sum_{j=0}^{n-1} f(j/n)\left(f_{Z_r}(j/n) \pm O(n^{-\delta})\right), \tag{2.276}$$

and since f is bounded,

$$=\; \frac{1}{n} \sum_{j=0}^{n-1} f(j/n)f_{Z_r}(j/n) \;\pm\; O(n^{-\delta}) \tag{2.277}$$

$$\underset{\text{Proposition 2.12–(b)}}{=}\; \int_0^1 f(z)f_{Z_r}(z)\,\mathrm{d}z \;\pm\; O(n^{-\min\{\phi,\zeta\}}) \;\pm\; O(n^{-\delta}) \tag{2.278}$$

$$=\; \mathbb{E}[f(Z_r)] \;\pm\; O(n^{-\min\{\delta,\phi,\zeta\}}). \tag{2.279}$$

With this lemma, we can conveniently approximate expectations over subproblem sizes that we need later.

Corollary 2.74: *For any $a \geqslant 0$ holds with $\varphi = \min\{\delta, \zeta, a\}$ that*

$$\sum_{r=1}^{s} \mathbb{E}\left[(J_r^{(n)})^a\right] \;=\; z(a) \cdot n^a \;\pm\; \begin{cases} O(n^{a-\varphi}), & \text{for } a > 0; \\ 0, & \text{for } a = 0. \end{cases}$$

Proof: The claim is vacuous for $a = 0$, since the expectation then does not depend on J_r: $z(0) = s = \sum_{r=1}^{s} \mathbb{E}[J_r^0]$. For $a > 0$, we have that $z \mapsto z^a$ is Hölder-continuous with exponent $\min\{a, 1\}$, so we find

$$\mathbb{E}[J_r^a] = n^a \mathbb{E}[(J_r/n)^a] \tag{2.280}$$

$$\underset{\text{Lemma 2.73}}{=} n^a \left(\mathbb{E}[Z_r^a] \pm O(n^{-\min\{\delta, \zeta, a\}}) \right) \tag{2.281}$$

$$= \mathbb{E}[Z_r^a] n^a \pm O(n^{a - \varphi}). \tag{2.282}$$

Summing over $r = 1, \ldots, s$ yields the claim. ∎

Corollary 2.75: *For any $a > 0$ holds with $\varphi = \min\{\delta, \zeta, a - \varepsilon\}$, for any $\varepsilon > 0$, that*

$$\sum_{r=1}^{s} \mathbb{E}\left[(J_r^{(n)})^a \ln(J_r^{(n)})\right] = z(a) \cdot n^a \ln(n) + z_{\ln}(a) \cdot n^a \pm O(n^{a - \varphi} \log n). \tag{2.283}$$

◀

Proof: By Lemma 2.14, $z \mapsto z^a \ln(z)$ is Hölder-continuous with exponent $a - \varepsilon$ for any $\varepsilon > 0$, so we have

$$\mathbb{E}[J_r^a \ln(J_r)] = n^a \mathbb{E}\left[\left(\frac{J_r}{n}\right)^a \left(\ln\left(\frac{J_r}{n}\right) + \ln(n) \right) \right] \tag{2.284}$$

$$\underset{\text{Lemma 2.73}}{=} n^a \left(\mathbb{E}[Z_r^a \ln(Z_r)] \pm O(n^{-\min\{\delta, \zeta, a - \varepsilon\}}) \right) + n^a \ln(n) \left(\mathbb{E}[Z_r^a] \pm O(n^{-\varphi}) \right) \tag{2.285}$$

$$= n^a \mathbb{E}[Z_r^a \ln(Z_r)] + n^a \ln(n) \mathbb{E}[Z_r^a] \pm O(n^{a - \varphi} \log n + n^{\varepsilon}). \tag{2.286}$$

Summing over all r, we obtain the claim. ∎

Note that in Corollary 2.75, we had to exclude the case $a = 0$. In this case the Hölder-continuity argument breaks down, since $\ln(z)$ is not Hölder-continuous; indeed, the convenient route we took above seems not to work for this corner case, at all. This is why we exclude the case $\alpha = c = 0$ from the statement of the theorem.

With these preparation, we can now put our plan for the proof of Theorem 2.71 into action.

☐ **Equilibrium Solution.** The relative subproblem sizes $Z_r^{(n)} = J_r^{(n)}/n$ converge to a limit variable $Z_r = Z_r^*$, and for large n, we might get away with simply substituting it for $Z_r^{(n)}$. What we obtain from replacing $J_r^{(n)}$ by nZ_r in Equation (2.271) is called the *equilibrium equation*. It is given by

$$\bar{c}(n) = Kn^\alpha + \sum_{r=1}^{s} \mathbb{E}[\bar{c}(Z_r n)], \qquad (n \in \mathbb{R}_{>0}). \tag{2.287}$$

We call the function in the equilibrium equation $\bar{c}(n)$, reserving $c(n)$ for solutions of the original recurrence. Note that unlike $c(n)$, $\bar{c}(n)$ has to be defined for all positive reals, since nZ_r can be any number in $[0, n]$. To be well-defined, we also require $\bar{c}(0)$ to exist. Note that Equation (2.287) is vacuous for $n = 0$; but the choice of $\bar{c}(0)$ is also immaterial: since Z_r is strictly positive almost surely, the single value $\bar{c}(0)$ has no influence on $\bar{c}(n)$ for $n > 0$. We therefore simply set $\bar{c}(0) = 0$. With $z(a)$ and $z_{\ln}(a)$ defined in Equation (2.272), the solution of the equilibrium equation is for $n > 0$ given by

$$\bar{c}(n) \;=\; \begin{cases} \dfrac{K}{1 - z(\alpha)} n^\alpha, & \text{if } z(\alpha) \neq 1; \\[2ex] -\dfrac{K}{z_{\ln}(\alpha)} n^\alpha \ln(n), & \text{if } z(\alpha) = 1. \end{cases} \tag{2.288}$$

To prove this, we simply plug the solution in and check that Equation (2.287) is fulfilled.

$z(\alpha) \neq 1$ For the first case we have

$$\frac{K}{1 - z(\alpha)} n^\alpha \;=\; K \cdot n^\alpha + \frac{K}{1 - z(\alpha)} n^\alpha \underbrace{\sum_{r=1}^{s} \mathbb{E}[Z_r^\alpha]}_{z(\alpha)} \tag{2.289}$$

$$\iff \quad 1 \;=\; (1 - z(\alpha)) + z(\alpha). \tag{2.290}$$

$z(\alpha) = 1$ In the second case we find

$$-\frac{K}{z_{\ln}(\alpha)} n^\alpha \ln(n) \;=\; K \cdot n^\alpha - \frac{K}{z_{\ln}(\alpha)} \sum_{r=1}^{s} \mathbb{E}[(Z_r n)^\alpha \ln(Z_r n)] \tag{2.291}$$

$$=\; K \cdot n^\alpha - \frac{K}{z_{\ln}(\alpha)} n^\alpha \left(\underbrace{\sum_{r=1}^{s} \mathbb{E}[Z_r^\alpha \ln(Z_r)]}_{z_{\ln}(\alpha)} + \ln(n) \underbrace{\sum_{r=1}^{s} \mathbb{E}[Z_r^\alpha]}_{z(\alpha)=1} \right) \tag{2.292}$$

$$=\; -\frac{K}{z_{\ln}(\alpha)} n^\alpha \ln(n). \tag{2.293}$$

This shows that $\bar{c}(n)$ fulfills the equilibrium equation for all $n \in \mathbb{R}_{>0}$. This equilibrium solution will be our candidate for an approximation of $c(n)$.

Note that for $z(\alpha) > 1$ the solution can be spurious, an artifact of passing to the limit: In that case $\bar{c}(n)$ is *negative,* if our original sequence $c(n)$ and K are positive. Intuitively, this tells us that no matter how little (positive) weight we assign to recursive calls, their contribution exceeds the toll function for large n; equilibrium is only reached for a negative weight. The equilibrium solution cannot be a valid approximation in this case, and indeed, we will see below that in this case the approximation error grows faster than the equilibrium solution.

$\boxed{II}$ **Equilibrium Solution Fulfills Recurrence Approximately.**   We now insert the equilibrium solution $\bar{c}(j)$ in the right-hand side of the recurrence for $c(n)$, Equation (2.271). The result is $\bar{c}(n)$ up to an error term. To be precise, we claim that for any $\varepsilon_\nu > 0$ holds

$$\bar{c}(n) \;=\; \mathbb{E}[T_n] + \sum_{r=1}^{s} \mathbb{E}\big[\bar{c}(J_r^{(n)})\big] \;\pm\; O(n^\nu), \qquad (n \to \infty), \tag{2.294}$$

where ν is given by

$$\nu \;=\; \begin{cases} \alpha - \min\{\delta, \zeta, \varepsilon\}, & \text{for } z(\alpha) \neq 1; \\ \alpha - \min\{\delta, \zeta, \varepsilon\} + \varepsilon_\nu, & \text{for } z(\alpha) = 1 \text{ and } \alpha > 0; \\ \infty, & \text{for } z(\alpha) = 1 \text{ and } \alpha = 0. \end{cases} \tag{2.295}$$

In the last case, we effectively make no statement.

To prove Equation (2.294), recall that $\mathbb{E}[T_n] = Kn^\alpha \pm O(n^{\alpha-\varepsilon})$ with $\alpha \geq 0$ by assumption. With the approximation for expectations over $J_r^{(n)}$ from above, Corollaries 2.74 and 2.75, this step is simple. We consider again the two cases for $\bar{c}(n)$.

$\boxed{z(\alpha) \neq 1}$ If we insert $\bar{c}(n) = \frac{K}{1-z(\alpha)}n^\alpha$ in the right-hand side of Equation (2.271), we find with $\varphi = \min\{\delta, \zeta, \varepsilon\}$

$$Kn^\alpha\big(1 \pm O(n^{-\varepsilon})\big) + \frac{K}{1-z(\alpha)} \sum_{r=1}^{s} \mathbb{E}[(J_r^{(n)})^\alpha] \tag{2.296}$$

$$\underset{\text{Corollary 2.74}}{=} \; Kn^\alpha + \frac{K}{1-z(\alpha)}z(\alpha)n^\alpha \;\pm\; O(n^{\alpha-\varphi}) \tag{2.297}$$

$$= \; \frac{K}{1-z(\alpha)}n^\alpha \;\pm\; O(n^{\alpha-\varphi}) \tag{2.298}$$

$$= \; \bar{c}(n) \;\pm\; O(n^{\alpha-\varphi}). \tag{2.299}$$

We get exactly the equilibrium solution, up to an error term; where we can set $\nu = \alpha - \varphi$ in this case.

$\boxed{\begin{array}{l} z(\alpha) = 1 \\ \alpha > 0 \end{array}}$ As above, we insert the equilibrium solution in the right-hand side of Equation (2.271). This time we find with $\varphi = \min\{\delta, \zeta, \varepsilon\}$

$$Kn^\alpha\big(1 \pm O(n^{-\varepsilon})\big) - \frac{K}{z_{\ln}(\alpha)} \sum_{r=1}^{s} \mathbb{E}[(J_r^{(n)})^\alpha \ln(J_r^{(n)})] \tag{2.300}$$

$$\underset{\text{Corollary 2.75}}{=} \; Kn^\alpha - \frac{K}{z_{\ln}(\alpha)}n^\alpha\big(z_{\ln}(\alpha) + z(\alpha)\ln(n)\big) \;\pm\; O(n^{\alpha-\varphi}\log n) \tag{2.301}$$

$$= \; -\frac{K}{z_{\ln}(\alpha)}n^\alpha \ln(n) \;\pm\; O(n^{\alpha-\varphi}\log n) \tag{2.302}$$

$$= \; \bar{c}(n) \;\pm\; O(n^{\alpha-\varphi}\log n). \tag{2.303}$$

Here, we have to pick a $\nu > \alpha - \varphi$, to get rid of the logarithmic factor.

This concludes the proof of Equation (2.294), and we can proceed to the last step.

III **Bounding the Difference.** Let us denote by $d(n) = |c(n) - \bar{c}(n)|$ the difference between the equilibrium solution and the actual sequence. With the results from above, we find that $d(n)$ fulfills a recurrence of the same shape as our original one, only with a different toll function: for $n \geqslant n_0$ we have

$$d(n) \quad = \quad |c(n) - \bar{c}(n)| \tag{2.304}$$

$$\underset{(2.271),\,(2.294)}{=} \quad \left| \sum_{r=1}^{s} \left(\mathbb{E}[c(J_r^{(n)})] - \mathbb{E}[\bar{c}(J_r^{(n)})] \right) \pm O(n^\nu) \right| \tag{2.305}$$

$$\leqslant \quad \sum_{r=1}^{s} \mathbb{E}\left[|c(J_r^{(n)}) - \bar{c}(J_r^{(n)})| \right] \pm O(n^\nu) \tag{2.306}$$

$$= \quad \sum_{r=1}^{s} \mathbb{E}\left[d(J_r^{(n)}) \right] \pm O(n^\nu), \tag{2.307}$$

where the constant ν is given by Equation (2.295). We now will show that

$$d(n) \quad = \quad \begin{cases} O(n^c), & \text{if } c > \nu \text{ and } c > 0; \\ O(n^\gamma), & \text{for any positive } \gamma \text{ with } \gamma > c \text{ and } \gamma > \nu. \end{cases} \tag{2.308}$$

Let us denote by t_d the toll function of the recurrence in Equation (2.307), $t_d(n) = d(n) - \sum_{r=1}^{s} \mathbb{E}[d(J_r^{(n)})] = O(n^\nu)$. We derive an explicit upper bound on $d(n)$ for the two cases.

$c > \nu$
$c > 0$ For the first case, let γ be a constant with $\max\{0, \nu, c - \delta, c - \zeta\} < \gamma < c$, e.g., $\gamma = (c + \max\{0, \nu, c - \delta, c - \zeta\})/2$. By Corollary 2.74 and the definition of γ, we find weakly positive constants μ_0, μ_1 and $\varepsilon_\gamma > 0$ so that for all n holds

$$t_d(n) + \sum_{r=1}^{s} \mathbb{E}\left[(J_r^{(n)})^c \right] - \sum_{r=1}^{s} \mathbb{E}\left[(J_r^{(n)})^\gamma \right] \leqslant z(c)n^c - z(\gamma)n^\gamma + \mu_1 n^{\gamma - \varepsilon_\gamma} + \mu_0.$$

$$\tag{2.309}$$

Recall that by definition, $z(c) = 1$; by Lemma 2.72 and since $\gamma < c$, we have that $\xi = z(\gamma) - 1 > 0$. This means that there is a constant $\tilde{n}_0$, so that

$$\mu_1 n^{\gamma - \varepsilon_\gamma} + \mu_0 - \xi n^\gamma \quad \leqslant \quad -1, \qquad \text{for } n > \tilde{n}_0, \tag{2.310}$$

since the left-hand side goes to negative infinity as $n \to \infty$. Given this threshold $\tilde{n}_0$, set

$$c_0 \quad = \quad \max_{n \leqslant \tilde{n}_0} d(n), \qquad \text{and} \qquad c_1 \quad = \quad \max\{c_0(s-1), 1\}.$$

We show by induction that for all $n \in \mathbb{N}_0$ holds $d(n) \leqslant \hat{d}(n) = c_1(n^c - n^\nu) + c_0$.

For the base cases $n < \tilde{n}_0$ we note that since $\gamma < c$, we have for all $n \in \mathbb{N}$ that $n^c \geqslant n^\nu$. By the choice of c_0, we have $\hat{d}(n) = c_1(n^c - n^\nu) + c_0 \geqslant c_0 \geqslant d(n)$ for all $n \leqslant \tilde{n}_0$.

For the inductive step, we assume for all $m \leqslant n-1$ holds $d(m) \leqslant \hat{d}(m)$ for an $n \geqslant n_0$. By the choice of c_1, we find

$$d(n) \underset{(2.307)}{\leqslant} t_d(n) + \sum_{r=1}^{s} \mathbb{E}\big[d(J_r^{(n)})\big] \tag{2.311}$$

$$\underset{\text{I.H.}}{\leqslant} c_1 \left(t_d(n) + \sum_{r=1}^{s} \mathbb{E}\big[(J_r^{(n)})^c\big] - \sum_{r=1}^{s} \mathbb{E}\big[(J_r^{(n)})^\gamma\big] \right) + c_0 s \tag{2.312}$$

$$\underset{(2.309)}{\leqslant} c_1 \Big(\underbrace{z(c)}_{=1}\, n^c - \underbrace{z(\gamma)}_{=1+\xi}\, n^\gamma + \mu_1 n^{\gamma - \varepsilon_\gamma} + \mu_0 \Big) + c_0 s \tag{2.313}$$

$$= \underbrace{c_1(n^c - n^\gamma) + c_0}_{=\hat{d}(n)} + c_1 \underbrace{\Big(\mu_1 n^{\gamma - \varepsilon_\gamma} + \mu_0 - \xi n^\gamma \Big)}_{\leqslant -1 \text{ since } n > \tilde{n}_0} + c_0(s-1) \tag{2.314}$$

$$\leqslant \hat{d}(n). \tag{2.315}$$

This completes the inductive step and the proof that $d(n)$ is upper bounded by $\hat{d}(n) = O(n^c)$.

$\gamma > c$
$\gamma > v$
$\gamma > 0$ We proceed with the second case; it is similar to the above, but we are "on the opposite side of c", so the bound is actually slightly simpler. As $\gamma > c$, we have by Lemma 2.72 that $\xi = 1 - z(\gamma) > 0$.

By Corollary 2.74 with $\gamma \geqslant 0$ and $\gamma > v$, we find weakly positive constants μ_0, μ_1 and $\varepsilon_\gamma > 0$ so that for all n holds

$$t_d(n) + \sum_{r=1}^{s} \mathbb{E}\big[(J_r^{(n)})^\gamma\big] \leqslant z(\gamma)n^\gamma + \mu_1 n^{\gamma - \varepsilon_\gamma} + \mu_0. \tag{2.316}$$

As $\gamma > 0$, there is an $\tilde{n}_0$, so that

$$\mu_1 n^{\gamma - \varepsilon_\gamma} + \mu_0 - \xi n^\gamma \leqslant -1, \qquad \text{for } n > \tilde{n}_0, \tag{2.317}$$

and as above, we set

$$c_0 = \max_{n \leqslant \tilde{n}_0} d(n), \qquad \text{and} \qquad c_1 = \max\{c_0(s-1), 1\}.$$

We now show by induction that $d(n) \leqslant \hat{d}(n) = c_1 n^\gamma + c_0$ for all $n \in \mathbb{N}_0$. For the base cases $n < \tilde{n}_0$ we have by the choice of c_0 that $\hat{d}(n) = c_1 n^\gamma + c_0 \geqslant d(n)$.

For the inductive step, we assume $d(m) \leqslant \hat{d}(m)$ for all $m \leqslant n-1$ for an $n \geqslant n_0$. Similar as above, we compute

$$d(n) \underset{(2.307)}{\leqslant} t_d(n) + \sum_{r=1}^{s} \mathbb{E}\big[d(J_r^{(n)})\big] \tag{2.318}$$

$$\underset{\text{I.H.}}{\leqslant} c_1 \left(t_d(n) + \sum_{r=1}^{s} \mathbb{E}\big[(J_r^{(n)})^\gamma\big] \right) + c_0 s \tag{2.319}$$

$$\underset{(2.316)}{\leqslant} \; c_1 \Big(\underbrace{z(\gamma)n^\gamma}_{1-\xi} + \mu_1 n^{\gamma-\varepsilon_\gamma} + \mu_0 \Big) + c_0 s \tag{2.320}$$

$$= \underbrace{c_1 n^\gamma + c_0}_{=\hat{d}(n)} + \underbrace{c_1 \Big(\mu_1 n^{\gamma-\varepsilon_\gamma} + \mu_0 - \xi n^\gamma \Big) + c_0(s-1)}_{\leqslant 0 \text{ by choice of } n_0 \text{ and } c_1} \tag{2.321}$$

$$\leqslant \; \hat{d}(n). \tag{2.322}$$

This completes the induction, and we have for all n that $d(n) \leqslant \hat{d}(n) = O(n^\gamma)$.

These are the two cases in Equation (2.308), so its proof is complete.

Putting Pieces Together. The statement of Theorem 2.71 follows from Equation (2.308) rather directly, but we have to sort out the possible cases.

$c < \alpha$ In this case $\bar{c}(n) = \frac{K}{1-z(\alpha)}n^\alpha$ is the leading term; the error bound depends on v. If $v < c$ and $c > 0$, it is $O(n^c)$ by the first case of Equation (2.308), otherwise it is $O(n^{\max\{v,c\}})$, where $v = \alpha - \min\{\delta, \zeta, \varepsilon\}$.

$c = \alpha$ This means $z(\alpha) = 1$, so we have $\bar{c}(n) = -\frac{K}{z_{\ln}(\alpha)}n^\alpha \ln n$ as the leading term. By assumption, we then have $c = \alpha > 0$ and $v < \alpha = c$, so the error term is $O(n^c)$ by Equation (2.308).

$c > \alpha$ In this case, $\bar{c}(n) = \Theta(n^\alpha)$ is dominated by the error term. If $c > 0$, it is $O(n^c)$ by Equation (2.308), since $v < \alpha < c$. If $c \leqslant 0$, we obtain the bound $O(n^\gamma)$ for any $\gamma = \tilde{\varepsilon} > 0$ from the second case of Equation (2.308).   ∎

What can be done with concentration? The technical core of the proof are Corollary 2.74 and Corollary 2.75; we can replace both with a simpler Chernoff-bound argument for the special case that $J^{(n)} \overset{\mathcal{D}}{=} \mathrm{Mult}(n, Z)$: with Lemma 2.36 (page 76) it directly follows for any $a > 0$ and $\varepsilon > 0$ that

$$\mathbb{E}[J_r^a] \;=\; n^a \mathbb{E}[Z_r^a] \pm O(n^{a/2+\varepsilon}), \tag{2.323}$$

$$\mathbb{E}[J_r^a \ln(J_r)] \;=\; n^a \mathbb{E}[Z_r^a \ln(Z_r)] + n^a \ln(n)\mathbb{E}[Z_r^a] \pm O(n^{a/2+\varepsilon}), \tag{2.324}$$

since both functions are Hölder-continuous with $h < a$. The resulting error bounds are slightly weaker, but we can drop the restriction to distributions of Z with a Hölder-continuous density. For example, Z might be a discrete variable in this case.

2.6.5 The Distributional Master Theorem

Theorem 2.70 has limited scope in that no coefficients in front of the costs of recursive calls are allowed. A more general setting is amenable to essentially the same methods. We consider one possible generalization of the distributional master theorem in this section.

Concerning the scope of this work, coefficients are needed in Chapter 8, but they also appear in the recurrence for the grand average of costs in Quickselect. There, the coefficient represents *guards* or *selectors* that determine whether a certain recursive call is present or not. The coefficients will then be indicator random variables.

> **Theorem 2.76 (Distributional Master Theorem (DMT) with coefficients):**
> Let $(C_n)_{n \in \mathbb{N}_0}$ *be a family of random variables that satisfies the distributional recurrence*
>
> $$C_n \overset{\mathcal{D}}{=} T_n + \sum_{r=1}^{s} A_r^{(n)} \cdot C_{J_r^{(n)}}^{(r)}, \qquad (n \geq n_0), \tag{2.325}$$
>
> *where* $(C_n^{(1)})_{n \in \mathbb{N}}, \ldots, (C_n^{(s)})_{n \in \mathbb{N}}$ *are independent copies of* $(C_n)_{n \in \mathbb{N}}$*, which are also independent of* $\mathbf{J}^{(n)} = (J_1^{(n)}, \ldots, J_s^{(n)}) \in \{0, \ldots, n-1\}^s$, $\mathbf{A}^{(n)} = (A_1^{(n)}, \ldots, A_s^{(n)}) \in \mathbb{R}_{\geq 0}^s$ *and* T_n*. Define* $\mathbf{Z}^{(n)} = \mathbf{J}^{(n)}/n$ *and assume that the components* $Z_r^{(n)}$ *of* $\mathbf{Z}^{(n)}$ *fulfill uniformly for* $z \in (0,1)$
>
> $$n \cdot \mathbb{P}[Z_r^{(n)} \in (z - \tfrac{1}{n}, z]] \;=\; f_{Z_r^*}(z) \pm O(n^{-\delta}), \qquad (n \to \infty), \tag{2.326}$$
>
> *for a constant* $\delta > 0$ *and a Hölder-continuous function* $f_{Z_r^*} : [0,1] \to \mathbb{R}$*. Then* $f_{Z_r^*}$ *is the density of a random variable* Z_r^* *and* $Z_r^{(n)} \overset{\mathcal{D}}{\longrightarrow} Z_r^*$.
>
> Let further
>
> $$\mathbb{E}[A_r^{(n)} \mid Z_r^{(n)} \in (z - \tfrac{1}{n}, z]] \;=\; a_r(z) \pm O(n^{-\delta}), \qquad (n \to \infty), \tag{2.327}$$
>
> *for a function* $a_r : [0,1] \to \mathbb{R}$ *and require that* $f_{Z_r^*}(z) \cdot a_r(z)$ *is also Hölder-continuous on* $[0,1]$*. Moreover, assume* $\mathbb{E}[T_n] \sim K n^\alpha \log^\beta(n)$*, as* $n \to \infty$*, for constants* $K \neq 0$, $\alpha \geq 0$ *and* $\beta > -1$*. Then, with* $H = 1 - \sum_{r=1}^{s} \mathbb{E}[(Z_r^*)^\alpha a_r(Z_r^*)]$*, we have the following cases.*
>
> **1** *If* $H > 0$*, then* $\mathbb{E}[C_n] \sim \dfrac{\mathbb{E}[T_n]}{H}$.
>
> **2** *If* $H = 0$*, then* $\mathbb{E}[C_n] \sim \dfrac{\mathbb{E}[T_n] \ln n}{\tilde{H}}$ *with* $\tilde{H} = -(\beta + 1) \sum_{r=1}^{s} \mathbb{E}[(Z_r^*)^\alpha a_r(Z_r^*) \ln(Z_r^*)]$.
>
> **3** *If* $H < 0$*, then* $\mathbb{E}[C_n] = O(n^c)$ *for the* $c \in \mathbb{R}$ *with* $\displaystyle\sum_{r=1}^{s} \mathbb{E}[(Z_r^*)^c a_r(Z_r^*)] = 1$. ◄

Proof of Theorem 2.76: We start by conditioning on $\mathbf{J}$ in the right-hand side of Equation (2.325) and then taking expectations on both sides. Exploiting independence and equality in distribution, we obtain

$$\mathbb{E}[C_n] \;=\; \mathbb{E}[T_n] + \sum_{j=0}^{n-1} w_{n,j} \mathbb{E}[C_j], \tag{2.328}$$

with weights $w_{n,j} := \sum_{r=1}^{s} w_{n,j}^{(r)}$, where $w_{n,j}^{(r)} := \mathbb{P}[J_r = j] \cdot \mathbb{E}[A_r^{(n)} \mid J_r = j]$. This is precisely the form (2.258) required for the CMT. In order to apply it, it remains to show that the condition (2.259) holds.

Let $r \in [s]$ and $z \in (0,1)$ be fixed. For $j = \lfloor zn \rfloor$ the unique integer in $(zn - 1, zn]$, we have

$$J_r^{(n)} = j \iff J_r^{(n)} \in (zn - 1, zn] \iff Z_r^{(n)} = (z - \tfrac{1}{n}, z], \tag{2.329}$$

and so Equations (2.326) and (2.327) imply

$$\begin{aligned} nw_{n,j}^{(r)} &= n \cdot \mathbb{P}\big[Z_r^{(n)} \in (\tfrac{j-1}{n}, \tfrac{j}{n}]\big] \cdot \mathbb{E}\big[A_r^{(n)} \mid Z_r^{(n)} \in (\tfrac{j-1}{n}, \tfrac{j}{n}]\big] \\ &= w_r(j/n) \pm O(n^{-\delta}), \end{aligned} \tag{2.330}$$

where $w_r(z) := f_{Z_r^*}(z) \cdot a_r(z)$. The function $w(z) = \sum_{r=1}^{s} w_r(z)$ is Hölder-continuous since $w_r(z)$ are so by assumption. Summing Equation (2.330) over $r = 1, \ldots, s$ yields Equation (2.260), so Equation (2.259) holds by Lemma 2.69. This shows that the recurrence (2.328) for $\mathbb{E}[C_n]$ is in fact a continuous recurrence in the sense of the CMT with shape function $w(z) = \sum_{r=1}^{s} f_{Z_r^*}(z) \cdot a_r(z)$.

Next, we briefly check that $f_{Z_r^*}$ is in fact a density function, so that we can speak of the limit random variable Z_r^* defined by $f_{Z_r^*}$. First, $f_{Z_r^*}(z)$ is weakly positive for $z \in [0,1]$; otherwise Equation (2.326) implied $\mathbb{P}[Z_r^{(n)} \in (z - \tfrac{1}{n}, z]] < 0$ for large n. Moreover, $f_{Z_r^*}$ Hölder-continuous by assumption and thus clearly integrable. It remains to check that $\int_0^1 f_{Z_r^*}(z)\, dz = 1$. This follows from the following more general statement by taking $u \to 1$. As $f_{Z_r^*}$ is Hölder-continuous with exponent h, say, for any $u \in (0,1)$ we find

$$\mathbb{P}\big[Z_r^{(n)} \leqslant u\big] = \sum_{j=0}^{\lfloor un \rfloor} \mathbb{P}\big[Z_r^{(n)} \in (\tfrac{j-1}{n}, \tfrac{j}{n}]\big] \tag{2.331}$$

$$\underset{(2.326)}{=} \sum_{j=0}^{\lfloor un \rfloor} f_{Z_r^*}(j/n) \pm O(n^{-\delta}) \tag{2.332}$$

$$\underset{\text{Proposition 2.12}}{=} \int_0^u f_{Z_r^*}(z)\, dz \pm O(n^{-h}) \pm O(n^{-\delta}). \tag{2.333}$$

This shows that the cumulative distribution functions (CDFs) converge point-wise—in fact even uniformly with guaranteed speed—and so $Z_r^{(n)} \xrightarrow{\mathcal{D}} Z_r^*$, as claimed.

The rest of the theorem is exactly the result of applying the CMT to Equation (2.328), where the various *"entropies,"* i.e., integrals $\int_0^1 g(z)w(z)\, dz$, have been rewritten as expectations:

$$\int_0^1 g(z)w(z)\, dz = \int_0^1 g(z) \sum_{r=1} s w_r(z)\, dz \tag{2.334}$$

$$= \sum_{r=1}^{s} \int_0^1 g(z) \cdot a_r(z) f_{Z_r^*}(z)\, dz \tag{2.335}$$

$$= \sum_{r=1}^{s} \mathbb{E}[g(Z_r^*) \cdot a_r(Z_r^*)]. \tag{2.336}$$

This concludes the proof of the distributional master theorem.   ■

◆   ◆   ◆

With the distributional master theorem, we close this chapter on mathematical tools. The ground is now prepared to turn to the main topic of this work: sorting. The mathematical tools of this chapter can only be applied in a formal mathematical model of reality. Before we describe in detail the sorting algorithms that we consider for analysis, the next chapter therefore introduces our models.

3 Models and Assumptions

Contents

THE ACADEMIC DISCIPLINE of computer science, in particular the field of algorithmics, lives in the intersection of mathematics and engineering. The bridge between these two worlds form *models*. Mathematical statements only apply to well-defined models of reality. Usually, the simpler and more elegant the model, the stronger statements can be derived. The engineer on the other hand has to base design decisions on these statements that work in the real world. Usually, the more aspects of real world behavior a model reflects, the closer its predictions will be to what can be observed. Good models are compromises between these requirements, they are tractable and expressive; *as simple as possible, but no simpler*.

In the natural sciences, researchers are painfully aware of the imperfection of their models. History is full of findings that lead to the rejection of previously established theories. As computer scientists, we are in fact a slight bit better off: computers are built by humans after all; we know their operating principles. Nevertheless have our machines reached a level of complexity that escapes detailed understanding. We have stacked many layers on top of each other, each of which is of manageable complexity in isolation, but we have lost intellectual control of the result as a whole.

I thus consider it unlikely that a single unifying model exists that is able to predict the running time of a program to sensible accuracy, and that is at the same time of manageable complexity for a mathematical analysis. However, we can capture certain aspects of execution in specialized models of cost; we discuss such models in Section 3.2. How different cost measures relate to each other is hard to predict and depends on the machine, but an expert can compare algorithms by looking at their costs w.r.t. different models and choose one that is a good mix.

Our analysis will consider the *expected* costs of different Quicksort variants. Besides measures of cost, we thus also need a model for input distributions. For the most part of this work, we confine ourselves to the *random-permutation model* discussed in Section 3.1.1. We also consider, but in much less detail, the *expected-profile model,* a natural model for inputs with equal keys. We briefly describe the model in Section 3.1.2.

3.1   Models of Input Distributions

Our input consists of n *elements* $U_1, \ldots, U_n$ from a totally ordered *universe*. We assume they are given in an *array* $A[1..n]$, where initially $A[i] = U_i$ for $i = 1, \ldots, n$. The array can be modified; in fact our algorithms are required to sort elements *in place*, i.e., by rearranging them in the array. While the contents of array cells $A[i]$ thus change over time, with $U_1, \ldots, U_n$ we always denote the elements in their initial order.

3.1.1   The Random-Permutation Model

As is usual for the average-case analysis of sorting algorithms, we assume the *random-permutation model* for the most part of this work: we assume that all elements are different and every ordering of them is equally likely.

For comparison-based sorting, the actual values do not matter; only their ranking is of significance. Traditionally one therefore assumes that $U_1, \ldots, U_n$ are the numbers 1 to n in a random order. There is however another, equivalent, choice that is much more convenient for the analysis of Quicksort, and potentially also other sorting algorithms: the *uniform model*. We assume that $U_1, \ldots, U_n$ are i.i.d. uniformly $\mathcal{U}(0,1)$ distributed. This assumption is without loss of generality as their ordering forms a random permutation almost surely.

Fact 3.1: Let $U_1, \ldots, U_n$ be n i.i.d. random variables uniformly drawn from $(0,1)$. Then

1 there are no duplicates, $U_i \neq U_j$ for $i \neq j$, almost surely and

2 the ranks of $U_1, \ldots, U_n$, i.e., the number of elements less or equal an element, form a random permutation of $[n]$. ◀

Proof: For $U \stackrel{\mathcal{D}}{=} \mathcal{U}(0,1)$, we have $\mathbb{P}[U = u] = 0$ for any fixed number u, likewise the event that any two if the i.i.d. elements are equal is a zero-measure event.

The second part is intuitively a consequence of the i.i.d. variables and the resulting symmetry, but I found it reassuring to explicitly compute the probability of a given rank sequence. So let $\pi_1, \ldots, \pi_n$ be a permutation of $[n]$ and denote by $a_1, \ldots, a_n$ its inverse, i.e., $a_j = i \iff \pi_i = j$. Intuitively, a_j is the index i of number j in the list π. Our elements $U_1, \ldots, U_n$ have the same relative ranking as $\pi_1, \ldots, \pi_n$ if and only if $U_{a_1} < U_{a_2} < \cdots < U_{a_n}$. The probability for that event is

$$
\mathbb{P}\big[U_{a_n} > U_{a_{n-1}} > \cdots > U_{a_2} > U_{a_1}\big]
$$
$$
= \int_{x_n=0}^{1} \int_{x_{n-1}=0}^{x_n} \cdots \int_{x_2=0}^{x_3} \int_{x_1=0}^{x_2} 1 \, dx_1 \, dx_2 \cdots dx_{n-1} \, dx_n. \quad (3.1)
$$

These integrals have a recursive structure; we have $\mathbb{P}[U_{a_n} > \cdots > U_{a_1}] = I_n(1)$ where

$$
I_1(x) \;:=\; \int_0^x 1 \, dx, \quad\quad\quad (3.2)
$$

$$
I_n(x) \;=\; \int_{y=0}^{x} I_{n-1}(y) \, dy, \quad (n \geqslant 2). \quad\quad\quad (3.3)
$$

One easily verifies inductively that $I_n(x) = x^n/n!$, so for any permutation π, the probability that $U_1, \ldots, U_n$ has the same relative ordering as π is $1/n!$. ■

The models are hence equivalent results-wise, and we use the established term *random-permutation model* throughout this work, but will mostly work in the uniform model from above.

Fact 3.1 actually holds for any continuous distribution; e.g., Mahmoud [113] discusses this general case. I think it is this fact that makes the random-permutation model a natural choice in the first place: Coming from a scientific or engineering application, data will usually consist of real numbers. Without further information, the *principle of maximum entropy* tells us to assume i.i.d. data then.

3.1.2 The Expected-Profile Model

For data from a continuous universe, exact duplicates are rare, even when real numbers are discretized to fixed-length floating-point numbers. In other application of sorting, it is sensible to assume a *finite universe*. For example, Knuth [103] lists as application of sorting what he calls solving the *togetherness* problem: bring elements together that share the same value of some attribute. We will consider an example in Section 8.1.

In many cases, this attribute has a finite domain a priori, e.g., the country of origin or the year of birth, or as an extreme example, the sex of a person. The time for sorting such inputs can differ significantly from what the random-permutation model predicts. Therefore, we consider an alternative model here, the *expected-profile model*.

The expected-profile model is a parametric model. On top of the length n of the inputs, we have as parameter the *universe size* $u \in \mathbb{N}$ and the *universe probabilities* $\mathbf{q} = (q_1, \ldots, q_u) \in (0,1)^u$ with $\Sigma \mathbf{q} = 1$. Recall that $\mathcal{D}(\mathbf{q})$ denotes the discrete distribution over $[u]$ with weights $\mathbf{q}$, i.e., with $U \stackrel{\mathcal{D}}{=} \mathcal{D}(\mathbf{q})$ we have $\mathbb{P}[U = v] = q_v$ for $v = 1, \ldots, u$. For the expected-profile model with parameters n, u and $\mathbf{q}$, we assume that $U_1, \ldots, U_n$ are i.i.d. $\mathcal{D}(\mathbf{q})$ distributed.

Unless specific information is available, a natural choice is $\mathbf{q} = (\frac{1}{u}, \ldots, \frac{1}{u})$, i.e., elements are chosen uniformly from the universe. We refer to this special case as the *random-u-ary-word model*, as it corresponds to the uniform distribution over all u^n words of length n over the alphabet $[u]$. Coming from the continuous uniform model above, random u-ary words are a natural modification: instead of n i.i.d. elements from a *continuous* uniform distribution, we now use n i.i.d. elements from a *discrete* uniform distribution. Unlike in the continuous case, the choice of the universe does matter in the discrete case, though.

3.1.3 The Exact-Profile Model

With parameter $\mathbf{q}$, we fix the expected number nq_v of occurrences of each value $v \in [u]$, i.e., the *expected profile* of the input, hence the name of the model. This is in contrast to the *exact-profile model*, where we fix the numbers x_v of occurrences of v in the input and then choose a random permutation of the corresponding multiset.

Both models have already been studied in the literature: Burge [27] considers the exact-profile model, without giving it a name. Sedgewick [160] calls the model *random permutation from a multiset*. Kemp [98] introduces the names multiset-model and probability-model, which are used also by Archibald and Clément [3]. Sedgewick [160] also explicitly studies the random-u-ary-word model, which he calls *n-ary file model;* Sedgewick writes N and n for our n and u.

3.1.4 Enforcing Random Order

The families of distributions for the initial input values introduced above are all comprised of i.i.d. elements with a certain universe distribution. Unless more is known, this might be a reasonable assumption but we certainly cannot rely on real-world data to be chosen i.i.d. This is not as severe a restriction as it might seem at first sight: we can actually *enforce* inputs to be in random order by first randomly *shuffling* it. This turns Quicksort into a Las Vegas algorithm, whose random costs follow precisely the distribution that we get for inputs that are chosen i.i.d. in first place.

The assumption that elements appear in random order is thus w.l.o.g. if we are willing to invest in the overhead for shuffling. In terms of memory bandwidth and caching, shuffling can be quite expensive. For Quicksort, we can reduce the cost by doing the shuffle *on demand:* whenever pivots are to be chosen from a sample, we pick the sample elements from random positions in the input. This has the same effect on the chosen pivot values as a complete a-priori shuffle: sample elements are chosen uniformly at random from the input. As array accesses are then restricted to the current subproblem, we get increasingly better locality of references as we proceed to sorting smaller subarrays.

3.2 Cost Models

In this section we discuss different models of cost for the execution of an algorithm. Some models only make sense for specific algorithms, e.g., the comparison model, others are more general.

3.2.1 Information Costs: The Comparison Model

In the *comparison model,* the cost of an execution of a program is the number of *key comparisons* it uses. This only makes sense with notions of "key" and "comparison." For our application we define that a *key comparison* is any operation that compares two elements U_i and U_j of the input w.r.t. the ordering relation on the elements. It can be only of the three forms $U_i \leqslant U_j$, $U_i < U_j$ or $U_i = U_j$, or their symmetric versions.

For conciseness one often says just *comparisons* instead of key comparisons. To avoid confusion let us make explicit here that even then other forms of comparisons, e.g., involving index variables, do *not* count as comparisons.

The comparison model is a valuable model for two reasons. First, the elements of the input can be complicated objects, and comparing their keys can be an expensive operation. The comparison model can then be seen as the limit case when these comparisons are so expensive that any other parts of the computation can be ignored. We remark however that usually we are not dealing with very expensive comparison functions, and if so the running time of a comparison often depends heavily on the objects compared, as, e.g., for the lexicographic order on strings. We should not rely on the comparison model in isolation to predict running times.

Lower Bounds. The second reason for the importance of the comparison model is that— unlike for most other cost models—we can prove nontrivial lower bounds for costs in the comparison model by information-theoretic arguments. In its simplest form, it has become folklore: at least $\mathrm{ld}(n!) \sim n\,\mathrm{ld}\,n$ (binary) comparisons, i.e., yes-no-questions, are needed to distinguish $n!$ different possibilities. If $U_1, \ldots, U_n$ are all different, we cannot sort them with less key comparisons.

3.2.2 Rearrangement Costs: Swaps and Write Accesses

It is not enough for a sorting method to *know* the permutation of the input, it also has to actually *apply* it—or rather its inverse—to the data. For in-place sorting methods it makes sense to compare the effort they need for rearranging the array into order. The rearrangement operations in classic versions of Quicksort are conveniently expressed in terms of *swaps,* where we exchange the values of two cells in the array. Therefore the number of swaps has become an established measure of rearrangement cost.

Not all rearrangement procedures are based on swaps, therefore we prefer a more elementary unit of cost: *write accesses* to the array. One swap entails exactly two write accesses, so all swap counts can simply be multiplied by two.

Discussion. Other elementary operations might come to mind; the choice to count write accesses might seem a bit arbitrary. Let us see why other operations are less well-suited: We could count read accesses, but every element will have to be compared, and to do so it has to be read first. Subsequent accesses can be cached in local variables, i.e., CPU registers. We would thus essentially only reproduce the comparison count.

We could also count *all* assignment operations, not only those targeted at the array. Local variables are likely to reside in CPU registers so that this assignment is relatively cheap. Write accesses to the array can also be cached, but unlike local variables they have to be written back to main memory at some point in time.

3.2.3 Primitive Instruction Counts

There is more to sorting than comparisons and write accesses, e. g., control flow statements and index increments. This is ignored by the above models. A refinement is to consider an actual implementation in a low-level language and to count the number of *executed instructions*. We refer to this as the *primitive instruction model.*

Many options for implementations exist, ranging from theoretical models like random-access machines (RAM) over ones inspired by real hardware like Knuth's MMIX [104], the successor of MIX, to real low-level instruction sets like x86 assembly or Java Bytecode.

Are Comparisons and Swaps Overrated? While swaps and comparisons together give a rough indication of efficiency, I think their importance has traditionally been over-rated. The reason is the following special property of classic Quicksort: All code locations with linearithmic execution frequencies—i.e., those that contribute to the leading term of costs—contain a comparison or a swap operation. Moreover, both inner loops are completely symmetric. Therefore, the instruction count of a reasonable implementation of classic Quicksort will simply be a *linear combination of the number of swaps and comparisons* [103, 162, 182].

This is no longer true for other variants of Quicksort, in particular not for dual-pivot Quicksort, as discussed in detail by Wild et al. [185]. It is still true that high-frequency blocks contain comparisons or write accesses to the array, but not all blocks have the same number of instructions. We therefore have to determine execution frequencies *separately*

> for all locations in the code where a comparison happens. This is not what is usually done when considering the comparison model.
>
> For classic Quicksort the number of comparisons and swaps are, coincidentally, exactly what determines the leading term of the number of executed instructions. Researchers might in the past have rightfully concluded that swaps and comparisons explain the running time of classic Quicksort, but this result does not carry over to other variants of Quicksort.

Its flexibility is actually a weakness of the primitive instruction model: results are specific to the given language and the given implementation. I determined exemplary instruction counts for MMIX and Java Bytecode implementations of classic Quicksort, YBB Quicksort and Kciwegdes partitioning [182] (the algorithms are discussed in Section 4.2). Running times and instruction counts showed *opposite* results: the implementations that ran faster executed *more* instructions at the same time. It is plausible that running time is heavily influenced by the modern hardware features discussed below, which the primitive instruction model does not take into account.

For the purpose of this work, the primitive instruction model only adds complexity without providing a significant gain in explanatory power. We will therefore not determine instruction counts in this work. Instead, we consider models for two aspects that the primitive-instruction model does not take into account: memory hierarchies and pipelined execution.

3.2.4 The Memory Hierarchy: Scanned Elements and Cache Misses

One of the aspects ignored by the primitive instruction model is the *memory hierarchy:* memory access costs are not uniform.

The Memory Hierarchy.   Accesses to main memory are roughly two orders of magnitude slower than CPU speed. To alleviate this discrepancy, current machines use two to three levels of *caches* with faster, but smaller memory, holding data that is close to previous accesses in time or location. They do so by keeping copies of a number of contiguous segment of main memory, called *blocks* or *cache lines*. Access to main memory always goes through the cache, so that after an access to an address the whole block containing the accesses location is in the cache. If the accessed element is already in the cache, the access is cheap. This situation is called a *cache hit*. Otherwise, we have a *cache miss* and have to load that element's block to the cache first; this is costly as it involves an access to the next level of the memory hierarchy, whose latency is usually an order of magnitude larger. As cache capacities are limited we must *evict* one old block to make room for the new one. The *cache replacement strategy* determines which block to select in this case. Level-one caches (L1) are closest to the CPU and offer access latencies at the order of a single instruction. At the other end of the memory hierarchy, we might have solid-state disks and hard-disk drives for data that is too large to fit in main memory. The latency of the latter is around *seven orders of magnitude* slower the CPU frequency. This sure has an influence on running time.

A matter of scale.   Such numbers are hard to grasp; it is important to translate them to relations we have a better feeling for.

Here are some:

- ► If a L1 cache access would takes a few seconds, a disk seek took a few *years*.
- ► A nanosecond, the time a usual CPU needs to execute one instruction, is also the time light needs to travel the distance from the paper or monitor to the reader's eyes. And light is fast.
- ► A classic spacial analogy for the orders of magnitude is shown in the graphic to the right by Nyberg et al. [142].

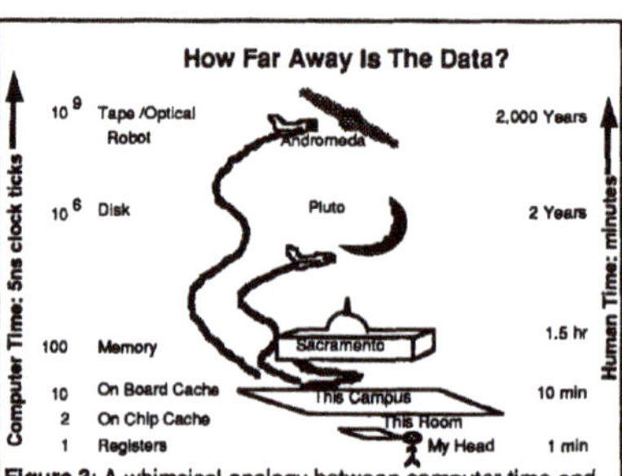

Figure 3: A whimsical analogy between computer time and human time as seen from San Francisco. The scale on the left shows the number of processor cycles to get to various levels of the memory hierarchy (measured in 5ns processor clock ticks). The scale on the right is a more human scale showing time based in human units (minutes).

The External-Memory Model.   There is a standard model for non-uniform memory costs, the *external-memory model* of Aggarwal and Vitter [1]. It was originally intended and described for the situation that inputs are so large that they do not fit into the main memory of size M at once and have to be held on disk, see, e.g., Section 2.2.1 of Mehlhorn and Sanders [127]. The cost of an algorithm is the number of *I/Os, (input/output operations)*, which are transfers of size-B blocks between memory and disk. The external-memory model also applies to lower levels of the memory hierarchy as they are conceptually similar. Despite its wide use, I am reluctant to use the external-memory terminology in this work, for several reasons:

- ► For our purposes *"a straightforward extension of the I/O model is inadequate for hierarchical memory systems"* (Wickremesinghe et al. [181], p. 2), as efficient in-memory *"algorithms need to be both instruction-conscious and cache-conscious"* ([181], p. 16). There is vast literature on *sorting in external memory,* describing algorithms with as little I/O cost as possible, potentially at the expense of excessive in-memory effort. The assumption there is that we are sorting *on disk,* so that *only* I/Os matter. This is a different regime and we should avoid confusion.

- ► Second, all our Quicksort variants are essentially *scanning-based:* memory accesses are sequential, even though several scans can work interleaved. The parameters M and B of the model do not add insight for Quicksort and similar algorithms.

  We may note here that as a scanning-based algorithm, Quicksort is *cache oblivious* in the sense of Frigo et al. [67]: it does not adapt its behavior to the actual values of M and B, but is reasonably cache-efficient for any parameters M and B.

- ► Moreover, the external-memory model (nominally) restricts attention to *cache misses,* the event that is equivalent to I/Os on lower levels of the memory hierarchy. But it is not a priori clear whether it is really the latency of the next level in the hierarchy that determines execution time. It might as well be the *bandwidth* of the bus to the next level of the hierarchy. In fact, CPUs can in restricted cases recognize a scan and issue *prefetching instructions* to load elements into the cache ahead of time; in the best case there are then no cache misses at all. Bandwidth still limits execution speed, whereas counting cache misses would be misleading in that case.

I hence prefer the more abstract terminology given below, which leaves open whether latency or bandwidth is the limiting factor.

The Iterator-Model: Scanned Elements. Our cost measure for assessing efficiency w.r.t. the use of the memory hierarchy is the number of *scanned elements*. We recently introduced this name [137] and it was taken up by Aumüller et al. [10], but the underlying ideas are older. Both LaMarca and Ladner [107] and Kushagra et al. [105] only speak of the approximate number of cache misses, but their analysis fits exactly the scanned-elements model.

We previously defined scanned elements as the *"total distance covered by all scanning indices"* (Nebel et al. [137], p. 3). We will complement this definition herein with an operational model that makes the notion of scanning indices explicit.

A *scanning index* is a *one-directional iterator,* i.e., an object pointing at one element of the array and having a *direction,* either forward or backward. The notion of iterators is widely used in programming libraries, e.g., in the Java runtime library and the standard template library of C++. Our iterators offer access to the array of elements through exactly the following interface:

read() returns the value at the current location,

write(x) writes new value x to current location,

advance() move the iterator one position in its direction,

clone(dir) creates a new iterator with same position and the given direction,

distance(iter) returns the number of cells between *iter* and this iterator;
     the result is negative if *iter* is to the left of this.

In the *iterator model,* algorithms may only use scanning indices to access the input. The input array is initially given by two indices pointing at $A[1]$ and $A[n]$, the left and right end of the array, respectively. The cost of an execution is the total number of advance-calls, i.e., each call of advance() is counted as one scanned element.

We assume that there is an fixed upper bound on the number of scanning iterators an algorithm uses at any point in time. This will be the case for all Quicksort variants studied in this work; if in another application this is not the case, one should probably also count the number of clone-calls as costs.

We demonstrated that scanned elements match the number of cache misses very well in an idealized fully associative LRU cache [137], and Aumüller et al. [10] found good correspondence to L1 cache misses also on actual hardware.

Classic Quicksort with Iterators.   To illustrate the iterator model, here is a Java implementation of classic Quicksort using the scanning index interface. The code is quite similar to a pointer-based implementation in a language like C.

```java
1   interface ScanningIndex {
2       int read();
3       void write(int newValue);
4       Direction direction();
5       ScanningIndex advance(); // returns this
6       ScanningIndex clone(Direction direction);
7       int distance(ScanningIndex other);
8       enum Direction { FORWARD, BACKWARD }
9   }

11  void quicksort(ScanningIndex start, ScanningIndex end) {
12      if (start.differenceTo(end) > 0) {
13          final int p = end.read(); // the pivot
14          ScanningIndex i =
          start.clone(BACKWARD).advance().clone(FORWARD);
15          ScanningIndex j = end.clone(BACKWARD);
16          while (true) {
17              do i.advance(); while (i.read() < p);
18              do j.advance(); while (j.read() > p);
19              if (i.distance(j) < 0) break;
20              int t = i.read(); i.write(j.read()); j.write(t);
21          }
22          // bring pivot to its final position i
23          end.write(i.read()); i.write(p);
24          quicksort(start, i.clone(BACKWARD).advance());
25          quicksort(i.advance(), end);
26      }
27  }
```

3.2.5 Pipelined Execution: Branch Mispredictions

A second aspect ignored by the primitive-instruction model is that branching statements, i.e., conditional jump instructions, have non-uniform cost because only mispredicted branches imply a pipeline stall.

Instruction pipelines.   Modern processors use *instruction pipelines* to speed up execution as follows: Inside the CPU, machine instructions are split into severals *phases* like, e.g.,

1 fetching the instruction,

2 decoding and loading data,

3 executing the instruction, and

4 writing back the results.

Each phase takes one CPU cycle. If there are L phases, a single instruction would take L cycles. Modern processors can execute different phases of different instructions in parallel, i.e., one can execute up to L instructions at once, each in a different phase. If the pipeline is completely filled we now finish the last stage of one command *in every cycle*; a speedup of L.

The downside of this idea comes with *conditional jumps*. For those, the CPU will have to decide the outcome *before* it has actually been computed. Otherwise it could not go on with the first phases of the subsequent commands. To alleviate that, processors try to predict the outcome and start executing, speculatively, the commands that will follow if the prediction is correct. Several *branch-prediction schemes* have been invented to guess the actual outcome, some of which we discuss below.

In case of a false prediction, a *branch misprediction (BM)* or *branch miss,* the CPU has to *undo* all erroneously executed steps (phases) and load the correct instructions instead (pipeline stall). A branch miss is thus a costly event, and we use their number as our costs measure.

Branch-Prediction Schemes.   Several branch prediction schemes have been invented to guess the actual outcome. In the simplest case each branch (conditional jump) is marked as *probably taken* or *probably not taken* at compile time and the CPU acts accordingly. Knuth's MMIX for example has two variants of each branch instruction, a probably-taken variant and a probably-not-taken variant.

When branch outcomes depend on data not known at compile time, this *static* strategy does not help much. We have to *adapt* predictions at runtime in such cases. Adaptive schemes are either local or global. Local schemes store for each branching instruction a history of past outcomes. Predictions for different branch locations are done on independent data, i.e., locally. If we allow ℓ bits of history, there are 2^ℓ different states. Each of these states corresponds to a prediction (taken or not taken). When the branch is executed the next time, its outcome triggers a state transition. We thus describe local schemes as finite-state machines. Figures 8–10 show the most common local predictors. The schemes are described in more detail, e.g., by Martínez et al. [117].

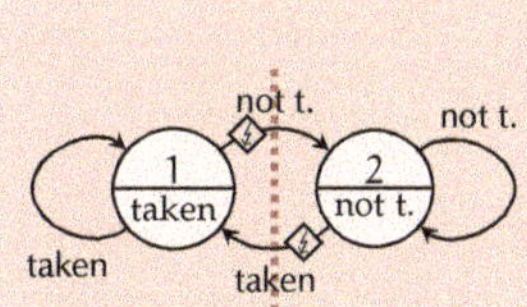

Figure 8: The finite-state automaton corresponding to a 1-bit branch predictor. The prediction for the next execution of the branch is given in the lower part of the nodes, and after the branch has been executed, the edge corresponding to the actual outcome is followed. Whenever an edge marked with ◈ is followed, we incur a branch miss.

Global schemes store a history table of size 2^ℓ, indexed by the outcome of the last ℓ branches, *no matter where they happened*. For example, if $\ell = 3$ and the outcomes of the last three branches were taken, taken and not-taken, we would access the history entry 110.

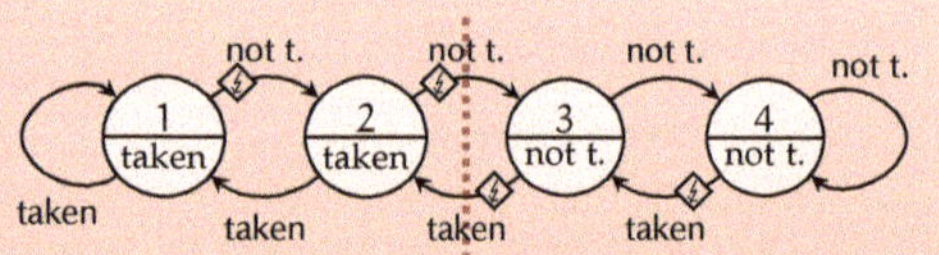

Figure 9: The finite-state automaton corresponding to a 2-bit saturating-counter predictor; see Figure 8 for an explanation.

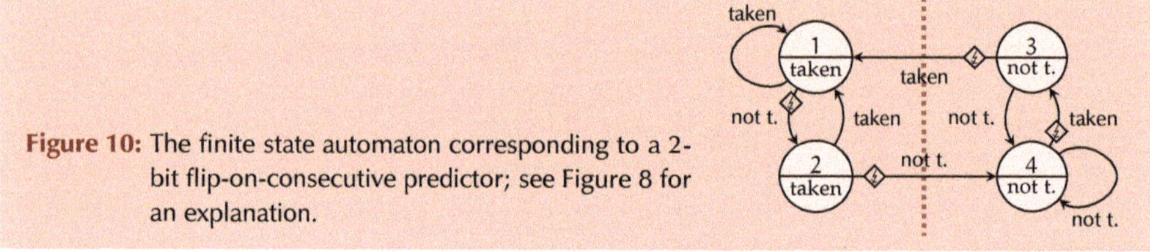

Figure 10: The finite state automaton corresponding to a 2-bit flip-on-consecutive predictor; see Figure 8 for an explanation.

Each entry of the history table is then a local predictor, usually a 2-bit saturating counter, which then determines the actual prediction.

Auger et al. [6] analyzed a global prediction scheme for a variant of binary search with two branch locations. Analysis becomes intractable quickly if the number of involved branch instructions grows.

Hardware Implementation of Prediction Schemes. Adaptive schemes require special hardware support. When it comes to actual implementations, the above descriptions are an idealized view. For the local 1-bit predictor as given above, the CPU would need one bit of storage for each branch in the code; other predictors require even more memory. It is impossible in practice to reserve even just a single bit of branch history for every possible branch-instruction location. Therefore actual hardware prediction units use hash tables of history storage, which means that all branch instructions whose addresses hash to the same value will share one history storage. The resulting *aliasing effects* have typically small, but rather chaotic influences on predictions in practice. We ignore those in our model.

The simple schemes described above have been used by the first CPUs with pipelining. Modern microprocessors implement more sophisticated heuristics, as the ones described by Fog [65]. They try to recognize common patterns in branching behavior, in particular, for-loops with known numbers of iteration. They also mix global and local predictors. Such schemes are probably too intricate for precise analysis. We will therefore focus on local schemes.

Discussion. Differences in the number of branch misses can make a big difference. As an extreme example, Kaligosi and Sanders [96] observed on a Pentium 4 Prescott CPU (a processor with an extremely long pipeline and thus a high cost per branch miss) that the running time penalty of a BM is so high that a very skewed pivot choice outperformed the typically optimal median pivot, even though the latter leads to much less executed instructions in total. The effect was not reproducible on the slightly different Pentium 4

Willamette [23]. Here two effects counteract: a biased pivot makes branches easier to predict but also gives unbalanced subproblem sizes.

We showed in earlier work that for the comparison of dual-pivot and classic Quicksort, branch misses do *not* seem to make the difference [117]; nevertheless, branch misses are analytically an interesting cost measure. We will thus show how to extend that analysis to generic one-pass partitioning in this work, but we will not discuss branch misses results in detail.

With these models for input distributions and costs of execution, the stage is set for the main part of this work: the analysis of Quicksort. We already gave a rough idea of Quicksort and multiway partitioning in the introduction, but a precise analysis needs a precise description of the object of study. This is the purpose of the next chapter.

4 Quicksort

Contents

The purpose of this chapter is to present our object of study: *Quicksort*. As the name suggests, it is a sorting algorithm: given a list of *elements* from a totally ordered *universe,* the task is to rearrange them into sorted order.

We assume that we have $n \in \mathbb{N}_0$ elements, given in an *array* $A[1..n]$. We can access array cells $A[i]$ by index i, $1 \leqslant i \leqslant n$, both for reading the current entry or for writing a new value to that cell. It is convenient to think of the values in A as numbers, and we will use numbers in examples, but our algorithms may only use pairwise comparisons between such values: we can ask whether $A[i] < A[j]$, $A[i] \leqslant A[j]$ etc. but nothing else; the values we sort can in general be arbitrarily complex objects.

Chapter Outline.   We begin this chapter with a short discussion of the abstract idea of Quicksort: partitioning recursively. We then present in Section 4.2 all practically relevant array-based implementations for the partitioning step. We also briefly discuss the most important optimizations that can be combined with any particular partitioning procedure. In Section 4.3 we present generic s-way one-pass partitioning, the synthesis of all the methods discussed before that we will analyze in this work. In Section 4.4 we detail the most important optimization of Quicksort: *pivot sampling.* We present a generalized version of it that covers all practically relevant variants. We discuss in Section 4.5 how to preserve randomness in Quicksort; a vital property for our analysis. Finally, Section 4.6 briefly states what is not covered by generic one-pass partitioning, and we relate our framework to related work.

4.1   From Partitioning to Sorting

Quicksort is a classic instance of the *divide-and-conquer paradigm:* the solution to the problem at hand consists of using the very same method on *parts* of the problem, so that at the end, the whole problem is solved magically. *The method to be described re(oc)curs in its own description.* It is one of the great achievements of computer science to take the mystery out of such recursive definitions, by formally settling the question when such a definition is vacuous and how to give it a precise meaning whenever it is not.

There is no magic in recursion; at some point we have to actually *do* something to the array. For Quicksort, this active part is called *partitioning:* We partition the elements in the input array into a finite number s of *segments* or *classes*, according to a partition of the universe into intervals. That means that either all elements in one segment are smaller than all elements of another segment, or they are all larger. We obtain this partition of the universe by selecting $s-1$ *pivot* elements from the array—let us call them $P_1 \leqslant \cdots \leqslant P_{s-1}$ in weakly increasing order—which serve as borderlines separating the segments. The rth segment for $r = 1, \ldots, s$ thus only contains elements between P_{r-1} and P_r, where we set $P_0 := -\infty$ and $P_s := +\infty$ for notational convenience. The segments form contiguous parts in the sorted array, and they can indeed by sorted independently of each other, e.g., by recursively using Quicksort.

An implementation of Quicksort consists of a partitioning method together with a frame of recursive-call logic. Several variants of the former, and a unifying parametric version will be discussed in detail in the remainder of this chapter. The latter is almost trivial nowadays, since programming languages have built-in recursion stack management.

◆   ◆   ◆

The concept of recursion is still a startling and fascinating one. I still remember vividly the *aha moment* when I first saw the recursive solution for the *Tower of Hanoi* problem. Of course, I was taught the modern version of recursion right away; as a *native recursionist* it is thus hard for me to imagine how it must have been to describe the idea of Quicksort without recursion. Let us hear a contemporary witness on that.

Dijkstra describes the relevance of recursion for Quicksort as follows: *"A major milestone of ALGOL 60 was its introduction of recursion into imperative programming. [. . .] it was crucial in enabling Tony Hoare to complete the design of one of computing's most famous algorithms, viz. Quicksort. Prior to knowing ALGOL 60, he had the idea, but it remained an elusive vision, a dream that defied formulation, but as soon as he saw ALGOL 60 offering him just what he needed, Quicksort materialized in all its glory"* [44].

ALGOL 60, Recursion and the Amsterdam Plot.   ALGOL 60 was the first imperative programming language to include recursive procedure calls with automatic call-stack management. How it came to be so is a story worth telling.

A novelty of ALGOL 60 is that it was specification-defined and vendor-independent: In the late 1950s an expert committee was formed to work out a specification for the language, based on which a reference compiler would be implemented. The committee was divided in the question whether recursive procedures should be explicitly allowed in ALGOL 60. One group around F. L. Bauer argued strongly against it as they deemed it impossible to be implemented efficiently.

At that time the standard was to statically allocate for each procedure one *fixed* portion of memory for the local variables of that procedure. This piece of memory was *globally shared among all* invocations of the procedure, which naturally limits the allowable number of invocations of any procedure to *one* at any given time. The idea of a call stack had not spread widely at that time. Even two years later, Hoare [82] found it adequate to start his Quicksort article with a detailed description of a data structure he called *nest*—nothing but a stack in modern terminology. This shows how little standardized these notions were at the time.

Another group in the ALGOL committee around A. van Wijngaarden and J. McCarthy, the creator of LISP, feared that excluding recursion would substantially limit ALGOL's usefulness and elegance. Wijngaarden was in contact with E. W. Dijkstra who, shortly after the report for ALGOL 60 was finished, published an article describing in detail an implementation of procedure calls with the modern version of stack frames etc. [42]. It can be taken for granted that he had these ideas already in mind when the issue of recursion was discussed in the ALGOL committee.

As ideas for the final report started to converge, a majority of the committee seemed to oppose recursion. Nevertheless, the final report allows recursive procedure calls *explicitly*.

Dijkstra remembers the inclusion of recursion in ALGOL 60 as *"almost an accident and certainly a coup. When the ALGOL 60 Report was nearing completion and circulated for final comments, it was discovered that recursion was nowhere explicitly excluded, and, just to be sure that it would be in, one innocent sentence was added at the end of the Section 5.4.4., viz. 'Any other occurrence of the procedure identifier within the procedure body denotes activation of the procedure.' Some committee members only noticed this sentence when it was too late to oppose, got very cross and refused to implement it. In more than one sense they were the losers"* [44]. The sneaky addition of this sentence, initiated by the Dutchmen Wijngaarden and Dijkstra, was called the *"Amsterdam plot on introducing recursivity"* by Bauer [135, p. 130].

◆   ◆   ◆

Personal controversy aside, the impact of this single sentence may seriously be questioned. In a recent article, van den Hove argues that even without that explicit mention of recursive calls, there are several means to force an ALGOL program to have several simultaneous invocations of one procedure: mutually recursive functions, procedure parameters with self-application and via the call-by-name mechanism [84]. Formulating syntactic rules to disallow recursive invocations—so that the static memory implementation remains possible—is quite hard, and not natural. Even more so for a language like ALGOL 60 that contains intricate constructs like call-by-name parameter. It may be for a reason that these constructs are hardly found in modern programming languages.

Though obscure the circumstances may have been, we must be happy in hindsight that recursion was, sneakily or not, indeed introduced in the ALGOL 60 report, as it fostered the wide adoption of recursion in programs and its reception as a core technique of computer science. Many algorithms are most elegantly specified recursively.

We close the history class by remarking that even though ALGOL 60 is hardly used any more, the widespread understanding of the concept of recursion is a lasting legacy. It is probably also rather this abstract idea than the specific implementation in ALGOL that enabled Hoare to bring Quicksort into our world.

4.2 Famous Quicksort Variants

The Quicksort version initially published by Hoare [80, 81, 82] used a single pivot and $s = 2$ segments. With some minor changes, it is to this day one of the most efficient sorting algorithms, so we shall describe this classic version of Quicksort in some detail.

4.2.1 Classic Quicksort

The classic partitioning method consists of letting two *indices* k and g scan the array from left resp. right until they finally meet. Invariantly, elements left of k are known to belong to the first segment and elements to the right of g belong to the second segment. Elements between the two indices are in an undecided state as of yet.

Whenever one index moves towards the other, a new element is considered. If it belongs to the corresponding segment—the first segment for k resp. the second segment for g—the invariant already holds again and we are done. So k moves right until an element

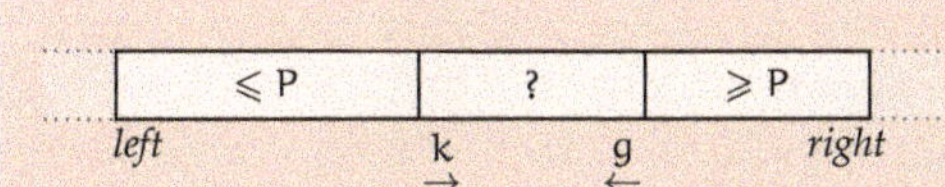

Figure 11: Invariant for Algorithm 2. Initially, the "?-area" covers the complete range, at the end it is empty.

greater than the pivot is found; this element belongs in the second segment. Then g moves left until an element smaller than the pivot is found. That element likewise belongs to the first segment, so we can reestablish the invariant by *swapping* the two elements $A[k]$ and $A[g]$.

Once k and g have met, we have found the boundary between small and large elements and partitioning is finished. We put the pivot element at this position, between the segments. The pivot has reached its final position in the sorted array now. The two segments are sorted recursively by the same procedure. To be concrete, Algorithm 2 gives a detailed implementation of this sorting method.

Algorithm 2: Classic Quicksort with Sedgewick-Hoare partitioning

CLASSICQUICKSORT$(A, \mathit{left}, \mathit{right})$

    // Sort the array A in index range $\mathit{left}, \ldots, \mathit{right}$ (both inclusive).

    // We assume a sentinel value $A[\mathit{left}-1] = -\infty$, i.e.

    // $\forall i \in \{\mathit{left}, \ldots, \mathit{right}\} : A[\mathit{left}-1] \leqslant A[i]$

1 **if** $\mathit{right} - \mathit{left} \geqslant 1$

2      $P := A[\mathit{right}]$ // Choose rightmost element as pivot

3      $k := \mathit{left} - 1; \; g := \mathit{right}$

4   **while** *true*

5   **do** $k := k+1$ **while** $A[k] < P$ **end while**

6   **do** $g := g-1$ **while** $A[g] > P$ **end while**

7   **if** $k \geqslant g$ **then break** while **end if**

8   Swap $A[k]$ and $A[g]$

9   **end while**

10   Swap $A[k]$ and $A[\mathit{right}]$ // Move pivot to final position

11   CLASSICQUICKSORT$(A, \mathit{left}, k-1)$

12   CLASSICQUICKSORT$(A, k+1, \mathit{right})$

13 **end if**

The implementation closely follows the description of and is due to Sedgewick [162, 161], but uses the rightmost element as pivot instead of the leftmost, as done in Program 1.2 of Sedgewick and Flajolet [165]. We call Algorithm 2 *classic Quicksort* in this work. Its brevity is appealing and it ranks among the fastest sorting methods as its inner loops are simple and short.

In light of this, we may forgive it the idiosyncrasy of requiring a sentinel value in $A[0]$ that is less or equal to all occurring elements. Sentinels allow us to omit array-boundary checks in inner loops, which gives a significant speed-up in practice. One can avoid this problem by only using the sentineled version in recursive calls that are not leftmost. Then elements of adjacent segments can serve as sentinels.

Rest in Peace, Loop-while-repeat.   For clever implementations of partitioning, we will often find the construct used in Algorithm 2: a while-true loop, that is exited using break statements. It would have been nice to have an explicit control statement for this:

loop		**while** *true*
⟨some code⟩		⟨some code⟩
while ⟨condition⟩	instead of	**if** ⟨condition⟩ **then break end if**
⟨more code⟩		⟨more code⟩
repeat		**end while**

Knuth [101] suggested the specific syntax on the left. A few programming languages indeed offer such control structures, e.g., Ada and ALGOL 68. Unfortunately, middle-conditioned loops never found widespread adoption and none of the modern languages support it directly. In fact, these loops are so uncommon nowadays that I did not even dare to use them in pseudocode; it must be feared that for many readers it would be unclear what the intended meaning is.

We will occasionally want to exit an outer loop directly from within an inner loop. In Java, this is possible using labeled break statements; in C/C++ we can resort to goto.

4.2.2 Lomuto's Partitioning

Hoare's partitioning method is among the most efficient ones, but certainly not the easiest to understand or implement correctly. Bentley, who certainly is (among other things) one of the most talented programmers of our time, commented on Hoare's partitioning: *"Although the basic idea of that code is simple, I have always found the details tricky—I once spent the better part of two days chasing down a bug hiding in a short partitioning loop"* [18, p. 117]. I can say I share Bentley's experience.

Figure 12: Invariant for Algorithm 3. Initially, the "?-area" covers the complete range, at the end it is empty.

Bentley [18] therefore advocates in his *Programming Pearls* to start with a conceptually simpler method that we attributes to Nico Lomuto. It is given in Algorithm 3.

Lomuto's partitioning scheme works unidirectional: instead of growing two segments from both ends, we have two segments on the left. This makes the termination condition simpler: we are done when k reaches *right*.

Algorithm 3: Quicksort with Lomuto's Partitioning [35, Chapter 7].

$\textsc{LomutoQuicksort}(A, \textit{left}, \textit{right})$

```
 1   if left < right
 2       P := A[right]; k₂ := left − 1
 3       for k := left, … , right − 1
 4           if A[k] ⩽ P
 5               k₂ := k₂ + 1
 6               Swap A[k₂] and A[k]
 7           end if
 8       end for
 9       k₂ := k₂ + 1
10       Swap A[k₂] and A[right]
11       LomutoQuicksort(A,  left  , k₂ − 1)
12       LomutoQuicksort(A, k₂ + 1,  right )
13   end if
```

◆　　◆　　◆

The history of Quicksort is full of eager suggestions for improvements of the basic algorithm. In the words of Sedgewick and Wayne, it *"is tempting to try to develop ways to improve quicksort: a faster sorting algorithm is computer science's 'better mousetrap,' and quicksort is a venerable method that seems to invite tinkering"* ([166], p. 295). An analysis of many variants of classic Quicksort is given by Sedgewick [162]. Many variations are indeed not helpful in all circumstances.

Some ideas did stand the test of time, most notably *pivot sampling,* i.e., choosing pivots as order statistics of a (small) sample of the input and truncating the recursion at some cut-off size, w, and using Insertionsort there. We include these in our study, see Section 4.2.6. Splitting the array into more than two parts at once, used to be counted among the unsuccessful ideas, but the success of the dual-pivot Quicksort introduced in Java 7 caused a sea change.

4.2.3 Yaroslavskiy-Bentley-Bloch Quicksort

Since Java 7, the reference implementation of the Java runtime library uses dual-pivot Quicksort as default sorting method for primitive-type arrays. At its core is the ternary partitioning method given in Algorithm 4 below.

The algorithm is due to V. Yaroslavskiy, J. Bentley and J. Bloch and will be referred to as *YBB Quicksort* for short. I previously called it *Yaroslavskiy's algorithm,* because it was him who first discovered that time is ripe for a Quicksort with two pivots. From personal

Figure 13: Invariant for Algorithm 4. Initially, the "?-area" covers the complete range, at the end it is empty.

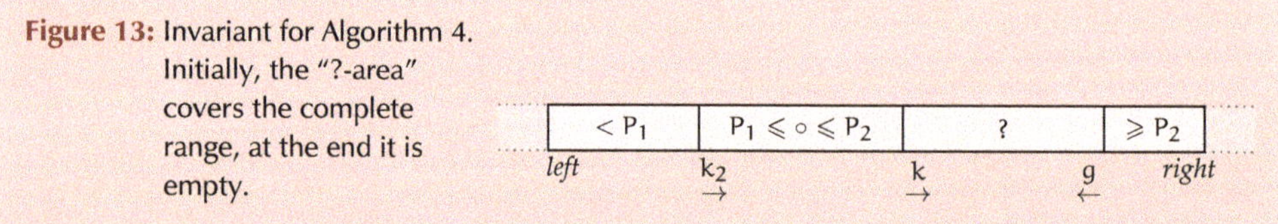

communication with the three I learned that YBB Quicksort is more appropriate since Bentley and Bloch were involved in early stages of the development of the algorithm.

Algorithm 4: Dual-pivot partitioning by V. Yaroslavskiy, J. Bentley and J. Bloch.

$\text{YBBPARTITION}\,(A, \mathit{left}, \mathit{right}, P_1, P_2)$

    // Assumes $\mathit{left} \leqslant \mathit{right}$ and $P_1 \leqslant P_2$.

    // Modifies A s.t. with return value (i_1, i_2) holds $\begin{cases} A[j] < P_1, & \text{for } \mathit{left} \leqslant j \leqslant i_1; \\ P_1 \leqslant A[j] \leqslant P_2, & \text{for } i_1 \ < j < i_2; \\ A[j] \geqslant P_2, & \text{for } i_2 \ \leqslant j \leqslant \mathit{right}. \end{cases}$

```
 1   k₂ := left;  k := k₂;  g := right
 2   while k ≤ g
 3       if A[k] < P₁
 4           Swap A[k₂] and A[k]
 5           k₂ := k₂ + 1
 6       else
 7           if A[k] ≥ P₂
 8               while A[g] > P₂ and k < g
 9                   g := g − 1
10               end while
11               if A[g] ≥ P₁
12                   Swap A[k] and A[g]
13               else
14                   CyclicShiftLeft₃(A; k, k₂, g)
15                   k₂ := k₂ + 1
16               end if
17               g := g − 1
18           end if
19       end if
20       k := k + 1
21   end while
22   return (k₂ − 1, g + 1)
```

The Dutch National Flag Problem. Partitioning an array around two pivots is similar to the *Dutch National Flag Problem (DNFP)* which Dijkstra [43] posed as a programming exercise in 1976:

> Given an array of n pebbles in the colors red, white and blue, rearrange them by swaps, such that the colors form the Dutch national flag: red, white and blue in contiguous regions. Each pebble may be inspected only once and only a constant amount of extra storage may be used.

Dijkstra assumes an operation "buck" that tells us an element's color in one shot, so any algorithm must use exactly n buck-operations. Performance differences only concern the number of swaps needed.

Interestingly, S. J. Meyer gave an algorithm for the DNFP that has essentially the structure of YBB partitioning and outperformed Dijkstra's original solution to the problem [126]! One may hence say that the partitioning scheme is not entirely novel; its effective use in Quicksort certainly is.

It is surprising how little was known about YBB Quicksort at the time it was included in the Java library. With my coauthors, I have devoted considerable effort to the mathematical analysis of this important algorithm to remedy that. In particular, my master's thesis [182] contains a detailed account of the inner workings of the algorithm and a meticulous discussion of certain details, e.g., why it makes sense to have a non-strict comparison in line 7. The reader is thus referred there for such details on YBB Quicksort.

Rotations and Cyclic Shifts. Single-pivot partitioning methods are naturally written in terms of swap operations. In multiway one-pass partitioning the need arises to move more than one element to make way for a single new element in its segment. The usual case is that we apply a *cyclic shift*, or *rotation* to the elements in question, e.g., the second element takes the position of the first one, the third element takes the position of the originally second and the originally first element now becomes the third one.

Algorithm 5: Cyclic shift operation on ℓ indices in an array.

$\textsc{CyclicShiftLeft}_\ell(A; i_1, \ldots, i_\ell)$

1   $tmp := A[i_1]$
2   **for** $r := 2, \ldots, \ell$
3      $A[i_{r-1}] := A[i_r]$
4   **end for**
5   $A[i_\ell] := tmp$

We can implement such a cyclic shift with a single temporary variable, generalizing binary swaps, see Algorithm 5. We will base our algorithms on this cyclic shift to the left; in fact we already do so for YBB Quicksort, see line 14 of Algorithm 4.

One could define a symmetric version that shifts to the right, but we can just as well reverse the indices. Aumüller et al. [10] also pursued this route and defined a generic "rotation" macro. I prefer the name (cyclic) shift, since it makes it easy to specify the direction unambiguously: we always shift to the *left*. The term cyclic shift is also commonly used for the corresponding operations on (bit) strings.

There is a little nuisance in working with a generic shifting macro: if some of the passed indices are equal, the order of the assignment becomes vital. Our algorithms will indeed call CyclicShiftLeft with equal indices if some segments are (still) empty. One thus has to choose the order of the indices carefully; the reader has been warned.

4.2.4 Sedgewick's Dual-Pivot Method and Kciwegdes Partitioning

Dual-pivot Quicksort was considered much earlier than the recency of YBB Quicksort might suggest. To the authors knowledge, Program 5.1 of Sedgewick [162] is the first full Quicksort implementation featuring two pivots. We reproduce it here as our Algorithm 6 and call it *Sedgewick's (dual-pivot) partitioning*.

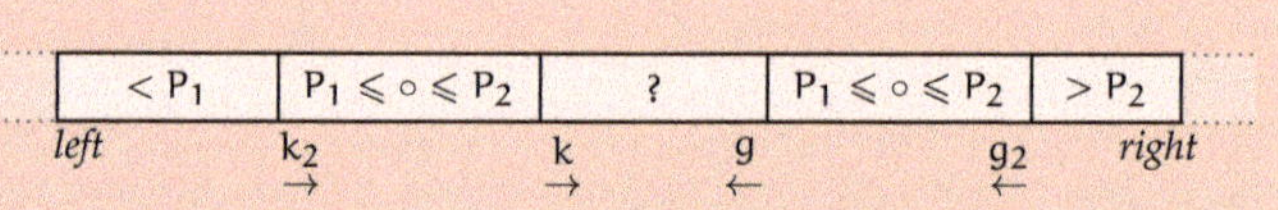

Figure 14: Invariant for Algorithm 6. Initially, the "?-area" covers the complete range, at the end it is empty.

A detailed discussion of this algorithm appears in my master's thesis [182]. We only emphasize one peculiarity of this algorithm that none of the aforementioned partitioning schemes has: the innermost indices, k and g, jointly scan the middle segment and when they meet, they do so somewhere in amidst this segment. We will later call partitioning methods with this characteristic *master-segment methods,* since there is one segment governing the overall movement of pointers. In the partitioning methods considered up to now, k and g always meet at the boundary of two segments, or equivalently stated, at the final position of one of the pivots. We call this pivot the *master pivot,* and the corresponding partitioning schemes *master-pivot methods.*

Kciwegdes. Sedgewick's dual-pivot Quicksort can quite easily be improved w.r.t. the expected comparison count: we have to *reverse* the order of comparisons with the two pivots. We refer to this modified version as *Kciwegdes partitioning,* Sedgewick reversed literally. The movement of pointers otherwise coincides with the original. I discussed this variation in my master's thesis [182]; Algorithm 7 shows pseudocode for this method.

Aumüller and Dietzfelbinger [9] independently discovered the idea of Kciwegdes partitioning, see their Algorithm 5.

Swaps vs. Hole-Moving. Sedgewick's dual-pivot partitioning employs a variation of how to rearrange elements. Classic Quicksort, Lomuto's Quicksort and YBB Quicksort are all based on *swaps resp. cyclic shifts.* If we consider swaps and rotations as atomic operations,

Algorithm 6: Sedgewick's dual-pivot partitioning.

$\textsc{DualPivotPartitionSedgewick}(A, \mathit{left}, \mathit{right})$

    // Assumes $\mathit{left} < \mathit{right}$ and $A[\mathit{left}] \leqslant A[\mathit{right}]$ are the two pivots.

```
 1   k := left;  k₂ := k ;   g := right;  g₂ := g
 2   P₁ := A[left];  P₂ := A[right]
 3   while true
 4       k := k + 1
 5       while A[k] ≤ P₂
 6           if k ≥ g then break outer while end if // pointers met
 7           if A[k] < P₁
 8               A[k₂] := A[k];  k₂ := k₂ + 1;  A[k] := A[k₂]
 9           end if
10           k := k + 1
11       end while
12       g := g − 1
13       while A[g] ≥ P₁
14           if A[g] > P₂
15               A[g₂] := A[g];  g₂ := g₂ − 1;  A[g] := A[g₂]
16           end if
17           if k ≥ g then break outer while end if // pointers met
18           g := g − 1
19       end while
20       A[k₂] := A[g];  A[g₂] := A[k]
21       k₂ := k₂ + 1;  g₂ := g₂ − 1
22       A[k] := A[k₂];  A[g] := A[g₂]
23   end while
24   A[k₂] := P₁ ;  A[g₂] := P₂
25   return (k₂, g₂)
```

Algorithm 7: Kciwegdes partitioning.

$\textsc{DualPivotPartitionKciwegdes}(A, \textit{left}, \textit{right})$

     // Assumes $\textit{left} < \textit{right}$ and $\mathrm{A}[\textit{left}] \leqslant \mathrm{A}[\textit{right}]$ are the two pivots.

```
 1   k := left;  k₂ := k;  g := right;  g₂ := g
 2   P₁ := A[left];  P₂ := A[right]
 3   while true
 4       k := k + 1
 5       while true
 6           if k ⩾ g then break outer while end if
 7           if A[k] < P₁
 8               A[k₂] := A[k]; k₂ := k₂ + 1; A[k] := A[k₂]
 9           else if A[k] ⩾ P₂ then break inner while end if
10           k := k + 1
11       end while
12       g := g − 1
13       while true
14           if A[g] > P₂
15               A[g₂] := A[g]; g₂ := g₂ − 1; A[g] := A[g₂]
16           else if A[g] ⩽ P₁ then break inner while end if
17           if k ⩾ g then break outer while end if
18           g := g − 1
19       end while
20       A[k₂] := A[g];  A[g₂] := A[k]
21       k₂ := k₂ + 1;  g₂ := g₂ − 1
22       A[k] := A[k₂];  A[g] := A[g₂]
23   end while
24   A[k₂] := P₁;  A[g₂] := P₂
25   return (k₂, g₂)
```

each element is stored at exactly one position in the array at any given time, including the pivots.

Algorithm 6 uses a *hole-moving* scheme instead. It initially creates two "holes" by copying the pivots to local variables. Like a juggler it keeps them flying in the air, writing other elements to the free positions. Only at the end, the pivots come down again, just in time to catch them and put them to their final positions. Algorithm 2 also copies the pivot to a local variable, but this is only for readability; we could have written A[*right*] each time, as well.

In general, hole-moving algorithms are a bit more efficient in that they directly reserve room for the pivots, so that no additional swapping is needed at the end. This difference exists only if there are several segments. If we pick pivots from a sample, segments should be initialized to include the elements from the sample that did not become pivots, which makes it slightly harder to logically separate pivot selection from partitioning. I hence find rotation-based methods a little easier to understand, so our new algorithm is formulated as such; we could easily convert it to use hole-moving.

4.2.5 Waterloo Quicksort

Kushagra et al. [105] were the first to note that it is likely that YBB Quicksort is faster than classic Quicksort in practice because of its more economical usage of the memory hierarchy. They propose a Quicksort version with three pivots to improve on that further. We will refer to their partitioning method as *Waterloo partitioning*; it is given as Algorithm 8. The structure and invariant of the algorithm, see Figure 15, are quite similar to Sedgewick's dual-pivot partitioning. But while the latter scans the middle segment with both k and g, so that they meet inside this segment, Waterloo partitioning uses them as boundary for *two* middle segments.

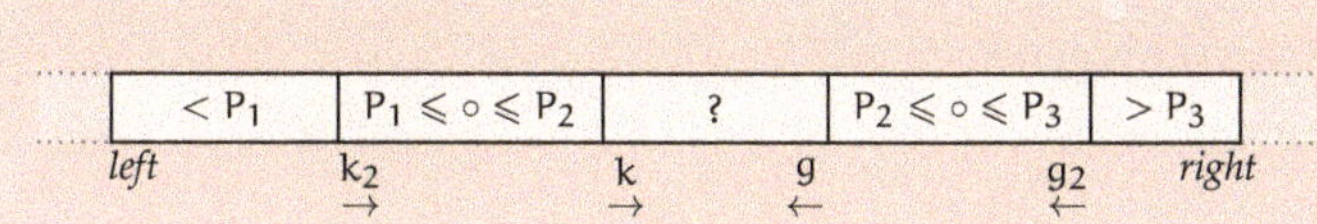

Figure 15: Invariant for Waterloo partitioning, variables have been renamed to match our scheme.

4.2.6 Algorithmic Improvements

A few optimizations are orthogonal to the choice of a partitioning scheme and can be combined with any of the above methods. We only mention here those that have stood the test of time and yield significant improvements in practice. It is noteworthy in this context how far-sighted Hoare's 1962 article on Quicksort [82] was: apart from the description and analysis of the basic algorithm, he anticipated all algorithmic improvements to Quicksort included in the following.

Algorithm 8: Waterloo Partitioning as given in Algorithm A.1.1 of Kushagra et al. [105]

WATERLOOPARTITION$(A, \mathit{left}, \mathit{right}, P_1, P_2, P_3)$

```
 1   k := left;  k₂ := left;  g := right;  g₂ := right;
 2   while k ⩽ g
 3       while A[k] < P₂ and k ⩽ g
 4           if A[k] < P₁
 5               Swap A[k₂] and A[k]
 6               k₂ := k₂ + 1
 7           end if
 8           k := k + 1
 9       end while
10       while A[g] > P₂ and k ⩽ g
11           if A[g₂] > P₃
12               Swap A[g] and A[g₂]
13               g₂ := g₂ − 1
14           end if
15           g := g − 1
16       end while
17       case distinction on the value of (A[k] > P₃, A[g] < P₁)
18           in case (true, true) do
19               CYCLICSHIFTLEFT₄(k, k₂, g, g₂);  k₂ := k₂ + 1;  g₂ := g₂ − 1
20           in case (true, false) do
21               CYCLICSHIFTLEFT₃(k, g, g₂);  g₂ := g₂ − 1
22           in case (false, true) do
23               CYCLICSHIFTLEFT₃(k, k₂, g);  k₂ := k₂ + 1
24           in case (false, false) do
25               Swap A[k] and A[g]
26       end cases
27       k := k + 1;  g := g − 1
28   end while
29   return (k₂, k, g, g₂)
```

Pivot Sampling.   Choosing pivots from a small sample is the improvement with the arguably highest potential. We present our generalized sampling scheme in Section 4.4 below.

Truncating Recursion.   Quicksort is very efficient on moderate-size inputs, but for very small subarrays, other methods are indeed superior. It is thus helpful to truncate the recursion at some threshold size w and sort subarrays of at most w elements with another sorting algorithm. We will assume in the analysis that w is a fixed constant. s-way partitioning does not make sense if the subarray is so small that we cannot even select our $s-1$ pivots. It is therefore convenient to require $w \geqslant s-1$. If we additionally choose pivots from a sample of size k, we assume $w \geqslant k$.

Insertionsort has consistently been found a good general-purpose choice as the base case sorting method [170, 161]. Other methods are also used successfully, recently also exploiting modern hardware features like vectorized instructions and predicated instructions [68, 33].

Manual Stacks and Logarithmic Space.   Quicksort is most conveniently stated using recursive procedure calls, but if memory is scarce, a manually handled explicit stack allows more economic storage usage.

The first important observation is that Quicksort is *tail-recursive:* nothing remains to be done for the current call after its child recursive calls have returned. There is no need then to keep memory blocked for the current stack frame, i.e., the local variables and return address, during execution of these child recursive calls.

With tail-recursion elimination and reordering of recursive calls, Quicksort can be implemented with only logarithmic stack height in the worst case. This has already been pointed out by Hoare [82] when he initially presented Quicksort and is exemplified in detail in Algorithm Q of Knuth [103] for single-pivot Quicksort.

The proof is often not even spelled out as it is quite elementary, see e.g., Exercise 5.2.2-20 of Knuth [103]). For s-way Quicksort, a similar result must be possible, but I could not find a source where this is made explicit. So even though it might be considered below the threshold of originality, I include here an extended argument for s-way Quicksort.

Fact 4.1 (Logarithmic Stack for s-Way Quicksort): Assume we maintain a stack of yet-to-be-sorted subranges (i, j) of the array. At the beginning of a partitioning step, we remove its pair from the stack and at the end, we push the s pairs for the created segments onto the stack. The order in which the segments are pushed is arbitrary except for the largest segment, which is always pushed on the stack first. Then the height of the stack never exceeds $\max\{0, (s-1)\lceil \mathrm{ld}(n/w)\rceil\}$, where recursion is truncated at ranges of size w. ◄

Proof: Let us denote the maximal stack height for sorting n elements as described in the claim by h_n and the bound by $f(n) = \max\{0, (s-1)\lceil \mathrm{ld}(n/w)\rceil\}$. We prove the claim by induction. If $n \leqslant w$, no partitioning and no recursion takes place, so $h_n = 0 \leqslant f(n)$.

For $n > w$, we partition the array into s parts and push all but one segment on the stack, starting with the largest one. The sth segment would be pushed and removed again immediately after anyway, so it does not contribute to stack height. As $f(n) \geqslant s - 1$ for $n > w$, we are in accordance with the bound. Now consider any of the segments that are now recursively partitioned.

The first case is that this segment is not the largest one. Then its length is at most $\frac{n-(s-1)}{2} \leqslant n/2$. By the induction hypothesis, we have $h_{n/2} \leqslant f(n/2) = f(n) - (s - 1)$. (The latter holds for $n > w$.) Together with the at most $s - 1$ segments still waiting to be handled, we never exceed stack size $f(n)$.

The second case is that we are now sorting the largest segment which has at most $n - (s - 1)$ elements. By assumption, all other top-level segments have been sorted by now already, and the stack is empty. That means, we only need a stack as high as required to sort the largest segment in isolation, which is by induction hypothesis at most $f(n - (s - 1)) \leqslant f(n)$.

So we never needed more than $f(n)$ stack entries, which concludes the inductive step and thus the proof. ∎

Remark: The given bound is almost tight for the given stack organization for large n, as the segment sizes assumed in the proof are attainable. We can improve the constant of proportionality if we sort subranges by size decreasingly, i.e., put the largest first onto the stack, then the second-largest etc. We can then show that a stack of size

$$\tilde{f}(n) \;=\; \max\left\{0, \frac{s-1}{\lfloor \mathrm{ld}(s) \rfloor} \lceil \mathrm{ld}(n/w) \rceil\right\} \tag{4.1}$$

actually suffices: As in the proof above, consider the situation for the subproblems of the topmost partitioning step. We now sort the rth largest subproblem of these, for $r = 1, \ldots, s$. The $r - 1$ larger subproblems are still present in the stack, so that we may use a stack of size at most $\tilde{f}(n) - (r - 1)$ for sorting the rth largest subproblem. This subrange can contain at most $\frac{n-(s-1)}{r} \leqslant \frac{n}{r}$ elements, for which we need at most $\tilde{f}(n/r)$ stack height by the inductive hypothesis. It is now easy to verify that indeed $\tilde{f}(n/r) \leqslant \tilde{f}(n) - (r - 1)$ for $r \geqslant 1$ and $n \geqslant 1$, so the claim follows by induction. ◄

4.3 Generic One-Pass Partitioning

The partitioning schemes described above cover all Quicksort variants that have been in wide-spread productive use. All of those have been analyzed mathematically, each one separately. Although they differ in details, when it comes to the average-case analysis, what unites them is stronger than what divides them. It is the purpose of this work to present a single framework to unite all the solitary analyses. The generic analysis will also cover as of yet unknown partitioning schemes sharing the same common features, and so will make analyses of future partitioning schemes much easier.

In this section, we describe the realm of analysis in this work: *generic one-pass partitioning*. It is a synthesis of the ideas underlying all of the aforementioned partitioning methods, which are recovered as special cases.

Common Properties: One-Pass and In-Place.   The main characteristic of all partitioning methods above is that partitioning proceeds in a *one-pass* fashion: we "consider" each element of the array exactly once and after all n elements have been considered, partitioning is finished.

It is not easy to come up with a sensible definition of what exactly "consider" means in this case, and we will not try to formalize the notion here. Note that an element might be further moved around in the array after it has officially been considered, in particular after it has been determined into which segment an element belongs. Such later movements happen when we have to make room for another element that is currently under consideration. For any given partitioning method, it is usually easy to say whether it proceeds in one pass over the array or not. A few notable examples for methods that do not work in one pass are discussed in Section 4.6. We will not cover those in our analysis.

The second common characteristic of all previous methods is that they partition the array *in place:* they use only a constant amount of temporary storage no matter how large the array is. I consider this a vital requirement for a good practical sorting algorithm. Quicksort needs logarithmic space even with in-place partitioning, but this is tolerable.

4.3.1 Master-Pivot Schemes

To describe our generic algorithm in detail, we introduce some notation that will also simplify language later in the analysis. In the main text, we successively add to this body of notations as we make our idea of generic one-pass partitioning more and more specific. Where it would have overly obscured explanations and formulas, we will first ignore later generalizations, e.g., the case of master-segment methods. I tried to meticulously collect all notations used in this work in Appendix A with definitions covering all cases. Code and figures also match these general definitions.

Memory Layout of Partitioning.   Assume we want to partition an array into a fixed given number, $s \geqslant 2$, of segments, which is the first parameter of the procedure. The segments are defined by $s - 1$ pivot values $P_1, \dots, P_{s-1}$. How can this be done in-place and in one pass? Without scratch memory to hold elements, we have to establish the partition by maintaining a partition for a *subset* of the array, to which we add elements step by step. To be able to do so, we certainly need a way to remember the boundaries between all segments.

As the sizes of the segments are not known a priori, the only method avoiding excessive swapping at the end is to grow segments from the ends of the array inwards; these are the only fixed points that we have. Therefore, we will have one contiguous region in the middle of the array that contains the elements yet to be partitioned, whereas partially filled segments will grow outside-in. Needless to say that we arrange the segments in order: the smallest elements to the left, followed by the segment of the second-smallest class etc.

How many partial segments should we grow from the left end and how many from the right? A priori it is not clear how to answer that question, so we leave this an open

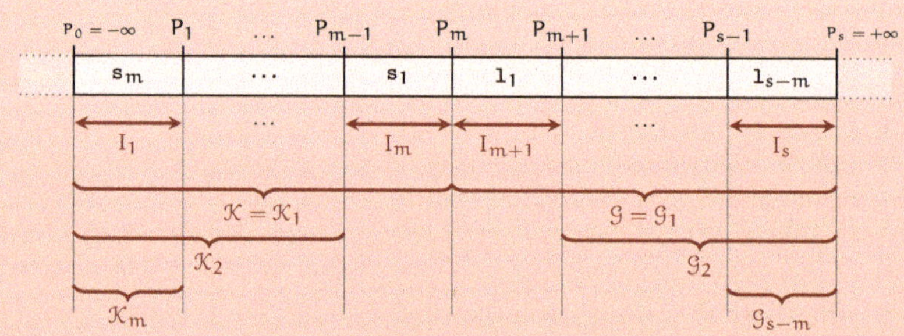

Figure 16: State of the array after partitioning. The figure illustrates naming conventions for pivots P_r (shown at their final position), classes s_i, l_j, segment sizes I_r (to be introduced in Section 5.2) and index ranges $\mathcal{K}_i$ and $\mathcal{G}_j$ for generic one-pass partitioning in the master-pivot case.

parameter of generic one-pass partitioning. We assume here for the moment that any segment is either a left or a right segment, i.e., we consider only *master-pivot methods*. In Section 4.3.2, we treat *master-segment schemes,* where the innermost segment is growing from both ends, coalescing only at the very end of the partitioning process.

Naming Convention for Index Variables and Classes.   Let us denote the number of left segments by m. We will also call m the *meeting point* of the left and right parts, more precisely, we put the mth pivot P_m at the boundary between left and right part after partitioning, and we call P_m the *master pivot*. The meeting point m can be any integer between 0 and s, endpoints included; the corner cases of only left or only right segments are explicitly allowed. If there are m segments on the left, $s - m$ segments grow from the right.

We use the m index variables $k_1, \ldots, k_m$ to mark the right boundaries of the m left segments. Likewise, the $s - m$ variables $g_1, \ldots, g_{s-m}$ demarcate the left boundaries of the $s - m$ right segments. The index variables are numbered in *inside-out order*, i.e., k_1 and g_1 are the two indices that eventually meet, the leftmost index is always k_m, the rightmost g_{s-m}. As k_1 and g_1 are the main indices that advance into the area of unclassified elements, we abbreviate them as $k \equiv k_1$ and $g \equiv g_1$, dropping the subscript. We already follow this somewhat unorthodox naming conventions for Algorithms $2-8$. The reader might find it helpful to consult these again.

In s-way partitioning, each element belongs to one of s different *classes*. Its class determines which segment an element is put in. We think of the classes as *labels* that are assigned to elements when they are *classified*. For classic Quicksort, elements can either be small or large, relative to the single pivot. In dual-pivot Quicksort, the classes are called small, medium and large in previous work. This convention does not scale up to larger s, though.

We will instead call all classes for left segments *small*, and all classes for right segments *large*. To further differentiate, we number the small and large classes, again in *inside-out order*. For example in Waterloo partitioning, we have $s = 4$ classes, $m = 2$ of which are small. In sorted order, the classes are *small of order 2, small of order 1, large of order 1* and *large of order 2*. In symbols, we call these classes s_2, s_1, l_1 and l_2, respectively.

If U is small of order 2, we write this as $U \in s_2$ etc. We mostly think of the classes as mere labels assigned to elements; if we want to interpret classes sets of values to which this label can be assigned, we can state $s_i \subseteq [P_{m-i}, P_{m-i+1}]$ for $1 \leqslant i \leqslant m$ and $l_j \subseteq [P_{m+j-1}, P_{m+j}]$ for $1 \leqslant i \leqslant s - m$. The question to which class the pivots themselves belong is discussed below. The vector of all classes is written as

$$\mathcal{C} = (s_m, \ldots, s_1, l_1, \ldots, l_{s-m}). \tag{4.2}$$

Finally, we use the *position sets* $\mathcal{K}_i$ resp. $\mathcal{G}_j$, which are the set of array indices accessed through index k_i resp. g_j for $i = 1, \ldots, m$ and $j = 1, \ldots, s - m$. They are also depicted in Figure 16. We abbreviate the two most important of those: $\mathcal{K} = \mathcal{K}_1$ and $\mathcal{G} = \mathcal{G}_1$.

Invariant for Partitioning. The actual partitioning process is governed by the memory layout sketched above. Amidst partitioning, the array is kept invariably in the form shown in Figure 17.

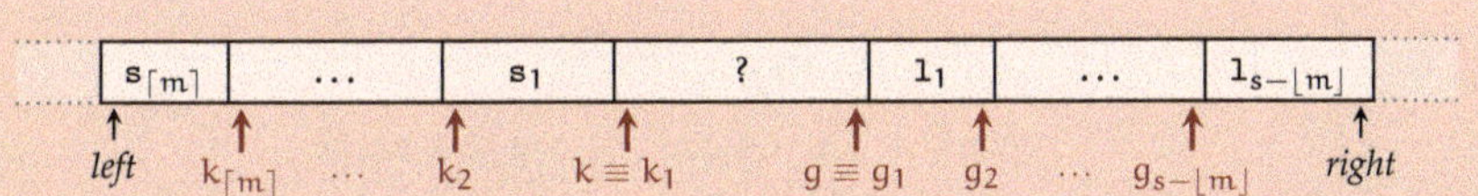

Figure 17: Invariant for Algorithm 9. Initially, the "?-area" covers all of A; partitioning is finished, when it has been consumed completely. The k_i-indices are initially equal to *left*, and all g_j-indices are initially *right*; partitioning is finished when k and g have met. Note that in the master-segment case, s_1 and l_1 are actually the same, and k and g meet somewhere inside the master segment.

Structure of Code. We are finally in the position to fix the structure of the partitioning procedure. The complete code is given in Algorithm 9. We use an outer loop that continues until the main indices k and g have met, that is until the area of unclassified elements has been consumed entirely. Two inner loops advance the indices. The first one handles the left side, the second one the right side.

The first inner loop, the k-loop, starts by classifying the element $A[k]$. If it is small of some order i, $A[k] \in s_i$, we do a rotational swap to put this element into its corresponding segment. In doing so we move all small segments with lesser order one position to the right: it is a cyclic shift to the right, see Figure 18. This is needed to make room in segment s_i to accommodate for the new element. Then we can advance k and repeat the procedure until $A[k]$ is instead large of order j, $A[k] \in l_j$. Then we pass control to the second loop.

Algorithm 9: Generic s-way one-pass partitioning (abstract pseudocode).

$\textsc{Partition}_{s,m}(\mathbf{A}, \textit{left}, \textit{right}, \mathbf{P})$

1 $k \equiv k_1, k_2, \ldots, k_{\lceil m \rceil} := \textit{left}, \qquad g \equiv g_1, g_2, \ldots, g_{s-\lfloor m \rfloor} := \textit{right}$
   // k and g will point at elements next to be classified.
2 **while** $k \leqslant g$
3   **while** *true*
4         $c_k :=$ classify $A[k]$ with λ_k w.r.t. $\mathbf{P}$
5   **if** $c_k == \mathbf{s}_i$ for some $i \in [1..\lceil m \rceil]$
6            $\textsc{CyclicShiftLeft}_i(A; k, k_2, \ldots, k_i)$
7   Increment $k, k_2, \ldots, k_i$ by one each.
8   **if** $k > g$ **then break** outer while **end if**
9   **else break** inner while **end if**
10   **end while** k-loop

   // We know here: $A[k]$ is already classified as $\mathbf{l}_j$ for some $j \in [1..s - \lfloor m \rfloor]$.

11   **while** *true*
12   **if** $k == g$ // Special case: $A[g]$ is last element to put in place.
13   Set j so that $c_k == \mathbf{l}_j$.
14           $\textsc{CyclicShiftLeft}_j(A; g, g_2, \ldots, g_j)$
15   Decrement $g \equiv g_1, g_2, \ldots, g_j$ by one each.
16   **break** outer while
17   **end if**
18        $c_g :=$ classify $A[g]$ with λ_g w.r.t. $\mathbf{P}$
19   **if** $c_g == \mathbf{l}_j$ for some $j \in [1..s - \lfloor m \rfloor]$
20           $\textsc{CyclicShiftLeft}_j(A; g, g_2, \ldots, g_j)$
21   Decrement $g, g_2, \ldots, g_j$ by one each.
22   **else break** inner while **end if**
23   **end while** g-loop

   // We know: c_k is large and c_g is small $\rightsquigarrow$ ∞-shape rotation.
24   Set i and j such that $c_k == \mathbf{l}_j$ and $c_g == \mathbf{s}_i$.
25    $\textsc{CyclicShiftLeft}_{i+j}(A; k, k_2, \ldots, k_i, g, g_2, \ldots, g_j)$
26   Increment $k, k_2, \ldots, k_i$ by one each.
27   Decrement $g, g_2, \ldots, g_j$ by one each.
28 **end while**
29 **return** $(k_{\lceil m \rceil}, k_{\lceil m \rceil - 1}, \ldots, k_1, g_1, g_2, \ldots, g_{s - \lfloor m \rfloor})$

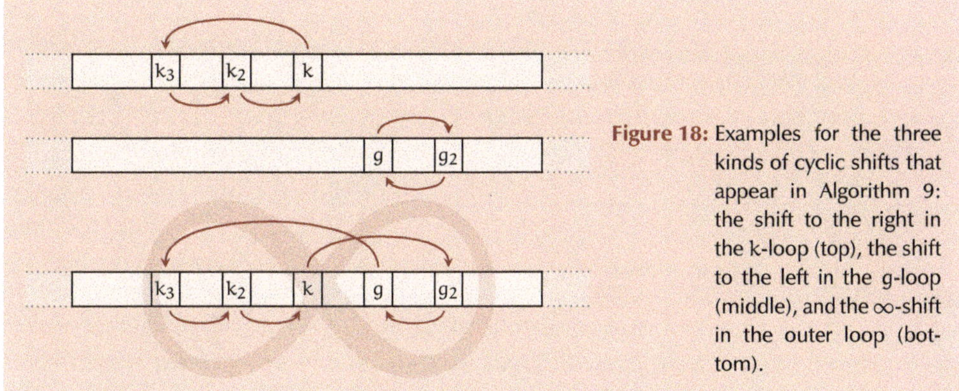

Figure 18: Examples for the three kinds of cyclic shifts that appear in Algorithm 9: the shift to the right in the k-loop (top), the shift to the left in the g-loop (middle), and the ∞-shift in the outer loop (bottom).

The second inner loop, the g-loop, determines the class of $A[g]$. If $A[g] \in 1_j$, we put it to its segment with cyclic shift to the left, decrement g and repeat. Once $A[g] \in s_i$, we move both $A[k]$ and $A[g]$ to their corresponding segments on the opposite side, again making room by moving intermediate segments towards the middle, see line 25. The rotation applied in this case has the twisted shape of the ∞-symbol, so we call this operation ∞-shift. Then we continue in the outer loop.

A Special Case of Termination.   The if-statement at the beginning of the g-loop (line 12) takes care of the special case that we found a large element in $A[k]$, but there is no small element left to participate as its partner in an ∞-shift. In such a case, we handle this element separately with an ordinary cyclic shift. Note that the outer loop is always exited afterwards, so this case can occur at most once.

Partitioning could be made to work without explicitly dealing with this special case, but then the last element would sometimes be classified *twice*, a nuisance for the analysis I prefer to avoid. Double classifications do occur, e.g., in YBB partitioning, and that has complicated its precise analysis [186]. When classifications are very costly, e.g., for large values of s or complicated comparison functions, it might also pay in terms of running time to avoid the unnecessary classifications.

There are several exit points for the outer loop in Algorithm 9, and it might be helpful to make explicit under which conditions each is taken. We have the following cases:

1 k becomes equal to g in the k-loop, and $A[k]$ is small.
Then we exit the outer loop via the break statement in line 8.

2 k becomes equal to g in the k-loop, and $A[k]$ is large.
Then we leave the k-loop (via line 9) with $k = g$ and immediately enter the special-case handler in line 12. We leave the outer loop through the break statement in line 16.

3 g becomes equal to k in the g-loop.

Then $A[g] = A[k]$ has already been classified as large, and the special-case handler kicks in. We leave the outer loop via line 16.

4 k and g cross each other simultaneously after an ∞-shift.

In this case, we exit the outer loop via the ordinary exit condition. For this situation to occur, we must have had $k = g - 1$ before the ∞-shift.

(We cannot have had $k = g$ since we would have ended up in cases 2 or 3 then.)

No matter which exit point is taken, at the end we have $k = g + 1$, and in particular, the invariant shown in Figure 17 still holds with an empty ?-area.

Unidirectional Cases. We include the cases $m = 0$ and $m = s$, where we do not have a crossing-pointer scheme at all, and the meeting point is on one of the two imaginary pivots P_0 resp. P_s, i.e., at the left resp. right boundary of the array.

Consider for example $m = s$. Lomuto's single-pivot partitioning scheme (Algorithm 3) is an example of such an algorithm, corresponding to $s = m = 2$. Formally, we then have zero index variables on the right side, but Algorithm 9 accesses g even for $m = s$. Our code still works correctly if we interpret g as an *alias* for *right* in this case; it is initialized to *right* and never changed afterwards.

For $m = s$, the whole partitioning is done in the k-loop; we only exit it via line 8 when k has reached *right* $= g$. A real implementation with these parameters would of course eliminate all the dead code after the k-loop. It is good to see we have found one abstract formulation that covers all possible choices of parameters.

Comparison Trees. There is a final aspect that we did not yet address: how to classify? We have to determine for each element U to which of the s classes it belongs. Assuming distinct elements for the moment, we do so by comparing U to pivot elements until we find an index r with $P_r < U < P_{r+1}$. The degrees of freedom in ordering these pivot comparisons are the most overlooked feature of multiway Quicksort; probably because in single-pivot Quicksort there is no such freedom: we simply compare each element to the single pivot. The new possibilities in multiway Quicksort were only very recently addressed by Aumüller et al. [10].

For our generic one-pass partitioning, we have two parameters: $\lambda_k, \lambda_g \in \Lambda_s$, the *comparison trees*, where Λ_s is the set of extended binary tree over s leaves. If we fill the $s - 1$ internal nodes of such a binary tree in in-order with our $s - 1$ pivots $P_1, \ldots, P_{s-1}$, and label the s leaves from left to right with our s classes, we obtain a bona fide *binary search tree (BST)*. Classification of an element U then consists of searching U in this BST. If the search ends in a leaf with label c, the class of U is c. We write this as $c(U) = c$.

Classes and Classification in Presence of Equal Keys. In the analysis of Algorithm 9, we will assume distinct elements, but a sensible sorting method of course has to cope with equal elements. In Chapter 8, we discuss partitioning methods that treat elements equal to one of the pivots as a class of their own; such methods are called *fat-pivot* schemes. For

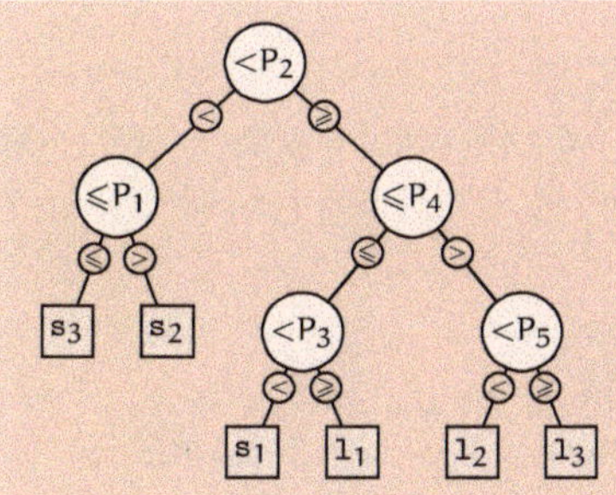

Figure 19: An exemplary comparison tree for $s = 6$ and $m = 3$ with different tie-breaking rules in the nodes. This tree induces the partition $s_3 \mathbin{\dot\cup} s_2 \mathbin{\dot\cup} s_1 \mathbin{\dot\cup} l_1 \mathbin{\dot\cup} l_2 \mathbin{\dot\cup} l_3$ of the universe with
$s_3 = (-\infty, P_1]$, $s_2 = (P_1, P_2)$, $s_1 = [P_2, P_3)$,
$l_1 = [P_3, P_4]$, $l_2 = (P_4, P_5)$, and $l_3 = [P_5, +\infty)$.

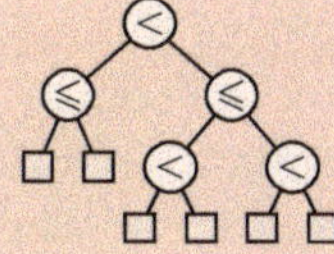

Figure 20: The comparison tree of Figure 19 in compact notation. The labels of the nodes are fully determined by $s = 6$ and $m = 3$, so there is no need to give them explicitly.

the remainder of this work, we confine ourselves to methods that only use the s classes introduces above; see Equation (4.2).

To deal with elements equal to one of the pivots, we require a tie breaking rule in each internal node of a comparison tree: in λ_k and λ_g, each node has to be marked with either "$<$" or "$\leqslant$", indicating that the left branch is to be pursued either for strictly smaller elements only, or for elements less or equal than the corresponding pivot; if that condition is not met, we pursue the right branch. With that convention, searching any element U in a comparison tree always ends in a leaf and returns one well-defined class $c(U)$. An example of a comparison tree is given in Figure 19; we will in the following also use the compact notation shown in Figure 20.

Note that the same element U might be assigned to different classes for different tie breaking rules, if U equals one of the pivots. We remark that such a difference is explicitly allowed for λ_k and λ_g. This means that even for $s = 2$, where only one tree shape is possible, we have two options for the single comparison: we can ask $U < P$ or $U \leqslant P$. The attentive reader might have noticed that we already used the two different types of comparisons in classic Quicksort (Algorithm 2).

The code in Algorithm 9 works just fine in that case, as well; since all elements are classified exactly once, either with λ_k or λ_g, we can consider classification as a black box. From the point of view of Algorithm 9, we do not notice if the two classification methods would have disagreed over the class of a certain element. In the invariant in Figure 17, we marked segments with their corresponding classes, which means that a segment contains only elements which have been assigned the corresponding label.

The resulting segmentation of the array is in general not a partition in the set-theoretic sense of the values in the universe since elements equal to pivots can end up in any of the two neighboring segments. For Quicksort this weaker form of a partition is fully sufficient; it is in fact to be encouraged: For many equal elements the possibility to spread equals out to two segments can mean the difference between quadratic and linearithmic complexity; see Section 8.1.1. This is why comparisons in classic Quicksort are chosen as in Algorithm 2.

To have a concrete algorithm to work with, let us fix a tie breaking rule for generic partitioning that generalizes this behavior. Unless explicitly stated otherwise, we always assume this rule in the following.

> ***Tie-breaking Rule:***
> *All nodes in λ_k are marked as '$<$', and all nodes in λ_g are marked as '$\leqslant$', i.e., elements equal to a pivot are always assigned to the smaller class in λ_k and to the larger class in λ_g.*

This rule distributes duplicates of pivots roughly equally over two segments, leading in particular to efficient behavior on inputs with all elements equal since it stops scanning in the k- and g-loop as soon as possible. This makes sure we do not go quadratic on inputs with many equals. The other extreme, making all nodes in λ_k '$\leqslant$' and all in λ_g '$<$' would result in a degenerate partition for such inputs and is clearly not desirable. A mixture of both extremes might have certain benefits.

Since we focus on random permutations in this work where no duplicates occur, all these variants behave the same. And if equal keys are to be expected, a fat-pivot scheme as discussed in Chapter 8 is superior to any of the above. We will thus not further explore the question of how to best assign '$<$'- and '$\leqslant$'-nodes in comparison trees.

4.3.2 Master-Segment Schemes

Some partitioning algorithms have a segment that is scanned from *both* left and right, so that the meeting point of k and g is somewhere in the middle of this segment. We call this segment the *master segment*. Sedgewick's dual-pivot partitioning method, Algorithm 6, is an example of this type: the two outer segments are scanned exclusively by one index, but k and g meet somewhere *inside* the middle segment.

We formally include this possibility in our generic partitioning scheme by allowing non-integral values: $m \in \{1, \ldots, s\} - \frac{1}{2}$. The Sedgewick dual-pivot method corresponds to $s = 3$ and $m = 1.5$, where *one and a half segments* grow from the left (and another one and a half from the right).

We name the classes of elements so that for non-integral m the two inner classes coincide: $s_1 = l_1$. When convenient, we refer to such elements also as *medium* elements and denote their class by $m = s_1 = l_1$. The medium elements are those that go to the master segment. Figure 21 shows the state of the array after partitioning with the corresponding naming conventions for indices and pivots. The master segment is the $\lceil m \rceil$th segment (counting from the left), and contains elements that lie between $P_{\lfloor m \rfloor}$ and $P_{\lceil m \rceil}$. The vector of classes is then

$$\mathfrak{c} \;=\; \begin{cases} (s_m, \ldots, s_1, l_1, \ldots, l_{s-m}), & \text{for } m \in [0..s]; \\[2mm] (s_{\lceil m \rceil}, \ldots, s_2, m, l_2, \ldots, l_{s-\lfloor m \rfloor}), & \text{for } m \in [1..s] - \frac{1}{2}. \end{cases} \qquad (4.3)$$

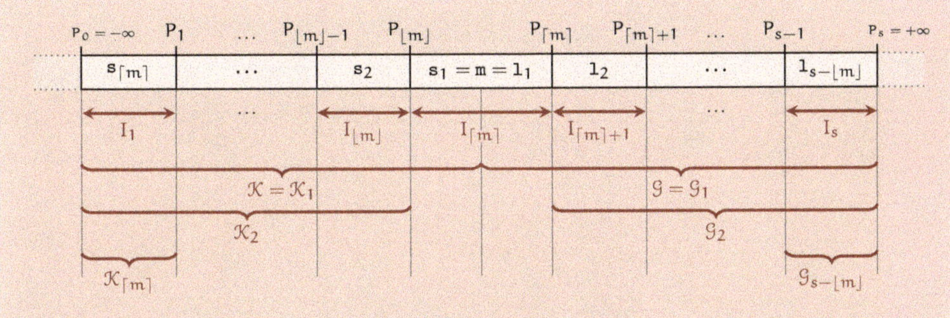

Figure 21: State of the array after partitioning in the master-segment case (cf. Figure 16.

With these conventions, the pseudocode in Algorithm 9 remains valid: we have a single formulation for both master-pivot and master-segment methods. Let us clarify that the condition $c_k == s_i$ in line 5 is considered fulfilled when $c_k = m$; in this case we have $i = 1$. Likewise, the condition $c_g == 1_j$ in line 19 is fulfilled when $c_g = m$, with $j = 1$. If you like, the medium class m is a wildcard that can play the role of both s_1 and 1_1, whichever is needed.

Our syntactical choice $m = 1.5$ might be mistaken to imply that the indices k and g in Sedgewick's algorithm meet exactly in the middle of the second segment; this is of course not the case. It depends on the classes of elements in that range of the array how far k and g proceed. I discussed the meeting point in detail for the special case of Sedgewick's algorithm in my master's thesis [182]. We will extend this in Section 5.5.2.

Master-segment methods might appear wasteful in their use of two indices to delimit the same segment. They can however be a natural choice, e.g., for symmetry reasons if s is odd. It is not a priori clear whether master-segment schemes are inferior in general, so we retain them as possible choice for the analysis.

4.3.3 Known Methods as Generic One-Pass Instances

Now that we have introduced generic one-pass partitioning, we can show how the methods from Section 4.2 fit into the framework. The parameter choices corresponding to these methods are shown in Table 1.

Upon inserting these values in Algorithm 9, we will *not* precisely obtain the hand-crafted code we presented earlier. For certain parameter choices, the generic code can be simplified, e.g., for Lomuto's partitioning method, where the g-loop is never executed. A subtler difference is that the hand-written multiway partitioning methods do not classify elements completely at one location in the code, but rather mix the comparisons with different pivots with code to move elements around. For example, Waterloo partitioning postpones comparisons with P_3 for elements that are reached by k until after the second inner loop (see line 17 in Algorithm 8).

Table 1: Famous Quicksort variants as special cases of generic s-way one-pass partitioning.

Method	Code	s	m	λ_k	λ_g
Classic	Algorithm 2	2	1		
Lomuto	Algorithm 3	2	2		
YBB	Algorithm 4	3	2	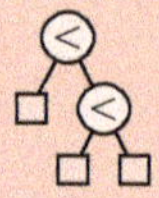	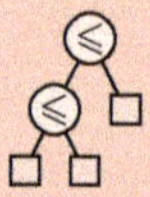
Sedgewick	Algorithm 6	3	1.5	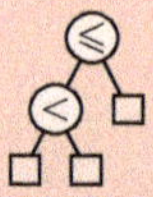	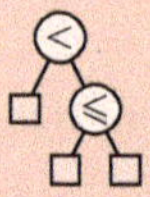
Kciwegdes	Algorithm 7	3	1.5	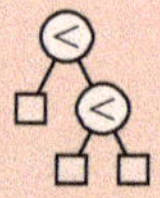	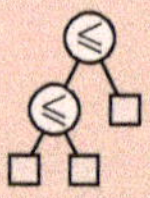
Waterloo	Algorithm 8	4	2	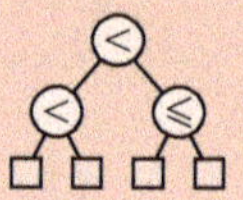	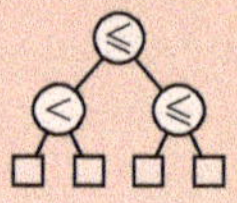

It is therefore clear that actual running times and detailed cost measures like the precise number of executed instructions will be slightly different for the methods presented in Section 4.2 when compared with generic one-pass partitioning with the parameter choices of Table 1. For the cost measures we consider in this work, though, they will perform exactly the same: the numbers of comparisons, scanned elements, swaps resp. cyclic shifts, write accesses to the array, and branch misses at comparison branches are cost measures abstract enough to not be influenced by minor differences in coding style.

4.4 Choosing Pivots From a Sample

A good partitioning method efficiently divides the array into segments for recursive calls, but it can only *react* to a given selection of pivots: if in the worst case, all elements fall into the same class, there is nothing a partitioning method could do about it. A good Quicksort implementation has to choose its pivots wisely.

4.4.1 Generalized Pivot Sampling

The question what exactly *wisely* means has no simple answer. We try to approach the answer from the analytic side, and leave the pivot selection method parametric. For consistency with existing literature [162, 77, 182], we use the *pivot-sampling parameter* $t = (t_1, \ldots, t_s) \in \mathbb{N}_0^s$ to specify the generic pivot sampling process. We remark in particular that our sampling scheme is precisely the same as the one used by Hennequin [77]. In some respects, the choice of this parameter is a little unfortunate and we will use $\sigma = (\sigma_1, \sigma_2, \ldots, \sigma_s) = t + 1$ whenever more convenient.

The $s - 1$ pivots $P_1 \leqslant P_2 \leqslant \ldots P_{s-1}$, are selected from a sample of $k = \Sigma\sigma - 1$ elements from A. For notational convenience we write $\kappa := k + 1 = \Sigma\sigma$; as for σ and $t + 1$, we use κ instead of $k + 1$ whenever more convenient.

The pivots are chosen as *quantiles* of the sample, according to the *quantiles vector* $\tau = \sigma/\kappa = \frac{t+1}{k+1}$: P_1 is the τ_1-quantile of the sample, P_1 the $(\tau_1 + \tau_2)$-quantile, and so on. P_{s-1} is the element with relative rank $\tau_1 + \cdots + \tau_{s-1} = 1 - \tau_s$. Note that $\Sigma\tau = 1$ by definition, so that τ is in fact a κ-discretized distribution in the sense of Definition 2.51 (page 89). The absolute ranks of the pivots are similarly described by σ: P_1 has rank σ_1 in the sample, P_2 has rank $\sigma_1 + \sigma_2$ etc.

We call the $k - (s - 1)$ sample elements which are not selected as pivots *sampled-out* elements. We assume they are excluded from partitioning since their classes are known after sampling anyway; hence the name. All elements that have not been part oft the sample are *ordinary* elements. In terms of t, we have t_1 sampled-out elements smaller than P_1; t_s is the number of sampled-out elements greater than P_{s-1} and, in general, t_i is the number of sampled-out elements between P_{i-1} and P_i, for $2 \leqslant i \leqslant s - 1$.

If no sampling is used then $k = s - 1$ and $t = 0$, the vector of s zeros. Note that $\tau = (\frac{1}{s}, \ldots, \frac{1}{s})$ is well-defined in this case. Median-of-three sampling for single-pivot Quicksort corresponds to $t = (1, 1)$, median-of-five would be $t = (2, 2)$. Similarly, the tertiles-of-five scheme for dual-pivot Quicksort has $t = (1, 1, 1)$.

All these sampling schemes pick pivots equidistantly from the sample and have $\tau = (\frac{1}{s}, \ldots, \frac{1}{s})$. A sampling parameter $t = (0, 1, 2)$ entails pivots with a systematic skew towards smaller elements. Here $\tau = (\frac{1}{6}, \frac{1}{3}, \frac{1}{2})$ and the expected value for the large pivot will be the median of the array.

Our notation has the advantage that we often desire to separate the influence of the quantiles vector τ and the sample size k, which we can now conveniently do. For example, we might want to hold τ fixed and observe the effect of varying k. We have to make sure that τ is $(k + 1)$-discretized, or define some rounding rule, but we have a clear separation of concepts. t specifies τ and k in one shot.

4.4.2 Random-Parameter Pivot Sampling

Allowing arbitrary quantiles of a sample already gives a lot of freedom, but it does not cover all sensible ways of how to select pivots. A widely used method in practice is the *ninther*, which is the median of three elements, each of which is the median of three other elements. It is a good approximation for the median of nine elements, but can be computed much more efficiently.

The ninther actually gives the exact median with probability $\frac{4}{7}$ if all permutations of the sample are equally likely; with probability $\frac{3}{14}$ each, the ninther is the forth or sixth largest element instead [49]. Result-wise, ninther sampling is thus equivalent to first randomly selecting t to be any of the three sampling vectors $(3,5)$, $(4,4)$, and $(5,3)$ with probabilities $\frac{3}{14}$, $\frac{4}{7}$, resp. $\frac{3}{14}$, and then using generalized pivot sampling with the selected sampling parameter as described above.

Of course, we would not like to really execute the method this way, as that would be at least as expensive as selecting the precise median. But we know that selecting the ninther as median of medians has the very same outcome distribution, and for the analysis the two-phase definition turns out much more convenient.

Random-Parameter Pivot Sampling. As a general model, we allow the sampling parameter t to be a random variable, then written as T, with a given, fixed distribution over sampling parameters. In theory, even the used sample size can be random if T attains values corresponding to different sample sizes. For such methods it is unlikely to find efficient shortcuts similar to ninther sampling, but there is no need to exclude them from our analysis.

The idea of random-parameter pivot sampling has been studied before, see, e.g., the doctoral theses of Sedgewick [162] and Hennequin [77], but the connection to ninther sampling was not pointed out by them. Chern et al. [30] gave some more examples of interesting distributions for T.

As we will show in Section 6.4, we can compute the expected costs of Quicksort with random-parameter pivot sampling by taking the expectation over T in the final results for a fixed t; hence most of the time, we will work only with a fixed sampling parameter t.

4.5 Randomness Preservation in the Presence of Pivot Sampling

For the analysis of Quicksort via recurrence equations, it is vital to ensure that subproblems for recursive calls follow the same input distribution as the initial input. We get this guarantee if we never compare two non-pivot elements directly [76], so any sensible partitioning method, including all those above, preserves randomness on ordinary elements.

However, we violate this condition in the pivot sampling step! Sampled-out elements have been compared and ordered, but did not end up being pivots. We therefore have to take special care of them. There are several viable options:

(a) Copy the complete sample to scratch memory, select pivots there as described above, and then discard that array again.

   The original elements have remained untouched and thus random. As we would like to exclude pivot elements from partitioning, we also have to swap them to the ends of the array before partitioning.

(b) Explicitly shuffle sampled-out elements before sorting segments recursively.

(c) Ensure that sampled-out elements are part of the sample in recursive calls.

If we use a sorting algorithm that can skip presorted prefixes or suffixes, e.g., Insertionsort, we can still precisely analyze the costs of sorting the sample and short subarrays. Details on this approach are given in [136] in the context of YBB Quicksort. This approach is easily generalized to any number of pivots, if we choose $t_s + 1$ elements from the right end of the array and the $k - (t_s + 1)$ other ones from the left end of the array.

For this work, it does mostly not matter which method is used. We assume in the analysis that randomness is preserved.

Both options should be considered primarily relevant for analysis purposes. In fact, practical implementations do usually not preserve randomness precisely. As long as sample sizes are small, the non-randomness due to sampling is negligible. A partitioning method that systematically violates randomness among ordinary elements can however be problematic [101, 162].

4.6 Other Partitioning Methods

Generic one-pass partitioning methods cover most (practically) relevant partitioning schemes, but of course there are other conceivable methods that do not fit our template. We briefly list them here for completeness.

4.6.1 Removing Duplicates

In presence of many equal keys, it can pay off to choose a partitioning method that singles out all elements that are equal to one of the pivots. We can directly put such elements to their final position in the sorted list, removing them from subproblems for recursive calls. We discuss such *fat-pivot* partitioning methods in Chapter 8; if carefully designed, their performance on random permutations does not differ very much from methods that do not remove all duplicates. To a good extent, our results and conclusions on generic one-pass partitioning apply to fat-pivot methods as well.

4.6.2 Linear Memory Or Several Passes

Result-wise, multiway partitioning can be seen as equivalent to several rounds of binary partitioning: we first partition around one of the $s - 1$ pivots and obtain two segments. If there still is one, we select a smaller pivot and partition the left segment around this smaller pivot; likewise we partition the right segment around a larger pivot, and so on, until all pivots have been used.

Tan made this idea of *iterative binary partitioning* the basis of the Quicksort framework he studied in his Ph.D. thesis [173]. He required s to be a power of two, so that in each binary-partitioning round, we can select the median of the remaining pivots; e.g., for $s = 8$, we have three rounds: First, we partition the whole list around P_4, yielding two segments. In the second round, we partition the first segment around P_2 and the second around P_6, leaving us with four segments. In the third and last round, we partition these around P_1,

P_3, P_5, and P_7, respectively, and so obtain eight segments. Result-wise, this is the same as an eight-way partitioning method that produces the same eight segments in one step.

Tan's multiway partitioning method works in place if the binary partitioning method it is based on does so; but it does clearly not operate in one pass: it scans the whole array $ld(s)$ times, considering every single element exactly $ld(s)$ times.

As we will discuss in depth in Section 7.3, iterative binary partitioning is equivalent in terms of costs to a single-pivot method with a properly chosen sampling method for the pivot. I therefore consider it not very interesting.

◆ ◆ ◆

More tricks can be applied to speed up partitioning if ample scratch storage is available. The *super scalar sample sort* algorithm of Sanders and Winkel [157] determines the classes of all elements and stores them in an array. In a second step, we use this information to copy elements to a new array, directly at the correct position. Super scalar sample sort fully decouples classification of elements from rearrangement into segments. This allows code that fosters instruction-level parallelism and branch-free code using predicated instructions.

Aumüller et al. [10] consider two related two-pass methods which they call *Permute* and *Copy*. Instead of storing all classes, they only keep the sizes of segments, which suffices to govern rearrangement. Copy is essentially super scalar sample sort, only that classes are recomputed in the rearrangement phase. Permute achieves partitioning by following cycles of the needed permutation. The algorithm is much more contrived as for Copy, but does not need additional storage.

These methods have the potential to speed up Quicksort, if the need for extra memory can be tolerated. Their analysis is beyond the scope of this work.

4.6.3 Hennequin's Generalized Quicksort

In his doctoral thesis [77], Hennequin studied a parametric framework for Quicksort that is quite similar to generic one-pass partitioning: Hennequin also considers partitioning into s segments around $s - 1$ pivots chosen as order statistics from a sample according to generalized pivot-sampling parameter t. This model of Quicksort is often simply called *generalized Quicksort* in the analysis-of-algorithms literature. We will built on Hennequin's work on the analytical side, namely for (asymptotically) solving recurrences; his algorithmic framework is, however, somewhat limited:

▶ Hennequin did not specify an array-based implementation of partitioning, but rather considered a simple method working on linked lists; I sketched Hennequin's generic partitioning method in Algorithm 5 of my master's thesis. For such an implementation, cost measures like counting swaps, write accesses and scanned elements are meaningless; Hennequin always focused on comparisons.

▶ Hennequin fixed comparison trees as almost-complete binary search tree. His method naturally uses only one comparison tree.

4.6.4 Relation to Work of Aumüller et al.

Aumüller et al. also study multiway Quicksort with a generic partitioning method in a recent preprint [10]; most results already appear in Aumüller's doctoral thesis [7]. That work has been done in parallel and independently of my work on this thesis. Due to the similarity of the approaches a detailed breakdown of the differences is in order.

The algorithm $Exchange_k$ of Aumüller et al. [10] is essentially equivalent to our generic one-pass partitioning with parameters $s = k + 1$, $m = \lceil s/2 \rceil$ and $\lambda_k = \lambda_g$. Aumüller et al. fix the choice $m = \lceil s/2 \rceil$, which means in particular that they do not consider master-segment methods. They further assume for their detailed analysis that a *single* comparison tree is used for all classifications.

The latter has implications for the analysis: with a single comparison tree, the number of comparisons is a *linear* function of the quantiles vector τ, and it is independent of the sample size k; this is no longer the case for two different trees. For other cost measures, e.g., the number of assignments, Aumüller et al. also deal with nonlinear functions, but they only study these without pivot sampling. They thus confine the discussion of pivot sampling to cost functions that are linear in τ, which simplifies analysis and interpretation. We do the analysis including pivot sampling for all our cost measures including two trees.

Note that with respect to comparisons, Aumüller et al. also analyze the much more general situation of an arbitrary classification strategy; see their Section 3. However it is not clear how to simplify their generic result for our case of partitioning with two trees. Also, their result is only given for random pivots, i.e., without using sampling.

The reader is encouraged to consult their sections on the very interesting experimental results. Aumüller et al. not only compare bare running times, but they also evaluate performance-counter measurements of the number of cache misses and branch misses, leading to a variety of noteworthy observations, e.g., that the number of L1 cache misses are (approximately) proportional to the number of scanned elements. Experimental validations are beyond the scope of this work.

5 Analysis of Generic Partitioning

Contents

THE ANALYSIS OF QUICKSORT parallels its glorious structure: We first analyze partitioning in isolation in this chapter, then we use the result in a recursive description of overall costs in Chapter 6. The parameters of generic one-pass partitioning now become parameters of the analysis; we have

- the *number of segments* $s \in \mathbb{N}_{\geq 2}$,
- the *meeting point* $m \in \{0, 0.5, 1, 1.5, \ldots, s - 0.5, s\}$, where we operate either in master-pivot mode if $m \in [0..s]$ or in master-segment mode for $s \in [1..s] - \frac{1}{2}$, and
- the *comparison trees* $\lambda_k, \lambda_g \in \Lambda_s$.
- Additionally, we have the *pivot-sampling parameter* t that influences the used pivot values.

Our analysis is valid for any valid combination of parameter values. Orthogonal to these options for the algorithm, there are several models of costs discussed in Chapter 3. Each of these is a sensible model, it depends on the machine which one will be more relevant. It is likely that no single model will suffice to explain performance differences, and it is to be expected that cost models change over time; they already did so in the past. The framework of *element-wise charging schemes* developed below generalizes the common parts of the analysis for all our cost measures. The resulting unified analysis of Quicksort can be instantiated for future cost measures, as well.

5.1 Toll-Function Notation

Quicksort means partitioning and recursing. The work for partitioning is the toll we have to pay to get to the next level of the recursion tree. In the recurrence equation for total sorting costs, the partitioning costs are the toll we have to pay for unfolding the recurrence once. It has become customary to call the non-recursive part of such a recurrence equation *toll function*.

We will use toll function and partitioning costs interchangeably to denote the cost of one execution of Algorithm 9. We write $T_M(n)$ for these costs, where M is the used cost measure:

- $T_C(n)$ for the number of *comparisons*,
- $T_{SE}(n)$ for the number of *scanned elements*,
- $T_{WA}(n)$ for the number of *write accesses* to the array and
- $T_S(n)$ for the number of *swaps resp. cyclic shifts*.

Whenever n is clear from the context, we write T_M instead of $T_M(n)$.

5.2 Stochastic Description of Partitioning Under Pivot Sampling

In this chapter, we study the expected costs of partitioning n randomly permuted distinct elements $U_1, \ldots, U_n$, i.e., we assume the *uniform model*. As discussed in Section 3.1.1, for comparison-based sorting this is equivalent to the random-permutation model (Fact 3.1). Let us repeat this important fact: *The values that we sort are stochastically independent of each other* and they are all uniformly in $(0,1)$ distributed.

We will introduce several random variables and notations in the following; their definitions are collected for convenience in Appendix A, see Section A.5 (page 341).

5.2.1 Class Probabilities

Assume we have picked the $s-1$ pivots, $\mathbf{P} = (P_1, \ldots, P_{s-1})$, where $P_1 \leqslant P_2 \leqslant \cdots \leqslant P_{s-1}$. They are chosen from our input elements $U_1, \ldots, U_n \in (0,1)$ and so lie in $(0,1)$; it is therefore convenient to set $P_0 = 0$ and $P_s = 1$. (We used a different convention, namely $P_0 = -\infty$ and $P_s = +\infty$ in Chapter 4; we replace that convention in the uniform model.) The pivots partition the unit interval into s intervals of lengths given by the successive differences

$$\mathbf{D} \;=\; \left(P_1 - P_0, P_2 - P_1, \ldots, P_s - P_{s-1}\right) \tag{5.1}$$

of the pivots, see Figure 22. (The reader might have noticed by now that I prefer notation for *parts* over notation for *separators*.)

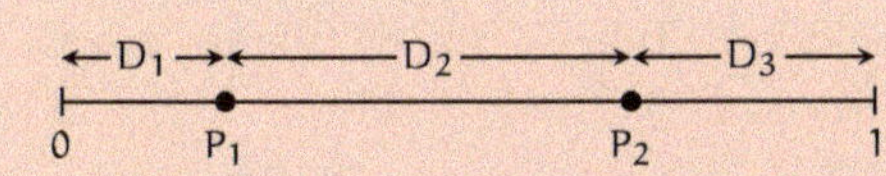

Figure 22: Partition of the unit interval induced by $\mathbf{P} = (P_1, P_2)$. The three intervals have lengths $\mathbf{D} = (P_1, P_2 - P_1, 1 - P_2)$.

If we *condition* on the pivot values, i.e., consider $\mathbf{P}$, or equivalently $\mathbf{D}$, fixed, an ordinary element U falls into the first segment, if $U \in (0, P_1)$, which happens with probability D_1, *independently* of all other ordinary elements. The same is true for all segments: the probability of an ordinary element to end up in the rth segment after partitioning is given precisely by D_r. It is a trivial consequence of our random model, but let us state this vital observation once again for reference.

Fact 5.1 (Class Probabilities): Let the input for generic one-pass partitioning be n i.i.d. $\mathcal{U}(0,1)$ variables. Conditional on $\mathbf{D}$, the probability of an ordinary element U to belong to a class $c \in \mathcal{C}$ is given by

$$\mathbb{P}[c(U) = c \mid \mathbf{D}] \;=:\; \mathbb{P}[c \mid \mathbf{D}] \;=\; D_{r(c)}, \tag{5.2}$$

where $r(c)$ denotes the index map $r : \mathcal{C} \to [1..s]$ given by

$$r(c) \;=\; \begin{cases} \lceil m \rceil - i + 1, & \text{for } c = s_i,\, 1 \leqslant i \leqslant \lceil m \rceil, \\ \lfloor m \rfloor + j, & \text{for } c = 1_j,\, 1 \leqslant j \leqslant s - \lfloor m \rfloor. \end{cases} \tag{5.3}$$

Conditional on $\mathbf{D}$, the classes of all ordinary elements are thus independent and identically distributed. ∎

Note that conditioning on $\mathbf{D}$ is important here: the unconditional class probabilities of two ordinary elements are *not* independent, exactly because they both depend on the pivot values.

5.2.2 Segment Sizes and Subproblem Sizes

Recall that we only have to partition the *ordinary* elements, i.e., the elements that have *not* been part of the sample. We denote by I_r the number of such ordinary elements that belong into the rth segment, $r = 1, \ldots, s$. The vector $\mathbf{I} = (I_1, \ldots, I_s)$ is the vector of *segment sizes* after partitioning (excluding sampled-out elements). We have $\Sigma\mathbf{I} = n - k$, the *number of ordinary elements*, which we will abbreviate as $\eta := n - k$.

> **In Lack of Letters.** I chose η and n because the two quantities are similar, so it makes sense to have their names look similar as well. Nevertheless I carefully distinguished them in the analysis. (Munsonius [132] independently used a corresponding convention for random split trees, which I take as sign that this naming scheme is acceptable.)

Recall from Fact 5.1 that the classes of ordinary elements are i.i.d. random variables if we condition on $\mathbf{D}$. The segment sizes $\mathbf{I}$ are then obtained as the collective outcome of η independent drawings from this distribution, so conditional on $\mathbf{D}$, $\mathbf{I}$ is multinomially $\mathrm{Mult}(\eta, \mathbf{D})$ distributed.

Subproblem Sizes. Before we call Quicksort recursively on the s segments, we have to add the sampled-out elements again. As discussed in Section 4.4, the number of sampled-out elements that belong to the rth segment is precisely t_r. Their number is not random. The number J_r of elements in the rth subproblem is thus $J_r = I_r + t_r$. So there is a close relation between the vectors of *segment* sizes $\mathbf{I}$ and *subproblem* sizes $\mathbf{J}$ that characterizes also the distribution of subproblem sizes: $\mathbf{J} = \mathbf{I} + t$.

5.2.3 Distribution of Pivot Values

The random variable $\mathbf{D} \in [0, 1]^s$ is a vector of *spacings* induced by order statistics from a sample of i.i.d. uniform variables in the unit interval, which is known to have a *Dirichlet* $\mathrm{Dir}(\sigma)$ distribution, see Proposition 2.28 (page 72):

$$\mathbf{D} \overset{\mathcal{D}}{=} \mathrm{Dir}(\sigma) \overset{\mathcal{D}}{=} \mathrm{Dir}(t + 1). \tag{5.4}$$

The distribution of $\mathbf{D}$ depends on the pivot-sampling scheme; this should not come as a surprise. It is however remarkable that the class probabilities and segment sizes $\mathbf{I}$ depend on t *only* via $\mathbf{D}$: The segment sizes $\mathbf{I}$ are multinomially distributed with a parameter that has a Dirichlet distribution. We know from Section 2.4.7 (page 78) that the unconditional distribution of $\mathbf{I}$ is then a Dirichlet-multinomial distribution,

$$\mathbf{I} \overset{\mathcal{D}}{=} \mathrm{DirMult}(\eta; \sigma). \tag{5.5}$$

> **Advertisement: The Strengths of the Uniform Model.**   The benefit of the i. i. d. uniform input model stems from exactly this fact that segment sizes I and class probabilities depend only indirectly on the pivot-sampling parameter t. We can determine partitioning costs conditional on D in a form that is valid for *any* pivot-sampling scheme. What is more, in determining the costs conditionally on D, we can exploit the (conditional) independence of classes.
>
> The classical approach to the analysis of Quicksort effectively conditions on the *ranks* of the pivots, or equivalently, the segment sizes I: if we assume the input to be a permutation of $\{1,\ldots,n\}$, the values and ranks of pivots *coincide*! Only with our alternative input model we can *decouple* pivot ranks from the pivot values.
>
> Apart from my work, this decoupling trick has (implicitly) been applied to the analysis of classic Quicksort earlier, e. g., by Neininger [139], but it had not yet gained currency.
>
> Of course there are other ways to analyze Quicksort. Our approach is admittedly somewhat heavier in notation and requires a little proficiency in stochastics. As long as we only use it to compute expected values, as in this work, it might feel like cracking a nut with a sledgehammer … but who does not like to operate a sledgehammer at times?

5.2.4 Random-Parameter Pivot Sampling

In the most general setting, we allow a *random* pivot-sampling parameter $T \in \mathbb{N}_0^s$ to be used, drawn according to some given distribution, see Section 4.4.2. In terms of the stochastic model, this merely means another level of mixing variables: D now is a mixture of Dirichlet variables and conditional on T, we have

$$D \;\overset{\mathcal{D}}{=}\; \mathrm{Dir}(T+1). \tag{5.6}$$

For example, ninther sampling yields

$$D \;\overset{\mathcal{D}}{=}\; \mathbb{1}_{\{X=1\}}\mathrm{Dir}(4,6) \;+\; \mathbb{1}_{\{X=2\}}\mathrm{Dir}(5,5) \;+\; \mathbb{1}_{\{X=3\}}\mathrm{Dir}(6,4) \tag{5.7.1}$$

$$\text{with } X \;\overset{\mathcal{D}}{=}\; \mathcal{D}\left(\tfrac{3}{14},\tfrac{4}{7},\tfrac{3}{14}\right). \tag{5.7.2}$$

We stress again that only the distribution of D is directly affected; conditional on D, the same analysis remains valid as before.

5.3 Generic Model: Element-wise Charging Schemes

In this section, we define our unifying framework to analyze cost measures: *element-wise charging schemes*. Element-wise means that overall costs for partitioning are the sum of contributions of all ordinary elements. These contributions may depend on the *class* of the element and the current *state* of the partitioning algorithm, and nothing else.

We will later, in Section 5.5, derive how many elements of a certain class occur in a certain state. Combined with the (constant) contributions per class and state for our cost measures discussed in Section 5.4, we obtain the partitioning cost w.r.t. all our cost measures.

5.3.1 General Charging Schemes

Our parametric algorithms unify the analysis of many practical partitioning methods by embedding them in a common framework. In this section, we will likewise set up a universal framework for studying different measures of cost using one generic analysis.

The framework embraces all *element-wise* cost measures, which intuitively means that overall partitioning costs are given as a sum of the costs for each (ordinary) element, where these per-element costs in turn depend only on the classes of the elements up to now. With the natural assumption that comparing with the pivots is the only allowed operation on ordinary elements in partitioning, this framework is quite comprehensive. Here comes the formal definition. Recall that we denote by $\mathcal{C}$ the vector of classes;

$$
\mathcal{C} \;=\; \begin{cases} (s_m,\ldots,s_1,l_1,\ldots,l_{s-m}), & \text{for } m \in [0..s]; \\ (s_{\lceil m \rceil},\ldots,s_2,m,l_2,\ldots,l_{s-\lfloor m \rfloor}), & \text{for } m \in [1..s] - \tfrac{1}{2}\,; \end{cases}
\qquad \text{(4.3) revisited}
$$

$\mathcal{C}^*$ denotes the set of all finite sequences of classes. Moreover, we write $c(U)$ for the class of an ordinary element U.

Definition 5.2 (Element-Wise Cost Measures): *An element-wise cost measure M consists of*

- ▶ *a (possible infinite) state set $\mathcal{Q}_M$,*

- ▶ *a next-state function $next_M : \mathcal{C}^* \to \mathcal{Q}_M$, where $next_M(c_1 \ldots c_j)$ denotes the state after processing j elements with respective classes $c_1 \ldots c_j$, and $next(\varepsilon)$ denotes the initial state, and*

- ▶ *a charging scheme $cost_M : \mathcal{C} \times \mathcal{Q}_M \to \mathbb{R}_{\geqslant 0}$, where $cost_M(c, q)$ is the cost of processing one element of type $c \in \mathcal{C}$, when the partitioning algorithm is currently in state $q \in \mathcal{Q}_M$.*

The M-cost T_M of partitioning the elements $U_1, \ldots, U_\eta$ (in that order) is defined as

$$
T_M \;=\; \sum_{i=1}^{\eta} cost_M\Big(c(U_i), next_M\big(c(U_1) \cdots c(U_{i-1}) \big) \Big). \tag{5.8}
$$

◀

One should think of the state as the internal state of the machine while executing the partitioning algorithm, in particular, the *program counter*, i.e., the location in the code is part of the state.

Note that even though $\mathcal{Q}_M$ may be infinite in general, for any fixed η, only the finitely many states $next_M(\mathcal{C}^{\leqslant \eta})$ are reachable, where $\mathcal{C}^{\leqslant \eta}$ is the set of all words over alphabet $\mathcal{C}$ with length at most η. In fact, for the general element-wise cost measures the *full-history* state set $\mathcal{Q}_M = \mathcal{C}^*$ is always a possible choice, but our analysis below becomes uninformative then.

We will later restrict that to the natural and analyzable class of next-state functions corresponding to finite automata. The first step in our analysis, however, works just as well for the more general setting of element-wise cost measures, so we will stick to it for the moment.

5.3.2 Relation to Classification Strategies

Our element-wise cost measures generalize the *classification strategies* introduced by Aumüller et al. [10], and the core idea of splitting state frequencies and per-state average costs is due to them. A classification strategy for $\eta = n - k$ (ordinary) elements around $s - 1$ given pivots $P_1, \ldots, P_{s-1}$ has to determine in each step

- ▶ an index $i \in \{1, \ldots, \eta\}$ of an element to classify next and
- ▶ a comparison tree λ to use for the next classification.

Both choices may depend on the *classes* of all previously classified elements.

This framework of classification strategies arguably contains the comparison costs of any reasonable partitioning method as special case. Aumüller et al. [10] in particular study cases where the comparison tree is changed after each classified element, e.g., so that it minimizes the total cost of classifying all elements seen up to now. We consider their comparison-optimal strategies in Section 5.7.

Clearly, the number of key comparisons under any given classification strategy, i.e., a rule how to choose the next comparison tree based on the classes of all previously classified elements, is an element-wise cost measure, whose states are the possible comparison trees.

5.3.3 Separating State Frequencies From Element Costs

In this section, we do the first step in the analysis of the expected costs of one partitioning step, for an arbitrary element-wise cost measure. We show that we can separately take expectations on the number of times partitioning is in a given state and on the cost of dealing with a random element in that state. Roughly speaking, the former depends on the algorithm and the latter on the cost measure, so with this separation, it suffices to analyze the partitioning algorithm once. Different cost measures are obtained by inserting corresponding charging schemes.

As discussed above, our element-wise cost measures generalize the classification strategies introduced by Aumüller et al. [10]. While the cost models and results are similar, the analyses differ. Aumüller et al. use concentration arguments, more precisely the *method of averaged bounded differences,* to show that even for fixed segment sizes $\mathbf{I}$, the probability for an element to fall in a certain class is close to being independent of the classes of all previously classified elements, unless only very few, a sublinear number, of elements are left (Lemma 2.2 of Aumüller et al. [10]). These last few elements can however be ignored for the leading term of costs. In the uniform model, we can get rid of this case distinction, since conditional of $\mathbf{D}$, classes of elements are i.i.d., *precisely*.

Let M be an arbitrary element-wise cost measure. To analyze (expected) costs, we consider again a random input, consisting of n i.i.d. $\mathcal{U}(0, 1)$ distributed elements $U_1, \ldots, U_n$. We partition the $\eta = n - k$ ordinary elements using pivots chosen by generalized pivot sampling with parameter $\mathbf{t} \in \mathbb{N}^s$.

In general, the elements in the array are not classified in a predefined order, e.g., in our one-pass partitioning methods it depends on their classes whether we continue scanning from the left or from the right (see Section 5.5 for more details). Let in general

$\Pi_1, \Pi_2, \ldots, \Pi_\eta$ be the (random) indices of the elements as they are classified, so that U_{Π_1} is the element classified first, U_{Π_2} is the second one, and so on. We assume that $\Pi_1, \ldots, \Pi_\eta$ is a permutation of the indices of all ordinary elements. If we denote with $c(U)$ the class of an ordinary element U, the (random) sequence of classes, as seen by the element-wise cost measure, is $c(U_{\Pi_1}), c(U_{\Pi_2}), \ldots, c(U_{\Pi_\eta})$. The next-state function transforms this to a (random) sequence of states $\mathbf{Q} = (Q_0, Q_1, Q_2, \ldots, Q_\eta)$, where $Q_j = next_M(c(U_{\Pi_1}) \ldots c(U_{\Pi_j}))$ for $j \in [0..\eta]$. We are in state Q_j *after* having classified U_{Π_j}. With this notation, the (random) total cost of the first partitioning step is

$$T_M(n) = \sum_{j=1}^{\eta} cost_M\big(c(U_{\Pi_j}), Q_{j-1}\big) \tag{5.9}$$

$$= \sum_{j=1}^{\eta} \sum_{q \in \mathcal{Q}_M} \sum_{c \in \mathcal{C}} \mathbb{1}_{\{c(U_{\Pi_j})=c\}} \mathbb{1}_{\{Q_{j-1}=q\}} \, cost_M(c, q) \tag{5.10}$$

$$= \sum_{q \in \mathcal{Q}_M} \sum_{c \in \mathcal{C}} cost_M(c, q) \sum_{j=1}^{\eta} \mathbb{1}_{\{c(U_{\Pi_j})=c\}} \mathbb{1}_{\{Q_{j-1}=q\}}. \tag{5.11}$$

Recall that both the classes of elements $c(U_{\Pi_j})$ and the states Q_{j-1} are random, and they are in general *not* stochastically independent. (Even for the restricted case introduced below, they are not: for the automaton in Section 5.4.1 (page 174), there will be a correlation between the probability of being in state q_k and the probability of an element to be small.)

What comes to our rescue is that upon *conditioning on* $\mathbf{D}$, the classes $c(U_{\Pi_j})$ of all ordinary elements are i.i.d., see Fact 5.1. The current state Q_{j-1} depends only on the classes of the *previous* elements, namely $Q_{j-1} = next_M(c(U_{\Pi_1}) \ldots c(U_{i_{\Pi-1}}))$. So for *fixed* $\mathbf{D}$, we find that Q_{j-1} and $c(U_{\Pi_j})$ are *conditionally independent*. We use this to simplify the conditional expectation

$$\mathbb{E}[T_M(n) \mid \mathbf{D}] = \sum_{q \in \mathcal{Q}_M} \sum_{c \in \mathcal{C}} cost_M(c, q) \sum_{j=1}^{\eta} \mathbb{E}\big[\mathbb{1}_{\{c(U_{\Pi_j})=c\}} \mathbb{1}_{\{Q_{j-1}=q\}} \mid \mathbf{D}\big] \tag{5.12}$$

$$= \sum_{q \in \mathcal{Q}_M} \sum_{c \in \mathcal{C}} cost_M(c, q) \sum_{j=1}^{\eta} \mathbb{E}\big[\mathbb{1}_{\{c(U_{\Pi_j})=c\}} \mid \mathbf{D}\big] \cdot \mathbb{E}\big[\mathbb{1}_{\{Q_{j-1}=q\}} \mid \mathbf{D}\big] \tag{5.13}$$

$$= \sum_{q \in \mathcal{Q}_M} \left(\sum_{c \in \mathcal{C}} cost_M(c, q) \cdot \mathbb{P}[c(U) = c \mid \mathbf{D}] \right) \left(\sum_{j=1}^{\eta} \mathbb{E}[\mathbb{1}_{\{Q_{j-1}=q\}} \mid \mathbf{D}] \right) \tag{5.14}$$

$$= \sum_{q \in \mathcal{Q}_M} \underbrace{\mathbb{E}_U\big[cost_M(c(U), q) \mid \mathbf{D}\big]}_{=:\overline{cost}_M(\mathbf{D}, q)} \cdot \underbrace{\mathbb{E}_Q\left[\sum_{j=1}^{\eta} \mathbb{1}_{\{Q_{j-1}=q\}} \,\middle|\, \mathbf{D}\right]}_{=:F_q^{(n)}}. \tag{5.15}$$

Both abbreviations have intuitive meanings. $F_q = F_q^{(n)}$ is the *frequency* of state q, i.e., the (random) number of elements that are classified while we are in state q. $\overline{cost}_M(\mathbf{D}, q)$ is the *expected cost* of an element *in state* q, when the class probabilities are given by $\mathbf{D}$ (Fact 5.1). We state the above result once more for reference.

Lemma 5.3: *Conditional on the pivot values, i.e., on* $\mathbf{D}$*, the expected cost of the first partitioning step in an element-wise cost measure* M *is given by*

$$\mathbb{E}[T_M(n) \mid \mathbf{D}] \;=\; \sum_{q \in \mathcal{Q}_M} \mathbb{E}[F_q \mid \mathbf{D}] \cdot \overline{cost}_M(\mathbf{D}, q), \tag{5.16}$$

with F_q *and* $\overline{cost}_M$ *as in Equation* (5.15). *The unconditional expectation can be written as*

$$\mathbb{E}[T_M(n)] \;=\; \sum_{q \in \mathcal{Q}_M} \sum_{c \in \mathcal{C}} cost_M(c, q) \cdot o_{c,q}^{(n)}, \tag{5.17}$$

where $o_{c,q}^{(n)} := \mathbb{E}_{\mathbf{D}}\big[\mathbb{E}[F_q^{(n)} \mid \mathbf{D}] \cdot \mathbb{P}[c \mid \mathbf{D}]\big]$ *is the expected number of co-occurrences of class* c *and state* q. ■

The class-state co-occurrences generalize and replace the hypergeometric terms "s@$\mathcal{K}$" (the number of small elements falling in k's range) etc. that we used in previous works [184, 186, 137].

◆   ◆   ◆

Lemma 5.3 is similar to Lemma 3.1 of Aumüller et al. [10] for the comparison case. (They write F^λ for the number of classifications with tree λ, and $c_{\mathrm{avg}}^\lambda(i)$ for the average comparison cost using that tree when the number of occurrences of each class is given by i.) The difference is that Aumüller et al. work with expectations conditional on segment sizes $\mathbf{I}$. These are usually easy to compute; but then we have to average over all pivot *ranks*. The resulting sums are quite inconvenient to deal with. A look at the lengthy computations in the proof of Theorem 7.1 of Aumüller et al. [10] might convince the reader of our point here — and that computation only deals with the case $\mathbf{t} = 0$.

In contrast, we split up costs at the level of fixed $\mathbf{D}$. The conditional state frequencies $\mathbb{E}[F_q \mid \mathbf{D}]$ are much easier to compute, even precisely, as we will see. Once we have them computing the unconditional co-occurrences is a mechanic task.

5.3.4 FSM-based Element-Wise Charging Schemes

We have shown in the last section that in the very general framework of element-wise cost measures, it suffices to separately compute how often we are in a certain state and of how much an average element costs us in that state (Lemma 5.3). This is only helpful if we can compute these two things. State frequencies can be very complicated in general, but we do not need this generality for most cost measures.

In generic one-pass partitioning, costs essentially depend on whether the element is reached by index k or by index g. Transitions between these two modes of operation only depend on the current state and the next element's class. They can thus be characterized by a *finite automaton*. This motivates the following definition.

Definition 5.4 (FSM-Based Cost Measure): *An element-wise cost measure* M *is finite-state-machine based (FSM-based) if* $next_M(c_1 \ldots c_j)$ *is the state of a finite automaton after reading* $c_1 \ldots c_j$*, for all sequences of classes* $c_1 \ldots c_j$*. More specifically, FSM-based means there is a* *finite automaton $\mathcal{A}_M = (\mathcal{Q}_M, \mathcal{C}, q_0, \delta_M)$, the state automaton, with (finite) state set $\mathcal{Q}_M$, initial state $q_0 \in \mathcal{Q}_M$, alphabet $\mathcal{C}$ (the set of classes of elements), and the transition function δ, so that $next_M(\varepsilon) = q_0$ (initial states agree), and for all $j \geqslant 1$ and all class sequences $c_1 \ldots c_j \in \mathcal{C}^j$ holds*

$$next_M(c_1 \ldots c_j) = \delta_M\big(next_M(c_1 \ldots c_{j-1}), c_j\big). \qquad \blacktriangleleft$$

5.4 Charging Schemes for Our Cost Measures

Except for branch misses, we can express all cost measures introduced in Chapter 3 as FSM-based charging schemes with a simple two-state automaton: costs only depend on whether we are in the first inner loop or in the second inner loop. We derive the corresponding state transition probabilities in Section 5.5. In this section, we give the charging schemes $cost_M$ for comparisons, scanned elements, swaps/shifts and write accesses. We treat branch misses separately in Section 5.8.

5.4.1 The State Automaton For One-Pass Partitioning

For generic one-pass partitioning, the state automaton is actually quite simple; and the same for all our cost measures; the only exception are branch misses, which are treated separately in Section 5.8.

From an ordinary element's point of view, there are only two basic alternatives: it can be reached with index k, i.e., while we are executing the first inner loop, or it can be reached with index g, while we are in the second inner loop. We will denote these two states by q_k and q_g, respectively. We initially start in state q_k. The new state depends on the class of the most recently classified element: if we found a small element, we go to state q_k, and if we found a large element, we go to state q_g.

Figure 23 shows the resulting automaton. Note that slight differences exist between the master-pivot case, ($m \in [0..s]$) and the master-segment case ($m \in [1..s] - \frac{1}{2}$). A detailed discussion of the state automaton is given in Section 5.5 below, in particular Lemma 5.5 and Lemma 5.8 show that the transitions in the automata are as given in Figure 23. In that section, we also determine the expected state frequencies (Corollary 5.7 and Lemma 5.9).

5.4.2 Key Comparisons

The number of comparisons to classify a single ordinary element U depends on the used comparisons tree, i.e., the order in which we compare the elements to the pivots, and the class of the element itself. Our algorithms use two comparison trees, where λ_k is used while in state q_k and λ_g is used in state q_g. We thus have for all classes $c \in \mathcal{C}$ that

$$cost_C(c, q_k) \;=\; \lambda_k(c) \quad \text{and} \quad cost_C(c, q_g) \;=\; \lambda_g(c), \qquad (5.18)$$

where $\lambda(c)$ is the depth of leaf c in the comparison tree λ. It is convenient to define the *leaf-depth profile* $\boldsymbol{\lambda}$ of a comparison tree λ as the vector

$$\boldsymbol{\lambda} \;=\; \lambda(\mathcal{C}) \;=\; \big(\lambda(\mathcal{C}_1), \ldots, \lambda(\mathcal{C}_s)\big), \qquad (5.19)$$

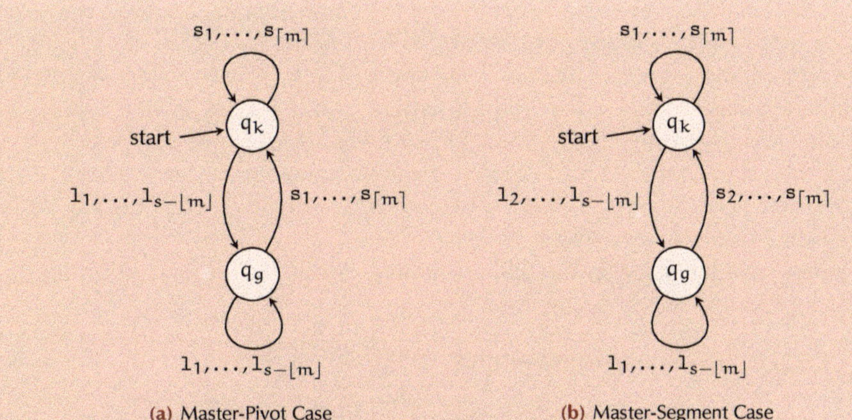

(a) Master-Pivot Case   (b) Master-Segment Case

Figure 23: State automata for the element-wise cost measures in our generic one-pass partitioning algorithm (Algorithm 9). There is a slight difference in the transitions between the master-pivot and the master-segment case; the reason is that in the master-segment case, the classes small and large of order one coincide, $s_1 = l_1 = m$, and do not trigger a state change.

i.e., λ is the vector of leaf depths in left-to-right order. Then average costs in a given state for a fixed $\mathbf{D}$ are a weighted external path length of the comparison tree:

$$\overline{cost}_C(\mathbf{D}, q_k) \;=\; \lambda_k^{\mathsf{T}} \cdot \mathbf{D} \;=\; \sum_{c \in \mathcal{C}} \mathbb{P}[c \mid \mathbf{D}] \cdot \lambda_k(c), \tag{5.20}$$

$$\overline{cost}_C(\mathbf{D}, q_g) \;=\; \lambda_g^{\mathsf{T}} \cdot \mathbf{D} \;=\; \sum_{c \in \mathcal{C}} \mathbb{P}[c \mid \mathbf{D}] \cdot \lambda_g(c). \tag{5.21}$$

Example. Consider for example $s = 6$, $m = 3$ and let λ_k be comparison tree from Figure 19 (page 155). Then we have $cost_C(s_3, q_k) = \lambda_k(s_3) = 2$, since the leaf with label s_3 is at depth 2. Similarly $cost_C(s_2, q_k) = 2$, and $cost_C(c, q_k) = 3$ for all other classes. We thus have the leaf-depth profile $\lambda_k = (2, 2, 3, 3, 3, 3)$.

5.4.3 Scanned Elements

If we are in q_k and the current element is small of order i, we rotate i elements down (line 6), which requires one (new) element scan with each of the indices $k_1, k_2, \ldots, k_i$. So we have $cost_{SE}(s_i, q_k) = i$. Symmetrically, in state q_g we rotate j elements up (line 20) if the current element is large of order j, so $cost_{SE}(l_j, q_g) = j$.

The remaining two cases are slightly more interesting. Consider first a s_i-type element in state q_g. A brief look at Algorithm 9 shows that we then have to end up in the ∞-shift in line 25. This operation involves a total of $i + j$ elements, accessed through the indices $k_1, \ldots, k_i$ and $g_1, \ldots, g_j$, where j is the order of the ∞-shift partner, i.e., $c_k = l_j$ there.

But we do not know c_k; are we in trouble here? The answer is no, since we can *split the bill:* the current element will pay for $cost_{SE}(q_g, s_i) = i$ of the $i + j$ scanned elements, say, for those through indices g (the element itself) and $k_2, \ldots, k_i$, the $i - 1$ elements that have been touched to make room for $A[g]$ in the s_i-region.

It is then clear that $cost_{SE}(q_k, l_j)$ must be j, if this element is put into position by the ∞-shift. Unlike above, we might also end up in the special case handler in line 14, namely if the current element is the last element classified by λ_k and $k = g$ holds. Luckily we need exactly j element scans in these cases, as well.

We summarize the result in the following table. Note that these numbers apply for both master-pivot and master-segment methods.

$cost_{SE}(c, q)$	$q = q_k$	$q = q_g$
$c = s_i$	i	i
$c = l_j$	j	j

The cost measure of scanned elements has a few noteworthy properties.

▶ First of all, as becomes obvious in the table above, the scanned elements charging scheme is state-less: $cost_{SE}(c, q)$ does not depend on state q. It is clear then that the number of scanned elements will only depend on the number of elements in each class, that is, the segment sizes $\mathbf{I}$. In fact, $T_{SE}(n)$ is by definition the distance scanned by the indices $k_1, \ldots, k_{\lceil m \rceil}$ and $g_1, \ldots, g_{s - \lfloor m \rfloor}$. It is immediate from the invariant after partitioning, Figure 16 (page 150), that the innermost segments are scanned only by k_1 resp. g_1; the next segment outwards is additionally scanned by k_2 resp. g_2, and so forth. We thus have

$$T_{SE}(n) \;=\; \boldsymbol{\alpha}_{SE}^{\mathsf{T}} \cdot \mathbf{I}, \tag{5.22}$$

the dot product or scalar product of the vectors $\boldsymbol{\alpha}_{SE}$ and $\mathbf{I}$, where coefficient vector $\boldsymbol{\alpha}_{SE}$ is given by

$$\boldsymbol{\alpha}_{SE} \;=\; \begin{cases} (\, m \,,\, m - 1, \ldots, 2, 1, 1, 2, \ldots, s - m \,), & \text{for } m \in \mathbb{N}_0; \\ (\lceil m \rceil, \lceil m \rceil - 1, \ldots, 2,\ 1,\ 2, \ldots, s - \lfloor m \rfloor), & \text{otherwise.} \end{cases} \tag{5.23}$$

▶ Comparing the two representations, the charging scheme and the explicit vector form above, it seems suspicious at first that one of them has to distinguish master-pivot and master-segment methods, whereas the other does not. Let us give two (redundant) arguments, why both are correct and equivalent. First, master-segment schemes differ from master-pivot schemes only in that medium elements, which coincide with s_1 and l_1 in this case, do not participate in ∞-shifts. These elements are charged only 1 scanned element, which is needed to read and classify them anyway.

The other reason is that the definition of $\mathbf{I}$ does not depend on m, but the definition of the classes does. In the master-segment case, both s_1- and l_1-elements go to the same segment, the master segment, which is jointly scanned by k_1 and g_1.

► Note that in some cases, we access the current location, $A[k]$ resp. $A[g]$ twice: Once for classifying the element, and a second time later, when the element is moved to the correct segment. In terms of scanned elements, these two references count as one, as they refer to the same location and happen through the same index variable, namely k resp. g. Usually, these accesses happen so shortly after each other that the second access will not cause a cache miss.

5.4.4 Write Accesses

By *write accesses*, we mean only write accesses to the array, assignments to local variables are not counted as they usually reside in registers and are discarded afterwards. Writes to the array, in contrast, have to be written back to main memory at some point in time, which is more costly. Write accesses are closely related to scanned elements, but differences exist in the details.

First note that an ordinary cyclic shift involving $i \geqslant 2$ elements needs exactly i write accesses to the array A, see Algorithm 5. Formally, CYCLICSHIFTLEFT$_1(i)$ would entail one write operation, but such a shift is actually vacuous and would of course be eliminated from real code. We will thus *not* count a write access for it.

For an element's share of the cost of an ∞-shift, we have to distinguish between master-pivot and master-segment methods. In the master pivot-case, the exception above does *not* apply, because even in the case that both i and j are 1, i.e., we have $c_k = l_1$ and $c_g = s_1$ in line 25 of Algorithm 9, we still have to swap these two elements, charging each of them 1 write access. For master-segment methods, the classes with order 1 do not participate in the ∞-shift, so elements of types s_1 and l_1 never entail a write access.

In summary, we obtain the following charging scheme for the number of write accesses. Note that in the master-segment case, the charging scheme is stateless, whereas states are needed in the master-pivot case.

<table>
<tr><th colspan="3">Master-Pivot Algorithms</th><th colspan="3">Master-Segment Algorithms</th></tr>
<tr><td>$cost_{WA}(c,q)$</td><td>$q = q_k$</td><td>$q = q_g$</td><td>$cost_{WA}(c,q)$</td><td>$q = q_k$</td><td>$q = q_g$</td></tr>
<tr><td>$c = s_i$</td><td>$i - [i = 1]$</td><td>i</td><td>$c = s_i$</td><td>$i - [i = 1]$</td><td>$i - [i = 1]$</td></tr>
<tr><td>$c = l_j$</td><td>j</td><td>$j - [j = 1]$</td><td>$c = l_j$</td><td>$j - [j = 1]$</td><td>$j - [j = 1]$</td></tr>
</table>

5.4.5 Swaps resp. Cyclic Shifts

Since one-pass partitioning methods usually have to move several elements around to make room for one new element in its segment, it is not efficient to implement the rearrangement based on (binary) swaps. Instead, we use cyclic shifts of a number of elements. We herein determine *how many* of these shift operations we execute. For single-pivot partitioning, this is the number of swaps, which is a widely used measure of cost in the literature.

In terms of running time, it is plausible that the contribution of one cyclic shift should be proportional to the number of involved elements, as is the case for counting write accesses. One should thus not expect the number of shift operations to be a suitable measure to predict running times for multi-pivot Quicksort variants; however, it may serve well in a compound cost measure: we can use the number of shifts to model constant overhead per shift.

To be precise, we define the *number of (cyclic) shifts* to be the number of times lines 6, 14, 20, and 25 of Algorithm 9 are executed. Cyclic shifts related to only one new element, i.e., all but the ∞-shift in line 25, are charged to that element. A cyclic shift there happens if and only if the same element is charged a positive amount of write accesses: $cost_S(s_i, q_k) = [cost_{WA}(s_i, q_k) \geqslant 1]$ and $cost_S(1_j, q_g) = [cost_{WA}(1_j, q_g) \geqslant 1]$. Costs of ∞-shifts are split equally between the two involved new elements, i.e., $cost_S(1_j, q_k) = \frac{1}{2}[cost_{WA}(1_j, q_k) \geqslant 1]$ and $cost_S(s_i, q_g) = \frac{1}{2}[cost_{WA}(s_i, q_g) \geqslant 1]$. We thus obtain the following charging scheme for the number of cyclic shifts:

<table>
<tr><th colspan="3">Master-Pivot Algorithms</th><th colspan="3">Master-Segment Algorithms</th></tr>
<tr><td>$cost_S(c, q)$</td><td>$q = q_k$</td><td>$q = q_g$</td><td>$cost_S(c, q)$</td><td>$q = q_k$</td><td>$q = q_g$</td></tr>
<tr><td>$c = s_i$</td><td>$[i > 1]$</td><td>$\frac{1}{2}$</td><td>$c = s_i$</td><td>$[i > 1]$</td><td>$\frac{1}{2}[i > 1]$</td></tr>
<tr><td>$c = 1_j$</td><td>$\frac{1}{2}$</td><td>$[j > 1]$</td><td>$c = 1_j$</td><td>$\frac{1}{2}[j > 1]$</td><td>$[j > 1]$</td></tr>
</table>

5.5 Execution Frequencies of Inner Loops

For our analyses it is vital to know how often each the two inner loops of Algorithm 9 are executed. As k is incremented in the first inner loop and g in the second, we will call the loop in lines 3 – 10 of Algorithm 9 the "k-loop" and the loop in lines 11 – 23 of the "g-loop." To be a little more precise, let F_k and F_g denote the (random) numbers of executions of line 4 respectively line 18, i.e., the number of classifications with λ_k respectively with λ_g, during the first partitioning step.

Stated in terms of our element-wise cost measures, F_k and F_g are the (random) numbers of elements that are classified while in state q_k resp. q_g of the state automaton (Section 5.4.1 on page 174). We have (slight) differences in transitions of the automaton when we use a master-pivot method as compared to a master-segment method, see Figure 23, so we consider these two cases separately.

5.5.1 Master-Pivot Algorithm

Let us first consider the master-pivot case $m \in [0..s]$. From the invariant after partitioning, see Figure 16, it is clear that $F_k + F_g$ must be the number of ordinary elements and that the meeting point of indices k and g is roughly after the first $I_1 + \cdots + I_m$ elements, since those appear left of k after partitioning is finished. We must have roughly $F_k \approx I_1 + \cdots + I_m$ executions of the k-loop and $F_g \approx I_{m+1} + \cdots + I_s$ of the g-loop.

Note however that there are several possible points at which the outer loop can be left, which causes slight (in particular, constant w.r.t. n) deviations from the above bird's eye view. Also note that the last update of pointers k and g has been carefully chosen so that after partitioning we always have $k = g + 1$ and the master pivot P_m belongs at position $k - 1 = g$; the final valuations of variables k and g do thus not directly reflect the number of classifications with λ_k and λ_g.

> **State Frequencies in YBB partitioning**   This is different for YBB Quicksort as studied in [186], where each increment of k corresponds exactly to one classification with λ_k, and likewise for each decrement of g we have a classification with λ_g. However, YBB partitioning occasionally classifies the same element *twice*, namely when the ranges of k and g overlap (see the "crossing-point lemma" in [186]). Our Algorithm 9 was tailored to avoid exactly this idiosyncrasy — which inevitably comes at the price of losing the one-to-one correspondence of pointer movements and classifications.

We can precisely characterize F_k and F_g despite the missing correspondence with final pointer values using the following observation.

Lemma 5.5: *Except for the very last element classified in the partitioning step, after each large element, we classify the following element using λ_g; likewise each small element entails a classification with λ_k for the next element.*   ◀

Proof: We briefly consider the possible cases and assume that we are *not* currently dealing with the element classified last, so we have $k \leqslant g - 1$. If we classified the current element using λ_k in line 4 as small, we execute the k-loop once more and thus use λ_k for the next element. If otherwise $A[k]$ is large, we do leave the loop and continue classification using λ_g, as claimed.

Now consider the case of classifying with λ_g in line 18. If the element is small, we leave the g-loop and the next classification must be with λ_k in the next iteration of the outer loop. (Recall that the current element is not the last one by assumption, so there will be a next iteration.) Otherwise, the element is large and we claim we then execute the g-loop at least once more, entailing a new classification with λ_g, as claimed. So towards a contradiction, assume we left the g-loop. We had $k \geqslant g$ then, because c_g is a large class and after the g-loop, we decrement g for sure so that afterwards $k > g$ would hold. But then, no further execution of the outer loop would follow and our current element would have been the last classified element in this partitioning step, contradiction our assumption that it is not.   ■

The automaton shown in Figure 23-(a) is nothing more than this simple rule of Lemma 5.5 expressed as finite-state machine.

As hinted at above, there does not seem to be a neat, concise characterization of the exact index of the element classified last (apart from that it is roughly $I_1 + \cdots + I_m$). But we can characterize the distribution of F_k and F_g.

Lemma 5.6: *Let the pivot value distances, $\mathbf{D}$, be fixed and denote by $\eta = n - k$ the number of ordinary elements. The numbers of elements classified using λ_k resp. λ_g satisfy*

$$(F_k, F_g) \overset{\mathcal{D}}{=} \mathrm{Mult}(\eta - 1; D_1 + \cdots + D_m, D_{m+1} + \cdots + D_s) + (1, 0). \qquad (5.24)$$

Proof: No matter what the input, Algorithm 9 always does the first classification using λ_k, hence the constant offset for F_k. For the remaining $\eta - 1$ classifications, the used tree depends on the outcome of the previous classification: we use λ_k if the last element was small and λ_g if it was large, see Lemma 5.5. Conditional on $\mathbf{D}$, the classes of elements are i.i.d., and an element is small with probability $D_1 + \cdots + D_m$ and large otherwise, i.e., with probability $D_{m+1} + \cdots + D_s$. ■

Corollary 5.7: *The expected numbers of elements classified using λ_k resp. λ_g in the first partitioning step using Algorithm 9, conditional on $\mathbf{D}$, are*

$$\mathbb{E}[F_k^{(n)} \mid \mathbf{D}] = (D_1 + \cdots + D_m)(n - k - 1) + 1, \qquad (5.25)$$
$$\mathbb{E}[F_g^{(n)} \mid \mathbf{D}] = (D_{m+1} + \cdots + D_s)(n - k - 1). \qquad (5.26)$$

The total expectations are

$$\mathbb{E}[F_k^{(n)}] = \frac{t_1 + \cdots + t_m + m}{k + 1}(n - k - 1) + 1, \qquad (5.27)$$
$$\mathbb{E}[F_g^{(n)}] = \frac{t_{m+1} + \cdots + t_s + s - m}{k + 1}(n - k - 1). \qquad (5.28)$$

■

5.5.2 Master-Segment Algorithms

The pointers k and g in Sedgewick's algorithm (Algorithm 6) do not always meet exactly in the middle of the second segment, even though our syntactical choice $m = 1.5$ might seem to imply that; rather it depends on the classes of elements in that range of the array [182]. This is true in general for master-segment methods. The numbers F_k and F_g of elements classified using λ_k resp. λ_g exhibit a more complex behavior than in the case of master-pivot partitioning. Recall that the s classes for master-segment methods are

$$\mathcal{C} = \left(s_{\lceil m \rceil}, \ldots, s_2, s_1 = m = l_1, l_2, \ldots, l_{s - \lfloor m \rfloor} \right).$$

Lemma 5.8: *All elements up to and including the first non-medium element are classified using λ_k. For all others holds: If the most recent non-medium element that has been classified was small of order at least two, the current classification uses λ_k, and if the most recent non-medium element was large of order at least two, we use λ_g.*

Proof: Following the code of Algorithm 9, we see that we initially classify using λ_k in the k-loop, and we stay there until we find an element that is large of order at least two. Likewise we classify with λ_g in the g-loop as long as no element is found that is small of order at least two. ■

This means that we can describe the state sequence in Algorithm 9 as the finite-state machine given in Figure 23-(b). After each classification, the edge containing the resulting class of the element then determines the new state.

If we consider a fixed $\mathbf{D}$, the probabilities for classes of ordinary elements are i.i.d., and so are the transition probabilities in the finite-state machine with the corresponding labels. It thus forms a Markov chain; it is shown in Figure 24.

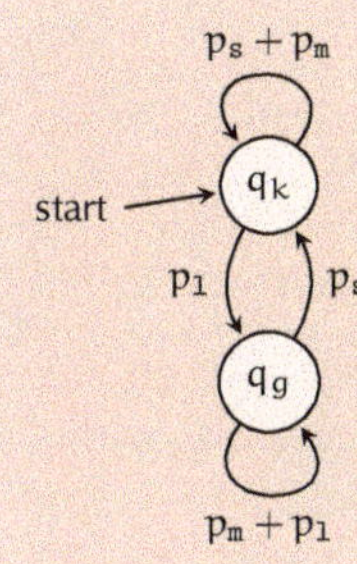

Figure 24: Markov chain of used classification trees in Algorithm 9. Nodes indicate the tree used for the next classification, the outcome of the classification determines the transition to be taken. The edge labels give the transition probabilities using the abbreviations of Equation (5.31); we assume $\mathbf{D}$ is fixed.

To determine $\mathbb{E}[F_k^{(n)} \mid \mathbf{D}]$, we have to count how often we *leave* the λ_k-state in a random run of length η of this Markov chain. To do so, we make use of the rich toolkit around generating functions for combinatorics on regular languages, see Section I.4 of *Analytic Combinatorics* [64]. We consider the generating function

$$F_k(z, u) \;=\; \sum_{\eta, i} \mathbb{P}\big[F_k^{(n)} = i \mid \eta, \mathbf{D}\big] \cdot z^\eta u^i \tag{5.29}$$

for words of element classes including their probabilities, where we encode the word length in the exponent of z and the number of visits of state λ_k in the exponent of u. The coefficient $[z^\eta u^i] F_k(z, u)$ is thus precisely $\mathbb{P}[F_k = i \mid \eta, \mathbf{D}]$ and $\mathbb{E}[F_k \mid \mathbf{D}] = [z^\eta] \frac{\partial}{\partial u} F_k(z, u)\big|_{u=1}$.

The following set of equations for $F_k(z, u)$ follows directly from the decomposition given by the automaton:

$$F_k(z, u) \;=\; (p_s + p_m) z u F_k(z, u) \,+\, p_1 z u F_g(z, u) \,+\, 1, \tag{5.30.1}$$

$$F_g(z, u) \;=\; (p_m + p_1) z F_g(z, u) \,+\, p_s z F_k(z, u) \,+\, 1, \tag{5.30.2}$$

where we abbreviate

$$p_s \;=\; D_1 + \cdots + D_{\lfloor m \rfloor}, \tag{5.31.1}$$

$$p_m \;=\; D_{\lfloor m \rfloor + 1} + \cdots + D_{\lceil m \rceil} \;=\; 1 - p_s - p_1, \tag{5.31.2}$$

$$p_1 \;=\; D_{\lceil m \rceil + 1} + \cdots + D_s. \tag{5.31.3}$$

Note that $p_s + p_m + p_1 = 1$ by definition. Solving the equations for $F_k(z, u)$ and rewriting, we find

$$F_k(z, u) \;=\; \frac{1 + \dfrac{p_1 z u}{1 - (p_m + p_1)z}}{1 - \dfrac{p_1 z u}{1 - (p_m + p_1)z} p_s z - (p_s + p_m) z u}. \tag{5.32}$$

As we are mainly interested in the expected values of F_k and F_g, we proceed with the derivative w.r.t. u

$$\frac{\partial}{\partial u} F_k(z, u)\Big|_{u=1} = \frac{z - (p_m + p_1)z^2}{(1 - p_m z)(1 - z)^2} \tag{5.33.1}$$

$$= \frac{p_s}{p_s + p_1} \frac{1}{(1 - z)^2} - \left(1 - \frac{p_1}{p_s + p_1} - \frac{p_1}{(p_s + p_1)^2}\right) \frac{1}{1 - z}$$

$$- \frac{p_1}{(p_s + p_1)^2} \frac{1}{1 - p_m z}. \tag{5.33.2}$$

In the last partial-fractions form, it is easy to precisely extract coefficients, yielding

$$\mathbb{E}[F_k \mid \mathbf{D}] = \frac{p_s}{p_s + p_1}(\eta + 1) - \left(1 - \frac{p_1}{p_s + p_1} - \frac{p_1}{(p_s + p_1)^2}\right) - \frac{p_1}{(p_s + p_1)^2} p_m^\eta. \tag{5.34}$$

Since each ordinary element is classified exactly once in Algorithm 9, we have $F_g = \eta - F_k$ and we need not compute $\mathbb{E}[F_g \mid \mathbf{D}]$ from the $F_g(z, u)$. We summarize the main result of this derivation in the following statement.

Lemma 5.9: *The expected numbers of elements classified using λ_k resp. λ_g in the first partitioning step using Algorithm 9 in the master-segment case, conditional on $\mathbf{D}$, are*

$$\mathbb{E}[F_k^{(n)} \mid \mathbf{D}] = \frac{D_1 + \cdots + D_{\lceil m \rceil - 1}}{1 - D_{\lceil m \rceil}} \cdot n \pm O(1), \tag{5.35}$$

$$\mathbb{E}[F_g^{(n)} \mid \mathbf{D}] = \frac{D_{\lceil m \rceil + 1} + \cdots + D_s}{1 - D_{\lceil m \rceil}} \cdot n \pm O(1). \tag{5.36}$$

∎

Remark: We actually know the terms hidden in the $O(1)$ precisely, see Equation (5.34), but they are rather unwieldy and will not contribute to leading-term coefficients. The statement of Lemma 5.9 is sufficient for our purpose. ◀

Ergodic Theory. Along the same lines as above, one can in principle compute the state frequencies of any Markov chain and thus any FSM-based element-wise cost measure. A possible shortcut is given by ergodic theory for Markov chains. It basically states that *the leading-term coefficient of the expected number of traversals of a certain edge in the chain is given by the weight of that edge in the stationary distribution of the Markov chain.* Biggar et al. [23], Kaligosi and Sanders [96], Martínez et al. [117] and Auger et al. [6] took this route for example.

Simple formulations of ergodic theorems, e.g., Proposition V.8 of Flajolet and Sedgewick [64], do not give a sufficiently strong error bound. Such a theorem can be proven, though. For the present work, I prefer the above elementary derivation as it does not need Markov chain theory.

◆   ◆   ◆

Unifying Master-Pivot and Master-Segment Case. The attentive reader will have noticed that the Markov chain in Figure 24 and its analysis are actually also valid in the master-pivot case. Inserting $p_m = 0$ and $p_s + p_1 = 1$ in Equation (5.34), we directly find

$$\mathbb{E}[F_k \mid \mathbf{D}] \;=\; p_s(\eta - 1) + 1,$$

from which Corollary 5.7 follows immediately. When we are only interested in the expected value, we can thus analyze both master-pivot and master-segment variants in one shot.

I think the observations made in Section 5.5.1 are helpful to better understand generic one-pass partitioning; the automaton-based approach is a little opaque in that sense. As briefly discussed in the next section, there is indeed a significant difference between master-pivot and master-segment methods when it comes to the distribution of costs.

5.5.3 A Note on Limit Distributions

For YBB Quicksort we derived limit distributions of costs in an article [186] with Ralph Neininger. YBB partitioning is a master-pivot method, and for such it is indeed relatively easy to generalize our contraction-method arguments. We do not explicitly cover the issue of limit distributions of costs in this work, but let us briefly sketch how this could be done.

One first has to determine the full distribution of class-state co-occurrences for that, and, as a first step the distribution of F_k and F_g *conditional* on $\mathbf{I}$. Lemma 5.6 gives the distribution when only fixing $\mathbf{D}$; this is not sufficient; but there is indeed a close connection between F_k, F_g, and $\mathbf{I}$ verbally expressed in Lemma 5.5:

$$(F_k, F_g) \;=\; (I_1 + \cdots + I_m, \, I_{m+1}, \ldots, I_s) \pm 1. \tag{5.37}$$

The term ± 1 is needed as we cannot be sure what the class of the element classified last is. This is a somewhat special element, so we cannot simply assume that the class probabilities conditional on being the last element are the same as for the unconditional case; for asymptotic statements, however, the ± 1 does not make a difference. The remainder of the analysis is along the same lines as for YBB Quicksort.

For master-segment methods, such a simple relation between $\mathbf{I}$ and (F_k, F_g) does *not* hold: not only the number of medium elements is important, but also their location in the array. Following the arguments for Sedgewick's partitioning (see Lemma 4.8 and Proposition 4.9 in my master's thesis [182]), we obtain

$$F_k \;\overset{\mathcal{D}}{=}\; I_1 + \cdots + I_{\lceil m \rceil - 1} + \mathrm{Bin}\left(I_{\lceil m \rceil}, \frac{I_1 + \cdots + I_{\lceil m \rceil - 1} + 1}{\eta - I_{\lceil m \rceil} + 1}\right) \pm 1, \tag{5.38.1}$$

$$F_g \;\overset{\mathcal{D}}{=}\; I_{\lceil m \rceil + 1} + \cdots + I_s + \mathrm{Bin}\left(I_{\lceil m \rceil}, \frac{I_{\lceil m \rceil + 1} + \cdots + I_s}{\eta - I_{\lceil m \rceil} + 1}\right) \pm 1. \tag{5.38.2}$$

It is not directly clear how to show stochastic convergence of the normalized partitioning costs to a limit distribution in this case; one would have to generalize, e.g., Lemmas 4.1 and 4.2 of Wild et al. [186]. For the present work, we leave this open.

Open Problem 5.10 (Limit Distributions for Master-Segment Methods): Compute limiting distributions of cost for Quicksort under a master-segment method. Sedgewick's dual-pivot partitioning method (Algorithm 6) may serve as prototypical example.   ◄

5.6   Class-State Co-Occurrences

By Lemma 5.3 we have for any FSM-based element-wise cost measure M the total expectation

$$\mathbb{E}[T_M(n)] \;=\; \sum_{q \in \mathcal{Q}_M} \sum_{c \in \mathcal{C}} cost_M(c, q) \cdot o_{c,q}^{(n)}, \qquad \text{(5.17) revisited}$$

where $o_{c,q}^{(n)} := \mathbb{E}_{\mathbf{D}}\big[\mathbb{P}[c \mid \mathbf{D}] \cdot \mathbb{E}[F_q^{(n)} \mid \mathbf{D}]\big]$. For our state frequencies (Corollary 5.7 and Lemma 5.9) these expectations are all of the form dealt with in the following lemma.

Lemma 5.11: *Let* $\mathbf{D} \stackrel{\mathcal{D}}{=} \mathrm{Dir}(\sigma)$ *for* $\sigma \in \mathbb{R}_{>0}^s$ *and let* $\mathcal{I} \subseteq \mathcal{J} \subseteq \{1, \dots, s\}$ *be index sets and* $r \in \{1, \dots, s\}$. *Then*

$$\mathbb{E}\left[D_r \cdot \frac{\sum_{i \in \mathcal{I}} D_i}{\sum_{i \in \mathcal{J}} D_i} \right] \;=\; \frac{\sigma_r}{\Sigma\sigma} \cdot \frac{[r \in \mathcal{I}] + \sum_{i \in \mathcal{I}} \sigma_i}{[r \in \mathcal{J}] + \sum_{i \in \mathcal{J}} \sigma_i}. \qquad (5.39)$$

   ◄

Proof: Recall that we denote by $\mathbb{1}_{\mathcal{J}}$ the *characteristic vector* of a subset, see (2.4) on page 40. We compute in the Dirichlet-calculus, see Section 2.4.5:

$$\mathbb{E}\left[D_r \cdot \frac{\sum_{i \in \mathcal{I}} D_i}{\sum_{i \in \mathcal{J}} D_i} \right] \;=\; \mathbb{E}_{D(\sigma)}\left[X_r \cdot \frac{\sum_{i \in \mathcal{I}} X_i}{\sum_{i \in \mathcal{J}} X_i} \right] \qquad (5.40)$$

$$\underset{\text{(P2P)}}{=} \frac{\sigma_r}{\Sigma\sigma} \mathbb{E}_{D(\sigma + \mathbb{1}_{(r)})}\left[\frac{\sum_{i \in \mathcal{I}} X_i}{\sum_{i \in \mathcal{J}} X_i} \right], \qquad (5.41)$$

aggregating components $i \in [s]$ according to the cases $i \in \mathcal{I}$, $i \in \mathcal{J} \setminus \mathcal{I}$ or $i \notin \mathcal{J}$ and setting $\tilde{\sigma}_1 := [r \in \mathcal{I}] + \sum_{i \in \mathcal{I}} \sigma_i$, $\tilde{\sigma}_2 := \big([r \in \mathcal{J}] + \sum_{i \in \mathcal{J}} \sigma_i\big) - \tilde{\sigma}_1$ and $\tilde{\sigma}_3 := [r \notin \mathcal{J}] + \sum_{i \notin \mathcal{J}} \sigma_i$, we continue

$$\underset{\text{(Agg)}}{=} \frac{\sigma_r}{\Sigma\sigma} \mathbb{E}_{D(\tilde{\sigma}_1, \tilde{\sigma}_2, \tilde{\sigma}_3)}\left[\frac{X_1}{X_1 + X_2} \right] \qquad (5.42)$$

$$\underset{\text{(Zoom)}}{=} \frac{\sigma_r}{\Sigma\sigma} \mathbb{E}_{D(\tilde{\sigma}_1, \tilde{\sigma}_2)}[X_1] \qquad (5.43)$$

$$= \frac{\sigma_r}{\Sigma\sigma} \cdot \frac{[r \in \mathcal{I}] + \sum_{i \in \mathcal{I}} \sigma_i}{[r \in \mathcal{J}] + \sum_{i \in \mathcal{J}} \sigma_i}. \qquad (5.44)$$

   ■

To allow concise notation, we write $\sigma = t + 1$ and $\kappa = k + 1 = \Sigma\sigma$. Moreover, we abbreviate the subrange totals of σ corresponding to the ranges scanned from the left, from the right, and, for master-segment algorithms, from both sides:

$$\sigma_\rightarrow \;=\; \sigma_1 + \cdots + \sigma_{\lfloor m \rfloor}, \qquad (5.45.1)$$

$$\sigma_\leftrightarrow \;=\; \sigma_{\lfloor m \rfloor + 1} + \cdots + \sigma_{\lceil m \rceil} \;=\; \sigma_{\lceil m \rceil} \cdot [m \notin \mathbb{Z}] \;=\; \Sigma\sigma - \sigma_\rightarrow - \sigma_\leftarrow, \qquad (5.45.2)$$

$$\sigma_\leftarrow \;=\; \sigma_{\lceil m \rceil + 1} + \cdots + \sigma_s. \qquad (5.45.3)$$

Table 2: Leading term coefficients for the class-state co-occurrences $o_{c,q}$. The main term is linear, and the error is in $O(1)$. For example, we have $o_{s_i,q_k}^{(n)} = (\sigma_{m-i+1}(\sigma_{\rightarrow}+1)/\kappa^2) \cdot n \pm O(1)$ for $i = 1,\ldots,m$ in the master-pivot case.

(a) Master-Pivot Algorithms

$o_{c,q}$	$q = q_k$	$q = q_g$
$c = s_i$	$\dfrac{\sigma_{m-i+1}(\sigma_{\rightarrow}+1)}{\kappa^{\overline{2}}}$	$\dfrac{\sigma_{m-i+1}\sigma_{\leftarrow}}{\kappa^{\overline{2}}}$
$c = l_j$	$\dfrac{\sigma_{m+j}\sigma_{\rightarrow}}{\kappa^{\overline{2}}}$	$\dfrac{\sigma_{m+j}(\sigma_{\leftarrow}+1)}{\kappa^{\overline{2}}}$

(b) Master-Segment Algorithms

$o_{c,q}$	$q = q_k$	$q = q_g$
$c = s_i,$ $(i \geqslant 2)$	$\dfrac{\sigma_{\lceil m \rceil - i + 1}(\sigma_{\rightarrow}+1)}{\kappa(\kappa - \sigma_{\leftrightarrow}+1)}$	$\dfrac{\sigma_{\lceil m \rceil - i + 1}\sigma_{\leftarrow}}{\kappa(\kappa - \sigma_{\leftrightarrow}+1)}$
$c = m$	$\dfrac{\sigma_{\lceil m \rceil}\sigma_{\rightarrow}}{\kappa(\kappa - \sigma_{\leftrightarrow})}$	$\dfrac{\sigma_{\lceil m \rceil}\sigma_{\leftarrow}}{\kappa(\kappa - \sigma_{\leftrightarrow})}$
$c = l_j,$ $(j \geqslant 2)$	$\dfrac{\sigma_{\lfloor m \rfloor + j}\sigma_{\rightarrow}}{\kappa(\kappa - \sigma_{\leftrightarrow}+1)}$	$\dfrac{\sigma_{\lfloor m \rfloor + j}(\sigma_{\leftarrow}+1)}{\kappa(\kappa - \sigma_{\leftrightarrow}+1)}$

With these preparations set up, we can count the class-state occurrences for our partitioning method. The leading terms for all $o_{c,q}$ are given in Table 2.

Note that the leading-term coefficients are mainly the product of the two components of the co-occurrence: For example for o_{s_i,q_k}, the term σ_{m-i+1}/κ is the expected fraction of s_i-type elements, and $\sigma_{\rightarrow}/\kappa$ is the expected fraction of time we spend in state q_k. However, there is a $+1$ whenever the considered class and state "co-vary": many elements of type s_i imply many visits to state q_k. The $+1$ is absent when this correlation is not present, e.g., many elements of type l_j do not imply many visits to state q_k; rather the contrary.

For our main cost measures—comparisons, scanned elements, write accesses and swaps—we now have all ingredients we need for the partitioning cost: We multiply the class-state occurrences by the corresponding cost from the charging scheme and sum up. This yields Theorem 7.1 in Chapter 7.

We devote the rest of this chapter to two further cases, where the simple automaton with two states from above is no longer sufficient.

5.7 Comparison-Optimal Partitioning

The first case that we consider where the above analysis is not sufficient is when the partitioning algorithm may choose comparison trees *depending on the current input*. Aumüller et al. [10] have shown that there is a partitioning method of this kind that achieves asymptotically the minimal possible expected comparison count of any s-way partitioning method. Our random model, and in particular the possibility to condition on **D**, offers an alternative route to compute this comparison lower bound on the s-way classification problem.

A Lower Bound On Classification with One Tree. Conceptually we analyze a partitioning algorithm that can ask an *oracle* before partitioning, how many elements of each class we have, i.e., the algorithm may use the value of $\mathbf{I}$. Based on that we select one comparison tree that minimizes the number of comparisons for this partitioning step: it is the binary tree over s leaves with minimal *weighted external path length,* where the access frequencies of the leaves are the segment sizes $I_1, \ldots, I_s$. (Recall that the s external nodes correspond exactly to the classes $\mathcal{C}$.) This optimal BST can actually be computed reasonably efficiently with the algorithms discussed in Section 7.7.3. We ignore the cost of this step in the analysis, since we regard s as constant.

To obtain an actual algorithm, we can replace the oracle by running counts of segment sizes and we switch dynamically the comparison tree, so that it is optimal w.r.t. the current counts. Aumüller et al. [10] have shown that this strategy's comparison count is asymptotically equivalent to using the optimal tree right away. What this cost is remains to a good extent open. A formula can be given for its leading-term coefficient, which is known to be a rational number, but Aumüller et al. [10] could only compute its exact value for $s \leqslant 4$. In this section, we will derive a formula for the leading-term coefficient in our framework, including generalized pivot sampling. We also contribute the exact value for one more term: $s = 5$.

Analysis of Oracle-Based Strategy. The overall number of comparisons for the first partitioning step using the comparison-optimal strategy is

$$T_C(n) \;=\; \min_{\lambda \in \Lambda_s} \sum_{j=1}^{n} \lambda(c(U_{i_j})) \tag{5.46}$$

$$=\; \min_{\lambda \in \Lambda} \left[\sum_{i=1}^{m} \lambda(s_i) \cdot I_{m-i+1} + \sum_{i=1}^{s-m} \lambda(l_i) \cdot I_{m+i} \right] \tag{5.47}$$

$$=\; \min_{\lambda \in \Lambda} \lambda^{\mathsf{T}} \cdot \mathbf{I}, \tag{5.48}$$

for λ the leaf-depth vector of the comparison tree λ, see Equation (5.19). $T_C(n)$ is the pointwise minimum of linear functions in $\mathbf{I}$. This expression is hard to simplify in general. Note that the minimum is over exponentially many BSTs as s increases—we have $|\Lambda_s| = \frac{1}{s}\binom{2s-2}{s-1}$, the sth Catalan number—and all trees contribute for some $\mathbf{I}$. We will therefore confine ourselves to computing the leading term of $\mathbb{E}[T_C(n)]$ for the first few values of s.

We start noting that by linearity

$$\frac{T_C(n)}{n} \;=\; \min_{\lambda \in \Lambda} \lambda^{\mathsf{T}} \cdot \frac{\mathbf{I}}{n}. \tag{5.49}$$

Now, by the *strong law of large numbers* $\frac{\mathbf{I}}{n}$ converges almost surely to $\mathbf{D}$, so we have

$$\mathbb{E}\left[\frac{T_C(n)}{n} \,\middle|\, \mathbf{D} \right] \;\sim\; \min_{\lambda \in \Lambda} \lambda^{\mathsf{T}} \cdot \mathbf{D} \tag{5.50}$$

by the *continuous mapping theorem.* (The right-hand side of Equation (5.49) is the pointwise minimum of linear functions and thus continuous.)

This already gives a means to compute the leading-term coefficient of $\mathbb{E}[T_C(n)]$; we shall see, however, that we need an error bound of $O(n^{1-\varepsilon})$, cf. our Theorem 6.1 (page 196). We can get such an error guarantee from Lemma 2.36 (page 76): we use it on $\mathbb{E}[f(I/\eta) \mid D]$ with

$$f(x) \;=\; \min_{\lambda \in \Lambda} \lambda^{\mathsf{T}} \cdot x, \tag{5.51}$$

which is certainly bounded and Lipschitz-continuous over all of $[0,1]^s$ with Lipschitz constant s w.r.t. $\|\cdot\|_\infty$, since all entries in λ are at most s. We thus have by Lemma 2.36

$$\mathbb{E}[f(I/\eta) \mid D] \;=\; f(D) \pm o(n^{-1/2+\varepsilon}) \tag{5.52}$$

for any $\varepsilon > 0$, where the error bound holds uniformly for $D \in (0,1)^s$. Taking expectations over D gives the desired result

$$\mathbb{E}[T_C(n)] \;=\; \left(\int_{\Delta_s} \min_{\lambda \in \Lambda} [\lambda^{\mathsf{T}} \cdot x] \cdot \frac{x_1^{t_1} \cdots x_s^{t_s}}{B(t+1)} \, dx \right) n \;\pm\; O(n^{1-\varepsilon}), \qquad (n \to \infty), \tag{5.53}$$

for any $\varepsilon < \frac{1}{2}$ as $n \to \infty$.

Some Values. Table 3 shows the leading-term coefficient for a few exemplary values. All were computed automatically by *Mathematica* from Equation (5.53). Sampling does not seem to complicate the computation of the integral significantly, but larger numbers of pivots do: The computation for $s = 5$ already took several days and used some tens of gigabytes of main memory. The computation for $s = 6$ failed with an out-of-memory exception on our compute server with 128 GB of main memory.

Table 3: Leading-term coefficients for comparison-optimal partitioning.

t	a	$a/\mathcal{H}$
(t_1, t_2)	1	$1/\mathcal{H}$
$(0,0,0)$	$3/2$	1.8
$(1,1,1)$	$37/24$	$1.6\overline{228070175438596491}$
$(0,1,2)$	$71/48$	$1.70\overline{67307692}$
$(0,0,0,0)$	$133/72$	$1.7\overline{051282}$
$(1,1,1,1)$	$44\,761/23\,328$	$1.57553\ldots$
$(0,2,2,0)$	$5785/2916$	$1.81532\ldots$
$(0,0,0,0,0)$	$2384/1125$	$1.65\overline{125541}$

Our integral representation is amenable to the usual approaches to approximate the integral numerically. Since the integrand has bounded derivative, one should be able to bound exactly the error resulting from numeric approximations, at least in the case without pivot sampling. Of course, we will feel the *curse of dimensionality* here as well. I did not pursue this route further.

We discuss crude upper and lower bounds in the digression on page 269; there we also discuss a relation to redundancy of prefix codes. Except for $s \leqslant 5$, a feasible method to compute the precise cost of comparison-optimal partitioning remains to be found.

Open Problem 5.12 (Analysis of Comparison-Optimal Partitioning):
Compute the leading-term coefficient of the expected number of comparisons for s-way Quicksort with comparison-optimal partitioning.

This is tantamount to computing the integral in Equation (5.53), or to compute the average redundancy of alphabetic codes a.k.a. Hu-Tucker codes, i.e., the difference of the expected leaf depth in an optimal alphabetic tree and the entropy of the leaf distribution, when the leaf probabilities are $\mathbf{D} \stackrel{\mathcal{D}}{=} \mathrm{Dir}(\mathbf{t}+1)$. ◀

5.8 Branch Misses

In this section, we express the expected number of branch misses as an FSM-based charging scheme. As is common in the literature, we consider only the local branch-prediction schemes introduced in Section 3.2.5 (page 128). This means that we can consider each branching location in the code in isolation, adding up the overall number of branch misses from different locations at the end.

Branching Locations. Algorithm 9 has several branching locations, but not all are interesting w.r.t. branch misses. For example, the outer while loop (line 2) is exited exactly once per partitioning step, so this will cause only a constant number of mispredictions with any predictor scheme. The conditional statements in lines 8 and 12 are likewise executed at most once and thus contribute $O(1)$ branch misses. All of these can be ignored for the leading term of costs.

There are two more types of branching locations. The first type occurs in lines 5 and 19, and in a hidden way also in line 24 to determine the values of i and j; the second type corresponds to the comparisons used in classifying elements by searching them in the comparison trees. We call this second type *comparison branches,* since their outcome is directly tied to a specific key comparison with a certain pivot.

The branching locations of the first type are actually *conceptual* branches only; implementations can usually avoid using additional branches to implement these steps by deferring comparison branches needed for classification anyway until we can react suitably to its outcome. For example, Waterloo partitioning (Algorithm 8) directly uses key comparisons to determine which swaps resp. cyclic shifts have to be executed, by deferring the comparison with P_3 from λ_k respectively the comparison with P_1 from λ_g until directly before the ∞-shift.

This works in general if we put the master pivot into the root of the comparison tree. We therefore ignore these branching locations, and it remains to analyze branch misses from comparison branches.

5.8.1 Conditional Independence

We know that conditional on $\mathbf{D}$, the classes of ordinary elements in partitioning are i.i.d. random variables, see Fact 5.1. For comparison branches during one partitioning step, this means that the *outcomes of subsequent executions of one branch location are also i.i.d. random variables.* This allows us to analyze the number of incurred branch misses under the local predictor schemes *precisely*, since the corresponding predictor automaton is a Markov chain.

Algorithm 10: Exemplary Insertionsort implementation.

$\textsc{Insertion}(A, n)$

    // Sorts $A[1, \ldots, n]$.

```
1   for i = 2, ..., n
2       j := i − 1;   v := A[i]
3       while j ⩾ 1 ∧ v < A[j]
4           A[j + 1] := A[j];   j := j − 1
5       end while
6       A[j + 1] := v
7   end for
```

Quicksort is Special!   That branch outcomes are i.i.d. directly follows from our random model, and the observation is trivial in hindsight. But we should appreciate what a lucky situation this is. If we think of a typical program and a branch location in the code, we often find dependencies between outcomes of past executions of this branch and how likely it is for this branch to be taken in the next execution. This naturally happens if a branch outcome is actually deterministic, e.g., the branch to enter a block in a loop body that is executed exactly every other iteration. But it can more subtly happen also in situations where outcomes are random.

Consider for example the comparison branch in Insertionsort, see line 3 of Algorithm 10. Since the insertion positions in a random permutation are uniformly distributed, it is easy to see that $v < A[j]$ holds with probability $1 - \frac{1}{i}$, independently of all previous branch outcomes. This means that at the beginning of an iteration of the outer loop, when $j = i - 1$ it is quite likely that $v < A[j]$, but with each iteration of the inner loop it becomes more and more unlikely to continue.

So even if the outcome of the next execution $v < A[j]$ was stochastically independent of the previous outcomes (which it is not), the outcomes cannot be identically distributed, and our machinery to analyze branch misses is not applicable. In fact, I am not aware of a precise, mathematical analysis of branch misses in Insertionsort; Biggar et al. [23] reported from experiments that we essentially get one branch miss for each execution of the inner loop, namely when it is exited. This would be exactly the result for a static predictor that always predicts $v < A[j]$.

> **Open Problem 5.13 (Branch Misses in Insertionsort):** Analyze the expected number of branch misses in Insertionsort on random permutations using the local branch predictor schemes. ◀

> Now that we brought to mind how beautiful Quicksort is compared to other algorithms, let us quickly get back to it.

5.8.2 A Generic Comparison-Branch Location

In this section, we always consider D to be fixed. We will take the expected value w.r.t. D only at the very end. We have a comparison branch for each node in the two comparison trees λ_k and λ_g, and each of these branches has different branching characteristics: the probability to take the branch depends on the probabilities of the two subtrees of the corresponding node in the comparison tree, and there is also a probability that this node is not reached at all during the classification of an element.

Notation. Let us now consider one fixed node, say the one corresponding to P_r, in comparison tree λ_k. If we classify an element U with λ_k, we denote the three possible events w.r.t. the comparison branch for P_r as follows:

- ▶ t denotes the event that we compare U with P_r and the branch was taken.
- ▶ n denotes the event that we compare U with P_r and the branch was not taken.
- ▶ – denotes the event that we did not (directly) compare U with P_r.

Additionally, we will use s, m, and l to denote the events that $c(U)$, the class of U, is small, medium resp. large. Of course, m never occurs for master-pivot methods. We always understand the three events as disjoint, so for master-segment methods, s then means $c(U) = s_i$ with $i \geq 2$, and l similarly means $c(U) = l_j$ with $j \geq 2$.

For notational convenience, we additionally introduce the wildcard event $*$ which simply occurs always. We now abbreviate with $p_{c,b} = \mathbb{P}[c \wedge b]$ the joint probability of events $c \in \{s, m, l, *\}$ and $b \in \{t, n, -, *\}$. Some of these probabilities will be zero, and we always have $p_{*,*} = 1$. The notation generalizes abbreviations we used before see Equation (5.31) in Section 5.5.2:

$$
\begin{aligned}
p_{s,*} &= p_s = D_1 + \cdots + D_{\lfloor m \rfloor}, & (5.54) \\
p_{m,*} &= p_m = D_{\lfloor m \rfloor + 1} + \cdots + D_{\lceil m \rceil} = 1 - p_s - p_l, & (5.55) \\
p_{l,*} &= p_l = D_{\lceil m \rceil + 1} + \cdots + D_s. & (5.56)
\end{aligned}
$$

Figure 25 shows an example for a comparison-branch and the corresponding probabilities. By varying the parameter m, it is clear that none of the $p_{c,b}$ probabilities is zero in all cases, even though for any fixed choice some probabilities are zero.

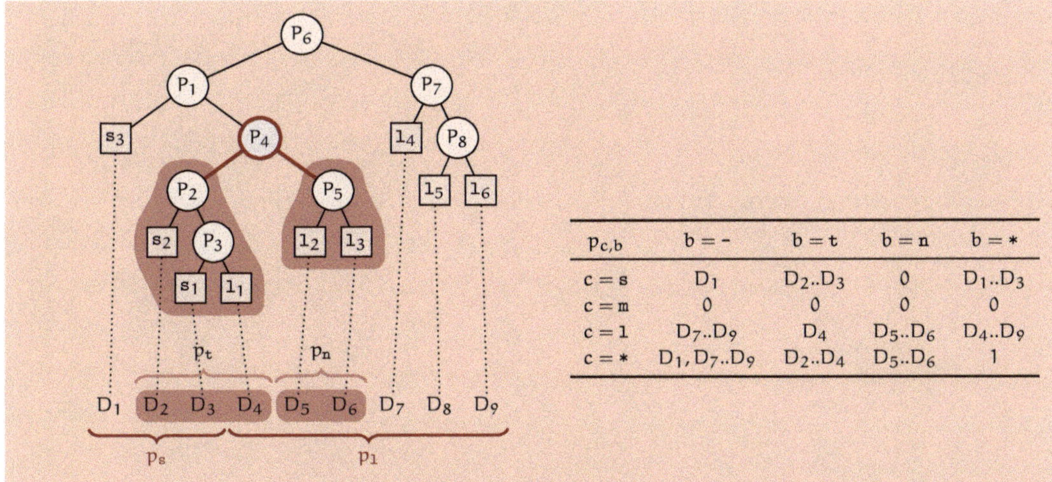

$p_{c,b}$	$b = \text{-}$	$b = t$	$b = n$	$b = *$
$c = s$	D_1	$D_2..D_3$	0	$D_1..D_3$
$c = m$	0	0	0	0
$c = 1$	$D_7..D_9$	D_4	$D_5..D_6$	$D_4..D_9$
$c = *$	$D_1, D_7..D_9$	$D_2..D_4$	$D_5..D_6$	1

Figure 25: An exemplary comparison branch for the comparison tree shown; we have $s = 9$, $m = 3$ and we consider the branch at the node corresponding to P_4. The table shows the probabilities $P_{c,b}$ for all combinations of classes $c \in \{s, m, 1, *\}$ and branch outcomes $b \in \{\text{-}, t, n, *\}$; here we write $D_k, D_i..D_j$ for $D_k + D_i + \cdots + D_j$.

Branch-Miss Automata.   The local branch-prediction schemes are given as a finite-state machine, whose states indicate the current prediction. After each execution of the branch, the state is updated. We will focus here on the *2-bit saturating-counter predictor;* its corresponding automaton is shown in Figure 9 (page 130). The techniques below apply equally well to other local branch-predictor schemes.

The outcomes of our comparison branch is positive (branch taken) with probability $p_{*,t}/(1 - p_{*,-})$ and negative (not taken) with probability $p_{*,n}/(1 - p_{*,-})$; that is, when it is executed at all: with probability $p_{*,-}$ we classify U without reaching this branch location. Additionally there is the second comparison tree in the partitioning algorithm, so for some classifications, we are for sure not reaching this branch location.

In a joint article on branch misses [117] we computed for each branch location separately how often it is reached and which fraction of its executions yield a branch miss. This requires to argue precisely why such a separation is legitimate; in fact there is also a more mechanical way to proceed that avoids this separation: we construct one big automaton, the *branch-miss automaton,* from the automata for comparison trees (Figure 24) and the branch-predictor automaton (Figure 9).

Its states are all pairs of states, i.e., (i, q) for $i \in [4]$ and $q \in \{q_k, q_g\}$. For q_g-states, i.e., states with q_g as second components, outgoing transitions are copied from the comparison-tree automaton, i.e., they ignore the first component of the state and leave it unchanged; in q_g, we do not execute the branch in λ_k. For q_k-states, we similarly leave i unchanged if we do not execute the branch; these transitions are labeled with a $-$ then. For the other transitions, we update i as in the predictor automaton, and at the same time

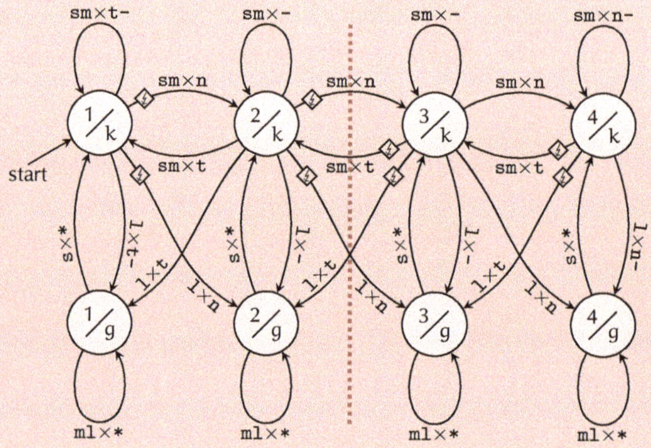

Figure 26: Branch-miss Markov chain for a generic comparison branch in λ_k. The edge labels encode the transition probabilities, where, e.g., "sm×t-" means $p_{s,t} + p_{s,-} + p_{m,t} + p_{m,-}$ (expand all combinations and add them up).

update q as in the comparison-tree automaton. This is where we need all the combinations of events s, m, l, resp –, t, and n. The resulting automaton is shown in Figure 26, labeled with the corresponding transition probabilities.

> **Product Automata.** The construction is similar to the idea of *product automata:* there also the states are all pairs of original states, and transitions are chosen so that the restriction to one component of the states gives the original transitions. Intuitively, the product automaton simulates running both original automata independently in parallel by keeping track of the current state of each. This is a classic construction in the field of formal languages; product automata accept the intersection of two languages, see e.g., Hopcroft et al. [83].
>
> Our construction looks similar, but the transitions are a bit different: we *pause* execution of the branch-predictor while we are in a q_g-state.

Since we consider **D** fixed, the automaton defines a Markov chain. All that remains to do is to determine the expected number of transitions using edges marked with a ◈ symbol in a random run of length η of this Markov chain.

This is possible with the technique described in Section 5.5.2: the transitions of the Markov chain induce a linear system of equations for the generating function $F_{1k}(z, u) = \sum_{\eta, i} b_{\eta, i} z^\eta u^i$ where $b_{\eta, i}$ is the probability for a random run of the Markov chain that starts in state $(1, k)$ and takes η transitions in total to use exactly i branch-miss transitions. Solving the system of equations and determining the coefficients $[z^\eta] \frac{\partial}{\partial u} F_{1k}(z, u)\big|_{u=1}$ gives the expected number of branch misses at a comparison branch location when classifying η ordinary elements.

Since the terms become large the use of computer algebra is unavoidable with this approach, and we skip the details here. Although the results can be obtained exactly in principle, the terms are so huge that *Mathematica* could not produce a result in a reasonable amount of time. Hence, I truncated precision already at the level of generating function by considering only a singular expansion around the dominant singularity $z = 1$; one finds

$$\frac{\partial}{\partial u}F_{1k}(z,u)\bigg|_{u=1} = \frac{A}{(1-z)^2} \pm O((1-z)^{-1}), \qquad (z \to 1), \tag{5.57}$$

for a constant A that depends on the probabilities $p_{c,b}$. By Theorem 2.19 we thus have $[z^\eta]\frac{\partial}{\partial u}F_{1k}(z,u)\big|_{u=1} = A(\eta+1) \pm O(1)$. (The function is clearly Δ-analytic since $z = 1$ is its only singularity.) After simplifying the term for A a bit, we find

$$A = \frac{p_{s,*}}{1-p_{m,*}}(1-p_{*,-}) \cdot \frac{p_{*,t}p_{*,n}}{p_{*,t}^2 + p_{*,n}^2} \tag{5.58}$$

$$= \underbrace{\frac{p_{s,*}}{1-p_{m,*}}(1-p_{*,-})}_{\substack{\text{\# executions} \\ \text{of branch}}} \cdot \underbrace{\frac{q}{1-2q}}_{\substack{\text{steady-state} \\ \text{miss rate}}}, \qquad \text{where } q = \frac{p_{*,t}p_{*,n}}{p_{*,t}+p_{*,n}}. \tag{5.59}$$

Note that for the leading term, the probabilities could be split again into terms that only depend on the events s, m and 1, and terms that only depend on the events t, n and -. In the latter form, we obtain as special cases our results on YBB Quicksort and classic Quicksort [117]; in particular the term $\frac{q}{1-2q}$ with $q = p(1-p)$ is the *steady-state miss-rate function*, i.e., the expected misprediction probability for a branch that is i.i.d. taken with probability p (after a long sequence of branch executions).

For any fixed comparison node, this is a function of $\mathbf{D}$, and we have to take expectation over $\mathbf{D}$ at the end. Here the rules of Dirichlet-calculus are useful; however, I could not find a nice closed form in the end; cf. the *geometric beta integrals* from Figure 4 of Martínez et al. [117]. We therefore leave the analysis of branch misses in this stage, remarking that it requires only a good portion of diligence and computer algebra to compute the expected number of branch misses for any given choice of parameters of generic s-way one-pass partitioning.

With this, we close our chapter on the analysis of partitioning. The notion of (FSM-based) element-wise charging schemes combined with the uniform input model has proven to be just the right tool to analyze partitioning algorithms for Quicksort, even for such complicated cost measures as branch misses.

Now that we understand what it costs to do a single step in the recursive Quicksort algorithm, we can turn to its overall costs, given by the Quicksort recurrence.

6 The Quicksort Recurrence

Contents

IMPLEMENTING QUICKSORT reduces to implementing a partitioning method and surrounding it with a recursive-call scaffold. Analyzing Quicksort reduces to analyzing the partitioning method and inserting the result into a recursive description of overall costs.

While recursion is deceptively simple to implement, its analysis can be challenging, and we are far from having a general automatic solution for that. We do have theorems of impressive generality, however, to solve many kinds of recursive equations, if we are willing to accept an *asymptotic* solution.

In this chapter, we derive such solutions for the generalized Quicksort recurrence, corresponding to the costs of s-way Quicksort with pivot sampling. Here is our main result of this chapter.

> **Theorem 6.1 (Total Expected Costs):**
> *The total expected costs $\mathbb{E}[C_n]$ for sorting a random permutation with a randomness-preserving Quicksort using a partitioning method that incurs expected costs $\mathbb{E}[T_n]$ of the form $\mathbb{E}[T_n] = an \pm O(n^{1-\varepsilon})$, with constants a and $\varepsilon > 0$, to produce s segments, and whose $s - 1$ pivots are chosen by generalized pivot sampling with parameter $\mathbf{t} \in \mathbb{N}^s$ are asymptotically*
>
> $$\mathbb{E}[C_n] \;=\; \frac{a}{\mathcal{H}} n \ln n \pm O(n),$$
>
> *where $\mathcal{H}$ is the discrete entropy of $\mathbf{t}$:*
>
> $$\mathcal{H} \;=\; \sum_{r=1}^{s} \frac{t_r + 1}{k + 1}(H_{k+1} - H_{t_r+1}). \qquad (2.193) \text{ revisited}$$
>
> *This result also holds if we truncate the recursion at subproblems of size at most w, for any constant w, and switch to another sorting method.* ◀

The solution to the recurrence underlying Theorem 6.1 has long been known, see also below. In fact, all technical results in this section, already appeared in previous work in one form or another; but there is no source that rigorously proves Theorem 6.1 in the form above, in particular with the weaker requirement $\mathbb{E}[T_n] - an = O(n^{1-\varepsilon})$ on the toll function.

This chapter contains two formal proofs as well as and some back-of-the-envelope ideas. Certainly it could have been shortened, but while researching on the Quicksort recurrence, I stumbled upon many interesting connections between recurrence, tools and techniques that are not pointed out in existing literature, and I feel that they deserve begin mentioned.

Chapter Outline. We discuss the Quicksort recurrence in Section 6.1; we give a distributional recurrence of total costs, from which one can derive the ordinary recurrence for expected costs easily. We then first discuss some non-rigorous, but insightful approaches to estimate the solution of the Quicksort recurrence in Section 6.2.

Hennequin [77, Proposition III.9] gave the first formal proof of (a slightly weaker form of) Theorem 6.1 using direct arguments on the Cauchy-Euler differential equations that the recurrence implies for the generating function of $\mathbb{E}[C_n]$. Sedgewick [162] used that method already in his Ph. D. thesis to analyze classic Quicksort with sampling. We retrace this path of arguments in Section 6.5.

Building on the toolbox of theorems developed by the analysis-of-algorithms community, the proof of Theorem 6.1 can be simplified significantly, and we present this straightened-out derivation first: Section 6.3 gives the proof using the *Continuous Master Theorem* of Roura [154]. Here we use our Distributional Master Theorem (Theorem 2.70) as a shortcut. The latter derivation nicely generalizes to the case of random-parameter sampling, see Section 6.4.

Constant-Coefficient Error Term.   We can strengthen the statement of Theorem 6.1 a little further: the $O(n)$ error term has a constant coefficient.

Lemma 6.2: *Under the conditions of Theorem 6.1 there is a constant $\mu \in \mathbb{R}$ so that*

$$\mathbb{E}[C_n] \;=\; \frac{a}{\mathcal{H}} n \ln n + \mu n + o(n). \qquad\qquad \blacktriangleleft$$

For direct applications this fact is not very relevant, unless we can get hold of that constant, as well. This is doable in principle, but the procedure is only tractable for special cases, and we will not pursue this path in this work. Even when the constant remains unspecified, the stronger result is very helpful in studying limit distributions with the contraction method, where a linear term with μn entails cancellation of the linear terms after normalization. This ensures the needed convergence of the toll function in the normalized recurrence; see, e.g., Wild et al. [186].

Not all methods provide enough detail to prove this stronger version; in fact there seems to be no shortcut around the detailed generating-function approach pursued by Hennequin [77]. To my knowledge, Hennequin's French thesis is the only source with a rigorous proof of Lemma 6.2 for the generalized Quicksort recurrence with Insertionsort cutoff, and we reproduce it in Section 6.5 for future reference.

6.1 Recursive Description of Costs

Fix one of our measures of cost from Chapter 3, e.g., the number of comparisons, and denote by C_n the (random) costs to sort a random permutation of size n. Further let T_n denote the (random) costs for the first partitioning step in doing so. It is immediate from the recursive structure of Quicksort that C_n can be written as T_n plus the costs for the recursive calls.

> **Additive Costs.**   We use here that all our cost measures are *additive:* costs of sequential executions add up. This is not the case in general; e.g., for memory usage, we would have to take the maximum.

Let $J_1^{(n)}, \ldots, J_s^{(n)}$ be the (random) sizes of the s subproblems. Since we assume that Quicksort preserves randomness in subproblems, the costs to sort a subproblem of size j has the same distribution as the costs to sort an initial input of size j, i.e., it has the same distribution as C_j. We can thus give a recursive description of the distribution of total costs.

The Distributional Recurrence. The total costs of Quicksort form a family $(C_n)_{n\in\mathbb{N}}$ of nonnegative random variables which satisfies the following distributional recurrence:

$$C_n \overset{\mathcal{D}}{=} T_n + \sum_{r=1}^{s} C_{J_r^{(n)}}^{(r)}, \qquad (n > w); \qquad\qquad (6.1.1)$$

$$C_n \overset{\mathcal{D}}{=} W_n, \qquad (n \leqslant w), \qquad\qquad (6.1.2)$$

where $(C_n^{(1)})_{n\in\mathbb{N}}, \ldots, (C_n^{(s)})_{n\in\mathbb{N}}$ are independent copies of $(C_n)_{n\in\mathbb{N}}$, which are also independent of $\mathbf{J}^{(n)} = (J_1^{(n)}, \ldots, J_s^{(n)}) \in \{0, \ldots, n-1\}^s$ and T_n. (For a more detailed description of what these side conditions mean, see Section 2.6.2.)

The distribution of the subproblem sizes $\mathbf{J}^{(n)}$ is discussed in Section 5.2 in detail; we only summarize the result here. Recall the abbreviations we introduced there: $\sigma = t + 1$, $\kappa = \Sigma\sigma = k + 1$, $\tau = \sigma/\kappa$, and $\eta = n - k$.

$$\mathbf{J}^{(n)} = \mathbf{I}^{(n)} + \mathbf{t}, \qquad\qquad (6.2.1)$$

$$\mathbf{I}^{(n)} \overset{\mathcal{D}}{=} \mathrm{Mult}(\eta, \mathbf{D}), \qquad\qquad (6.2.2)$$

$$\mathbf{D} \overset{\mathcal{D}}{=} \mathrm{Dir}(\sigma). \qquad\qquad (6.2.3)$$

(For a description of the multinomial distribution and the Dirichlet distribution, see Section 2.4.) We will drop the superscripts when n is clear from the context.

For arrays of length at most w, which is the (constant) Insertionsort threshold $w \geqslant k$, we have the initial values W_n, the cost to sort a random permutation of length n with Insertionsort. Of course, Insertionsort can be replaced with other sorting methods; the choice does not matter: the careful reader will have noticed that the initial values do not appear in Theorem 6.1 since they do not contribute to the leading term of costs.

As in the theorem, we assume from now on that

$$\mathbb{E}[T_n] = an \pm O(n^{1-\varepsilon}) \qquad\qquad (6.3)$$

for constants $\varepsilon > 0$ and a. The leading-term coefficient a eventually depends on the parameters of the partitioning algorithm, namely, s, m and our pivot selection scheme as described by t.

6.1.1 Nitpicks on Generalized Pivot Sampling

If we sort samples to select pivots in place, Equation (6.1) is not 100 % accurate. The costs of sorting the sample then depend on whether the current call is a topmost invocation or an rth child recursive call. The reason is that the ranges of the sample from the parent call are already sorted.

For an earlier article, I worked out a detailed implementation of YBB Quicksort that actually exploits this presortedness and maintains randomness [137], which is vital for the analysis. The basic idea is to use Insertionsort, but skip the first few iterations corresponding to the sorted part. I refer the reader to reference [137] for details. The same ideas work for generic s-way one-pass partitioning.

For most interesting cost measures, the resulting savings only depend on the length ℓ of the sorted part, not on the length of the whole array. If we denote these savings by E_ℓ, we pay E_{t_r} less for calls to an rth subproblem, regardless of n: We either save in sorting the sample or in sorting the whole subarray if there are at most w elements. We assume that the *same* algorithm is used for sorting both samples and small subarrays.

Using the following simple *charging scheme*, we can then still write total costs in the form of Equation (6.1), with a reduced toll function $\tilde{T}_n$: We simply discount the future savings $E_t := E_{t_1} + \cdots + E_{t_s}$ of all recursive calls directly in the current call. Then each partitioning step adds the reduced toll costs of $\tilde{T}_n := T_n - E_t$, where T_n contains the cost of fully sorting the sample, and all subarrays shorter than w pay the full price of Insertionsorting their elements.

Since t is considered a constant, the savings described above will not affect the leading term of costs. We will thus ignore these in the rest of this work. The reader who prefers so may imagine that we instead use another one of the methods to preserve randomness discussed in Section 4.5. For the purpose of this work, the result will be the same.

6.1.2 Recurrence for Expected Costs

From the practitioner's point of view, we are primarily interested in the average behavior of Quicksort. We easily obtain an (ordinary) recurrence for the sequence $(\mathbb{E}[C_n])_{n \in \mathbb{N}_0}$ of expected costs $\mathbb{E}[C_n]$ from the distributional recurrence for C_n by taking expectations, circumventing thereby the error-prone task of coming up with probabilities for subproblem sizes anew.

A little care is needed in doing so, because the right-hand side involves several random quantities, namely T, C and $\mathbf{J}$:

$$T_n + \sum_{r=1}^{s} C^{(r)}_{J_r^{(n)}}.$$

Our aim is a recurrence in $\mathbb{E}[C_n]$, i.e., we would like to express the expected value of this as a function of terms $\mathbb{E}[C_j]$ for (deterministic) numbers j. Taking expectations $\mathbb{E}[C_{J_r}]$ would result in a "mix" of $\mathbb{E}[C_j]$ for different values of j.

We can apply a trick here called *conditioning* to get the terms in the shape we need. In general, if $\mathbf{X}$ is a discrete random variable, taking values in the countable set $\mathcal{X}$, and $f(\mathbf{X})$ is a term depending on $\mathbf{X}$, we have

$$f(\mathbf{X}) \;=\; \sum_{x \in \mathcal{X}} \mathbb{1}_{\{\mathbf{X}=x\}} f(x). \tag{6.4}$$

In our sum over subproblems, we condition on $\mathbf{J}$ to find

$$\sum_{r=1}^{s} C_{J_r^{(n)}}^{(r)} \;=\; \sum_{j \in \mathbb{N}_0^s} \mathbb{1}_{\{\mathbf{J}^{(n)}=j\}} \sum_{r=1}^{s} C_{j_r^{(n)}}^{(r)}\,, \tag{6.5}$$

which is of the form we need for a proper recurrence. So finally taking expectations on both sides of Equation (6.1) gives

$$\mathbb{E}[C_n] \;=\; \mathbb{E}[T_n] + \mathbb{E}\left[\sum_{j \in \mathbb{N}_0^s} \mathbb{1}_{\{\mathbf{J}^{(n)}=j\}} \sum_{r=1}^{s} C_{j_r^{(n)}}^{(r)} \right], \qquad (n > w), \tag{6.6}$$

and since $\mathbf{J}$ and $C_{j_r}^{(r)}$ are independent, and $C_{j_r}^{(r)} \overset{\mathcal{D}}{=} C_{j_r}$, we obtain an ordinary recurrence for the sequence of numbers $(\mathbb{E}[C_n])_{n \in \mathbb{N}_0}$ that we can approach with the usual machinery:

$$\mathbb{E}[C_n] \;=\; \mathbb{E}[T_n] + \sum_{j \in \mathbb{N}_0^s} \mathbb{P}\big[\mathbf{J}^{(n)}=j\big] \sum_{r=1}^{s} \mathbb{E}[C_{j_r}], \qquad (n > w). \tag{6.7}$$

Note that the sum over j in Equation (6.7) is finite for all n, as $\mathbb{P}\big[\mathbf{J}^{(n)}=j\big] = 0$ unless $\Sigma j = n - (s-1)$. We can therefore safely exchange the order of summation to collect all terms with the same subproblem size:

$$\mathbb{E}[C_n] \;=\; \mathbb{E}[T_n] + \sum_{j=0}^{n-(s-1)} \left(\sum_{r=1}^{s} \mathbb{P}\big[J_r^{(n)}=j\big] \right) \cdot \mathbb{E}[C_j], \qquad (n > w). \tag{6.8}$$

This is a second useful representation of our recurrence, one that very explicitly shows its *full-history* nature.

6.1.3   Relation to Combinatorial Form for Subproblem Size Probabilities

We can directly argue *combinatorially* that

$$\mathbb{P}[\mathbf{J}=j] \;=\; \begin{cases} \dfrac{\binom{j_1}{t_1} \cdots \binom{j_s}{t_s}}{\binom{n}{k}}, & \text{if } j_1 + \cdots + j_s = n - (s-1); \\[2ex] 0, & \text{otherwise.} \end{cases} \tag{6.9}$$

The representation via binomial coefficients holds because for a fixed j, there are $\binom{j_1}{t_1}$ ways to choose exactly t_1 elements from the smallest group, $\binom{j_2}{t_2}$ ways to choose from the second smallest, etc. Combining all these yields the number of possible size-k samples compatible with a given j, which we divide by the overall number of samples.

    The following lemma gives an arithmetic proof that both models are really the same.

Lemma 6.3: *Let* $t \in \mathbb{N}_0^s$ *be given and let* $\mathbf{J} \in \{0, \dots, n\}$ *be a random variable so that* $\mathbb{P}[\mathbf{J}=j]$ *is given by Equation (6.9). Then* $\mathbf{I} = \mathbf{J} - t \overset{\mathcal{D}}{=} \mathrm{DirMult}(n-k, t+1)$.   ◀

Proof: We compute using $\eta = n - k$ and $i = j - t$

$$\frac{\binom{j_1}{t_1} \cdots \binom{j_s}{t_s}}{\binom{n}{k}} = \frac{\Gamma(k+1)\Gamma(n-k+1)}{\Gamma(n+1)} \prod_{r=1}^{s} \frac{\Gamma(j_r+1)}{\Gamma(t_r+1)\Gamma(j_r-t_r+1)} \tag{6.10}$$

$$= \frac{\Gamma(k+1)\Gamma(\eta+1)}{\Gamma(\eta+k+1)} \prod_{r=1}^{s} \frac{\Gamma(i_r+t_r+1)}{\Gamma(t_r+1)\Gamma(i_r+1)} \tag{6.11}$$

$$= \frac{\Gamma(\eta+1)}{\prod_{r=1}^{s}\Gamma(i_r+1)} \cdot \frac{\Gamma(k+1)}{\prod_{r=1}^{s}\Gamma(t_r+1)} \cdot \frac{\prod_{r=1}^{s}\Gamma(i_r+t_r+1)}{\Gamma(\eta+k+1)} \tag{6.12}$$

$$= \binom{\eta}{i_1,\ldots,i_s} \frac{B((t+1)+i)}{B(t+1)}, \tag{6.13}$$

which is the probability weight of a Dirichlet-multinomial distribution with parameters $\eta = n - k$ and $t + 1$. ∎

6.2 Back-of-the-Envelope Approaches

Before tackling formal proofs, let us first devise a *guess-timate* for $\mathbb{E}[C_n]$ following gut instinct, ignoring any cumbersome technicalities in our way. Such informal reasoning is dangerous since we might arrive at wrong results. Not pursuing the path of intuition altogether is just as dangerous, though, because interesting results might not be found at all: they might be too deep in the jungle to be seen from our current camp of rigorous knowledge.

Therefore, we first explore some back-of-the-envelope computations, and back them up later with rigorous proofs. To make this very clear here is my explicit disclaimer: *This section is not intended to prove Theorem 6.1, it is there to convey intuitions.* That said, let us start. Since we seek an approximation for large n, let us consider n to be large, in particular $n > w$, throughout this section.

6.2.1 Van Emden's Entropy-Reduction Argument

Van Emden [55] was the first researcher to analytically compute the number of comparisons for classic Quicksort with median-of-$(2t + 1)$. He attributes the formula to F. E. J. Kruseman Aretz, who did not publish it however.

Van Emden's derivation builds on an intuitive entropy argument, which is not fully rigorous, but definitely deserves to be mentioned here, not only because it is the historically first published argument, but also because it conveys another enlightening perspective on the Quicksort recurrence.

Sorting is a process of learning about the input: initially, we do not know anything about the relative order of input elements, at the end, we have (maybe implicitly) fully identified the initial permutation. In order to get there, we thus have to overcome $\mathrm{ld}(n!)$ bits of uncertainty or *entropy*. By comparing two elements, we learn at most one bit, since the outcome is binary. If we knew the (average) amount of information gain per comparison, we could invert that to compute how many such trials, i.e., how many comparisons, we need to learn the whole permutation.

The amount of information gained is hard to tell on this individual basis, but we can determine it for a whole partitioning step. If after partitioning, the pivot has rank I, all $(I-1)!(n-I)!$ permutations of the remaining elements are still possible, leaving us with uncertainty of $\mathrm{ld}((I-1)!) + \mathrm{ld}((n-I)!)$ bits. The *information yield* of the first partitioning step then is $\mathrm{ld}(n!) - \mathrm{ld}((I-1)!) - \mathrm{ld}((n-I)!)$; since we used n comparisons for that, the average information gain per comparison is that divided by n. Asymptotically for large n, we have $\mathrm{ld}(n!) \sim n\,\mathrm{ld}(n)$, so this information gain H is roughly

$$H \;=\; \frac{1}{n}\Big(n\,\mathrm{ld}(n) - I\,\mathrm{ld}(I) - (n-I)\,\mathrm{ld}(n-I)\Big) \tag{6.14}$$

$$=\; -\frac{I}{n}\,\mathrm{ld}\!\left(\frac{I}{n}\right) - \frac{n-I}{n}\,\mathrm{ld}\!\left(\frac{n-I}{n}\right) \tag{6.15}$$

$$\approx\; -Z\,\mathrm{ld}(Z) - (1-Z)\,\mathrm{ld}(1-Z) \tag{6.16}$$

for $Z = I/n$. Now, for large n and a pivot chosen as median of $2t+1$ sample elements, we have $Z \overset{\mathcal{D}}{=} \mathrm{Beta}(t+1, t+1)$; we then obtain (Proposition 2.54 on page 90)

$$\mathbb{E}[H] \;\approx\; -2\mathbb{E}[Z\,\mathrm{ld}(Z)] \;=\; -\frac{H_{t+1} - H_{2t+2}}{\ln(2)} \;=\; \frac{\mathcal{H}}{\ln(2)}. \tag{6.17}$$

The expected number of comparisons is then $\mathrm{ld}(n!)/\mathbb{E}[H] \approx \frac{1}{\mathcal{H}} n \ln(n)$. Van Emden's argument can be extended to multiway Quicksort and asymmetric sampling; the only change is that in our general model $\mathbb{E}[H] = -\sum_{r=1}^{s} \mathbb{E}[D_r\,\mathrm{ld}(D_r)]$, leading to the general formula for $\mathcal{H}$ from Equation (2.193).

♦   ♦   ♦

The two steps, using the asymptotic approximation of $\mathrm{ld}(n!)$ for I and $n - I$, and replacing I/n by Z, require formal justification, to bound the resulting error term. We essentially follow this route in Section 6.3 below. The key to get back to firm grounds is to argue along the formal description of costs that we have: the recurrence. So we try to get it into a form that is easier to reason about.

6.2.2 A Continuous Recurrence

We start with the recurrence for $\mathbb{E}[C_n]$ in Equation (6.8), where we ignore the constant offsets in $n - (s-1)$ and the error term for $\mathbb{E}[T_n] = an \pm O(n^{1-\varepsilon})$

$$\mathbb{E}[C_n] \;\approx\; an + \sum_{j=0}^{n} \mathbb{E}[C_j] \underbrace{\sum_{r=1}^{s} \mathbb{P}[J_r = j]}_{=:w_{n,j}}. \tag{6.18}$$

The sum over *all* previous terms makes things a little involved; in particular the dependence of the weights $w_{n,j}$ on the current value of n is a pain in the neck. Let us get rid of those then. We first symbolically substitute $z \cdot n$ for j, so that $z \in [0,1]$ becomes the *relative subproblem size*:

$$\mathbb{E}[C_n] \;\approx\; an \;+\; \sum_{zn=0}^{n} \mathbb{E}[C_{zn}] \sum_{r=1}^{s} \mathbb{P}\left[\frac{J_r}{n} = z\right]. \tag{6.19}$$

In the sum over zn, of course n remains unchanged while z goes from 0 to 1, in discrete steps of $\frac{1}{n}$. As often, things get simpler when discreetness is thrown overboard. When n gets larger and larger, z "scans" the unit interval more and more densely, so that it is plausible to replace the sum by an integral:

$$\sum_{zn=0}^{n} \mathbb{E}[C_{zn}] \sum_{r=1}^{s} \mathbb{P}\left[\frac{J_r}{n} = z\right] \;\approx\; \int_{z=0}^{1} \mathbb{E}[C_{zn}] \sum_{r=1}^{s} \mathbb{P}\left[\frac{J_r}{n} \in (z-dz, z]\right] dz. \tag{6.20}$$

J_r is essentially $\mathrm{Bin}(n-k, D_r) \approx \mathrm{Bin}(n, D_r)$ distributed when we fix $\mathbf{D}$. For n large, J_r/n is thus very close to its expectation D_r, so we continue with

$$\approx \int_{z=0}^{1} \mathbb{E}[C_{zn}] \sum_{r=1}^{s} \mathbb{P}\left[D_r \in (z-dz, z]\right] dz. \tag{6.21}$$

$\mathbb{P}\left[D_r \in (z-dz, z]\right]$ is nothing else than the density $f_{D_r}(z)$ of D_r. This means that the *relative subproblem size* follow a beta distribution, namely $\mathrm{Beta}(t_r + 1, k - t_r)$ for the rth subproblem ($r = 1, \ldots, s$). This does not depend on n any more. Hooray!

Recapitulating our steps up to now, we obtain a *continuous* recurrence

$$\mathbb{E}[C_n] \;\approx\; an \;+\; \int_0^1 w(z)\mathbb{E}[C_{zn}]\,dz, \tag{6.22}$$

where $w(z)$ is the *shape function* of the recurrence, i.e.,

$$w(z) \;=\; \sum_{r=1}^{s} f_{D_r}(z) \;=\; \sum_{r=1}^{s} \frac{z^{t_r}(1-z)^{k-t_r-1}}{B(t_r+1, k-t_r)}. \tag{6.23}$$

6.2.3 Explicit Solution of Continuous Recurrence

Equation (6.22) is what we called the *equilibrium equation* of the original recurrence in Section 2.6.4. There we made an educated guess for a solution and prove it correct; we will repeat that process for our specific recurrence in Section 6.2.5. But let us take a step back and try to justify this guess purely analytically.

Equation (6.22) is an integral equation for the unknown function $\phi(x) = \mathbb{E}[C_x]$ of the form

$$\phi(x) \;=\; ax \;+\; \int_0^1 w(z)\phi(zx)\,dz. \tag{6.24}$$

The term $\phi(zx)$ might look scary, but we can substitute $z = u/x$ to get rid of it

$$\phi(x) \;=\; ax + \int_0^x \underbrace{\frac{w(u/x)}{x}}_{K(x,u)} \phi(u)\,du. \tag{6.25}$$

Equations of this form are called *Volterra integral equations of the second kind,* they are discussed, e.g., by Arfken and Weber [5]. General solutions are not available for such integral equations, but there is hope if they have a *separable kernel,* i.e., if the part $K(x,u) = \frac{w(u/x)}{x}$ of the integrand without the unknown function, can be written as $K(x,u) = \sum_i M_i(x) \cdot N_i(u)$. As our $w(z)$ is a polynomial, such a separation is possible, more precisely, we have

$$K(x,u) \;=\; \frac{w(u/x)}{x} \;=\; \sum_{i=1}^{k} \lambda_i \frac{u^{i-1}}{x^i} \tag{6.26}$$

by expanding. The coefficients λ_i can be computed explicitly, but we leave them for now symbolically. Inserting into Equation (6.25), exchanging the order of integration and summation, and finally multiplying by x^k gives

$$\phi(x)x^k \;=\; ax^{k+1} + \sum_{i=1}^{k} \lambda_i x^{k-i} \underbrace{\int_0^x u^{i-1}\phi(u)\,du}_{``\frac{d^{-1}}{dx^{-1}}x^{i-1}\phi(x)"}. \tag{6.27}$$

Now in this form, the integrals are precisely in form of the *fundamental theorem of calculus,* so by differentiating k times on both sides, we do away with all integrals and obtain a linear differential equation of order k. Moreover, all terms involving ϕ are products with powers of x (or u inside the integral, but after taking the derivative of the integral, u turns into x) *with like powers.* After taking the kth derivative, these terms are sums of terms of the form $x^i\phi^{(i)}(x)$, so that the resulting differential equation is actually a Cauchy-Euler equation. It can therefore be solved explicitly for a given sampling parameter t.

Example. Let us quickly illustrate the process for $t = (1,1)$, median-of-three Quicksort. The kernel then is $K(x,u) = -12\frac{u^2}{x^3} + 12\frac{u}{x^2}$, which is already in the separated form. We have $k = 3$ and the constants in the expansion are $(\lambda_1, \lambda_2, \lambda_3) = (0, 12, -12)$. Inserting into Equation (6.27) and differentiating thrice, we obtain the Cauchy-Euler differential equation

$$x^3\phi'''(x) + 9x^2\phi''(x) + 6x\phi'(x) - 6\phi(x) \;=\; 24ax\,. \tag{6.28}$$

With the differential operator $\Theta f(x) = xf'(x)$ the equation can be written as $(\Theta + 6)(\Theta + 1)(\Theta - 1).\phi(x) = 24ax$, and successively solved to

$$\phi(x) \;=\; \frac{12}{7}ax\ln x + \left(c_1 - \frac{54}{49}a\right)x + \frac{c_2}{x} + \frac{c_3}{x^6}\,. \tag{6.29}$$

> The integration constants c_1, c_2 and c_3 depend on the initial conditions; they do not affect the leading term though, and its coefficient is correct!

One might try to derive a closed form for the operator polynomial, which will always have a root $\Theta = 1$ contributing the $\ln x$ factor. If we obtain the corresponding summand of the solution, that would give another derivation of $\mathcal{H}$.

With this approach, we can determine the general solution of the equilibrium equation. We will verify in Section 6.2.5 that there is always a particular solution of the form $\phi(x) = \frac{\alpha}{\beta} x \ln x$; and we will see later that the difference between the equilibrium solution and the solution of the original recurrence dominates the contribution of any other summands of the general solution. We will therefore not pursue this path further; but it is interesting that the continuous recurrence for the total cost function leads to structurally very similar differential equations as for the *generating function* of the cost sequence, see Section 6.5.1.

The analytic solution of Equation (6.22) is doable, but cumbersome to carry out. Maybe we can throw in some algorithmic insight to get to its solution without the rote calculations on differential equations? Let us again take a step back and consider how we would roughly bound the effort of a divide-and-conquer algorithm.

6.2.4 A Master-Theorem-Style Argument

In the classical *master theorem* for divide-and-conquer recurrences, there are three cases to distinguish depending on the toll function:

1 If the toll function grows very slowly with n, the current subproblem size is not very relevant, but the *number* of considered subproblems is important. In terms of a recursion tree, the major contribution comes from the leaves of the tree. This also means that initial conditions of the recurrence are important.

2 If the toll function has just the right rate of growth, the toll for treating one subproblem is (roughly) the same as the tolls of treating all its direct child subproblems. This means that on each level of the recursion tree, the toll costs sum up to (roughly) the same cost and the overall solution is given by this sum of costs times the recursion depth. In a classical divide-and-conquer recurrence, this depth is logarithmic.

3 Finally, if the toll function grows very fast with n, the first step essentially dominates overall costs, as the toll costs of subproblems are small in relation to the first step. The first two cases need no further restriction on the toll function, but in this last case we have to assume a technical regularity condition.

Binary search and Mergesort are prime examples of the second case; in the analysis of Karatsuba's integer multiplication or Strassen's matrix multiplication, we end up in the first case, and in the *Median-of-Medians* selection algorithm, the initial call is asymptotically dominating, so we get the third case (see, e.g., Cormen et al. [35] for these examples).

The classical master theorem distinguishes these cases by comparing, for large n, the toll of the topmost call with the total tolls of all its immediate child recursive calls. If there is an (asymptotic) imbalance to the one or the other side, this imbalance will eventually dominate for large n.

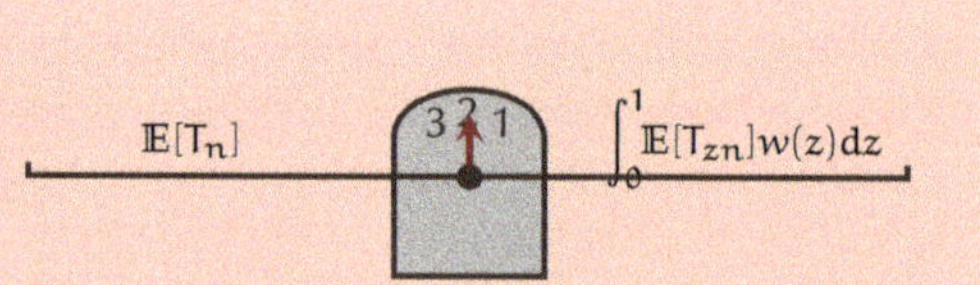

Figure 27: Balance scale of asymptotics. Depending on which side outweighs the other, we have one of the three cases of the master theorem.

Quicksort is a paragon of divide and conquer, should not its recurrence be similar to those well-conducted divide-and-conquer recurrences then? In fact, it is, only that we have to consider the *expected* toll cost of the child subproblems to make the above case distinction. So let us compare the toll of the first call $\mathbb{E}[T_n]$ to the total tolls of its child recursive calls, i.e., how

$$\int_0^1 \mathbb{E}[T_{zn}]\,w(z)\,dz \tag{6.30}$$

relates to $\mathbb{E}[T_n]$, as illustrated by Figure 27. Upon inserting the leading term $\mathbb{E}[T_n] = a \cdot n$, we find

$$\int_0^1 azn\,w(z)\,dz \;=\; an, \tag{6.31}$$

so the balanced case applies: The total cost of the child subproblems is (asymptotically) the *same* as the cost of the initial call. In analogy with the classical master theorem, the overall costs $\mathbb{E}[C_n]$ are thus the toll cost of the initial call times the number of levels in the recursion tree.

6.2.5 Leading Term by Ansatz

Guessing that the number of recursion levels will be logarithmic as in the case of the classical master theorem, we make the *ansatz* $\mathbb{E}[C_n] = \frac{a}{\beta}n\ln n$ with an unknown constant β. Inserting into Equation (6.22) yields

$$\frac{a}{\beta}n\ln n \;=\; an + \int_0^1 w(z)\,\frac{a}{\beta}zn\ln(zn)\,dz\,. \tag{6.32}$$

Multiplying by $\frac{\beta}{an}$ and rearranging, we find

$$\beta \;=\; \ln n \cdot \left(1 - \int_0^1 zw(z)\,dz\right) - \int_0^1 z\ln(z)w(z)\,dz, \tag{6.33}$$

where the first integral is 1, we just computed it in Equation (6.31). This is good; otherwise we would be left with a $\ln n$ term. The second integral turns out to be precisely $-\mathcal{H}$

(Proposition 2.54 on page 90). Recall that $\mathcal{H} = \mathcal{H}(\mathbf{t})$ is the discrete entropy of $\mathbf{t}$ defined in Equation (2.193). So we find that

$$\mathbb{E}[C_n] \;=\; \frac{a}{\mathcal{H}} n \ln n$$

fulfills the continuous recurrence (6.22) exactly.

$$\blacklozenge \qquad \blacklozenge \qquad \blacklozenge$$

Great, our somewhat sketchy arguments all yield the correct leading term! Now that we have gained confidence in this result, let us dive into the formal proofs. We start with what is the most convenient one in my opinion, and then work our way through the more elaborate methods that are needed to get more refined results.

6.3 Solution with the Distributional Master Theorem

Our first formal proof of Theorem 6.1 is based on the *Distributional Master Theorem (DMT)*, our Theorem 2.70 (page 106), which in turn builds on the *Continuous Master Theorem* of Roura [154]. Because of its generality, the proof for Roura's theorem is rather lengthy; the concerned reader might appreciate that the simplified version, Theorem 2.71, also suffices here. For the latter we gave a self-contained proof in Section 2.6.4.

Proof of Theorem 6.1: The random costs for Quicksort fulfill Equation (6.1), which is of the form required by Theorem 2.70. Note that C_n is a *linear* function of the toll function T_n: upon fully expanding recursive uses of C_n, we obtain for any n a large, but finite sum of terms T_j with $j \leqslant n$. This is obvious from Equation (6.7), but let us state it for reference here.

Fact 6.4: $\mathbb{E}[C_n]$ is a linear combination of terms $\mathbb{E}[T_j]$ with $j \leqslant n$, i.e., we can write $\mathbb{E}[C_n] = \sum_{j=0}^{n} \tau_{n,j} \cdot \mathbb{E}[T_j]$ for some numbers $\tau_{n,j} \geqslant 0$. ∎

We can therefore apply the DMT separately to each summand of the toll function, in our case the main term an and the error term $O(n^{1-\varepsilon})$. We will in total apply the DMT three times:

1. to the main term an of $\mathbb{E}[T_n]$, which gives the leading term $\mathbb{E}[C_n] \sim \frac{a}{\mathcal{H}} n \ln n$;

2. to the error term $O(n^{1-\varepsilon})$, which contributes an $O(n)$ term; and

3. to $\mathbb{E}[C_n] - \frac{a}{\mathcal{H}} n \ln n$ to bound the error of the leading-term approximation. This will contribute another $O(n)$ term.

Before we can do so, we have to show that Equation (2.269), the *density convergence condition*, holds for the relative subproblem sizes $\mathbf{Z}^{(n)} = \mathbf{J}^{(n)}/n$. What is the limiting behavior of $\mathbf{J}/n$? For large n, we have $\mathbf{J} \approx \mathbf{I}$ and for a fixed $\mathbf{D}$ this is $\mathbf{I} \overset{\mathcal{D}}{=} \mathrm{Mult}(n-k, \mathbf{D})$. In other words, $I_r^{(n)}/n$ is the average of n i.i.d. drawings and thus converges almost surely to its expectation, D_r for $r = 1, \ldots, s$.

Our educated guess for the limiting marginal densities is

$$f_{Z_r^*}(z) \;=\; f_{D_r}(z) \;=\; \frac{z^{t_r}(1-z)^{k-t_r-1}}{B(t_r+1,k-t_r)}, \tag{6.34}$$

the density of $D_r \overset{\mathcal{D}}{=} \mathrm{Beta}(t_r+1, k-t_r)$. We guess that $Z_r^* \overset{\mathcal{D}}{=} D_r$. This limit density has the required smoothness: it is Lipschitz-continuous by Lemma 2.29 (page 73) (and thus Hölder-continuous by Proposition 2.9).

To show the required speed of convergence, recall that $I_r \overset{\mathcal{D}}{=} \mathrm{BetaBin}(\eta, t_r+1, k-t_r)$, and by Lemma 2.38 (page 80), I_r/n converges in density to D_r. We only have to take care of the little nuisance that our subproblem sizes J are $J = I + t$, and thus not directly Dirichlet-multinomially distributed. The small offset is harmless, though, since the limit density is smooth enough: with $\tilde z$ so that $z = \tilde z + \frac{t_r - \tilde z k}{n}$, i.e., $\tilde z = \frac{zn - t_r}{\eta} = z + \frac{zk - t_r}{\eta}$, we have

$$n\mathbb{P}\!\left[Z_r^{(n)} \in (z - \tfrac{1}{n}, z]\right] \;=\; n\mathbb{P}\!\left[Z_r^{(n)} \in \left(\tilde z + \frac{t_r - \tilde z k}{n} - \frac{1}{n}, \tilde z + \frac{t_r - \tilde z k}{n}\right]\right] \tag{6.35}$$

$$=\; n\mathbb{P}\!\left[Z_r^{(n)} \in \left(\frac{\tilde z(n-k)+t_r}{n} - \frac{1}{n}, \frac{\tilde z(n-k)+t_r}{n}\right]\right] \tag{6.36}$$

$$=\; n\mathbb{P}\!\left[nZ_r^{(n)} - t_r \in (\tilde z\eta - 1, \tilde z\eta]\right] \cdot \frac{n-k}{n-k} \tag{6.37}$$

$$=\; \eta\mathbb{P}\!\left[I_r = \lfloor \tilde z\eta \rfloor\right] \cdot \left(1 + \frac{k}{\eta}\right) \tag{6.38}$$

$$\overset{\text{Lemma 2.38}}{=}\; \left(f_{D_r}(\tilde z) \pm O(\eta^{-1})\right) \cdot \left(1 + \frac{k}{\eta}\right) \tag{6.39}$$

$$=\; f_{D_r}(\tilde z) \pm O(\eta^{-1}) \tag{6.40}$$

$$=\; f_{D_r}\!\left(z + \frac{zk - t_r}{\eta}\right) \pm O(\eta^{-1}), \tag{6.41}$$

and since f_{D_r} is Lipschitz-continuous (Lemma 2.29) and $\frac{zk-t_r}{\eta} = O(\eta^{-1})$ uniformly in $z \in (0,1)$, we conclude with Proposition 2.12–(a) that this is

$$=\; f_{D_r}(z) \pm O(\eta^{-1}). \tag{6.42}$$

This proves Equation (2.269). So, we have shown that the distributional recurrence in Equation (6.1) fulfills the requirements of the DMT; we proceed with the three announced applications of the DMT for different toll functions.

1 To obtain the main term, we use as toll function $\mathbb{E}[T_n] = an$, i.e., parameters $K = a$, $\alpha = 1$, $\beta = 0$. As $\sum_{r=1}^{s} D_r = 1$, we have $H = 1 - \sum_{r=1}^{s} \mathbb{E}[D_r] = 0$, so we are in case 2 of the DMT. Thus $\mathbb{E}[C_n] \sim \frac{\mathbb{E}[T_n]\ln n}{\tilde H}$ with $\tilde H = -\sum_{r=1}^{s} \mathbb{E}[D_r \ln(D_r)] = \mathbb{E}[\mathcal{H}_{\ln}(\mathbf{D})]$, which is the expected entropy of the distribution induced by $\mathbf{D}$. Proposition 2.54 (page 90) yields $\tilde H = \mathcal{H}_{hd_\kappa}(\boldsymbol{\tau}) = \mathcal{H}(\mathbf{t})$ and $\mathbb{E}[C_n] \sim \frac{a}{\mathcal{H}} n \ln n$, as claimed.

2 Next, we consider the error term $O(n^{1-\varepsilon})$ in the expansion of $\mathbb{E}[T_n]$. By definition, there is a constant K with $\mathbb{E}[T_n] \leqslant Kn^{1-\varepsilon}$ for large enough n, so we set $\mathbb{E}[T_n] =$

$Kn^{1-\varepsilon}$. Consequently, we have to compute $H = 1 - \sum_{r=1}^{s} \mathbb{E}[D_r^{1-\varepsilon}]$. Since $x^{1-\varepsilon} > x$ for all $x \in (0,1)$, we must have $\sum_{r=1}^{s} \mathbb{E}[D_r^{1-\varepsilon}] > \sum_{r=1}^{s} \mathbb{E}[D_r] = 1$, thus $H < 0$. We are therefore in case 3 of the DMT. We already know that we have $\sum_{r=1}^{s} \mathbb{E}[D_r^c] = 1$ for $c = 1$, so the contribution from the toll function $\mathbb{E}[T_n] = Kn^{1-\varepsilon}$ is in $O(n)$. We thus get an overall contribution of $O(n)$ for tolls in $O(n^{1-\varepsilon})$.

3 Finally, we consider the remainder $R_n := C_n - \frac{a}{\mathcal{H}} n \ln n$ in order to bound the second-order term in the asymptotic approximation of $\mathbb{E}[C_n]$. From Equation (6.1) for $n \geqslant k$, we find

$$R_n \overset{\mathcal{D}}{=} T_n + \sum_{r=1}^{s} R_{J_r}^{(r)} + \sum_{r=1}^{s} \frac{a}{\mathcal{H}} J_r \ln(J_r) - \frac{a}{\mathcal{H}} n \ln n \tag{6.43}$$

$$=: T_R(n) + \sum_{r=1}^{s} R_{J_r}^{(r)}, \tag{6.44}$$

so R_n also fulfills a recurrence of the shape (2.268) and the DMT is applicable. If we can show that $\mathbb{E}[T_R(n)] = O(n^{1-\varepsilon})$, we know from above that $\mathbb{E}[R_n] = O(n)$ and we are done. So let us work on

$$T_R(n) = T_n - \frac{a}{\mathcal{H}}\left(n \ln n - \sum_{r=1}^{s} J_r \ln J_r \right) \tag{6.45}$$

a little more. The main idea is that second summand can be written (details follow) as

$$an \cdot \frac{\sum_{r=1}^{s} \mathbb{E}\left[\frac{J_r}{n} \ln\left(\frac{J_r}{n}\right) \right]}{\sum_{r=1}^{s} \mathbb{E}[D_r \ln D_r]},$$

which converges to an since $J_r/n \to D_r$. However, we have to explicitly deal with the error to prove our claim $\mathbb{E}[T_R(n)] = O(n^{1-\varepsilon})$, so we have to look a little closer. Again, it is inconvenient that I, and not directly $J = I + t$, has a Dirichlet-multinomial distribution, but the small offset does not matter in the end:

$$T_R(n) - T_n = \frac{a}{\mathcal{H}}\left(\sum_{r=1}^{s} J_r \ln J_r - n \ln n \right) \tag{6.46}$$

(using $J = I + t$ and splitting $n = I_1 + \cdots + I_s + k$ in the $n \ln n$ term)

$$= \frac{a}{\mathcal{H}}\left(\sum_{r=1}^{s} I_r (\ln J_r - \ln n) + \sum_{r=1}^{s} t_r \ln J_r - k \ln n \right) \tag{6.47}$$

$$= \frac{a}{\mathcal{H}} \sum_{r=1}^{s} I_r \big(\ln J_r \underbrace{- \ln I_r + \ln I_r - \ln \eta + \ln \eta}_{=0} - \ln n \big) \pm O(\log n) \tag{6.48}$$

$$= \frac{a}{\mathcal{H}}\left(\sum_{r=1}^{s} I_r \left(\ln\left(\frac{I_r}{\eta}\right) + \ln\left(\frac{J_r}{I_r}\right) \right) + \eta \ln\left(\frac{\eta}{n}\right) \right) \pm O(\log n) \tag{6.49}$$

$$
= \left(1 - \frac{k}{n}\right) \frac{an}{\mathcal{H}} \sum_{r=1}^{s} \frac{I_r}{\eta} \ln \frac{I_r}{\eta}
$$

$$
+ \underbrace{\frac{a}{\mathcal{H}} \eta \ln\left(1 - \frac{k}{n}\right)}_{= O(1)} + \underbrace{\frac{a}{\mathcal{H}} \sum_{r=1}^{s} I_r \ln\left(1 + \frac{t_r}{I_r}\right)}_{= O(1)} \pm O(\log n) \qquad (6.50)
$$

(using $\ln(1 + x) \leqslant x$ twice and $\frac{k}{n} = \Theta(n^{-1})$)

$$
= \frac{an}{\mathcal{H}} \sum_{r=1}^{s} \frac{I_r}{\eta} \ln \frac{I_r}{\eta} \pm O(\log n). \qquad (6.51)
$$

Now, we take expectations and insert $\mathcal{H} = - \sum_{r=1}^{s} \mathbb{E}[D_r \ln D_r]$, see the proof for the main term above, to get

$$
\mathbb{E}[T_R(n)] = an - an \cdot \frac{\sum_{r=1}^{s} \mathbb{E}[\frac{I_r}{\eta} \ln \frac{I_r}{\eta}]}{\sum_{r=1}^{s} \mathbb{E}[D_r \ln D_r]} \pm O(\log n). \qquad (6.52)
$$

We can apply Lemma 2.36 on the *conditional* expectation $\mathbb{E}\left[\frac{I_r}{\eta} \ln \frac{I_r}{\eta} \mid D_r\right]$ because $x \mapsto x \ln x$ is Hölder-continuous for any exponent $h \in (0, 1)$ on $x \in [0, 1]$ by Lemma 2.13. We get for any $\varepsilon' > 0$

$$
\mathbb{E}[T_R(n)] = an - an \cdot \frac{\sum_{r=1}^{s} \mathbb{E}[D_r \ln D_r] + o(n^{-1/2+\varepsilon'})}{\sum_{r=1}^{s} \mathbb{E}[D_r \ln D_r]} \pm O(\log n) \qquad (6.53)
$$

$$
= O(n^{1/2+\varepsilon'}). \qquad (6.54)
$$

Thus, by the DMT with arguments just as in the second step above, we find $\mathbb{E}[R_n] = \mathbb{E}[C_n] - \frac{a}{\mathcal{H}} n \ln n = O(n)$.

Putting these three results together concludes the proof of Theorem 6.1.   ■

6.4   Random-Parameter Pivot Sampling

The proof using the distributional master theorem extends very nicely to the random-parameter pivot-sampling case, e.g., ninther sampling; see Section 4.4.2 for details. The recurrence, Equation (6.1), remains valid literally, the only thing that changes is that now the distributions in Equation (6.2) only hold conditionally on the event $T = t$. We can thus copy Theorem 6.1 almost literally.

> **Theorem 6.5 (Total Expected Costs (Random-Parameter Sampling)):**
> The total expected costs $\mathbb{E}[C_n]$ for sorting a random permutation with a randomness-preserving Quicksort using a partitioning method that incurs expected costs $\mathbb{E}[T_n]$ of the form $\mathbb{E}[T_n] = an \pm O(n^{1-\varepsilon})$, with constants a and $\varepsilon > 0$, to produce s segments and whose s − 1 pivots are chosen by generalized pivot sampling with the finitely supported

random parameter $\mathbf{T} \in \mathbb{N}^s$ *are asymptotically*

$$\mathbb{E}[C_n] = \frac{a}{\mathbb{E}[\mathcal{H}(\mathbf{T})]} \, n \ln n \pm O(n).$$

This result holds also if we truncate the recursion at subproblems of size at most w, for any constant w, and switch to another sorting method. ◄

By "finitely supported" we mean that $\mathbf{T}$ can take only finitely many different values. This is probably not necessary for the statement of the theorem to hold, but it spares us from dealing with convergence issues in the proof.

Proof: We can extend the arguments used in Section 6.3 for the case of a fixed $\mathbf{T}$, and we will only consider the difference to that case in detail.

Let us assume that $\mathbf{T}$ takes the values $\mathbf{t}^{(1)}, \ldots, \mathbf{t}^{(b)} \in \mathbb{N}_0^s$ for some $b \in \mathbb{N}$. Conditional on $\mathbf{T}$ we have $\mathbf{D} \stackrel{\mathcal{D}}{=} \mathrm{Dir}(\mathbf{T}+1)$, i.e., $\mathbf{D}$ is a mixture of Dirichlet variables; see Section 5.2.4. Its density is then a convex combination of Dirichlet densities:

$$f_{D_r}(z) = \sum_{i=1}^{b} \mathbb{P}[\mathbf{T} = \mathbf{t}^{(i)}] \cdot \frac{z^{t_r^{(i)}}(1-z)^{k - t_r^{(i)} - 1}}{B(t_r^{(i)} + 1, k - t_r^{(i)})}; \tag{6.55}$$

it is Hölder-continuous as it is the sum of Hölder-continuous functions, see Lemma 2.11–(a). Since all $\mathbf{t}^{(i)}$ are constant, by Equation (6.42) we have that uniformly in $z \in (0,1)$ holds

$$n \mathbb{P}\left[Z_r^{(n)} \in (z - \tfrac{1}{n}, z] \,\Big|\, \mathbf{T} = \mathbf{t}^{(i)} \right] = \frac{z^{t_r^{(i)}}(1-z)^{k^{(i)} - t_r^{(i)} - 1}}{B(t_r^{(i)} + 1, k^{(i)} - t_r^{(i)})} \pm O(\eta^{-1}). \tag{6.56}$$

Unconditioning using the *law of total probability* yields

$$n \mathbb{P}\left[Z_r^{(n)} \in (z - \tfrac{1}{n}, z] \right] = \underbrace{\sum_{i=1}^{b} \mathbb{P}[\mathbf{T} = \mathbf{t}^{(i)}] \cdot \frac{z^{t_r^{(i)}}(1-z)^{k^{(i)} - t_r^{(i)} - 1}}{B(t_r^{(i)} + 1, k^{(i)} - t_r^{(i)})}}_{= f_{D_r}(z)} \pm O(\eta^{-1}). \tag{6.57}$$

So the DMT is applicable; as in Section 6.3, we apply it three times.

1. We still have $\Sigma \mathbf{D} = 1$ by definition, so we are in Case 2. Conditionally on $\mathbf{T} = \mathbf{t}^{(i)}$, we have $\mathbb{E}[\mathcal{H}_{\ln}(\mathbf{D}) \mid \mathbf{T} = \mathbf{t}^{(i)}] = \mathcal{H}(\mathbf{t}^{(i)})$ and by the law of total expectation $\tilde{H} = \mathbb{E}[\mathcal{H}(\mathbf{T})]$, as claimed.

2. The arguments for the bound on the influence of the lower term of $\mathbb{E}[T_n]$ remains valid literally.

3. Likewise, the proof of the bound on the difference between exact solution and leading term remains literally the same; all arguments consider a fixed $\mathbf{D}$.

This concludes the proof. ∎

Sedgewick [162] and Hennequin [77] considered a scenario equivalent to random-parameter sampling in their respective theses, and it is certainly possible to prove Theorem 6.5 without the stochastic detour that we took. However, the stochastic formulation allows an elegant solution of the Quicksort recurrence that naturally suggests and supports the extension to random-parameter sampling.

On the other hand, if we require more than the leading term, for example as in Lemma 6.2, the master-theorem-style arguments are too coarse. We thus present the more algebraic route to solve the Quicksort recurrence in the following section.

6.5 Solution with Generating Functions

The arguments in this section follow the presentation in the French doctoral thesis of Hennequin [77], and are a generalization of the analysis for the single-pivot case given in Sedgewick's Ph.D. thesis [162]. We rederive and detail some of Hennequin's results here for the reader's convenience and for future reference as a "community service."

We restrict our attention to solving the recurrence of expected costs. Hennequin additionally considers properties of the distribution of C_n and gives a description of Quicksort in terms of combinatorial structures as discussed by Flajolet and Sedgewick [64] in depth. This latter part is covered for single-pivot Quicksort in an English article by Hennequin [76], as well.

We start with introducing the ordinary generating function

$$C(z) \;=\; \sum_{n \geqslant 0} \mathbb{E}[C_n] z^n \tag{6.58}$$

for the sequence $(\mathbb{E}[C_n])_{n \in \mathbb{N}_0}$. We will show that the recurrence on the coefficients implies a *Cauchy-Euler differential equation* for $C(z)$. Such equations can in principle be solved explicitly using the *differential-operator method,* as discussed in Section 2.3.2. As the degree of the differential equation depends on k, the explicit solution has to remain symbolic, though. In particular, determining the integration constants is a challenging task in general.

It can luckily be shown that the integration constants are irrelevant for the leading term of the coefficients. Using the *O-transfer theorems* of Flajolet and Odlyzko [62], also given in *Analytic Combinatorics* [64], we can directly translate the partially determined generating function into a truncated asymptotic expansion for the coefficients, i.e., our sequence of costs $\mathbb{E}[C_n]$.

6.5.1 A Differential Equation for the Generating Function

We will often need to sum over all feasible vectors of subproblem sizes $\mathbf{j}$, so we define the abbreviation $\mathcal{J}_n := \{\mathbf{j} \in \mathbb{N}_0^s : \Sigma\mathbf{j} = n - (s-1)\}$. We start with Equation (6.7) and insert

Equation (6.9) for $\mathbb{P}[J = j]$ to obtain

$$
\mathbb{E}[C_n] = \begin{cases} \mathbb{E}[T_n] + \displaystyle\sum_{j\in\mathcal{J}_n} \frac{\prod_{r=1}^{s}\binom{j_r}{t_r}}{\binom{n}{k}} \sum_{r=1}^{s} \mathbb{E}[C_{j_r}], & n > w; \\[2ex] \mathbb{E}[W_n], & n \leqslant w. \end{cases}
\tag{6.59}
$$

Multiplying both sides by $\binom{n}{k}z^n$ and summing over all $n \geqslant 0$, we obtain

$$
\sum_{n\geqslant 0} \binom{n}{k} \mathbb{E}[C_n]z^n =
$$

$$
\sum_{n>w} \left[\binom{n}{k}\mathbb{E}[T_n]z^n + \sum_{j\in\mathcal{J}_n}\left[\prod_{r=1}^{s}\binom{j_r}{t_r}\right]\sum_{l=1}^{s}\mathbb{E}[C_{j_l}]z^n\right] + \sum_{n=0}^{w}\binom{n}{k}\mathbb{E}[W_n]z^n .
\tag{6.60}
$$

Our goal is to express this equation in terms the generating functions $C(z)$ and $T(z) = \sum_{n\geqslant 0} \mathbb{E}[T_n]z^n$. The left-hand side is easily expressed in terms of derivatives of $C(z)$ using

$$
\sum_{n\geqslant 0} \binom{n}{k} \mathbb{E}[C_n]z^n = \frac{z^k C^{(k)}(z)}{k!},
\tag{6.61}
$$

which follows from $C^{(k)}(z) = \sum_{n\geqslant 0} n^{\underline{k}}\mathbb{E}[C_n]z^{n-k}$ by multiplying with $z^k/k!$. The first of the three parts on the right is similar, but since the sum excludes sizes $n = 1,\ldots,w$, we have to subtract $\sum_{n=0}^{w}\binom{n}{k}\mathbb{E}[T_n]z^n$ again. For the remaining terms, we have to work a little harder. Exchanging the order of summations we can split the middle terms into s summands dealing with $\mathbb{E}[C_{j_1}],\ldots,\mathbb{E}[C_{j_s}]$, respectively. Let us consider the term for $\mathbb{E}[C_{j_1}]$. With the abbreviations $\hat{\jmath} = (j_2,\ldots,j_s)$ and $\hat{\rho} = (s-1)+\Sigma\hat{\jmath} = j_2 + \cdots + j_s + s - 1$, so that $j_1 = n - \hat{\rho}$, we find:

$$
\sum_{n\geqslant 0}\sum_{j\in\mathcal{J}_n}\left[\prod_{r=1}^{s}\binom{j_r}{t_r}\right]\mathbb{E}[C_{j_1}]z^n
\tag{6.62}
$$

$$
= \sum_{n\geqslant 0}\sum_{j\in\mathcal{J}_n}\left[\prod_{r=2}^{s}\binom{j_r}{t_r}\right]\cdot\binom{j_1}{t_1}\mathbb{E}[C_{j_1}]z^n
\tag{6.63}
$$

$$
= \sum_{\hat{\jmath}\in\mathbb{N}_0^{s-1}}\left[\prod_{r=2}^{s}\binom{j_r}{t_r}\right]\sum_{n\geqslant\hat{\rho}}\binom{n-\hat{\rho}}{t_1}\mathbb{E}[C_{n-\hat{\rho}}]z^n
\tag{6.64}
$$

$$
= \sum_{\hat{\jmath}\in\mathbb{N}_0^{s-1}}z^{\hat{\rho}}\left[\prod_{r=2}^{s}\binom{j_r}{t_r}\right]\sum_{n\geqslant 0}\binom{n}{t_1}\mathbb{E}[C_n]z^n
\tag{6.65}
$$

$$
\underset{(6.61)}{=} z^{(s-1)+t_2+\cdots+t_s}\sum_{\hat{\jmath}\in\mathbb{N}_0^{s-1}}\left[\prod_{r=2}^{s}\binom{j_r}{t_r}z^{j_r-t_r}\right]\cdot\frac{z^{t_1}C^{(t_1)}(z)}{t_1!}
\tag{6.66}
$$

$$
= \frac{z^k C^{(t_1)}(z)}{t_1!}\prod_{r=2}^{s}\sum_{j_r=0}^{\infty}\binom{j_r}{t_r}z^{j_r-t_r}
\tag{6.67}
$$

$$\underset{(2.64)}{=} \frac{z^k C^{(t_1)}(z)}{t_1!} \prod_{r=2}^{s} \frac{1}{(1-z)^{t_r+1}} \tag{6.68}$$

$$= \frac{z^k C^{(t_1)}(z)}{t_1!(1-z)^{k-t_1}} \, . \tag{6.69}$$

Similar computations with $\mathbb{E}[C_{j_2}], \ldots, \mathbb{E}[C_{j_s}]$ yield corresponding results. Using this representation in Equation (6.60) for the generating functions, we find

$$\frac{z^k C^{(k)}(z)}{k!} = \frac{z^k T^{(k)}(z)}{k!} + \sum_{r=1}^{s} \left[\frac{z^k C^{(t_r)}(z)}{t_r!(1-z)^{k-t_r}} - \sum_{n=0}^{w} \sum_{j \in \mathcal{J}_n} \left[\prod_{r=1}^{s} \binom{j_r}{t_r} \right] \mathbb{E}[C_{j_r}] z^n \right]$$

$$+ \sum_{n=0}^{w} \binom{n}{k} \left(\mathbb{E}[W_n] - \mathbb{E}[T_n] \right) z^n \tag{6.70}$$

$$= \frac{z^k T^{(k)}(z)}{k!} + \sum_{r=1}^{s} \frac{z^k C^{(t_r)}(z)}{t_r!(1-z)^{k-t_r}}$$

$$+ \sum_{n=k}^{w} z^n \underbrace{\left[\binom{n}{k} \left(\mathbb{E}[W_n] - \mathbb{E}[T_n] \right) - \sum_{j \in \mathcal{J}_n} \left[\prod_{r=1}^{s} \binom{j_r}{t_r} \right] \sum_{r=1}^{s} \mathbb{E}[W_{j_r}] \right]}_{=:\sigma_n} . \tag{6.71}$$

Multiplying both sides by $(1-z)^k/z^k$ finally yields a Cauchy-Euler differential equation for $C(z)$:

$$\frac{(1-z)^k C^{(k)}(z)}{k!} - \sum_{r=1}^{s} \frac{(1-z)^{t_r} C^{(t_r)}(z)}{t_r!} =$$

$$\frac{(1-z)^k T^{(k)}(z)}{k!} + (1-z)^k \sum_{n=0}^{w-k} \sigma_{n+k} z^n . \tag{6.72}$$

This equation corresponds to Equation (III.12) of Hennequin [77]. Note that the only summand involving the unwieldy coefficients σ_n is a *polynomial* of degree $w - k$ when viewed as a function of z. W_n thus only contributes to a polynomial part of the right-hand side, and the leading term of the asymptotic expansion of $\mathbb{E}[C_n]$, the coefficients of $C(z)$, is thus independent of the strategy for sorting small subarrays.

6.5.2 Differential-Operator Transformation

For solving the differential equation, it is convenient to make the change of variable $x = 1 - z$ and denote by $\bar{C}(x) := C(1-x)$ and $\bar{T}(x) := T(1-x)$ the correspondingly changed generating functions. Hennequin uses $\tilde{C}(x)$ instead of $\bar{C}(x)$; our notation is meant to resemble the minus sign in $1 - x$. We can then rephrase Equation (6.72) using a *differential operator* Θ, defined by

$$\Theta f(x) = x \frac{\mathrm{d}}{\mathrm{d}x} f(x) . \tag{6.73}$$

As discussed in Section 2.3.2, Θ is a linear operator, and with powers Θ^i understood as i successive applications, we can extend the notation to $P(\Theta)[f(x)]$ for arbitrary polynomials P. Recall that

$$\binom{\Theta}{k} f(x) \;=\; \frac{1}{k!}\Theta(\Theta-1)\cdots(\Theta-k+1)f(x) \;=\; \frac{x^k f^{(k)}(x)}{k!}, \qquad \text{(2.98) revisited}$$

so we can write Equation (6.72) as

$$P_t(\Theta)\bar{C}(x) \;=\; (-1)^k \binom{\Theta}{k}\bar{T}(x) \;+\; x^k \sum_{n=0}^{w-k} \sigma_{n+k}\,(1-x)^n \qquad (6.74)$$

$$\text{with } P_t(\Theta) \;=\; (-1)^k \binom{\Theta}{k} \;-\; \sum_{r=1}^{s}(-1)^{t_r}\binom{\Theta}{t_r}. \qquad (6.75)$$

The -1 factors come from the inner derivate of the original functions:

$$\frac{d}{dx}\bar{C}(x) \;=\; \frac{d}{dx}C(1-x) \;=\; -\frac{d}{dz}C(z)\Big|_{z=1-x}. \qquad (6.76)$$

For the rest of the section, we will only work with $\bar{C}(x)$ and $\bar{T}(x)$, and thus avoid further trouble with -1 factors.

The main benefit of writing our differential equation in terms of Θ, however, is that it unleashes the power to apply algebraic transformations to the operator polynomial P_t; the prime trick of the trade being to *factorize* P_t. This allows us to reduce the differential equation to a sequence of ordinary *first-order* equations, which are easy to solve using *integrating factors*. In order to do so, we need the roots of P_t, which depend on t in a non-obvious way.

Luckily, we can obtain the main terms of the solution without computing all roots. In fact, Hennequin showed that all contributions to coefficients up to the linear term come from the single root -2. Following his argument for the symmetric case $t = (t,\ldots,t)$, we will solve Equation (6.74) up to linear terms for coefficients. The following lemma collects the needed properties of P_t.

Lemma 6.6: *The polynomial $P_t(y)$ given in Equation (6.75) has a simple root at $y = -2$ and all other roots have real part strictly greater than -2. The value of the derivative at $y = -2$ is given by*

$$P_t'(-2) \;=\; -(k+1)H_{k+1} + \sum_{r=1}^{s}(t_r+1)H_{t_r+1} \;=\; (k+1)\cdot\mathcal{H}(t). \qquad (6.77)$$

◄

The first part of Lemma 6.6 corresponds to Lemme B.8 of Hennequin [77] and we follow his arguments in the proof.

Proof: To check that -2 is a root, we negate the upper index with Equation (2.63)

$$(-1)^m\binom{-2}{m} \;=\; (-1)^{2m}\binom{m+1}{m} \;=\; m+1, \qquad \text{for integer } m, \qquad (6.78)$$

hence $P_t(-2) = k + 1 - \sum_{l=1}^{r}(t_r + 1) = 0$. Next, we compute the derivative at -2, considering the summands in isolation. For any integer m, we have by the product rule

$$\frac{d}{dy}(-1)^m \binom{y}{m}\Bigg|_{y=-2} = \frac{(-1)^m}{m!} \sum_{i=0}^{m-1} \frac{y^{\underline{m}}}{y - i}\Bigg|_{y=-2} \tag{6.79}$$

$$= -\frac{2^{\overline{m}}}{m!} \sum_{i=0}^{m-1} \frac{1}{2 + i} \tag{6.80}$$

$$= -(m + 1)(H_{m+1} - 1), \tag{6.81}$$

which proves Equation (6.77). If $y = -2$ was a multiple root of P_t, we would have $P_t'(-2) = 0$, however, we easily find by monotonicity of H_n and since $t_r \leqslant k - (s - 1)$

$$P_t'(-2) < -(k + 1)H_{k+1} + \sum_{r=1}^{s}(t_r + 1)H_{k+1} \tag{6.82}$$

$$= H_{k+1}\left(\sum_{r=1}^{s}(t_r + 1) - (k + 1)\right) = 0. \tag{6.83}$$

It remains to show that all other roots of P_t have real part no smaller than -2. For that, we write P_t as

$$P_t(y) = (-1)^k \binom{y}{k}\left(1 - \sum_{r=1}^{s} B_{t_r}(y)\right) \tag{6.84}$$

$$\text{with } B_t(y) = (-1)^{k-t}\binom{y}{t} \Big/ \binom{y}{k} \tag{6.85}$$

$$= (-1)^{k-t}\frac{k!\, y^{\underline{t}}}{t!\, y^{\underline{k}}} \tag{6.86}$$

$$= \frac{k^{\underline{k-t}}}{(t - y)^{\overline{k-t}}} \tag{6.87}$$

$$= \frac{t + 1}{k + 1} \cdot \frac{k + 1}{k - 1 - y}\frac{k}{k - 2 - y}\frac{k - 1}{k - 3 - y} \cdots \frac{t + 2}{t - y}. \tag{6.88}$$

Let $y = a + ib$ be an arbitrary complex number with $\Re(y) = a \leqslant -2$ and $y \neq -2$. Then we have for $c \geqslant 0$

$$\left|\frac{c - y}{c + 2}\right| = \sqrt{\left(\frac{c - a}{c + 2}\right)^2 + \left(\frac{b}{c + 2}\right)^2} > 1, \tag{6.89}$$

since we have $\frac{c-a}{c+2} \geqslant 1$ with equality for $a = -2$; and if $a = -2$, we have $b \neq 0$ by assumption. This means that all fractions $\frac{k+1-i}{k-1-y-i}$, for $i = 0, 1, \ldots, k - t$, are of modulus strictly less than 1, so we have $|B_t(y)| < \frac{t+1}{k+1}$ and thus

$$\left|\sum_{r=1}^{s} B_{t_r}(y)\right| < 1. \tag{6.90}$$

From the representation of P_t in Equation (6.84), it is clear that then $|P_t(y)| \neq 0$, so y is not a root. $\blacksquare$

By Lemma 6.6, we can write P_t as

$$P_t(y) \;=\; Q_t(y)(y+2) \;=\; \frac{(-1)^k}{k!}(y-\alpha_1)(y-\alpha_2)\cdots(y-\alpha_{k-1})(y+2) \qquad (6.91)$$

for a polynomial $Q_t(y)$ of degree $k-1$ with (not necessarily distinct) roots $\alpha_1,\ldots,\alpha_{k-1}$, for which we know that $\Re(\alpha_i) > -2$, for $i = 1,\ldots,k-1$. The factor $(-1)^k/k!$ comes from equating coefficients: the common factor must be the coefficient of the highest power y^k.

For any fixed k, we can find $\tilde{\varepsilon} = \tilde{\varepsilon}(k) > 0$ such that $\Re(\alpha_i) \geqslant -2+\tilde{\varepsilon}$ for all roots α_i and also $-1 > -2+\tilde{\varepsilon}$.

6.5.3 A General Solution to the Differential Equation

We discussed how to solve Euler equations in Section 2.3.2; with the knowledge about the roots of the operator polynomial this is a simple application of Theorem 2.23 (page 66). We still have to take care of the right-hand side of Equation (6.74).

By assumption, our toll function is $\mathbb{E}[T_n] = an \pm O(n^{1-\varepsilon})$ for some constants a and $\varepsilon > 0$. We would like to translate the error term for $\mathbb{E}[T_n]$ into a corresponding error term for $T(z)$ as $z \to 1$, the dominant singularity of $T(z)$.

Translating O-terms from a generating function to its coefficients is an intensely studied and well-understood operation. It is formally justified by so-called *transfer theorems*, a term originally coined by Flajolet and Odlyzko [62]. O-transfers are at the core of the process of *singularity analysis* of generating functions, which is comprehensively described in *Analytic Combinatorics* [64, Chapter VII].

For our scenario above, we would need the *inverse* direction, from coefficients to generating functions. This case is not covered by the standard O-transfer theorems, e.g., Theorem VI.3 of Flajolet and Sedgewick [64].

Inverse O-Transfers.   It might often be the case that we would like to translate a known sequence to generating functions to apply a certain transformation that is conveniently done in the world of series, and then extract coefficients again. If that first sequence is only known in the form of an asymptotic approximation, the first step corresponds to an "inverse O-transfer."

It is certainly possible to deduce some properties of the generating function from bounds on its coefficients, e.g., that the radius of convergence must be at least 1 if coefficients grow sub-exponentially. Other properties are simply not available from a coarse asymptotic bound on coefficients, most notably the location of dominant singularities. Assume we know that $f_n = O(n)$ as $n \to \infty$ and $f(z) = \sum f_n z^n$. We can conclude that $f(z) = O((1-z)^{-2})$ as $z \to 1$ inside the unit disk; otherwise we would get faster-growing coefficients.

We cannot, however, extend the validity of the bound $|f(z)| \leqslant K|1-z|^{-2}$ beyond a neighborhood of 1 in general, as f might have additional singularities at any point z_0 on the unit circle. To make the discussion concrete, take $g(z) = (1-z)^{-2}(z_0-z)^{-2}$, whose coefficients satisfy by ordinary O-transfer (Theorem VI.5 of Flajolet and Sedgewick [64]) $[z^n]g(z) = O(n)$, as well.

If we cannot locate the dominant singularities, the usual approaches to extract precise bounds for coefficients are not available, and the detour to the generating functions world remains fruitless.

I spent a few days on proving properties of functions and their singular expansions if we only have analyticity *inside* the unit disk. A weak form of an inverse O-theorem can be obtained, and differentiation and integration of singular expansions can be justified. However as indicated above, the obtained analyticity properties for the functions are too weak in the end to obtain useful error bounds on the coefficients again.

An unfortunate formulation of Flajolet and Odlyzko [62] in their Theorem 4 had fueled my hopes to succeed on this route. They wrote *"Assume that $f(z)$ is analytic in $|z| < 1$. Assume further that as $z \to 1$ in this domain, $f(z) = O(|1 - z|^\alpha)$, for some real number $\alpha < -1$."* In the limiting sense used also in this work, the O-term is only concerned with a neighborhood around 1, but what they mean here is that we have $|f(z)| \leqslant K|1 - z|^\alpha$ "in this domain," i.e., for *all* z with $|z| < 1$—the bound has to hold in the whole open unit disk! This of course excludes the possibility of any singular points other than 1 in whose neighborhood f becomes unbounded. Flajolet and Sedgewick [64] briefly mentioned this in their Note VI.10, stating more clearly that *"in the whole open unit disc it [the function] satisfies $f(z) = O((1 - z)^{-\alpha})$".*

Using only an asymptotic approximation for the coefficients, such a uniform bound for the generating function in the whole open unit disk seems impossible to obtain, and the idea of inverse O-transfer turns out to be a dead end. May posterity be warned.

To avoid the troubles of inverse O-transfers, we will work with concrete functions instead. This is essentially made possible by Fact 6.4, which implies that we can solve our recurrence using an upper and lower bound on $\mathbb{E}[T_n]$ and obtain an upper and lower bound on $\mathbb{E}[C_n]$. This monotonicity of the transformation of toll costs into total costs relieves us of dealing with generating functions of a sequence that we only know as asymptotic approximation.

Our toll terms are given as the asymptotic approximation $\mathbb{E}[T_n] = an \pm O(n^{1-\varepsilon})$. We can well assume that $1 - \varepsilon > 0$, i.e., $1 < \varepsilon < 2$; otherwise we weaken our error bound slightly. The asymptotic approximation means that there are constants n_0 and C so that for all $n \geqslant n_0$ holds $|\mathbb{E}[T_n]| \leqslant an + Cn^{1-\varepsilon} \leqslant an + C\binom{n+1-\varepsilon}{n}$, where the last inequality follows by Lemma 2.15 (page 56). Let K be the maximum of C and $\max_{0 \leqslant n < n_0} |\mathbb{E}[T_n]|$. Then we have for all $n \in \mathbb{N}_0$ the following corridor for our toll costs

$$a(n+1) - K\left(\binom{n+1-\varepsilon}{n} + 1\right) \;\leqslant\; \mathbb{E}[T_n] \;\leqslant\; a(n+1) + K\left(\binom{n+1-\varepsilon}{n} + 1\right). \qquad (6.92)$$

Multiplying by z^n and summing over all n, we find

$$\frac{a}{(1-z)^2} - K\left(\frac{1}{(1-z)^{2-\varepsilon}} + \frac{1}{1-z}\right) \;\leqslant\; T(z) \;\leqslant\; \frac{a}{(1-z)^2} + K\left(\frac{1}{(1-z)^{2-\varepsilon}} + \frac{1}{1-z}\right).$$
$$(6.93)$$

Note that the only singularities of the upper and lower bounds are at $z = 1$; in particular we can analytically continue both bounds to the whole complex plane slit along $[1, +\infty)$, so that they are Δ-analytic. We continue our derivation with the upper and lower bounds instead of $T(z)$, knowing that this will give us a sandwich for the coefficients in the end.

By truncating the precision to the point where the bounds differ, we can handle the lower and upper bound in one shot. So let us set

$$T(z) \; := \; \frac{a}{(1-z)^2} \; \pm \; K\left(\frac{1}{(1-z)^{2-\varepsilon}} + \frac{1}{1-z}\right) \tag{6.94}$$

$$= \; \frac{a}{(1-z)^2} \pm O((1-z)^{-2+\varepsilon}), \quad (z \to 1). \tag{6.95}$$

The singular expansion for $z \to 1$ follows from $1 < \varepsilon < 2$.

Next, we have to apply the differential-operator polynomial to $\bar{T}(x) = T(1-x)$. Taking term-wise derivatives of $\bar{T}(x)$ is justified by Proposition 2.20 (page 62), where we use that $T(z)$ is Δ-analytic. The result of applying operator polynomial $(-1)^k\binom{\Theta}{k}$ to $\bar{T}(x)$ then fulfills

$$(-1)^k\binom{\Theta}{k}\bar{T}(x) \; = \; (-1)^k\binom{\Theta}{k}\left(ax^{-2} \pm O(x^{-2+\varepsilon})\right) \tag{6.96}$$

$$\underset{\text{Proposition 2.21}}{=} \; a(-1)^k\binom{-2}{k}x^{-2} \pm O(x^{-2+\varepsilon}) \tag{6.97}$$

$$\underset{(2.63)}{=} \; \frac{a(k+1)}{x^2} \pm O(x^{-2+\varepsilon}). \tag{6.98}$$

Inserting into Equation (6.74) yields the Euler equation

$$Q_t(\Theta)(\Theta+2)\bar{C}(x) \; = \; \frac{a(k+1)}{x^2} \pm O(x^{-2+\varepsilon}), \tag{6.99}$$

where the O-term considers the limit as $x \to 0$.

Solving this equation is a simple application of Theorem 2.23, where we weaken the error bound $O(x^{-2+\varepsilon})$ so that $-2 + \varepsilon$ is smaller than the real part of any of the roots of Q_t; this is possible for any fixed k by Lemma 6.6. We thus obtain that $\bar{C}(1-z)$ is Δ-analytic and admits for $x \to 0$ the singular expansion

$$\bar{C}(x) \; = \; \frac{a(k+1)}{Q_t(-2)}x^{-2}\ln(x) + \lambda x^{-2} \pm O(x^{-2+\varepsilon}), \quad (x \to 0), \tag{6.100}$$

where λ is an integration constant that depends on the initial conditions of the differential equation and thus on the initial conditions for $\mathbb{E}[C_n]$.

6.5.4 Coefficient Asymptotics

Observing that

$$P_t'(-2) \; = \; \frac{d}{dy}(y+2)Q_t(y)\Big|_{y=-2} \; = \; Q_t(-2), \tag{6.101}$$

we can use Lemma 6.6 and substitute back $x = 1 - z$ to get the generating function for the total costs as

$$C(z) \; = \; \frac{a}{\mathcal{H}(t)}\frac{\ln\left(\frac{1}{1-z}\right)}{(1-z)^2} + \frac{\lambda}{(1-z)^2} \pm O\left(\frac{1}{(1-z)^{2-\varepsilon}}\right), \tag{6.102}$$

where the error bound considers the limit $z \to 1$. As $C(z)$ is Δ-analytic we can translate the error bound on the generating function to an appropriate error bound on coefficients using Theorem 2.19. The coefficients of the first two summands are from the standard function scale, see Equation (2.93); so we finally find

$$\mathbb{E}[C_n] \;=\; \frac{a}{\mathcal{H}}(H_{n+1} - 1)(n+1) \;+\; \lambda(n+1) \;\pm\; O(n^{1-\varepsilon}), \tag{6.103}$$

where λ is an unknown constant. Inserting the well-known asymptotic approximation for the harmonic numbers $H_n = \ln n + \gamma \pm O(n^{-1})$, see Equation (2.70), concludes the proof of Lemma 6.2 and Theorem 6.1.

With this second proof, we close our study of the Quicksort recurrence, and this also completes the technical part of our analysis of Quicksort under the random-permutation model. It only remains to put the pieces together, and to see what algorithmic conclusions we can draw from our findings; this is our plan for the next chapter.

7 Results and Discussion

Contents

THIS CHAPTER IS DEVOTED to the discussion of the results of our analysis. The analysis was carried out in a setting as general as tractable, keeping a parameter for as many choices for the algorithm as possible, to not exclude any potentially interesting variant. In its full glory, the statement for the average cost is presented in Section 7.1. Merely stating this result in a concise way requires creative abbreviations. We will spend the most part of this chapter to get a feeling for what it *means* algorithmically by looking at the result from various angles.

7.1 Average Costs

We are finally in the position to state the main result of this work: the expected costs of Quicksort with generic s-way one-pass partitioning, symbolically in all its parameters, and in several cost measures.

> **Theorem 7.1 (Expected Costs of s-way Quicksort):**
> *Consider Quicksort with generic one-pass partitioning (Algorithm 9), splitting the input into $s \in \mathbb{N}_{\geq 2}$ segments at once, with meeting point $m \in \{0, 0.5, 1, 1.5, \ldots, s - 0.5, s\}$ of main scanning indices, pivot-sampling parameters $t \in \mathbb{N}_0^s$, comparison trees $\lambda_k, \lambda_g \in \Lambda_s$, and Insertionsort cutoff $w \geq k$.*
>
> *Sorting a random permutation of n elements with Quicksort costs on average $C_n = \frac{a_C}{\mathcal{H}} n \ln n \pm O(n)$ key comparisons and $SE_n = \frac{a_{SE}}{\mathcal{H}} n \ln n \pm O(n)$ scanned elements, where the leading-term coefficients are given by*
>
> $$a_C = \sum_{c \in \mathcal{C}} \tau_{r(c)} \frac{\lambda_k(c) \cdot (\sigma_{\rightarrow} + [c = s]) + \lambda_g(c) \cdot (\sigma_{\leftarrow} + [c = 1])}{\kappa - \sigma_{\leftrightarrow} + [c \neq m]}, \tag{7.1}$$
>
> $$a_{SE} = \sum_{i=1}^{\lceil m \rceil} i \cdot \tau_{\lceil m \rceil - i + 1} + \sum_{j=1}^{s - \lfloor m \rfloor} j \cdot \tau_{\lfloor m \rfloor + j} - \frac{\sigma_{\leftrightarrow}}{\kappa}. \tag{7.2}$$
>
> *(We use the abbreviations in Table 4 for concise notation.)*
>
> *Moreover, s-way Quicksort uses $S_n = \frac{a_S}{\mathcal{H}} n \ln n \pm O(n)$ (cyclic) shifts / swaps, which cause $WA_n = \frac{a_{WA}}{\mathcal{H}} n \ln n \pm O(n)$ write accesses to the array where*
>
> $$a_{WA} = a_{SE} - M, \tag{7.3}$$
>
> $$a_S = 1 - \frac{\sigma_{\rightarrow} \sigma_{\leftarrow}}{\kappa (\kappa - \sigma_{\leftrightarrow} + 1)} - M, \tag{7.4}$$
>
> *where we have*
>
> $$M = \begin{cases} \tau_m \dfrac{\sigma_{\rightarrow} + 1}{\kappa + 1} + \tau_{m+1} \dfrac{\sigma_{\leftarrow} + 1}{\kappa + 1}, & \text{for the master-pivot case;} \\[2ex] \dfrac{\sigma_{\leftrightarrow}}{\kappa} & \text{for the master-segment case.} \end{cases} \tag{7.5}$$
> ◄

Table 4: This table collects notations and abbreviations used in Theorem 7.1.

Symbol	Definition
τ	$(t+1)/(k+1) = \sigma/\kappa$
σ	$t+1$
κ	$k+1 = \sigma_1 + \cdots + \sigma_s$
$\sigma_\rightarrow$	$\sigma_1 + \cdots + \sigma_{\lfloor m \rfloor}$
$\sigma_\leftrightarrow$	$\sigma_{\lfloor m \rfloor + 1} + \cdots + \sigma_{\lceil m \rceil}$; (0 for $m \in \mathbb{N}$ and $\sigma_{\lceil m \rceil}$ otherwise)
$\sigma_\leftarrow$	$\sigma_{\lceil m \rceil + 1} + \cdots + \sigma_s$
$r(c)$	index in $[s]$ corresponding to c, see (5.3) on page 167
$\lambda_k(c)$	number of comparisons to classify c-type element with λ_k
$\lambda_g(c)$	as $\lambda_k(c)$, but using tree λ_g
$[c = s]$ etc.	1 if c is a small class, 0 otherwise; see Table 5

Table 5: Which classes count as small, medium resp. large. Note that for master-segment algorithms, s_1 and 1_1 coincide, and are written as m. Such elements are neither regarded small nor large then.

"$c = s/m/1$"	$c = s_2 \ldots s_{\lceil m \rceil}$	$c = s_1$	$c = m$	$c = 1_1$	$c = 1_2 \ldots 1_{s - \lfloor m \rfloor}$
Master Pivot	y/n/n	y/n/n	—	n/n/y	n/n/y
Master Segment	y/n/n	n/y/n	n/y/n	n/y/n	n/n/y

Proof: For the proof, we only have to put the pieces together: By Lemma 5.3 (page 173) (Equation (5.17)), we know that the partitioning costs can be expressed via class-state co-occurrences and the constants from the cost-measure-specific charging schemes. The latter are listed in the tables in Section 5.4 (page 174) for the four cost measures covered by Theorem 7.1. The leading terms of the class-state co-occurrences are listed in Table 2 (page 185). Together, we obtain the partitioning costs as $\mathbb{E}[T_n] = an \pm O(1)$, where a depends on the parameters of the algorithm and the cost measure. We finally obtain the total costs using Theorem 6.1. ■

The formulas in Theorem 7.1 are a bit hard to digest, and we will discuss them extensively in the rest of this chapter. Before we dive into this, let us look at a few concrete numbers first. To keep things simple, let us set $t = 0$, i.e., we do not use pivot sampling.

Table 6 shows the leading-term coefficients $a/\mathcal{H}$ for all cost measures and the parameter choices corresponding to the Quicksort variants we discussed in Section 4.2; see also Table 1 (page 158). They coincide with known results from the literature [82, 162, 24, 182, 105]. Note that many previous works counted the number of binary swaps [162, 182, 105]. Since our generic partitioning method is not based on binary swaps, this cost measure does not appear in the table. In particular, it is not the same as the number of cyclic shifts.

Table 6: Leading-term coefficients of costs for parameter choices corresponding to famous Quicksort variants, and a few more. All results are for $t = 0$, i.e., without sampling. The numbers are all rational, and where feasible we give exact representations as (repeating) decimals.

s	m	λ_k	λ_g	$a_C/\mathcal{H}$	$a_{SE}/\mathcal{H}$	$a_{WA}/\mathcal{H}$	$a_S/\mathcal{H}$
2	1	(tree)	(tree)	2	2	$0.\overline{6}$	$0.\overline{3}$
2	2	(tree)	(tree)	2	3	2	1
3	2	(tree)	(tree)	1.9	1.6	1.1	0.5
3	1.5	(tree)	(tree)	$2.1\overline{3}$	2	1.6	$0.\overline{6}$
3	1.5	(tree)	(tree)	$1.8\overline{6}$	2	1.6	$0.\overline{6}$
3	3	(tree)	(tree)	2	2.4	2	0.8
4	2	(tree)	(tree)	$1.\overline{846153}$	$1.\overline{384615}$	$1.\overline{1076923}$	$0.\overline{461538}$
6	3	 (tree)	 (tree)	1.80624...	1.37931...	1.24795...	0.410509...
6	6	 (tree)	 (tree)	1.87192...	2.41379...	2.29885...	0.574713...
8	4	 (tree)	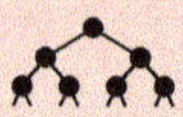 (tree)	$1.\overline{746361}$	$1.\overline{455301}$	$1.\overline{374451}$	$0.\overline{371910}$

Chapter Outline. A few observations are immediate from the values in Table 6. For example, using more pivots seems beneficial for the number of comparisons. Hennequin [77] already noted this in his thesis. We will see in Section 7.7.6, however, that part of this improvement is spurious in a certain sense.

Multiway partitioning is also beneficial for the number of scanned elements, in fact, the savings are even more pronounced; but unlike for comparisons, there seems to be a finite optimal s w.r.t. scanned elements. We consider this in detail in Section 7.6. Scanned elements are also very sensitive to parameter m, and so are write accesses and shifts. We consider choices for m in Section 7.4.

From the few examples it is hard to tell what the influence of λ_k and λ_g will be. For $s = 3$ it is clearly important to choose them wisely, and having two different trees helps, for $s = 6$ the differences in the number of comparisons are smaller. Section 7.7 sheds light on that.

The numbers in Table 6 are without pivot sampling. How to choose t is the subject of Section 7.5, but we will see throughout this chapter that pivot sampling can change the picture dramatically. We close this chapter with a word of caution in Section 7.8: as the *jellyfish paradox* shows, intuitions for optimal parameter choices can be misleading when pivot sampling is taken into account.

7.2 Disclaimer

All discussions in this chapter consider the leading-term coefficient of the average costs in the random-permutation model. It has to be taken into account that the given optimal choices need not be best possible for small n. Our goal is to provide an academic discussion of good values for the parameters and why they are so. This provides guidelines for identifying promising Quicksort variants for practice; but the choices need further empirical evaluation before they are used in production code.

The parameter space is vast. Even for the leading term of costs we can still play with

- ▶ s, the number of segments,

- ▶ k, the sample size,

- ▶ τ, the quantiles vector, (which together with k determines $\mathbf{t} = \tau(k+1) - 1$),

- ▶ λ_k and λ_g, the comparison trees that determine to which pivots we compare an element, and

- ▶ m, the meeting point of the main scanning indices k and g, which also determines whether we use a *master-pivot* or a *master-segment method.*

An implementation also has to decide for a threshold w, i.e., when to stop recursion, and which algorithm to use for the base cases; Insertionsort is the classical choice, but others are possible. We will have to concentrate on certain restricted regions of the parameter space.

In the following, we will mostly try to identify good choices for all the parameters of generic s-way Quicksort in isolation; i.e., in Sections 7.4 – 7.7, we focus on one of the parameters, namely the meeting point m, the pivot-sampling parameter $\mathbf{t}$, the number of segments s and the comparison trees λ_k and λ_g, respectively, and consider the other parameters as given. Even though this does not in general reveal what the optimal combination of parameters is (see Section 7.8), it seems the only manageable approach to me.

Moreover, we will focus on comparisons and scanned elements. The former is the classical cost measure for sorting, and of interest because of the connections to information theory. If we sort complex objects, comparisons are an expensive operation, and might in fact dominate running time. For simple types like numbers, the number of scanned elements is more likely to be a good predictor for running time on modern machines, so this is the cost measure of practical interest.

In contrast, the number of cyclic shifts is not likely to predict running time well, since shifts of different length contribute the same; the number of write accesses is more appropriate in this respect. Write accesses, however, are of minor importance in practice, since all array cells we ever write to were read immediately before, so that the write access is cached for sure.

7.3 Simulating Multiway Partitioning by Binary Partitioning

A reason why multiway Quicksort might not have been considered interesting in the past is that it can be simulated by several rounds of binary partitioning. We will discuss below what exactly can be gained by multiway partitioning; not much in terms of comparisons, but quite a lot in terms of scanned elements.

The situation is reminiscent of folklore results about Mergesort: a heap-based multiway merge can also be simulated by iterative binary merging, and the comparison costs are very similar. In terms of I/Os, however, multiway merging is far superior. What makes the situation in Quicksort much more interesting is the choices of the pivots.

7.3.1 Waterloo vs. Classic

Let us first consider a simple example. Consider Waterloo Quicksort without sampling, i.e., the parameter choice $s = 4$, $\mathbf{t} = (0,0,0,0)$ $m = 2$, and $\lambda_k = \lambda_g = \text{⋀}$. What one execution of four-way partitioning does in a single step can also be achieved by first partitioning the input around P_2, and then partitioning only the left segment around P_1, and likewise only the right segment around P_3.

Each (ordinary) element will have participated in exactly two binary partitioning rounds, so the overall number of comparisons for the latter is 2η. (Recall that $\eta = n - k = n - 3$ is the number of ordinary elements). Similarly, classifying an element using ⋀ also requires exactly two comparisons per element, yielding costs 2η also for the single round of four-way partitioning. Does that mean that four-way Quicksort and classic Quicksort use the same number of comparisons in total?

The answer is no; Theorem 7.1 tell us that classic Quicksort needs $2n \ln n \pm O(n)$ comparisons, while four-way Quicksort needs only $\frac{24}{13} n \ln n \pm O(n)$. Why does classic Quicksort need $8.\overline{3}\,\%$ more comparisons in the asymptotic average?

Apples and Oranges. The difference is that even though the three pivots for four-way Quicksort are randomly selected, they are then *sorted*, so P_2 is effectively chosen as the *median of three* elements. The first round of partitioning gets a higher-quality pivot, and produces more balanced subproblems on average.

That Waterloo Quicksort without sampling outperforms classic Quicksort without sampling seems to speak in favor of multiway partitioning, but we are really comparing apples and oranges: we effectively allow one method to sample pivots but not the other. Recall that we effectively disregard the costs for sampling since it only contributes to the $O(n)$ error term; that is not a fair comparison then.

Towards a Fair Race. To make the competition fair, we have to allow sampling for classic Quicksort, as well. Is four-way Quicksort then equivalent to median-of-three classic Quicksort? Again no; the costs for the latter would be $\frac{12}{7} n \ln n \pm O(n)$, roughly another $2.2\,\%$ better than four-way Quicksort. The reason is that the second level of partitioning, where we use P_1 resp. P_3 as pivots, does not get a median-of-three pivot, but rather a random one. (A moments reflection shows that P_1 is indeed uniformly selected among the elements smaller than P_2, i.e., those in the left segment, and similarly for P_3.)

If we want to simulate four-way Quicksort without sampling using binary partitioning, we have to *alternate* between the two pivot selection modes: initially, we pick the median-of-three, for the child recursive calls we switch to no sampling, for their child calls again back to median-of-three, and so on. For this simple example, it is easy to see that the two methods perform exactly the same comparisons if sampled-out elements of a median-of-three round become the pivots of the child calls.

The main result of this section is that, for the leading term of costs, we can consider a randomized version of this alternating scheme: In each round, we flip a (fair) coin and depending on its outcome we either choose the pivot at random or as median of three elements. That is to say, we use a *random-parameter pivot-sampling scheme* (cf. Section 4.4.2) whose parameter T takes the values $t = (0,0)$ and $t = (1,1)$ with probability one half each. On average, we will use median-of-three in half of the partitioning steps, as in the strictly alternating version, so it is plausible that the costs should be similar.

7.3.2 Entropy-Equivalent Sampling

In this section, we show that for *any* pivot-sampling parameter $t \in \mathbb{N}_0^s$, we can indeed find a binary random-parameter scheme $T = (T_1, T_2)$, so that choosing a single pivot according to T is equivalent to sampling $s - 1$ pivots according to t w.r.t. the reduction in entropy. To make precise what we mean by this statement, we need some notation.

Bisection Trees.   To simulate s-way partitioning, we have to choose pivots for the binary partitioning rounds: for $s = 3$, we may first use P_1 and then partitioning the right segment around P_2, or we first use P_2 and partition the left segment around P_1 afterwards. It is in general inevitable that not all elements participate in the same number of rounds.

To describe one possible way to organize rounds, we fix a *bisection tree* $\lambda_b \in \Lambda_s$. The levels of this BST correspond to the rounds of binary partitioning, and the labels of inner nodes indicate the pivots to use in these rounds. Leaves correspond to one of the s classes resp. segments produced by s-way partitioning. A natural choice for λ_b is to pick a comparison tree used for classification; but recall that λ_k and λ_g need not be equal. For the statements below, λ_b may be an entirely different tree.

Let the internal nodes of λ_b be $v_1, \ldots, v_{s-1}$, indexed in in-order, so that node v_r corresponds to a binary partitioning step using pivot P_r. Further, let the s leaves be labeled by $\sigma_1, \ldots, \sigma_s$, the parameter $\sigma = t + 1$ of the pivot-sampling scheme of the s-way Quicksort. We then denote for each inner node v by $\kappa(v)$ the sum of leaf weights in its subtree; for the root, this is simply $\kappa = \Sigma\sigma$. Moreover, we write $p(v) = \frac{\kappa(v)}{\kappa}$, which is the probability to pass node v in a search for a random leaf, and $p_L(v)$ resp. $p_R(v) = 1 - p_L(v)$ are the probabilities to go to the left respectively right child of v in such a search. Finally, we denote the expected depth of a random leaf by

$$b \;=\; \sum_{r=1}^{s-1} p(v_r) \;=\; \lambda_b^{\mathsf{T}} \cdot \tau. \tag{7.6}$$

Proposition 7.2 (Equivalent Binary Sampling-Parameter Distribution):
Let $\tau \in (0,1)^s$, $\kappa > 0$, and a bisection tree $\lambda_b \in \Lambda_s$ be given. With the notation introduced above, let

$$
\mathsf{T} \;=\; \sum_{r=1}^{s-1} \mathbb{1}_{\{X=r\}} \cdot \underbrace{\Big(\kappa(v_r) \cdot (p_L(v_r), p_R(v_r)) - 1 \Big)}_{\rightsquigarrow\; \text{local } (t_1, t_2)\text{-sampling at } v} ,
\tag{7.7}
$$

$$
\text{with } X \overset{\mathcal{D}}{=} \mathcal{D}\!\left(\frac{p(v_1)}{b}, \ldots, \frac{p(v_{s-1})}{b} \right).
\tag{7.8}
$$

Then holds

$$
\mathbb{E}\big[\mathcal{H}(\mathsf{T})\big] \;=\; \frac{\mathcal{H}(\mathbf{t})}{b} ,
\tag{7.9}
$$

and we will call that number the effective bisection entropy of $\mathbf{t}$ w.r.t. λ_b.   ◄

Proof: With the corresponding lemma from our discussion of discrete entropy, see Section 2.5 (page 89), the proof is actually trivial:

$$
\mathbb{E}\big[\mathcal{H}(\mathsf{T})\big] \;=\; \sum_{r=1}^{s-1} \frac{p(v_r)}{b} \cdot \mathcal{H}\!\Big(\kappa(v_r) \cdot (p_L(v_r), p_R(v_r)) - 1 \Big)
\tag{7.10}
$$

$$
\;=\; \frac{1}{b} \sum_{r=1}^{s-1} \frac{\kappa(v_r)}{\kappa} \mathcal{H}_{\mathrm{hd}_{\kappa(v_r)}}(p_L(v_r), p_R(v_r))
\tag{7.11}
$$

$$
\underset{\text{Lemma 2.67}}{=} \frac{1}{b} \cdot \mathcal{H}_{\mathrm{hd}_\kappa}(\tau)
\tag{7.12}
$$

$$
\;=\; \frac{\mathcal{H}(\mathbf{t})}{b}.
\tag{7.13}
$$

∎

Our notation hides an important fact that deserves to be noticed: if τ is κ-discretized in the sense of Definition 2.51, then all local probabilities $\tau(v) = (p_L(v), p_R(v))$ will be $\kappa(v)$-discretized. This means that $\mathsf{T} \in \mathbb{N}_0^s$ holds, and the resulting sampling scheme is implementable.

Entropy-Equivalent Sample Sizes. With Proposition 7.2 we can compare two otherwise incomparable sampling schemes, for example: is $\mathbf{t} = (0, 1, 2)$ yielding higher-quality pivots than $\mathbf{t} = (0, 0, 0, 0, 0, 0)$? Note that both schemes use a sample of five elements.

For both, we first select bisection trees, and we will in the following always pick the best such, i.e., the ones with minimal values for b. These are simply optimal BSTs with leaf weights τ; we discuss properties of such trees in depth in Section 7.7.3. For $\mathbf{t} = (0, 1, 2)$, the optimal b is $\frac{3}{2}$, for $\mathbf{t} = (0, 0, 0, 0, 0, 0)$, we have $\frac{8}{3}$. Proposition 7.2 says that we should compare the effective bisection entropy of the two, which here is

$$
\frac{26}{45} = 0.5\overline{7} \quad \text{vs.} \quad \frac{87}{160} = 0.54375 ,
\tag{7.14}
$$

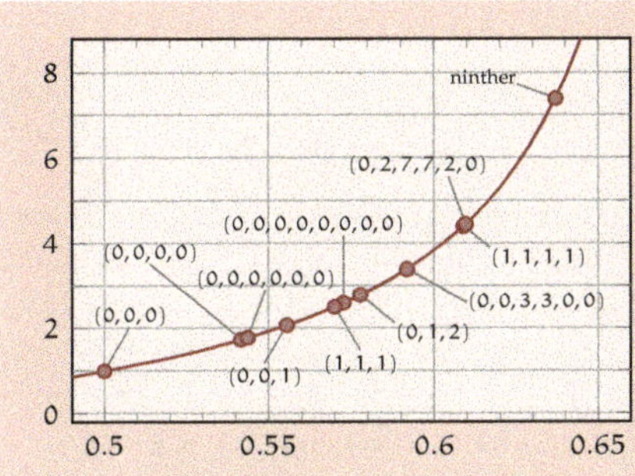

Figure 28: Entropy-equivalent median-of-k sampling. The x-axis gives the discrete entropy per binary partitioning round, i.e., the x-coordinate for the given points is computed as $\mathcal{H}(t)/b^*(\tau)$; the y-axis shows the value of k, so that median-of-k sampling has this entropy, i.e., x- and y-values are related as $x = \mathcal{H}_{\mathrm{hd}_{y+1}}(\frac{1}{2}, \frac{1}{2})$.

so $t = (0, 1, 2)$ yields higher-quality pivots.

But is this difference significant? The effective bisection entropy is not a very intuitive scale to judge that. We can always translate it to a (not necessarily integral) sample size $\hat{k}$, so that it has the same entropy-value as median-of-$\hat{k}$ sampling. To do so, we (numerically) solve the equation

$$\mathcal{H}_{\mathrm{hd}_{\hat{k}+1}}\left(\tfrac{1}{2}, \tfrac{1}{2}\right) \;=\; -\mathrm{hd}_{\hat{k}+1}\left(\tfrac{1}{2}\right) \;=\; \frac{\mathcal{H}(t)}{b}. \tag{7.15}$$

Figure 28 shows $\hat{k}$ as a function of the right-hand side, and also includes the values of a few exemplary sampling parameters. For our two from above, we find that the quality of pivots using $t = (0, 1, 2)$ corresponds approximately to "median-of-2.778," whereas pivots using $t = (0, 0, 0, 0, 0, 0)$ correspond to "median-of-1.776."

7.3.3 s-Way vs. Binary Partitioning

Recall that the overall costs of generalized Quicksort are given by $\frac{a}{\mathcal{H}} n \ln n \pm O(n)$, where we understand $\mathcal{H}$ either as $\mathcal{H}(t)$ for a fixed t, or as $\mathbb{E}[\mathcal{H}(T)]$ for random-parameter sampling; see Theorem 6.5. Proposition 7.2 then simply says that we can *exactly* simulate the effect of drawing $s - 1$ pivots according to the sampling parameter t in a Quicksort variant that uses only binary partitioning with a suitably chosen random-parameter sampling scheme $T = (T_1, T_2)$.

More importantly, Proposition 7.2 allows to assess the *relative* efficiency of an s-way partitioning method w.r.t. classic binary partitioning *in isolation*, without the different shapes of the recurrences getting in our way: we simulate s-way partitioning by b rounds of binary partitioning, where b depends on the bisection tree λ_b and on τ; these b rounds of binary partitioning each have cost $n \pm O(1)$, independent of sampling. If the s-way method cannot beat this cost of $bn \pm O(1)$, there is no incentive to use multiway partitioning.

The value b depends on the bisection tree λ_b, which we are free to choose; for a fair comparison we should choose the best possible such tree as above. Since b is the weighted external path length of λ_b, when we assign the probabilities $\tau_1, \ldots, \tau_s$ to the leaves, b is nothing but the expected search costs of λ_b, which are lower-bounded by the entropy:

$b \geqslant \mathcal{H}_{\mathrm{ld}}(\boldsymbol{\tau})$, see Proposition 2.49 (page 86). We can thus advise for $\boldsymbol{\tau}$ the quantiles vector of our pivot selection method:

> *If multiway-partitioning is more than $\mathcal{H}_{\mathrm{ld}}(\boldsymbol{\tau})$ times as expensive as binary partitioning, i.e., if $a \geqslant \mathcal{H}_{\mathrm{ld}}(\boldsymbol{\tau})$, better use classic Quicksort with median-of-$\hat{k}$.*

Assume we use only one comparison tree $\lambda_k = \lambda_g$. The entropy bound then also holds for comparison-costs there, so we have $a \geqslant \mathcal{H}_{\mathrm{ld}}(\boldsymbol{\tau})$, and by the above rule, we are *always* at least as good with iterated binary partitioning. With respect to the average comparison count, *there is absolutely no savings possible from multiway partitioning with a single (fixed) comparison tree.* Zero.

Any apparent advantage of multiway methods is due to comparing apples and oranges: we effectively allow the multiway methods to sample higher-quality pivots. If we are fair enough to grant classic Quicksort the entropy-equivalent amount of sampling, it is at least as good.

But this is not the end of the story; multiway partitioning does have intrinsic qualities:

1. We can use two different comparison trees in generic one-pass partitioning, and this indeed allows us to break the entropy bound (or circumvent it rather).

2. For practical purposes the number of scanned elements is more important than comparisons; for those there is no lower bound that spoils the game, and indeed, significant savings are possible.

In the following sections, we will quantify what is possible, and which parameter choices reap the most benefits from multiway partitioning.

7.4 The Optimal Meeting Point for Indices

Recall that our generic s-way partitioning method consists of repeatedly moving the scanning indices towards each other, k to the right or g to left, putting the newly encountered element into the corresponding segment. One parameter of this method is the meeting point of the scanning indices k and g; more precisely m is the number of segments to the left of the point where k and g finally meet. We allow non-integral values like $m = 1.5$, which means that k and g jointly scan one segment, in this case the second one, counting from the left. Such a partitioning method is of the *master-segment* type, those with $m \in \mathbb{N}$ are called *master-pivot* methods.

The flexibility in parameter m allows us to give one general analysis that covers many special cases of existing partitioning methods, see Chapter 4. It does not complicate analysis too much, so we kept it symbolically. Aumüller et al. [10] also use the value m, but they fix it to $m = \lceil s/2 \rceil$. They do not consider master-segment methods.

For interpreting results, every additional parameter complicates matters significantly. If we can, we will fix parameters to values that are good for most, if not all, choices of all other parameters. This is not possible, since the parameters interact and influence each other; but as we will see in this section, $m = \lceil s/2 \rceil$ is often a good choice.

7.4.1 Comparisons

With respect to comparisons, m essentially influences how many elements are classified with λ_k and how many with λ_g. If $\lambda_k = \lambda_g$, the number of comparisons does not depend on m at all. So assume $\lambda_k \neq \lambda_g$. To put the difference between the two trees to good use, $m \approx s/2$ intuitively is a good choice. It is a recurrent theme of this chapter that things are a little more involved than they might appear at first glance, and this case is no exception. Let us look at a few examples to get a feeling of the influence of m.

We focus on simple choices for the other parameters, in particular let us assume we do not use pivot sampling, i.e., $\mathbf{t} = 0$, and we pick for each parameter set the optimal pair of comparison trees (λ_k, λ_g). When s is an integer-power of two, the best pick for both trees is the complete binary search tree; we discuss this in more detail in Section 7.7. In that case, the choice of m is immaterial to the number of comparisons; this is a boring case. Figure 29 shows all possible choices for m for a few exemplary values of s that are not powers of two.

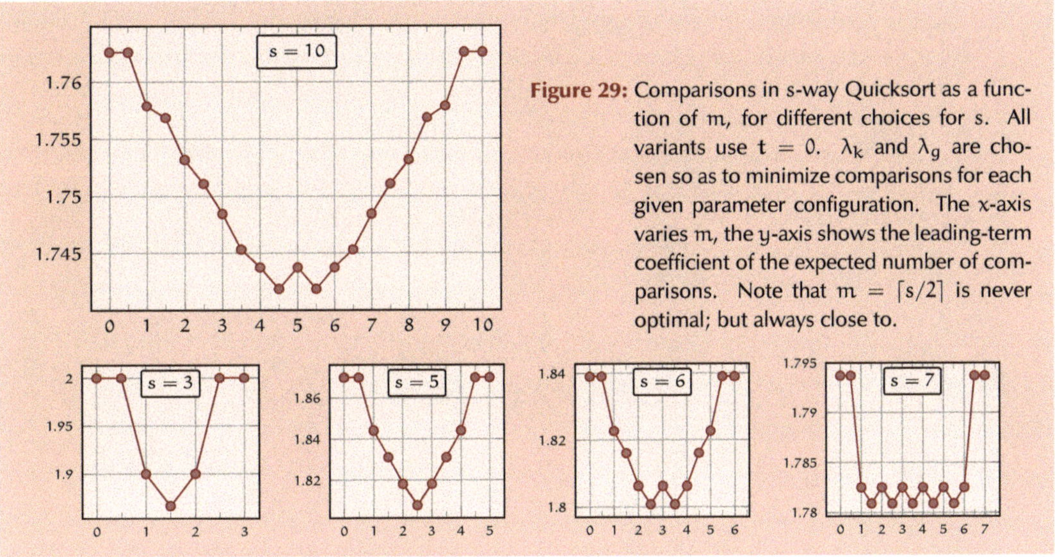

Figure 29: Comparisons in s-way Quicksort as a function of m, for different choices for s. All variants use $\mathbf{t} = 0$. λ_k and λ_g are chosen so as to minimize comparisons for each given parameter configuration. The x-axis varies m, the y-axis shows the leading-term coefficient of the expected number of comparisons. Note that $m = \lceil s/2 \rceil$ is never optimal; but always close to.

Our general intuition to pick m roughly at $s/2$ is confirmed, but the patterns that emerge are interesting. Note in particular that neither $m = s/2$, $m = \lceil s/2 \rceil$, nor $m = \lfloor s/2 \rfloor$ are optimal for all s, even though they always come close. With a little more diligence, we can characterize the choices for m that contribute the lowest two levels of points in Figure 29, in particular also for cases like in $s = 7$.

Proposition 7.3: *Assume s is fixed and let $\mathbf{t} = 0$. Further let (λ_k, λ_g) be the optimal trees w.r.t. the number of comparisons, for given s, m and $\mathbf{t}$. Among $m \in \{0, 0.5, 1, 1.5, \ldots, s\}$, an optimal choice is $m^* = \lceil s/2 \rceil - \frac{1}{2}$. Unless s is a power of two, no master-pivot method, i.e., no choice $m \in \mathbb{N}_0$, achieves optimal cost.*

Moreover, let $lll = lll(s) = 2\left(s - 2^{\lfloor ld(s) \rfloor}\right)$ *be the number of leaves on the lower level of a maximally balanced binary tree with s leaves. Write* $ls = \min\{lll, s - lll\}$ *and* $ls_2 = \max\{lll, s - lll\}$. *All of the following choices for* m *are optimal, and they are the only optimal choices unless s is a power of two:*

$$\left\{ ls + \tfrac{1}{2},\ ls + \tfrac{1}{2} + 1, \ldots, ls_2 - \tfrac{1}{2} \right\}. \tag{7.16}$$

Finally, for any $m \in (ls, ls_2)$ *holds*

$$a_C = \lfloor ld(s) \rfloor + 1 - \left[lll < \tfrac{s}{2}\right] \cdot \frac{s - 2\,lll}{s} - ls \cdot \left(1 + \frac{1}{s - [m \notin \mathbb{N}_0] + 1}\right). \tag{7.17}$$

(Note that $ls = 0$ *for s a power of two.)*   ◀

Proof: The optimal choice of comparison trees in this scenario uses for λ_k a maximally balanced binary search tree on s leaves whose leftmost $s - lll(s)$ leaves are at depth $\lfloor ld(s) \rfloor$ and the remaining $lll(s)$ leaves are on level $\lfloor ld(s) \rfloor + 1$. As we do not use sampling, the access probabilities for all leaves of the trees are almost uniform, with a slight overhang on the left, so the above tree is a plausible choice. We refer the reader to our detailed discussion of optimal trees, in particular Section 7.7.6 (page 271), for formal arguments for the optimality of this tree.

We thus have $\lambda_k(c) = \lfloor ld(s) \rfloor$ for all $c \in \mathcal{C}$ with $r(c) \leqslant s - lll$, and $\lambda_k(c) = \lfloor ld(s) \rfloor + 1$ otherwise. Similarly, λ_g is the maximally balanced BST where the leaves on the lesser level are at the very right, i.e., $\lambda_g(c) = \lfloor ld(s) \rfloor$ for $r(c) > lll$, and $\lambda_g(c) = \lfloor ld(s) \rfloor + 1$ otherwise.

Inserting this and our other parameters into the expression for a_C from Theorem 7.1, we find after rearranging

$$
\begin{aligned}
a_C = {}& \lfloor ld(s) \rfloor + 1 - \left[lll < \tfrac{s}{2}\right] \frac{s - 2\,lll}{s} \\[4pt]
& - \frac{1}{s} \cdot \begin{cases} \dfrac{\lfloor m \rfloor(\lfloor m \rfloor + 1)}{s - [m \notin \mathbb{Z}] + 1} + \dfrac{[m \notin \mathbb{Z}] \cdot \lfloor m \rfloor}{s - [m \notin \mathbb{Z}]} + \dfrac{(ls - \lceil m \rceil)\lfloor m \rfloor}{s - [m \notin \mathbb{Z}] + 1}, & m \leqslant ls, \\[10pt] \dfrac{ls(\lfloor m \rfloor + 1)}{s - [m \notin \mathbb{Z}] + 1}, & m > ls, \end{cases} \\[10pt]
& - \frac{1}{s} \cdot \begin{cases} \dfrac{(s - \lceil m \rceil)(s - \lceil m \rceil + 1)}{s - [m \notin \mathbb{Z}] + 1} + \dfrac{[m \notin \mathbb{Z}](s - \lceil m \rceil)}{s - 1} + \dfrac{(ls - s + \lfloor m \rfloor)(s - \lceil m \rceil)}{s - [m \notin \mathbb{Z}] + 1}, & m \geqslant ls_2, \\[10pt] \dfrac{ls(s - \lceil m \rceil + 1)}{s - [m \notin \mathbb{Z}] + 1}, & m < ls_2. \end{cases}
\end{aligned}
\tag{7.18}
$$

The terms are a bit unwieldy, but the representation is telling. The terms in the first line do not depend on m, so we can ignore them for optimizing. In the case distinctions one easily checks that the first alternative is smaller in both cases, and as we subtract it, we should thus pick the second alternative to minimize a_C. This already shows that $m^* \in (ls, ls_2)$. For all such m, adding up the two terms from the case distinctions yields the representation of Equation (7.17).

It remains to show that $\lceil s/2 \rceil - \tfrac{1}{2} \in (ls, ls_2)$, in particular that interval had better not be empty. So, assume towards a contradiction that $ls = ls_2$ for some $s \in \mathbb{N}$. Unfolding definitions, that would mean $\mathrm{lll}(s) = s - \mathrm{lll}(s)$, i.e.,

$$s \;=\; 2\,\mathrm{lll}(s) \;=\; 4\big(s - 2^{\lfloor \mathrm{ld}(s)\rfloor}\big) \tag{7.19}$$

$$\implies s \;=\; \frac{2^{\lfloor \mathrm{ld}(s)\rfloor}}{3} \;\notin\; \mathbb{Z}, \tag{7.20}$$

so $ls_2 - ls \geq 1$. For the claim that master-pivot methods are not optimal unless s is a power of two, it suffices to note that in Equation (7.17), only the last term depends on m, namely via $[m \notin \mathbb{N}_0]$. ∎

7.4.2 Scanned Elements

Scanned elements are simpler to deal with than comparisons: we do not have to take different trees into account. To keep things simple, let us again consider the case without pivot sampling, i.e., $t = 0$. Then $\kappa = s$, $\sigma = 1$, and $\tau = (\frac{1}{s}, \ldots, \frac{1}{s})$, so the leading-term coefficient from Theorem 7.1 becomes

$$a_{SE} \;=\; \frac{1}{s} \sum_{i=1}^{\lceil m \rceil} i + \frac{1}{s} \sum_{j=1}^{s - \lfloor m \rfloor} j - \frac{[m \notin \mathbb{Z}]}{s} \tag{7.21}$$

$$=\; \frac{\lceil m \rceil^{\overline{2}} + (s - \lfloor m \rfloor)^{\overline{2}}}{2s} - \frac{[m \notin \mathbb{Z}]}{s}. \tag{7.22}$$

Figure 30 shows a few exemplary values, similarly as Figure 29 above for comparisons. Values around $s/2$ seem to be good. With a quick second look, we can again characterize optimal choices precisely.

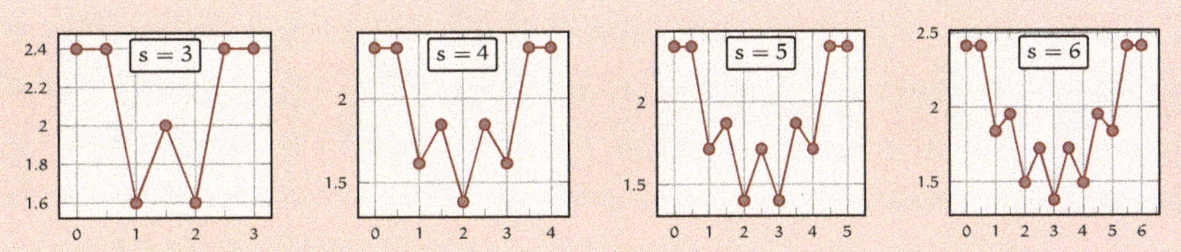

Figure 30: Scanned elements in s-way Quicksort as a function of m, for different choices for s. All variants use $t = 0$. The x-axis varies m, the y-axis shows the leading-term coefficient of the expected number of scanned elements.

Proposition 7.4: *Assume s is fixed and let $t = 0$. Among $m \in \{0, 0.5, 1, 1.5, \ldots, s\}$, the optimal choices are exactly $m^* = \lceil s/2 \rceil$ and $m^* = \lfloor s/2 \rfloor$, for which*

$$a_{SE} \;=\; \frac{\lceil s/2 \rceil}{2}\Big(1 + \frac{1}{s}\Big). \tag{7.23}$$

In particular, no master-segment method, i.e., no choice $m \notin \mathbb{N}_0$, achieves optimal cost. ◄

Proof: We first show that among all master-pivot methods, those with m closest to $s/2$ must be optimal. If $m \in \mathbb{N}_0$, we have by Equation (7.22)

$$a_{SE} \;=\; \frac{m^{\overline{2}} + (s-m)^{\overline{2}}}{2s}, \tag{7.24}$$

and upon settings $m = \mu s$ for $\mu \in [0,1]$ and rearranging, this is

$$=\; s \cdot \left(\frac{1}{2} - \mu(1-\mu) \right) + \frac{1}{2}. \tag{7.25}$$

a_{SE} is obviously minimal for $\mu = 1/2$, and increasing monotonically from there. The integer values closest to $s/2$ are optimal among all master-pivot choices.

Next, we show that for any master-segment method, the adjacent integer m is strictly better. Rewriting the term for a_{SE} lets us see why that is the case:

$$a_{SE} \;=\; \frac{1}{s} \sum_{i=1}^{\lceil m \rceil} i + \frac{1}{s} \sum_{j=1+[m \notin \mathbb{Z}]}^{s-\lfloor m \rfloor} j \tag{7.26}$$

$$=\; \frac{1}{s} \sum_{i=1}^{\lceil m \rceil} i + \begin{cases} \dfrac{1}{s} \displaystyle\sum_{j=1}^{s-\lceil m \rceil} j, & \text{for } m \in \mathbb{N}_0, \\[2em] \dfrac{1}{s} \displaystyle\sum_{j=1}^{s-\lceil m \rceil} (j+1), & \text{for } m \notin \mathbb{N}_0. \end{cases} \tag{7.27}$$

Thus we can strictly improve a_{SE} for any $m \in \{1.5, 2.5 \ldots, s-0.5\}$ by using $m-0.5 \in \mathbb{N}_0$ instead, since $\lceil m \rceil = \lceil m-0.5 \rceil = m-0.5$. ∎

7.4.3 Summary

The meeting point m of the indices is a rather simple parameter in its influence on overall costs. For our cost measures it is always optimal to use $m \in \left\{ \frac{s-1}{2}, \frac{s}{2}, \frac{s+1}{2} \right\}$, and all three choices are usually close to the optimum. We will in the following mostly use $m = \lceil s/2 \rceil$ since this choice is always optimal w.r.t. scanned elements and master-pivot methods also feel more natural to me. For odd s, the resulting method is thus asymmetric: there is one more segment that is scanned from the left than there are segments on the right; YBB Quicksort is the instantiation of this scheme for $s = 3$.

Other measures of quality might well lead to other choices of m. As vividly discussed by Bentley [18], code simplicity, ease of implementation and maintenance favor Lomuto's partitioning scheme ($s = 2$, $m = 2$) over Hoare's scheme ($s = 2$, $m = 1$). One deliberately compromises on efficiency then, which may be appropriate in a given situation. The analysis in this work tells us how much we pay for simplicity; in this case 50 % additional scanned elements.

7.5 Optimal Pivot Sampling

While choosing pivots from a sample of the input has been used in Quicksort since its child days, people mostly focused on *equidistant* choices for the pivots. For single-pivot Quicksort, the *median-of-three* strategy has become a classic trick to speed up Quicksort, and its generalization, median-of-$(2t + 1)$, has been studied extensively.

The possibility to choose other order statistics of the sample has been considered, but was not found very helpful [162, 77]: the studied Quicksort versions were highly symmetric—either single-pivot Quicksort, or multiway Quicksort, but with a single, balanced comparison tree and no one-pass in-place partitioning—therefore skewed pivots only increased the entropy $\mathcal{H}$, but did not lower the comparison count per partitioning step.

There are scenarios where, even for the symmetric, classic Quicksort, a skewed pivot can yield benefits over median of $(2t + 1)$: the number of swaps and the number of branch misses *increase* in single-pivot Quicksort when using sampling, unless skewed order statistics are used [116, 96]. However, these cost measures do not usually dominate practical performance.

Only with the advent of the truly asymmetric YBB Quicksort has skewed sampling entered the limelight [185, 137]. In this section, we extend these results to our generic s-way Quicksort and try to find optimal ways to pick pivots from a sample.

We start by briefly discussing the parameter k, the sample size. For the rest of the section, we assume k is already given; either as some concrete value or as the limiting behavior for $k \to \infty$, where pivots are chosen as precise quantiles of the input. We then give conditions for optimality, starting with the simplest ones and working onwards to more general statements. In particular, we first consider the limit case $k \to \infty$. We conclude the section with examples of optimal sampling vectors.

7.5.1 Optimal Sample Sizes?

In our discussion, we confine ourselves to the leading terms of costs. For these leading terms, the cost of pivot sampling is completely *neglected*: If we consider the sample size k a fixed, constant parameter, we have only constant effort per partitioning step. The number of partitioning steps remains linear in n, since we exclude in each step the constant number of pivots from further consideration. Together this means that pivot sampling only affects the linear term of overall costs. When we only consider leading terms, we can increase k *for free*.

An interesting theoretic model is to let k be a function of n. This has been studied for classic Quicksort [123, 116]. We do not cover that case in this work.

For most cost measures, larger sample sizes improve overall costs in the leading term, because $\mathcal{H}_{\mathrm{hd}_\kappa}$ is decreasing with κ, and *there is no finite optimal sample size*.

We will consider the limiting case $k \to \infty$ in more detail in the following, for two reasons. First, because it corresponds to the best sample size, even though we cannot expect to achieve this costs with finite k. Second, because in the limit any stochastic vector is a feasible quantiles vector τ, which simplifies the process of finding optimal quantiles.

We will then at the end of this section try to translate back from optimal continuous quantiles to the κ-discretized choices for a finite sample size k.

The actual value of k in practice has to be chosen to yield good performance on reasonably sized inputs. Our leading-term analysis is not very helpful in doing so, but it clearly states how the theoretical cost measures are affected, and how much can be gained from using larger samples.

7.5.2   Entropy-Tight Pairs

For certain cases, it is simple to show that a given sampling vector τ must be optimal w.r.t. comparisons, because it achieves the information-theoretic lower bound for comparison-based sorting. For a single comparison tree and the exact-quantile limit $k \to \infty$, we can in fact *characterize* the optimal parameters: they are precisely the *entropy-tight pairs* of comparison trees and quantiles vectors.

Proposition 7.5: *Assume s and $\lambda_k = \lambda_g$ and τ are fixed. Then the leading-term coefficient of the expected number of comparisons converges to $1/\ln(2)$ as $k \to \infty$ if and only if*

$$\tau_r \;=\; \frac{1}{2^{\lambda_k(r)}}, \qquad \text{for } r = 1,\ldots,s, \qquad\qquad \text{(2.192) revisited}$$

where $\lambda_k(r)$ denotes the depth of the rth leaf of λ_k.

Parameters (s,λ_k,τ) that fulfill Equation (2.192) are called exact-quantiles comparison-optimal: no other parameter configuration can have a strictly smaller limiting value as $k \to \infty$ for the leading-term coefficient of the expected number of comparisons. ◀

Proof: For a single comparison tree we have independent of k that

$$a_C \;=\; \sum_{r=1}^{s} \tau_r \lambda_k(r) \tag{7.28}$$

$$\;=\; \mathbb{E}[\lambda_k(I)] \tag{7.29}$$

for $I \overset{\mathcal{D}}{=} \mathcal{D}(\tau)$. By Fact 2.50 (page 88) and Proposition 2.49 this is

$$\geqslant \; \mathcal{H}_{\mathrm{ld}}(\tau), \tag{7.30}$$

and equality holds exactly under the given assumption, Equation (2.192). The overall number of comparisons in the limit $k \to \infty$ is then $\sim \frac{\mathcal{H}_{\mathrm{ld}}(\tau)}{\mathcal{H}_{\mathrm{ln}}(\tau)} n \ln n = \frac{1}{\ln 2} n \ln n$, which is up to first order the information-theoretic lower bound for comparison-based sorting. So the given parameter configuration is asymptotically optimal. ■

There are a lot of exact-quantiles comparison-optimal choices (s,λ,τ). The probably most well-known is $s = 2$ and $\tau = (\frac{1}{2},\frac{1}{2})$, which is the limit case of median-of-k Quicksort for $k \to \infty$. For a single pivot, there is only one comparison tree with both classes on level 1, so we have $a_C = 1$ regardless of τ. For the entropy $\mathcal{H}_{\mathrm{ln}}(\tau)$, we have the unique maximum of $\ln(2)$ at $\tau = (\frac{1}{2},\frac{1}{2})$ (Corollary 2.44), so for single-pivot Quicksort, this is the only comparison-optimal sampling vector.

For more pivots, there are many different comparison trees to choose from. If we fix any of them, $\lambda_k = \lambda_g = \lambda$ and define a quantiles vector $\boldsymbol{\tau}$ according to Equation (2.192), the so obtained triple $(s, \lambda, \boldsymbol{\tau})$ is exact-quantiles comparison-optimal, and it is the only such for the given λ.

Arguing for optimality w.r.t. comparisons is facilitated by entropy bounds: whenever an algorithm needs asymptotically $n\,\mathrm{ld}(n)$ comparisons, we know it must be optimal to first order, irrespective of any alternative parameter choices. Similarly, we could lower-bound partitioning costs with entropy arguments. One can extend these arguments a little further, however, even for other cost measures.

7.5.3 Linear Costs With Exact-Quantile Pivots

Aumüller et al. [10] noticed that we can use *Gibb's inequality*, stated as Lemma 2.43 in this work, to cook up a rather general optimality criterion for the exact-quantiles case. We give here a slightly stronger version of Lemma 8.1 of Aumüller et al., adding uniqueness of the optimum.

Proposition 7.6 (Optimality Criterion for $k \to \infty$): *Let $a = a(\boldsymbol{\tau}) = \boldsymbol{\alpha}^\mathsf{T} \boldsymbol{\tau} = \sum_{r=1}^{s} \alpha_r \tau_r$, for a vector $\boldsymbol{\alpha} \in \mathbb{R}_{>0}^s$ with $s \geqslant 2$. Then the unique minimum of $a(\boldsymbol{\tau})/\mathcal{H}_{\ln}(\boldsymbol{\tau})$ over all $\boldsymbol{\tau} \in [0,1]^s$ with $\Sigma\boldsymbol{\tau} = 1$ is attained for $\boldsymbol{\tau}^* = x^{\boldsymbol{\alpha}} = (x^{\alpha_1}, \ldots, x^{\alpha_s})$ and has value $a(\boldsymbol{\tau}^*)/\mathcal{H}_{\ln}(\boldsymbol{\tau}^*) = 1/\ln(1/x)$, where x is the unique value in $(0,1)$ so that $\Sigma\boldsymbol{\tau}^* = 1$.* ◀

Proof: Let us briefly check that x as claimed exists and is unique. $\Sigma(x^{\boldsymbol{\alpha}})$ is non-negative and continuous, and goes from 0 at $x = 0$ to s at $x = 1$, so it must cross the value 1 in between by the *intermediate value theorem*. Moreover, $\Sigma(x^{\boldsymbol{\alpha}})$ is strictly increasing on $(0,1)$, so the crossing point is unique.

Let now $\boldsymbol{\tau} \in [0,1]^s$ with $\Sigma\boldsymbol{\tau} = 1$ be arbitrary. Using Lemma 2.43 with $\mathbf{p} = \boldsymbol{\tau}$ and $\mathbf{q} = \boldsymbol{\tau}^*$, we find

$$\mathcal{H}_{\ln}(\boldsymbol{\tau}) \;\leqslant\; -\sum_{r=1}^{s} \tau_r \ln(\tau_r^*) \tag{7.31}$$

$$= \; -\sum_{r=1}^{s} \tau_r \ln(x^{\alpha_r}) \tag{7.32}$$

$$= \; -\ln(x) \sum_{r=1}^{s} \alpha_r \tau_r \tag{7.33}$$

$$= \; \ln(1/x)\,a(\boldsymbol{\tau}), \tag{7.34}$$

so $a(\boldsymbol{\tau})/\mathcal{H}_{\ln}(\boldsymbol{\tau}) \geqslant 1/\ln(1/x)$. As in Lemma 2.43, equality holds only for $\boldsymbol{\tau} = \boldsymbol{\tau}^*$, so the minimum of $1/\ln(1/x)$ is attained only for $\boldsymbol{\tau}^*$. ■

Proposition 7.6 offers an analytic method to determine the optimal sampling parameter in the exact-quantile limit. It applies, however, only to cost measures for which the leading-term coefficient of partitioning costs is a *linear* function of τ. For our selection of measures, this is the number of scanned elements and the number of comparisons when $\lambda_k = \lambda_g = \lambda$.

Comparisons. For comparisons, the coefficient vector α is simply $(\lambda(1), \ldots, \lambda(s))$, the sequence of leaf depths in λ. We already know that the value for which $(x^{\lambda(1)}, \ldots, x^{\lambda(s)})$ sums to one is $x = \frac{1}{2}$: $\tau^* = \left(\frac{1}{2}\right)^{\alpha}$ is just the entropy-tight distribution for tree λ, and the minimal value for $a/\mathcal{H}_{\ln}$ is $1/\ln(2)$. For comparisons, Proposition 7.6 reduces exactly to Proposition 7.5.

A Generalized Lower Bound. For comparisons, we knew a priori that the leading-term coefficient cannot undercut $1/\ln(2)$. With Proposition 7.6, we can generalize this property, as well: In the given form, the partitioning cost coefficient $a(\tau)$ does not depend on the sample size k at all. As the discrete entropy of any $\tau \in [0, 1)^s$ is always strictly larger than its base-e Shannon entropy (Lemma 2.63 on page 96), we obtain the following corollary from Proposition 7.6.

Corollary 7.7 (Lower Bound for Finite k): *Let $a = a(\tau) = \alpha^{\mathsf{T}}\tau$ for a vector $\alpha \in \mathbb{R}^s_{>0}$ and x^* be the unique solution of $\Sigma(x^{\alpha}) = 1$ in $(0, 1)$. For any finite $\kappa \geqslant s$ and $\tau \in [0, 1)^s$ with $\Sigma\tau = 1$ holds $a(\tau)/\mathcal{H}_{\mathrm{hd}_\kappa}(\tau) > 1/\ln(1/x^*)$. In particular, for any sampling vector $t \in \mathbb{N}^s_0$ holds $a(\tau)/\mathcal{H}(t) > 1/\ln(1/x^*)$.*   ■

For the number of comparisons, Corollary 7.7 shows that *it is impossible to achieve the lower bound of $1/\ln(2)$ with fixed-size sampling* for any choice of the parameters for our generic s-way Quicksort, as long as we use a single comparisons tree. This fact has probably been known before, but I am not aware of an explicit proof in earlier work.

7.5.4 Scanned Elements

The optimality criterion from Proposition 7.6 allows us to characterize the optimal quantile vectors w.r.t. the number of scanned elements in the limit $k \to \infty$.

Proposition 7.8: *Let s, $\tau \in [0, 1]^s$ with $\Sigma\tau = 1$ and $m \in \mathbb{N}_0$ and be fixed, i.e., we use a master-pivot method. Let us denote with $x^* = x^*(s, m)$ the unique number in $(0, 1)$ satisfying*

$$\sum_{i=1}^{m} x^i + \sum_{j=1}^{s-m} x^j \; = \; 1. \tag{7.35}$$

Then the leading-term coefficient of the expected number of scanned elements is $a_{SE}/\mathcal{H} > 1/\ln(1/x^*)$. This coefficient converges to $1/\ln(1/x^*)$ as $k \to \infty$ if and only if

$$\tau \; = \; \left((x^*)^m, (x^*)^{m-1}, \ldots, (x^*)^2, x^*, x^*, (x^*)^2, \ldots, (x^*)^{s-m-1}, (x^*)^{s-m} \right). \tag{7.36}$$

◀

Proof: By Theorem 7.1, $a_{SE} = \alpha_{SE}^\mathsf{T}\tau$ for

$$\alpha_{SE} = \alpha_{SE}(s,m) = (m, m-1, \ldots, 2, 1, 1, 2, \ldots, s-m) \tag{7.37}$$

when m is an integer. The claim then follows from Proposition 7.6 and Corollary 7.7. ■

Unlike for comparisons, the basis x^* depends on s and m, therefore the behavior of the lower bound and τ^* is a little opaque. Equation (7.35) can be simplified: $x^*(s,m)$ is the unique solution in $(0,1)$ of

$$x^{m+1} + x^{s-m+1} - 3x + 1 = 0. \tag{7.38}$$

Obviously, the behavior is symmetric: $s^*(s,m) = s^*(s, s-m)$.

Table 7: $x^*(s,m)$ for scanned elements from Proposition 7.8 for small values of s and exemplary choices for m. All solutions are polynomial roots, so they can easily be computed to arbitrary precision. In a few special cases they can be expressed explicitly as radicals: $x^*(2,0) = (\sqrt{5}-1)/2$, $x^*(3,1) = x^*(3,2) = \sqrt{2}-1$, $x^*(4,2) = (\sqrt{3}-1)/2$ and $x^*(s,1) \to (\sqrt{5}-3)/2$.

s	2	3	4	5	6	7	16	$s \to \infty$
$m = 0$	0.618	0.544	0.519	0.509	0.504	0.502	0.500	0.5
$m = 1$	0.5	0.414	0.393	0.386	0.383	0.383	0.382	0.382
$m = \lceil s/4 \rceil$	0.5	0.414	0.393	0.353	0.349	0.348	0.335	$0.\overline{3}$
$m = \lceil s/2 \rceil$	0.5	0.414	0.366	0.353	0.343	0.339	0.333	$0.\overline{3}$

Table 7 shows some concrete values for small s, and the limit value for $s \to \infty$. Even for very small s, x^* is very close to these limit values. Therefore a reasonably good choice for the quantiles vector is $\tau \propto x^{\alpha_{SE}}$ for $x = \lim_{s\to\infty} x^*$, which is $\frac{1}{3}$, unless m is held constant. This means that a good quantiles vector should assign about one third of all weight to each of the two innermost segments, corresponding to classes s_1 and l_1, then one ninth to classes s_2 and l_2 and so on. The resulting distribution is extremely skewed, essentially a (truncated) geometric distribution.

Figure 31 shows that for all but the most extreme values of m, we are close to the case $m = \lceil s/2 \rceil$. With sampling, less centered meeting points can well be compensated for. In contrast, we find a parabolic shape in Figure 30 (page 233), which shows corresponding numbers without pivot sampling.

How does the lower bound $1/\ln(1/x^*)$ look like as a function of s? For ease of discussion, let us now concentrate on $m = \lceil s/2 \rceil$. If we compare the overall number of scanned elements of τ^* to the quantiles vector proportional to $\left(\frac{1}{3}\right)^{\alpha_{SE}}$, we find for $s = 3$ that the latter implies $0.00344n \ln n$ additional scanned elements, on top of the $1.13459n \ln n$ for τ^*. For larger s, the difference is even smaller. So it is legitimate to consider quantiles vectors of the form $C \cdot \left(\frac{1}{3}\right)^{\alpha_{SE}}$.

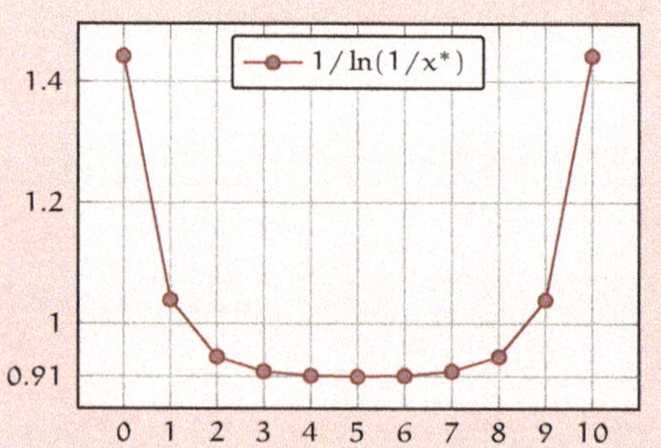

Figure 31: Lower bound from Proposition 7.8 for the leading-term coefficient of the number of scanned elements in s-way Quicksort for $s = 10$ and $m = 0, 1, \ldots, 10$. The minimum is at $m = 5$ and has value 0.912553; the corresponding x^* is $x^*(10, 5) \approx 0.334263$. For the other extreme, we have $x^*(10, 0) \approx 0.500245$.

We can complement this observation with an asymptotic approximation for $x^*(s, s/2)$. Rewriting Equation (7.38) for $s = 2m$ as

$$x \;=\; \frac{1}{3} + \frac{2}{3} \cdot x^{m+1}, \tag{7.39}$$

we immediately see that $x = \frac{1}{3}$ is a solution for $m \to \infty$. Starting with a rough asymptotic approximation, we can *bootstrap* a complete expansion:

Lemma 7.9: *The solution of Equation (7.39) admits the following asymptotic approximation:*

$$x^*(2m, m) \;=\; \frac{1}{3} + \frac{2}{9} \cdot 3^{-m} + \frac{4}{81}(m+1) \cdot 3^{-2m} \;\pm\; O(3^{-3m}), \qquad (m \to \infty). \tag{7.40}$$

◀

Proof: By comparing the two sides of Equation (7.39), we see that for $m \in \mathbb{N}$, x^* always lies between $\frac{1}{3}$ and $\frac{1}{2}$. Inserting $x \leqslant \frac{1}{2}$ into Equation (7.39), we find $x^* \leqslant \frac{1}{3} + \frac{1}{3} \cdot 2^{-m}$, and inserting this again yields

$$x^* - \frac{1}{3} \;\leqslant\; \frac{2}{3} \cdot 3^{-m-1} \underbrace{\left(1 + 2^{-m}\right)^{m+1}}_{\to 1} \;=\; O(3^{-m}). \tag{7.41}$$

This is the term with which we now "prime the pump" in the words of Greene and Knuth [73]: starting with $x^* = \frac{1}{3} \pm O(3^{-m})$, we can pump out a full asymptotic expansion of x^* by repeatedly inserting into Equation (7.39). The results of the first two rounds of pumping are

$$\frac{1}{3} \;\pm\; O(3^{-m}), \tag{7.42}$$

$$\frac{1}{3} + \frac{2}{9} \cdot 3^{-m} \;\pm\; O(3^{-m}), \tag{7.43}$$

$$\frac{1}{3} + \frac{2}{9} \cdot 3^{-m} + \frac{4}{81}(m+1)3^{-2m} \;\pm\; O(3^{-m}). \tag{7.44}$$

■

Corollary 7.10: *Let s be even and* $m = s/2$. *The lower bound* $1/\ln(1/x^*)$ *for* $a_{SE}/\mathcal{H}$ *from Proposition 7.8 fulfills*

$$1\Big/\ln\!\left(\frac{1}{x^*(s,s/2)}\right) = \frac{1}{\ln(3) - \frac{2}{3}\cdot 3^{-s/2}} \pm O(3^{-s}), \qquad (s\to\infty). \tag{7.45}$$

◀

Proof: Using $\ln(1+x) = x \pm O(x^2)$ as $x\to 0$ we find

$$1\Big/\ln\!\left(\frac{1}{x^*(s,s/2)}\right) = -\frac{1}{\ln\big(\frac{1}{3}\cdot(1+\frac{2}{3}3^{-m}\pm O(3^{-2m}))\big)} \tag{7.46}$$

$$= \frac{1}{\ln(3) - \frac{2}{3}3^{-m} \pm O(3^{-2m})} \tag{7.47}$$

$$= \frac{1}{\ln(3) - \frac{2}{3}3^{-m}} \pm O(3^{-2m}). \tag{7.48}$$

■

7.5.5 An Optimality Criterion for Finite Sample Sizes and Gibb's Gap

If we seek a sorting method that is fast also for moderate sized inputs, we cannot afford to use very large sample sizes for selecting the pivots in each partitioning step. Among the algorithms that are or have been in productive use, the largest sample size is nine. We cannot assume the results of the last sections to apply with great accuracy there. In this section, we derive an optimality criterion similar to Proposition 7.6 that explicitly addresses finite sample sizes.

If we stick to the restriction $a = \alpha^\mathsf{T}\tau$, the sample size only affects the entropy: we replace $\mathcal{H}_{\ln}$ by $\mathcal{H}_{hd_\kappa}$, and use the corresponding version of Gibb's inequality that we derived in Section 2.5. Unfortunately, Gibb's inequality for $\mathcal{H}_{hd_\kappa}$ (Lemma 2.66) does not hold for all vectors, and much of the elegance of Proposition 7.6 is lost thereby. Still, the resulting criterion is a useful tool.

Proposition 7.11 (Optimality Criterion for Finite k): *Let* $s \geqslant 2$ *and* $\kappa = k+1 \geqslant s$ *be fixed, and assume* $a = a(\tau) = \alpha^\mathsf{T}\tau = \sum_{r=1}^{s}\alpha_r\tau_r$, *for a vector* $\alpha \in \mathbb{R}^s_{>0}$. *A sampling vector* t^* *with* $\Sigma(t^*+1) = \kappa$ *is the unique optimum if there is a constant* $c > 0$ *such that for all* $r \in [s]$ *holds* $hd_\kappa(\tau_r^*) = -c\cdot\alpha_r$ *with* $\tau^* = \frac{t^*+1}{\kappa}$. *In this case, the value of the leading-term coefficient is* $a(\tau^*)/\mathcal{H}(t^*) = 1/c$.

Moreover, if no such c exists, but we have $c' > 0$ *with* $hd_\kappa(\tau_r^*) \geqslant -c'\cdot\alpha_r$ *for* $r = 1,\ldots,s$, *then holds* $a(\tau)/\mathcal{H}(t) > 1/c'$ *for all sampling vectors* t.

◀

Proof: Let t be an arbitrary sampling vector for sample size k, i.e., $t \in \mathbb{N}_0^s$ with $\Sigma(t+1) = \kappa = k+1$. As usual, denote by $\tau = \frac{t+1}{\kappa}$ the corresponding quantiles vector.

Towards a unified proof of both parts of the claim, assume that $hd_\kappa(\tau_r^*) \geqslant -c\alpha_r$ for a $c > 0$. Both τ^* and τ are κ-*discretized* vectors/distributions in the sense of Definition 2.51, so we can apply Gibb's inequality for the discrete entropy (Lemma 2.66). This gives

$$\mathcal{H}_{\mathrm{hd}_\kappa}(\boldsymbol{\tau}) \;\leqslant\; -\sum_{r=1}^{s} \tau_r\, \mathrm{hd}_\kappa(\boldsymbol{\tau}_r^*) \tag{7.49}$$

$$\leqslant\; \sum_{r=1}^{s} \tau_r \cdot c\alpha_r \tag{7.50}$$

$$=\; c \cdot a(\boldsymbol{\tau}), \tag{7.51}$$

and so

$$\frac{a(\boldsymbol{\tau})}{\mathcal{H}_{\mathrm{hd}_\kappa}(\boldsymbol{\tau})} \;\geqslant\; \frac{1}{c}. \tag{7.52}$$

The first inequality, Equation (7.49), holds with equality only if $\boldsymbol{\tau} = \boldsymbol{\tau}^*$, see Lemma 2.66. For the first part of the claim, we also have equality in the second line (7.50), so in fact $\frac{a(\boldsymbol{\tau}^*)}{\mathcal{H}_{\mathrm{hd}_\kappa}(\boldsymbol{\tau}^*)} = \frac{1}{c}$. For any $\boldsymbol{\tau} \neq \boldsymbol{\tau}^*$, the first inequality is strict and so is Equation (7.52) as a whole. This proves the first part.

For the moreover-part, we have by assumption strict inequality in Equation (7.50), so Equation (7.52) is strict even for $\boldsymbol{\tau}^*$. ∎

Proposition 7.11 bears a blemish: the first part is hardly ever applicable; for integral t and $\boldsymbol{\alpha}$ it is not usually the case that a c exists with $\mathrm{hd}_\kappa(\boldsymbol{\tau}) = -c \cdot \boldsymbol{\alpha}$.

> **How likely is it for integral t to be optimal?** For a fixed t, we can compute a cost vector $\boldsymbol{\alpha}$ so that the optimality criterion from Proposition 7.11 is satisfied: it simply says $\boldsymbol{\alpha} \propto -\mathrm{hd}_\kappa(\boldsymbol{\tau})$. If we consider w.l.o.g. only normalized $\boldsymbol{\alpha}$, then for each $\boldsymbol{\tau}$ there is *exactly one* cost function so that the criterion is fulfilled, namely $\boldsymbol{\alpha} = \frac{-\mathrm{hd}_\kappa(\boldsymbol{\tau})}{\|\mathrm{hd}_\kappa(\boldsymbol{\tau})\|}$. If we now assume that $\boldsymbol{\alpha}$ is, say, uniformly distributed over the set of all normalized vectors over $\mathbb{R}_{>0}$, the probability of hitting one of the finitely many choices is zero.
>
> I hope the reader did not have the impression up to now that the cost measures studied in this work are *random*. The above result thus has no direct implications. But it makes clear that it is an exceptionally lucky case, if we can apply the optimality criterion of Proposition 7.11.

If the optimality criterion is not applicable, we can only resort to the lower bound $1/c'$ for $c' := \max_{r \in [s]} \frac{-\mathrm{hd}_\kappa(\boldsymbol{\tau}_r)}{\alpha_r}$. Then a gap remains between the value of the optimal t and $1/c'$: *Gibb's gap*. We consider a few examples below. Unfortunately, Gibb's gap is often quite large.

Still, to my knowledge, it is the only rigorous tool to judge the quality of sampling vectors for finite sample sizes; besides exhaustively exploring the design space, of course. It can be useful as an inexpensive way to show that no other sampling vector can improve over a given one by too much.

Balanced Comparisons Trees. We consider once more the number of comparisons with $\lambda_k = \lambda_g = \lambda$. If s is a power of two and λ is the complete BST, we have $a_C = \mathrm{ld}(s) = \boldsymbol{\alpha}^\mathsf{T}\boldsymbol{\tau}$ for $\boldsymbol{\alpha} = (\mathrm{ld}(s), \ldots, \mathrm{ld}(s))$. If further κ is a multiple of s, say, $\kappa = s(t+1)$ for $t \in \mathbb{N}_0$, a feasible sampling vector is the symmetric choice $\mathbf{t}^* = (t,\dots,t)$. Indeed, this vector must be optimal since $\mathrm{hd}_\kappa(\tau_r^*) = \mathrm{hd}_\kappa(\tfrac{1}{s}) = -c\alpha_r$ for $c = -\frac{\mathrm{hd}_\kappa(\tfrac{1}{s})}{\mathrm{ld}(s)}$, so the first part of Proposition 7.11 applies!

This result is long known, of course, see, e.g., Hennequin's doctoral thesis [77]; yet it is always reassuring to see new theorems reproduce old results. For the symmetric tree, partitioning costs are completely independent of τ, so we only have to maximize the discrete entropy, and we know already that the discrete entropy is maximal for $\tau = (\tfrac{1}{s},\dots,\tfrac{1}{s})$, see Corollary 2.48 (page 85).

Much to my displeasure, this degenerate example is the *only* situation I could find among our cost measures where the first part of Proposition 7.11 could be applied.

◆   ◆   ◆

If κ is not an integer multiple of s, there is no balanced integral $\mathbf{t}$, but it is intuitive that the entries in $\mathbf{t}$ should only differ by 1, i.e., an optimal choice is $\mathbf{t} = (t+1,\dots,t+1,t,\dots,t)$ or obtained by permuting the components of this vector. In fact, this follows directly from Schur-concavity of $\mathcal{H}_{\mathrm{hd}_\kappa}(\tau)$, (Corollary 2.48 (page 85) with Lemma 2.59): the given vector $\mathbf{t}$ is majorized by any other integral vector with the same total.

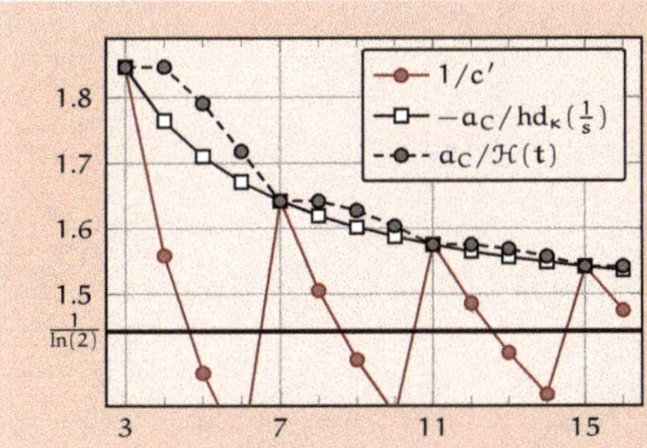

Figure 32: Quality of the lower bound $1/c'$ from Proposition 7.11 for $s = 4$ and λ the complete BST. The sample size k is given on the x-axis, the y-axis shows the leading-term coefficient of the expected number of comparisons. We also show the actual cost $a_C/\mathcal{H}(\mathbf{t})$ of the optimal $\mathbf{t}$, and the value $-a_C/\mathrm{hd}_\kappa(\tfrac{1}{s})$ of the symmetric, but possibly non-integral choice $\tau = (\tfrac{1}{s}, \tfrac{1}{s}, \tfrac{1}{s}, \tfrac{1}{s})$.

Figure 32 shows the quality of the error bound from Proposition 7.11 for this case. The result is quite disappointing. In half of the cases, the $1/c$ bound lies even below $1/\ln(2)$, the one from Corollary 7.7. This does not change much if we increase s.

Scanned Elements. Maybe, Gibb's gap is particularly large for balanced α; let us try a skewed one then. For the number of scanned elements in YBB Quicksort, i.e., $s = 3$ and $m = 2$, we have $\alpha = (2,1,1)$, so the cost of the first segment is twice as much as for the other two segments.

Figure 33 shows the resulting lower bound $1/c'$ together with the actual cost of the optimal $\mathbf{t}^*$ for the first values of k. $\mathbf{t}^*$ is determined by exhaustive search. Again, for around half of the values of k, the lower bound $1/c'$ is even below the continuous bound from Corollary 7.7; only for a few lucky cases is it informative.

We conclude this section with the observation that the lower bound from Proposition 7.11 is not often helpful: Gibb's gap is too large.

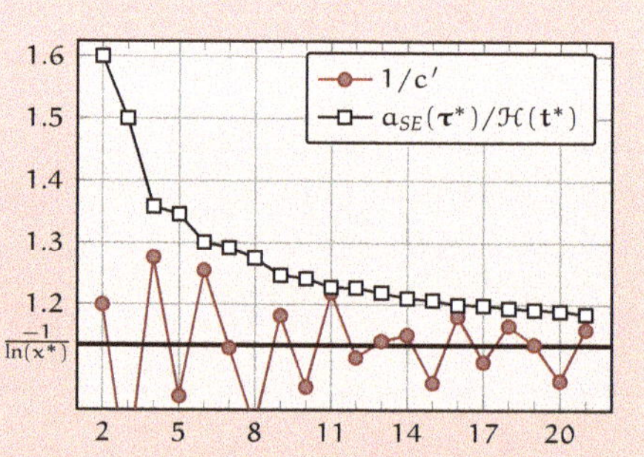

Figure 33: Quality of the lower bound $1/c'$ from Proposition 7.11 for scanned elements in YBB Quicksort, i.e., $s = 3$ and $m = 2$. The sample size k is given on the x-axis, the y-axis shows the leading-term coefficient of the expected number of scanned elements. We also show the actual cost $a_{SE}(\tau^*)/\mathcal{H}(t^*)$ of the optimal t^*. The fat black line gives the lower bound from Corollary 7.7; here $x^* = \sqrt{2} - 1$.

7.5.6 Two Comparisons Trees: Non-Linear Costs

The optimality criteria discussed in this section only apply to cost measures where the leading-term coefficient of the toll cost is a linear function in τ, the quantiles vector, and independent of the sample size k. When we use two comparison trees $\lambda_k \neq \lambda_g$, a_C is neither linear, nor independent of k.

YBB Quicksort. For example in YBB Quicksort, we have

$$
a_C = a_C(\tau, \kappa) = 2\tau_2 + \frac{\kappa}{\kappa+1}\left(\tau_1(\tau_1 + \tau_2)\frac{\tau_1 + \tau_2 + \frac{1}{\kappa}}{\tau_1 + \tau_2} + 2(2\tau_1 + \tau_2)\tau_3 + \tau_3^2\frac{\tau_3 + \frac{1}{\kappa}}{\tau_3}\right)
\tag{7.53}
$$

$$
\rightarrow \quad 2\tau_2 + \tau_1(\tau_1 + \tau_2) + 2(2\tau_1 + \tau_2)\tau_3 + \tau_3^2, \qquad (\kappa \to \infty),
\tag{7.54}
$$

$$
= 1 + (\tau_2 + 2\tau_3)(1 - \tau_3).
\tag{7.55}
$$

It is an open problem even in the limit case to find the optimal τ, i.e., to analytically minimize

$$
\frac{1 + (\tau_2 + 2\tau_3)(1 - \tau_3)}{-\tau_1 \ln(\tau_1) - \tau_2 \ln(\tau_2) - \tau_3 \ln(\tau_3)}.
\tag{7.56}
$$

in the closed simplex. Numerically, the minimum is located at

$$
\tau^* \approx (0.42884\,60207,\ 0.26877\,31696,\ 0.30238\,08097),
\tag{7.57}
$$

with a leading-term coefficient of $1.49309\,53723$. Notably, this optimal leading-term coefficient is strictly larger than the lower bound $1/\ln(2) \approx 1.44270$ that we do achieve in the limit with a single comparison tree using an entropy-tight pair.

Kciwegdes. For Kciwegdes partitioning, i.e., $s = 3$, $m = 1.5$ we obtain

$$
a_C \rightarrow 1 + \tau_2 + 2\tau_1\left(1 - \frac{\tau_1}{1 - \tau_2}\right),
\tag{7.58}
$$

and we seek that minimum of $a_C/\mathcal{H}_{\ln}(\boldsymbol{\tau})$. The minimum is located roughly at

$$\boldsymbol{\tau}^* \;\approx\; (0.36809\,73350,\, 0.26380\,53300,\, 0.36809\,73350) \tag{7.59}$$

with value $1.50088\,87099$; again this is strictly larger than $1/\ln(2)$. Because Kciwegdes is a symmetric algorithm, it is plausible that $\tau_1^* = \tau_3^*$, as is in fact the case in the numerical solution. Starting with this assumption, it is easy to check using computer algebra that $\boldsymbol{\tau} = (q, 1-2q, q)$ with q the unique root of $q^4 + 8q^3 - 12q^2 + 6q - 1$ in $(0,1)$ is a stationary point of $a_C/\mathcal{H}_{\ln}(\boldsymbol{\tau})$.

Six-Way Quicksort. For six-way Quicksort with $s = 6$, $m = 3$ and comparisons as in Figure 43 (page 273), we obtain numerically

$$\boldsymbol{\tau}^* \;=\; (0.18430,\, 0.18430,\, 0.13141,\, 0.13141,\, 0.18430,\, 0.18430) \tag{7.60}$$

with a leading-term coefficient of 1.47823.

7.5.7 Optimal t: Heuristics and Tables

It turned out quite hard to identify optimal sampling vectors for a finite sample size k, and for partitioning costs that are not linear in $\boldsymbol{\tau}$, we cannot even find the optimal quantiles for the limit case $k \to \infty$. It is time to admit defeat.

Open Problem 7.12 (Characterize Optimal Sampling Vectors): Find a characterization, or at least a useful sufficient condition, for sampling vectors $\mathbf{t} \in \mathbb{N}_0^s$ that minimize the function $a(\mathbf{t})/\mathcal{H}(\mathbf{t})$. A result restricted to the case where $a(\mathbf{t})$ is linear in $\boldsymbol{\tau} = (\mathbf{t}+1)/(k+1)$ would already be valuable. ◀

Let us see what we can still do. Assume, we know, precisely or approximately, the optimal quantiles vector $\boldsymbol{\tau}^*$ for the limit case $k \to \infty$. Intuitively, a sampling vector $\mathbf{t}$ that resembles this quantiles vector, i.e., one that is close to $\mathbf{t} \approx \boldsymbol{\tau}^* \cdot \kappa - 1$, should not be too bad. So, we could try to simply round that quantity to nearest integers. Of course, we have to avoid negative entries in $\mathbf{t}$, and the total might not directly give the intended sample size.

We can correct for that by locally adapting, until $\Sigma t = \kappa - s$. A rule that works well in many cases is implemented in Algorithm 11: *always round away from extreme values*.

> **Proportional Apportionment** The problem of assigning exactly h indivisible, identical items to n entities proportional to some (fractional) weight vector v occurs in many applications. In the context of political systems it is known as *proportional apportionment*. It arises when after an election, seats in parliament are to be assigned to parties according to their relative share of votes. It also rises after a census in federate states where each state is to be represented proportionally to its population count, e.g., in the U.S. House of Representatives.
>
> Here also, simply rounding the relative shares does not in general assign the right total of seats. A variety of rules have been invented with the goal to solve this problem as fairly as possible, and to this day several of them remain in use. Balinski and Young [13] give a comprehensive overview of these rules—and in particular their prob-

---

Algorithm 11: Heuristic to compute a sampling vector close to given quantiles vector.

$\textsc{GoodTByRounding}(\boldsymbol{\tau}^*, \kappa)$

```
 1   t := max(round(κ · τ* − 1), 0)
 2   while Σt ≠ κ − s
 3       if Σt > κ − s
 4           m := max_{r∈[s]} t_r
 5           i := arg min_{r∈[s]}{τ_r : t_r = m}
 6           t_i := t_i − 1
 7       else
 8           m := min_{r∈[s]} t_r
 9           i := arg max_{r∈[s]}{τ_r : t_r = m}
10           t_i := t_i + 1
11       end if
12   end while
13   return t
```

lems and paradoxes. These are illustrated with examples from the eventful history of U. S. Congress, where any thinkable corner case of what could possibly go wrong seems to have happened some time in the past.

For our problem of finding a good t, we could employ any of the known apportionment rules, but they tend to be inferior to our heuristic. The reason is probably that apportionment methods aim at fairness, but entropy is not fair: costs typically improve if we move slightly towards the middle of the simplex, and they increase if make sampling slightly less balanced, that is, unless $a(\boldsymbol{\tau})$ shows a strong opposite tendency.

When fed with the optimal quantiles vector for infinite k, or a decent numerical approximation of it, Algorithm 11 in fact computes the *optimal* t in many cases. Tables 8, 9 and 10 demonstrate this by example.

It is quite remarkable how often the simple heuristic gives the precise optimum, in particular since it does not at all take the shape of partitioning costs into account. The intuition that rounding $\boldsymbol{\tau}^*$ gives a good t is thus not totally wrong.

It is reassuring that the precise details of the rounding rule are also not vitally important. When we change Algorithm 11 to modify a *random* entry in each iteration, we still get optimal t in more than half of the considered cases. We perform a little worse, though.

7.6 The Optimal Number of Pivots

The number of pivots to use is the parameter with the arguably largest impact on how an implementation will look like. Changing the number of pivots will significantly influence most parts of the code: obviously the partitioning procedure and the recursion skeleton,

Table 8: Optimal sampling vectors w.r.t. comparisons in YBB Quicksort for $k \leqslant 29$. The optimal vector $\mathbf{t}^*$ was determined by exhaustive search. The resulting leading-term coefficient of the expected number of comparisons is given, as well. A number in column "heu. (%)" indicates that our rounding heuristic (Algorithm 11) computed a suboptimal $\mathbf{t}$, which is worse by given percentage. The quantiles vector used for Algorithm 11 is $\boldsymbol{\tau}^* = (0.42878, 0.26880, 0.30242)$.

k	$\mathbf{t}^*$	$a_C(\mathbf{t}^*)/\mathcal{H}(\mathbf{t}^*)$	heu. (%)	k	$\mathbf{t}^*$	$a_C(\mathbf{t}^*)/\mathcal{H}(\mathbf{t}^*)$	heu. (%)
2	(0,0,0)	1.9	—	16	(6,4,4)	1.55971	—
3	(1,0,0)	1.8	—	17	(6,4,5)	1.55535	0.027
4	(1,0,1)	1.73585	—	18	(7,4,5)	1.55007	—
5	(1,1,1)	1.70426	—	19	(8,4,5)	1.54933	—
6	(2,1,1)	1.65414	—	20	(8,5,5)	1.54646	—
7	(2,1,2)	1.63592	—	21	(8,5,6)	1.54254	—
8	(3,1,2)	1.62274	—	22	(9,5,6)	1.54041	—
9	(3,2,2)	1.60701	—	23	(9,5,7)	1.53955	0.052
10	(4,2,2)	1.59693	—	24	(9,6,7)	1.53750	—
11	(4,2,3)	1.58485	—	25	(10,6,7)	1.53459	—
12	(5,2,3)	1.58378	—	26	(11,6,7)	1.53401	—
13	(5,3,3)	1.57304	—	27	(11,6,8)	1.53275	0.034
14	(5,3,4)	1.56623	—	28	(11,7,8)	1.53059	—
15	(6,3,4)	1.56217	—	29	(12,7,8)	1.52921	—

Table 9: Optimal sampling vectors w.r.t. scanned elements in YBB Quicksort for $k \leqslant 29$. The setup is as for Table 8. The vector for Algorithm 11 is $\boldsymbol{\tau}^* = (0.17158, 0.41421, 0.41421)$.

k	$\mathbf{t}^*$	$a_{SE}(\mathbf{t}^*)/\mathcal{H}(\mathbf{t}^*)$	heu. (%)	k	$\mathbf{t}^*$	$a_{SE}(\mathbf{t}^*)/\mathcal{H}(\mathbf{t}^*)$	heu. (%)
2	(0,0,0)	1.6	—	16	(2,6,6)	1.19959	—
3	(0,0,1)	1.5	—	17	(2,6,7)	1.19869	0.409
4	(0,1,1)	1.35849	—	18	(2,7,7)	1.19427	—
5	(0,1,2)	1.34615	4.261	19	(3,7,7)	1.19191	—
6	(0,2,2)	1.30081	—	20	(3,7,8)	1.18959	—
7	(1,2,2)	1.29151	—	21	(3,8,8)	1.18488	—
8	(1,2,3)	1.27501	—	22	(3,8,9)	1.18395	—
9	(1,3,3)	1.24701	—	23	(3,9,9)	1.18092	—
10	(1,3,4)	1.24180	—	24	(3,9,10)	1.18091	0.005
11	(1,4,4)	1.22751	—	25	(3,10,10)	1.17905	—
12	(1,4,5)	1.22699	0.243	26	(4,10,10)	1.17581	—
13	(1,5,5)	1.21934	—	27	(4,10,11)	1.17492	—
14	(2,5,5)	1.21021	—	28	(4,11,11)	1.17265	—
15	(2,5,6)	1.20699	—	29	(4,11,12)	1.17242	0.108

Table 10: Optimal sampling vectors w.r.t. scanned elements in six-way Quicksort with $m = 3$ for $k \leqslant 24$. For the general setup, see Table 8. The quantiles vector used for Algorithm 11 is $\tau^* = (0.04019, 0.11731, 0.34249, 0.34249, 0.11731, 0.04019)$.

k	t^*	$a_{SE}(t^*)/\mathcal{H}(t^*)$	heu. (%)	k	t^*	$a_{SE}(t^*)/\mathcal{H}(t^*)$	heu. (%)
5	$(0,0,0,0,0,0)$	1.37931	—	15	$(0,1,4,4,1,0)$	1.03189	—
6	$(0,0,0,1,0,0)$	1.28079	—	16	$(0,1,4,5,1,0)$	1.02645	—
7	$(0,0,1,1,0,0)$	1.19221	—	17	$(0,1,5,5,1,0)$	1.01913	—
8	$(0,0,1,2,0,0)$	1.15734	—	18	$(0,1,5,6,1,0)$	1.01668	—
9	$(0,0,2,2,0,0)$	1.11969	—	19	$(0,1,6,6,1,0)$	1.01248	—
10	$(0,0,2,3,0,0)$	1.10495	—	20	$(0,1,6,6,2,0)$	1.00832	1.625
11	$(0,0,3,3,0,0)$	1.08618	—	21	$(0,2,6,6,2,0)$	1.00320	—
12	$(0,0,3,3,1,0)$	1.07095	0.515	22	$(0,2,6,7,2,0)$	1.00013	—
13	$(0,1,3,3,1,0)$	1.05489	—	23	$(0,2,7,7,2,0)$	0.99598	—
14	$(0,1,3,4,1,0)$	1.04434	—	24	$(0,2,7,8,2,0)$	0.99445	—

the sampling method to choose pivots, potentially even the handling of small subproblems as the efficiency of Quicksort on short lists is sensitive to the number of pivots as well.

We discuss in this section how the parameter s, the number of segments, affects overall costs of our generalized s-way Quicksort. As we will see below it heavily depends on the employed cost model which choices of s are favorable. We would like to study the influence of s separately from that of other parameters, but this is not always possible: many parameter domains depend on s. For example, we must have $k \geqslant s - 1$ (we have to sample at least the $s - 1$ pivots), so fixing, say, $k = 10$ also means $s \leqslant 11$.

7.6.1 Key Comparisons

For comparisons, the choice of the two comparison trees λ_k and λ_g is vital. We cannot fix a given tree, of course, as the trees have to contain exactly $s - 1$ inner nodes, one for each pivot. So let us assume that we have two sequences of such trees, $(\lambda_k^{(s)})_{s \in \mathbb{N}_{\geqslant 2}}$ and $(\lambda_g^{(s)})_{s \in \mathbb{N}_{\geqslant 2}}$. To state the behavior of the number of comparisons as s grows, the sequences of comparison trees have to *converge* in a certain sense, so that the trees for s-way Quicksort are *not totally different* from the trees for $(s - 1)$-way Quicksort. Proposition 7.13 below hints at the required form of convergence: a specific weighted external path length of λ_k and λ_g dictates overall costs. Before we consider this general statement, let us consider two simple special cases as a warm-up.

No sampling and One Tree. The simplest case is $\lambda_k = \lambda_g$, i.e., elements are always classified using one fixed comparison tree, and we do not use pivot sampling, i.e., $t = (0, \ldots, 0)$. Then many things become symmetric and simple. For example, the expected fraction of elements that belong to a certain class $c \in \mathcal{C}$ is simply $\tau_{r(c)} = 1/s$. The term from Theorem 7.1 for a_C, the leading-term coefficient of comparisons in one partitioning step, reduces to the average depth of a leaf in λ_k, which is just the external path length divided by s. The latter is minimized by the *almost complete binary tree,* for which we have

$$a_C \;=\; \lceil \operatorname{ld} s \rceil + 1 - \frac{2^{\lceil \operatorname{ld} s \rceil}}{s} \;\geqslant\; \operatorname{ld}(s), \tag{7.61}$$

see Equation 5.3.1–(34) of Knuth [103]. For $\mathbf{t} = (0,\dots,0)$, we have $\mathcal{H} = H_s - 1$ and so the leading-term coefficient of the overall number of comparisons *converges* to $\frac{a_C}{\mathcal{H}} \to \frac{1}{\ln 2} \approx 1.4427$ and fulfills

$$\frac{a_C}{\mathcal{H}} \;\geqslant\; \frac{\operatorname{ld} s}{H_s - 1} \;\underset{(2.70.1)}{\geqslant}\; \frac{\operatorname{ld} s}{\ln s - 1} \;=\; \frac{1}{\ln 2} \cdot \frac{1}{1 - \frac{1}{\ln s}} \;>\; \frac{1}{\ln 2}, \tag{7.62}$$

so it approaches the limit from above. Therefore, there is *no optimal s*; picking more pivots *always* improves the leading term in this case. Note that $\frac{1}{\ln 2} n \ln n = n \operatorname{ld} n$ is the leading term of the information-theoretic lower bound on comparisons, so it is clear a priori that the convergence must be from above.

Equidistant Sampling.   If we fix a number $t \in \mathbb{N}_0$ and set $\mathbf{t} = (t, t, \dots, t)$, we pick as pivots the s-quantiles of the sample of $k = s(t+1) - 1$ elements. While $t > 0$ improves the "quality" of the pivots, it does not change their relative location, in particular we still have $\boldsymbol{\tau} = (\frac{1}{s}, \dots, \frac{1}{s})$ and $\tau^*(z) = 1$, so Equation (7.61) remains valid. The discrete entropy changes to $\mathcal{H} = -\operatorname{hd}_{s(t+1)}(\frac{1}{s})$, which converges to $-\ln(\frac{1}{s}) = \ln(s)$ (Equation (2.207)), but remains $\mathcal{H} < -\ln(\frac{1}{s}) = \ln s$ (Lemma 2.61). The leading term of the overall number of comparisons hence still converges from above to the information-theoretic lower bound if we choose the maximally balanced comparison trees; the convergence will be faster though. Again there is no (finite) optimal s. This observation has been made by Hennequin [77], as well.

It is quite well-known and intuitively clear that classic single-pivot Quicksort with median-of-$(2t+1)$ sampling approaches the comparison lower bound in the limit for $t \to \infty$. We consider this limit in Section 7.5. Note that even though the limiting values of the leading-term coefficients are the same, this is an entirely different limiting process from the case $s \to \infty$ considered above.

7.6.2 Sampling with a Limit Density

The two appetizer examples above barely scratch the surface of our vast parameter space. In this section, we consider a whole class of parameters and study their costs as s increases. The characteristic property of this class is that the pivot-sampling parameters $\boldsymbol{\tau}$ converge to a smooth limiting density. This rules out some degenerate cases. In particular, we will have that $\|\boldsymbol{\tau}\|_\infty = \Theta(s^{-1})$, i.e., the $s-1$ pivots are selected roughly uniformly. Thus (many of) the s segments receive a fraction of all elements, and we make effective use of the growing number of segments.

Under this model, the number of comparisons behaves for large s as one might expect (see Proposition 7.13 below): The *Iverson brackets* in a_C as given in Theorem 7.1, $[c = s]$

etc., can be ignored, and overall costs are a convex combination of the weighted path lengths of the two comparison trees.

Proposition 7.13: *Let* $\tau^* : [0,1] \to \mathbb{R}_{\geq 0}$ *be a Lipschitz-continuous probability density function. Let* $(\mathbf{t}^{(s)})_{s \in \mathbb{N}_{\geq 2}}$, $\mathbf{t}^{(s)} \in \mathbb{N}_0^s$, *be a sequence of sampling vectors, so that we have uniformly for* $z \in (0,1)$ *that*

$$s \cdot \tau^{(s)}_{\lceil zs \rceil} \;=\; s \cdot \frac{t^{(s)}_{\lceil zs \rceil} + 1}{k^{(s)} + 1} \;=\; \tau^*(z) \,\pm\, O(s^{-\varepsilon}), \qquad (s \to \infty). \tag{7.63}$$

Moreover, let $\mu \in (0,1)$ *be fixed and assume either* $m = m^{(s)} = \lceil \mu s \rceil$ *for the master pivot case or* $m = m^{(s)} = \lceil \mu s \rceil - \frac{1}{2}$ *for the master-segment case. We define the "limit-weighted" (external) path lengths*

$$PL_k(s) \;:=\; \sum_{r=1}^{s} \lambda_k^{(s)}(\mathcal{C}_r) \cdot \int_{(r-1)/s}^{r/s} \tau^*(z) \, dz \; ; \tag{7.64}$$

$PL_g(s)$ *is similar but with* $\lambda_g(c)$. *(These are the expected depths of an external node drawn according to the (discretized) limiting density.) With the constants*

$$\tau^*_{\to} \;:=\; \int_0^\mu \tau^*(z) \, dz \qquad \text{and} \qquad \tau^*_{\leftarrow} \;:=\; \int_\mu^1 \tau^*(z) \, dz \,, \tag{7.65}$$

we have for the leading-term coefficient of the number of comparisons per partitioning step

$$a_C \;=\; \Big(\tau^*_{\to} \cdot PL_k(s) + \tau^*_{\leftarrow} \cdot PL_g(s) \Big) \big(1 \pm O(s^{-\varepsilon}) \big) \tag{7.66}$$

as $s \to \infty$. ◄

The condition (7.63) is essentially the same as in Lemma 2.69, which concerns the continuous master theorem (CMT). There the subproblem size probabilities converge to a shape function, which is nothing more than a limiting density with certain smoothness requirements.

Proof: By Equation (7.63), there is a constant C so that $\tau^{(s)}_r \leq \frac{C}{s}$ for $r = 1, \ldots, s$ and s large enough. We trivially have $\kappa = \Omega(s)$. We start noting for reference that

$$\frac{\sigma_{\to}}{\kappa} \;=\; \sum_{r=1}^{\lfloor m \rfloor} \frac{\sigma_r}{\kappa} \tag{7.67}$$

$$\underset{(7.63)}{=} \sum_{r=1}^{\lfloor m \rfloor} \frac{\tau^*(r/s)}{s} \,\pm\, O(s^{-\varepsilon}) \tag{7.68}$$

$$\underset{\text{Proposition 2.12}}{=} \int_0^\mu \tau^*(z) \, dz \,\pm\, O(s^{-\varepsilon}) \tag{7.69}$$

$$=\; \tau^*_{\to} \,\pm\, O(s^{-\varepsilon}). \tag{7.70}$$

Similarly $\frac{\sigma_{\leftarrow}}{\kappa} = \tau^*_{\leftarrow} \pm O(s^{-\varepsilon})$. We also have $\frac{\sigma_{\leftrightarrow}}{\kappa} \leq \tau_{\lceil \mu s \rceil} = O(s^{-1})$.

We prove the claim by expanding the expression for a_C given in Theorem 7.1:

$$a_C = \frac{\sigma_\rightarrow}{\kappa - \sigma_\leftrightarrow + 1} \sum_{c \in \mathcal{C}} \overbrace{\tau_{r(c)} \lambda_k(c)}^{\pi_k} + \frac{\sigma_\leftarrow}{\kappa - \sigma_\leftrightarrow + 1} \sum_{c \in \mathcal{C}} \overbrace{\tau_{r(c)} \lambda_g(c)}^{\pi_g}$$

$$+ \underbrace{\frac{1}{\kappa - \sigma_\leftrightarrow + 1}}_{O(s^{-1})} \underbrace{\left(\sum_{\substack{c \in \mathcal{C} \\ c \text{ small}}} \tau_{r(c)} \lambda_k(c) + \sum_{\substack{c \in \mathcal{C} \\ c \text{ large}}} \tau_{r(c)} \lambda_g(c) \right)}_{\leqslant \pi_k + \pi_g = O(s)}$$

$$+ [m \notin \mathbb{N}_0] \cdot \underbrace{\tau_{r(m)}}_{O(s^{-1})} \underbrace{\left(\frac{1}{\kappa - \sigma_\leftrightarrow} - \frac{1}{\kappa - \sigma_\leftrightarrow + 1} \right) \left(\lambda_k(m) \sigma_\rightarrow + \lambda_g(m) \sigma_\leftarrow \right)}_{O(s)} \tag{7.71}$$

$$= \frac{\sigma_\rightarrow}{\kappa - \sigma_\leftrightarrow + 1} \cdot \pi_k + \frac{\sigma_\leftarrow}{\kappa - \sigma_\leftrightarrow + 1} \cdot \pi_g \ \pm\ O(1). \tag{7.72}$$

It remains to show that $\pi_k \sim PL_k(s)$:

$$\pi_k = \sum_{c \in \mathcal{C}} \tau_{r(c)} \lambda_k(c) \tag{7.73}$$

$$\underset{(7.63)}{=} \sum_{r=1}^{s} \frac{\tau^*(r/s)}{s} \lambda_k(\mathcal{C}_r) \ \pm\ O(s^{-\varepsilon}) \tag{7.74}$$

$$\underset{\text{Proposition 2.12}}{=} \sum_{r=1}^{s} \lambda_k(\mathcal{C}_r) \int_{(r-1)/s}^{r/s} \tau^*(z)\, dz \ \pm\ O(s^{-\varepsilon}); \tag{7.75}$$

a similar relation holds for π_g. Using this in the above equation for a_C, we finally obtain

$$a_C = \frac{\sigma_\rightarrow}{\kappa - \sigma_\leftrightarrow + 1} \cdot PL_k(s) + \frac{\sigma_\leftarrow}{\kappa - \sigma_\leftrightarrow + 1} \cdot PL_g(s) \ \pm\ O(1) \tag{7.76}$$

$$\underset{(7.70)}{=} \left(\tau^*_\rightarrow PL_k(s) + \tau^*_\leftarrow PL_g(s) \right) \left(1 \pm O(s^{-\varepsilon}) \right). \tag{7.77}$$

■

The second ingredient for the overall costs is the discrete entropy. We can approximate it for limit-density sampling as follows.

Proposition 7.14: *Under the conditions of Proposition 7.13, we have for $s \to \infty$*

$$\mathcal{H}(\mathbf{t}^{(s)}) = \ln s \ \pm\ O(1). \tag{7.78}$$

◄

Proof: A simple calculation using $\ln(1 + x) = O(x)$ for $x \to 0$ shows that for a sequence (a_n) with $a_n = \frac{a}{n} \pm O(n^{-1-\varepsilon})$, $a \neq 0$ a constant, holds $a_n \ln(a_n) = \frac{a}{n} \ln\left(\frac{a}{n}\right) \pm O\left(\frac{\log(n)}{n^{1+\varepsilon}}\right)$.

Since $\tau^*(z)$ is Lipschitz-continuous in $[0,1]$, it is bounded, say $\tau^*(z) \leqslant M$. Moreover, $x \ln x$ is Hölder-continuous for any exponent $\alpha \in (0,1)$ on the unit interval $x \in [0,1]$ (Lemma 2.13) and for $x \in [1, M]$ it has bounded derivative. So it is Hölder-continuous on all of $[0, M]$ (Propositions 2.9 and 2.10). The composition of Hölder-continuous functions is again Hölder-continuous, where the exponents multiply (Lemma 2.11–(c) on page 52). So we find that $\tau^*(z)\ln(\tau^*(z))$ is Hölder-continuous on $[0,1]$ for any exponent $\alpha \in (0,1)$.

Using these two facts, we obtain for the base-e entropy

$$\mathcal{H}_{\ln}(\boldsymbol{\tau}^{(s)}) \;=\; -\sum_{r=1}^{s} \tau_r \ln(\tau_r) \tag{7.79}$$

$$=\; -\sum_{r=1}^{s}\left(\frac{\tau^*(r/s)}{s}\ln\!\left(\frac{\tau^*(r/s)}{s}\right) \pm O\!\left(\frac{\log(s)}{s^{1+\varepsilon}}\right)\right) \tag{7.80}$$

$$=\; -\frac{1}{s}\sum_{r=1}^{s}\tau^*(r/s)\ln(\tau^*(r/s)) \;+\; \ln(s)\cdot\frac{1}{s}\sum_{r=1}^{s}\tau^*(r/s) \;\pm\; O\!\left(\frac{\log(s)}{s^{\varepsilon}}\right) \tag{7.81}$$

$$\underset{\text{Proposition 2.12–(b)}}{=}\; -\int_0^1 \tau^*(z)\ln(\tau^*(z))\,dz \pm O(s^{-1+\varepsilon})$$

$$+\; \ln(s)\underbrace{\left(\int_0^1 \tau^*(z)\,dz \pm O(s^{-1})\right)}_{=1} \;\pm\; O\!\left(\frac{\log(s)}{s^{\varepsilon}}\right) \tag{7.82}$$

$$=\; \ln(s) - \int_0^1 \tau^*(z)\ln(\tau^*(z))\,dz \;\pm\; O\!\left(\frac{\log(s)}{s^{\varepsilon}}\right). \tag{7.83}$$

For s and hence κ large enough, we will have τ_i as required for Lemma 2.65, so we can apply Lemmas 2.63 and 2.65 to get $\mathcal{H}(\mathbf{t}^{(s)}) = (1+\delta)\cdot\mathcal{H}_{\ln}(\boldsymbol{\tau}^{(s)})$ where $-\frac{1}{2\ln(\kappa)} \leqslant \delta \leqslant 0$. With that we finally find

$$\mathcal{H}(\mathbf{t}^{(s)}) \;=\; \mathcal{H}_{\ln}(\boldsymbol{\tau}^{(s)}) \pm O\!\left(\frac{\log(s)}{\log(\kappa)}\right) \tag{7.84}$$

$$=\; \ln(s) - \int_0^1 \tau^*(z)\ln(\tau^*(z))\,dz \;\pm\; O\!\left(\frac{\log(s)}{s^{\varepsilon}} + \frac{\log(s)}{\log(\kappa)}\right), \tag{7.85}$$

and since $\kappa = \Theta(s)$ this is

$$=\; \ln(s) \pm O(1). \tag{7.86}$$

It is certainly remarkable that the leading term of the entropy does not depend on the actual limit distribution. The reason is that the information-theoretic entropy does not generalize nicely to continuous distributions: The limiting value of the entropy of almost-uniform discrete distributions over larger and larger support, as in our case, goes to infinity like $\ln(s)$. Intuitively speaking, the information content of a non-degenerate continuous distribution is infinite, because we can encode any (countable) number of bits in any single real number, say. Of course, one could define an entropy for the continuous distribution with density f similarly to the discrete case as $\int f(z)\,\mathrm{ld}(f(z))\,dz$; but the resulting quantity does not carry the same information-theoretic meaning.

◆   ◆   ◆

Proposition 7.13 shows that under the given scenario with growing s, the possibility to use different comparison trees $\lambda_k \neq \lambda_g$ only offers negligible savings over enforcing $\lambda_k = \lambda_g$:

the difference to using a "mixture tree," whose cost is a convex combination of the costs for λ_k and λ_g, vanishes in the error term. The question whether and when two trees are helpful is taken up in Section 7.7 again. We will see there that the benefit of two distinct trees drops very rapidly with s, so that for the present section we can assume $\lambda_k = \lambda_g$ without noticeably affecting results. As $\tau_{\rightarrow}^* + \tau_{\leftarrow}^* = 1$ under the conditions of Proposition 7.13, we have $a_C \sim PL(s) = PL_k(s)$.

With Propositions 7.13 and 7.14, we get

$$\frac{a_C}{\mathcal{H}} \;=\; \frac{PL(s)}{\ln(s)}\left(1 \pm O\!\left(\frac{1}{\log s}\right)\right), \tag{7.87}$$

where $PL(s)$ is the limit-weighted path length given in Equation (7.64).

> **Mind the Error Terms.** A general statement as Equation (7.87) is very helpful for discussions of limiting behaviors. It should be noted, however, that the convergence rate is extremely slow, so that it might take really huge values of s to come close to the limit. To get a feeling for what this means, assume the constant hidden by $O(\circ)$ in (7.87) is 1. Then for $s = 1000$, we still get a relative error of over 14 %!
>
> We only prove an upper bound in Proposition 7.14, but considering the proof, it will in most cases be a Θ-bound.
>
> There are other limiting processes around Quicksort that have been deemed "slowly converging." For example the leading-term coefficient of the number of comparisons for classic Quicksort with median-of-$(2t+1)$ converges to $\frac{1}{\ln(2)}$. The relative savings are only worthwhile for the first few values of t. Here, the convergence rate is actually $\Theta(t^{-1})$.
>
> So, without curtailing our enthusiasm, let us remind ourselves of what the disclaimer above already stated: Direct practical implications of Equation (7.87) and our corresponding discussion are limited.

Let us briefly reconsider the special cases from above in light of the framework of limit-density sampling.

No sampling and One Tree. If we do not use sampling at all we get $\tau^*(z) = 1$, the density of the uniform distribution and the number of comparisons reduces to the ordinary external path length $PL(s)$.

For the almost complete binary trees, we have $PL(s) \sim \mathrm{ld}(s)$ and hence $\frac{a_C}{\mathcal{H}} \to \frac{1}{\ln 2} \approx 1.4427$, which is to first order the information-theoretic lower bound for comparison-based sorting.

Equidistant Sampling. If we fix a number $t \in \mathbb{N}_0$ and set $\mathbf{t} = (t, t, \ldots, t)$, we pick as pivots the s-quantiles of the sample of $k = s(t+1) - 1$ elements. While $t > 0$ improves the "quality" of the pivots, it does not change their relative location, in particular we still have $\tau = (\frac{1}{s}, \ldots, \frac{1}{s})$ and $\tau^*(z) = 1$ remains valid. Therefore the behavior for $s \to \infty$ remains the *same* as if we do not sample at all.

Sample Size. The above observation is in fact a general one: as the limiting behavior of the discrete entropy does not depend on the sampling parameter *at all,* the only thing that reflected the influence of different sample size is gone: Any sampling parameter with the same τ yields the same result then; the sample size has no influence whatsoever on the limiting behavior for $s \to \infty$.

Other comparison trees. As long as we pick a balanced comparison tree, we thus always have $PL(s) \sim \mathrm{ld}(s)$ and $\mathcal{H} \sim \ln(s)$ as $s \to \infty$; no matter how we sample pivots. This means in particular that in all these cases, there is no finite optimal choice for s: we always improve by using even more pivots. We say $s^* = \infty$ then.

If we decide not to pick completely balanced comparison trees for some reason, but instead any family of trees and sampling vectors, so that $PL(s) \sim c \cdot \ln(s)$ as $s \to \infty$, the same reasoning as above shows that the optimal pick still is $s^* = \infty$.

If, however, our comparison trees exhibit superlogarithmic expected node depths, i.e., $PL(s) = \omega(\log s)$, overall costs are asymptotically *increasing* and there will be finite values s^* minimizing the number of comparisons. Let us look at one specific family of trees, the *extremal trees* studied by Aumüller et al. [10].

Definition 7.15 (Extremal Trees): *The extremal tree for parameters $s \in \mathbb{N}_{\geq 2}$ and $m \in \{0.5, 1, 1.5, \ldots, s-1, s-0.5\}$, is the comparison tree we obtain by putting the $\lceil m \rceil$-smallest pivot in the root and appending all other pivots as linear lists to the root: in decreasing order for the pivots smaller than the root and in increasing order for those larger than the root.* ◀

See Figure 34 for an example.

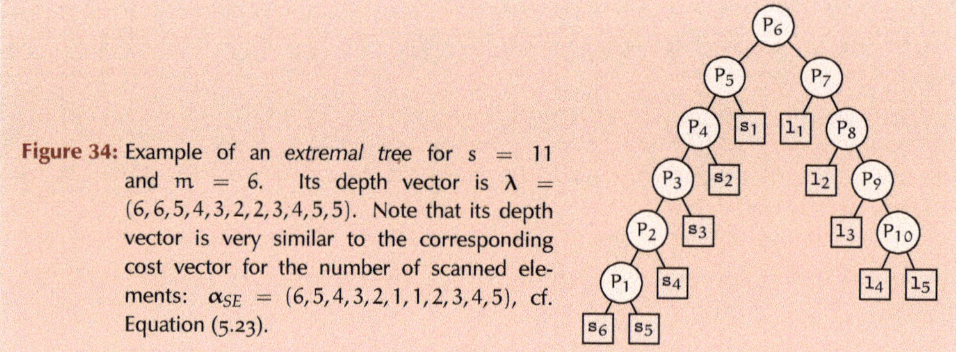

Figure 34: Example of an *extremal tree* for $s = 11$ and $m = 6$. Its depth vector is $\lambda = (6, 6, 5, 4, 3, 2, 2, 3, 4, 5, 5)$. Note that its depth vector is very similar to the corresponding cost vector for the number of scanned elements: $\alpha_{SE} = (6, 5, 4, 3, 2, 1, 1, 2, 3, 4, 5)$, cf. Equation (5.23).

These trees are *deficient* in the sense that under a uniform class distribution, their expected (external) node depth is *linear:*

$$PL(s) \;=\; \frac{1}{s}\left(\left\lceil \frac{s}{2} \right\rceil + \sum_{r=1}^{\lceil s/2 \rceil - 1}(r+1)\right) + \frac{1}{s}\left(\left\lfloor \frac{s}{2} \right\rfloor + \sum_{r=1}^{\lfloor s/2 \rfloor - 1}(r+1)\right) \qquad (7.88)$$

$$= \frac{s}{4} + \frac{3}{2} - \frac{7 + [s \text{ even}]}{4s} \tag{7.89}$$

$$\sim \frac{1}{4} \cdot s. \tag{7.90}$$

The extremal trees are thus asymptotically only twice as good as the worst-case tree for comparisons, and far away from the more balanced ones with logarithmic depth. It is clear that large values of s will not be helpful in this case, since $\frac{s/4}{\ln(s)} \to \infty$. For small values of s, things are not so clear, however. Here are the first few values when we choose $\mathbf{t} = 0$, i.e., do not sample pivots.

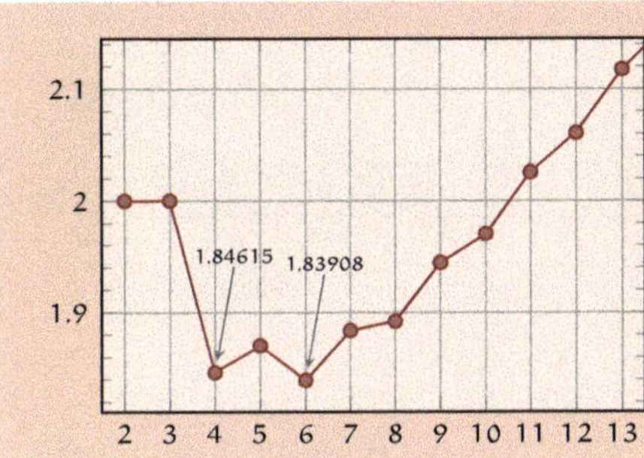

Figure 35: Leading-term coefficient of the number of comparisons using the extremal tree for s and $m = \lceil s/2 \rceil$. s is given on the x-axis.

The optimal choice in this setting is $s^* = 6$. A slightly closer look reveals that exactly up to (including) $s = 6$, the extremal tree *coincides* with an almost complete binary search tree. Stated otherwise, as soon as s becomes large enough for the extremal tree to live up to its name, the comparison count starts increasing.

The picture changes little if we choose pivots equidistantly from a sample, i.e., with $\mathbf{t} = (t, \dots, t)$ for $t \in \mathbb{N}$. Then $s^* = 4$ for all $t \geqslant 1$. Of course, the absolute values keep improving upon increasing t, but the relative ranking does not change further. That is a first indication that more than five pivots may be not too helpful, at least without tricky sampling schemes.

7.6.3 Scanned Elements

We have discussed at length how the number of comparisons in s-way Quicksort behaves when we let s tend to infinity. In practice, however, other cost measures are likely to be important, as well; in particular the number of *scanned elements*. As always, let us start simple.

No Sampling. Without pivot sampling, i.e., with $\mathbf{t} = 0$, we have $\boldsymbol{\tau} = (\frac{1}{s}, \dots, \frac{1}{s})$ and Proposition 7.4 (page 233) shows that in fact the optimal choice for m is $\lceil s/2 \rceil$, in particular optimal choices are always master-pivot methods. The resulting costs for $m \in \mathbb{N}_0$ are

$$a_{SE} = \frac{m^2 + (s - m)^2}{2s}, \tag{7.91}$$

for the special case of even s with $m = s/2$, this reduces to $a_{SE} = \frac{1}{4}s + \frac{1}{2}$—as simple as it gets. The partitioning costs are to be divided by $\mathcal{H} = H_s - 1$ to get overall costs. As $\mathcal{H} \sim \ln(s)$, it is obvious that $a_{SE}/\mathcal{H}$ *goes to infinity* for $s \to \infty$! With respect to scanned elements, it is therefore not advisable to make s larger and larger. For the simple function above, we expect a unique global minimum on $\mathbb{R}_{\geqslant 2}$. Figure 36 shows the function for small values of s.

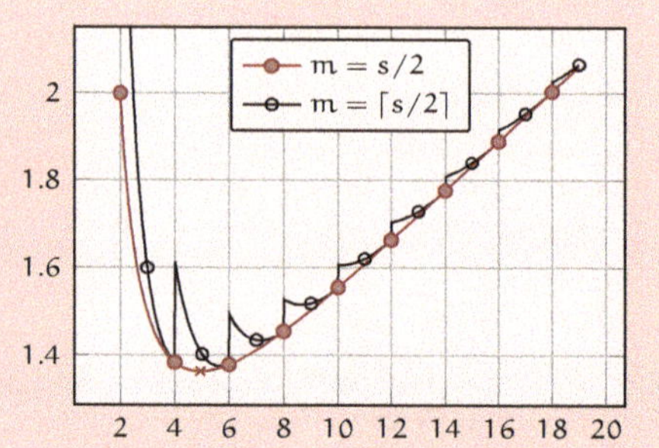

Figure 36: Scanned elements for s-way Quicksort, when $t = 0$ and $m = s/2$ or $m = \lceil s/2 \rceil$. s is given in the x-axis, the y-axis shows the leading-term coefficient for the average number of scanned elements. For $m = s/2$, the function is simply $\frac{s/4 + 1/2}{H_s - 1}$; it only has algorithmic meaning for *even* s, where it coincides with the $m = \lceil s/2 \rceil$ case. The cross marks the minimum of the red curve.

The continuous minimum is at $s \approx 4.94$; but recall that the simple form shown in Figure 36 is only valid for even s. With $m = \lfloor s/2 \rfloor$, the values in the vicinity of this continuous minimum are 1.38462 for $s = 4$, 1.4026 for $s = 5$, 1.37931 for $s = 6$ and 1.43498 for $s = 7$, so $s^* = 6$ here; see also the black line in Figure 36.

Five-pivot Quicksort is thus the optimal choice w.r.t. scanned elements when we do not sample pivots. But note that three-pivot Quicksort, in particular the "Waterloo-Quicksort" by Kushagra et al. [105] needs only 0.4 % more scanned elements in the asymptotic average.

Equidistant Sampling. Now assume $t = (t, \dots, t)$ for a fixed $t \in \mathbb{N}_0$. We still have $\tau = (\frac{1}{s}, \dots, \frac{1}{s})$ and a_{SE} is as without sampling, but $\mathcal{H}$ changes to $H_{(t+1)s} - H_{t+1} = \mathrm{hd}_{(t+1)s}(\frac{1}{s})$. The qualitative features of the number of scanned elements are the same as without sampling, i.e., for $t = 0$, but the numbers change.

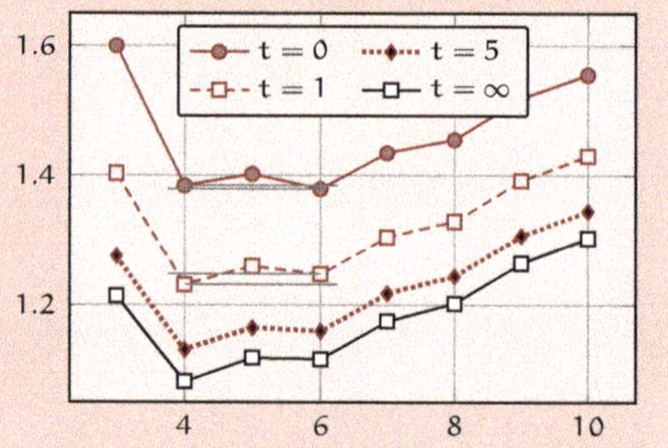

Figure 37: Scanned elements for s-way Quicksort, when $t = (t, \dots, t)$ and $m = \lceil s/2 \rceil$, for several choices of t. s is given in the x-axis, the y-axis shows the leading-term coefficient for the average number of scanned elements. Minimal scanned elements are achieved for $s = 4$, except for the case $t = 0$, then $s = 6$ is optimal.

Figure 37 shows that in fact $s^* = 4$ for all variants shown there except $t = 0$. In fact, $s^* = 4$ for *any* $t \geqslant 1$; the case without sampling is the sole exception, where $s = 6$ is very slightly better. As long as our pivots are chosen without skew, the Waterloo-Quicksort is a very good choice.

Limit-Density Sampling. Even though the practical motivation behind counting scanned elements is different from that for counting comparisons, the two cost measures are analytically quite similar to deal with. In fact, the techniques used in Section 7.6.2, in particular Propositions 7.13 and 7.14 do not make use of the fact that the numbers $\lambda_k^{(s)}(c)$ for a class $c \in \mathcal{C}$ actually are depths of leaves in a binary search tree. We obtain analogous results for scanned elements, by setting $\lambda_k(s_i) = \lambda_g(s_i) = i$ and $\lambda_k(1_j) = \lambda_g(1_j) = j$; recall Section 5.4.3 (page 175). The "path length" $PL(s)$ which appears in Proposition 7.13 is thus given by $PL(s) = a_{SE}$ from Theorem 7.1, i.e.,

$$a_{SE}(s) \;=\; \sum_{i=1}^{\lceil m^{(s)} \rceil} i \cdot \tau^{(s)}_{\lceil m^{(s)} \rceil - i + 1} \;+\; \sum_{j=1}^{s - \lfloor m^{(s)} \rfloor} j \cdot \tau^{(s)}_{\lfloor m^{(s)} \rfloor + j} \;-\; \frac{\sigma_{\leftrightarrow}}{\kappa}, \tag{7.92}$$

where we define for all $s \geqslant 2$ the vector $\boldsymbol{\tau} = \boldsymbol{\tau}^{(s)}$ via

$$\tau^{(s)}_r \;=\; \int_{(r-1)/s}^{r/s} \tau^*(z)\,dz, \qquad \text{for } r = 1,\ldots,s. \tag{7.93}$$

Again, the formulas might look daunting, but the scenario is in fact quite simple: We pick a $\boldsymbol{\tau}$ from a limit density by picking the average value of the density in the corresponding $\frac{1}{s}$-strip of the unit interval.

Now, assume a family of sampling vectors as in Proposition 7.13, i.e., we sample with a limit density $\tau^*(z)$. By continuity τ^* is bounded on $[0,1]$, and it integrates to 1; hence there must be a nonempty interval $(\zeta, \zeta + \varepsilon) \subset [0,1]$ and a $\delta > 0$ such that $\tau^*(z) \geqslant \delta$ for all $z \in (\zeta, \zeta + \varepsilon)$. Then, even if we only consider classes in this interval, we have

$$a_{SE}(s) \;\geqslant\; \sum_{r=1}^{s} \lambda^{(s)}(\mathcal{C}_r) \cdot \int_{(r-1)/s}^{r/s} \delta \cdot \big[z \in (\zeta, \zeta + \varepsilon)\big] \tag{7.94}$$

$$\geqslant\; (\varepsilon s - 1) \cdot \frac{\varepsilon s - 1}{4} \cdot \frac{\delta}{s}, \tag{7.95}$$

$$=\; \Omega(s), \qquad (s \to \infty), \tag{7.96}$$

since at least $(\varepsilon s - 1)$ classes get an integral contribution of δ/s from the ε-strip $(\zeta, \zeta + \varepsilon)$, and $\lambda(c)$ is at least $\frac{\varepsilon s - 1}{4}$ on average in any interval of $(\varepsilon s - 1)$ classes. So when sampling with a limit density, the number of scanned elements eventually *increases* with the number of pivots and there will be a finite optimal choice s^*.

Let us consider the following scenario: We pick a smooth limiting density $\tau^*(z)$ and set $\boldsymbol{\tau}^{(s)}$ as in Equation (7.93) above. Moreover, we consider the limit case $k \to \infty$. Then the overall number of scanned elements is $a_{SE}(s)/\mathcal{H}_{\ln}(\boldsymbol{\tau}^{(s)})$.

Equidistant sampling as considered above corresponds to a uniform limit density $\tau^*(z) = 1$, and we have $s^* = 4$ there. In fact, $s = 4$ performed exceptionally well for all sample sizes there, not only in the limit $k \to \infty$. There is nothing "magical" in this number, though, as the examples below show.

In order to save scans, we should try a limit density with a peak towards $\frac{1}{2}$, since elements in "outermost" segments are more expensive than those towards the middle. There are many such choices; let us, arbitrarily, pick as limit distribution the Beta(α, α) distribution with $\alpha \geqslant 1$, i.e., $\tau^*(z) \propto \big(z(1-z)\big)^{\alpha-1}$. The larger α is, the more peaky the distribution becomes, and we expect less scanned elements than in the uniform case for s large enough.

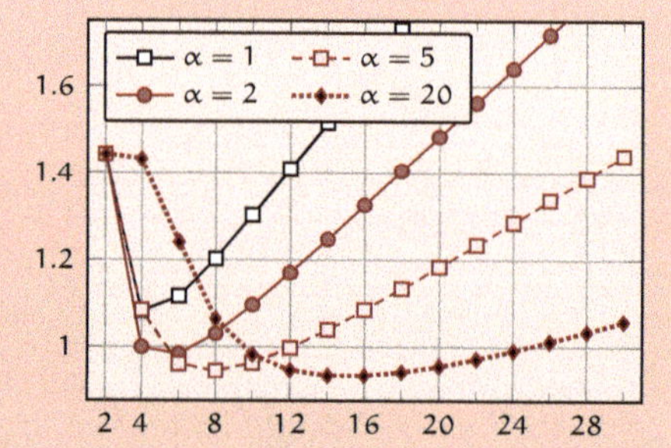

Figure 38: Scanned elements for s-way Quicksort, for even s and $m = \lceil s/2 \rceil$, where pivots are sampled with limit Beta(α, α) density, see (7.93). s is given in the x-axis, the y-axis shows the leading-term coefficient for the average number of scanned elements. Different values for α are shown. The minima are at $s = 4$, $s = 6$, $s = 8$ and $s = 14$, respectively.

Figure 38 shows corresponding values for exemplary choices of α. Note that $\alpha = 1$ yields $\tau^*(z) = 1$, the uniform case again. With increasing α, scanned element counts do improve for large s. For sensible values of s, extremely peaky distributions are not helpful, though, because the resulting entropy is extreme low there. The optimal value for s thus increases with α, and it is larger than 4 for $\alpha \geqslant 2$.

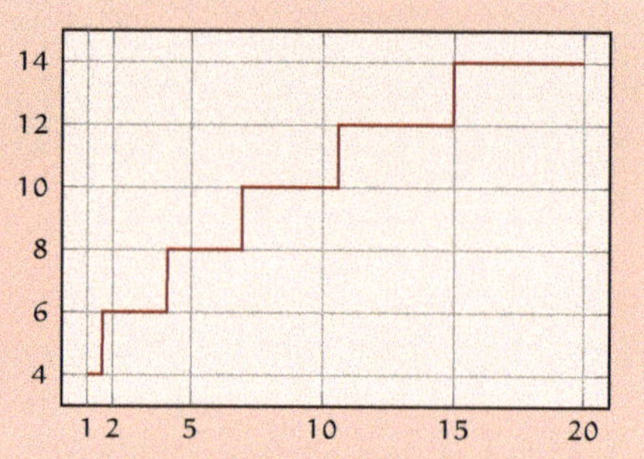

Figure 39: Optimal choice for s w.r.t. scanned elements for $m = \lceil s/2 \rceil$ when pivots are sampled with limit Beta(α, α) density. α is given on the x-axis, the y-axis shows s^*.

Figure 39 shows explicitly how s^* changes when we increase α. In essence, we can make any even number the optimal s by choosing the right α. But for any fixed α, or any other fixed limit density, we have a finite optimal s^*.

7.6.4 Exponential-Decay Sampling

The above scenario for the limiting behavior of the sampling parameters $\mathbf{t}^{(s)}$, formally described in Propositions 7.13 and 7.14, is quite general in that it covers any smooth limiting density. However, the mere *existence* of a smooth limiting density is a limiting assumption itself. In this section, we consider a special case where no such density exists and how overall costs behave when we vary s.

For scanned elements, we have seen for fixed s that in the limit of $k \to \infty$, the optimal sampling distribution weights τ^* are *geometrically decreasing* when we move away from the master pivot, see Proposition 7.8 (page 238). This means that a constant *fraction* of all probability mass is concentrated in a constant number of segments around the meeting point m—irrespective of the number of segments s. The limiting distribution of these geometrically decreasing weights is the degenerate distribution that has value μ almost surely. Its density is degenerate, as well, and can only be written using the *Dirac delta function*; it is certainly not smooth. This scenario is hence not covered by Propositions 7.13 and 7.14.

For $m = \lceil s/2 \rceil$, Corollary 7.10 already tells us that the overall leading-term coefficient for scanned elements in this case is

$$\frac{a_{SE}(\tau^*)}{\mathcal{H}_{\mathrm{hd}_\kappa}(\tau^*)} = \frac{1}{\ln(3) - \frac{2}{3} \cdot 3^{-s/2}} \pm O(3^{-s}), \qquad (s \to \infty), \tag{7.97}$$

and it is always strictly larger than $1/\ln(3)$. This means that there is *no* finite optimal s^*! When we sample pivots optimally w.r.t. scanned elements for each given s, increasing s improves the number of scanned elements in the asymptotic average.

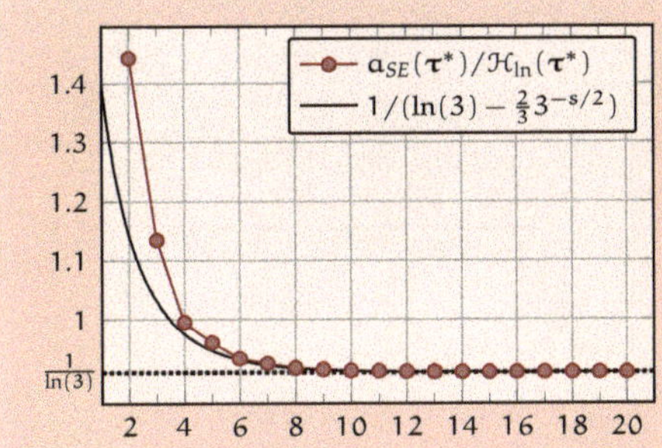

Figure 40: Scanned elements for s-way Quicksort with $m = \lceil s/2 \rceil$ and exact-quantiles pivots sampled with scanned-element optimal τ^*, see Proposition 7.8. s is given in the x-axis, the y-axis shows the leading-term coefficient for the average number of scanned elements. The asymptotic approximation from Corollary 7.10 is also shown.

While the fact that $s^* = \infty$ is similar to the results for the number of comparisons using balanced comparison trees above, the type of convergence is very different. For comparisons, we had extremely slow convergence of the costs to their limit: the error bound in Equation (7.87) gives a relative error rate of $1/\log(s)$. In contrast, the number of scanned elements under exponential-decay sampling converges *exponentially fast* towards its lower bound. This means that even more so than for comparisons, the largest improvements happen for small s, and increasing the number of segments further delivers rapidly diminishing returns.

Relation to Extremal Trees. The costs vector α_{SE} (Equation (5.23) on page 176) that assigns each class the number of scanned elements is very similar to the leaf-depth vector λ of the corresponding extremal tree, see also Figure 34 (page 254). It is therefore not surprising that the optimal quantiles vector w.r.t. comparisons using the extremal tree is similar to τ^* from above: it is also an exponential-decay vector, and the conclusions from above apply accordingly.

7.6.5 Optimal s for fixed k

As argued several times in this work, the leading term of costs does not reflect the cost of pivot sampling. We can thus increase k *for free* in our model. Extremely large values for k or s will clearly not be efficient for practical input sizes. The conclusion from our analysis to make both s and k as large as possible are not really helpful.

In this section, we take a different perspective: Assume we have decided for a (maximum) sample size k, what is the best way to exploit it? For any fixed k, the compatible parameter space is finite, even though its size quickly explodes. In particular we have $s \leqslant \kappa = k + 1$.

The idea of this section is similar to Section 7.3, where we discussed how to compare the entropy-reducing effect of different sampling schemes. Instead of fixing k, it might seem fairer to fix an entropy-reduction value instead. However, for any $\tau \neq (\frac{1}{s}, \ldots, \frac{1}{s})$ we get in the limit $k \to \infty$ a *finite* limit value for $\hat{k}$, the sample size so that median-of-$\hat{k}$ is entropy-equivalent to sampling with $t = \tau \cdot (k+1) - 1$. Optimal sampling schemes w.r.t. scanned elements are quite skewed, and we would get insanely large samples with moderate entropy reduction, see Figure 41. If we allowed sampling with the quality of median-of-9, *no* restriction on the sample size for Waterloo Quicksort would result whatsoever. Therefore, we fix the sample size k instead.

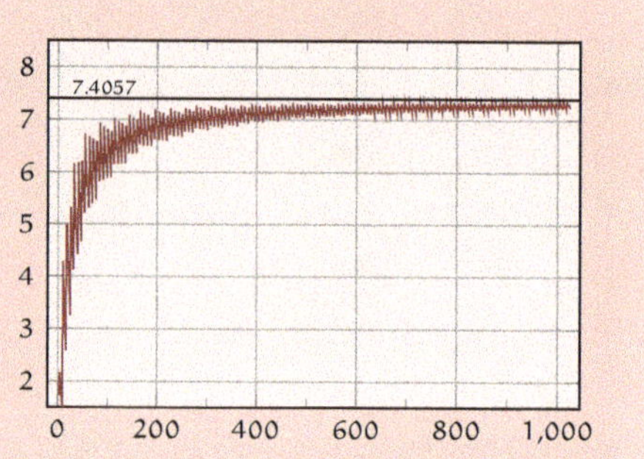

Figure 41: Entropy-equivalent sample sizes for sampling with scanned-elements-optimal t. The x-axis shows the original sample size k, the y-axis shows $\hat{k}$ computed as follows: First, we determine the optimal sampling parameter t^* for Waterloo Quicksort ($s = 4$, $m = 2$) for sample size k using the heuristic from Section 7.5.7. Then $\hat{k}$ is the sample size, so that median-of-$\hat{k}$ has the same entropy-reducing effect as sampling with t^*.

Scanned Elements. Optimal quantiles vector for scanned elements have been derived in Proposition 7.8: they are geometrically decreasing from the meeting point outwards with a basis close to $\frac{1}{3}$. Unless we have an extremely large sample size—namely exponentially large in s—we are not able to express the tiny differences in the probabilities for the outermost segments. More specifically, if we use Algorithm 11 (page 246), our rounding heuristic to find good sampling vectors, the outermost entries of t are often 0. This is already the case for $s = 6$ for reasonable sample sizes, see Table 10.

Intuitively, these low-probability segments cannot be very helpful overall. We have seen in Section 7.5.7 that t^* is usually close to $\text{round}(\tau^* \cdot \kappa) - 1$. For scanned elements with $m = s/2$ and even s, the smallest entry in τ^* is $(x^*)^m$, which is very close to 3^{-m}. If now $s \geqslant 2\log_3(\kappa)$, then the outermost entry of t^* is at most $\text{round}(\kappa \cdot 3^{-m}) = \text{round}(\kappa\frac{1}{\kappa}) = 1$, which is the limit of precision for sampling. Any further entries should receive less than a $\frac{1}{\kappa}$ fraction of elements, but we cannot express a smaller class probability with the given sample size.

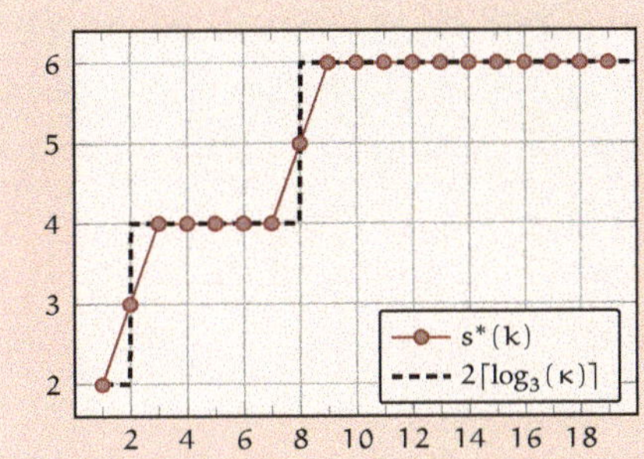

Figure 42: Optimal $s^* = s^*(k)$ w.r.t. scanned elements when k is fixed. $s^*(k)$ is determined by exhaustive search among all choices for s, m and t with sample size k. The dashed line shows a heuristic explanation for $s^*(k)$, namely $2\lceil\log_3(k+1)\rceil$. This is (roughly) the number of non-zero entries in t chosen by Algorithm 11 based on the optimal quantiles vector τ^* w.r.t. scanned elements.

For a given κ, we thus expect $s \gg 2\log_3(\kappa)$ to perform worse than $s \approx 2\log_3(\kappa)$. In fact, Figure 42 shows that this back-of-the-envelope computation very accurately predicts the optimal number of segments: $s^*(k) \approx 2\lceil\log_3(k+1)\rceil$. The optimal choice of m is always $m = \lceil s^*/2\rceil$ and the sampling vector is as discussed in Section 7.5.7.

It is quite reassuring that for realistic choices for k in practice, say $3 \leqslant k \leqslant 27$, we have either $s^* = 4$ or $s^* = 6$, which both still allow reasonably simple partitioning code. The case $s = 4$ corresponds to Waterloo partitioning, and this discussion is another indication that this algorithm has favorable characteristics.

Comparisons. Let us now we ask the same question as above for comparisons: what is the optimal choice of parameters w.r.t. the number of comparisons, when k is fixed to a given value? In addition to the s, m and t, for comparisons can also change the comparisons trees λ_k and λ_g.

Unlike for scanned elements and despite the many degrees of freedom, the optimal choice for s is unspectacular: two. It is best to put all the stakes on one card and select a single pivot very precisely, namely as close to the median of the input as possible.

7.7 Optimal Comparison Trees

With one pivot, all we can do is to compare each ordinary element to that pivot. For s-way partitioning, we have much more freedom, we can choose from many different *comparison trees.* Most previous work on Quicksort with more than one pivot does not explore this design space, in particular Hennequin [77] only considers maximally balanced trees; Tan [173] implicitly does so as well. Sedgewick [162] and Kushagra et al. [105] study specific implementations with two respectively three pivots and do not explicitly discuss the chosen order of comparisons.

Aumüller et al. [10], who worked concurrently on multi-pivot Quicksort, were the first to explicitly describe the idea of comparison trees and to explore the possibility to choose one that is not maximally balanced. They also discuss the most general setting of generic classification strategies that we considered in Section 5.3.2. The used comparison tree was there allowed to change after every single classification. For practical algorithms, the overhead of dynamically adapting the order in which to compare elements to pivots is usually too big, see the experiments of Aumüller et al. [8, 10]. Aumüller et al. therefore consider the simplest strategy in more detail: A priori choose one tree $\lambda = \lambda_k = \lambda_g$ for good.

We first revisit this strategy here in our more general setting and extend a few results of Aumüller et al. [10]. Then we consider the benefit of dropping the restriction to use the same comparisons tree for both λ_k and λ_g.

7.7.1 The Single-Tree Case

If we use the same comparison tree $\lambda = \lambda_k = \lambda_g$ to classify all elements, the number of comparisons in one partitioning step has leading-term coefficient (Theorem 7.1)

$$a_C = \sum_{c \in \mathcal{C}} \lambda(c) \cdot \tau_{r(c)} \frac{\sigma_{\rightarrow} + \sigma_{\leftarrow} + [c = 1] + [c = s]}{\sigma_{\rightarrow} + \sigma_{\leftarrow} + [c \neq m]} = \sum_{c \in \mathcal{C}} \lambda(c) \cdot \tau_{r(c)} = \lambda^{\mathsf{T}} \tau, \quad (7.98)$$

which is the expected depth of the leaf for the random class C, where $\mathbb{P}[C = \mathcal{C}_r] = \tau_r$ for $r = 1, \ldots, s$. As noted already in Section 7.5.3, a_C is a linear function in τ, which is not the case in general for $\lambda_k \neq \lambda_g$.

By Equation (7.98), the access probabilities of leaves in the comparison tree are simply τ and thus determined by the sampling parameter t as $\tau = \frac{t+1}{\kappa}$, where $\kappa = \Sigma(t+1)$.

Legitimate Expectations?   In a given partitioning step, the actual leaf access frequencies in the comparison tree are *random:* they are given by $\mathbf{I}$. We might consider the expectation of $\mathbf{I}$, as classes of elements are i.i.d., but even then, the leaf access *probabilities* are still random; they are given by $\mathbf{D}$. Of course, the expected value of the latter is $\mathbb{E}[\mathbf{D}] = \tau$; but is it legitimate to simply *insert* that expected value in our cost function?

Of course, the general answer is no. But for a fixed comparison tree, the number of comparisons for sorting with that tree is a *linear* function in $\mathbf{I}$ and $\mathbf{D}$, and we obtain expected a_C by taking expectations first on $\mathbf{I}$, then on $\mathbf{D}$ by the linearity of the expectation.

Note that this simple relation does no longer hold for two different trees: the usage frequencies of the trees and the access frequencies of leaves/classes are *not* independent. Therefore, we need the more elaborate machinery of Chapter 5 to compute the expected comparison count. Luckily, we did that once and for all there.

If the sampling parameter t is fixed, we can ask for the optimal choice λ^* for the comparison tree, namely the binary search tree (BST) on $s-1$ internal nodes whose weighted external path length with weights τ is minimal. This optimization problem is a classic scenario, known as the *optimal alphabetic tree problem*. Section 7.7.3 briefly surveys what is known for this problem, with a focus on properties that help characterize optimal trees for important special cases for the weights. But before we consider in more detail how to find such optimal trees, let us drop the restriction $\lambda_k = \lambda_g$.

7.7.2 Two Comparison Trees

Aumüller et al. [10] did not study the possibility of having two different trees, their setting thus corresponds to the one of the last section. We hence consider the two-tree case in more detail in this work.

When we allow two different comparison trees, we have to find the best possible *pair* of trees. This might seem a much harder problem than the single-tree case above, but it is actually not. The key observation is that the total costs are a *sum* of two terms, where one is influenced only by λ_k, the other only by λ_g. We can hence optimize for the two trees separately; we only have to determine the weights according to which we should choose λ_k and λ_g. The weights are contained in the term for a_C from Theorem 7.1, we just have to dig them out:

$$a_C \;=\; \sum_{c \in \mathcal{C}} \lambda_k(c) \cdot \frac{\tau_{r(c)}(\sigma_\rightarrow + [c = s])}{\kappa - \sigma_\leftrightarrow + [c \neq m]} \;+\; \sum_{c \in \mathcal{C}} \lambda_g(c) \cdot \frac{\tau_{r(c)}(\sigma_\leftarrow + [c = 1])}{\kappa - \sigma_\leftrightarrow + [c \neq m]}. \qquad (7.99)$$

Unlike for a single tree, master-pivot and master-segment methods differ in the leaf weights for two trees. The case distinction is hidden in the $\sigma_\rightarrow$ etc. notation (see Table 4).

As the formula is a little opaque with all the abbreviations, let us consider a concrete example. The parameter choices are rather nonsensical and meant for illustrative purposes only. Set $s = 6$ and $m = 2.5$, then the classes are $\mathcal{C} = (s_3, s_2, m, 1_2, 1_3, 1_4)$. Let us pick $t = (0, 5, 1, 3, 1, 4)$, i.e., we have $\kappa = 20$ and $\tau = \left(\frac{1}{20}, \frac{3}{10}, \frac{1}{10}, \frac{1}{5}, \frac{1}{10}, \frac{1}{4}\right)$. The leaf weights for λ_k then are

$$\left(\frac{2}{95}, \frac{12}{95}, \frac{7}{180}, \frac{7}{95}, \frac{7}{190}, \frac{7}{76}\right) \;\approx\; (0.021, 0.126, 0.039, 0.074, 0.037, 0.092), \qquad (7.100)$$

and for λ_g we have

$$\left(\frac{11}{380}, \frac{33}{190}, \frac{11}{180}, \frac{12}{95}, \frac{6}{95}, \frac{3}{19}\right) \;\approx\; (0.029, 0.174, 0.061, 0.126, 0.063, 0.158). \qquad (7.101)$$

Note that the weights sum to $\frac{7}{18} \approx 0.389$ resp. $\frac{11}{18} \approx 0.611$, which makes 1 in *total*, not per tree. The optimal choices for λ_k and λ_g are given in Figure 43 (page 273); they are coincidentally the same as for the symmetric case discussed there. The weighted external path lengths are $\frac{581}{570} \approx 1.02$ and $\frac{919}{570} \approx 1.61$, so that we get $a_C = \frac{50}{19} \approx 2.63$. The expected leaf depth in the trees, i.e., the weighted path lengths after normalizing so that weights sum to one per tree, is $\frac{249}{95} \approx 2.62$ and $\frac{2757}{1045} \approx 2.64$ for λ_k and λ_g, respectively. They differ only very slightly.

7.7.3 The Optimal Alphabetic Tree Problem

The problem of computing λ^* from the weights τ is known as the *optimal alphabetic tree problem*. It is a special case of computing *optimal binary search trees,* for which the internal nodes may have weights, as well, and a stricter variant of the *coding tree problem,* where we look for any binary tree with the given leaves, but the leaves need not appear in the input order. The term *alphabetic* exactly refers to the fact that we require leaves to remain in order in binary search trees. Nagaraj [134] gives a comprehensive overview of all three problems. We herein only discuss a few facts relevant for our further discussion of optimal comparison trees in Quicksort.

Algorithms.   The coding tree problem is solved exactly and optimally—w.r.t. the Θ-class of the number of comparisons—by the classic greedy algorithm due to Huffman [90]. Interestingly, the true complexity of finding optimal BSTs is still open in both variants of the problem.

Huffman's algorithm starts with a list of all leaves with their weights. It then iteratively replaces a pair of nodes with minimal sum of weights, by a new internal node with the sum as its weight. The two removed nodes become the children of this newly created node. When only one node is left, the process terminates and the last node is the root of the constructed tree, which can be shown to have minimal expected external path length.

A neat implementation of Huffman's algorithm first sorts the leaves by weight—needless to say it should use Quicksort for that—and then uses an ordinary queue for created nodes, see Rytter [156] for details. Excluding the sorting step, Huffman's algorithm then runs in linear time.

For the more general optimal binary search tree problem, there is a conceptually simple dynamic-programming algorithm, see Knuth [103, Section 6.2.2]. It has quadratic time and space complexity. This algorithm can of course be used to compute optimal alphabetic trees, and it is fast enough for reasonable values of s.

Specialized methods for the alphabetic tree problem are much more efficient for large inputs: The *Hu-Tucker algorithm* [87] and the *Garsia-Wachs algorithm* [70] both compute optimal alphabetic trees in linearithmic time. The algorithms and even more so their correctness proofs are more involved [134, 103]. Even though we do not make use of the algorithms themselves in this work, we use insights gained from their correctness proofs to establish optimality of certain trees. We thus describe the idea of the Hu-Tucker algorithm, following Mumey [131, 99] and Nagaraj [134]. A well accessible description is also given by Shor [169].

The Hu-Tucker algorithm first computes a binary tree that is not necessarily alphabetic, i.e., leaves might appear out of order. The cost of this tree can be shown to be optimal in a restricted class of coding trees containing all alphabetic trees. Moreover a procedure is known to create an alphabetic tree of the same cost, which thus is optimal. We only describe the first step, see Nagaraj [134] for the construction of the alphabetic tree.

The first phase is similar to Huffman's algorithm; it also starts with the list of leaves and successively merges pairs of nodes until a single root remains. Unlike for Huffman's algorithm, the order of nodes is important, so we keep them in a list. A newly created node takes a place between the two just removed nodes, e.g., the position of its left son. Also, we do not simply merge nodes with minimal weight sum, but so-called *local minimum compatible pairs (LMCP)*. Two nodes are *compatible* if there is *no leaf between them* in the current list of nodes—*internal* nodes may be crossed over, though—and such a pair of nodes (u, v) is *locally minimal* if u has minimal weight among all nodes compatible to v and the other way round, i.e., u and v are mutually minimum compatible nodes. It may happen that several compatible nodes have the same weight; in that case a tie-breaking rule is needed to single out the LMCP. We use the position in the list to strictly order nodes of equal weight. One can show that there always is such a construction where we merge only LMCPs.

Conditions for Optimality.   The following statement is then an immediate consequence of the correctness of the Hu-Tucker algorithm, see, e.g., Nagaraj [134], and provides the basis of the proofs of following statements for weights with specific properties.

Proposition 7.16: *Let $w \in \mathbb{R}_{>0}^n$ be a vector of weights and λ a BST with leaves $1, \dots, n$. If the expected leaf depth $\mathbb{E}[\lambda(I)]$ for $I \stackrel{\mathcal{D}}{=} \mathcal{D}(w)$ equals the weighted external path length of a tree formed by merging local minimum compatible pairs on $w_1, \dots, w_n$, then λ is an optimal alphabetic tree w.r.t. w.* ■

For special cases shortcuts are possible to the optimal alphabetic tree. These cover many choices of interest for sampling vectors t, so we list some here for reference.

Corollary 7.17 (Theorem 5.1 of Hu and Tan [86]): *Let $0 < w_1 \leqslant w_2 \leqslant \cdots \leqslant w_n$ be sorted weights. Then the costs of optimal alphabetic trees and Huffman trees coincide.* ◄

Proof: We show that Huffman's algorithm never merges incompatible node pairs; as it chooses sum-of-weight-minimal pairs, all combinations are LMCP and we are done.

Consider the queue-based implementation of Huffman's algorithm, i.e., we have one queue Q_l initially holding the leaves in sorted order, increasing by weight, and a second queue Q_i to which we add newly created internal nodes. We only ever remove minimal-weight leaves from Q_l and Q_i contains only internal nodes, so Q_l and Q_i invariantly contain exactly all leaves resp. all internal nodes, sorted by nondecreasing weight. If the two weight-minimal leaves and internal nodes are l_1, l_2 and i_1, i_2, respectively, the next merge must combine (l_1, l_2), (l_1, i_1) or (i_1, i_2). All are compatible pairs since i_1 is the leftmost inner node. ■

With Corollary 7.17, one can show that optimal alphabetic trees can be computed in linear time for sorted leaf weights: the LMCP-merging step is the only part in the Hu-Tucker algorithm that need super-linear time. It is intriguingly still open, whether it is possible to compute optimal alphabetic trees in linear time, if the weights are only linear-time *sortable;* of course, for *alphabetic* trees this is a much weaker requirement than having leaves with weights in order also in the final tree.

Proposition 7.18 (Theorem 3.1 of Klawe and Mumey [99]):

Assume the weights w are "within a factor of two," i.e., there is a constant c such that $c \leqslant w_i < 2c$ for $i = 1, \ldots, s$. Then there is an optimal alphabetic tree with all leaves on at most two consecutive levels. ◄

Proof: We first show that after merging "one level," we again have weights within a factor of two.

Starting with s weights within a factor of two, the first $\lfloor s/2 \rfloor$ LMCP merges each combine two leaves, as any created internal node weighs at least $2c$ and thus more than any leaf. If s is even, all nodes are pairs of leaves and thus have weights in $[2c, 4c)$, so the sequence is again within a factor of two. Also, after this round of merges, all leaves are at level 1.

If s is odd, a largest-weight leaf will be left over; Klawe and Mumey somewhat aptly call it the *wallflower* of the leaves. Let $w_{wf} = \max w_i$ be its weight.

The next LMCP must combine the wallflower and the cheapest of the previously formed internal nodes, which has weight, say, $c' \in [2c, 4c)$. All other internal nodes have weight at least c', and less than $2c'$ because $2c' \geqslant 4c$, so they all fall into $[c', 2c')$. The triple that is formed by including the wallflower, of course, has weight greater than c', but not more than $2c'$ as the wallflower contributes $w_{wf} < 2c$, but $c' \geqslant 2c$. Hence, after the wallflower merge we have, as in the even case, $\lfloor s/2 \rfloor$ nodes and their weights are within a factor of two.

After this round of LMCP merges, most leaves are at level 1, except for the pair that had to include the wallflower, those two leaves are at level 2. Joining the wallflower pushes them down one level.

We finally observe that the wallflower triple has the unique maximal weight of all $\lfloor s/2 \rfloor$ nodes in the current list:

$$c' + w_{wf} \; \geqslant \; 2c + w_{wf} \; > \; 2w_{wf} \; \geqslant \; \max w_i + w_j. \tag{7.102}$$

It is thus guaranteed that the root of the wallflower subtree will be the wallflower of any subsequent rounds (unless we have an even number of nodes then). Joining the wallflower not only pushes you one level down, it makes the clique *become* the new wallflower. On the other hand, once a leaf is part of the wallflower subtree we will never see its level increase by two again in future rounds, so any one leaf has in the end as level the number of rounds or the number of rounds plus one. Of course, the number of rounds is simply $\lfloor \mathrm{ld}(s) \rfloor$. ∎

If the number of leaves is a power of two, we can even precisely characterize the weight vectors that make the complete BST optimal:

Proposition 7.19 (Lemma 4.4 of Ramanan [147]): *Let s be a power of two. The complete binary search tree with all s leaves on level $\mathrm{ld}(s)$ is an optimal alphabetic tree w.r.t. leaf weights $\boldsymbol{w}$ if and only if*

$$\forall i \in \{1,3,5,\ldots,s-3\} : \forall j > i : \; w_i \leqslant w_j + w_{j+1}, \quad (7.103.1)$$

$$\forall i \in \{4,6,8,\ldots,s\} : \forall j < i : \; w_i \leqslant w_{j-1} + w_j, \quad (7.103.2)$$

$$\forall i \in \{1,3,\ldots,s-1\} : \forall j \in \{i+1,i+3,\ldots,s\} : \forall q \geqslant p+2 \; :$$

$$(p > j \vee q+1 < i) \implies w_i + w_j \leqslant w_p + w_{p+1} + w_q + w_{q+1} . \quad (7.103.3)$$

◆ ◆ ◆

Another extreme case that is also easy to handle is when weights are exponentially spaced. More specifically, if the ratio between any two nodes is at least two, i.e., $w_i \geqslant w_j$ implies $|w_i/w_j| \geqslant 2$, then only adjacent nodes will ever be merged; see Lemma 3.3 of Mumey [131].

This very situation is not so useful for our purposes, but a particular shape of weights with locally exponential spacing is. The precise conditions are somewhat technical, but essentially they require the weights to increase exponentially up to some index m, and then they decrease exponentially, a prototypical example would be $\boldsymbol{w} = (c^5, c^4, c^3, c^2, c, c, c^2, c^3)$ for a $c \leqslant \frac{1}{2}$. Weights of such shape are used if we sample so that the number of scanned elements is optimized.

Proposition 7.20: *Assume the weights $\boldsymbol{w} \in (0,1)^s$ fulfill*

$$w_1 < w_3 , \qquad\qquad \text{if } m \geqslant 3, \qquad\qquad (7.104.1)$$

$$w_{s-2} > w_s , \qquad\qquad \text{if } m \leqslant s-2, \qquad\qquad (7.104.2)$$

$$\phi \cdot w_i < w_{i+1} , \qquad\qquad \text{for } i = 2,\ldots,m-1, \qquad\qquad (7.104.3)$$

$$w_i > \phi \cdot w_{i+1} , \qquad\qquad \text{for } i = m+1,\ldots,s-2, \qquad\qquad (7.104.4)$$

$$\sum_{i=1}^{m-1} w_i < w_{m+1} , \qquad\qquad\qquad\qquad\qquad\qquad (7.104.5)$$

$$w_m > \sum_{i=m+2}^{s} w_i , \qquad\qquad\qquad\qquad\qquad\qquad (7.104.6)$$

◀

for $\phi = (\sqrt{5}+1)/2 \approx 1.61803$ the golden ratio and an index $m \in [1..s-1]$. Then the optimal alphabetic tree for weights $\boldsymbol{w}$ has as root the node with key $m+0.5$, separating leaves w_m and w_{m+1}. The left subtree of the root consists of a linear list of the leaves in decreasing order of the indices and likewise the right subtree is a linear list with leaves in increasing index order.

In other words, under the conditions of Proposition 7.20, the *extremal tree* is optimal, see Definition 7.15 on page 254.

Proof: We argue inductively that LMCPs are always the two first or the two last elements. The resulting Hu-Tucker tree is then already alphabetic and hence an optimal BST.

If $s = 2$, we have $m = 1$ and there is only one merge possible, which gives a tree as claimed.

Now assume $s \geqslant 3$ and consider first the case $m \geqslant 2$. Then (w_1, w_2) is a LMCP since $w_1 < w_3$, either by Equation (7.104.1) if $m \geqslant 3$ or by Equation (7.104.5) if $m = 2$, so we merge w_1 and w_2. Next, we show that the resulting weight sequence $w' \in (0,1)^{s-1}$ with $w'_i = w_{i+1}$ for $i \geqslant 2$ and $w'_1 = w_1 + w_2$ again fulfills Equation (7.104) with $s' = s - 1$ and $m' = m - 1$. Equations (7.104.2), (7.104.3) and (7.104.4) only concern elements that did not change, so they remain valid. $w'_{m'} \geqslant w_m$ as no elements can shrink, and the right-hand side did not change, so Equation (7.104.6) still holds. Similarly, the sum in Equation (7.104.5) has not changed; we only summed up two summands up front. It remains to check Equation (7.104.1) if $m' \geqslant 3$, i.e., $m \geqslant 4$

$$w'_1 \;=\; w_1 + w_2 \underset{(7.104.1)}{<} w_3 + w_2 \underset{(7.104.3)}{<} \left(1 + \frac{1}{\phi}\right) w_3 \;=\; \phi w_3 \underset{(7.104.3)}{<} w_4 \;=\; w'_3.$$

$$(7.105)$$

So, indeed, for the case $s \geqslant 3$ and $m \geqslant 2$, we can merge the LMCP (w_1, w_2) and get the tree of the claimed form by the induction hypothesis.

It remains to consider the case $s \geqslant 3$ and $m = 1$, but since the conditions are symmetric, we obtain by the same line of arguments that (w_{s-1}, w_s) is a LMCP and that we get a sequence of the same form again after merging these two nodes. ∎

Note that all conditions in Equation (7.104) are *linear* inequalities in the weights $\boldsymbol{w}$. So if $\boldsymbol{w}$ and $\boldsymbol{v}$ fulfill Equation (7.104), so does *any conic combination* $\alpha \boldsymbol{w} + \beta \boldsymbol{v}$ with $\alpha, \beta > 0$.

This section was mainly concerned with *relative* quality: how to find the best tree *among all that are possible*, or how to recognize a given tree as optimal. The next section complements this with bounds on its absolute quality: how good can trees possibly be?

7.7.4 Entropy-Bounds for Comparison Trees

Apart from the well-known information-theoretic lower bound on the number of comparisons needed to sort, we can also put entropy arguments to good use in analyzing a *single classification* step in multi-pivot Quicksort.

As noted above, even in the two-trees case, we can analyze and optimize costs separately for the two trees. In this section, we therefore consider a single classification with one comparison tree λ whose leaves are accessed with probabilities $\mathbf{q} \in [0,1]^s$. As the leaves are associated to classes $c \in \mathcal{C}$, $\mathbf{q}$ really gives a distribution over $\mathcal{C}$. The expected number of comparisons to classify a random class $C \in \mathcal{C}$, distributed according to this distribution, is then given by $\mathbb{E}[\lambda(C)]$, where $\lambda(c)$ denotes the depth of the leaf c. Proposition 2.49 (page 86) relates this to the entropy of the distribution of C, in particular we have the following *lower bound* on the expected number of comparisons to classify one element:

$$\mathbb{E}[\lambda(C)] \;\geqslant\; \mathcal{H}_{\mathrm{ld}}(\mathbf{q}) \tag{7.106}$$

for any tree λ. Moreover, we can always find a tree with $\mathbb{E}[\lambda(C)] < \mathcal{H}_{\mathrm{ld}}(q) + 2 \leqslant \mathrm{ld}(s) + 2$.

The lower bound is precisely attainable for some distributions q, namely those that admit an entropy-tight tree (see Algorithm 1).

Single-Tree Case. If we enforce $\lambda_k = \lambda_g$, we directly have $a_C = \mathbb{E}[\lambda(C)]$. Also, the weights are simply $q = \tau$. So for the single-tree case, we always have

$$a_C \;\geqslant\; \mathcal{H}_{\mathrm{ld}}(\tau), \tag{7.107}$$

and the optimal tree λ^* achieves $a_C < \mathcal{H}_{\mathrm{ld}}(\tau) + 2$.

Bounds for Comparison-Optimal Partitioning. In Section 5.7 on comparison-optimal partitioning, we have seen that it suffices for the leading term to consider a classification strategy that chooses the optimal comparisons tree for a given D. We need not know the actual segment sizes I, because for large n, they do not deviate much from $D \cdot n$.

Now for a fixed D, the best conceivable strategy would cut the range of possible values of an element in half with each comparison. If that is possible precisely, we need exactly $\mathcal{H}_{\mathrm{ld}}(D)$ per ordinary element on average. In general, we will need a few more comparisons, but never more than $\mathcal{H}_{\mathrm{ld}}(D) + 2$.

If we could achieve the entropy bound for each D, the expected number of comparisons per partitioning step would be

$$\mathbb{E}[\mathcal{H}_{\mathrm{ld}}(D)] \;=\; -\frac{1}{\ln 2} \sum_{r=1}^{s} \mathbb{E}[D_r \ln D_r] \;=\; \frac{1}{\ln 2}\mathcal{H}(t), \tag{7.108}$$

where the second equality follows by Proposition 2.54. The overall number of comparisons is then precisely $n\,\mathrm{ld}\,n \pm O(n)$, the information-theoretic lower bound for comparison-based sorting. Of course, we knew that lower bound already.

We also get the upper bound $a_C < \mathbb{E}[\mathcal{H}_{\mathrm{ld}}(D)] + 2$, but this bound is not very helpful. A precise statement about the quality of comparison-optimal partitioning would require the expected value of the weighted external path length of the optimal alphabetic tree, when the leaf weights are $\mathrm{Dir}(t+1)$ distributed, i.e., uniformly for $t = 0$. To my knowledge, this average redundancy is not known. It is hence included in Open Problem 5.12.

Redundancy has been studied in more detail for Huffman codes, starting with Gallager [69], but also with a focus on upper bounds. To the author's knowledge, even for Huffman codes the average redundancy is not known in this model.

Open Problem 7.21 (Average Redundancy of Huffman Codes): Let $P \overset{\mathcal{D}}{=} \mathrm{Dir}(1,\dots,1)$ be an s-dimensional random vector, drawn uniformly among all stochastic vectors. Let $\lambda_H = \lambda_H(P)$ be a Huffman tree for the leaf weights P, and define the redundancy of λ_H as $R = \sum_{r=1}^{s} P_r \lambda_H(r) - \mathcal{H}_{\mathrm{ld}}(P)$. Compute $\mathbb{E}[R]$, as a function in s. Results for special s (small values) or nontrivial lower and upper bounds would already be interesting. ◄

A related problem has been solved by Szpankowski [172]: There, alphabet symbols are *blocks of bits* of length n, generated by a memoryless source where $p < 0.5$ is the probability for 0 in the block. The average redundancy of different codes, including Huffman's, are computed for large n. Here the symbol probabilities are *fixed*, and so is the redundancy;

the *average* here means average redundancy over all symbols, not over random symbols weights.

7.7.5 Optimal Choices for A Single Tree

For any given τ, we can use the algorithms discussed in Section 7.7.3 to determine an optimal comparison tree. However, running the algorithm as black box does not give much insight into what parameters allow for good trees. For two sensible special cases of families of weights, we can explicitly give optimal trees, so that we can analytically compare costs.

Let us start simple: We do not use sampling, i.e., $t = 0$ and $\tau = (\frac{1}{s}, \ldots, \frac{1}{s})$, and assume s is a power of two. Then the complete binary tree is optimal: all s leaves are at depth $\mathrm{ld}(s)$, i.e., $\tau_i = 2^{-\lambda(i)}$, so the tree is entropy-tight by Fact 2.50 (page 88), and thus optimal. The same remains true if $t = (t, \ldots, t)$ for any $t \in \mathbb{N}_0$.

If s is not a power of two, there is no perfectly balanced tree, but as discussed already in Section 7.6, the almost complete BST is optimal and has the cost given in Equation (7.61) on page 249.

Exponential-Decay Sampling. Things get more interesting if we sample pivots with a systematic skew. To save comparisons, it might not help to deviate much from equidistant sampling, but we have seen in Section 7.5.4 that extremely skewed sampling is needed to optimize the number of scanned elements. Aumüller et al. [10] show that this remains true at least for small s and k, when we optimize the sum of comparisons and scanned elements. So let us assume τ is the optimal quantiles vector w.r.t. scanned elements for $m \in \mathbb{N}_0$, that means

$$\tau = (x^m, x^{m-1}, \ldots, x^2, x, x, x^2, \ldots, x^{s-m}), \tag{7.109}$$

with $x = x^*(s, m)$, see Proposition 7.8. It is easy to check that τ fulfills the conditions (Equation (7.104)) of Proposition 7.20 (page 267). For scans-optimal sampling, the optimal comparison tree is thus the *extremal tree* with the master pivot P_m as root. We can generalize this statement to a class of quantiles vectors.

Proposition 7.22: *For $\chi \in [0, 1]$ and $x \in (0, \frac{1}{2}]$ set*

$$\alpha = (m - \chi, m - 1, m - 2, \ldots, 2, 1, 1, 2, 3, \ldots, s - m - 2, s - m - 1, s - m - \chi), \tag{7.110}$$

and assume $\tau \propto x^\alpha = (x^{\alpha_1}, \ldots, x^{\alpha_s})$. If $1 - x - x^\chi \geqslant 0$, we require additionally that $3 \leqslant m \leqslant s - 3$. Then the optimal comparison tree λ^* is the extremal tree with P_m in the root. ◀

Proof: Conditions $(7.104.1)-(7.104.4)$ trivially hold because $1/\phi > \frac{1}{2}$. For $(7.104.5)$, we compute

$$\sum_{i=1}^{m-1} \tau_i \;=\; x^{m-x} + \sum_{i=2}^{m-1} x^i \tag{7.111}$$

$$=\; \frac{x^2}{1-x} + x^{m-x} \cdot \frac{1-x-x^x}{1-x}; \tag{7.112}$$

for the case $1 - x - x^x < 0$, we can simply drop that term and continue

$$<\; \frac{x^2}{1-x} \tag{7.113}$$

$$\underset{(x \leqslant 1/2)}{\leqslant}\; x \tag{7.114}$$

$$=\; \tau_{m+1}. \tag{7.115}$$

If $1 - x - x^x \geqslant 0$, we have $m \geqslant 3$ by assumption. Moreover, $1 - x - x^x \geqslant 0$ implies $x \geqslant \log_x(1-x)$, so if $x = \frac{1}{2}$, then we must have $x = 1$. Then $\tau = \left(\frac{1}{2}\right)^{\alpha+1}$ is precisely the entropy-tight distribution for the extremal tree, so it must be optimal by Proposition 2.49. Otherwise we have $x < \frac{1}{2}$ and continue the estimate from above

$$\sum_{i=1}^{m-1} \tau_i \;=\; \frac{x^2}{1-x} + x^{m-x} \cdot \frac{1-x-x^x}{1-x} \tag{7.116}$$

$$\underset{(m \geqslant 3)}{\leqslant}\; \frac{x^2}{1-x} + x^{3-x} \cdot \frac{1-x-x^x}{1-x} \tag{7.117}$$

$$=\; x^2 + x^{3-x} \tag{7.118}$$

$$\leqslant\; 2x^2 \tag{7.119}$$

$$\underset{(x < 1/2)}{<}\; x \tag{7.120}$$

$$=\; \tau_{m+1}. \tag{7.121}$$

That proves condition $(7.104.5)$. Condition $(7.104.6)$ is similar. Therefore, all requirements of Proposition 7.20 are fulfilled and the extremal tree with root P_m is optimal. $\blacksquare$

7.7.6 The Benefit of Two Trees

We can rewrite the term for a_C from Equation (7.99) to make the influence of the two trees λ_k and λ_g more transparent:

$$a_C \;=\; \underbrace{\sigma_\rightarrow \sum_{c \in \mathcal{C}} \lambda_k(c)\rho_c + \sigma_\leftarrow \sum_{c \in \mathcal{C}} \lambda_g(c)\rho_c}_{\text{symmetric in } \lambda_k \text{ and } \lambda_g} \;+\; \sum_{\substack{c \in \mathcal{C} \\ c=s}} \lambda_k(c)\rho_c + \sum_{\substack{c \in \mathcal{C} \\ c=1}} \lambda_g(c)\rho_c , \tag{7.122}$$

where

$$\rho_c \;=\; \frac{\tau_{r(c)}}{\kappa - \sigma_\leftrightarrow + [c \neq m]}. \tag{7.123}$$

The first part of this expression for a_C is symmetric in the sense that the value of this part does not change if we simultaneously swap λ_k and λ_g, as well as $\sigma_\rightarrow$ and $\sigma_\leftarrow$. It is a linear combination of weighted path lengths of λ_k and λ_g, with the same weights ρ_c. Stated otherwise it represents a *mixture* of the cost of the two trees, where the cost of λ_k contribute $\sigma_\rightarrow$ parts of the cost and λ_g contributes $\sigma_\leftarrow$ parts. If we choose trees so that they minimize the overall comparison count, there often are several choices with the same overall path length and any combination of these has the same value for this symmetric part.

The asymmetry of the partitioning algorithm manifests in the second two sums. Each considers only a part of the tree, and those parts are *disjoint*. Thereby the contribution of these two sums can be smaller than the path length of any single tree. This is where comparisons can be saved.

Dual-Pivot Quicksort. The simplest case to see the above remark in action is dual-pivot Quicksort, i.e., $s = 3$. We only have two trees to choose from, which makes four different combinations for λ_k and λ_g

Let us first assume that $m = 2$ like in the YBB Quicksort. Without sampling, all combinations then yield $\frac{5}{4}$ in the symmetric part of a_C. The reason is that the two trees have the same external path length, namely 5. For the asymmetric part, however, they differ. In the order from above, the four combinations yield additionally

$$\frac{5}{12}, \qquad \frac{1}{3} = \frac{4}{12}, \qquad \frac{1}{2} = \frac{6}{12}, \qquad \frac{5}{12}. \tag{7.124}$$

The clear winner is the second pair of trees, where we have $\lambda_k \neq \lambda_g$. This is indeed the choice of trees used in YBB Quicksort, with an overall number of $\frac{19}{12}n$ comparisons in the asymptotic average for partitioning n elements, saving $5\,\%$ of the comparisons over using one tree.

A most remarkable feature is that this is *less than the entropy bound*! Without sampling, the three leaves all have probability $\frac{1}{3}$, and entropy of this distribution is

$$\mathcal{H}_{\mathrm{ld}}\left(\tfrac{1}{3}, \tfrac{1}{3}, \tfrac{1}{3}\right) \;=\; \mathrm{ld}(3) \;=\; 1.58496\ldots \;>\; 1.58\overline{3} \;=\; \frac{19}{12}. \tag{7.125}$$

Of course, the above entropy considers the overall distribution of leaves, and is only a valid lower bound for a *single* comparison tree. There is nothing fishy in beating lower bounds that are not applicable.

We do get a valid lower bound for the two trees scenario be computing the *conditional* leaf distributions, given that we classify with λ_k resp. λ_g. In our example, these distributions are

$$\left(\frac{3}{8}, \frac{3}{8}, \frac{1}{4}\right) \quad \text{for } \lambda_k, \qquad \text{resp.} \qquad \left(\frac{1}{4}, \frac{1}{4}, \frac{1}{2}\right) \quad \text{for } \lambda_g. \tag{7.126}$$

The entropy of these distributions is $1.56128\ldots$ and 1.5, which we should compare to the expected leaf depths in λ_k and λ_g, namely 1.625 and 1.5, respectively. None is smaller than the entropy, but λ_g is in fact entropy-tight.

Dual-Pivot Quicksort with Kciwegdes-Partitioning. In terms of comparisons, we can slightly improve upon YBB Quicksort if we switch to a master segment method with $m = 1.5$. The symmetric part rises to $\frac{4}{3}$ for all tree pairs and the asymmetric part becomes

$$\frac{1}{3} = \frac{3}{9}, \qquad \frac{2}{9}, \qquad \frac{4}{9}, \qquad \frac{1}{3} = \frac{3}{9}. \tag{7.127}$$

The differences between the tree pairs becomes even more pronounced; we save $6.\overline{6}\%$ of the comparisons by using two different trees; if we use the right pair. The classification strategy corresponds exactly to *Kciwegdes partitioning* (Algorithm 7).

Intuitively the optimal choice of trees profits from the following fact: The left tree λ_k is advantageous for inputs with many small elements, as it needs only one comparison to identify these. Likewise, λ_g is good for many large ones. How often each of the two trees is used for classification is *coupled* to the number of small and large elements in the input by the way our partitioning proceeds. If there are exceptionally many small elements, we use λ_k more often than λ_g, and likewise for many large elements, λ_g is used more often. That way, we automatically use that tree more often which is better for the current input. In the formula for a_C from Equation (7.122), this shows in the asymmetric part, where we only add the costs of λ_k on the small classes and the costs of λ_g on the large classes.

The benefit of two trees is quite striking in the example above. Yet we argued in Section 7.6 and Section 7.5, that the use of two trees has negligible effect; how does that fit together? The answer is that the relative contribution of the asymmetric part of Equation (7.122) soon becomes very small when we increase the number of pivots or the sample size. To get a feeling for what "soon very small" means, let us consider another concrete example from the realistic range of parameters.

Six-way Quicksort. Let us set $s = 6$ and $m = 3$ and again assume we do not sample pivots. The optimal choice of trees is given in Figure 43; with a complete enumeration of all possibilities, we find that it is in fact the unique optimal choice.

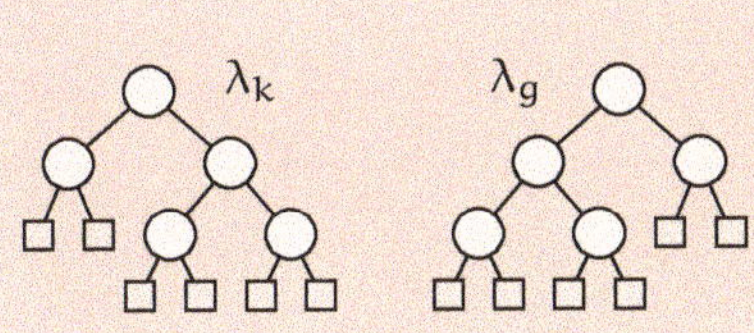

Figure 43: The optimal comparison trees λ_k (left) and λ_g (right) for $s = 6$ and $m = 3$ under equidistant sampling. The second part of Equation (7.122) considers the leftmost three leaves of λ_k and the right most three leaves of λ_g, and thus combines the inexpensive part of each tree.

Both trees have minimal path length; but there are *four more* trees with the same path length. All of these six trees would be optimal choices if we enforced $\lambda_k = \lambda_g$, but allowing two trees only the given pair is optimal. The intuitive reason is that only this pair minimizes the asymmetric contribution in Equation (7.122), by putting the high-hanging leaves all the way to the left for λ_k resp. to the right for λ_g.

The overall expected number of comparisons in one partitioning step is then $\sim \frac{55}{21}n$, whereas using any of the two trees for both λ_k and λ_g yields the coefficient $\frac{8}{3} = \frac{56}{21}$. If we swap λ_k and λ_g, we even need $\sim \frac{57}{21}n$ comparisons. The difference is clearly there, but it is small; below 2 % in this case. If we include pivot sampling, the differences become even less pronounced; the three cases above for $\mathbf{t} = (1,1,1,1,1,1)$ are $\frac{103}{39}$, $\frac{104}{39}$ resp. $\frac{105}{39}$, differing by less than 1 %.

General Perspective: Varying s. In the above examples we found that the benefit of allowing $\lambda_k \neq \lambda_g$ drops when we make s and/or k larger. The general picture is somewhat richer, so let us examine it in a little more detail. Figure 44 shows the savings from using the optimal pair of comparison trees, where two different trees are allowed, over the optimal choice for a single tree, in a range of practical values for s. Here, we assume that no sampling is used to pick pivots. Also, we let $m = s/2$, which means that λ_k and λ_g are each used for half of the classifications in expectation, maximizing the effect of two trees.

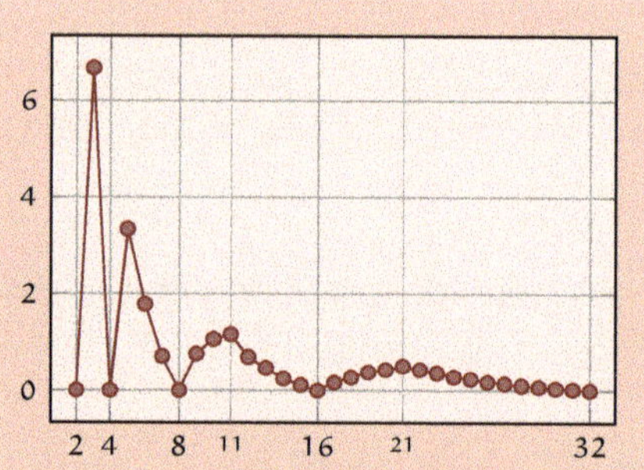

Figure 44: Improvement by using the optimal pair of comparison trees over the optimal choice upon enforcing $\lambda_k = \lambda_g$. The x axis shows s in the range from 2 to 32, the y axis the savings of two trees in percent when pivots are chosen at random, i.e., with $\mathbf{t} = 0$, and we choose $m = s/2$.

Indeed, the overall picture is that for $s \geqslant 12$, less than 1 % is gained from using two trees, which might be deemed as unobservable in practice. Moreover, there are no savings at all if s is a power of two in the given range. With symmetric sampling, the complete binary search tree is the optimal choice for both λ_k and λ_g, even if they are allowed to differ. Between two consecutive powers of two, savings first increase and then drop again.

Let us see whether we can transfer the above observations to all s and give a rigorous proof. With $\mathbf{t} = 0$ and $m = s/2$, Equation (7.99) simplifies to

$$a_C = \sum_{c \in \mathcal{C}} \lambda_k(c) \cdot \frac{\frac{1}{s}(\lfloor s/2 \rfloor + [c = s])}{s - [m \notin \mathbb{N}] + [c \neq m]} + \sum_{c \in \mathcal{C}} \lambda_g(c) \cdot \frac{\frac{1}{s}(\lfloor s/2 \rfloor + [c = 1])}{s - [m \notin \mathbb{N}] + [c \neq m]} . \tag{7.128}$$

For simplicity let us confine ourselves to even s, then we have $m \in \mathbb{N}$, i.e., a master-pivot method. In this case, we get the following weights for λ_k:

$$w^{(k)} = \left(\overbrace{\frac{s/2+1}{s(s+1)}, \ldots, \frac{s/2+1}{s(s+1)}}^{s/2 \text{ terms}}, \overbrace{\frac{s/2}{s(s+1)}, \ldots, \frac{s/2}{s(s+1)}}^{s/2 \text{ terms}} \right)$$

$$\propto \left(1 + \tfrac{2}{s}, \ldots, 1 + \tfrac{2}{s}, 1, \ldots, 1 \right).$$

For λ_g we get the same weights reversed, $w^{(g)} \propto (1, \ldots, 1, 1 + \tfrac{2}{s}, \ldots, 1 + \tfrac{2}{s})$. The weights are very close to uniform, but with a slight surplus in one half. In particular, they are within a factor of two for any $s \geqslant 4$, so that we know by Proposition 7.18 that there is an optimal almost complete binary search tree. In any almost complete binary tree on s leaves, we have the same number of leaves on the lower level, namely $\mathit{lll} = \mathit{lll}(s) := 2(s - 2^{\lfloor \mathrm{ld}(s) \rfloor})$ many: starting with a complete binary tree for the last power of two, each additional leaf lands in the lower level *and* it pushes one of old leaves down.

As our weights are sorted, the best we can do for λ_k obviously is to have cheap leaves as far to the left as possible. More specifically, λ_k^* is the tree where the rightmost $\mathit{lll}(s)$ nodes are at depth $\lfloor \mathrm{ld}(s) \rfloor + 1$ and the remaining $s - \mathit{lll}(s)$ are at depth $\lfloor \mathrm{ld}(s) \rfloor$. λ_g^* similarly has *leftmost* $\mathit{lll}(s)$ nodes at depth $\lfloor \mathrm{ld}(s) \rfloor + 1$ and the others at depth $\lfloor \mathrm{ld}(s) \rfloor$. For the single-tree case, any of these maximally balanced trees are optimal, so we can compare the comparison count of $(\lambda_k^*, \lambda_g^*)$ to say $\lambda_k = \lambda_g = \lambda_k^*$.

It is immediately clear from the above discussion that if s is a power of two, i.e., $\mathit{lll}(s) = 0$, both λ_k^* and λ_g^* are the complete binary tree, and indeed no savings over the single-tree case are achieved. For other values of s, the costs of the single-tree choice are

$$a_C^{(1)} = \lfloor \mathrm{ld}(s) \rfloor + \frac{\mathit{lll}}{s}. \tag{7.129}$$

For two trees with even s, overall costs are by symmetry twice the weighted path length for λ_k^*, which after some computation yields

$$a_C^{(2)} = \lfloor \mathrm{ld}(s) \rfloor + \frac{\mathit{lll}}{s+1} + \left[\mathit{lll} > \tfrac{s}{2} \right] \cdot \frac{2\frac{\mathit{lll}}{s} - 1}{s+1}, \tag{7.130}$$

and for the difference we get

$$a_C^{(1)} - a_C^{(2)} = \frac{\mathit{lll}}{s(s+1)} - \frac{[\mathit{lll} > \tfrac{s}{2}](2\frac{\mathit{lll}}{s} - 1)}{s+1} \tag{7.131}$$

$$= \begin{cases} \dfrac{\mathit{lll}}{s(s+1)}, & \mathit{lll} \leqslant s/2; \\[2mm] \dfrac{s - \mathit{lll}}{s(s+1)}, & \mathit{lll} > s/2. \end{cases} \tag{7.132}$$

The absolute benefit of using two trees is maximal for $\mathit{lll} = s/2$, where we save $\frac{1}{2(s+1)}$ comparisons per element on average, which is rapidly shrinking with s.

The two coefficients $a_C^{(1)}$ and $a_C^{(2)}$ are compared in Figure 45; they are divided by the common scale $\mathrm{ld}(s)$. While the two functions differ substantially for small s, they soon

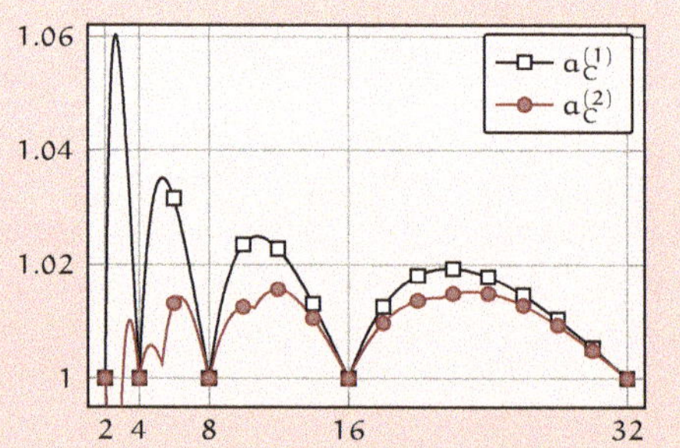

Figure 45: Leading term coefficient a_C of the number of comparisons in one s-way partitioning step with $m = s/2$ and $t = 0$, normalized by $\mathrm{ld}(s)$, i.e., the plot shows the functions given in Equations (7.129) and (7.130) divided by $\mathrm{ld}(s)$. Only even integer values are algorithmically meaningful, but it is interesting to see the behavior of the function also in between.

look very similar. When comparing this to Figure 44, note that there we show the *relative* savings, which is the difference from Equation (7.132) divided by $a_C^{(1)}$. The relative savings thus even drop at a rate of $O(\frac{1}{s\log s})$.

Strictly speaking, we have only considered the case of even s in detail here, but it is intuitively clear that the odd case will not differ by much, in particular if s becomes large.

General Perspective: Varying k.   We discussed at some length how savings decrease with growing s, while keeping $t = 0$ fixed. Let us now also consider the effect of sampling, for the value of s where the largest benefits are to be expected, namely for dual-pivot Quicksort. We thus fix $s = 3$ and $m = 1.5$ here. Let us start by expressing the leading-term coefficient a_C for the number of comparisons in one partitioning step in terms of κ and $\tau = (\tau_1, \tau_2, \tau_3)$. We find

$$
\begin{aligned}
a_C \;=\;\; & \tau_1 \frac{\tau_1 \kappa + 1}{(1 - \tau_2)\kappa + 1} \cdot \lambda_k(s_2) + \tau_2 \frac{\tau_1}{1 - \tau_2} \cdot \lambda_k(m) + \tau_3 \frac{\tau_1 \kappa}{(1 - \tau_2)\kappa + 1} \cdot \lambda_k(1_2) \\
+\;& \tau_1 \frac{\tau_3 \kappa}{(1 - \tau_2)\kappa + 1} \cdot \lambda_g(s_2) + \tau_2 \frac{\tau_3}{1 - \tau_2} \cdot \lambda_g(m) + \tau_3 \frac{\tau_3 \kappa + 1}{(1 - \tau_2)\kappa + 1} \cdot \lambda_g(1_2).
\end{aligned}
$$

$$(7.133)$$

Note the asymmetries between the weights for λ_k and λ_g, indicating that in general, $\lambda_k^* \neq \lambda_g^*$ is possible. The asymmetries vanish in the limit, though, when the vector $\tau \in (0, 1)^3$ is fixed:

$$
\begin{aligned}
a_C \;=\;\; & \frac{\tau_1}{1 - \tau_2}\big(\tau_1 \lambda_k(s_2) + \tau_2 \lambda_k(m) + \tau_3 \lambda_k(1_2)\big) \\
+\;& \frac{\tau_3}{1 - \tau_2}\big(\tau_1 \lambda_g(s_2) + \tau_2 \lambda_g(m) + \tau_3 \lambda_g(1_2)\big) \;\pm\; O(\kappa^{-1}), \qquad (\kappa \to \infty). \quad (7.134)
\end{aligned}
$$

Thus, when the sample size goes to infinity, there is an optimal choice $(\lambda_k^*, \lambda_g^*)$ with $\lambda_k^* = \lambda_g^*$ and the benefit of allowing two trees is zero. Note that this is not a special feature of dual-pivot Quicksort: we get the same weights for both trees for *any* s when we fix τ and let $\kappa \to \infty$.

Let us therefore consider in some detail how the benefit changes when we keep a sample size k fixed, but choose different order statistics of this sample as pivots. For two

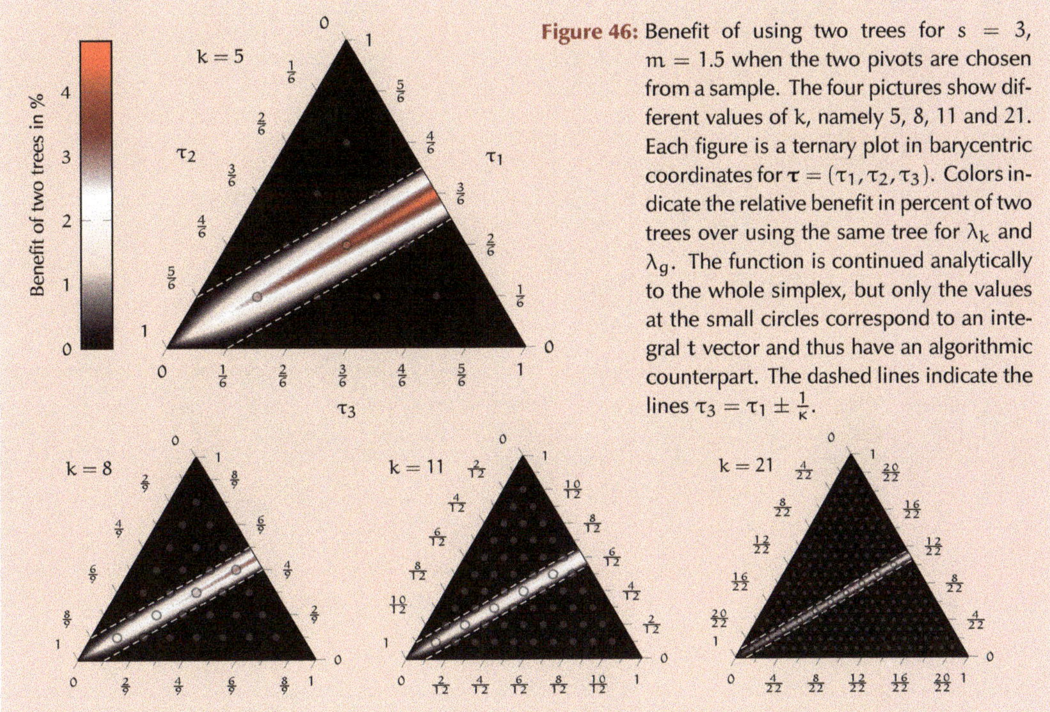

Figure 46: Benefit of using two trees for $s = 3$, $m = 1.5$ when the two pivots are chosen from a sample. The four pictures show different values of k, namely 5, 8, 11 and 21. Each figure is a ternary plot in barycentric coordinates for $\boldsymbol{\tau} = (\tau_1, \tau_2, \tau_3)$. Colors indicate the relative benefit in percent of two trees over using the same tree for λ_k and λ_g. The function is continued analytically to the whole simplex, but only the values at the small circles correspond to an integral t vector and thus have an algorithmic counterpart. The dashed lines indicate the lines $\tau_3 = \tau_1 \pm \frac{1}{\kappa}$.

pivots the sampling vectors $\boldsymbol{\tau}$ lie in a two-dimensional simplex, so we can still sensibly visualize their effect. Figure 46 does this for the benefit of two trees. The first impression probably is black dominates the picture: for a large region of possible sampling vectors, there is no (visible) benefit.

In fact, a moments reflection on Equation (7.133) shows that if $\tau_1 \geqslant \tau_3 + \frac{1}{\kappa}$, we have a larger weight for s_2 than for l_2 not only for λ_k, but also for λ_g. Hence, the tree with the smaller pivot P_1 in the root is optimal for both, and there is no advantage in allowing two different trees. Similarly we get twice the tree with root P_2, whenever $\tau_3 \geqslant \tau_1 + \frac{1}{\kappa}$. So the whole region outside the dashed lines in Figure 46 does not only look dark, it is perfectly black: the benefit is precisely zero there.

It is intuitive that the maximal savings are achieved for $\boldsymbol{\tau} = (\frac{1}{2}, 0, \frac{1}{2})$. Medium elements need two comparisons in any comparison tree, so their presence only weakens savings from two trees. This matches the behavior shown in Figure 46. The dashed lines there approach each other if κ, i.e., the sample size, grows, and so the margin for two trees shrinks. And also, the absolute value of savings seems to drop rapidly with the sample size.

Figure 47 confirms this claim. It shows the behavior of the savings for two points of the simplex, namely $\boldsymbol{\tau} = (\frac{1}{3}, \frac{1}{3}, \frac{1}{3})$ and $\boldsymbol{\tau} = (\frac{1}{2}, 0, \frac{1}{2})$, as k varies. The benefit is rapidly dropping with k, but for reasonable sample sizes, it is still over 2%. By inserting into

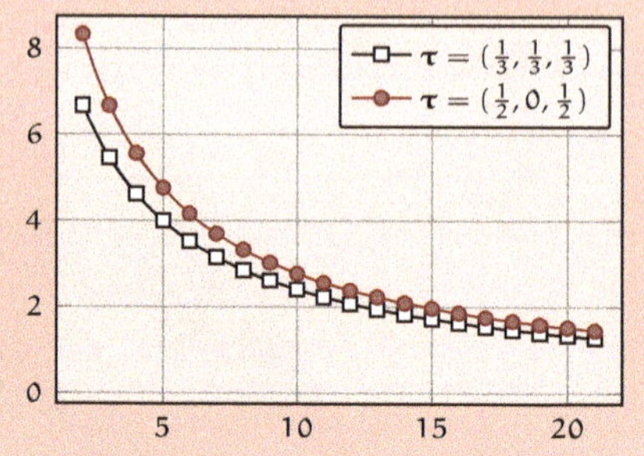

Figure 47: Benefit of two trees for $s = 3$ and $m = 1.5$ when sampling with $\tau = (\frac{1}{3}, \frac{1}{3}, \frac{1}{3})$ or $\tau = (\frac{1}{2}, 0, \frac{1}{2})$. The x-axis shows the sample size k, the y-axis shows relative savings in percent. In fact, the two shown functions are $\frac{60}{2k+5}$ and $\frac{100}{3k+6}$.

Equation (7.133), one finds that with $\tau = (\frac{1}{3}, \frac{1}{3}, \frac{1}{3})$ two trees save us, per element and partitioning step, precisely $\frac{1}{2k+5}$ comparisons in expectation; for $\tau = (\frac{1}{2}, 0, \frac{1}{2})$ it is slightly more, namely $\frac{1}{2k+4}$.

Enforcing Different Trees Can Hurt.   We have seen that there is some potential for savings with using two different trees, but it quickly becomes insignificant for growing sample sizes. Moreover it is a narrowing region for quantiles vectors τ, for which the option to use two trees helps, at all, see Figure 46. Things are even worse, if we fix instead of τ the trees that we use:

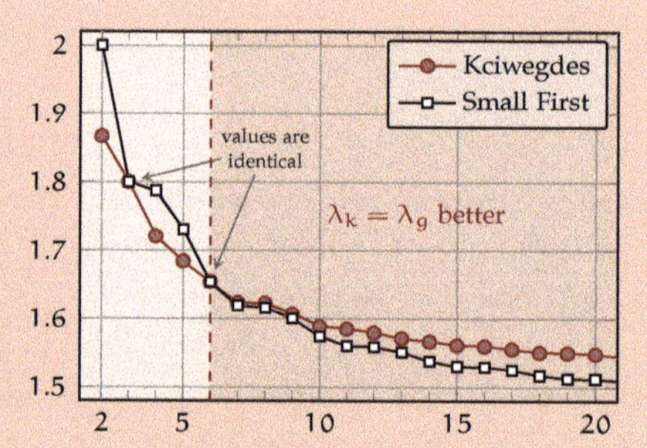

Figure 48: Comparison counts for Kciwegdes partitioning and $\lambda_k = \lambda_g =$ (Small First) with optimal sampling. The x-axis shows the sample size k, the y-axis the leading-term coefficient of the number of comparisons, where for each algorithm and k, the comparison-optimal τ is chosen. For $k \geqslant 6$, enforcing two trees as in Kciwegdes is *worse*.

Figure 48 shows that when we choose the best sampling vector t separately for the two strategies $(\lambda_k, \lambda_g) = ($, $)$ and $(\lambda_k, \lambda_g) = ($, $)$, we find savings only for $k \leqslant 5$; for larger sample sizes, it actually *hurts* to enforce the use of two different trees! We already noticed that we do not achieve the information-theoretic lower bound for YBB Quicksort in the exact-quantiles limit; but it is still surprising how little a sample suffices to outperform classification with two trees.

Figure 48 shows the situation only for $s = 3$ and $m = 1.5$. The plot for YBB Quicksort looks very similar, and also for larger s, choosing $\lambda_k \neq \lambda_g$ is better only for the first few values of k, even if we compare with a method that uses a single, but very unbalanced tree. If we can sample with sufficient accuracy, tuning the quantiles vector to *one* tree seems to outweigh by far what we save by beating the entropy using two trees.

7.7.7 Concluding Remarks on Optimal Comparison Trees

In this section, we considered how to choose the two comparisons trees. Roughly speaking, there are two regimes that require different choices:

If either the number of segments s is relatively large, say $s \geqslant 6$, or if the sample size k is relatively large, say $k \geqslant 5$, or both are relatively large, then the choice of two different trees is not rewarding. If the sample size is really large, it is important to *not* use two different trees, but which tree is chosen is not important, if we can choose the corresponding quantiles vector $\boldsymbol{\tau}$. In these cases, we should let other cost measures guide the choice for $\boldsymbol{\tau}$, and then choose a single comparison tree that fits the sampling vector. We recapitulated algorithms for finding such trees in Section 7.7.3.

In the practically relevant regime of small s and k, the option to use two different trees can be helpful; it depends on the sampling vector then. Again a good advise is to choose a **t** so that other cost measures are optimized, and then consider which trees are best. As shown in Section 7.7.2, we can use the same algorithms to independently find the best choices for λ_k and λ_g. This may save a few comparisons without increasing costs.

7.8 Interactions between Parameters: The Jellyfish Paradox

Humans seem to strive for symmetry whenever they can. In Quicksort that means equidistant $\mathbf{t} = (t, \ldots, t)$ for a $t \in \mathbb{N}_0$, $m = s/2$ and comparison trees λ_k and λ_g as close to complete binary trees as possible. Symmetric parameter choices have been used in many works on Quicksort without discussing alternatives. This is often legitimate; after all, comparison costs are highly symmetric among the classes, only restricted by classes being ordered.

If s is not a power of two, we cannot get perfect symmetry in trees, but we expect optimal comparison trees to be almost balanced and **t**-vectors that are almost equidistant. Mimicking the tree, **t** will slightly deviate from perfect symmetry to exploit the inevitable tiny asymmetries in the tree. Also **t** has to be an integer vector, so for certain sample sizes, we will have inevitable asymmetries due to rounding.

If, however, s is a power of two and κ is a multiple of s, no such obstacles exist and I expected at least the following statement to be true.

Plausibe Statement 7.23: Assume, we require $\lambda_k = \lambda_g$ and consider $s = 2^h$ with $h \in \mathbb{N}$. The sample size is $k = (s-1) + ts$, so that $(t, \ldots, t)$ is a possible sampling vector. If we are free to choose the comparison tree λ_k and **t**, so that the overall number of comparisons is minimized (in the asymptotic average), then the optimal choice is equidistant sampling $\mathbf{t}^* = (t, \ldots, t)$ and the complete binary search trees (for both λ_k^* and λ_g^*). ◄

It was surprisingly hard to prove this statement; which is, mostly, because it is not correct. As the statement seems so natural, I had been willing to believe it for some time, even though it resisted all attempts to prove it. This belief had been reinforced by the fact that for any reasonable choices for the parameters, it is in fact the case that symmetric tree and **t** are optimal: For $h = 1, \ldots, 8$, Statement 7.23 is true. Intriguingly, in general it is not.

Before we consider counterexamples, let us recapitulate evidence for the plausibility of Statement 7.23. First, the statement is true in the limit for $t \to \infty$: balanced tree and quantiles vector form an *entropy-tight pair*, so they achieve the information-theoretic lower bound for $k \to \infty$ (Proposition 7.5 on page 236). For finite k, we have $\mathbf{t}^* = (t, \ldots, t)$ if we fix λ_k and λ_g to both the complete tree. Likewise if we fix the equidistant sampling vector, the optimal choice for the comparison trees is the complete BST. The symmetric choice thus forms a *Nash equilibrium*: no unilateral change can improve the outcome. Should that not imply that it is an optimal choice then?

Well, no. As for the famous example in game theory, the *prisoner's dilemma,* a Nash equilibrium is not necessarily a global optimum. The two prisoners could both improve their situation if both decided—simultaneously!—to not betray each other.

So how shall we escape the trap of symmetry? Proposition 7.5 provides guidance: the local optima of the parameter landscape are precisely the entropy-tight pairs of trees and quantiles vectors; but in the limit $k \to \infty$, they all have the same value and are *all* global optima.

So let us start with the equidistant sampling vector $\mathbf{t}_{ed} = (1, \ldots, 1)$ and tinker with it locally—just enough to jump to the next entropy-tight pair, i.e., the next comparison tree. We consider for $s = 2^h$ the sampling vector $\tilde{\mathbf{t}} = (3, 1, 0, 0, 1, 1, 1, 1, \ldots)$, i.e., the first four entries are special, the remaining ones are 1. The corresponding sample size is $k = 2s - 1$.

For the trees, we also start with $\lambda_{\text{complete}}$, the complete binary search tree. For $s \geqslant 4$ it contains the subtree with root P_2 and children P_1 and P_3, that is the leftmost subtree of three internal nodes. This subtree is replaced in $\tilde{\lambda}$ by the tree with root P_1 followed by P_2 and P_3. This process is shown in Figure 49.

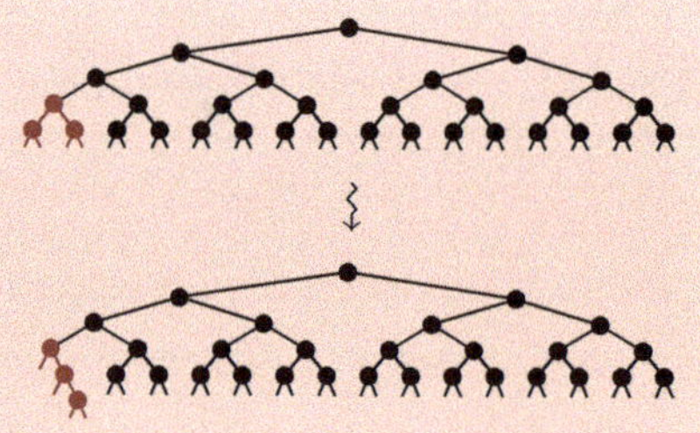

Figure 49: The tinkered-with tree $\tilde{\lambda}$ for $s = 2^5 = 32$ and how it results from the corresponding complete BST. The depth vector of the resulting tree is $\tilde{\lambda} = (4, 5, 6, 6, 5, 5, 5, \ldots, 5)$ instead of 5 for all classes.

Let us compute the number of comparisons we get with $\tilde{\mathbf{t}}$ and $\tilde{\lambda}$. Recall that $\kappa = 2s$ and that $a_C = \lambda^{\mathsf{T}}\tau$, so

$$a_C(\tilde{\lambda}, \tilde{\mathbf{t}}) \;=\; \mathrm{ld}(s) - \frac{4}{2s} + 2 \cdot \frac{1}{2s} \;=\; \mathrm{ld}(s) - \frac{1}{s}. \tag{7.135}$$

For the discrete entropy we find

$$\mathcal{H}(\tilde{\mathbf{t}}) \;=\; -\mathrm{hd}_\kappa\!\left(\tfrac{1}{s}\right) - \frac{4}{\kappa}\left(\mathrm{hd}_\kappa\!\left(\tfrac{4}{\kappa}\right) - \mathrm{hd}_\kappa\!\left(\tfrac{1}{s}\right)\right) - 2 \cdot \frac{1}{\kappa}\left(\mathrm{hd}_\kappa\!\left(\tfrac{1}{\kappa}\right) - \mathrm{hd}_\kappa\!\left(\tfrac{1}{s}\right)\right) \tag{7.136}$$

$$=\; -\mathrm{hd}_\kappa\!\left(\tfrac{1}{s}\right) - \frac{2}{3s} \tag{7.137}$$

$$= H_{2s} - \frac{2}{3s} - \frac{3}{2}. \tag{7.138}$$

For the overall number of comparisons, we thus make both numerator and denominator slightly smaller. When we compare the quotient to the corresponding one for t_{ed} and $\lambda_{complete}$, $-\mathrm{ld}(s)/\mathrm{hd}_\kappa(1/s)$, we find that the symmetric choice needs very slightly more comparisons for $s \geqslant 402$, see Figure 50.

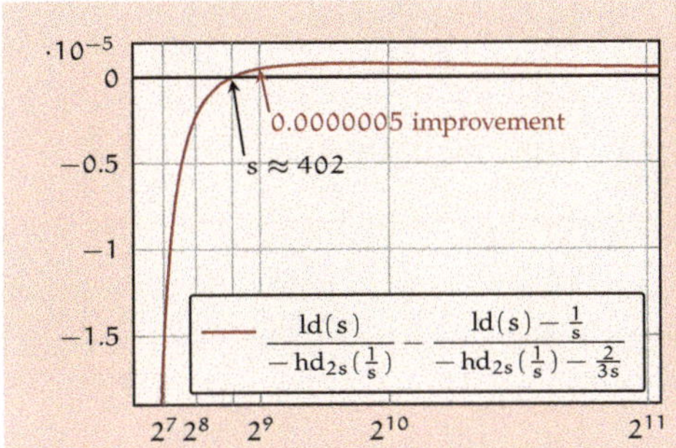

Figure 50: Benefit of using the tinkered with comparison tree and sampling vector $(\tilde{\lambda}, \tilde{t})$ over the symmetric choice $(\lambda_{complete}, t_{ed})$. For $s \geqslant 401$ the function is positive.

Of course, the above formula is only valid for s a power of two. The smallest s for which our tinkered pair is in fact better than the symmetric choice is thus $s = 512$: we reduce the leading-term coefficient by *half of a millionth*! This improvement, no matter how ridiculously small, clearly disproves our Plausible Statement 7.23. Our intuitions about the value of symmetry have been ruthlessly shattered to pieces.

◆　　◆　　◆

The tinkered tree from above is better than the complete BST; but can we do even better? Let us see if we can come up with a maybe less plausible, but more true statement than our first attempt about the optimal pair of tree and sampling vector. The essence of the above construction was to apply the rule

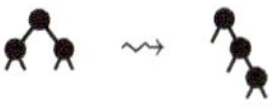

on the lowest level of the complete binary search tree. If *one* application of that rule could do good, how much better will repeated application on *all* three-node-subtrees do? The resulting tree is shown in Figure 51; we will call it the *jellyfish tree*.

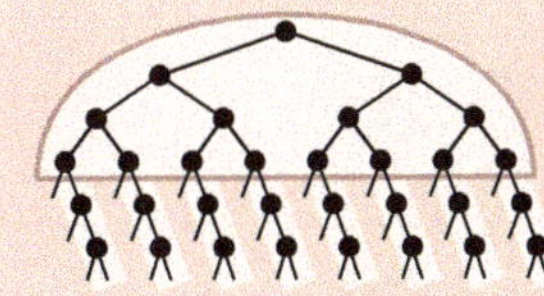

Figure 51: The jellyfish tree for $s = 2^5 = 32$. It results from replacing all balanced three-node trees on the lower level by a linear list of the three nodes. The depth vector is always of the form $\lambda = \mathrm{ld}(s) + (-1, 0, 1, 1, -1, 0, 1, 1, \ldots)$

The jellyfish tree and the sampling vector $(3, 0, 1, 1,\ 3, 0, 1, 1, \ldots)$ form an entropy-tight pair. Using these, the expected number of comparisons is

$$a_C \;=\; \mathrm{ld}(s) - \frac{s}{4} \cdot \frac{1}{s} \;=\; \mathrm{ld}(s) - \frac{1}{4} \tag{7.139}$$

and

$$\mathcal{H} \;=\; -\mathrm{hd}_\kappa\!\left(\tfrac{1}{s}\right) - \frac{s}{4} \cdot \frac{2}{3s} \;=\; -\mathrm{hd}_\kappa\!\left(\tfrac{1}{s}\right) - \frac{1}{6}. \tag{7.140}$$

The behavior of the quotient of these two is very similar to Figure 50, in fact we again get an improvement when $s \geqslant 402$. For $s = 512$, the leading term is smaller than for the symmetric tree and sampling by 0.00007; better than above, even though still negligible. Is the jellyfish optimal?

To find a definitive answer for at least the special case $s = 512$ and $\kappa = 2s$, let us consider all possibilities; it is just a finite problem. The number of BSTs on n internal nodes is C_n, the nth Catalan number. The number of $\mathbf{t}$ vectors is $\binom{\kappa-1}{s-1}$ because $\sigma = \mathbf{t} + 1$ is isomorphic to the integer compositions of κ with exactly s nonzero summands. We obtain these compositions, in unary notation, by laying out κ ones in a row and then throwing in $s - 1$ commas at a random subset of the $\kappa - 1$ gaps between the ones. For our parameter values, we had better not wait for a dull enumeration of all cases to finish in this life: there are roughly $2.19 \cdot 10^{303}$ search trees to consider, *times* $2.24 \cdot 10^{306}$ sampling vectors.

We can of course do better than that. First, we need not enumerate all trees, it suffices to consider the best tree for each $\mathbf{t}$. We can *compute* this tree with the algorithms described in Section 7.7.3. Moreover, there is a lot of symmetry in the problem that we can exploit.

Lemma 7.24 (Sorted leaf-depth trees): *Let $\lambda \in \mathbb{N}^s$. If there exists an extended binary tree λ whose leaves are at depths λ, then there is also an extended binary tree λ_{sort} with leaves at depth λ_{sort}, where λ_{sort} results from sorting λ ascendingly.* ◀

Proof: Imagine we construct λ bottom-up and level-wise according to the sequence of leaf depths λ. By assumption, there is a way to pair adjacent leaves for all maximal depth entries, otherwise there would remain a dangling leaf. Each of these pairs forms the two children of a new internal node. For the remaining construction, these internal nodes are regarded as leaves of depth one less, and we apply the same procedure again. This constructs the unique extended binary tree for a given leaf-depth profile—if one exists. Otherwise it fails at some stage to form pairs, either because the number is odd, or because maximal depth nodes are not adjacent.

In essence, the latter can never happen for sorted depth profiles, so finding a tree is only easier there. Formally, we prove by induction on the number of different leaf depths that we can mimic the construction on λ for λ_{sort}.

If all leaves are at the same level, the tree already has sorted leaf-depths. Otherwise, we can merge maximal-depth nodes in pairs by assumption, in particular their number is even, and obtain a new depth profile λ' with fewer different depths. By the inductive hypothesis, we can construct a sorted-depth tree on λ'_{sort}.

Now for our original depth vector λ_{sort}, we can thus perform the same merges of maximal-depth leaves and then obtain λ'_{sort}. We then obtain λ_{sort}, the tree with leaf-depths λ_{sort} from tree λ'_{sort} by adding the maximal-depth leaves as children of the rightmost leaves in λ'_{sort}. This concludes the inductive step. ∎

By Lemma 7.24 it suffices to consider *sorted* sampling vectors, as for any tree with a given depth profile, an equivalent one with sorted depths exists. Sorted vectors σ correspond to integer partitions of κ into exactly s summands; for our example there are $4\,453\,575\,699\,570\,940\,947\,378 \approx 4.45 \cdot 10^{21}$ such partitions [188]; better, but still way too many to consider all.

The next observation is that many of these sampling vectors will now make a comparison tree optimal, for which they do not form an entropy-tight distribution. Given that tree, we can do strictly better with another sampling vector, and the first vector cannot possibly be optimal. In light of Fact 2.50 (page 88), we can *restrict entries in σ to be powers of two*; other sampling vectors cannot yield entropy tight distributions τ. The number of partitions of $2 \cdot 512$ into 512 summands from the set $\{1, 2, 4, 8, 16, 32, 64, 128, 256, 512\}$ is $1\,139\,328$. That is a number we can deal with.

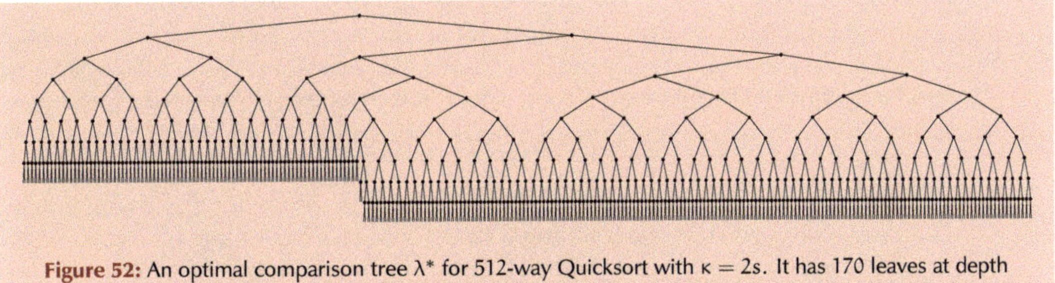

Figure 52: An optimal comparison tree λ^* for 512-way Quicksort with $\kappa = 2s$. It has 170 leaves at depth 8, 2 leaves at depth 9 and the remaining 340 leaves at depth 10. (The reader is cordially invited to verify these numbers in the picture.) The corresponding complete BST has all leaves at depth 9.

A hardly optimized implementation with symbolic computation in *Mathematica* took two days to finally find the optimal tree and sampling vector pair: the tree is shown in Figure 52, the corresponding sampling vector is $(3, \ldots, 3, 1, 1, 0 \ldots, 0)$, where we have 170 times a 3, two ones and 340 times a 0. The overall number of comparisons for these parameters is $1.49762\,19880n \ln n$, which improves the leading-term coefficient by 0.000088 over the symmetric case, only a tiny bit better than the jellyfish tree.

Of course, the found pair is merely a representative for a whole class of trees and vectors that share the same profile. We can freely permute the leaf-depth vector and t simultaneously without changing costs, as long as a binary tree with such leaf depths exists.

◆   ◆   ◆

Even with the above tricks, the exhaustive search becomes infeasible for larger values of s or k. The given parameters $s = 512$ and $k = 1023$ are the smallest where the symmetric choice is no longer optimal, but at the same time, it is the largest that we can deal with using our current methods. I am therefore reluctant to utter a conjecture based on so little reliable information, and prefer to leave this problem open.

Open Problem 7.25 (Characterize Optimal Comparison Trees and Sampling Vectors):
Let s and sample size k be fixed. Consider the family of s-way Quicksort variants with parameter λ, where we set $\lambda_k = \lambda_g = \lambda$ and **t** so that the overall number of comparisons for the given comparison tree is minimized. Find a characterization for optimal comparison trees λ. A result for the simplifying assumptions $s = 2^h$ for $h \in \mathbb{N}$ and $\kappa = k + 1 = s2^q$ for $q \in \mathbb{N}$, is already welcome. Here we can choose τ as the entropy-tight distribution for λ. ◄

Summary.   In the exact-quantiles case, the interaction of sampling vectors and comparison trees reduces to optimality of *all* entropy-tight pairs. This changes for finite sample sizes. Even Quicksort experts might find it surprising that the complete binary search tree is *not* optimal in general with finite-size sampling. The actual optimal pairs deviate locally quite a bit from symmetric choices. Their characterization remains an open problem.

Intriguing though it may be, the advantage of asymmetry kicks in only for astronomic parameter values: we need $s \geqslant 512$ segments and sample size $k \geqslant 1023$. Moreover its net effect is so tiny that it will most probably not be detectable even in targeted experiments.

With the intriguing comments on the jellyfish paradox we close our discussion of s-way Quicksort with generic one-pass partitioning. We have shown that through careful analysis, we can learn a lot about an algorithm, and that sometimes, intuitive algorithmic choices can be wrong. Then it is good to have mathematical tools to support our decisions.

There is a danger of getting lost in the details of analysis. In Chapter 9, we will zoom out a little and try to give concrete recommendations for practical parameter choices.

Before we do so, however, we consider the practically important situation of inputs with equal keys. If our findings in this chapter were valid only for the case of random permutations, they would be of limited value. Fortunately, we will see that many properties carry over, if some additional precautions are taken.

8

Equal Keys

Contents

Efficient handling of equal keys in the input is a relevant issue in practice, so relevant that productive-use implementations employ a partitioning method tailored specifically to cope well with duplicates. Our study up to now completely ignored this: under the random-permutation model all keys are distinct. We found that multiway Quicksort has great potential to speed up future library sorting methods on distinct keys, but unless we can make them perform similarly well on inputs with equal keys, practitioners will not accept them: when Bentley and McIlroy designed their Quicksort version for the C library, they found *"that it was unthinkable to replace a library routine with a program that was inferior on a common class of inputs: many users sort precisely to bring together equal elements"* ([20], p. 1256). It is the purpose of this chapter to study the average behavior of Quicksort in sensible models of inputs with equal keys.

Chapter Overview.   We briefly motivate the study of equal keys (Section 8.1) and present models for random inputs with equal keys (Section 8.2). Next, we review previous work on the analysis of Quicksort on inputs with equal keys in Section 8.3.

In Section 8.4 we discuss fat-pivot partitioning methods, i.e., methods that collect elements equal to pivots in a separate segment. We analyze the costs of the proposed methods in Section 8.5. To obtain the total costs, we again set up a distributional recurrence (Section 8.6) that we solve asymptotically using the correspondence between Quicksort and search trees; this connection is detailed in Section 8.7 and applied to the Quicksort recurrence in Section 8.8. Finally, Section 8.9 contains a few comments on the algorithmic implications of our analysis.

8.1 Introduction

The *togetherness problem* consists in grouping a list of elements w.r.t. a certain attribute. This task arises for example in a database system serving an SQL query with a GROUP BY clause. Consider for example the following query (taken from the SQL tutorial of *w3school.com*, see `http://www.w3schools.com/sql/sql_groupby.asp`)

```
SELECT Shippers.ShipperName, COUNT(Orders.OrderID) AS NumberOfOrders
FROM Orders LEFT JOIN Shippers ON Orders.ShipperID=Shippers.ShipperID
GROUP BY ShipperName;
```

This query returns a list of all shippers and the number of orders they served. The result is produced in three steps:

1. first, we produce the list of all pairs of shippers and corresponding orders (using the JOIN operation);

2. then, we GROUP these pairs BY their first component, the shipper name; and

3. finally, we determine in one pass the length of each block of pairs with the same shipper (COUNT). These lengths are the sought numbers of orders.

Unless we know up front which shippers we have, or that there will be only very few shippers in total, the second step is most conveniently and efficiently done by *sorting* the list of pairs according to their first component. In this sorting process, we expect to see a lot of equal keys.

One might try to find a sorting method that handles such inputs particularly well, but it is not so unlikely, and quite sensible in terms of development costs, that a general-purpose sorting method like Quicksort is used also for such applications instead; the quote from above supports this point.

Quicksort is extremely well-understood under the random-permutation model; in comparison, its behavior on inputs with equal keys is a terra incognita. This not to say that nothing has been done; we review previous work on Quicksort with equal keys in Section 8.3. But we can still give a comprehensive overview of all relevant work on the analysis of Quicksort with equals in those few pages.

One reason for this fact probably is that unlike for random permutations, there are several sensible models for inputs with equal keys. The most natural model in my eyes is that we have a *random u-ary word,* i.e., a uniformly chosen word over the alphabet $\{1,\ldots,u\}$ of length n. This is the model we will focus on in this chapter.

Most previous works consider what we call the *exact-profile model:* the input is a random permutation of a *fixed* multiset of size n, taken from the numbers $\{1,\ldots,u\}$. In the analysis, we then have to deal with a vector of parameters, namely the multiplicities of the u numbers, and this seems only tractable for the simplest cases.

For drawing algorithmic conclusions, the exact-profile model is a bit unwieldy, and in fact, researchers mostly used those results to derive the behavior in the random-u-ary-word model. Skipping this detour in our analysis, we will, for the first time ever, be able to analyze s-way Quicksort with pivot sampling on inputs with equal keys.

As a result we are able to confirm in part a conjecture of Sedgewick and Bentley [163] from 1999; see Conjecture 8.5 (page 292).

8.1.1 Ignoring Equals

We have carefully designed partitioning methods that excel on random permutations, and we might be unwilling to change these; how bad can the performance on an average input with equal keys get? The quick answer is: really bad in general, but not too bad, if we are a bit careful. We will not give a rigorous analysis of this case here, but discuss the order of growth.

Assume first a method where all duplicates of a pivot end up in the same subproblem. This is the case for all methods that use a single comparison tree, and hence (implicitly) for methods with $m = 0$ or $m = s$ like Lomuto partitioning. If we consider a random input of size n under the random-u-ary-word model, there is at least one value $v \in [u]$ that occurs $X_v \geqslant \frac{n}{u}$ times in the input. This block of equal keys is never split across two segments by assumption; so we reduce the size of the v-block by at most $s - 1$ copies in each partitioning step, namely only when a pivot has value v. We thus need at least $\frac{n}{u(s-1)}$ partitioning steps to put all v-copies in place. Since s is constant, this implies cost of at least $\Omega\big((n/u)^2\big)$.

If u is constant, this is quadratic in n; a catastrophe. Later, we consider the case where u grows with n, but not too quickly: $u = O(n^{1/3})$. Then the above arguments still imply costs $\Omega(n^{4/3})$. For large n it is very likely that we will have roughly n/u copies of *all* values v, and so the true costs are probably closer to $\Theta(n^{5/3})$. We certainly need something better than that.

We can substantially improve the behavior on equal keys, if we distribute duplicates over two segments. Generic one-pass partitioning with its two comparison trees offers a natural way to achieve that without any overhead. We discussed this in Section 4.3, and the tie-breaking rule given there achieves that duplicates classified by λ_k go to the larger of the two possible classes, and those classified by λ_g go to the smaller of two possible classes. This generalizes Singleton's idea to *stop on equals* [170].

The precise analysis of such partitioning schemes under the random-u-ary-word model is challenging; note in particular that subproblems in this case are *not* random u-ary words again, but tend to have fewer copies of the smallest and largest values which potentially served as pivot in the previous partitioning step. Sedgewick [160] managed to analyze single-pivot variants without sampling using the detour to exact-profile inputs, but nobody has yet succeeded in generalizing these arguments to multiway partitioning or Quicksort with pivot sampling.

Generic one-pass partitioning puts exactly the $s - 1$ pivot elements to their final place; the sum of the sizes of the s subproblems is always $n - (s - 1)$. Ignoring Insertionsort cutoffs for the moment, this means that we need $\Omega(n)$ partitioning steps, and $\Omega(\log n)$ recursion depth. Even in the perfectly balanced case, this yields total costs in $\Omega(n \log n)$. One can show that the average costs are indeed linearithmic for reasonable methods.

A random permutation cannot be sorted using comparisons in less than linearithmic time; but this bound only holds when all $n!$ permutations of the input are different. If $u \leqslant n/e$, the number of u-ary words, u^n is smaller than that, and only $\mathrm{ld}(u^n) = n\,\mathrm{ld}(u)$ bits of information are to be acquired. To get close to this cost in Quicksort, we obviously have to explicitly deal with duplicates during partitioning.

In the following we focus on the case that *all* elements equal to a pivot are removed before recursive calls.

8.2 Input Models with Equal Keys

We already defined models for random inputs with equal keys in Chapter 3: the expected-profile model, the special case of random u-ary words, and the exact-profile model. Let us briefly recapitulate and fix the notation.

In general we call two elements x and y *equal* if both $x \leqslant y$ and $y \leqslant x$ holds. In the context of one partitioning step, we call an ordinary element a *duplicate*, if it is equal to one of the pivot elements. If we say a partitioning method removes all duplicates, we mean that it singles out all elements that are equal to one of the pivots, so that they are not part of the input for any recursive call. Of course, a single such partitioning step does not remove all equal elements from the input, only the duplicates of the current pivots.

Expected-Profile Model. In the *expected-profile model* with parameters $u \in \mathbb{N}$ and $q \in (0,1)^u$ with $\Sigma q = 1$, a random input of size n consists of n i.i.d. random variables $U_1, \ldots, U_n$ with $U_i \overset{\mathcal{D}}{=} \mathcal{D}(q)$ for $i = 1, \ldots, n$. The domain $[u]$ is called the *universe,* and q the (probability vector of the) *universe distribution.* For $q = (\frac{1}{u}, \ldots, \frac{1}{u})$ the model is called *random-u-ary-word model.*

We denote by X_v, for $v \in [1..u]$, the number of elements U_j that have value v; the vector $X = (X_1, \ldots, X_u)$ of all these *multiplicities* is called the *profile* of the input $U = (U_1, \ldots, U_n)$. Clearly, $X \overset{\mathcal{D}}{=} \mathrm{Mult}(n, q)$ and $\mathbb{E}[X] = nq$. This explains the name of the model: We do not fix the profile, but the expectation of the profile.

The distribution function of the universe distribution is $F_U(v) = \mathbb{P}[U \leqslant v] = \sum_{i=1}^{\lfloor v \rfloor} q_i$ for $v \in [0, u+1)$, and we denote its (generalized) inverse by $F_U^{-1} : (0,1) \to [1..u]$ with $F_U^{-1}(x) = \inf\{v \in [1..u] : F_U(v) \geqslant x\}$. If we abbreviate by $c_j := \sum_{i=1}^{j} q_i$ for $j = 0, \ldots, u$ the cumulative sums of q, we have

$$F_U(v) \;=\; c_{\lfloor v \rfloor}, \qquad 0 \leqslant v < u+1, \tag{8.1}$$

$$F_U^{-1}(x) = v \;\iff\; x \in (c_{v-1}, c_v], \qquad 0 < x < 1, \; v \in [1..u]. \tag{8.2}$$

The expected-profile model is a natural complement of the random-permutation model: we draw elements i.i.d. from a *discrete* distribution in the former instead of a *continuous* distribution in the latter. This adds the feature of equal elements, but not much more; in particular for any given multiset of values, any ordering is equally likely to appear, since elements are still drawn i.i.d.

Gaming the Random u-ary Word Model. Random u-ary words are a rather special model and it is true that one can "game" the model: by exploiting its properties we can speed up sorting or partitioning. In a random u-ary word of length $n \gg u$, we have very close to n/u occurrences of each letter with high probability. We can use this as a good guess of where boundaries between segments will end up, so we *start* building our segments from there. If one segment would reach into an adjacent one, we use cyclic shifts to move the segments by a few places. The latter is costly, but happens not so often in expectation.

This strategy will thus be very effective w.r.t. scanned elements on an average random u-ary word. However, it performs poorly on many other input distributions, in particular, it will not be very successful on random permutations, unless we excessively sample to get very good pivots.

If it can be exploited by such a simple strategy, one might question the relevance of the random-u-ary-word model. But we should not forget that the random-permutation model just as well has its particularities, not to say peculiarities. Sorting algorithms have traditionally been tweaked for random permutations, at times shamefully neglecting other possibilities. The absence of equal keys in random permutations once lead even practitioners to overlook that the sorting method of BSD UNIX had quadratic running time on inputs consisting of few different values [20].

We should strive for sorting algorithms that perform reasonably on all inputs, and excel on the most frequent ones. In many applications of sorting, equal keys occur naturally. For Quicksort implementations that are not obviously flawed on other types of inputs, an analysis in the random-u-ary-word model will give a good indication of how gracefully they handle equal keys in general; that is, unless we explicitly make algorithmic use of the special structure of random u-ary words.

Exact-Profile Model. The second model is the exact-profile model. It has parameters $u \in \mathbb{N}$, the *universe size*, and $x \in \mathbb{N}^u$, the fixed *profile*. An input under this model always has size $n = \Sigma x$, and is formed as a uniformly chosen random permutation of

$$\underbrace{1,\ldots,1}_{x_1 \text{ copies}}, \underbrace{2,\ldots,2}_{x_2 \text{ copies}}, \ldots, \underbrace{u,\ldots,u}_{x_u \text{ copies}},$$

i.e., the multiset with x_v copies of number v for $v = 1, \ldots, u$.

A Note on Notation.   In the literature on Quicksort with equal keys, the universe size u is commonly called n, whereas the number of elements in the input is denoted by N. I have always found the use of the capital N typographically less pleasing, and in the context of this work capital letters are used for random variables, so n is the input size throughout. I hope the reader will find <u>u</u>niverse size u mnemonically enough to forgive the deviation from tradition.

8.3 Related Work

A brief overview of previous work on Quicksort with equal keys appeared already in Section 1.7; here we give some more technical details and also state a few results for later reference.

Burge's Trees.   The earliest relevant work for Quicksort with equal keys appeared in 1976, and it does not deal with Quicksort at all. Burge [27] analyzed the expected depth of nodes in a binary search tree (BST) built from successively inserting elements from an exact-profile input. Burge set up recurrences in $x_1, \ldots, x_u$ for the (left- and right-going) depth of a key and used an ingenious differencing trick to obtain telescoping recurrences: drop the first resp. the last component of the profile vector.

Burge's BSTs used the peculiar convention that equal keys *are kept in the tree:* upon insertion, keys greater *or equal* to the key of the current node are passed on to the right subtree.

Sedgewick's Lower Bound.   Although Burge's BSTs are a little different in their handling of duplicates, the well-known connection between binary search trees and Quicksort allowed Sedgewick, to transfer Burge's techniques to Quicksort [160] in 1977: he analyzed Quicksort under the exact-profile model, and additionally looked at random u-ary words (he calls them n-*ary files*). Once we have the results for exact-profiles, the behavior on u-ary words is obtained by suitably averaging over all multisets of size n with elements from $[u]$.

Sedgewick then studied the number of comparisons for *fat-pivot partitioning methods*, i.e., methods that collect all elements equal to the pivot and remove them from recursive calls. He argued that this is the most desirable situation and thus calls the corresponding results lower bounds for any Quicksort program, that is, *"any program which sorts by recursively subdividing files of more than one element into three subfiles: a (nonempty) middle subfile whose elements are all equal to some value* j; *a left subfile with no elements* > j; *and a right subfile with no elements* < j. *The only further restrictions are that the value* s *[the pivot] must be chosen by examining one element from the file, and that if the input file is randomly ordered, so must be the subfiles"* (Sedgewick [160], p. 244). Assuming *ternary* comparisons, i.e., comparisons that tell us in one shot whether an element is strictly smaller, strictly larger, or equal to another element, he obtained the following result.

> **Theorem 8.1 (Theorem 1 (Lower Bound) of Sedgewick [160]):**
> *Assume we use a fat-pivot partitioning method that needs* $n-1$ *comparisons to split the input into three segments with elements strictly less, equal to and strictly larger than the pivot. Quicksort with this method and a random pivot requires on average*
>
> $$n - u + 2 \cdot \sum_{1 \leqslant i < j \leqslant u} \frac{x_i x_j}{x_i + \cdots + x_j} \tag{8.3}$$
>
> *(ternary) key comparisons under the exact-profile model with parameters* u *and* x, *and*
>
> $$2n\left(1 + \frac{1}{u}\right) H_u - 3(n + u) \tag{8.4}$$
>
> *(ternary) key comparisons to sort a random* u-*ary word of length* n. ◀

The Origins of Quicksort Entropy.   The sum in Equation (8.3) also appeared in a different context: one year after Sedgewick's article appeared, Allen and Munro published a paper [2] on the *move-to-root heuristic* for self-organizing BSTs, in which they effectively studied BSTs built from successive insertions under an expected-profile model.

Proposition 8.2 (Theorems 3.1 and 3.4 of Allen and Munro [2]): *Let* $u \in \mathbb{N}$ *and* $q \in (0, 1)^u$ *with* $\Sigma q = 1$ *be given. Assume we build a BST by repeatedly inserting i.i.d.* $\mathcal{D}(q)$ *distributed elements into an initially empty BST, until all* u *values appear in the tree. Then we search a* $\mathcal{D}(q)$ *distributed element in this tree. The expected search costs to find this element are exactly*

$$\mathbb{E}[A_q] \;=\; 1 + 2 \cdot \mathcal{H}_Q(q), \tag{8.5}$$

$$\text{with } \mathcal{H}_Q(q) \;=\; \sum_{1 \leqslant i < j \leqslant u} \frac{q_i q_j}{q_i + \cdots + q_j}. \tag{8.6}$$

◀

(The connection between these two results will become obvious in Section 8.7.)

Following Sedgewick and Bentley [163, 164], we will call $\mathcal{H}_Q$ the *Quicksort entropy;* the reason for this name is another result from the paper of Allen and Munro [2], which they attributed to Kurt Mehlhorn:

Lemma 8.3 (Quicksort-Entropy Bound, Theorem 3.2 of Allen and Munro [2]):
For any $q \in (0,1)^u$ with $\Sigma q = 1$ holds

$$\mathcal{H}_Q(q) \;\leqslant\; \mathcal{H}_{\ln}(q) \;=\; \ln(2) \cdot \mathcal{H}_{\mathrm{ld}}(q). \tag{8.7}$$

◀

Quicksort is Optimal. In two presentations [163, 164] given in 1999 and 2002, respectively, Sedgewick reported from joint work with Bentley on Quicksort. They showed a lower bound for comparison-based sorting under the exact-profile model:

Theorem 8.4 (Information-Theoretic Lower Bound for Exact Profile [163, 164]):
To sort a permutation of the multiset $\{x_1 \times 1, \dots, x_u \times u\}$ of n numbers from $[u]$ with profile $x = (x_1, \dots, x_u)$ requires at least $\mathcal{H}_{\mathrm{ld}}(\frac{x}{n}) \cdot n - n$ comparisons. ◀

Combining Theorem 8.1, Lemma 8.3 and Theorem 8.4, Sedgewick concluded that the average performance of *classic fat-pivot Quicksort without sampling is optimal, up to a constant factor of $2\ln 2 \approx 1.3863$, on any distribution of keys.* Sedgewick further conjectured that this constant can be brought down to one using pivot sampling.

Conjecture 8.5 (Sedgewick-Bentley Conjecture [163, 164]):
Let $\mathbb{E}[C_n^{(k)}]$ be the expected number of comparisons used by classic Quicksort with fat-pivot partitioning and median-of-k sampling under an exact-profile model with parameters u and x with $\Sigma x = n$. Then holds

$$\frac{\mathbb{E}[C_n^{(k)}]}{n} \;\to\; \mathcal{H}_{\mathrm{ld}}\left(\frac{x}{n}\right), \qquad (k \to \infty). \tag{8.8}$$

◀

Sedgewick's Upper Bound. Sedgewick [160] further observed that the behavior of a Quicksort variant (single-pivot, no sampling) on random u-ary words is determined to a good deal by its behavior on *binary inputs.*

Proposition 8.6 (Corollaries on p. 251 and 255 of Sedgewick [160]):
If a Quicksort program (as in Theorem 8.1) requires on average more than $\alpha\binom{n}{2} = \frac{\alpha}{2}n^2$ comparisons on a random binary word, $u = 2$, then it will require on average at least

$$\left(1 - \frac{1}{u}\right)\frac{\alpha}{u}\binom{n}{2} - n \;+\; 2n\left(1 + \frac{1}{u}\right)H_u - 3(n+u)$$

$$= \;\Omega\left(\frac{n^2}{u}\right), \qquad \text{as } n \to \infty \text{ with } u = O\left(\frac{n}{\log n}\right), \tag{8.9}$$

comparisons on random u-ary words. Conversely, if the average number of comparisons on a random binary word is less than $2nH_n$, then it will require at most

$$\frac{6}{u}nH_n + \left(2\left(1-\frac{1}{u}\right)H_{u-1} - 4 + \frac{39}{2u}\right)n \;=\; O\left(\frac{n\log n}{u} + n\log u\right), \qquad (n \to \infty), \quad (8.10)$$

comparisons for a random u-ary word. ◀

Hennequin's Analysis. Hennequin [77] included a chapter on equal keys in his doctoral thesis. Like Sedgewick, he focused on single-pivot methods without sampling. Hennequin studied three variants of partitioning methods:

1. *unilateral* methods (unilatéral) put all duplicates in one segment,

2. *central* methods correspond to our fat-pivot schemes, and

3. *bilateral* methods (bilatéral) distribute duplicates to the two segments, so that the number of duplicates that go to the left segment is uniformly distributed.

Hennequin rephrased Sedgewick's analysis of unilateral and fat-pivot methods in the language of combinatorial structures and multivariate generating functions. He observed that for fat-pivot methods, one can directly consider the random-u-ary-word model.

Hennequin shows that bilateral methods that preserve randomness have *exactly* the same costs as for random permutations. This is in fact quite easy to see, since we effectively choose the meeting point of k and g there uniformly among all positions of the array: For a given profile x, we first chose the pivot value v with probability proportional to x_v, then the actual splitting point uniformly among the x_v copies. This is a very nice observation, but we should note that the bilateral scheme does not correspond to a natural partitioning method; in particular, this is not the distribution we get from generic one-pass partitioning with the tie-breaking rule.

Wegner's Algorithms. Wegner [178] discussed several variants of Quicksort intended to deal smoothly with equals. In particular the idea to collect equal keys at the outsides of the array should be attributed to him. He called this partitioning scheme *Head & Tail-Sort*; it uses the same invariant as the method of Bentley and McIlroy [20].

Wegner presented his ideas mainly as invariants and a table of how different cases are dealt with, which unfortunately leaves some details of the algorithms unclear. He gave a more detailed description in retrospect to a talk series of his on Quicksort [180]. He discussed his methods mainly for the case of constant repetition factor $x_1 = \cdots = x_u = M$, with a focus on $M = 1$, i.e., the random permutation case. While it is important to not get much worse for random permutations, the derivation of results for random u-ary words would have been more interesting.

More on BSTs from Equal Keys. Kemp [98] studied binary search trees built from successive insertions in both the exact-profile and expected-profile model. Unlike Burge, he considered the reasonable BST variant where insertion of keys already in the tree have no effect. Kemp computed *exact* expressions for the expected values of various parameters of the trees: the left- and right-going depth of the ith internal node, the depth of the ith external node (level), the size of the subtree rooted at the ith internal node (frontier), as well as internal and external path lengths.

Kemp [98] also studied all these parameters in the expected-profile model. Similar to Sedgewick's study of the special case of random u-ary words, Kemp averaged over all possible multisets and their costs, to obtain their values under the expected-profile model. He gave exact expressions for the average left- and right-going depths. For the other parameters, the formulas became unmanageably large, so he gave asymptotic approximations instead.

Archibald and Clément [4, 3] re-derive part of Kemp's result, namely the left- and right-going depth of certain nodes, by giving regular expressions for the languages of insertion sequences that expose the number of left-to-right maxima resp. minima, which they then count with generating functions. The depth of an arbitrary node can be obtained by a shuffle product of the regular expressions for maxima among smaller keys and minima among larger keys. With this approach they could also compute the variance of this quantity.

8.4 Fat-Pivot Partitioning

In this section, we will sketch the design space of partitioning methods that remove all duplicates from the input, i.e., methods that identify all elements equal to one of the pivots and put them in a separate segment between the corresponding subproblem segments. These segments of duplicates can then be excluded from recursive calls.

In terms of the memory layout pictures that we used in Chapter 4, the rectangles labeled with pivots become wider, since they represent the segment of all duplicates of this pivot. We will thus call partitioning methods that remove all duplicates *fat-pivot methods*. In the context of single-pivot Quicksort this is often called *three-way partitioning*; in the context of this work, however, three-way partitioning means a dual-pivot method; we will thus exclusively use the term fat-pivot.

8.4.1 Existing Methods

In Chapter 4, we had a sizable collection of known partitioning methods. In contrast, I could not find any genuine multiway fat-pivot partitioning methods in the literature. For single-pivot Quicksort, there are mainly two sensible fat-pivot partitioning methods.

Dijkstra Partitioning. Sedgewick and Wayne [166, p. 299] present elegant code for a fat-pivot partitioning method that grows the segments for small elements and another one for duplicates from the left; the segments for large elements grows from the right. This memory layout is one of schemes that Wegner [178] proposed: he calls this one *Slidesort*. The memory layout has the structure of YBB Quicksort, but the segments have a different meaning. That method is known as solution for Dijkstra's *Dutch National Flag problem;* Dijkstra presents a very similar method as a first solution in his book [43, p. 114]; we will therefore call this method *Dijkstra partitioning.* It is not used very much in Quicksort, since it causes a dramatic increase in the number of swaps for the also common case of no duplicates.

Bentley-McIlroy Partitioning. The most widely used fat-pivot partitioning method is *Bentley-McIlroy partitioning* [20]. The memory layout was again given by Wegner [178] before—he calls it Head & Tail-Sort—but it was the implementation of Bentley and McIlroy that popularized the scheme. Bentley-McIlroy partitioning is an extension of Hoare's (thin-pivot) partitioning scheme that collects elements equal to the pivot in two additional outermost segments. After partitioning is finished, these segments have to be swapped to the middle. This overcomes the above drawback, even though it seems expensive: the method has hardly any overhead for inputs without duplicates, and with many duplicates the additional swapping is well-invested effort.

Java 7 Quicksort. We certainly expect to find the first industrial implementation of dual-pivot Quicksort to perform well on inputs with equal keys, otherwise its developers would have done a poor job; and indeed, precautions have been taken. But if the reader expected to find a three-way fat-pivot method there, he or she will be disappointed: the Quicksort implementation in Java 7's runtime library checks whether the two pivot values are equal, and if so, it switches to Bentley-McIlroy partitioning using this single pivot value.

This is probably a pretty clever choice; and not only because it reuses a well-tested method. That the two pivot values are equal is a good signal for an input with many equals, where a fat-pivot method excels, and it avoids any overhead of such a method if the pivots are not equal. It is not a genuine multiway method, though, and we reserve the analysis of this hybrid method for future work.

In this work, we are interested in the potential of multiway partitioning for speeding up Quicksort. Since there are no existing such methods to guide us, we will try to set up a framework that remains as flexible as possible.

8.4.2 New Concepts and Notations

We can take generic one-pass partitioning as starting point also for fat-pivot methods. With duplicates, we have a few more degrees of freedom, and that requires a few terms and notations. Recall that we list all introduced notations in Appendix A.

Pivot Classes. We extend the set of classes by $s - 1$ *pivot classes* $p_1, \ldots, p_{s-1}$, where p_r is the class of all (ordinary) elements classified as equal to P_r. Small, large and medium classes are understood as open intervals then, i.e., $s_i = (P_{\lceil m \rceil - i}, P_{\lceil m \rceil - i + 1})$ for $1 \leqslant i \leqslant \lceil m \rceil$; $l_j = (P_{\lfloor m \rfloor + j - 1}, P_{\lfloor m \rfloor + j})$ for $1 \leqslant j \leqslant s - \lfloor m \rfloor$; for master-segment algorithms, i.e.,

$m \in [1..s] - \frac{1}{2}$, we also have medium elements $m = (P_{\lfloor m \rfloor}, P_{\lceil m \rceil})$. The vector of classes in sorted order now is

$$
\mathcal{C} = \begin{cases}
(s_m, p_1, s_{m-1}, p_2, \ldots, s_1, p_m, l_1, p_{m+1}, \ldots, p_{s-1}, l_{s-m}), & \text{for } m \in [1..s]; \\
(s_{\lceil m \rceil}, p_1, \ldots, s_2, p_{\lfloor m \rfloor}, m, p_{\lceil m \rceil}, l_2, p_{\lceil m \rceil+1}, \ldots, p_{s-1}, l_{s-\lfloor m \rfloor}), & \text{for } m \in [1..s] - \frac{1}{2}.
\end{cases}
$$

$$(8.11)$$

This looks more complicated than it is; the new $\mathcal{C}$ is the old one, but with pivot classes inserted between the other classes. As before, we write s without index to mean small of any order; likewise l is any large element and p is an element equal to any one of the pivots without specifying which. The p-elements are exactly the *duplicates*.

Different Flavors of Comparisons. (Thin-pivot) generic one-pass partitioning used the extended binary search trees $\lambda_k, \lambda_g \in \Lambda_s$ to classify elements by searching them in the tree. We allowed nodes to specify whether the comparison is strict ($<$) or non-strict ($\leqslant$). The search ended in a leaf labeled with one of the classes given in Equation (4.3) on page 156. With the pivot classes, new types of operations are thinkable. Lookup in a search tree can be implemented based on

- ► *ternary comparisons,* which tell us the outcome $<, =$ or $>$ in one shot; on

- ► *binary queries,* asking any yes-no-question regarding the relative order of two elements, i.e., $x \leqslant y$, $x < y$, or their reverse cousins, and in particular $x = y$; or on

- ► *binary comparisons,* allowing only $\leqslant$- or $<$-queries.

All models appear in the literature and it depends on the application which is more appropriate. Ternary comparisons are the default comparison interface (for objects) in Java and for comparator functions in C, whereas the sorting algorithms of the C++ STL are based solely on $<$-queries.

    At the level of usual CPU instructions, one typically—at least for MMIX, x86 and MIPS—has a compare instruction that subtracts two numbers and yields the result *smaller,* *equal* or *larger;* this corresponds to a ternary comparison. To react with changed control flow to such a result, usually conditional branches are used, and those are inherently binary: if some condition holds, jump to a different address, otherwise stay. However multiway branches are also possible with jump-register instructions, as used, e.g., to implement switch-case statements of high-level languages. We will try not to hastily choose one model over the other, and keep the analysis as general as possible.

Generalized Classification Trees.   A search in an extended binary search tree, where pivot classes correspond to the internal nodes of the tree, is a sensible and natural method for classification in presence of equals. It is by far not the only possible choice, though. In full generality, any procedure that determines the class of an element by comparisons is viable; we might even mix binary queries and ternary comparisons.

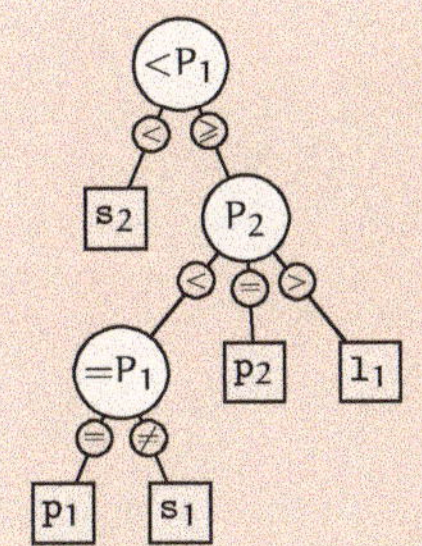

Figure 53: Example of a generalized comparison tree for $s = 3$ and $m = 2$ to determine the class $c(U) \in \{s_2, p_1, s_1, p_2, l_1\}$. The method mixes binary queries and ternary comparisons; it first compares $U < P_1$, and unless this is so, executes a ternary comparison of U and P_2. If U is strictly smaller than P_2, the last step checks $U = P_1$. Note that in the degenerate case $P_1 = P_2$, all duplicates are classified as p_2, even though they are first compared with P_1.

All such methods can be described by a *generalized comparison tree*, where internal nodes represent either a ternary comparison or a binary query with one of the pivot elements, and classes appear in the leaves. An example is given in Figure 53. Note that these trees are not search trees any more: the same pivot can appear several times and leaves might appear out of order.

The only thing we require is that for any possible element U and all possible values of the pivots, there must be a unique path from the root to a leaf with a valid class for that element. If several pivots happen to have the same value, several pivot classes are possible for one value; a generalized comparison tree will assign a uniquely defined class in that case, as well. As before, we think of classes as labels assigned to an element; we do no require the classes to form a partition of the universe in the set-theoretic sense.

We can use two different generalized comparison trees λ_k and λ_g for elements reached by index k resp. g.

Class and Subproblem Sizes. Each of the $\eta = n - k$ ordinary elements belongs to one of the classes given in Equation (8.11). As before, we denote small and large ordinary element counts by $\mathbf{I}$; more specifically, the number of elements of class c is $I_{r(c)}$ with

$$r(c) \;=\; \begin{cases} \lceil m \rceil - i + 1, & \text{for } c = s_i, \; 1 \leqslant i \leqslant \lceil m \rceil, \\ \lfloor m \rfloor + j, & \text{for } c = l_j, \; 1 \leqslant j \leqslant s - \lfloor m \rfloor. \end{cases} \qquad \text{(5.3) revisited}$$

For the number of duplicates, we use the vector $\mathbf{E}$, with E_r the number of elements in class p_r, for $r = 1, \ldots, s - 1$. Recall that if all pivot values are distinct, this is simply the number of elements equal to P_r; if some pivots are equal, though, the generalized comparison trees decide which pivot class is chosen, and there is not simple relation between E_r and the number of ordinary elements that are equal to P_r in general.

With a single comparison tree λ, all such elements count for a single pivot class, leaving some other pivot classes empty, but which one is chosen depends on λ. If we use more than one comparison tree, $\mathbf{E}$ will additionally depend on how many elements are classified with each tree, if the trees disagree over the class to be assigned to a certain value.

In total, $\mathbf{I}$ and $\mathbf{E}$ are all ordinary elements, i.e., $\Sigma I + \Sigma E = \eta$. Before recursive calls, we have to add again the sampled-out elements. For the rth subproblem, there are t_r sampled-out elements, but some of them might be equal to P_{r-1} or P_r. These are put in place, so that a potentially smaller random number, $B_r \in [0..t_r]$, of sampled-out elements adds to the size $J_r = I_r + B_r$ of the subproblem.

8.4.3   Generic Multiway Fat-Pivot Partitioning

Recall generic one-pass partitioning from Chapter 4. From the perspective of the code (Algorithm 9 on page 152), the classes are simply labels assigned to elements that indicate in which segments they belong. Apart from the distinction between small and large labels, Algorithm 9 does not use further information, e.g., that the segments are arranged in sorted order; Algorithm 9 does not explicitly use the pivot values, either.

We can therefore use Algorithm 9 also as basis for a generic fat-pivot partitioning method; we only have to define a *mapping* from the actual classes $\mathcal{C}$ including the pivot classes to *virtual classes* that we use in the code. We leave the details of an all-embracing general setup for future work. Instead, we consider the two concrete methods from above and sensible ways to generalize them.

8.4.4   Fat-Separator Methods

Dijkstra partitioning as described by Sedgewick and Wayne [166, p. 299] corresponds to $s = 2$ and the following mapping of classes:

Actual Class	s_1	p_1	l_1
Virtual Class	$\tilde{s}_2$	$\tilde{s}_1$	$\tilde{l}_1$

We thus use Algorithm 9 with parameters $\tilde{s} = 3$ and $\tilde{m} = 2$. λ_k and λ_g both consist of a single ternary-comparison node.

We will call methods like Dijkstra partitioning that leave the pivot-class segments in place between the subproblem segments *fat-separator methods*.

Clearly this scheme can be extended to multiway partitioning right away. We will always have $\tilde{s} = 2s - 1$ and we are free to choose an $\tilde{m} \in \{0, 0.5, \dots, \tilde{s} - 0.5, \tilde{s}\}$, so we can characterize fat-separator methods by giving s, $\tilde{m}$, λ_k, and λ_g.

8.4.5   Fat-Outsides Methods

The method discussed by Bentley and McIlroy [20] collects all duplicates of the pivot at the outsides of the array, so we call it a *fat-outsides method*. Although it is a binary partitioning method that creates two subproblems, Bentley-McIlroy partitioning uses a total of $\tilde{s} = 4$ segments during partitioning, $\tilde{m} = 2$ of which grow from the left. The method is also a *split-pivot method:* for the pivot used as master-pivot in partitioning, we have two segments, one on each side. We obtain this behavior in Algorithm 9 with the following definition of virtual classes:

<table>
<tr><td colspan="4" align="center">Mapping for λ_k</td><td></td><td colspan="4" align="center">Mapping for λ_g</td></tr>
<tr><td>Actual Class</td><td>p_1</td><td>s_1</td><td>l_1</td><td></td><td>Actual Class</td><td>s_1</td><td>l_1</td><td>p_1</td></tr>
<tr><td>Virtual Class</td><td>$\tilde{s}_2$</td><td>$\tilde{s}_1$</td><td>$\tilde{l}_1$</td><td></td><td>Virtual Class</td><td>$\tilde{s}_1$</td><td>$\tilde{l}_1$</td><td>$\tilde{l}_2$</td></tr>
</table>

Note that elements at λ_k are never classified as l_2, likewise at λ_g there is no s_2. The comparison trees are again both a single ternary node.

When Algorithm 9 has done its work, the array is partitioned according to the virtual classes; but they are not in order w.r.t. the actual classes. Therefore, a cleanup phase after partitioning is needed to bring the segments into order. In the case of Bentley-McIlroy partitioning this can be done by simply swapping blocks.

We can generalize the fat-outsides idea easily to multiway partitioning: we collect all pivot-class segments at the outsides of the array. Instead of the somewhat complicating split-pivot scheme of Bentley-McIlroy partitioning, we will use only one segment per pivot class. Then we have again $\tilde{s} = 2s - 1$.

We can in principle freely choose how many pivot segments we put to the left, and how many non-pivot segments grow from the left. To have a specific framework to work with, we will in the following always assume that for an s-way fat-outsides method we use

$$\tilde{m} = \lceil \tilde{s}/2 \rceil = s \qquad \text{and}$$

$$\lfloor \tilde{m}/2 \rfloor = \lfloor s/2 \rfloor \quad \text{pivot segments grow at the left outside;}$$

we thus determine all parameters by s. The analyses in this chapter do not need this assumption, and future work might consider a more general framework, but for the sake of a concise discussion, we refrain from doing so at the moment. Similarly, let us focus here on comparison trees built solely from ternary-comparison nodes. Comparison trees are then (isomorphic to) simple BSTs, as in the thin-pivot case.

Let us consider two simple examples to illustrate our convention.

Fat-Outsides YBB Partitioning. The rules above for $s = 3$ imply $\tilde{s} = 5$, $\tilde{m} = 3$; moreover the p_1-segment is at the left outside, that for p_2 is at the right outside. For classification, we use $(\lambda_k, \lambda_g) = (\text{⋏}, \text{⋏})$, where each node is a ternary-comparison node. After classification we apply the following mapping to the classes:

<table>
<tr><td>Actual Class</td><td>p_1</td><td>s_2</td><td>s_1</td><td>l_1</td><td>p_2</td></tr>
<tr><td>Virtual Class</td><td>$\tilde{s}_3$</td><td>$\tilde{s}_2$</td><td>$\tilde{s}_1$</td><td>$\tilde{l}_1$</td><td>$\tilde{l}_2$</td></tr>
</table>

After partitioning, we have the two pivot-class segments that have to be swapped with parts of the s_2- resp. l_1-segments.

Fat-Outsides Waterloo Partitioning. For $s = 4$, we get $\tilde{s} = 7$, $\tilde{m} = 4$. As for Algorithm 8, we use $(\lambda_k, \lambda_g) = (\text{⋏⋏}, \text{⋏⋏})$. The virtual-class mapping looks as follows.

Actual Class	p_1	p_2	s_2	s_1	l_1	l_2	p_3
Virtual Class	$\tilde{s}_4$	$\tilde{s}_3$	$\tilde{s}_2$	$\tilde{s}_1$	$\tilde{l}_1$	$\tilde{l}_2$	$\tilde{l}_3$

In the cleanup phase, we first rotate the p_2-elements over the s_2- and s_1-segments using cyclic shifts of three elements each. After that, we swap the p_1-elements with the rightmost s_2-element, and do likewise for p_3 and l_2 on the right side.

8.5 Partitioning Costs

In this section, we discuss the costs of partitioning using the methods sketched above under the expected-profile model. Since we build on generic one-pass partitioning for doing the actual work in partitioning, we can build on Chapter 5 for the actual results on the costs of partitioning. Of course, all formulations in that chapter are for the virtual parameters, and in the uniform input model. Therefore a few things are different in this chapter:

▶ The *class probabilities* are more complicated than in the uniform model. We have to separately deal with pivot classes and non-pivot classes. This is done in Section 8.5.2.

▶ The solution of the recurrence will only be given for so-called *stateless cost measures*. We introduce that notion in Section 8.5.1. From our cost measures, only scanned elements and comparisons with $\lambda_k = \lambda_g$ are stateless.

▶ Most work in partitioning is done using Algorithm 9, but not everything; for fat-outsides methods we also have a cleanup phase that does not come for free.

8.5.1 Stateless Cost Measures

Recall the notion of element-wise cost measures from Definition 5.2 (page 170): for all our cost measures, the partitioning costs were a sum of costs for single elements, which in turn depend only on the *class* of that element and the current *state* of the partitioning algorithm. In the simplest cases, element costs are the same for all states, so that costs depend only on the classes.

Definition 8.7 (Stateless Cost Measure): *If the partitioning costs $T_M(n, q)$ w.r.t. cost measure M fulfill*

$$T_M(n, q) \;=\; \beta^\mathsf{T} E + \gamma^\mathsf{T} I \tag{8.12}$$

for two constant coefficient vectors $\beta \in \mathbb{R}_{>0}^{s-1}$ and $\gamma \in \mathbb{R}_{>0}^{s}$, we call M stateless cost measure. ◀

Here I and E are the number of elements in ordinary and pivot classes, see Section 8.4.2. Two examples of stateless cost measures are the number of scanned elements and the number of comparisons with a single (generalized) comparison tree, i.e., when $\lambda_k = \lambda_g$.

In the following, we always assume a stateless cost measure, and in particular, we assume that the same generalized comparison tree $\lambda = \lambda_k = \lambda_g$ is used to classify all elements.

8.5.2 Stochastic Model

In this section, we introduce notation for fat-pivot Quicksort under an expected-profile input. In particular, we build on the notation from Section 8.2.

Distribution of Pivot Values. The distribution of the pivot values determines sizes and universes for subproblems and is thus an important ingredient for the analysis. As in the rest of this work, we assume pivots are chosen by generalized pivot sampling with parameter t, see Section 4.4. We can express the distribution of the *pivot values* $\mathbf{P}$ in terms of an underlying continuous vector $\mathbf{\Pi}$: we define the following random variables depending on the pivot-sampling parameter t, respectively, $\sigma = t + 1$.

$$\mathbf{D} \stackrel{\mathcal{D}}{=} \mathrm{Dir}(\sigma), \tag{8.13}$$

$$\mathbf{\Pi} = \mathbf{\Pi}(\mathbf{D}) = \left(\sum_{i=1}^{r} D_i\right)_{r=0}^{s}. \tag{8.14}$$

The subvector $\mathbf{\Pi}_{1,s-1} = (\Pi_r)_{r=1}^{s-1}$ is exactly the vector of pivot values in the uniform model studied in the rest of this work. We add the sentinel elements $\Pi_0 = 0$ and $\Pi_s = 1$ for notational convenience.

To obtain the actual pivot values, which are chosen as the appropriate order statistics of k elements i.i.d. from $[u]$, we can apply the *inversion method of random sampling,* i.e., we apply the (generalized) inverse distribution function to uniform order statistics, see, e.g., Devroye [38, Section V.3.4]. The latter are precisely given by $\mathbf{\Pi}$, so we find

$$\mathbf{P} = \mathbf{P}^{(q)} = F_u^{-1}(\mathbf{\Pi}) = \left(F_u^{-1}(\Pi_r)\right)_{r=0}^{s}, \tag{8.15}$$

with the convention that $P_0 = F_u^{-1}(0) = 0$ and $P_s = F_u^{-1}(1) = u + 1$.

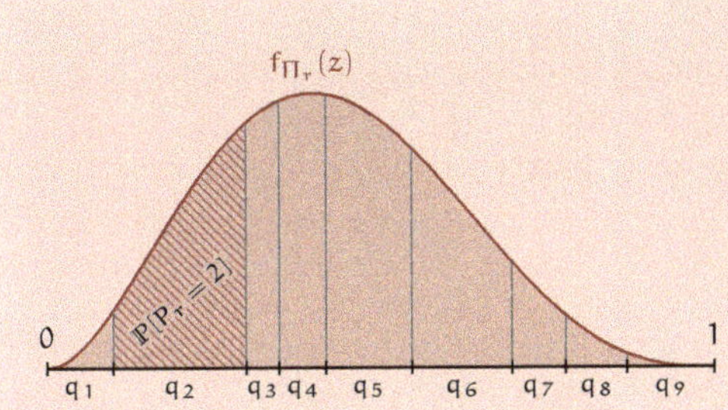

Figure 54: Illustration of pivot sampling under an expected-profile model with $u = 9$. We have $P_r = f_u^{-1}(\Pi_r)$, where $\Pi_r \stackrel{\mathcal{D}}{=} \mathrm{Beta}(\sigma_1 + \cdots + \sigma_r, \sigma_{r+1} + \cdots + \sigma_s)$, so Π_r is the x-coordinate of point uniformly chosen in the area under the curve, and P_r is the index of the interval this point lies in.

Class Probabilities. As indicated above, the class probabilities are considerably more complex than in the random-permutation case. First, we denote for two values $\underline{p}, \overline{p} \in [u]$ the probability to fall *strictly* between them by

$$v(\underline{p}, \overline{p}) = \mathbb{P}\big[U \in (\underline{p}, \overline{p})\big] = \sum_{r=\underline{p}+1}^{\overline{p}-1} q_r = \max\{c_{\overline{p}-1} - c_{\underline{p}}, 0\}. \tag{8.16}$$

Since all elements equal to any of the pivots are put in place during partitioning, the probability of an ordinary element to end up in the rth recursive call is exactly $v(P_{r-1}, P_r)$ conditional on $\mathbf{P}$, for $r = 1, \ldots, s$. We denote the vector of these probabilities by

$$\mathbf{V} \;=\; \mathbf{V}^{(q)} \;=\; \big(v(P_{r-1}, P_r)\big)_{r=1}^{s} . \tag{8.17}$$

The counter-probability $1 - \Sigma\mathbf{V}$ to all these is the probability to hit one of the pivot values, which in the random permutation case was zero, so that each element fell almost surely into one of the s regular classes. Here we additionally have the pivot classes $p_1, \ldots, p_{s-1}$ as introduced in Section 8.4.2. There we also defined E_r as the (random) number of elements in p_r, and $\mathbf{E} = (E_1, \ldots, E_{r-1})$ as the vector of those.

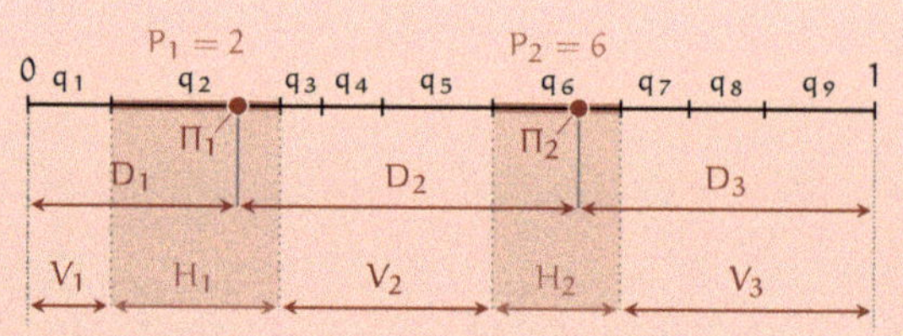

Figure 55: Relation of the quantities introduced in our stochastic model for $s = 3$.

To specify the distribution of $\mathbf{E}$, we have to determine the *hitting probabilities* H_r which is the probability that an ordinary element U is of type p_r. The hitting probabilities are determined by the generalized comparison tree λ and the pivot values $\mathbf{P}$.

$$\mathbf{H} \;=\; \mathbf{H}^{(q)}(\mathbf{P}, \lambda) \;=\; (H_1, \ldots, H_{r-1}) \tag{8.18.1}$$

$$\text{with} \quad H_r \;=\; \begin{cases} q_{P_r}, & \text{if } P_r \text{ is classified as } p_r \text{ by } \lambda \text{ w.r.t. } \mathbf{P}; \\ 0, & \text{otherwise.} \end{cases} \tag{8.18.2}$$

The second case applies if a P_r is equal to another pivot, say P_l and is *dominated* by it in λ, i.e., elements equal to $P_r = P_l$ are classified as p_l instead of p_r.

Class Probabilities with Two Trees. At this point, it becomes evident that using two different generalized comparison trees $\lambda_k \neq \lambda_g$ would make the analysis very complicated. Assume the two trees disagree over the class of a certain element $U = P_r$ for a certain choice of pivot values $\mathbf{P} \in [u]^{s-1}$. Then the hitting probabilities $\mathbf{H}(\mathbf{P}, \lambda_k)$ at λ_k are *different* from those at λ_g. All of our analysis in Chapter 5 was based on the idea that conditioning on the pivot values fixes the class probabilities. This is no longer true in this case.

Note that the probability to hit any one of the pivots, $\Sigma\mathbf{H} = 1 - \Sigma\mathbf{V}$, is itself a *random* quantity, even in the uniform case $q = (\frac{1}{u}, \ldots, \frac{1}{u})$, since the number of distinct pivot values is random.

Segment Sizes. The classes of all (ordinary) elements are i.i.d. by definition, so the cardinalities of the segment sizes $\mathbf{I}$ of elements falling between the pivots $\mathbf{P}$ together with the number E of duplicates has a multinomial distribution:

$$(\mathbf{I}, \mathbf{E}) \;\overset{\mathcal{D}}{=}\; \mathrm{Mult}(\eta; \mathbf{V}, \mathbf{H}), \tag{8.19}$$

where as usual $\eta = n - k$ is the number of ordinary elements.

Most of the random variables introduced here implicitly depend on $\mathbf{q}$, and $\mathbf{I} = \mathbf{I}^{(n,\mathbf{q})}$ and $\mathbf{E} = \mathbf{E}^{(n,\mathbf{q})}$ depend additionally on n. We usually omit that dependence, to keep the notation readable.

Expected Stateless Toll Costs. Conditional on the pivot values $\mathbf{P}$, we have by Equation (8.19) the expectations $\mathbb{E}[E_r \mid P_r] = H_r \cdot \eta = H_r \cdot n \pm O(1)$, and similarly, for the non-pivot segments $\mathbb{E}[I_r \mid V_r] = V_r \cdot n \pm O(1)$. We can thus state

$$\mathbb{E}[T_{n,\mathbf{q}} \mid \mathbf{P}] \;=\; R_{\mathbf{q}} \cdot \eta \;=\; R_{\mathbf{q}} \cdot n \pm O(1), \tag{8.20.1}$$

$$\text{with}\quad R_{\mathbf{q}} \;=\; \boldsymbol{\beta}^{\mathsf{T}} \cdot \mathbf{H} + \boldsymbol{\gamma}^{\mathsf{T}} \cdot \mathbf{V}. \tag{8.20.2}$$

Unconditional Expectations. Upon unconditioning in Equation (8.20.2), we find

$$\mathbb{E}[T_{n,\mathbf{q}}] \;=\; a_{\mathbf{q}} \cdot n \pm O(1), \tag{8.21.1}$$

$$\text{with}\quad a_{\mathbf{q}} \;=\; \mathbb{E}[R_{\mathbf{q}}] \;=\; \boldsymbol{\beta}^{\mathsf{T}} \cdot \mathbb{E}[\mathbf{H}] + \boldsymbol{\gamma}^{\mathsf{T}} \cdot \mathbb{E}[\mathbf{V}]; \tag{8.21.2}$$

but the latter expectations, $\mathbb{E}[\mathbf{H}]$ and $\mathbb{E}[\mathbf{V}]$, are quite unwieldy in general. For example, consider the term for H_r if it is not dominated:

$$\mathbb{E}[q_{P_r}] \;=\; \sum_{v=1}^{u} q_v \cdot \mathbb{P}[P_r = v] \tag{8.22}$$

$$\underset{(8.2)}{=} \sum_{v=1}^{u} q_v \cdot \mathbb{P}\big[\Pi_r \in (c_{v-1}, c_v]\big] \tag{8.23}$$

$$= \sum_{v=1}^{u} q_v \cdot \int_{c_{v-1}}^{c_v} \frac{x^{\sigma_1 + \cdots + \sigma_r - 1}(1-x)^{\sigma_{r+1} + \cdots + \sigma_s}}{B(\sigma_1 + \cdots + \sigma_r, \sigma_{r+1} + \cdots + \sigma_s)}\, dx \tag{8.24}$$

$$= \sum_{v=1}^{u} q_v \cdot I_{c_{v-1}, c_v}(\sigma_1 + \cdots + \sigma_r, \sigma_{r+1} + \cdots + \sigma_s), \tag{8.25}$$

with $I_{x,y}(\alpha, \beta)$ the incomplete regularized beta function. Luckily, we can get asymptotic results without dealing explicitly with these terms.

8.5.3 (Ternary) Comparisons

Recall that we assume $\lambda = \lambda_k = \lambda_g \in \Lambda_s$, i.e., we use the same comparison tree λ for both classification locations in Algorithm 9. We further restrict ourselves here to nodes with ternary comparisons only. Then λ is (isomorphic to) an ordinary BST. The number of comparisons is a stateless cost measure with $\boldsymbol{\gamma} = \lambda$, the vector of leaf depths, and $\boldsymbol{\beta}$ is the vector of internal node depths, where in both cases we define depth as the number of internal nodes on the path from the root to a node, including the node itself. Figure 56 gives an example. Note that we draw explicit leaves for the pivot classes, which one would omit for an ordinary BST.

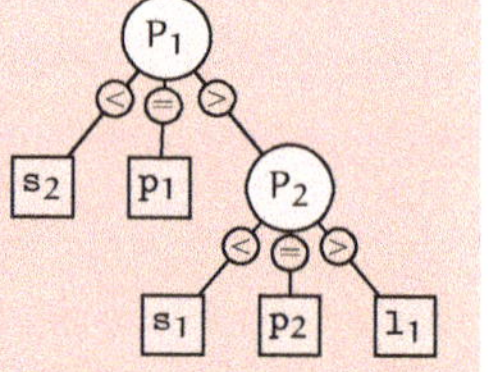

Figure 56: Exemplary generalized comparison tree for a simple dual-pivot Quicksort. The five classes $\mathcal{C} = (s_2, p_1, s_1, p_2, l_1)$ have (ternary) comparison costs $\beta = (1, 2)$ and $\gamma = (1, 2, 2)$; these correspond to the depths in the tree.

8.5.4 Scanned Elements (Partitioning)

The scanned-elements costs of an execution of Algorithm 9 depends only on the final sizes of the classes and thus is a stateless cost measure. The coefficient vectors β and γ are easy to derive from the mapping of classes to virtual classes and the charging scheme from Section 5.4.3. Let us consider some examples.

Fat-Separator Three-Way Partitioning.   For the fat-separator method with $s = 3$ and $\tilde{m} = 3$ we have the following classes mapping:

Original Class	s_2	p_1	s_1	p_2	l_1
Segment Size	I_1	E_1	I_2	E_2	I_3
Virtual Class	$\tilde{s}_3$	$\tilde{s}_2$	$\tilde{s}_1$	$\tilde{l}_1$	$\tilde{l}_2$
Scanned Elements	3	2	1	1	2

We can read off $\beta = (2, 1)$ and $\gamma = (3, 1, 2)$. It is obvious at this level that this method will incur significantly more scanned elements than (thin-pivot) YBB partitioning if there are no equal elements, since we still have to keep track of both start and end of the two (empty) pivot segments.

> **Scanned Elements vs. Cache Misses.**   For the extreme case sketched above, the number of scanned elements will not sensibly predict the number of cache misses: if there are no duplicates whatsoever, having the second scanning index does not really cost anything since its element is for sure in the cache.
>
> The above statement probably holds just as well if we have just enough duplicates to fill a cache line, and then having the almost-empty pivot-segment around is costly.

Fat-Outsides YBB.   If we instead put the pivot-segments to the outsides, we have to add the cleanup costs that we discuss below. Ignoring them for a moment, we find that for the partitioning process alone we get $(\beta^{(p)})^{\mathsf{T}}\mathbf{E} + \gamma^{\mathsf{T}}\mathbf{I}$ scanned elements, where $\beta^{(p)} = (3,2)$ and $\gamma = (2,1,1)$. The scanned elements-cost for partitioning are then *exactly* the same as for (thin-pivot) YBB partitioning if no equal keys are present.

General Fat-Outsides Methods. The latter is true in general: for fat-outsides methods, we always have $\gamma = \alpha_{SE}$, where the latter was given in Equation (5.23) on page 176.

8.5.5 Scanned Elements (Cleanup)

For fat-outsides methods, we have to perform a cleanup phase. We assume that we do so using cyclic shifts, element by element, working inside-out. (That way, we avoid touching any duplicate more than once.)

For a p_r-segment at the left end of the array, i.e., for $r = 1,\ldots,\lfloor s/2 \rfloor$, we have to move each p_r-element over exactly r segments to the right, i.e., with a cyclic shift involving $r+1$ elements. Afterwards, we have to advance the corresponding $r+1$ scanning indices, so one such operation has costs of $r+1$ scanned elements.

Similarly, for p_r with $r = \lfloor s/2 \rfloor + 1,\ldots,s-1$ its segment grows from the right, and each such duplicate is put into place with a cyclic shift of $s-r+1$ elements, contributing $s-r+1$ scanned elements. In total, the costs of the cleanup step for fat-outsides methods in terms of scanned elements are $(\beta^{(c)})^{\mathsf{T}}\mathbf{E}$ with

$$\beta^{(c)} \;=\; (2,3,\ldots,\lfloor s/2 \rfloor + 1,\ \ s - \lfloor s/2 \rfloor, s - \lfloor s/2 \rfloor - 1,\ldots,2). \tag{8.26}$$

Fat-Outsides YBB. Continuing the example from above, we thus find that the total number of scanned elements incurred in a partitioning round with the fat-outsides method for $s = 2$ is $\beta^{\mathsf{T}}\mathbf{E} + \gamma^{\mathsf{T}}\mathbf{I}$ scanned elements, where $\beta = \beta^{(p)} + \beta^{(c)} = (5,4)$ and $\gamma = (2,1,1)$.

Building on our work on generic one-pass partitioning, it was quite easy to analyze the cost of fat-pivot partitioning. We are now ready to proceed to the technically challenging part of Quicksort with equal keys: the solution of the recurrence for total costs.

8.6 Recurrence for Expected-Profile Inputs

In this section we assume the expected-profile model for inputs and a *fat-pivot* partitioning method, i.e., all elements equal to a pivot are moved to their final landing positions and are not part of a recursive call.

Randomness Preservation. In this scenario, subproblems for recursive calls correspond to a subrange of the universe, and the elements that are part of this subproblem are i.i.d. distributed from the corresponding *subdistribution:* this distribution is simply the original universe distribution, conditioned on the event that the element lies is this subproblem's slice of the universe. This means that inputs for recursive calls follow again an expected-profile model, so that we can set up a recurrence relation for the costs of Quicksort.

Note that the assumption that all duplicates of pivots are removed is vital: If some duplicates were allowed to remain in the subproblem inputs, the new probability of this value in the subproblem would change, and it will depend on n.

On top of that, we require the used partitioning method to have the usual form of randomness preservation as discussed in Section 4.5; all methods discussed in Section 8.4 do so.

8.6.1 Distributional Recurrence

As for the random-permutation model, we can formulate a recurrence for the random costs of Quicksort. Here is the recurrence; explanations of occurring terms will follow:

$$C_{n,q} \stackrel{\mathcal{D}}{=} T_{n,q} + \sum_{r=1}^{s} C^{(r)}_{J_r, Z_r}, \qquad (n > w, \ \Sigma q = 1), \qquad (8.27.1)$$

$$C_{n,q} \stackrel{\mathcal{D}}{=} W_{n,q}, \qquad (n \leqslant w, \ \Sigma q = 1), \qquad (8.27.2)$$

$$C_{0,()} = 0, \qquad (8.27.3)$$

where the independence assumptions are as for Equation (6.1), i.e., the $C^{(r)}_{n,q}$ are independent copies of $C_{n,q}$ for all n and q, which are also independent of $J = J^{(n)}$, $Z = Z^{(n)}$ and $T_{n,q}$. The base cases for $n \leqslant w$ are the sorting cost with Insertionsort; as we consider w a constant, their value will not influence the leading term.

The distributional recurrence is visually quite similar to Equation (6.1) for the random-permutation case, but the second parameter q introduces some additional features. Also, the distribution of J is different. We have $I \leqslant J \leqslant I + t$, but J is random even for fixed I. The reason is that the t_r sampled-out elements between P_{r-1} and P_r might be equal to P_{r-1}, equal to P_r, or lie between the two. Only the latter ones are included in the array segment for the recursive call. The contribution of sampled-out elements to J_r is thus binomially distributed:

$$J = J^{(n,q)} = I^{(n,q)} + B^{(q)}, \qquad (8.28)$$

$$B = B^{(q)} \stackrel{\mathcal{D}}{=} \left(\mathrm{Bin}\left(t_r, \frac{V_r}{q_{P_{r-1}} + V_r + q_{P_r}} \right) \right)_{r=1}^{s}. \qquad (8.29)$$

Z is the vector of "zoomed-in" distributions for the subproblems. The entries Z_r are themselves vectors, namely the (potentially empty) subranges of q for values between P_{r-1} and P_r. Z is formally given by

$$Z = Z^{(q)} = \left(z(P_{r-1}, P_r) \right)_{r=1}^{s}, \qquad (8.30)$$

$$z(\underline{p}, \overline{p}) = \frac{1}{v(\underline{p}, \overline{p})} \cdot q_{\underline{p}+1, \overline{p}-1} = \left(\frac{q_r}{v(\underline{p}, \overline{p})} \right)_{r=\underline{p}+1}^{\overline{p}-1}. \qquad (8.31)$$

We have $z(0, u+1) = q$, the initial distribution. There are two special cases where two adjacent pivots do not allow for elements in between them: if they are equal, and if they differ by exactly 1. For this degenerate case $P_r - P_{r-1} \leqslant 1$, our Z_r is not well-defined since the sub-universe size is 0. Luckily, also the corresponding segment size is $I_r = 0$ and $J_r = 0$ since the t_r sampled-out elements must equal P_{r-1} or P_r, as well. These degenerate recursive calls thus always concern an empty segment and simply do nothing. Their costs are handled by the initial values of the recurrence.

Back-of-the-Envelope Remarks.   Even though nicely hidden in the notation for J and Z in Equation (8.27), the inner workings are somewhat involved; after all we needed a page of text to introduce all constituents. Let us thus complement this with a very rough order-of-growth estimate of $\mathbb{E}[C_{n,q}]$.

A fat-pivot method removes in each partitioning step at least one value from the universe, so we can have at most u partitioning steps. Any reasonable partitioning method has costs linear in the number of elements it is applied to, so the overall costs for sorting are $\Theta(u \cdot n)$ in the worst case. This, of course, depends crucially on our assumption that all equal elements are removed, which means that each partitioning step removes in expectation a $\Theta(\frac{1}{u})$-fraction of the input. It is no wonder then that overall costs are linear in n. If we are lucky with pivot choices, we divide the universe into s sub-universes of approximately equal size in each step, and we are done in roughly $\log_s(u)$ steps, yielding $\Theta(n \log(u))$ overall cost in the best case.

As in the random-permutation model, we expect the worst-case complexity to be rare enough, so that costs are in $\Theta(n \log(u))$ also in the average case. Of course, we are interested in the constant of proportionality to be able to compare algorithms.

Outlook.   The best one can hope for is an explicit solution for $\mathbb{E}[C_{n,q}]$, in terms of n and q, as well as s and t. Given the complex nature of the recurrence, it seems hard to obtain such a solution, and we will resort to asymptotic approximations. This is easier said than done since we have two parameters in the recurrence.

What comes to our rescue here is that for large n, we can *separate* parts in $\mathbb{E}[C_{n,q}]$ that depend on q from those that depend on n, and investigate them in isolation. This trick comes at the price of two arguably bearable restrictions: The first one limits the ways how q may vary with n, in particular, u may not grow to fast w.r.t. n. The second restriction concerns the allowable cost measures; in the present form, the separation trick only works for stateless cost measures (Definition 8.7).

The separation of n and q depends on the connection between Quicksort costs and search costs in corresponding search trees. In the following section we present the general class of search trees corresponding to s-way Quicksort with pivot sampling and Insertion-sort cutoff.

8.7 Quicksort Recursion Trees

At first sight, Quicksort and search trees are two very different things, one being a sorting method, the other a data structure to implement dictionaries. But there is a close relationship between the cost of sorting an array with Quicksort and the cost of building a search tree of the elements in the array: *"Goethe famously said that 'architecture is frozen music.' In exactly that sense, I assert that 'data structures are frozen algorithms.' And if we freeze the Quicksort algorithm, we get the data structure of a binary search tree"* (Bentley [19], p. 37). In less flowery words, to each execution of Quicksort we can associate a *recursion tree*, which turns out to be a search tree. Moreover, the process of growing the recursion tree during execution mimics exactly the growth of a corresponding search tree upon insertion of new elements.

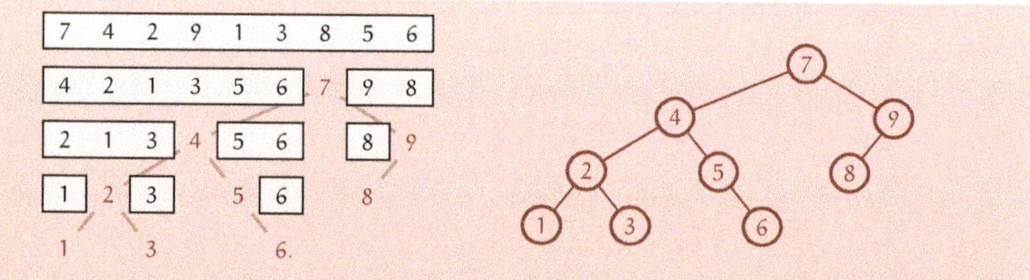

Figure 57: Execution trace of a simple Quicksort variant and its corresponding recursion tree. Here we assume that the first element is selected as pivot and the relative order of elements in subproblems is retained from the original input. The recursion tree then coincides with the BST that results from successively inserting the original input.

The correspondence is obvious for a most basic Quicksort implementation: single-pivot Quicksort with pivots selected as first elements of the list, and where partitioning is done so that the relative order of elements smaller resp. larger than the pivot is unaltered. Then the recursion tree is exactly the binary search tree that results from successively inserting the elements in the order they appear in the original input, see Figure 57. Moreover a moment's reflection shows that the very *same* comparisons are used in both processes, even though in a different order. This allows us to analyze whichever structure is more convenient, and the number of comparisons is then the same in the other.

Section Outline.   The analogy extends to our generic s-way Quicksort with a generalization of BSTs. It is the purpose of this section to make this generalization explicit, and to do some groundwork used later in our analysis of Quicksort with equal keys.

We formally define the notion of recursion trees for Quicksort in Section 8.7.1, and then introduce a corresponding class of search trees in Section 8.7.2: t-fringe-balanced s-ary search trees with leaf-buffer size w, or $(s, \mathbf{t}, w, \lambda)$-trees for short.

As nice as the correspondence between Quicksort and search trees may be, it has its limits: as we will discuss in detail in Section 8.8, the equivalence in costs of Quicksort and search trees only holds under *stateless* cost measures. In Section 8.7.4, we introduce a generic model for search costs in (s, t, w, λ)-trees that corresponds to stateless cost measures for Quicksort. In the remainder of this section, we then study these search costs for trees built from expected-profile inputs.

8.7.1 Recursion Trees

In the following, we always assume a generic s-way Quicksort with pivot-sampling parameter t and Insertionsort cutoff w. We further assume to simplify presentation that the k sample elements are chosen *deterministically*, say, as the first k elements in the input; under our input models, this assumption is w.l.o.g. for the distribution of costs of Quicksort.

We first define a superclass of recursion trees, which are simply s-ary search trees that allow an arbitrary number of elements in leaves.

Definition 8.8 (s-Ary Search Trees with Big Leaves): *An s-ary search tree (with big leaves) $\mathcal{T}$ for a (potentially empty) multiset of keys $\{U_1, \ldots, U_n\}$ from an ordered universe is either*

- *a leaf labeled with the sequence $U_1, \ldots, U_n$ (in some order), or*

- *an inner node labeled with $\mathbf{P} = (P_1, \ldots, P_{s-1})$ that has s child subtrees $\mathcal{T}_1, \ldots, \mathcal{T}_s$ attached to it.*

   We require $P_1 = U_{i_1} \leqslant \cdots \leqslant P_{s-1} = U_{i_{s-1}}$ for a subset $\{i_1, \ldots, i_{s-1}\} \subseteq [n]$ of the indices, and for $r = 1, \ldots, s-1$, $\mathcal{T}_r$ must be an s-ary search tree (with big leaves) for the multiset of all U_i with $P_{r-1} < U_i < P_r$, where we set $P_0 = -\infty$ and $P_s = +\infty$. ◄

We now define recursion trees for a given Quicksort implementation.

Definition 8.9 (Recursion Tree): *The recursion tree $\mathcal{T}(\mathbf{U})$ on an input $\mathbf{U} = (U_1, \ldots, U_n)$ is defined as follows.*

- *If $n \leqslant w$, $\mathcal{T}(\mathbf{U})$ is a single leaf containing $\mathbf{U}$.*

- *If $n > w$, let $\mathbf{P} = (P_1, \ldots, P_{s-1})$ denote the $s-1$ chosen pivot values, in ascending order. Then $\mathcal{T}(\mathbf{U})$ consists of the internal node containing $\mathbf{P}$, with the s children $\mathcal{T}(\mathbf{U}^{(1)}), \ldots, \mathcal{T}(\mathbf{U}^{(s)})$, where $\mathbf{U}^{(r)}$ is the input for the rth recursive call.* ◄

Note that the leaves remain unsorted. It is an immediate observation that $\mathcal{T}(\mathbf{U})$ for a fat-pivot Quicksort is an s-ary search tree with big leaves: all values in a subtree left of a pivot value x are strictly smaller than x, and all values in subtrees right of x are strictly larger.

For Quicksort with pivot sampling, certain s-ary search tree shapes cannot arise as recursion trees. If the input consists of distinct elements for example, the sampled-out elements guarantee a minimum size for subtrees. In the following, we define a subclass of s-ary search trees that corresponds exactly to the recursion trees of Quicksort.

8.7.2 t-Fringe-Balanced s-Ary Search Trees with Leaf-Buffer Size w

In recursion trees, the keys of inner nodes are the pivot values from the corresponding partitioning steps of Quicksort, so we have to simulate the sampling process of Quicksort in search trees. Upon constructing a search tree by inserting elements one at a time, we thus cannot decide immediately if a new element becomes a key in an inner node or not. We therefore *collect* a number of elements in the leaves and wait for an appropriate number of elements to arrive. If a leaf has collected enough elements, it is *split:* From the sample of elements now available, we select pivots with the same procedure as in Quicksort. These become the keys of a new inner node, and stay so for good. New child leaves of this new node hold the elements that did not become pivots.

Algorithm 12: Procedure to insert a key x into an (s, t, w, λ)-fringe-balanced tree $\mathcal{T}$.

```
STWLTREEINSERT⟨s,t,w,λ⟩(𝒯, x)
 1   if 𝒯 is Leaf(U)
 2       Append x to U
 3       if |U| ⩽ w
 4           return Leaf(U)
 5       else    // Split the leaf
 6           P := PIVOTSFROMSAMPLE⟨t⟩(U₁,...,Uₖ)
 7           C₁,...,Cₛ := new empty list
 8           for each U in U \ P    // all elements except pivots
 9               c := classify x with comparison tree λ w.r.t. P
10               if not c == pᵣ  for some r ∈ [1..s − 1]
11                   Add U to C_r(c)
12               end if
13           end for
14           return Inner(P; Leaf(C₁),...,Leaf(Cₛ))
15       end if
16   else 𝒯 is Inner(P; 𝒯₁,...,𝒯ₛ)
17       c := classify x with comparison tree λ w.r.t. P
18       if c == pᵣ  for some r ∈ [1..s − 1]
19           return "Already present as Pᵣ."
20       else
21           𝒯_r(c) := STWLTREEINSERT(𝒯_r(c), x)    // Continue insertion in subtree.
22           return Inner(P; 𝒯₁,...,𝒯ₛ)
23       end if
24   end if
```

We formalize this procedure as an insertion algorithm for s-ary search trees with big leaves, see Algorithm 12. Growing trees with Algorithm 12 enforces certain shapes upon the lowest subtrees, i.e., at the *fringe* of the tree. The resulting class of search trees is hence called *fringe-balanced*.

Definition 8.10 ((s, t, w, λ)-Fringe-Balanced Trees): *Let $s \in \mathbb{N}_{\geq 2}$, $t \in \mathbb{N}_0^s$, $w \in \mathbb{N}$ with $w \geq k - 1 = \Sigma(t + 1) - 2$ and λ a generalized comparison tree over $s - 1$ pivots.*
The t-fringe-balanced s-ary search tree with leaf-buffer size w and interior comparison tree λ, for short (s, t, w, λ)-fringe-balanced tree, for a sequence of elements $U_1, \ldots, U_n$ is the extended s-ary search tree, whose leaves can hold up to w elements, and that is built by inserting $U_1, \ldots, U_n$ successively into an initially empty tree using STWLTREEINSERT$_{(s,t,w,\lambda)}$ *(Algorithm 12).* ◀

Subclasses of these search trees have been studied extensively in the literature, unfortunately under varying names: *locally balanced search trees* [176], *fringe-balanced trees* [145], *diminished trees* [74], and *iR/SR trees* [88, 89]. Section 1.7.6 contains an overview of previous work. I will always say *fringe-balanced trees*, since it is the most vivid term and has been widely adopted in the analysis-of-algorithms community. In usual definitions of fringe-balanced, see, e.g., Drmota [47], the leaves hold up to $k - 1$ elements, just enough so that a sample of k is available for splitting. Sampling is usually restricted to equidistant choices $t = (t, \ldots, t)$. We extended the usual definition slightly; to avoid confusion, we call our generalized version (s, t, w, λ)-trees in the following.

Note that in our insertion procedure, we use λ to classify elements, and for splitting leaves, we use the very same procedure to select pivots as in Quicksort.

Algorithm 13: Procedure to search a key x in a (s, t, w, λ)-tree $\mathcal{T}$.

STWLTREESEARCH$_{\langle s,t,w,\lambda \rangle}(\mathcal{T}, x)$

```
 1   if 𝒯 is Leaf(U)
 2       Search x linearly in U
 3   else 𝒯 is Inner(P; 𝒯₁,…,𝒯ₛ)
 4       c := classify x with comparison tree λ w.r.t. P
 5       if c == pᵣ  for some r ∈ [1..s − 1]
 6           return "Found as Pᵣ."
 7       else
 8           stwlTreeSearch(𝒯_r(c), x)    // Continue in subtree.
 9       end if
10   end if
```

To define search costs precisely, we assume the procedure given in Algorithm 13 is used. Searching in an (s, t, w, λ)-tree works as in an ordinary s-ary search tree, but there are two small differences compared to s-ary trees as described, e.g., by Mahmoud [112]: First, elements in our leaves are not sorted, so we have to sequentially search through all elements in a leaf. The second difference is in how search proceeds "inside" inner nodes. Usually, one strategy is fixed for good, e.g., binary searching among the keys. We keep some flexibility here and allow a generalized comparison tree λ to be specified.

Equal Keys. As for Quicksort, search trees are usually studied under the random-permutation model. We there effectively ask for parameters of a tree that results form inserting n *distinct* keys in random order. Recalling that we are in the equal-keys chapter, we have to be clear about the behavior of our trees for duplicate insertions. When we insert an element x with STWLTREEINSERT that was already inserted before, what happens depends on where the element is: If x is a key in one of the inner nodes, the new insertion is without effect. Insertion will end in line 19 of Algorithm 12. If x appears in a leaf, however, the new duplicate is added to that leaf no matter what; see line 2.

This different handling of duplicates might seem peculiar at first sight, but it is the right way for our purposes: duplicates do play a role for selecting pivots—elements of the universe with higher probability contribute more duplicates in a random sample and are thus more likely selected as pivot—but once pivots have been selected, all its duplicates are put in place in this partitioning step, no matter how many of them we have.

8.7.3 Recursion Trees and stwl-Trees

We now show a generalization of the classic correspondence between Quicksort and search trees.

Proposition 8.11: *Consider generic s-way Quicksort with pivot-sampling parameter t, Insertionsort cutoff w, and a fat-pivot partitioning method using a single (generalized) comparison tree $\lambda = \lambda_k = \lambda_g$. Moreover, assume that elements for recursive calls retain their relative order during partitioning and that the first k elements are chosen as sample. Then for any input $U = (U_1, \dots, U_n)$ holds: Sorting U with Quicksort and inserting U successively into an initially empty (s, t, w, λ)-tree executes the same set of classification calls.*   ◄

Proof: We prove the claim by induction on n. If $n \leqslant w$, Quicksort passes control directly to Insertionsort, which does no classifications. In the tree, all elements are gathered in the single leaf and no classifications happen. So assume the claim holds for inputs with less than n elements.

If now $n > w$, Quicksort chooses pivots P from the first k elements, and classifies all other elements w.r.t. P. It partitions the input into segments $U^{(1)}, \dots U^{(s)}$ of all elements that are strictly between the pivots.

Now consider what happens upon inserting the $(w+1)$st element in the tree. This is the first time a leaf will overflow and we now split it. The keys for the inner node, the root of the tree, are chosen from the first k inserted elements using pivot sampling, so we get the same values P as were chosen as pivots in Quicksort. The other elements from the leaf are classified w.r.t. P and inserted into new leaves. Also, any later insertions must first consider the root, so each of these elements is classified w.r.t. P. So we execute the same set of classifications in both processes.

Towards applying the inductive hypothesis for recursive calls resp. subtrees, we only have to note that the relative order of elements is retained in both processes, so the elements inserted in the rth child of the root are exactly $U^{(r)}$, in the same order. The claim thus follows by induction.   ■

The assumption that partitioning maintains the relative order among segments is not fulfilled for usual in-place partitioning methods. How they affect this relative order is, indeed, rather opaque. We can avoid this complication by only considering a distributional equivalence.

Proposition 8.12: *Consider generic s-way Quicksort with pivot-sampling parameter t, Insertionsort cutoff w, and a fat-pivot partitioning method using a single (generalized) comparison tree $\lambda = \lambda_k = \lambda_g$. Let $\mathbf{U} = (U_1, \ldots, U_n)$ be n i.i.d. (real) random variables, and denote by $\mathcal{T} = \mathcal{T}(\mathbf{U})$ the random recursion tree of Quicksort on this input. Further, denote by $\mathcal{T}'$ the (s, t, w, λ)-tree for $\mathbf{U}$. Then holds $\mathcal{T} \overset{\mathcal{D}}{=} \mathcal{T}'$.* ◄

Remark: One could extend the above result to the set of classifications used during construction of the two trees, as in Proposition 8.11, but we will not need that. Since the shapes of the final trees do not depend on λ, the above equality in distribution also holds if different comparison trees are used in Quicksort and the search tree. ◄

Proof: Conditional on the multiset of values in $\mathbf{U}$, i.e., conditional on the profile of the input, $\mathbf{U}$ is uniformly distributed among all permutations of this multiset. This is a consequence of elements being chosen i.i.d. We will show that for a fixed tree and conditional on a fixed profile of the input, the same number of permutations of the multiset of values leads to this tree in both worlds. The tree thus has the same probability to occur as recursion tree and as (s, t, w, λ)-tree conditional on any profile; it then does so in particular after unconditioning, i.e., when the profile is not fixed, and the claim follows.

So let $\mathcal{T}$ be an arbitrary fixed s-ary search tree with leaf-buffer size w and let $\mathbf{X}$ be a multiset of values. We show inductively that the same number of permutations of $\mathbf{X}$ generate $\mathcal{T}$ as recursion tree and as (s, t, w, λ)-tree.

For $n \leqslant w$, $\mathcal{T}$ must be a single leaf containing the n unsorted values. In the (s, t, w, λ)-tree, the leaf collects elements in insertion order, so only the single permutation giving elements in this order generates $\mathcal{T}$. For recursion trees, we similarly have elements in input order, so there is also just this single permutation leading to $\mathcal{T}$.

Now assume the claim holds for inputs of up to $n - 1$ elements and let $n > w$. Then $\mathcal{T}$ consists of a root node with keys $\mathbf{P} = (P_1, \ldots, P_{s-1})$ and children $\mathcal{T}_1, \ldots, \mathcal{T}_s$. Subtree $\mathcal{T}_r$, for $r = 1, \ldots, s$, contains only keys from the open interval (P_{r-1}, P_r), where we set $P_0 = -\infty$ and $P_s = +\infty$ for notational convenience.

A permutation of $\mathbf{X}$ yields key values $\mathbf{P}$ in the root if and only if generalized pivot sampling on the first k elements, which form the sample both for recursion trees and (s, t, w, λ)-trees, yields the pivots $P_1, \ldots, P_{s-1}$, i.e., when the $(\sigma_1 + \cdots + \sigma_r)$th smallest element is P_r for $r = 1, \ldots, s - 1$. The precise number of such permutations for inputs with duplicates is inconvenient to describe, but obviously the same number results for both tree processes, since they do the same thing. This suffices for our claim.

Now for $r = 1, \ldots, s$ define $\mathbf{X}^{(r)} = \mathbf{X} \cap (P_{r-1}, P_r)$ as the multiset of values in the range of the rth subtrees. The profile of the input from which $\mathcal{T}_r$ is constructed is exactly $\mathbf{X}^{(r)}$: for recursion trees, because all such elements are put in the segment for the rth subproblem, and for (s, t, w, λ)-trees because exactly these elements are recursively inserted in this subtree.

Each element U now belongs to exactly one class: either $U \in (P_{r-1}, P_r)$ or $U = P_r$ for some r. As long as we keep the relative order of elements *within* one class and do not change the set of sample elements, we can permute elements without affecting the outcome: in both worlds still the same pivots are chosen and the same subproblem inputs are generated. Again, determining the precise number of these permutations that lead to $\mathcal{T}$ is cumbersome, but surely their number is the same for recursion trees and $(s, \mathbf{t}, w, \lambda)$-trees.

Finally, since pivots are not passed to subproblems, it holds $|\mathbf{X}^{(r)}| \leqslant n - 1$ and by the inductive hypothesis we have the same probability to obtain $\mathcal{T}_1, \ldots, \mathcal{T}_s$ as our subtrees for recursion trees as for $(s, \mathbf{t}, w, \lambda)$-trees, conditional on the pivot values $\mathbf{P}$. Together with the above observations, we find that the same number of permutations of $\mathbf{X}$ results in the recursion tree $\mathcal{T}$ as do generate $(s, \mathbf{t}, w, \lambda)$-tree $\mathcal{T}$ with successive insertion. This concludes the inductive step, and thus the proof. ∎

The equality in distribution allows us to study recursion trees of Quicksort by analyzing instead a randomly grown $(s, \mathbf{t}, w, \lambda)$-tree.

8.7.4 Generic Search Costs

Recall that a search in an s-ary search tree has to use a comparison tree λ "inside" the nodes to find the class of an element. Depending on the class, we can announce that an element is present, or that we have to continue searching in a subtree, cf. Algorithm 13. In general, classification costs may differ a lot depending on the resulting class: in lucky cases, we know the class after a single query, in other cases we might have to compare with all $s - 1$ pivots.

To account for this, we let search costs depend on all classes of the searched element on the path from the root down the tree; to be precise, the search costs are the sum of contributions of nodes on the path from the root, where following an rth child edge contributes γ_r, ending search as rth pivot in an internal node yields a summand β_r, and terminating the search in a leaf adds ζ. Formally, we express this in terms of search-cost vectors.

Definition 8.13 (Search-Cost Vector): *Let $\beta \in \mathbb{R}_{>0}^{s-1}$ and $\gamma \in \mathbb{R}_{>0}^{s}$ and $\zeta \in \mathbb{R}_{>0}$ be given, and let $\mathcal{T}$ be an s-ary search tree with leaf-buffers, containing keys in $[1..u]$. The search-cost vector $\Gamma = \Gamma(\mathcal{T}) \in \mathbb{R}^u$ w.r.t. (β, γ, ζ) is defined inductively for each $v \in [1..u]$ as*

$$\Gamma_v(\mathcal{T}) = \begin{cases} \zeta, & \text{if } \mathcal{T} \text{ is a single leaf;} \\ \displaystyle\sum_{r=1}^{s-1} \beta_r \mathbb{1}_{\{v \in P_r\}} + \sum_{r=1}^{s} \mathbb{1}_{\{v \in (P_{r-1}, P_r)\}} \big(\gamma_r + \Gamma_v(\mathcal{T}_r)\big), & \begin{array}{l}\text{if } \mathcal{T} \text{ is a root with keys } \mathbf{P} \\ \text{and subtrees } \mathcal{T}_1, \ldots, \mathcal{T}_s.\end{array} \end{cases}$$

$$(8.32)$$

◀

This definition allows us to express costs conveniently. If we search, one after another, for a sequence of elements that has the profile $\mathbf{X} \in \mathbb{N}_0^u$ in a tree with search-cost vector Γ, the total search costs are $\Gamma^{\mathsf{T}}\mathbf{X}$. A single search for $U \stackrel{\mathcal{D}}{=} \mathcal{D}(\mathbf{q})$ has expected costs $\mathbb{E}[\Gamma_U] = \Gamma^{\mathsf{T}}\mathbf{q}$.

8.7.5 Search Costs in Expected-Profile Models

Consider a universe distribution $q \in (0,1)^u$. Let $\Gamma(n, q)$ denote the search-cost vector of a random (s, t, w, λ)-tree built from n i.i.d. $\mathcal{D}(q)$ distributed elements $U = (U_1, \ldots, U_n)$. By Proposition 8.12, we may also interpret the tree as a recursion tree of Quicksort, so we can set up a recurrence equation similar to Equation (8.27), in particular using the same random variables J and Z:

$$\Gamma_v(n, q) \overset{\mathcal{D}}{=} \sum_{r=1}^{s-1} \mathbb{1}_{\{v \in P_r\}}\beta_r + \sum_{r=1}^{s} \mathbb{1}_{\{v \in (P_{r-1}, P_r)\}}\big(\gamma_r + \Gamma_v(J_r, Z_r)\big), \qquad (n > w), \quad (8.33.1)$$

$$\Gamma_v(n, q) = \zeta, \qquad (n \leqslant w), \tag{8.33.2}$$

$$\Gamma_v(0, ()) = 0. \tag{8.33.3}$$

The number n of elements inserted to create $\mathcal{T}$ occurs only as argument of Γ_v; all other quantities do not depend on n. With a fixed q, we can therefore hope for $\Gamma_v(n, q)$ to converge to a well-defined limit $\Gamma_v(q)$ as $n \to \infty$.

In fact, the creation process of $\mathcal{T}$ becomes *stationary* once all elements of $[u]$ appear in an internal node: further insertions are then ignored as duplicates. Let us assume we continue the insertion process until saturation. For simplicity, we may assume a process that never inserts duplicates of elements that already appear in internal nodes, then the tree is stationary after at most $u(w+1)$ insertions. In the resulting tree $\mathcal{T}^*$, all leaves are empty, because all elements $v \in [u]$ appear in an internal node. Let $\Gamma_v(q)$ denote the random search costs for element v in $\mathcal{T}^*$. They fulfill a recurrence very similar to $\Gamma_v(n, q)$, namely by formally letting $n \to \infty$:

$$\Gamma_v(q) \overset{\mathcal{D}}{=} \sum_{r=1}^{s-1} \mathbb{1}_{\{v \in P_r\}}\beta_r + \sum_{r=1}^{s} \mathbb{1}_{\{v \in (P_{r-1}, P_r)\}}\big(\gamma_r + \Gamma_v(Z_r)\big), \tag{8.34.1}$$

$$\Gamma_v(()) = 0. \tag{8.34.2}$$

We will later bound the probability for $\Gamma(n, q) \neq \Gamma(q)$ when n is much larger than u, which effectively shows that $\Gamma(n, q)$ converges in probability to $\Gamma(q)$. Note that $\Gamma(q)$ does not depend on ζ, but only on β and γ.

8.7.6 Distributional Recurrence for Weighted Path Length

To analyze the average-case behavior of Quicksort, we will not need search-cost vectors in full, but the product $\Gamma(q)^\top q$. This is the *expected* search cost when searching a random element $U \overset{\mathcal{D}}{=} \mathcal{D}(q)$. As we will work with this quantity a lot later, we give it a name: $A_q = \Gamma(q)^\top q = \mathbb{E}_U[\Gamma_U(q)]$. In other words, A_q is a weighted internal *path length* of random recursion trees: we sum up the costs of all paths from the root to any key in the tree, weighted by the corresponding key's probability, and for the cost of a path, an rth child edge contributes γ_r and ending as rth pivot in a node yields a summand β_r. Starting with Equation (8.34), we find for the random path length A_q the recurrence

$$A_q \;\overset{\mathcal{D}}{=}\; T_q \;+\; \sum_{r=1}^{s} V_r A_{Z_r}^{(r)}, \tag{8.35.1}$$

$$A_{()} \;=\; 0, \tag{8.35.2}$$

$$\text{with} \quad T_q \;=\; \boldsymbol{\beta}^{\mathsf{T}} \cdot \mathbf{H} + \boldsymbol{\gamma}^{\mathsf{T}} \cdot \mathbf{V}, \tag{8.35.3}$$

where $(A_q^{(r)})$ are independent copies of (A_q), which are also independent of $(\mathbf{V}, \mathbf{Z}, T_q)$. Note that $\mathbb{E}_u[\mathbb{1}_{\{u \in (P_{r-1}, P_r)\}}] = v(P_{r-1}, P_r) = V_r$ by definition.

The recurrence is written in this deceptively concise form by hiding complexity in the quantities $\mathbf{V}$ and $\mathbf{Z}$, whose distribution is given in Sections 8.5.2 and 8.6.1.

8.7.7 Expected Weighted Path Length for Random U-ary Words

A general solution for the expected weighted path length $\mathbb{E}[A_q]$ seems hard to obtain. For the special case $s = 2$, $t = (0,0)$ and $w = 1$, i.e., for ordinary binary search trees, the solution is known (Proposition 8.2 on page 291). This case is simpler since we never ever have more than one copy of any value in the tree; this is no longer true for any other parameter choice.

We derive an asymptotic result for the special case of a uniform universe distribution.

> **Theorem 8.14:**
>
> *Assume $\mathcal{T}^*$ is a random $(s, \mathbf{t}, w, \lambda)$-fringe-balanced tree built from inserting i.i.d. uniformly in $\{1, \ldots, u\}$ distributed elements until saturation, i.e., until each value $v \in \{1, \ldots, u\}$ occurs as key in an internal node. Let A_u be the average search cost in $\mathcal{T}^*$, averaged over the values v, where following an rth child edge contributes a summand γ_r and terminating the search as rth pivot in an internal node yields a summand β_r. Then holds*
>
> $$\mathbb{E}[A_u] \;=\; \frac{\boldsymbol{\gamma}^{\mathsf{T}} \boldsymbol{\tau}}{\mathcal{H}} \ln(u) \;\pm\; O(1). \tag{8.36}$$
>
> *The discrete entropy $\mathcal{H}$ is given by Equation (2.193), and $\boldsymbol{\tau} = \frac{t+1}{k+1}$ as usual.* ◀

The proof will use our *distributional master theorem*, Theorem 2.76 (page 116); indeed, were it not for *vector*-parameter q, also the general Equation (8.35) would be in the required form. Before we take on the proof, let us briefly see which restrictions are necessary to get rid of the vector-valued parameter.

Self-Similar Families of Distributions. Let us restrict allowable universe distributions to a family of distributions with a *fixed* number of parameters. One parameter will be the size of the universe u; the limit $u \to \infty$ is a natural choice for asymptotic statements. For general universe distributions, sub-distributions can differ vastly even if their sub-universe is of the same size. If A_q may only depend on u, we need that, except for maybe a few global parameters that remain the same throughout the recursion, *sub-distributions are fully determined by* u. Such families of distributions have a strong *self-similarity*; in particular, all sub-distributions over $u = 2$ elements have to be the same, i.e., $q_{i+1}/q_i = \mu$ for any i. This already determines the shape of q as

$$q \;=\; q(\mu, u) \;\propto\; (\mu, \mu^2, \ldots, \mu^{u-1}, \mu^u), \tag{8.37}$$

for a $\mu > 0$, properly rescaled so that $\Sigma q = 1$. By symmetry, we can require $\mu \in (0, 1]$, i.e., probabilities are decreasing with the index. For a fixed $\mu > 0$, we define $A_u := A_{q(\mu, u)}$. Note that $\mathcal{D}(q(\mu, u))$ is a *truncated geometric distribution* with parameter μ, and these are the only distributions where we can hope for a simple recurrence for A_u.

Assume q fulfills Equation (8.37), for a $\mu > 0$. Then $\mathbb{P}[Z_r = z(\underline{p}, \overline{p})] = \mathbb{P}[V_r = v(\underline{p}, \overline{p})]$ and the recurrence for A_u becomes

$$A_u \;\overset{\mathcal{D}}{=}\; T_u + \sum_{r=1}^{s} V_r\, A_{P_r - P_{r-1} - 1}, \qquad (u \geqslant 1) \tag{8.38.1}$$

$$A_0 \;=\; A_{-1} \;=\; 0, \tag{8.38.2}$$

$$\text{with } T_u \;=\; \beta^{\mathsf{T}} H + \gamma^{\mathsf{T}} V, \tag{8.38.3}$$

with the same independence assumptions as before. For $\mu \neq 1$, we can only conclude that $\mathbb{E}[A_u] = O(1)$ with the master theorem.

Random u-ary Words. Let us study in detail the case $\mu = 1$, so that $q = (\frac{1}{u}, \ldots, \frac{1}{u})$ and $\mathcal{D}(q) = \mathcal{U}[1..u]$ is a uniform distribution. We refer to this case as the random-u-ary-word model, because inputs are formed from i.i.d. uniformly chosen *letters* from the alphabet $[u]$. When duplicates are allowed, this is arguably the most natural model to assume, unless further knowledge is available; it is certainly the one with maximal entropy. As we expect the cost of Quicksort to scale with the entropy of the input (Conjecture 8.5), the uniform distribution is the worst case among all the choices for universe distributions.

The additional symmetry in the uniform case allows further simplifications of Equation (8.38). Since $c_p = \sum_{i=1}^{p} q_i = p \cdot u$ and $\frac{\lceil u \cdot \Pi \rceil}{u} = \Pi + [0, \frac{1}{u})$, we have the stochastic representations

$$P \;=\; F_u^{-1}(\Pi) \tag{8.39}$$

$$\underset{(8.2)}{=}\; \lceil u \cdot \Pi \rceil, \tag{8.40}$$

$$H_r \;=\; \begin{cases} \frac{1}{u}, & \text{if } P_r \text{ is classified as } p_r\,; \\ 0, & \text{otherwise,} \end{cases} \tag{8.41}$$

$$=\; O(u^{-1}), \qquad (u \to \infty), \tag{8.42}$$

and using interval-arithmetic notation

$$
V_r \; = \; \max\{c_{P_r-1} - c_{P_{r-1}}, 0\} \tag{8.43}
$$

$$
= \; \max\left\{ \frac{P_r}{u} - \frac{P_{r-1}}{u} - \frac{1}{u}, 0 \right\} \tag{8.44}
$$

$$
\underset{(8.40)}{=} \; \Pi_r - \Pi_{r-1} \; + \; [0, \tfrac{1}{u}) - [0, \tfrac{1}{u}) - \tfrac{1}{u} \tag{8.45}
$$

$$
= \; D_r \; + \; (-\tfrac{2}{u}, 0) \tag{8.46}
$$

$$
= \; D_r \; \pm \; O(u^{-1}), \qquad (u \to \infty). \tag{8.47}
$$

All error bounds hold uniformly for all realizations of random variables. Inserting these into Equation (8.38) we can simplify the recurrence for A_u

$$
A_u \; \overset{\mathcal{D}}{=} \; T_u + \sum_{r=1}^{s} V_r \, A_{uV_r}, \tag{8.48.1}
$$

$$
A_0 \; = \; A_{-1} \; = \; 0, \tag{8.48.2}
$$

and we obtain an asymptotic approximation for the toll function

$$
T_u \; = \; \gamma^{\mathsf{T}} D \; \pm \; O(u^{-1}), \tag{8.49}
$$

$$
\mathbb{E}[T_u] \; = \; \gamma^{\mathsf{T}} \tau \; \pm \; O(u^{-1}). \tag{8.50}
$$

With these preparations we can start.

Proof of Theorem 8.14: Equation (8.48) has the form (Equation (2.325)) required for Theorem 2.76 (page 116), our DMT with coefficients, with parameters $K = \gamma^{\mathsf{T}} \tau$, $\alpha = 0$, $\beta = 0$, $Z_r = D_r$ and $A_r(z) = V_r$. From Equation (8.48) one might be tempted to choose $Z_r = V_r$, but recall that $V = V^{(q(u))}$ depends on u and is thus no viable choice. Towards applying Theorem 2.76, we have to establish Equations (2.326) and (2.327). The latter is very simple:

$$
\mathbb{E}\big[V_r \,\big|\, V_r \in [z, z + \tfrac{1}{u})\big] \; \in \; [z, z + \tfrac{1}{u}) \; = \; z \pm O(\tfrac{1}{u}), \tag{8.51}
$$

so the coefficients condition (2.327) is fulfilled with $a_r(z) = z$ and $\delta = 1$. The same error bound is obtained for the density-convergence condition (2.326).

Lemma 8.15: *For $1 \leqslant r \leqslant s$ and uniformly for $z \in (0, 1)$ holds that*

$$
u \cdot \mathbb{P}\big[V_r \in (z - \tfrac{1}{u}, z]\big] \; = \; f_{D_r}(z) \pm O(u^{-1}), \qquad (u \to \infty), \tag{8.52}
$$

where $f_{D_r}(z) = z^{t_r}(1 - z)^{k - t_r - 1}/B(t_r + 1, k - t_r)$ is the (marginal) density of D_r. ◄

The proof is essentially by computing. We give the steps in detail below as the lemma is central to the analysis and since some of the transformations are instructive; the casual reader might prefer to skip these. Note that simply by inserting definitions, we already have $V_r = D_r \pm O(u^{-1})$, which even holds always, not only in distribution; see Equation (8.47). This is essentially what we need to show; only that the error bound is just too weak for the density-convergence condition. To get Equation (2.326), we have to work a little harder.

Proof of Lemma 8.15: The density of our Beta resp. Dirichlet distributed variables is Lipschitz-continuous, see Lemma 2.29 (page 73). By Proposition 2.12–(a) on page 52, it suffices to consider $z \in \{\frac{0}{u}, \frac{1}{u}, \frac{2}{u}, \ldots, \frac{u-1}{u}\}$ instead of all $z \in (0,1)$ to prove the claim. For the remainder of this proof, we therefore assume $z = \frac{v}{u}$ for $v \in [0..u-1]$. For these values of z, we simply have $\mathbb{P}\big[V_r \in [z, z + \frac{1}{u})\big] = \mathbb{P}[V_r = z]$.

We deal separately with the different cases for r. The border case $r = 1$ and $r = s$ are somewhat simpler, so let us start with those. Starting with Equation (8.44), we find that uniformly for $z \in (0,1)$ holds

$$
\begin{aligned}
\mathbb{P}[V_1 = z] \;&=\; \mathbb{P}[P_1 - 1 = zu] & (8.53)\\
&\underset{(8.40)}{=}\; \mathbb{P}\big[\lceil u\Pi_1 \rceil = u(z + \tfrac{1}{u})\big] & (8.54)\\
&=\; \mathbb{P}\big[\Pi_1 \in (z, z + \tfrac{1}{u}]\big] & (8.55)\\
&=\; \mathbb{P}\big[D_1 \in (z, z + \tfrac{1}{u}]\big] & (8.56)\\
&=\; \int_z^{z+1/u} \frac{x^{t_1}(1-x)^{k-t_1-1}}{B(t_1+1, k-t_1)}\, dx & (8.57)\\
&\underset{\text{Proposition 2.12–(c)}}{=}\; \frac{f_{D_1}(z)}{u} \pm O(u^{-2}), \qquad (u \to \infty). & (8.58)
\end{aligned}
$$

Similarly, we find

$$
\begin{aligned}
\mathbb{P}[V_s = z] \;&=\; \mathbb{P}[u + 1 - P_{s-1} - 1 = zu] & (8.59)\\
&=\; \mathbb{P}\big[\lceil u\Pi_{s-1} \rceil = u(1 - z)\big] & (8.60)\\
&=\; \mathbb{P}\big[\Pi_{s-1} \in (1 - z - \tfrac{1}{u}, 1 - z]\big] & (8.61)\\
&=\; \mathbb{P}\big[D_s \in [z, z + \tfrac{1}{u})\big] & (8.62)\\
&=\; \frac{f_{D_s}(z)}{u} \pm O(u^{-2}), \qquad (u \to \infty). & (8.63)
\end{aligned}
$$

That was simple enough; for the middle subproblems, $2 \leqslant r \leqslant s - 1$, the difference of two random pivot values is involved. In essence, we again use the smoothness of densities, namely that Dirichlet-densities are Lipschitz-continuous for integral parameters, to get an approximation for the difference of two *discrete* pivot values, P_{r-1} and P_r, in terms of the difference of the *continuous* relative ranks Π_{r-1} and Π_r, whose difference is by definition $D_r = \Pi_r - \Pi_{r-1}$, i.e., Beta distributed. Unlike above, fixing the difference of P_{r-1} and P_r still allows many different choices p for, say, P_{r-1}, that we have to sum over. To get this under control, we will need one more detour of translating from continuous to discrete and back again. Here are the details; all error bounds are understood uniformly in $z \in (0,1)$.

$$
\begin{aligned}
\mathbb{P}[V_r = z] \;&=\; \mathbb{P}[P_r - P_{r-1} - 1 = zu] & (8.64)\\
&=\; \sum_{p=1}^{u} \mathbb{P}\big[P_{r-1} = p \,\wedge\, P_r = p + zu + 1\big] & (8.65)\\
&=\; \sum_{p=1}^{u-zu-1} \mathbb{P}\big[\lceil u\Pi_{r-1} \rceil = p \,\wedge\, \lceil u\Pi_r \rceil = p + zu + 1\big] & (8.66)
\end{aligned}
$$

$$= \sum_{p=1}^{u-zu-1} \mathbb{P}\big[\Pi_{r-1} \in (\tfrac{p}{u} - \tfrac{1}{u}, \tfrac{p}{u}] \wedge \Pi_r \in (\tfrac{p}{u} + z, \tfrac{p}{u} + z + \tfrac{1}{u}]\big], \tag{8.67}$$

and with the aggregated Dirichlet vector $\mathbf{D}^{(r)} = (D_1 + \cdots + D_{r-1}, D_r, D_{r+1} + \cdots + D_s)$, with distribution $\mathbf{D}^{(r)} \overset{\mathcal{D}}{=} \mathrm{Dir}(\boldsymbol{\sigma}^{(r)})$ for the correspondingly aggregated parameter vector $\boldsymbol{\sigma}^{(r)} = (\sigma_1 + \cdots + \sigma_{r-1}, \sigma_r, \sigma_{r+1} + \cdots + \sigma_s)$, we continue,

$$= \sum_{p=1}^{u-zu-1} \mathbb{P}\big[D_1^{(r)} \in (\tfrac{p}{u} - \tfrac{1}{u}, \tfrac{p}{u}] \wedge D_1^{(r)} + D_2^{(r)} \in (\tfrac{p}{u} + z, \tfrac{p}{u} + z + \tfrac{1}{u}]\big] \tag{8.68}$$

$$= \sum_{p=1}^{u-zu-1} \int_{x=\frac{p}{u}-\frac{1}{u}}^{\frac{p}{u}} \int_{y=\frac{p}{u}+z}^{\frac{p}{u}+z+\frac{1}{u}} \frac{x^{\sigma_1^{(r)}-1}(y-x)^{\sigma_2^{(r)}-1}(1-y)^{\sigma_3^{(r)}-1}}{B(\boldsymbol{\sigma}^{(r)})}\, dy\, dx, \tag{8.69}$$

$$\overset{\text{Proposition 2.12–(c)}}{=} \sum_{p=1}^{u-zu-1} \left(\frac{(\tfrac{p}{u})^{\sigma_1^{(r)}-1} z^{\sigma_2^{(r)}-1}(1-z-\tfrac{p}{u})^{\sigma_3^{(r)}-1}}{u^2 \cdot B(\boldsymbol{\sigma}^{(r)})} \pm O(u^{-3})\right) \tag{8.70}$$

$$= \frac{z^{\sigma_2^{(r)}-1}}{u \cdot B(\boldsymbol{\sigma}^{(r)})} \cdot \frac{1}{u}\sum_{p=1}^{(1-z)u-1} (\tfrac{p}{u})^{\sigma_1^{(r)}-1}\big(1-z-\tfrac{p}{u}\big)^{\sigma_3^{(r)}-1} \pm O(u^{-2}); \tag{8.71}$$

and by Proposition 2.12–(b), with $a = 0$, $b = 1 - z$, $n = (1-z)u$, this is

$$= \frac{z^{\sigma_2^{(r)}-1}}{u \cdot B(\boldsymbol{\sigma}^{(r)})} \cdot \left(\int_{\rho=0}^{1-z} \rho^{\sigma_1^{(r)}-1}(1-z-\rho)^{\sigma_3^{(r)}-1} \pm O\big((1-z)u^{-1}\big)\right) \pm O(u^{-2}), \tag{8.72}$$

with the substitution $x = \tfrac{\rho}{1-z}$, i.e., $\rho = (1-z)x$, the integral becomes

$$= \frac{z^{\sigma_2^{(r)}-1}}{u \cdot B(\boldsymbol{\sigma}^{(r)})} \cdot \int_{x=0}^{1} \big((1-z)x\big)^{\sigma_1^{(r)}-1}\big((1-z)(1-x)\big)^{\sigma_3^{(r)}-1}(1-z)\, dx \pm O(u^{-2}) \tag{8.73}$$

$$= \frac{z^{\sigma_2^{(r)}-1}}{u \cdot B(\boldsymbol{\sigma}^{(r)})}(1-z)^{\sigma_1^{(r)}+\sigma_3^{(r)}-1} \cdot B(\sigma_1^{(r)}, \sigma_3^{(r)}) \pm O(u^{-2}) \tag{8.74}$$

$$= \frac{z^{t_r}(1-z)^{k-t_r-1}}{u \cdot B(t_r+1, k-t_r)} \pm O(u^{-2}) \tag{8.75}$$

$$= \frac{f_{D_r}(z)}{u} \pm O(u^{-2}). \tag{8.76}$$

This concludes the proof of Lemma 8.15   ■

With Lemma 8.15 the conditions of the DMT are fulfilled and we are ready to apply it. We start by computing the constant H as

$$H = 1 - \sum_{r=1}^{s} \mathbb{E}[D_r^0 \cdot D_r] = 0, \tag{8.77}$$

so we are in Case 2. With Proposition 2.54 (page 90), we find

$$\tilde{H} \;=\; -\sum_{r=1}^{s} \mathbb{E}[D_r^0 \cdot D_r \ln D_r] \;=\; \mathcal{H}(t), \tag{8.78}$$

and thus $\mathbb{E}[A_u] \sim \frac{\gamma^\mathsf{T}\tau}{\mathcal{H}} \ln u$ by Theorem 2.76.

To get the claimed error term $O(1)$ we proceed as in Section 6.3 for the ordinary Quicksort recurrence and apply the DMT two more times: First, the error term $O(u^{-1})$ in the asymptotic approximation for our toll function $\mathbb{E}[R_u]$ does not cause larger errors: Any toll function in $O(u^{-\varepsilon})$ yields $H < 0$ and thus a contribution in $O(1)$ overall; this with the very same computations as in Section 6.3.

The second application is on $R_u := A_u - \frac{\gamma^\mathsf{T}\tau}{\mathcal{H}} \ln u$. Unfolding the recurrence, we find

$$R_u \;\overset{\mathcal{D}}{=}\; T_R(u) + \sum_{r=1}^{s} V_r R_{uV_r} \tag{8.79}$$

$$\text{with} \quad T_R(u) \;=\; T_u + \sum_{r=1}^{s} V_r \cdot \frac{\gamma^\mathsf{T}\tau}{\mathcal{H}} \ln(uV_r) - \frac{\gamma^\mathsf{T}\tau}{\mathcal{H}} \ln(u), \tag{8.80}$$

so the remainder R_u fulfills a recurrence of the same shape, only with a different toll function. If $\mathbb{E}[T_R(u)] = O(u^{-\varepsilon})$ for a constant $\varepsilon > 0$, we know from above that $\mathbb{E}[R_u] = O(1)$. With Equations (8.47) and (8.50) we find

$$\mathbb{E}[T_R(u)] \;=\; \gamma^\mathsf{T}\tau \pm O(u^{-1}) + \frac{\gamma^\mathsf{T}\tau}{\mathcal{H}} \sum_{r=1}^{s} \mathbb{E}\Big[D_r \cdot \underbrace{\ln\big(u(D_r \pm O(u^{-1}))\big)}_{=\ln(u)+\ln(D_r)\pm O\left(\frac{\log u}{u}\right)}\Big] \pm O\left(\frac{\log u}{u}\right)$$
$$\qquad\qquad -\; \frac{\gamma^\mathsf{T}\tau}{\mathcal{H}} \ln(u) \tag{8.81}$$

$$=\; \gamma^\mathsf{T}\tau\left(1 - \frac{\sum_{r=1}^{s} \mathbb{E}[D_r \ln(D_r)]}{\mathcal{H}}\right) \;\pm\; O\left(\frac{\log u}{u}\right) \tag{8.82}$$

$$\underset{\text{Proposition 2.54}}{=}\; 0 \;\pm\; O\left(\frac{\log u}{u}\right) \tag{8.83}$$

$$=\; O(u^{-\varepsilon}), \tag{8.84}$$

for any $\varepsilon \in (0,1)$. So indeed, $\mathbb{E}[R_u] = O(1)$.

Together, this shows that indeed $\mathbb{E}[A_u] = \frac{\gamma^\mathsf{T}\tau}{\mathcal{H}} \pm O(1)$ as $u \to \infty$, and the proof of Theorem 8.14 is complete. ∎

We have seen that we can extend the connection between Quicksort and search trees to our s-way Quicksort with sampling by considering fringe-balanced search trees. We then analyzed search costs in the latter when generated from inputs with equal keys. In the next section, we close the remaining gap between this result on search trees and the analysis of Quicksort.

8.8 Quicksort Under Stateless Cost Measures

In this section, we derive an asymptotic approximation of $C_{n,q}$ for large n. The key idea is to separate the influence of n from that of q; intuitively speaking, we can approximate the costs of Quicksort by the costs of *searching* n random elements from the universe distribution in a random recursion tree of Quicksort. The general result in Theorem 8.16 below remains implicit, but for random u-ary words we state an explicit result in Theorem 8.17.

The concepts of expected-profile models with many duplicates and degenerate inputs are formally introduced below.

> **Theorem 8.16 (Expected-Profile Quicksort Recurrence):**
> *Consider Quicksort with an s-way fat-pivot partitioning method and pivot-sampling parameter t, under an expected-profile model with many duplicates, in the sense of Definition 8.18. Further assume a stateless cost measure, i.e., partitioning costs are $T_{n,q} = \beta^{\mathsf{T}}E + \gamma^{\mathsf{T}}I$, where $\beta \in \mathbb{R}^{s-1}_{>0}$ and $\gamma \in \mathbb{R}^{s}_{>0}$ are constant vectors. Denote by $C_{n,q}$, for $n \in \mathbb{N}$, the (random) costs to sort an input of size n with universe distribution q.*
>
> $\boxed{1}$ *The expected costs satisfy*
>
> $$\mathbb{E}[C_{n,q}] \;=\; \mathbb{E}[A_q] \cdot n \;\pm\; O(n^{1-\varepsilon}), \qquad (n \to \infty), \tag{8.85}$$
>
> *for a constant $\varepsilon > 0$ and the coefficient $\mathbb{E}[A_q]$ as given (recursively) by Equation (8.35). Note that $\mathbb{E}[A_q]$ depends only on the universe distribution $q = q^{(n)}$ and t, but not on n.*
>
> $\boxed{2}$ *Conditional on the event that the input is not degenerate (in the sense of Definition 8.20), we have the following stochastic representation:*
>
> $$C_{n,q} \;\overset{\mathcal{D}}{=}\; \Gamma^{\mathsf{T}} \cdot X \;\pm\; O(n^{1-\varepsilon}), \qquad (n \to \infty), \tag{8.86}$$
>
> *where $\Gamma = \Gamma(q^{(n)}) \in \mathbb{R}^{u_n}_{>0}$ and $X \in \mathbb{N}^{u_n}_0$ are independent, $X \overset{\mathcal{D}}{=} \mathrm{Mult}(n, q^{(n)})$, and the distribution of Γ is given recursively by Equation (8.34). The error term holds uniformly for all values of the random variables.*
>
> *If $\mu_n = \min_r q_r^{(n)} = \Omega(n^{-\rho})$, the error bounds hold for all $\varepsilon \in (0, 1-3\rho)$.*   ◄

Remark (Limit Distribution): Assume we fix a universe distribution q independent of n. Then holds for non-degenerate inputs

$$C_{n,q}/n \;\overset{\mathcal{D}}{=}\; \Gamma^{\mathsf{T}}X/n \;\pm\; O(n^{-\varepsilon}) \;\overset{\text{a.s.}}{\longrightarrow}\; \Gamma^{\mathsf{T}}q \;=\; A_q \tag{8.87}$$

by the *strong law of large numbers* and the *continuous mapping theorem*. Asymptotically for non-degenerate inputs and *fixed* q, the *distribution* of $C_{n,q}$ is thus determined by A_q. It is basically dominated by a few elements at the beginning, and highly concentrated.

Also note that A_q is a discrete distribution as there are only finitely many different recursion trees for a fixed universe size. This reflects the discrete nature of expected-profile models, as opposed to the continuous nature of the uniform model (random-permutation model). ◄

8.8.1 Random u-Ary Words

In the uniform case $q^{(u)} = (\frac{1}{u}, \ldots, \frac{1}{u})$, i.e., the random-u-ary-word model, we know an asymptotic approximation for $\mathbb{E}[A_q]$ (Theorem 8.14). Combining this with Theorem 8.16 yields our main analysis result. (We state it as another theorem, even though it is technically a direct corollary.)

> **Theorem 8.17 (Quicksort on Random u-ary Words):**
> *Consider Quicksort with an s-way fat-pivot partitioning method and pivot-sampling parameter* t, *under the random-u-ary-word model, where* $u = u_n$ *depends on* n, *so that* $u_n = \omega(1)$ *and* $u_n = O(n^{1/3-\varepsilon})$ *as* $n \to \infty$. *Further assume a stateless cost measure (in the sense of Definition 8.7) and denote by* C_n *the costs to sort a random* u_n*-ary word of length* n. *Then*
>
> $$\mathbb{E}[C_n] = \frac{\gamma^\mathsf{T}\tau}{\mathcal{H}} \cdot n\ln(u_n) \pm O(n), \qquad (n \to \infty), \qquad (8.88)$$
>
> *with discrete entropy* $\mathcal{H}$ *given by Equation (2.193), and* $\tau = \frac{t+1}{k+1}$ *as usual.* ∎

The rest of this section is devoted to the proof of Theorem 8.16; before we start, we formally introduce expected-profile models with many duplicates and degenerate inputs (Section 8.8.3), and how they relate to search costs in recursion trees (Section 8.8.2).

8.8.2 Quicksort Costs Value-Wise

A stateless cost measure effectively allows us to *reorder* parts of the input freely without affecting costs, as long as no pivot choices are affected: such a shuffling only affects the relative order of ordinary elements during partitioning, whose cost contribution is determined by their class only; it does not depend on their position in the input. We can thus state the costs of Quicksort in an alternative form. The usual Quicksort recurrence expresses total costs *partition-wise:* as the sum of partitioning costs over all partitioning stages. In terms of the recursion tree of Quicksort, we sum the contribution $\beta^\mathsf{T}E + \gamma^\mathsf{T}I$ over all nodes. Under a stateless cost measure, we can instead express costs also *value-wise,* i.e., summing over all elements of the universe.

This "transposition" of cost contributions allows then to further exploit the i.i.d. assumption for our input model. Before we proceed to the formal statement of this alternative representation of costs, let us first see it work on an example.

Example. In the recursion tree of Quicksort (Definition 8.9), we create a node with the used pivot values for each partitioning step, and a leaf for subproblems with size at most w, containing the remaining elements. Assume for this example that the universe size is $u = 8$ and n is large. It is then very likely that $\mathbf{X} \geqslant w + 1$, i.e., each of the eight values occurs at least $w + 1$ times. Let us assume this for the rest of the example.

Then each of the eight values is used as a pivot in *exactly* one partitioning step; all duplicates of this element will be removed in this step, and only there. Leaves will thus always be empty, i.e., Insertionsort is always called for empty subranges.

Assume that we use a dual-pivot Quicksort with the single comparison tree shown in Figure 56 (page 304). One possible outcome for the recursion tree is shown in Figure 58.

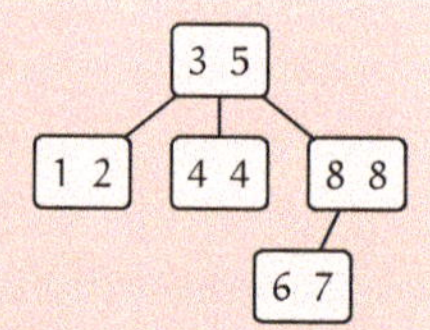

Figure 58: Exemplary recursion tree of a dual-pivot Quicksort with universe size $u = 8$. Each node represents a partitioning step, with the two pivot values given in the node. Child links correspond to child recursive calls, where subranges of the array appear in the order of the tree. Empty leaves are not shown.

The cost of a partitioning step are $\boldsymbol{\beta}^{\mathsf{T}}\mathbf{E} + \boldsymbol{\gamma}^{\mathsf{T}}\mathbf{I}$, for $\mathbf{I}$ and $\mathbf{E}$ the number of ordinary elements with the given classes. If we count as costs the number of ternary comparisons, we have $\boldsymbol{\beta} = (1,2)$ and $\boldsymbol{\gamma} = (1,2,2)$. The segment sizes $\mathbf{I}$ and $\mathbf{E}$ are essentially given by the profile $\mathbf{X}$ of the input, but the number of ordinary elements can be a little smaller due to sampled-out elements. This offset cannot exceed the sample size k, which is a constant.

For the first partitioning step, corresponding to pivots $(3,5)$, we have $\mathbf{E} = (X_3, X_5) \pm (k-1)$ and $\mathbf{I} = (X_1 + X_2, X_4, X_6 + X_7 + X_8) \pm t$. In total, we will overestimate the costs of each partitioning step by at most $c \cdot k$ for a constant c, if we include sampled-out elements in our computation. The (random) total costs for sorting, conditional on the recursion tree from Figure 58, are then

$$
C_n = \begin{cases}
(X_1 + X_2)\gamma_1 + X_3\beta_1 + X_4\gamma_2 + X_5\beta_2 + (X_6 + X_7 + X_8)\gamma_3 & \pm c \cdot k \\
\quad + X_1\beta_1 \qquad\qquad\qquad + X_2\beta_2 & \pm c \cdot k \\
\quad + X_4\beta_1 & \pm c \cdot k \\
+ (X_6 + X_7)\gamma_1 + X_8\beta_1 & \pm c \cdot k \\
\quad + X_6\beta_1 \qquad\qquad + X_7\beta_2 & \pm c \cdot k.
\end{cases}
\tag{8.89}
$$

Here each line corresponds to one partitioning step and each column corresponds to one class, in order s_2, p_1, s_1, p_2, l_1. Note that the used comparison tree decides that in case $P_1 = P_2$, all elements are treated as p_1, see Figure 56; that is why, e.g., the third line says $X_4\beta_1$. By re-aligning rows so that each X_i gets a column of its own this is the same as

$$
C_n = \begin{cases}
X_1\gamma_1 + X_2\gamma_1 + X_3\beta_1 + X_4\gamma_2 + X_5\beta_2 + X_6\gamma_3 + X_7\gamma_3 + X_8\gamma_3 & \pm c \cdot k \\
+ X_1\beta_1 + X_2\beta_2 & \pm c \cdot k \\
\qquad\qquad\qquad\qquad + X_4\beta_1 & \pm c \cdot k \\
\qquad\qquad\qquad\qquad\qquad\qquad\qquad + X_6\gamma_1 + X_7\gamma_1 + X_8\beta_1 & \pm c \cdot k \\
\qquad\qquad\qquad\qquad\qquad\qquad\qquad + X_6\beta_1 + X_7\beta_2 & \pm c \cdot k.
\end{cases}
\tag{8.90}
$$

If we read this sum column-wise, we find that, up to the given error terms, *overall sorting costs are the cost of searching each element in the recursion tree*, where following an rth child pointer costs γ_r and ending in a node as an rth pivot costs β_r. For example, when searching 6 in the tree from Figure 58, we first go right, then left and then find 6 as the first pivot. The costs are thus $\gamma_3 + \gamma_1 + \beta_1$, and this is coefficient of X_6 in overall costs, since there are X_6 occurrences of the value 6 in the input. In vector form, we can write search costs as $\Gamma^T X$, where in the above example

$$\Gamma \;=\; (\gamma_1 + \beta_1, \;\; \gamma_1 + \beta_2, \;\; \beta_1, \;\; \gamma_2 + \beta_1, \;\; \beta_2, \;\; \gamma_3 + \gamma_1 + \beta_1, \;\; \gamma_3 + \gamma_1 + \beta_2, \;\; \gamma_3 + \beta_1).$$
$$(8.91)$$

Of course, Γ is just the search-cost vector corresponding to our recursion tree; cf. Section 8.7.4. Note that the above transformation is exact except for the given error term; in particular, it holds for any realization of the random variables, not only in distribution.

General Case. The arguments used in the example extend to the general case, but a few issues need to be addressed:

1. The recursion tree was fixed in the example, but it is really a random object, that depends on the input, as well.

2. We have to bound the error we make by charging costs for sampled-out elements.

3. We have to bound the probability of degenerate cases, where not all elements occur at least w times.

8.8.3 Many Duplicates and Degeneracy

To address the above issues, we consider the following rather general model for how q, and thus u, may evolve with growing n.

Definition 8.18 (Expected-Profile Model with Many Duplicates):
Let $(q^{(n)})_{n\in\mathbb{N}}$ be a sequence of stochastic vectors, where $q^{(n)}$ has u_n entries, i.e., $q^{(n)} \in (0,1)^{u_n}$ and $\Sigma q^{(n)} = 1$, for all $n \in \mathbb{N}$. An input of size $n \in \mathbb{N}$ under the expected-profile model for $(q^{(n)})$ consists of the n i.i.d. $\mathcal{D}(q^{(n)})$ distributed random variables $U = (U_1, \ldots, U_n)$.
    The expected-profile model is said to have *many duplicates* if for $\mu_n := \min_r q_r^{(n)}$ holds $\mu_n = \Omega(n^{-1/3+\varepsilon})$ with a constant $\varepsilon > 0$. ◄

The condition for *many duplicates* is a little unintuitive, but the lower bound on μ_n is effectively an upper bound on u_n, as stated below. Bounding the universe size surely means many equal elements.

Fact 8.19: In any expected-profile model holds $u_n \leqslant \frac{1}{\mu_n}$ for all n. In particular, an expected-profile model with many duplicates has $u_n = O(n^{1/3-\varepsilon})$. ◄

Proof: Since μ_n is the smallest entry of $q^{(n)}$ we have $1 = \Sigma q^{(n)} \geqslant u_n \mu_n$, so $u_n \leqslant 1/\mu_n$. The second part follows directly from the definition. ∎

The converse is of course not true: even if the universe size remains fixed, distributions over it can assign some values arbitrarily little weight. We have to exclude this case, so we state the bound on μ_n. In light of this, it would be more appropriate to call our condition *many duplicates of each kind;* for conciseness, we refrain from doing so.

The precise value of the bound is chosen so that *degenerate* inputs, in the sense of the following definition, are rare enough.

Definition 8.20 (Degenerate Inputs): *Let $v \in [0,1)$ and $k \in \mathbb{N}$. An input vector $\mathbf{U} = (U_1, \ldots, U_n) \in [1..u]^n$ of size n is called (v, k)-degenerate if not all u elements of the universe appear at least k times in the first $n_T = \lceil n^v \rceil$ elements $U_1, \ldots, U_{n_T}$ of $\mathbf{U}$. If the parameters are clear from the context or not important, we call $\mathbf{U}$ simply degenerate.* ◄

The idea behind this definition is that, in general, the recursion tree and the profile of the input are *not independent:* if we fix a recursion tree, we have a slightly higher expected number of duplicates of the pivots higher up in the tree than those further down in the tree. For non-degenerate inputs, however, the recursion tree will depend only on the first n_T elements, and the (asymptotically) larger portion of the profile is indeed independent of the tree.

Choosing n_T large enough so that the first k occurrences of all values are among the first n_T elements with high probability, and at the same time small enough to not make a large error in ignoring these elements' cost for the search costs, we obtain our main result for stateless cost measures and expected-profile inputs with many duplicates.

8.8.4 Proof of Theorem 8.16

The proof will basically have to address the three issues listed above. We first show that degenerate inputs are so unlikely that we can basically ignore them, and use this to separate the distribution of recursion trees and search costs. We then address the sampled-out elements, and put the results together.

Probability of Degenerate Profiles. Bounding the probability of degenerate profiles is essentially a standard application of the Chernoff bound (our Lemma 2.35). To obtain a meaningful statement, we give an asymptotic result.

Lemma 8.21 (Non-Degenerate With High Probability): *Assume an expected-profile model with $\mu_n = \min_r q_r^{(n)} = \Omega(n^{-\rho})$ for $\rho \in [0, \frac{1}{2})$ and let $k \in \mathbb{N}$ and $v \in (2\rho, 1)$. Then holds: the probability of an input of size n to be (v, k)-degenerate is in $o(n^{-c})$ for any constant c.* ◄

Proof: Let $\rho \in [0, \frac{1}{2})$, k and $v \in (2\rho, 1)$ by given. Set $\varepsilon = v - 2\rho > 0$ and denote by $Y = Y^{(n)}$ the profile of the first $n_T = \lceil n^v \rceil$ elements of the input. Clearly $Y^{(n)} \overset{\mathcal{D}}{=} \text{Mult}(n_T; q^{(n)})$. Assume w.l.o.g. that the minimal probability is always $q_1^{(n)} = \mu_n$. A standard application of the *union bound* and the *Chernoff bound* yields

$$\mathbb{P}\big[\neg\mathbf{Y}^{(n)} \geqslant k\big] \;=\; \mathbb{P}\left[\bigvee_{r=1}^{u_n} Y_r^{(n)} < k\right] \tag{8.92}$$

$$\leqslant\; \sum_{r=1}^{u_n} \mathbb{P}\big[Y_r^{(n)} < k\big] \tag{8.93}$$

$$\leqslant\; u_n \cdot \mathbb{P}\big[Y_1^{(n)} < k\big]\,; \tag{8.94}$$

with $\delta = \mu_n - \frac{k}{n_T}$, this is

$$=\; u_n \cdot \mathbb{P}\left[\frac{X_1}{n_T} < \mu_n - \delta\right] \tag{8.95}$$

$$\underset{\text{Lemma 2.35}}{\leqslant}\; 2u_n \exp\left(-2\left(\mu_n - \frac{k}{n_T}\right)^2 n_T\right). \tag{8.96}$$

By assumption $\mu_n = \Omega(n^{-\rho})$, so for some constants n_μ and $c_\mu > 0$ we have $\mu_n \geqslant c_\mu n^{-\rho}$ for $n \geqslant n_\mu$, and by definition is $n_T = \lceil n^\nu \rceil = n^{2\rho+\varepsilon} \pm O(1)$. Inserting these, we find

$$\left(\mu_n - \frac{k}{n_T}\right)^2 n_T \;\geqslant\; \left(c_\mu n^{-\rho}(1 \pm O(n^{-\rho-\varepsilon}))\right)^2 n^\nu (1 \pm O(n^{-\nu})) \tag{8.97}$$

$$=\; c_\mu^2 n^\varepsilon (1 \pm O(n^{-\rho-\varepsilon})). \tag{8.98}$$

By Fact 8.19, also $u_n = O(n^\rho)$, so $\ln(u_n) = O(\log n)$, and we obtain for any $c \geqslant 0$ that

$$n^c \cdot \mathbb{P}\big[\neg\mathbf{Y}^{(n)} \geqslant k\big] \;\underset{(8.96)}{\leqslant}\; 2\exp\left(c\ln(n) + \ln(u_n) - 2\left(\mu_n - \frac{k}{n_T}\right)^2 n_T\right) \tag{8.99}$$

$$\underset{(8.98)}{=}\; 2\exp\left(-2c_\mu^2 n^\varepsilon (1 \pm o(1))\right) \tag{8.100}$$

$$\to\; 0, \qquad (n \to \infty). \tag{8.101}$$

This concludes the proof of the lemma. ∎

In Theorem 8.16, we assume an expected-profile model with many duplicates, i.e., $\frac{1}{\mu_n} = O(n^\rho)$ with $\rho \in [0, \frac{1}{3})$. For given $\varepsilon \in (0, 1-3\rho)$, we set

$$\nu \;:=\; 1-\varepsilon-\rho \;\in\; (2\rho, 1-\rho). \tag{8.102}$$

Then, by Lemma 8.21, an input is $(\nu, w+1)$-degenerate with probability in $o(n^{-c})$ for all c. This also means that the overall cost contribution of degenerate inputs to expected costs is in $o(n^{-c})$ for all c, and hence covered by the error term in Equation (8.85), since costs for any input are at most quadratic.

We will thus, for the remainder of this proof, assume that the input is not $(\nu, w+1)$-degenerate, i.e., each of the values of the universe appears at least $w+1 \geqslant k$ times among the first $n_T = \lceil n^\nu \rceil$ elements.

Independence of Recursion Trees.   We now turn to the distribution of the recursion trees. By Proposition 8.12 (page 313), recursion trees for s-way Quicksort with sampling parameter t have the same distribution as naturally grown t-fringe-balanced s-ary search tree with leaf-buffer size w.

The shape of the recursion tree is determined by at most $u \cdot k$ elements: we have at most u partitioning rounds since each of the u elements of the universe becomes a pivot in at most one partitioning step, and each of these chooses pivots after inspecting k elements.

Also, for each of the u values in the universe, at most the first $w + 1$ occurrences in the input, reading from left to right, can influence the tree. If a value $v \in [u]$ is already contained in an inner node, all further duplicates of v are ignored. Otherwise, all occurrences of v are collected in a single leaf, which can hold up to w values, so there are never more than w copies of v in the tree. At the latest upon inserting the $(w + 1)$st occurrence of a value v will the leaf overflow and a new internal node containing a pivot v is created; this might also happen earlier if other values make the leaf overflow and v is chosen as pivot.

In our non-degenerate input, the first $w + 1$ duplicates appear among the n_T first elements $U_1, \ldots, U_{n_T}$ of the input, so all pivots are chosen based on these elements only. Moreover, after these n_T insertions, *all* u elements appear for sure in inner nodes, so all leaves must be empty. The recursion tree has reached a stationary state, and cannot change any further.

As before, we denote by $\Gamma = \Gamma(q)$ the search-costs vector for the final recursion tree, and further, by $\tilde{X}$ the profile of $U_{n_T+1}, \ldots, U_n$. Since they are derived from disjoint ranges of the i.i.d. input, Γ and $\tilde{X}$ are stochastically independent.

Contribution of Sampled-Out Elements.   With a non-degenerate profile $X \geqslant w + 1$, where each element of the universe appears at least $w + 1$ times, the transformation shown on the example works for any fixed recursion tree. With the search costs $\Gamma^T X$, we overestimate the actual costs by at most $c \cdot k$ for each partitioning step, as we include the k sample elements. Here c is the maximum of all entries in β and γ. As argued above, we have at most u partitioning steps, so overall cost are $C_{n,q} = \Gamma^T X \pm O(u)$.

Result.   We now have all ingredients to compute the overall costs of Quicksort. Recall that $u_n = O(n^\rho)$ and $n_T \sim n^\nu$ with $\nu < 1 - \rho$. Since $\Gamma \leqslant cu$ for a constant c, we have for non-degenerate inputs the claimed stochastic representation:

$$
\begin{aligned}
C_{n,q} \;&=\; \Gamma^T X \;\pm\; O(u) & (8.103)\\
&=\; \Gamma^T \tilde{X} \;\pm\; O(u \cdot n_T) & (8.104)\\
&=\; \Gamma^T \tilde{X} \;\pm\; O(n^{1-\varepsilon}) & (8.105)\\
&\overset{\mathcal{D}}{=}\; \Gamma^T \hat{X} \;\pm\; O(n^{1-\varepsilon}), & (8.106)
\end{aligned}
$$

where $\hat{X}$ is independent of Γ and $\hat{X} \overset{\mathcal{D}}{=} \mathrm{Mult}(n, q^{(n)})$. Taking expectations over all non-degenerate inputs and exploiting independence yields

$$
\mathbb{E}[C_{n,q}] \;=\; \mathbb{E}[\Gamma^T \hat{X}] \;\pm\; O(n^{1-\varepsilon}) \tag{8.107}
$$

$$= \quad \mathbb{E}[\Gamma]^{\mathsf{T}} \cdot \mathbb{E}[\hat{X}] \quad \pm \quad O(n^{1-\varepsilon}) \tag{8.108}$$

$$= \quad \underbrace{\left(\mathbb{E}[\Gamma]^{\mathsf{T}} \cdot q^{(n)}\right)}_{\mathbb{E}[A_q]} \cdot n \quad \pm \quad O(n^{1-\varepsilon}), \tag{8.109}$$

with A_q as given in Section 8.7.6. As argued above, the contribution of degenerate inputs is in $o(n^{-c})$ for any c and thus covered by $O(n^{1-\varepsilon})$, so Equation (8.109) holds also for the unconditional expectation. This concludes the proof of Theorem 8.16.

◆   ◆   ◆

Hibbard [78] described the intimate connection of Quicksort and search trees in 1962; it was one of first nontrivial results on Quicksort in its history. We used it in the last technical section of this work to show that for large expected-profile inputs, we can express the costs of Quicksort as n times a path length of a search tree. With the results on path lengths from Section 8.7, we obtain the first average-case analysis of Quicksort on an input model with equal keys beyond the case of single-pivot Quicksort without sampling.

8.9 Discussion

The main analytical result of this chapter is Theorem 8.17 on page 323, which allows us to obtain total costs from partitioning costs of any fat-pivot method in the random-u-ary-word model. A technical restriction remains, namely that u must be in the range $u = \omega(1)$ and $u = O(n^{1/3-\varepsilon})$ as $n \to \infty$ for an $\varepsilon > 0$, but this covers the interesting range where we have many equal keys.

Bentley-McIlroy vs. Dijkstra. As a warmup, let us apply our result to compare the two well-known fat-pivot partitioning methods using a single pivot. What makes the widely used Bentley-McIlroy method superior in practice to the much simpler Dijkstra partitioning?

Theorem 8.17 tell us that the only property of the partitioning method that influences the leading term of costs is the costs per element of the s non-pivot classes; in terms of stateless cost measures (Definition 8.7), this is the coefficient vector γ. We discussed the values of γ in Section 8.5. For the number of (ternary) comparisons, both methods have $\gamma = (1,1)$, so they both perform

$$\mathbb{E}[C_{n,u}] \quad = \quad \frac{1}{\mathcal{H}} n \ln(u) \ \pm \ O(n), \qquad (n \to \infty, u = \omega(1), u = O(n^{1/3-\varepsilon})), \tag{8.110}$$

comparisons on average to sort a random u-ary word of length n. The number of comparisons will not make the difference.

How about scanned elements? Dijkstra partitioning is a *fat-separator method* and has $\gamma = (2,1)$; the segment for small elements is scanned by indices k and k_2; Bentley-McIlroy partitioning in contrast is a *fat-outsides method* and has $\gamma = (1,1)$. As long as we do not sample skewed pivots, Dijkstra partitioning incurs 50 % more scanned elements in the asymptotic average. This is reasonable explanation for its practical superiority on inputs with many equal keys.

The Conjecture of Sedgewick and Bentley.   With the results of this chapter, we made progress on Conjecture 8.5 of Sedgewick and Bentley: We confirmed that on random u-ary words, median-of-k Quicksort is entropy-optimal up to the leading term for $k \to \infty$, in the range of validity for u of our results. This directly follows from inserting $1/\mathcal{H} \to 1/\ln(2)$ as $k \to \infty$ in Equation (8.110) and from noting that $\mathcal{H}_{\mathrm{ld}}(\frac{1}{u}, \dots, \frac{1}{u}) = \mathrm{ld}(u)$.

The same is true for s-way Quicksort with a balanced comparison tree as $s \to \infty$, and in fact, for any family of Quicksort algorithms that in the limit attains the lower-bound on random permutations.

The Potential of Multiway Partitioning.   Our analysis has the aforementioned idiosyncrasies of requiring a stateless cost measure and a certain range for u; but apart from that Theorem 8.17 is a very fine result. Its true beauty lies in its simplicity and similarity to the solution for the Quicksort recurrence on random permutations (cf. Theorem 6.1 on page 196): *we merely have to replace* $\ln(n)$ *by* $\ln(u)$. Intuitively, this makes sense: instead of $\ln(n)/\mathcal{H}$ levels in the recursion tree, we now have $\ln(u)/\mathcal{H}$, because in each step, not a c/n fraction of the input is removed, but a c/u fraction. Yet I find it surprising that this simplistic reasoning gives the exact result.

If we consider the number of (ternary) comparisons as cost measure, any choice of parameters $(s, m, \mathbf{t}, \lambda)$ for generic one-pass partitioning with a single comparison tree λ can be used as basis for a corresponding fat-pivot method; the simplest choice is a fat-separator method as discussed in Section 8.4. Then Quicksort needs

$$\mathbb{E}[C_n] \;=\; \frac{\lambda^{\mathsf{T}}\tau}{\mathcal{H}} n \ln(n) \;\pm\; O(n) \tag{8.111}$$

comparisons to sort a random permutation of length n, and

$$\mathbb{E}[C_{n,u}] \;=\; \frac{\lambda^{\mathsf{T}}\tau}{\mathcal{H}} n \ln(u) \;\pm\; O(n) \tag{8.112}$$

comparisons to sort a random u-ary word as $n \to \infty$, with $u = \omega(1)$ and $u = O(n^{1/3-\varepsilon})$. *Simply replace* $\ln(n)$ *by* $\ln(u)$.

When we compare the number of scanned elements, it becomes important where we collect duplicates. We have seen in the competition between Dijkstra partitioning and Bentley-McIlroy partitioning that fat-outsides methods are superior w.r.t. scanned elements, so let us focus on these. As discussed in Section 8.5, with such a partitioning method Quicksort needs with α_{SE} given in Equation (5.23) on page 176

$$\mathbb{E}[SE_n] \;=\; \frac{\alpha_{SE}^{\mathsf{T}}\tau}{\mathcal{H}} n \ln(n) \;\pm\; O(n) \tag{8.113}$$

comparisons to sort a random permutation of length n, and

$$\mathbb{E}[SE_{n,u}] \;=\; \frac{\boldsymbol{\alpha}_{SE}^{\mathsf{T}}\,\boldsymbol{\tau}}{\mathcal{H}} n \ln(u) \;\pm\; O(n) \tag{8.114}$$

comparisons to sort a random u-ary word as $n \to \infty$, with $u = \omega(1)$ and $u = O(n^{1/3-\varepsilon})$. *Simply replace* $\ln(n)$ *by* $\ln(u)$.

This means that the two most effective optimizations of Quicksort—pivot sampling and multiway partitioning—are also effective for inputs with equal keys: in fact, they yield the very *same* relative speedup over basic Quicksort under the random-permutation model and under the random-u-ary-word model. For the most parts, our conclusions in Chapter 7 from the random-permutation results transfer directly to random u-ary words. *The same tricks help, and they even help the same.*

9 Conclusion

THE THESIS OF MY DISSERTATION has been that *multiway partitioning is a major improvement for Quicksort,* to be named in the same breath as pivot sampling and using Insertionsort for small subproblems, and not merely a gimmicky extension to keep Ph.D. students busy. To make my thesis verifiable, I described the design space of one-pass in-place partitioning algorithms, keeping as many design decisions open as possible. To demonstrate its generality I showed that all known such methods fit into my framework of *generic s-way one-pass partitioning*.

I am too much of a theoretician to trust in running time studies to give a reliable answer to my algorithmic question; so to test my thesis I conducted a mathematical average-case analysis of Quicksort with generic one-pass partitioning. I am also too much of a practitioner to believe that simple models for the cost of the execution of an algorithm can accurately predict its running time on modern computers. I do believe, however, that substantial improvements in running time that are stable across different machines, must have a cause observable also in a model that abstracts substantially from reality and allows a mathematical analysis.

As described in the introduction, memory speed has not fully kept pace with improvements in processing power. This growing imbalance forces us to economize on memory accesses in algorithms that were almost entirely CPU-bound in the past, and calls for new cost models for the analysis of algorithms. For sorting algorithms that build on sequential scans over their input, the proposed cost measure scanned elements serves as such a model and gives a good indication of the amount of memory traffic caused by an algorithm. It is exactly the amount of scanned elements where the dual-pivot Quicksort used in Java outclasses classic Quicksort.

I showed in this work what further improvements w.r.t. scanned elements are possible with multiway Quicksort. As has been demonstrated for particular implementations, it is likely that these improvements will also lead to better running time in practice.

9.1 The Optimal Quicksort?

Sedgewick finished his thesis with the remark that *"the final choice of implementation obviously depends on circumstances under which the program will be used, and the reader that has persisted this far should have little difficulty making the proper choices for his application."* ([162], p. 344). This applies equally well to my work, yet in light of the many parameters of generic one-pass partitioning, it is natural to ask for more specific advise on how to choose them.

First of all, it seems plausible to consider as cost measure a convex combination of all our cost measures. The relative weights are the relative importance of the cost measures, and depend on the target machine; on current machines the weight of scanned elements will be much larger than all others.

Combining hints from Chapter 7, I propose the following method to choose parameters. Here, we assume that the sample size k is given; this will have to be optimized over in running time studies, because the best value for k is very sensitive to the targeted input size. The larger the inputs to sort, the larger k will get. For given k, a good choice is

$$s = 2\lceil \log_3(k+1) \rceil, \tag{9.1}$$

$$m = \lceil s/2 \rceil, \tag{9.2}$$

$$\mathbf{t} = \text{optimal sampling vector w.r.t. scanned-elements}, \tag{9.3}$$

$$\lambda_k = \lambda_g = \text{extremal tree for } s \text{ and } m. \tag{9.4}$$

We defined extremal trees in Definition 7.15 (page 254). Finding a close to optimal $\mathbf{t}$ can be done with Algorithm 11 (page 246); Table 10 (page 248) contains optimal choices $\mathbf{t}$ for $s = 6$. The outcome of our procedure to choose the parameters for the first few values of k is shown in Table 11.

Table 11: Parameter choices resulting form the described procedure for the first values of k.

k	s	m	t	$\lambda_k = \lambda_g$
1	2	1	(0,0)	
2	2	1	(0,1)	
3	4	2	(0,0,0,0)	
4	4	2	(0,0,1,0)	
5	4	2	(0,1,1,0)	
6	4	2	(0,1,2,0)	
7	4	2	(0,2,2,0)	
8	4	2	(0,2,3,0)	

k	s	m	t	$\lambda_k = \lambda_g$
9	6	3	(0,0,2,2,0,0)	
10	6	3	(0,0,2,3,0,0)	
11	6	3	(0,0,3,3,0,0)	
12	6	3	(0,0,3,3,1,0)	
13	6	3	(0,1,3,3,1,0)	
14	6	3	(0,1,3,4,1,0)	
15	6	3	(0,1,4,4,1,0)	

When a good k has been found and s, m, $\mathbf{t}$ and λ_k/λ_g have been set appropriately, a second running time study should be used to find a good Insertionsort cutoff w.

Note that dual-pivot Quicksort is never chosen by this scheme. The choices above are quite strongly biased towards saving scanned elements on large inputs; in practice, the number of executed instructions will also be important. Counting individual instructions is too implementation-dependent to analyze in the style of this work, but it is possible that the Java 7 implementation is more efficient in that respect than using more pivots. Nevertheless, I consider it likely that we will eventually see a clever implementation of four- or six-way Quicksort outperform Java's current implementation.

9.2 Open Problems and Future Work

The following directions for future research seem interesting.

▶ The code we gave for generic one-pass partitioning was intended to describe the method precisely, so that we can refer to it in the analysis. But for any specific choice of its parameters, more elegant and efficient code can be found.

It seems promising to develop such implementations for the parameter choices listed above and see if we can make them competitive with Java's dual-pivot Quicksort.

▶ Quicksort is related to search trees as we discussed in Chapter 8. If it is nowadays advisable to use multiway Quicksort, it might also be advisable to use multiway search trees for dictionary data structures.

Of course, search trees with large fanout have been used successfully for decades, in particular in scenarios where the data is too large fit into main memory. General-purpose implementations in programming libraries, however, still use binary-search-tree based implementations. For such smaller in-memory scenarios, a B-tree or similar structures might add too much overhead, but a simpler implementation based on s-ary search trees with, say $s = 4$, might perform very well.

▶ On the analysis-side, a feasible method to determine (or approximate) the linear term of costs is still lacking.

▶ Moreover, the analysis of Quicksort on equal keys covers only the random-u-ary-word case because I could not determine $\mathbb{E}[A_q]$ in general, i.e., the expected node depth in fringe-balanced search trees built from i.i.d. keys. For ordinary BSTs, this problem has long been solved, and I determined an (asymptotic) solution for keys that are uniformly distributed in a universe. This problem is much easier than the analysis of Quicksort, and an asymptotic analysis might be possible for general q.

Shortly after finishing this dissertation, I found an asymptotic approximation of $\mathbb{E}[A_q]$ at least for *binary* fringe-balanced trees [183]. The method was to show lower and upper bounds for $\mathbb{E}[A_q]$ in terms of the universe entropy $\mathcal{H}_{\ln}(q)$ that coincide asymptotically as $\mathcal{H}_{\ln}(q) \to \infty$. We then obtain $\mathbb{E}[A_q] \sim \frac{1}{\mathcal{H}} \cdot \mathcal{H}_{\ln}(q)$. Once again, we find the *same* relative speed-up by sampling, and finally a proof of Conjecture 8.5!

The proof heavily depends on the fact that the toll function does not depend on q in binary trees; it is unfortunately not directly applicable to the multiway case.

List of Open Problems. On top of these broad directions for future work, a few more well-separated problems appeared as open problems when we encountered them in this work. Since they are scattered throughout the text, we link them here for convenience.

Index of Notation

IN THIS SECTION, we collect the notations used in this work. Some might be seen as standard, but I prefer including a few more than necessary to a potential misunderstanding caused by omitting them. Others are specifically chosen to build a convenient language to express the statements to made herein.

A.1 Generic Mathematical Notation

$\mathbb{N}, \mathbb{N}_0, \mathbb{Z}, \mathbb{Q}, \mathbb{R}, \mathbb{C}$ . . natural numbers $\mathbb{N} = \{1, 2, 3, \ldots\}$, $\mathbb{N}_0 = \mathbb{N} \cup \{0\}$, integers
$\mathbb{Z} = \{\ldots, -2, -1, 0, 1, 2, \ldots\}$, rational numbers $\mathbb{Q} = \{p/q : p \in \mathbb{Z} \wedge q \in \mathbb{N}\}$,
real numbers $\mathbb{R}$, and complex numbers $\mathbb{C}$.

$\mathbb{R}_{>1}, \mathbb{N}_{\geqslant 3}$ etc. . . . . . restricted sets $X_{\mathrm{pred}} = \{x \in X : x \text{ fulfills pred}\}$.

$0.\overline{3}$ . . . . repeating decimal; $0.\overline{3} = 0.333\ldots = \frac{1}{3}$;
numerals under the line form the repeated part of the decimal number.

$\Re z, \Im z$ . . . . real and imaginary part of $z \in \mathbb{C}$.

$\ln(n), \mathrm{ld}(n)$ . . . . . . natural and binary logarithm; $\ln(n) = \log_e(n)$, $\mathrm{ld}(n) = \log_2(n)$.

x . . . . to emphasize that x is a vector, it is written in **bold**;
components of the vector are not written in bold: $x = (x_1, \ldots, x_d)$;
we write $y \in x$ also for vectors to mean $y \in \{x_1, \ldots, x_d\}$;
unless stated otherwise, all vectors are column vectors.

X . . . . to emphasize that X is a random variable it is Capitalized.

$[a, b)$ . . . . real intervals, the end points with round parentheses are excluded, those
with square brackets are included.

$[m..n], [n]$ . . . . integer intervals, $[m..n] = \{m, m+1, \ldots, n\}$; $[n] = [1..n]$.

$[\mathrm{stmt}], [x = y]$ . . . . . Iverson bracket, $[\mathrm{stmt}] = 1$ if stmt is true, $[\mathrm{stmt}] = 0$ otherwise.

$x + 1, 2^x, f(x)$ . . . . . element-wise application on vectors; $(x_1,\ldots,x_d) + 1 = (x_1 + 1,\ldots,x_d + 1)$ and $2^x = (2^{x_1},\ldots,2^{x_d})$; for any function $f : \mathbb{C} \to \mathbb{C}$ write $f(x) = (f(x_1),\ldots,f(x_d))$ etc.

Σx . . . . "total" of a vector; for $x = (x_1,\ldots,x_d)$, we have $\Sigma x = \sum_{i=1}^{d} x_i$.

$x^\mathsf{T}, x^\mathsf{T} y$ . . . . "transpose" of vector/matrix x; for $x, y \in \mathbb{R}^n$, we write $x^\mathsf{T} y = \sum_{i=1}^{n} x_i y_i$.

$B_{<\varepsilon}(z), B_{\leqslant\varepsilon}(z)$ . . . . open resp. closed ε-neighborhood of z (in $\mathbb{C}$ if not stated otherwise), also called ε-ball around z; $B_{<\varepsilon}(z) := \{z' \in \mathbb{C} : |z' - z| < \varepsilon\}$, $B_{\leqslant\varepsilon}(z) := \{z' \in \mathbb{C} : |z' - z| \leqslant \varepsilon\}$.

$\mathbb{1}_{\mathcal{J}}^{(s)}$ . . . . characteristic vector of a subset $\mathcal{J} \subseteq [s]$, see Equation (2.4) on page 40; if s is clear from the context we write $\mathbb{1}_{\mathcal{J}}$ only.

H_n . . . . nth harmonic number; $H_n = \sum_{i=1}^{n} 1/i$.

$O(f(n)), \pm O(f(n)), \Omega, \Theta, \sim$

asymptotic notation; see Section 2.1.1.

$x \pm y$ . . . . x with absolute error $|y|$; formally the interval $x \pm y = [x - |y|, x + |y|]$; as with O-terms, we use one-way equalities $z = x \pm y$ instead of $z \in x \pm y$.

Δ_d . . . . $(d-1)$-dimensional standard open simplex, see Equation (2.16).

$x \propto y$ . . . . x is proportional to y, $\exists \lambda > 0 : x = \lambda \cdot y$.

$\Gamma(z)$ . . . . the gamma function, see Equation (2.8).

$\psi(z)$ . . . . the digamma function, see Equation (2.12).

$B(\alpha_1,\ldots,\alpha_d)$ . . . . . d-dimensional beta function; defined in Equation 2.19 (page 47).

$a^{\underline{b}}, a^{\overline{b}}$ . . . . factorial powers notation of Graham et al. [72]; "a to the b falling resp. rising."

A.2 Stochastics-related Notation

$\mathbb{P}[E], \mathbb{P}[X = x]$ . . . . . probability of an event E resp. probability for random variable X to attain value x.

$\mathbb{E}[X]$ . . . . expected value of X; we write $\mathbb{E}[X \mid Y]$ for the conditional expectation of X given Y, and $\mathbb{E}_X[f(X)]$ to emphasize that expectation is taken w.r.t. random variable X.

$X \stackrel{\mathcal{D}}{=} Y$ . . . . equality in distribution; X and Y have the same distribution.

$\mathbb{1}_E, \mathbb{1}_{\{X \leqslant 5\}}$ . . . . . . indicator variable for event E, i.e., $\mathbb{1}_E$ is 1 if E occurs and 0 otherwise; $\{X \leqslant 5\}$ denotes the event induced by the expression $X \leqslant 5$.

$B(p)$ . . . . Bernoulli distributed random variable; $p \in [0, 1]$.

$\mathcal{U}(a, b)$ . . . . uniformly in $(a, b) \subset \mathbb{R}$ distributed random variable.

$\mathcal{D}(\mathbf{p})$ . . . . discrete random variable with weights $\mathbf{p}$; for $\mathbf{p} \in [0, 1]^d$, for $I \stackrel{\mathcal{D}}{=} \mathcal{D}(\mathbf{p})$, we have $I \in [1..d]$ and $\mathbb{P}[I = i] = p_i$ for $i \in [d]$ and 0 otherwise.

$\text{Beta}(\alpha, \beta)$ . . . . Beta distributed random variable with shape parameters $\alpha \in \mathbb{R}_{>0}$ and $\beta \in \mathbb{R}_{>0}$; $X \overset{\mathcal{D}}{=} \text{Beta}(\alpha, \beta)$ is equivalent to $(X, 1-X) \overset{\mathcal{D}}{=} \text{Dir}(\alpha, \beta)$.

$\text{Dir}(\boldsymbol{\alpha})$ . . . . Dirichlet distributed random variable; $\boldsymbol{\alpha} \in \mathbb{R}_{>0}^{d}$; see Section 2.4.4.

$\text{Bin}(n, p)$ . . . . binomial distributed random variable with $n \in \mathbb{N}_0$ trials and success probability $p \in [0, 1]$;
$X \overset{\mathcal{D}}{=} \text{Bin}(n, p)$ is equivalent to $(X, n-X) \overset{\mathcal{D}}{=} \text{Mult}(n; p, 1-p)$.

$\text{Mult}(n, \mathbf{p})$ . . . . . . multinomially distributed random variable; $n \in \mathbb{N}_0$ and $\mathbf{p} \in [0, 1]^d$ with $\Sigma \mathbf{p} = 1$, see Section 2.4.6.

$\text{Gamma}(k, \theta)$, $\text{Gamma}(k)$
         Gamma distributed random variable with shape parameter $k \in \mathbb{R}_{>0}$ and scale parameter $\theta \in \mathbb{R}_{>0}$; $\text{Gamma}(k) = \text{Gamma}(k, 1)$; see Section 2.4.3.

$\text{BetaBin}(n, \alpha, \beta)$ . . . . beta-binomial distributed random variable; $n \in \mathbb{N}_0$, $\alpha, \beta \in \mathbb{R}_{>0}$;
$X \overset{\mathcal{D}}{=} \text{BetaBin}(n, \alpha, \beta)$ is equivalent to $(X, n-X) \overset{\mathcal{D}}{=} \text{DirMult}(n; \alpha, \beta)$.

$\text{DirMult}(n, \boldsymbol{\sigma})$ . . . . . Dirichlet-multinomial distributed random variable; $n \in \mathbb{N}_0$, $\boldsymbol{\sigma} \in \mathbb{R}_{>0}^{s}$, see Section 2.4.7.

$X_{(i)}$ . . . . ith order statistic of a set of random variables $X_1, \ldots, X_n$, i.e., the ith smallest element of $X_1, \ldots, X_n$.

$\mathcal{H}_f(\mathbf{p})$ . . . . generalized entropy-like function; for $\mathbf{p} \in [0, 1]^s$ we have $\mathcal{H}_f(\mathbf{p}) = \sum_{r=1}^{s} p_r \cdot f(p_r)$.

$\mathcal{H}_{\ln} = \mathcal{H}_{\ln}(\mathbf{p})$ . . . . . base e (Shannon) entropy; $\mathcal{H}_{\ln}(p_1, \ldots, p_d) = -\sum_{r=1}^{d} p_r \ln p_r$.

$\mathbb{E}_{D(\boldsymbol{\alpha})}[f(\mathbf{X})]$ . . . . . . items of Dirichlet-calculus; $\mathbb{E}_{D(\boldsymbol{\alpha})}[f(\mathbf{X})] = \mathbb{E}[f(\mathbf{X})]$ with $\mathbf{X} \overset{\mathcal{D}}{=} \text{Dir}(\boldsymbol{\alpha})$; see Section 2.4.5.

A.3 Input to the Algorithm

n . . . . length of the input array, i.e., the input size.

A . . . . input array containing the items $A[1], \ldots, A[n]$ to be sorted; initially, $A[i] = U_i$.

U_i . . . . ith element of the input, i.e., initially $A[i] = U_i$.
         Except for Chapter 8, we assume $U_1, \ldots, U_n$ are i.i.d. $\mathcal{U}(0, 1)$ distributed (the uniform model).

A.4 Notation for the Algorithm

s . . . . number of segments, $s \geqslant 2$; determines the number of pivots to be $s - 1$.

$t, \boldsymbol{\sigma}, T$ . . . . pivot-sampling parameter, see Section 4.4; $t \in \mathbb{N}^s$, $\boldsymbol{\sigma} = t + 1$; for random-parameter pivot sampling, we write T instead of t to emphasize that it is a random variable.

k, κ . . . . sample size $k \in \mathbb{N}_{\geqslant s-1}$; $\kappa = k + 1$ (abbreviation for convenience), $\kappa = \Sigma(t + 1) = \Sigma\boldsymbol{\sigma}$.

τ . . . . quantiles vector for sampling, $\tau = \frac{\sigma}{\kappa} = \frac{t+1}{k+1}$; τ is a κ-discretized distribution.

w . . . . Insertionsort threshold $w \geqslant k$; for $n \leqslant w$, Quicksort recursion is truncated and we sort the subarray by Insertionsort.

m . . . . the meeting point of scanning indices k and g;
$m \in \{0, 0.5, 1, 1.5, \ldots, s - 0.5, s\}$;
for $m \in \{0, \ldots, s\}$ we have a master-pivot method, m segments grow from the left end of A and k and g meet on the final position of the master pivot P_m;
for $m \in \{1, \ldots, s\} - \frac{1}{2}$ we have a master-segment method, k and g meet inside the master segment, which is the $\lceil m \rceil$-th from the left.

$P_1, \ldots, P_{s-1}; P_0, P_s$. (random) values of chosen pivots in the first partitioning step, ordered by value $0 \leqslant P_1 \leqslant P_2 \leqslant \cdots \leqslant P_{s-1} \leqslant 1$;
$P_0 := 0$ and $P_s := 1$ are used for notational convenience.

$k = k_1; k_2, \ldots, k_{\lceil m \rceil}$. scanning indices (index variables) used to separate (partial) segments that start growing from the left end of the array.
NB: The main pointer $k = k_1$ is the *innermost* pointer, so in terms of their index values, we always have $k_{\lceil m \rceil} \leqslant k_{\lceil m \rceil - 1} \leqslant \cdots \leqslant k_1$;
for notational convenience, we define $k_{m+1} := \textit{left}$;
for $m = 0$, we understand k as a constant $k = \textit{left}$.

$g = g_1; g_2, \ldots, g_{s-\lfloor m \rfloor}$
index variables used to separate (partial) segments that start growing from the right end of the array. The main pointer $g = g_1$ is the *innermost* pointer, in terms of index values, we have $g_1 \leqslant \ldots \leqslant g_{s-\lfloor m \rfloor}$. For notational convenience, we define $g_{s-\lfloor m \rfloor + 1} := \textit{right}$; for $m = s$, we understand g as a constant $g = \textit{right}$.

$s_1, \ldots, s_{\lceil m \rceil}$ . . . . . . s_i is the class of elements that are "small of order i";
under the uniform model $s_i \subseteq [P_{\lceil m \rceil - i}, P_{\lceil m \rceil - i + 1}] \subseteq (0, 1)$ for $1 \leqslant i \leqslant \lceil m \rceil$;
we say element $U \in s_i$ is of type s_i.

$l_1, \ldots, l_{s-\lfloor m \rfloor}$ . . . . l_j is the class of elements that are "large of order j";
under the uniform model $l_j \subseteq [P_{\lfloor m \rfloor + j - 1}, P_{\lfloor m \rfloor + j}] \subseteq (0, 1)$ for $1 \leqslant j \leqslant s - \lfloor m \rfloor$;
we say element $U \in l_j$ is of type l_j.

$\mathfrak{m}$ . . . . (master-segment case only) class of medium elements;
for $m \in [1..s] - \frac{1}{2}$ used as alternative name $\mathfrak{m} := s_1 = l_1$.

$p_1, \ldots, p_{s-1}$ . . . . . . (Chapter 8 only) p_r is the class of elements equal to rth pivot P_r.

$\mathcal{C}$ . . . . the vector of all classes;
for $m \in [0..s]$, we have $\mathcal{C} = (s_m, \ldots, s_1, l_1, \ldots, l_{s-m})$ and
for $m \in [1..s] - \frac{1}{2}$, it is $\mathcal{C} = (s_{\lceil m \rceil}, \ldots, s_2, \mathfrak{m}, l_2, \ldots, l_{s-\lfloor m \rfloor})$;
in Chapter 8, we extend $\mathcal{C}$ to contain the pivot classes, see Equation (8.11);
we write $\sum_{c \in \mathcal{C}}$ etc. to iterate over all classes.

$\lambda_k, \lambda_g, \lambda(c)$ . . . . $\lambda_k, \lambda_g \in \Lambda_s$; comparison trees for the left and right main indices k and g. We write $\lambda(c)$ for a class $c \in \mathcal{C}$ to denote the number of comparison needed to identify an element as belonging to this class.

$\boldsymbol{\lambda}$ . . . . vector of leaf depths; for comparison tree λ, we write $\boldsymbol{\lambda}$ for the vector of the depths of all leaves in left-to-right order; $\lambda(c)$ equals the $r(c)$th component of $\boldsymbol{\lambda}$; in vector notation, we have $\boldsymbol{\lambda} = \lambda(\mathcal{C})$.

Λ, Λ_s . . . . Λ_s is the set of (shapes of) extended binary trees over s leaves, we omit s if clear from context; upon assigning values $P_1 \leqslant \cdots \leqslant P_{s-1}$ to the $s-1$ internal nodes in in-order, we obtain a binary search tree.

A.5 Notation Specific to the Analysis (Uniform Model)

η . . . . $\eta = n - k$, the number of ordinary elements in the first partitioning step for an input array of length n.

$\mathcal{K}_1, \ldots, \mathcal{K}_{\lceil m \rceil}$ . . . . . $\mathcal{K}_i$ is the set of all index values attained by variable k_i during the first partitioning step; note that like the index variables k_i, the position sets $\mathcal{K}_i$ are numbered starting from the middle of the array.

$\mathcal{G}_1, \ldots, \mathcal{G}_{s-\lfloor m \rfloor}$ . . . . $\mathcal{G}_i$ is the set of all (index) values attained by variable g_i during the first partitioning step.

W_n . . . . (random) costs of sorting a random permutation of size n with Insertionsort.

$c(U)$ . . . . $c(U)$ is class assigned to U during classification; we write $U \in c(U)$; the class in general depends on the used comparison tree.

sampled-out element the $k - (s-1)$ elements of the sample that are *not* chosen as pivots.

ordinary element . . . the $n - k$ elements that have not been part of the sample.

F_k, F_g . . . . the (random) number of ordinary elements that are classified using λ_k resp. λ_g during the first partitioning step; $F_k + F_g = \eta$; see Section 5.5.

C_n, S_n, BC_n, SE_n . . (random) number of comparisons / swaps / Bytecodes / scanned elements of Quicksort on a random permutation of size n; in Chapter 6, C_n is used as general placeholder for any of the above cost measures.

T_C, T_S, T_{BC}, T_{SE} . . . . (random) number of comparisons / swaps / Bytecodes / scanned elements of the first partitioning step on a random permutation of size n; we write $T_C(n)$ etc. when we want to emphasize dependence on n.

T_n . . . . generic placeholder for one of $T_C(n), T_S(n), T_{BC}(n), T_{SE}(n)$.

a_C, a_S, a_{BC}, a_{SE} . . . coefficient of the linear term of $\mathbb{E}[T_C(n)], \mathbb{E}[T_S(n)], \mathbb{E}[T_{BC}(n)]$ and $\mathbb{E}[T_{SE}(n)]$; see Theorem 7.1 (page 222).

$hd_\kappa(x)$ . . . . the harmonic-difference function, $hd_\kappa(x) = H_{x\kappa} - H_\kappa$; see Section 2.5.2.

$\mathcal{H} = \mathcal{H}(t)$ . . . . discrete entropy; $\mathcal{H}(t) = \mathcal{H}_{hd_\kappa}(\tau)$ where $\kappa = \Sigma(t+1)$ and $\tau = \frac{t+1}{\kappa}$.

$\mathbf{J} \in \mathbb{N}^s$ . . . . (random) vector of subproblem sizes for recursive calls;
for initial size n, we have $\mathbf{J} \in \{0,\ldots,n-(s-1)\}^s$ with $\Sigma \mathbf{J}\mathbf{1} = n-(s-1)$.

$\mathbf{I} \in \mathbb{N}^s$ . . . . (random) vector of segment sizes, i.e., the number of *ordinary* elements of
the s classes; for initial size n, we have $\mathbf{I} \in \{0,\ldots,n-k\}^s$ with $\Sigma \mathbf{I} = n-k$;
$\mathbf{J} = \mathbf{I} + \mathbf{t}$ and $\mathbf{I} \stackrel{\mathcal{D}}{=} \mathrm{DirMult}(\eta,\boldsymbol{\sigma})$; conditional on $\mathbf{D}$ we have
$\mathbf{I} \stackrel{\mathcal{D}}{=} \mathrm{Mult}(\eta,\mathbf{D})$.

$\mathbf{D} \in [0,1]^s$ . . . . (random) spacings of the unit interval $(0,1)$ induced by the pivots
$P_1 \ldots, P_{s-1}$, i.e., $D_i = P_i - P_{i-1}$ for $1 \leqslant i \leqslant s$; $\mathbf{D} \stackrel{\mathcal{D}}{=} \mathrm{Dir}(\boldsymbol{\sigma}) \stackrel{\mathcal{D}}{=} \mathrm{Dir}(\mathbf{t}+1)$.

A.6 Notation for the Analysis with Equal Keys

The notations in this section are specific to the analysis in Chapter 8.

u . . . . universe size $u \in \mathbb{N}$.

q . . . . universe probabilities/distribution; $\mathbf{q} \in (0,1)^u$ with $q_i \geqslant 0$ and $\Sigma \mathbf{q} = 1$;
we assume $U_1,\ldots,U_n \in [1..u]$ are i.i.d. $\mathcal{D}(\mathbf{q})$ distributed.

$c_0,\ldots,c_u$ . . . . cumulative sums of $\mathbf{q}$; $c_j := \sum_{i=1}^{j} q_i$ for $j = 0,\ldots,u$.

$\mathbf{D}$ . . . . continuous spacings;
same as for uniform model, see Section A.5.

$\boldsymbol{\Pi}$ . . . . continuous pivot values, cumulative sums of $\mathbf{D}$:
$\boldsymbol{\Pi} = \boldsymbol{\Pi}(\mathbf{D}) = \left(\sum_{i=1}^{r} D_i\right)_{r=0}^{s}$.

$\mathbf{P}$ . . . . pivot values $\mathbf{P} = F_U^{-1}(\boldsymbol{\Pi}) = \left(F_U^{-1}(\Pi_r)\right)_{r=0}^{s}$, for F_U the cumulative
distribution function of $\mathcal{D}(\mathbf{q})$.

$v(\underline{p},\overline{p})$ . . . . probability to fall strictly between $\underline{p}$ and $\overline{p}$; see Equation (8.16).

$\mathbf{V}$ . . . . non-pivot class probabilities $\mathbf{V} = \left(v(P_{r-1},P_r)\right)_{r=1}^{s}$.

$z(\underline{p},\overline{p})$ . . . . subdistribution for elements between $\underline{p}$ and $\overline{p}$; see Equation (8.31).

$\mathbf{Z}$ . . . . zoomed-in distributions; see Equation (8.30).

$\mathbf{H}$ . . . . hitting probabilities, H_r, $1 \leqslant r \leqslant s-1$ is the probability of an ordinary
element to belong to class p_r; see Equation (8.18).

$\mathbf{E}$ . . . . E_r is the number of ordinary elements equal to P_r for $r = 1,\ldots,s-1$;
$\mathbf{E} = (E_1,\ldots,E_{s-1})$.

$\mathbf{I}$ . . . . segment sizes as for uniform model, but with probabilities $\mathbf{V}$;
$(\mathbf{I},\mathbf{E}) \stackrel{\mathcal{D}}{=} \mathrm{Mult}(\eta;\mathbf{V},\mathbf{H})$.

$\mathbf{B}$ . . . . $B_r \in [0..t_r]$ for $r \in [1..s]$ is the number of sampled-out elements U from
the rth segment that are not equal to a pivot, i.e., $U \in (P_{r-1},P_r)$.

$\mathbf{J}$ . . . . subproblem sizes for recursive calls; $\mathbf{J} = \mathbf{I} + \mathbf{B}$.

$\boldsymbol{\beta}, \boldsymbol{\gamma}$ . . . . $\boldsymbol{\beta} \in \mathbb{R}_{\geqslant 0}^{s-1}$, $\boldsymbol{\gamma} \in \mathbb{R}_{\geqslant 0}^{s}$; constant coefficient vectors for stateless cost
measures; in a stateless cost measure, partitioning costs are
$T_n = \boldsymbol{\beta}^\mathsf{T}\mathbf{E} + \boldsymbol{\gamma}^\mathsf{T}\mathbf{I}$.

Γ . . . . $\Gamma \in \mathbb{R}^u_{\geq 0}$; search-costs vector in recursion tree; Γ_v is the random cost of searching value $v \in [u]$ in the random recursion tree of Quicksort; see Equation (8.34).

A_q . . . . random path length of recursion tree, with the cost for paths as described in Section 8.7.6; $A_q = \Gamma_U$ for $U \overset{\mathcal{D}}{=} \mathcal{D}(q)$; see Equation (8.35).

B
Bibliography

[1] A. Aggarwal and J. S. Vitter. The input/output complexity of sorting and related problems. *Communications of the ACM*, 31(9):1116–1127, August 1988. doi: 10.1145/48529.48535. (Cited on pages 29 and 126.)

[2] B. Allen and I. Munro. Self-organizing binary search trees. *Journal of the ACM*, 25(4):526–535, October 1978. doi: 10.1145/322092.322094. (Cited on pages 291 and 292.)

[3] M. Archibald and J. Clément. Average depth in a binary search tree with repeated keys. In *Colloquium on Mathematics and Computer Science*, volume 0, pages 309–320, 2006. (Cited on pages 26, 122, and 294.)

[4] M. L. Archibald. *Combinatorial problems related to sequences with repeated entries*. Ph.D. thesis, University of the Witwatersrand, Johannesburg, South Africa, 2005. (Cited on page 294.)

[5] G. B. Arfken and H. J. Weber. *Mathematical Methods for Physicists*. Academic Press, 6th edition, 2005. (Cited on page 204.)

[6] N. Auger, C. Nicaud, and C. Pivoteau. Good predictions are worth a few comparisons. In N. Ollinger and H. Vollmer, editors, *Symposium on Theoretical Aspects of Computer Science (STACS)*, volume 47 of *Leibniz International Proceedings in Informatics (LIPIcs)*, pages 12:1–12:14. Schloss Dagstuhl–Leibniz-Zentrum fuer Informatik, 2016. ISBN 978-3-95977-001-9. doi: http://dx.doi.org/10.4230/LIPIcs.STACS.2016.12. (Cited on pages 130 and 182.)

[7] M. Aumüller. *On the Analysis of Two Fundamental Randomized Algorithms*. Doktorarbeit (Ph. D. thesis), TU Ilmenau, 2015. (Cited on pages 25, 33, and 163.)

[8] M. Aumüller and M. Dietzfelbinger. Optimal partitioning for dual pivot Quicksort. In F. V. Fomin, R. Freivalds, M. Kwiatkowska, and D. Peleg, editors, *International Colloquium on Automata, Languages and Programming (ICALP)*, volume 7965 of *LNCS*, pages 33–44. Springer, 2013. (Cited on pages 7, 33, and 262.)

[9] M. Aumüller and M. Dietzfelbinger. Optimal partitioning for dual-pivot Quicksort. *ACM Transactions on Algorithms*, 12(2):1–36, November 2015. doi: 10.1145/2743020. (Cited on pages 7, 30, 31, 33, and 142.)

[10] M. Aumüller, M. Dietzfelbinger, and P. Klaue. How good is multi-pivot Quicksort?, 2015. URL http://arxiv.org/abs/1510.04676. (Cited on pages 33, 127, 142, 154, 162, 163, 171, 173, 185, 186, 230, 237, 254, 262, 263, and 270.)

[11] M. Aumüller, M. Dietzfelbinger, C. Heuberger, D. Krenn, and H. Prodinger. Counting zeros in random walks on the integers and analysis of optimal dual-pivot Quicksort. February 2016. URL http://arxiv.org/abs/1602.04031. (Cited on pages 33 and 79.)

[12] J. Backus. Can programming be liberated from the von neumann style? A functional style and its algebra of programs. *Communications of the ACM*, 21(8):613–641, August 1978. doi: 10.1145/359576.359579. (Cited on page 8.)

[13] M. L. Balinski and H. P. Young. *Fair Representation*. Brookings Institution Press, 2nd edition, 2001. ISBN 978-0-8157-0111-8. (Cited on page 245.)

[14] N. Batir. On some properties of digamma and polygamma functions. *Journal of Mathematical Analysis and Applications*, 328(1):452–465, apr 2007. doi: 10.1016/j.jmaa.2006.05.065. (Cited on page 94.)

[15] P. J. Bayer. *Improved Bounds on the Cost of Optimal and Balanced Binary Search Trees*. Master's Thesis, Massachusetts Institute of Technology, 1975. (Cited on page 91.)

[16] C. J. Bell. *An Investigation into the Principles of the Classification and Analysis of Data on an Automatic Digital Computer*. Doctoral dissertation, Leeds University, 1965. (Cited on page 18.)

[17] J. Bentley. Programming pearls: how to sort. *Communications of the ACM*, 27(4):287–291, April 1984. (Cited on page 13.)

[18] J. Bentley. *Programming Pearls*. Addison-Wesley, 2nd edition, 2000. ISBN 0201657880. (Cited on pages 10, 138, and 234.)

[19] J. Bentley. The most beautiful code I never wrote. In *Beautiful Code*, chapter 3, pages 29–40. O'Reilly, 2007. ISBN 13: 978-0-596-51004-6. (Cited on page 308.)

[20] J. L. Bentley and M. D. McIlroy. Engineering a sort function. *Software: Practice and Experience*, 23(11):1249–1265, 1993. (Cited on pages 9, 11, 15, 17, 26, 286, 289, 293, 295, and 298.)

[21] J. L. Bentley and R. Sedgewick. Fast algorithms for sorting and searching strings. In *Symposium on Discrete Algorithms (SODA)*, pages 360–369, 1997. (Cited on page 26.)

[22] H. Bergeron, E. M. F. Curado, J. P. Gazeau, and L. M. C. S. Rodrigues. A note about combinatorial sequences and Incomplete Gamma function. page 6, September 2013. URL http://arxiv.org/abs/1309.6910. (Cited on page 54.)

[23] P. Biggar, N. Nash, K. Williams, and D. Gregg. An experimental study of sorting and branch prediction. *Journal of Experimental Algorithmics*, 12:1, June 2008. (Cited on pages 31, 131, 182, and 189.)

[24] H. Bing-Chao and D. E. Knuth. A one-way, stackless quicksort algorithm. *BIT*, 26(1):127–130, March 1986. doi: 10.1007/BF01939369. (Cited on pages 13, 33, and 223.)

[25] G. Brassard. Crusade for a better notation. *ACM SIGACT News*, 17(1):60–64, June 1985. (Cited on page 41.)

[26] G. Brodal and G. Moruz. Tradeoffs between branch mispredictions and comparisons for sorting algorithms. In *Workshop on Algorithms and Data Structures (WADS)*, volume 3608 of *LNCS*, pages 385–395. Springer, 2005. (Cited on page 31.)

[27] W. H. Burge. An analysis of binary search trees formed from sequences of nondistinct keys. *Journal of the ACM*, 23(3):451–454, July 1976. doi: 10.1145/321958.321965. (Cited on pages 26, 122, and 290.)

[28] D. Cantone and G. Cincotti. QuickHeapsort, an efficient mix of classical sorting algorithms. *Theoretical Computer Science*, 285(1):25–42, August 2002. doi: 10.1016/S0304-3975(01)00288-2. (Cited on page 32.)

[29] H.-H. Chern and H.-K. Hwang. Phase changes in random m-ary search trees and generalized quicksort. *Random Structures & Algorithms*, 19(3-4):316–358, October 2001. (Cited on pages 17 and 22.)

[30] H.-H. Chern, H.-K. Hwang, and T.-H. Tsai. An asymptotic theory for Cauchy–Euler differential equations with applications to the analysis of algorithms. *Journal of Algorithms*, 44(1): 177–225, 2002. (Cited on pages 16, 17, 22, 63, and 160.)

[31] J. Clément, J. A. Fill, T. H. Nguyen Thi, and B. Vallée. Towards a realistic analysis of the QuickSelect algorithm. *Theory of Computing Systems*, August 2015. doi: 10.1007/s00224-015-9633-5. URL http://link.springer.com/10.1007/s00224-015-9633-5. (Cited on page 29.)

[32] J. Clément, T. H. Nguyen Thi, and B. Vallée. Towards a realistic analysis of some popular sorting algorithms. *Combinatorics, Probability and Computing*, 24(01):104–144, January 2015. doi: 10.1017/S0963548314000649. (Cited on page 29.)

[33] M. Codish, L. Cruz-Filipe, M. Nebel, and P. Schneider-Kamp. Applying sorting networks to synthesize optimized sorting libraries. In *International Symposium on Logic-Based Program Synthesis and Transformation (LOPSTR)*, pages 127–142, May 2015. doi: 10.1007/978-3-319-27436-2_8. (Cited on page 147.)

[34] R. M. Corless, G. H. Gonnet, D. E. G. Hare, D. J. Jeffrey, and D. E. Knuth. On the Lambert W function. *Advances in Computational Mathematics*, 5(1):329–359, December 1996. doi: 10.1007/BF02124750. (Cited on page 97.)

[35] T. H. Cormen, C. E. Leiserson, R. L. Rivest, and C. Stein. *Introduction to Algorithms*. MIT Press, 3rd edition, 2009. ISBN 978-0-262-03384-8. (Cited on pages 15, 27, 41, 139, and 205.)

[36] T. M. Cover and J. A. Thomas. *Elements of Information Theory*. Wiley, September 2005. ISBN 978-0-471-74882-3. (Cited on page 83.)

[37] H. A. David and H. N. Nagaraja. *Order Statistics*. Wiley-Interscience, 3rd edition, 2003. ISBN 0-471-38926-9. (Cited on page 72.)

[38] L. Devroye. *Non-Uniform Random Variate Generation*. Springer New York, 1986. (Cited on pages 71, 72, and 301.)

[39] L. Devroye. On the expected height of fringe-balanced trees. *Acta Informatica*, 30(5):459–466, May 1993. doi: 10.1007/BF01210596. (Cited on page 18.)

[40] L. Devroye. Universal limit laws for depths in random trees. *SIAM Journal on Computing*, 28 (2):409–432, January 1998. ISSN 0097-5397. doi: 10.1137/S0097539795283954. (Cited on page 19.)

[41] L. Devroye and P. Kruszewski. The botanical beauty of random binary trees. pages 166–177. 1996. doi: 10.1007/BFb0021801. (Cited on page 19.)

[42] E. W. Dijkstra. Recursive programming. *Numerische Mathematik*, 2(1):312–318, December 1960. doi: 10.1007/BF01386232. (Cited on page 135.)

[43] E. W. Dijkstra. *A Discipline of Programming*. Prentice Hall PTR, 1st edition, 1976. ISBN 0-13-215871-X. (Cited on pages 141 and 295.)

[44] E. W. Dijkstra. Computing science: achievements and challenges. *ACM SIGAPP Applied Computing Review*, 7(2):2–9, 1999. (Cited on pages 135 and 136.)

[45] E. W. Dijkstra. The notational conventions I adopted, and why. circulated privately, July 2000. URL `https://www.cs.utexas.edu/users/EWD/transcriptions/EWD13xx/EWD1300.html`. (Cited on page xi.)

[46] DLMF. NIST Digital Library of Mathematical Functions. Release 1.0.10; Release date 2015-08-07. URL `http://dlmf.nist.gov`. (Cited on pages 44, 45, 47, 48, 53, 54, 58, 59, 60, and 93.)

[47] M. Drmota. *Random Trees*. Springer, 2009. ISBN 978-3-211-75355-2. (Cited on pages x, 18, and 311.)

[48] M. Durand. Holonomie et applications en l'analyse d'algorithmes et combinatoire. Mémoire de DEA (Master's Thesis), École Polytechnique, 2000. URL `http://algo.inria.fr/durand`. (Cited on page 17.)

[49] M. Durand. Asymptotic analysis of an optimized quicksort algorithm. *Information Processing Letters*, 85(2):73–77, 2003. (Cited on pages 15, 17, and 160.)

[50] W. F. Eddy and M. J. Schervish. How many comparisons does Quicksort use? *Journal of Algorithms*, 19(3):402–431, November 1995. doi: 10.1006/jagm.1995.1044. (Cited on pages 21 and 22.)

[51] F. Eggenberger and G. Pólya. Über die Statistik verketteter Vorgänge. *Zeitschrift für Angewandte Mathematik und Mechanik*, 3(4):279–289, 1923. doi: 10.1002/zamm.19230030407. (Cited on page 79.)

[52] B. Eisenbarth, N. Ziviani, G. H. Gonnet, K. Mehlhorn, and D. Wood. The theory of fringe analysis and its application to 2–3 trees and b-trees. *Information and Control*, 55(1-3):125–174, October 1982. doi: 10.1016/S0019-9958(82)90534-4. (Cited on page 18.)

[53] A. Elmasry and J. Katajainen. Lean programs, branch mispredictions, and sorting. In E. Kranakis, D. Krizanc, and F. Luccio, editors, *International Conference on Fun with Algorithms (FUN)*, volume 7288 of *LNCS*, pages 119–130, 2012. doi: 10.1007/978-3-642-30347-0_14. (Cited on page 31.)

[54] A. Elmasry, J. Katajainen, and M. Stenmark. Branch mispredictions don't affect mergesort. In *International Symposium on Experimental Algorithms (SEA)*, pages 160–171, 2012. doi: 10.1007/978-3-642-30850-5{_}15. (Cited on page 31.)

[55] M. H. van Emden. Increasing the efficiency of quicksort. *Communications of the ACM*, pages 563–567, 1970. (Cited on pages 14, 16, and 201.)

[56] Encyclopedia of Mathematics. Laplace theorem, 2012. URL `http://www.encyclopediaofmath.org/index.php?title=Laplace_theorem&oldid=26551`. (Cited on page 81.)

[57] M. A. Ertl. The memory wall fallacy, 2001. URL `https://www.complang.tuwien.ac.at/anton/memory-wall.html`. (Cited on page 9.)

[58] J. A. Fill and S. Janson. The number of bit comparisons used by Quicksort: An average-case analysis. In *Symposium on Discrete Algorithms (SODA)*, pages 300–307. SIAM, January 2004. ISBN 0-89871-558-X. (Cited on pages 27 and 29.)

[59] J. A. Fill and S. Janson. The number of bit comparisons used by Quicksort: An average-case analysis. *Electronic Journal of Probability*, 17:1–22, 2012. doi: 10.1214/EJP.v17-1812. (Cited on pages 27, 28, and 29.)

[60] J. A. Fill, P. Flajolet, and N. Kapur. Singularity analysis, Hadamard products, and tree recurrences. *Journal of Computational and Applied Mathematics*, 174(2):271–313, February 2005. doi: 10.1016/j.cam.2004.04.014. (Cited on pages 16 and 63.)

[61] P. Flajolet. $D \cdot E \cdot K = (100)_8$. *Random Structures & Algorithms*, 19(3-4):150–162, October 2001. doi: 10.1002/rsa.10022. (Cited on page 6.)

[62] P. Flajolet and A. Odlyzko. Singularity analysis of generating functions. *SIAM Journal on Discrete Mathematics*, 3(2):216–240, 1990. (Cited on pages 16, 212, 217, and 218.)

[63] P. Flajolet and R. Sedgewick. Mellin transforms and asymptotics: Finite differences and Rice's integrals. *Theoretical Computer Science*, 144(1-2):101–124, jun 1995. ISSN 03043975. doi: 10.1016/0304-3975(94)00281-M. (Cited on page 27.)

[64] P. Flajolet and R. Sedgewick. *Analytic Combinatorics*. Cambridge University Press, 2009. ISBN 978-0-52-189806-5. URL `http://algo.inria.fr/flajolet/Publications/book.pdf`. (Cited on pages ix, 28, 42, 54, 60, 61, 62, 181, 182, 212, 217, and 218.)

[65] A. Fog. The microarchitecture of Intel, AMD and VIA CPUs, 2014. URL `http://www.agner.org/optimize/#manuals`. (Cited on page 130.)

[66] W. D. Frazer and A. C. McKellar. Samplesort: A sampling approach to minimal storage tree sorting. *Journal of the ACM*, 17(3):496–507, July 1970. (Cited on page 14.)

[67] M. Frigo, C. E. Leiserson, H. Prokop, and S. Ramachandran. Cache-oblivious algorithms. *ACM Transactions on Algorithms*, 8(1):1–22, January 2012. doi: 10.1145/2071379.2071383. (Cited on page 126.)

[68] T. Furtak, J. N. Amaral, and R. Niewiadomski. Using SIMD registers and instructions to enable instruction-level parallelism in sorting algorithms. In *Symposium on Parallel Algorithms and Architectures (SPAA)*, pages 348–357. ACM Press, 2007. doi: 10.1145/1248377.1248436. (Cited on page 147.)

[69] R. Gallager. Variations on a theme by Huffman. *IEEE Transactions on Information Theory*, 24(6):668–674, November 1978. doi: 10.1109/TIT.1978.1055959. (Cited on page 269.)

[70] A. M. Garsia and M. L. Wachs. A new algorithm for minimum cost binary trees. *SIAM Journal on Computing*, July 1997. doi: 10.1137/0206045. (Cited on page 264.)

[71] I. Gradshteyn and I. Ryzhik. *Table of Integrals, Series, and Products*. Academic Press, 7th edition, 2007. ISBN 978-0-12-373637-6. (Cited on page 48.)

[72] R. L. Graham, D. E. Knuth, and O. Patashnik. *Concrete Mathematics: A Foundation For Computer Science*. Addison-Wesley, 1994. ISBN 978-0-20-155802-9. (Cited on pages 43, 56, 57, 62, and 338.)

[73] D. H. Greene and D. E. Knuth. *Mathematics for the Analysis of Algorithms*. Modern Birkhäuser classics. Birkhäuser, 3rd edition, 1990. ISBN 9780817635152. (Cited on pages ix and 240.)

[74] D. H. Greene. *Labelled formal languages and their uses*. Ph.D. thesis, Stanford University, January 1983. (Cited on pages 18 and 311.)

[75] Y. Gurevich. What does O(n) mean. *ACM SIGACT News*, 17(4):61–63, March 1986. (Cited on page 42.)

[76] P. Hennequin. Combinatorial analysis of Quicksort algorithm. *Informatique théorique et applications*, 23(3):317–333, 1989. (Cited on pages 20, 23, 160, and 212.)

[77] P. Hennequin. *Analyse en moyenne d'algorithmes : tri rapide et arbres de recherche*. Thèse (Ph. D. Thesis), Ecole Politechnique, Palaiseau, 1991. (Cited on pages 4, 9, 17, 19, 20, 22, 23, 64, 159, 160, 162, 197, 212, 214, 215, 224, 235, 243, 249, 262, and 293.)

[78] T. N. Hibbard. Some combinatorial properties of certain trees with applications to searching and sorting. *Journal of the ACM*, 9(1):13–28, January 1962. doi: 10.1145/321105.321108. (Cited on pages 13, 17, and 329.)

[79] C. A. R. Hoare. Algorithm 65: Find. *Communications of the ACM*, 4(7):321–322, July 1961. (Cited on page 4.)

[80] C. A. R. Hoare. Algorithm 64: Quicksort. *Communications of the ACM*, 4(7):321, July 1961. (Cited on pages 13 and 136.)

[81] C. A. R. Hoare. Algorithm 63: Partition. *Communications of the ACM*, 4(7):321, July 1961. (Cited on page 136.)

[82] C. A. R. Hoare. Quicksort. *The Computer Journal*, 5(1):10–16, January 1962. (Cited on pages 4, 10, 13, 16, 22, 135, 136, 145, 147, and 223.)

[83] J. E. Hopcroft, R. Motwani, and J. D. Ullman. *Introduction to Automata Theory, Languages, and Computation*. Pearson, 2nd edition, 2001. (Cited on page 192.)

[84] G. van den Hove. On the Origin of Recursive Procedures. *The Computer Journal*, 58(11): 2892–2899, November 2015. doi: 10.1093/comjnl/bxu145. (Cited on page 136.)

[85] R. R. Howell. On asymptotic notation with multiple variables. Technical report, Kansas State University, 2007. URL `http://people.cis.ksu.edu/~rhowell/asymptotic.pdf`. (Cited on page 42.)

[86] T. C. Hu and K. C. Tan. Path length of binary search trees. *SIAM Journal on Applied Mathematics*, 22(2):225–234, March 1972. doi: 10.1137/0122024. (Cited on page 265.)

[87] T. C. Hu and A. C. Tucker. Optimal computer search trees and variable-length alphabetical codes. *SIAM Journal on Applied Mathematics*, 21(4):514–532, December 1971. doi: 10.1137/0121057. (Cited on page 264.)

[88] S.-H. S. Huang and C. K. Wong. Binary search trees with limited rotation. *BIT*, (4):436–455, December 1983. doi: 10.1007/BF01933619. (Cited on pages 18 and 311.)

[89] S.-H. S. Huang and C. K. Wong. Average number of rotations and access cost in iR-trees. *BIT*, 24(3):387–390, September 1984. doi: 10.1007/BF02136039. (Cited on pages 18 and 311.)

[90] D. Huffman. A method for the construction of minimum-redundancy codes. *Proceedings of the IRE*, 40(9):1098–1101, September 1952. doi: 10.1109/JRPROC.1952.273898. (Cited on page 264.)

[91] H.-K. Hwang and R. Neininger. Phase change of limit laws in the Quicksort recurrence under varying toll functions. *SIAM Journal on Computing*, 31(6):1687–1722, January 2002. doi: 10.1137/S009753970138390X. (Cited on page 22.)

[92] V. Iliopoulos and D. B. Penman. Dual pivot Quicksort. *Discrete Mathematics, Algorithms and Applications*, 04(03):1250041, September 2012. doi: 10.1142/S1793830912500413. (Cited on page 25.)

[93] E. L. Ince. *Ordinary Differential Equations*. Longmans, Green & Co London, 1927. (Cited on page 63.)

[94] Java Core Library Development Mailing List. Replacement of quicksort in java.util.arrays with new dual-pivot quicksort, 2009. URL `http://permalink.gmane.org/gmane.comp.java.openjdk.core-libs.devel/2628`. (Cited on page 24.)

[95] N. L. Johnson and S. Kotz. *Urn Models and Their Application*. John Wiley & Sons, 1977. ISBN 0-471-44630-0. (Cited on page 79.)

[96] K. Kaligosi and P. Sanders. How branch mispredictions affect quicksort. In T. Erlebach and Y. Azar, editors, *ESA 2006*, volume 4168 of *LNCS*, pages 780–791. Springer, 2006. (Cited on pages 31, 130, 182, and 235.)

[97] R. Kemp. *Fundamentals of the Average Case Analysis of Particular Algorithms*. Wiley-Teubner, Stuttgart, 1984. ISBN 3-519-02100-5. (Cited on page ix.)

[98] R. Kemp. Binary search trees constructed from nondistinct keys with/without specified probabilities. *Theoretical Computer Science*, 156(1-2):39–70, March 1996. doi: 10.1016/0304-3975(95)00302-9. (Cited on pages 26, 122, 293, and 294.)

[99] M. Klawe and B. Mumey. Upper and lower bounds on constructing alphabetic binary trees. *SIAM Journal on Discrete Mathematics*, 8(4):638–651, November 1995. doi: 10.1137/S0895480193256651. (Cited on pages 264 and 266.)

[100] D. E. Knuth. *The Art of Computer Programming: Sorting and Searching*, volume 3 of *Computer Science and Information Processing*. Addison-Wesley, 1973. ISBN 0-201-03803-X. (Cited on pages 14 and 18.)

[101] D. E. Knuth. Structured programming with go to statements. *ACM Computing Surveys*, 6(4):261–301, December 1974. doi: 10.1145/356635.356640. (Cited on pages 14, 138, and 161.)

[102] D. E. Knuth. Big Omicron and big Omega and big Theta. *ACM SIGACT News*, 8(2):18–24, April 1976. ISSN 01635700. (Cited on page 41.)

[103] D. E. Knuth. *The Art Of Computer Programming: Searching and Sorting*. Addison Wesley, 2nd edition, 1998. ISBN 978-0-20-189685-5. (Cited on pages ix, 4, 13, 18, 19, 20, 24, 33, 87, 91, 99, 122, 124, 147, 249, and 264.)

[104] D. E. Knuth. *The Art of Computer Programming: Volume 1, Fascicle 1. MMIX, A RISC Computer for the New Millennium*. Addison-Wesley, 2005. ISBN 0-201-85392-2. (Cited on page 124.)

[105] S. Kushagra, A. López-Ortiz, A. Qiao, and J. I. Munro. Multi-pivot Quicksort: Theory and experiments. In *Meeting on Algorithm Engineering and Experiments (ALENEX)*, pages 47–60. SIAM, 2014. (Cited on pages 7, 10, 25, 30, 34, 127, 145, 146, 223, 256, and 262.)

[106] A. LaMarca and R. E. Ladner. The influence of caches on the performance of sorting. In *Symposium on Discrete algorithms (SODA)*, pages 370–379, January 1997. (Cited on page 29.)

[107] A. LaMarca and R. E. Ladner. The influence of caches on the performance of sorting. *Journal of Algorithms*, 31(1):66–104, April 1999. doi: 10.1006/jagm.1998.0985. (Cited on pages 29, 30, 31, 34, and 127.)

[108] A. G. LaMarca. *Caches and Algorithms*. Ph. D. Thesis, University of Washington, 1996. (Cited on page 29.)

[109] E. Landau. *Handbuch der Lehre von der Verteilung der Primzahlen*. Teubner, 1909. URL https://archive.org/stream/handbuchderlehre011landuoft. (Cited on pages 41 and 42.)

[110] O. Lau. Was lange währt .... *c't*, 17:172–177, 2011. URL http://shop.heise.de/katalog/was-lange-wahrt-5. (Cited on pages 4 and 5.)

[111] M. van Leeuwen. Why do we use "non-increasing" instead of decreasing? Mathematics Stack Exchange, 2012. URL http://math.stackexchange.com/q/115951. version: 2012-03-03. (Cited on page 40.)

[112] H. M. Mahmoud. *Evolution of Random Search Trees*. Wiley, 1992. ISBN 0-471-53228-2. (Cited on pages x, 19, and 311.)

[113] H. M. Mahmoud. *Sorting: A distribution theory*. John Wiley & Sons, 2000. ISBN 1-118-03288-8. (Cited on pages x, 22, 86, 105, and 121.)

[114] H. M. Mahmoud. *Pólya Urn Models*. Chapman & Hall, 2008. ISBN 978-1-4200-5983-0. (Cited on pages 18, 79, and 80.)

[115] A. W. Marshall, I. Olkin, and B. C. Arnold. *Inequalities: Theory of Majorization and Its Applications*. Springer Series in Statistics. Springer, 2011. ISBN 978-0-387-40087-7. doi: 10.1007/978-0-387-68276-1. (Cited on page 85.)

[116] C. Martínez and S. Roura. Optimal sampling strategies in Quicksort and Quickselect. *SIAM Journal on Computing*, 31(3):683–705, 2001. (Cited on pages 16, 33, 102, and 235.)

[117] C. Martínez, M. E. Nebel, and S. Wild. Analysis of branch misses in Quicksort. In R. Sedgewick and M. D. Ward, editors, *Meeting on Analytic Algorithmics and Combinatorics (ANALCO)*, pages 114–128. SIAM, 2015. doi: 10.1137/1.9781611973761.11. (Cited on pages xvii, 31, 36, 129, 131, 182, 191, and 193.)

[118] J. D. McCalpin. Sustainable memory bandwidth in high performance computers. Technical report, University of Virginia, Charlottesville, Virginia, 1991-2007. URL `http://www.cs.virginia.edu/~mccalpin/papers/bandwidth/bandwidth.html`. continually updated technical report. (Cited on page 8.)

[119] J. D. McCalpin. Memory bandwidth and machine balance in current high performance computers. *IEEE Computer Society Technical Committee on Computer Architecture (TCCA) Newsletter*, pages 19–25, December 1995. URL `http://www.cs.virginia.edu/~mccalpin/papers/balance/index.html`. (Cited on page 8.)

[120] C. J. H. McDiarmid. Concentration. In M. Habib, C. McDiarmid, J. Ramirez-Alfonsin, and B. Reed, editors, *Probabilistic Methods for Algorithmic Discrete Mathematics*, pages 195–248. Springer, Berlin, 1998. (Cited on page 76.)

[121] C. J. H. McDiarmid and R. B. Hayward. Strong concentration for Quicksort. In *Symposium on Discrete Algorithms (SODA)*, pages 414–421. SIAM, September 1992. (Cited on page 20.)

[122] C. J. H. McDiarmid and R. B. Hayward. Large deviations for Quicksort. *Journal of Algorithms*, 21(3):476–507, November 1996. doi: 10.1006/jagm.1996.0055. (Cited on page 20.)

[123] C. C. McGeoch and J. D. Tygar. Optimal sampling strategies for quicksort. *Random Structures & Algorithms*, 7(4):287–300, December 1995. (Cited on pages 33 and 235.)

[124] M. D. McIlroy. A killer adversary for quicksort. *Software: Practice and Experience*, 29(4):341–344, April 1999. doi: 10.1002/(SICI)1097-024X(19990410)29:4<341::AID-SPE237>3.0.CO;2-R. (Cited on page 15.)

[125] S. A. McKee. Reflections on the memory wall. In *Conference on Computing Frontiers (CF)*, pages 162–167, 2004. (Cited on pages 7 and 9.)

[126] C. L. McMaster. An analysis of algorithms for the Dutch National Flag Problem. *Communications of the ACM*, 21(10):842–846, October 1978. (Cited on page 141.)

[127] K. Mehlhorn and P. Sanders. *Algorithms and Data Structures – The Basic Toolbox*. Springer, Berlin, Heidelberg, 2008. ISBN 978-3-540-77977-3. (Cited on page 126.)

[128] M. Merkle. Logarithmic convexity and inequalities for the gamma function. *Journal of Mathematical Analysis and Applications*, 203(2):369–380, October 1996. doi: 10.1006/jmaa.1996.0385. (Cited on page 93.)

[129] U. Meyer, P. Sanders, and J. Sibeyn, editors. *Algorithms for Memory Hierarchies*, volume 2625 of *LNCS*. Springer Berlin Heidelberg, Berlin, Heidelberg, 2003. ISBN 978-3-540-00883-5. doi: 10.1007/3-540-36574-5. (Cited on page 29.)

[130] D. Motzkin. A stable quicksort. *Software: Practice and Experience*, 11(6):607–611, June 1981. doi: 10.1002/spe.4380110604. (Cited on page 32.)

[131] B. M. Mumey. *Some new results on constructing optimal alphabetic binary trees*. M. Sc. Thesis, University of British Columbia, 1992. (Cited on pages 264 and 267.)

[132] G. O. Munsonius. On the asymptotic internal path length and the asymptotic wiener index of random split trees. *Electronic Journal of Probability*, 16, June 2011. doi: 10.1214/EJP.v16-889. (Cited on page 168.)

[133] D. R. Musser. Introspective Sorting and Selection Algorithms. *Software: Practice and Experience*, 27(8):983–993, 1997. (Cited on pages 15 and 32.)

[134] S. Nagaraj. Optimal binary search trees. *Theoretical Computer Science*, 188(1-2):1–44, November 1997. doi: 10.1016/S0304-3975(96)00320-9. (Cited on pages 87, 264, and 265.)

[135] P. Naur. The European side of the last phase of the development of ALGOL 60. pages 92–139, June 1978. doi: 10.1145/800025.1198353. (Cited on page 136.)

[136] M. E. Nebel and S. Wild. Pivot sampling in dual-pivot Quicksort. In M. Bousquet-Mélou and M. Soria, editors, *International Conference on Probabilistic, Combinatorial and Asymptotic Methods for the Analysis of Algorithms (AofA)*, volume BA of *DMTCS-HAL Proceedings Series*, pages 325–338, 2014. (Cited on pages xvii, 7, 34, and 161.)

[137] M. E. Nebel, S. Wild, and C. Martínez. Analysis of pivot sampling in dual-pivot Quicksort. *Algorithmica*, 75(4):632–683, August 2016. doi: 10.1007/s00453-015-0041-7. (Cited on pages xvii, 7, 9, 31, 34, 35, 127, 173, 199, and 235.)

[138] R. Neininger. On a multivariate contraction method for random recursive structures with applications to Quicksort. *Random Structures & Algorithms*, 19(3-4):498–524, October 2001. doi: 10.1002/rsa.10010. (Cited on page 21.)

[139] R. Neininger. On a multivariate contraction method for random recursive structures with applications to Quicksort. *Random Structures & Algorithms*, 19(3-4):498–524, 2001. (Cited on page 169.)

[140] R. Neininger and L. Rüschendorf. A general limit theorem for recursive algorithms and combinatorial structures. *The Annals of Applied Probability*, 14(1):378–418, 2004. (Cited on page 21.)

[141] K. W. Ng, G.-L. Tian, and M.-L. Tang. *Dirichlet and Related Distributions*. Wiley, 2011. ISBN 978-0-470-68819-9. (Cited on pages 46 and 47.)

[142] C. Nyberg, T. Barclay, Z. Cvetanovic, J. Gray, and D. Lomet. AlphaSort: A RISC machine sort. *ACM SIGMOD Record*, 23(2):233–242, June 1994. doi: 10.1145/191843.191884. (Cited on page 126.)

[143] F. W. J. Olver, D. W. Lozier, R. F. Boisvert, and C. W. Clark, editors. *NIST Handbook of Mathematical Functions*. Cambridge University Press, 2010. (Cited on page 45.)

[144] V. V. Petrov. *Sums of Independent Random Variables*. Springer, 1975. ISBN 3-540-06635-7. (Cited on page 81.)

[145] P. V. Poblete and J. I. Munro. The analysis of a fringe heuristic for binary search trees. *Journal of Algorithms*, 6(3):336–350, September 1985. doi: 10.1016/0196-6774(85)90003-3. (Cited on pages 18 and 311.)

[146] S. T. Rachev and L. Rüschendorf. Probability metrics and recursive algorithms. *Advances in Applied Probability*, 27(3):770–799, 1995. (Cited on page 21.)

[147] P. Ramanan. Testing the optimality of alphabetic trees. *Theoretical Computer Science*, 93(2): 279–301, February 1992. doi: 10.1016/0304-3975(92)90334-C. (Cited on page 267.)

[148] M. Regnier. A limiting distribution for Quicksort. *Informatique théorique et applications*, 23(3): 335–343, 1989. (Cited on page 20.)

[149] A. W. Roberts and D. E. Varberg. *Convex Functions*. Academic Press, 1973. (Cited on pages 49 and 85.)

[150] U. Rösler and L. Rüschendorf. The contraction method for recursive algorithms. *Algorithmica*, 29(1-2):3–33, February 2001. doi: 10.1007/BF02679611. (Cited on page 21.)

[151] U. Rösler. A limit theorem for "Quicksort". *Informatique théorique et applications*, 25(1):85–100, 1991. (Cited on page 20.)

[152] U. Rösler. A fixed point theorem for distributions. *Stochastic Processes and their Applications*, 42(2):195–214, September 1992. doi: 10.1016/0304-4149(92)90035-O. (Cited on page 21.)

[153] S. Roura. *Divide-and-Conquer Algorithms and Data Structures*. Tesi doctoral (Ph. D. thesis, Universitat Politècnica de Catalunya, 1997. (Cited on pages 15, 100, and 102.)

[154] S. Roura. Improved Master Theorems for Divide-and-Conquer Recurrences. *Journal of the ACM*, 48(2):170–205, 2001. (Cited on pages 15, 38, 100, 102, 197, and 207.)

[155] K. Rutanen, G. Gómez-Herrero, S.-L. Eriksson, and K. Egiazarian. A general definition of the Big-Oh notation for algorithm analysis. 1(1):1–39, September 2013. URL http://arxiv.org/abs/1309.3210. (Cited on page 42.)

[156] W. Rytter. Trees with minimum weighted path length. In D. P. Mehta and S. Sahni, editors, *Handbook Of Data Structures And Applications*, chapter 14. Chapman & Hall, 2004. ISBN 158-488435-5. (Cited on page 264.)

[157] P. Sanders and S. Winkel. Super scalar sample sort. In S. Albers and T. Radzik, editors, *European Symposium on Algorithms (ESA)*, LNCS, pages 784–796. Springer Berlin/Heidelberg, 2004. (Cited on page 162.)

[158] R. Sedgewick. *Quicksort*. Ph. D. thesis, Stanford University, 1975. (Cited on page 14.)

[159] R. Sedgewick. The analysis of Quicksort programs. *Acta Informatica*, 7(4):327–355, 1977. (Cited on pages 15, 17, and 25.)

[160] R. Sedgewick. Quicksort with equal keys. *SIAM Journal on Computing*, 6(2):240–267, 1977. (Cited on pages 15, 26, 122, 288, 290, 291, and 292.)

[161] R. Sedgewick. Implementing Quicksort programs. *Communications of the ACM*, 21(10):847–857, 1978. (Cited on pages 10, 15, 137, and 147.)

[162] R. Sedgewick. *Quicksort*. Reprint of the author's Ph. D. thesis, 1980. (Cited on pages x, 4, 10, 14, 15, 17, 23, 124, 137, 139, 142, 159, 160, 161, 197, 212, 223, 235, 262, and 334.)

[163] R. Sedgewick and J. Bentley. New research on theory and practice of sorting and searching (talk slides), 1999. URL http://www.cs.princeton.edu/~rs/talks/Montreal.pdf. (Cited on pages 26, 287, and 292.)

[164] R. Sedgewick and J. Bentley. Quicksort is optimal (talk slides), 2002. URL http://www.cs.princeton.edu/~rs/talks/QuicksortIsOptimal.pdf. (Cited on pages 26 and 292.)

[165] R. Sedgewick and P. Flajolet. *An Introduction to the Analysis of Algorithms*. Addison-Wesley-Longman, 1996. ISBN 978-0-201-40009-0. (Cited on pages ix and 137.)

[166] R. Sedgewick and K. Wayne. *Algorithms*. Addison-Wesley, 4th edition, 2011. ISBN 978-0-32-157351-3. (Cited on pages 139, 294, and 298.)

[167] R. Seidel. Data-specific analysis of string sorting. In *Symposium on Discrete Algorithms (SODA)*, pages 1278–1286. SIAM, January 2010. ISBN 978-0-898716-98-6. (Cited on pages 28 and 29.)

[168] C. E. Shannon. A mathematical theory of communication. *Bell System Technical Journal*, 27(3): 379–423, July 1948. doi: 10.1002/j.1538-7305.1948.tb01338.x. (Cited on page 82.)

[169] P. W. Shor. My explanation of the Hu-Tucker algorithm, 2004. URL `http://www-math.mit.edu/~shor/PAM/hu-tucker_algorithm.html`. Accessed: 2015-11-01. (Cited on page 264.)

[170] R. C. Singleton. Algorithm 347: an efficient algorithm for sorting with minimal storage [M1]. *Communications of the ACM*, 12(3):185–186, March 1969. (Cited on pages 13, 15, 147, and 288.)

[171] H. H. Sohrab. *Basic Real Analysis*. Springer Birkhäuser, 2nd edition, 2014. ISBN 978-1-4939-1840-9. (Cited on pages 50, 51, 52, and 73.)

[172] W. Szpankowski. Average Redundancy for Known Sources: Ubiquitous Trees in Source Coding. 0(1), 2008. (Cited on page 269.)

[173] K.-H. Tan. *An asymptotic analysis of the number of comparisons in multipartition quicksort*. Ph.D. thesis, Carnegie Mellon University, January 1993. (Cited on pages 4, 9, 22, 23, 161, and 262.)

[174] K. H. Tan and P. Hadjicostas. Some properties of a limiting distribution in Quicksort. *Statistics & Probability Letters*, 25(1):87–94, October 1995. (Cited on pages 22 and 24.)

[175] B. Vallée, J. Clément, J. A. Fill, and P. Flajolet. The number of symbol comparisons in Quick-Sort and QuickSelect. In S. Albers, A. Marchetti-Spaccamela, Y. Matias, S. Nikoletseas, and W. Thomas, editors, *International Colloquium on Automata, Languages and Programming (ICALP)*, volume 5555 of *LNCS*, pages 750–763. Springer, 2009. (Cited on page 29.)

[176] A. Walker and D. Wood. Locally balanced binary trees. *The Computer Journal*, 19(4):322–325, April 1976. doi: 10.1093/comjnl/19.4.322. (Cited on pages 18 and 311.)

[177] L. M. Wegner. Sorting a linked list with equal keys. *Information Processing Letters*, 15(5): 205–208, December 1982. doi: 10.1016/0020-0190(82)90118-1. (Cited on page 32.)

[178] L. M. Wegner. Quicksort for equal keys. *IEEE Transactions on Computers*, C-34(4):362–367, April 1985. doi: 10.1109/TC.1985.5009387. (Cited on pages 26, 293, 294, and 295.)

[179] L. M. Wegner. A generalized, one-way, stackless quicksort. *BIT*, 27(1):44–48, March 1987. doi: 10.1007/BF01937353. URL `http://link.springer.com/10.1007/BF01937353`. (Cited on page 32.)

[180] L. M. Wegner. Sorting – the Turku lectures, 2014. ISBN 978-952-12-3020-2. URL `http://tucs.fi/publications/view/?pub_id=bWegner_LutzMx14a`. (Cited on page 293.)

[181] R. Wickremesinghe, L. Arge, J. S. Chase, and J. S. Vitter. Efficient sorting using registers and caches. *Journal of Experimental Algorithmics*, 7:9, December 2002. doi: 10.1145/944618.944627. (Cited on page 126.)

[182] S. Wild. Java 7's Dual Pivot Quicksort. Master's Thesis, University of Kaiserslautern, 2012. URL `http://nbn-resolving.de/urn/resolver.pl?urn:nbn:de:hbz:386-kluedo-34638`. (Cited on pages 5, 7, 33, 124, 125, 141, 142, 157, 159, 180, 183, and 223.)

[183] S. Wild. Sorting discrete i.i.d. inputs: Quicksort is optimal, 2016. URL `https://arxiv.org/abs/1608.04906`. (Cited on pages x and 335.)

[184] S. Wild and M. E. Nebel. Average case analysis of Java 7's dual pivot Quicksort. In L. Epstein and P. Ferragina, editors, *European Symposium on Algorithms (ESA)*, volume 7501 of *LNCS*, pages 825–836. Springer, 2012. URL `http://arxiv.org/abs/1310.7409`. (Cited on pages xvii, 7, 10, 24, 34, and 173.)

[185] S. Wild, M. E. Nebel, R. Reitzig, and U. Laube. Engineering Java 7's dual pivot Quicksort using MaLiJAn. In P. Sanders and N. Zeh, editors, *Meeting on Algorithm Engineering and Experiments (ALENEX)*, pages 55–69. SIAM, 2013. (Cited on pages xvii, 34, 124, and 235.)

[186] S. Wild, M. E. Nebel, and R. Neininger. Average case and distributional analysis of Java 7's dual pivot Quicksort. *ACM Transactions on Algorithms*, 11(3):22:1–22:42, 2015. (Cited on pages xvii, 22, 34, 153, 173, 179, 183, and 197.)

[187] S. Wild, M. E. Nebel, and H. Mahmoud. Analysis of Quickselect under Yaroslavskiy's dual-pivoting algorithm. *Algorithmica*, 74(1):485–506, 2016. doi: 10.1007/s00453-014-9953-x. (Cited on pages xvii and 35.)

[188] WolframAlpha. partitions of 1024 with 512 parts, 2015. URL `http://www.wolframalpha.com/share/clip?f=d41d8cd98f00b204e9800998ecf8427e494e9cmads`. (Cited on page 283.)

[189] W. A. Wulf and S. A. McKee. Hitting the memory wall: Implications of the obvious. *ACM SIGARCH Computer Architecture News*, 23(1):20–24, March 1995. (Cited on pages 7 and 9.)

[190] A. C.-C. Yao. On random 2-3 trees. *Acta Informatica*, 9(2):159–170, 1978. doi: 10.1007/BF00289075. (Cited on page 18.)

[191] V. Yaroslavskiy. Dual-Pivot Quicksort. 2009. URL `http://iaroslavski.narod.ru/quicksort/DualPivotQuicksort.pdf`. (Cited on pages 10, 24, and 25.)

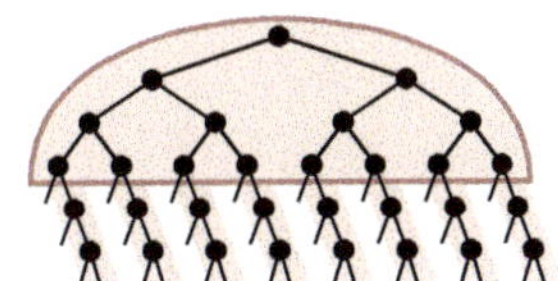